Unseasonable Truths

Also by Harry S. Ashmore

THE NEGRO AND THE SCHOOLS

AN EPITAPH FOR DIXIE

THE OTHER SIDE OF JORDAN

MISSION TO HANOI: A CHRONICLE OF DOUBLE DEALING
IN HIGH PLACES *(with William C. Baggs)*

THE MAN IN THE MIDDLE

FEAR IN THE AIR

ARKANSAS: A HISTORY

THE WILLIAM O. DOUGLAS INQUIRY INTO
THE STATE OF INDIVIDUAL FREEDOM *(editor)*

HEARTS AND MINDS:
A PERSONAL CHRONICLE OF RACE IN AMERICA

Unseasonable Truths

The Life of
Robert Maynard Hutchins

by

HARRY S. ASHMORE

Little, Brown and Company
Boston · Toronto · London

FIRST EDITION

The author is grateful for permission to include excerpts from the following publications:

Court of Reason: Robert Hutchins and the Fund for the Republic, by Frank K. Kelly. Copyright © 1981 by Frank K. Kelly. Reprinted with permission of The Free Press, a Division of Macmillan, Inc.

The Lives of William Benton, by Sidney Hyman. Copyright © 1969 by The University of Chicago. All rights reserved. Reprinted by permission of The University of Chicago Press.

"Very Simple But Thoroughgoing," by Reuben Frodin, published in *The Idea and Practice of General Education,* F. Champion Ward, ed. Copyright 1950 by The University of Chicago. All rights reserved. Reprinted by permission of The University of Chicago Press.

Freedom and the Foundation: The Fund for the Republic in the Era of McCarthyism, by Thomas Reeves. Copyright © 1969 by Thomas Reeves. Reprinted by permission of Alfred A. Knopf, Inc.

The Ford Foundation: The Men and the Millions, by Dwight Macdonald. Copyright © 1956 by Dwight Macdonald. Reprinted by permission of William Morrow and Co.

Library of Congress Cataloging-in-Publication Data

Ashmore, Harry S.
    Unseasonable truths: the life of Robert Maynard Hutchins /
by Harry S. Ashmore — 1st ed.
      p.   cm.
    Includes index.
    1. Hutchins, Robert Maynard, 1899–1977. 2.
Educators — United States — Biography. I. Title.
LB875.H9753A84 1989
370'.92'4 — dc19
[B]
        89–30715
        CIP

10 9 8 7 6 5 4 3 2 1

MV-PA

Designed by Jacques Chazaud

*Published simultaneously in Canada
by Little, Brown & Company (Canada) Limited*

PRINTED IN THE UNITED STATES OF AMERICA

*For the Hutchinses,
past and present*

I discovered in Scotland that in 1648 the General Assembly of the Kirk, in adopting the larger catechism, addressed itself, in Question 145, to the sins included in the Ninth Commandment. One of them is "speaking the truth unseasonably." You will recognize this as a sin I have been committing all my life.

— Robert M. Hutchins to
Thornton Wilder, 1954

Contents

LIST OF ILLUSTRATIONS   *xiii*

PREFACE   *xv*

1. Life on a Puritan Island   *3*
2. "Over There, Over There . . ."   *16*
3. "Bright College Years, with Pleasure Rife . . ."   *25*
4. The Genesis of an Educator   *36*
5. The Ebullient Experimentalist   *45*
6. "A Gamble on Youth and Brilliancy . . ."   *57*
7. The Harper Legacy   *66*
8. "A Hell of a Good Time . . ."   *77*
9. Of Habits and Morals   *88*
10. The Great Conversation   *98*
11. "Debonair, Fluent, Logical, Provocative . . ."   *108*
12. Impolitic Politics   *120*
13. "More Than Pious Hopes . . ."   *133*
14. "No Friendly Voice"   *142*
15. Facts vs. Ideas   *153*

16. Inflammable Gases   *165*

17. The Madison Avenue Touch   *176*

18. No Place to Go   *187*

19. A Not So Happy Birthday   *200*

20. "Drifting into Suicide . . ."   *210*

21. "An Instrumentality of Total War . . ."   *221*

22. "A Moral, Intellectual and Spiritual Revolution . . ."   *233*

23. "The Good News of Damnation"   *244*

24. Looking Toward the Apocalypse   *254*

25. "A Stuffed Shirt on Roller Skates"   *264*

26. A Proposal to History   *275*

27. Chancellor at Large   *287*

28. "A Return to 'Normalcy' "   *299*

29. "How Firm a Foundation . . ."   *311*

30. Trouble in Paradise   *323*

31. "A Herculean Effort . . ."   *333*

32. Attack and Counterattack   *343*

33. "Too Intellectually Arrogant . . ."   *354*

34. Innocence by Association   *365*

35. Back to Basics   *374*

36. "On the Mountain Eucalyptic . . ."   *386*

37. Raising the Encyclopaedic Roof   *397*

38. New Faces and New Issues   *408*

39. In Search of Survival   *417*

40. "An Extraordinary Gathering . . ."   *428*

41. Conflicting Priorities   *438*

42. Public Relations for Peace   *451*

43. " . . . Like Peevish Children"   *461*

44. The Center Refounded   *471*

45. The Search for a Successor   *482*

46. "As Well Settled As Could Be Expected . . ."   *492*

47. An Unsuccessful Succession   *503*

48. "Huddled in Dirt the Reasoning Engine Lies . . ."   *515*

49. Post Mortem   *528*

   NOTES   *543*

   BIBLIOGRAPHIC NOTES   *581*

   ACKNOWLEDGMENTS   *585*

   INDEX   *587*

List of Illustrations

Robert Hutchins's grandfather, the Reverend Robert Grosvenor Hutchins
Francis, William, and Robert Hutchins
Robert, Will, Anna, and William Hutchins, Jr., in Oberlin
New recruits William and Robert at the Allentown, Pennsylvania, Fairgrounds
"Hooch" Hutchins's Yale graduation picture
Robert and Maude arriving in Chicago, fall 1929
Hutchins with Acting President Frederick Woodward and Board Chairman Harold Swift
Hutchins with Egyptologist James Henry Breasted
Hutchins after receiving an honorary degree at Lafayette College, 1936
Maude with Mortimer Adler
Hutchins with Floyd Reeves and John T. McCloy on NBC's "Roundtable of the Air"
Robert and William at the Asheville School, May 1944
Will and Anna Hutchins
Robert and Maude, 1946
Robert and Vesta Hutchins
Hutchins with William Hocking at the Goethe Bicentennial, Aspen, Colorado, 1949
Hutchins after his farewell address, Chicago, 1951
Hutchins with Ford Foundation Chairman Paul Hoffman and William Benton of Encyclopaedia Britannica

Encyclopaedia Britannica's board of editors, 1965
The Center for the Study of Democratic Institutions, Santa Barbara
Hutchins with William O. Douglas
Hutchins with the author and Rexford Guy Tugwell
Hutchins with Linus Pauling
John Birch Society pickets outside the Center for the Study of Democratic
    Institutions
Hutchins with the author
Hutchins with Henry Kissinger
Center Dean Norton Ginsburg with Hans Morgenthau
Hutchins with Morris Levinson, chairman of the board of the Fund for the
    Republic
Vesta with Senator George McGovern
Hutchins with Nelson Rockefeller
Hutchins with Malcolm Moos, his successor as president of the Center

Preface

After plowing through the collection of Robert Hutchins's papers at the University of Chicago Library, a young English professor observed, "One of the things that continually amazes me is the variety of publications his educational and cultural criticism permeated. He turns up in everything from the *International Journal of Ethics* to newspapers and middlebrow magazines like *Time*. This fact, and his general attraction to journalists and public relations men, seems to be almost without parallel today."[1]

There are several reasons why this was so.

Hutchins was a man of ideas, and his effectiveness in propagating them was reflected in the public record he compiled in the course of a long career as a legal scholar, political philosopher, educational reformer, and civil libertarian. Tall, preternaturally handsome, equipped with a quick and penetrating mind, he began attracting attention with his wit and eloquence when he was very young. In his twenties, as the precocious dean of the Yale Law School, he became a prominent figure in academic circles; in his thirties, as president of the University of Chicago, he was recognized as a media star a generation before that dubious term was coined.

This kind of celebrity was essential to his lifelong effort to rally support for the changes he sought to effect in the nation's educational structure. "I have come to regard educators as a lost cause," he wrote. "I have felt that the only chance is to carry the public, of whom educators

xv

live in deathly fear. When I am conciliatory nobody pays any attention. Everybody sits nursing his vested interests. When I am vicious, the teachers at least have to answer the questions of their constituency."[2]

Hutchins had no need of popular adulation to bolster his considerable ego; he treated his public role as a sometimes rewarding but usually unpleasant necessity. He was interested in publicizing his ideas, not himself. It followed that he firmly refused to consider writing an autobiography to sum up the career that had made him a leading figure in the intellectual history of his time.

I was one of those who importuned him on that score. His not entirely facetious response was that he had been brought up to tell the truth and to respect the sensibilities of his friends and associates, and it was not possible to do both. His only regret, he said, was that this meant he would have no use for the title he had conceived for a chronicle of his life and times: "The Skunk at the Garden Party."

The title would have been fitting, and in keeping with the irony that usually marked Hutchins's references to himself. All his adult life he moved among the wellborn and those whose talent had earned them status, and in one way or another he outraged a substantial number of them. The potential harvest of anecdotes about the rich and famous a first-person account could have provided caused a number of leading publishers to approach him in his latter years.

He dismissed them with the same kind of irony he had accorded me. If it was suggested that he owed an accounting to posterity, he told Storer Lunt of W. W. Norton, he always responded, What has posterity ever done for me? But when Lunt persisted, he admitted that there was another, deeply personal reason: "What could I say about my first marriage?"[3]

That was his union with the darkly beautiful, egocentric artist Maude Phelps McVeigh, shortly after his graduation from Yale in 1921. The marriage endured until 1948 and produced three daughters before it ended in divorce. But its failure had long been made evident by Maude's behavior, which was erratic enough to become a cause célèbre in the close-knit University of Chicago community. Hutchins concealed the trauma of those years behind a reserve that was rarely penetrated even by his few intimates.

In part this reticence was a product of his Puritan heritage. He was reared to consider it unthinkable to discuss one's private affairs in public, and he was appalled to see a rising generation accept the revelation of the most brutish aspects of human nature as a laudable display of candor. When television began to dominate journalism and emphasis shifted from substance to style, Hutchins was effectively ruled off the course.

Celebrity had become the product of a cult of personality, no longer a mark of accomplishment but an end in itself.

He could not, of course, rule out a biography. The extensive public record that charted the development of his ideas, and the institutional applications he sought for them, was readily available. But he firmly rebuffed those who sought to go beyond that. He told Frank Keegan, a philosopher who had worked with him as a research assistant, that he was flattered by Keegan's proposal to write his life story, but he added:

> To the two or three publishers who have asked me to write my autobiography I have replied that I have no time. . . . So, I have no objection to your writing my biography, or any part of it, on condition that you use only published sources and don't engage me in extensive researches into the past, a past, incidentally, that I deplore and do not want to think about.[4]

He made essentially the same reply to two other associates, Frank Kelly and Milton Mayer, and to George Dell, a speech professor who was interested in Hutchins principally as a master of rhetoric. He did accede to three lengthy interviews with Mayer, a witty friend from his Chicago days, but these became an intellectual sparring match when his interrogator attempted to draw him out on his personal relationships and inner motivations. Mayer wryly termed him an "artless dodger."

Despite Hutchins's demurrers, his family and friends remained convinced that a biography was in order, and a decade after his death I was persuaded to undertake it. The object was not merely to erect a monument to the memory of a notable American, but to call attention to the means Hutchins had proposed for dealing with the unresolved issues he identified as basic to a nation beset by unprecedented social, economic, and demographic change.

Unlike many of his academic contemporaries, Hutchins never dealt in abstractions. He conceived of the university as a center of independent thought and criticism, but he also insisted that the task of defining the issues affecting society carried with it an obligation to develop and propagate the means of resolving them. The means, by definition, would have to be political, and they could not be pursued in an ivory tower.

I had gained some insight into the patterns of Hutchins's thought and action during an association that had its tentative beginnings in 1948, when I first encountered him in person. He had come to Louisville to address the founding session of the National Conference of Editorial Writers, and I found that his presence added a telling dimension to the trenchant Hutchins I had known only in print. Chastising the editors as failed pedagogues, he administered "a big dose of medicine to the press," as the *Louisville Courier-Journal* put it. "And his audience swallowed the dose without undue outcry, if they did not exactly lick the spoon."[5]

At the instigation of his Yale classmate Henry Luce, Hutchins had headed a Commission on Freedom of the Press, which accused the media of falling far short of providing the responsible public-affairs reporting envisioned in their First Amendment guarantee of press freedom. The proposal for a continuing independent commission to appraise and report on their performance had been rejected by the great majority of newspaper publishers and derided by most of the editorial writers present. After citing some of the most egregious misrepresentations of the Commission's findings, Hutchins made a characteristic charge, in keeping with his contention that education was not, and could not be, confined to the formal educational system:

> If the press wishes to repudiate the Report and silence me, it can attack my major premise. It may deny that its function is to teach. If, however, newspaper editors and writers are not teachers, what are they? They are either entertainers or the hired hands and voices of men who happen to have enough money to own newspapers. In neither case would they have any serious claim to public attention.[6]

I was then executive editor of the *Arkansas Gazette,* one of the few major dailies to applaud the report. Five years later the Fund for the Advancement of Education, established by Hutchins after he became associate director of the Ford Foundation, drafted me to head a team of academic experts charged with appraising the effects of the pending Supreme Court decision on school desegregation. In 1954, after I became embroiled in the resulting constitutional confrontation at Little Rock, he invited me to join the board of directors of the Fund for the Republic, the civil-rights organization he headed, which had been created by Ford.

In 1959, when the Fund founded the Center for the Study of Democratic Institutions, I resigned from the *Gazette* to join Hutchins full-time at his new headquarters in Santa Barbara. I expected to be there for a sabbatical year, but as chairman of the board of editors of *Encyclopaedia Britannica,* he arranged for my appointment as editor in chief to work with him in the preparation of a pioneering new edition. Later I became executive vice president of the Center, and our day-to-day association continued until his death in May 1977.

Our compatibility was largely a matter of temperament. We both came from WASP backgrounds, but his, rooted in New England, was one hundred proof abolitionist, while I am a South Carolinian with two Confederate grandfathers. His intellectual status derived from his standing as a scholar; I am a journalist and therefore suspect in academic circles. I was more familiar with the harsh realities of contemporary life than he was, and perhaps more tolerant of human frailty. But I found that I could share his faith that Americans, given time and a proper education, might yet create a truly democratic polity within the framework of their republican constitution.

So it was that I came to enjoy a close-up view of Robert Hutchins in action during the last third of his life. But to write his biography I also needed a more intimate knowledge of his career in the years when he was developing the philosophical tenets that were firmly in place by the time I came to know him. While he was studiedly informal with his close associates, and while his private conversation was colored by his often derisive wit, that was all part of the wall of reserve that cloaked his inner thoughts and effectively censored the recollections he chose to expose. When I cited the derelictions of those who had worked with him and, as he usually did, he said he wasn't able to confirm or deny, I accused him of using the lawyer's dodge of claiming a lapse of memory to avoid perjury. He only grinned and said, well, after all, he should have derived some benefit from his legal education.

It will be seen that in my account of Hutchins's life through World War II, I have been limited to the third person, relying on documentary sources and interviews with the few remaining survivors who were closely associated with him in those years. Beginning with my election as a director of the Fund for the Republic in 1954, the narrative shifts into the first person, but I have tested my recollections against many other sources.

At the end of the book I acknowledge my debt to those who encouraged me to undertake this work and provided funding for the extensive research it entailed. But it should be noted here that a biography of this scope would not have been possible without the active cooperation of Hutchins's widow, Vesta, his surviving brother, Francis, his daughters Clarissa and Barbara, and his nephew Francis, Jr., who made themselves and their family papers available.

It is only in this limited sense that this might be considered an authorized biography; none of these was given an opportunity to review the content prior to publication, and none bears any responsibility for the invasions of Robert Hutchins's privacy I considered necessary to round out the portrait and complete the record, or for the judgments I have made. Since I am certain that he would never have approved a hagiography, I can hope that he, as well as his relatives, might have finally conceded that such an undertaking was in order.

Santa Barbara
June 1989

Unseasonable Truths

CHAPTER ONE

Life on a
Puritan Island

It was Robert Hutchins's custom to deprecate his patrician persona by pointing out that he had been born in plebeian Brooklyn and shared his birthday with another native of the borough who also came to prominence in Chicago — Al Capone. Like all of his ironic asides, this one was technically correct: both infants first saw the light of day there on January 17, 1899. But the hereditary distance between them could not have been greater had Capone's parents remained in Italy and Hutchins's in New England.

The future gangster was a child of the tenements, the future educator a child of the parsonage. His mother had intended to name him Maynard, the given name borne by her father and her beloved brother, but the minister at the christening inverted Maynard Robert, and thus the latter came first on his baptismal record. His father reduced this to "Bobs," and so he was called when he first ventured forth from the residence provided at 73 Herkimer Street for the pastor of Bedford Presbyterian Church. He emerged into a sedate suburban neighborhood, a section of Brooklyn so quiet the local wags considered it appropriate that the trolley cars said Greenwood Cemetery.

"I was born in the dying century," Hutchins recalled, "before the open gas flame was superseded by the Welsbach burner, before the horsecars had disappeared, before the telephone was commonplace, and when the iceman was one of the mainstays of our lives. Although everybody went to school, almost nobody went to college. But everybody

3

went to church. Since my father was a minister, my brothers and I went to church at least three or four times as often as other people.''[1]

Among the few who enjoyed the benefits of higher education were his parents — the Reverend William James Hutchins at Oberlin, Yale, and Union Theological Seminary, his wife, Anna Laura Murch, at Oberlin and Mount Holyoke. Their happy marriage represented the convergence of two family lines going back to the earliest settlement of the seaboard colonies. The first American Hutchins, Nicholas, arrived from England in 1670 and settled at Groton, Massachusetts; the Murches were not far behind and put down roots in Maine. Across the generations, the collateral branches of the family tree bore many of the surnames to be found in the Puritan pantheon — Fell, Hartley, Hale, Dodge, Maynard, Jewett, Hardy, Pierce, Grosvenor, James, Townsend, Scarborough, and Wyman.

The Bedford pastorate was the young minister's first and, as it turned out, his last. The church he took over in 1896 was housed in a small frame building and counted only eighty-four members in its congregation. In short order Will Hutchins's eloquence in the pulpit, and the energy and compassion he brought to his pastoral duties, began attracting additional members of the Presbyterian elect. A solid brick church was built at Dean Street and Nostrand Avenue, and the Hutchinses moved into a more capacious parsonage at 1080 Prospect Place, a welcome change since the older boy, William Grosvenor, and Robert were soon to be joined by a younger brother, Francis Stevenson.

The Hutchinses maintained a religious household, but it was not unduly pious. Its head was a warmhearted, considerate father whose sons accorded him an affection that did not flag throughout his lifetime. A devoted husband, Will tolerated and even encouraged the sometimes irreverent observations of his young wife, whose interests extended beyond the parochial environment. "My mother was very good for all her sons," Robert wrote after her death in 1960. "She was witty and satirical to the last and kept reminding us that her opinion of us was not exactly the same as the opinions we had of ourselves."[2]

Thornton Wilder, the novelist and playwright who became a familiar of the family during his undergraduate years, continued his connection with the senior Hutchinses after they relocated to the Kentucky mountains, where Will headed Berea College. He recalled an even lighter side of Anna Laura in a letter to Robert:

> You know that your mother and I were particular chums — it
> flowered mostly during my two trips to Berea. Driving along the
> "pikes" and "knobs" with her was sheer hilarity. We saw so

many things in the same light — we never had to cross the *t*'s or dot the *i*'s. We were unimpressed by the same things; we were wearied by the same things. It was like driving in an oxygen tank — we were liberated.[3]

The sons recalled that under the tutelage of their parents, they had been imbued with the Protestant ethic without undue pain and suffering. This included devotion to duty, civic as well as religious, along with an ambition to succeed in life. On both counts the Reverend Hutchins provided an impeccable role model. Robert would recall that every morning after family prayers he had gazed at the Phi Beta Kappa key appended to his father's pocket watch, lying on the breakfast table beside his plate to insure that the young minister embarked promptly on his appointed rounds. Robert, an omnivorous reader before he entered kindergarten, was destined to do well in the public schools of Brooklyn and all the others he later attended.

When he was eight, this somewhat diluted metropolitan exposure was terminated by his father's call to a professorship at Oberlin Theological Seminary. The family may well have considered the summons predestined. Oberlin was in the heart of the Western Reserve, the Ohio territory that had once been part of Connecticut. The town and the College had been established in 1833 by Calvinists who believed they were ordained to provide a base from which preachers and teachers could carry the gospel to the raw new settlements on the western frontier.

The Reverend Hutchins left his pastorate with an easy conscience. In the eleven years of his tenure the membership of Bedford Presbyterian had grown to 748, with 920 enrolled in the Sunday school. He summarized his stewardship in a valedictory sermon:

Our official boards are absolutely united. There is no faction in the church. There is not even the slightest trace of friction. Every organization is in a thoroughly healthy condition. For the first time in thirteen years the church is free of every kind of financial encumbrance. Sums amounting, all told, to $34,000 have been paid and pledged toward the building of our greater church.[4]

He was, he told the congregation, answering a call to a higher duty. At the Seminary he would serve as professor of homiletics, the pulpit oratory for which he was already becoming famous within his denomination. As such, he would meet daily with each of his students throughout his seminary course, and thus would reach a new generation every three years. "These men," he said, "are to become the leaders of churches in the home land and in the foreign mission field. To influence them is to affect a great stream at its source."[5]

Oberlin Seminary professors also had close contact with the under-graduates in the College. He would be in charge of the Bible class and the prayer meeting required of all freshmen. Thus he "might hope to help mold the lives of at least two thousand of the future leaders in the social, civic and ecclesiastical life of our country." And he added a note that may have left a special impression on his son Robert: "I have been influenced by the remembrance that many of the most significant movements of the world have originated in the colleges."[6]

Finally, by way of demonstrating his purity of purpose, he told the congregation, "I need scarcely say that no monetary consideration has weighed with me. The salary at Oberlin will be absolutely and relatively less than my present salary."[7]

The Puritan tradition produced men who made their success in the secular world as well as men who committed themselves to the church or pursued the life of the mind. Often there was a blending of the two strains, as was the case with the missionaries to Hawaii who went to the islands to do good and, it was said, remained to do well. Robert Hutchins's ancestry included notable examples of both types.

His maternal grandfather, Captain Maynard Hale Murch, was a seafaring man who at age eleven circumnavigated the globe aboard a sailing ship under his father's command. Robert found it "amazing how our forebears put out to sea in those little sailboats, got blown to pieces, split on rocks, and carried off by scurvy, and still survived."[8] Captain Murch left the sea in middle age and settled at Ellsworth, Maine, where he ran a prospering shipyard.

In due course he transferred his talents to the Western Reserve, establishing a yard at Cleveland to build Great Lakes ore boats for James C. Hill, the railroad tycoon. His grandsons recalled the captain fondly as a teller of tall tales, and Francis was not surprised when, on a visit to Ellsworth, he heard his grandfather's former neighbors describe him as a "great liar." His son Maynard, however, was a model of probity who became a leading Cleveland financier.

The paternal grandfather, Robert Grosvenor Hutchins, a graduate of Andover Theological Seminary ordained in the Congregational branch of the Calvinist faith, was a powerful and popular evangelical preacher who filled pulpits in Columbus, Minneapolis, Los Angeles, and Honolulu. An inveterate traveler and something of a bon vivant, he once returned from London to wryly report that when he had identified himself as a member of the founding family at Grosvenor House, a servant had responded,

"Yes, some stayed here and got rich, while others went to America and flashed out."[9]

In 1886 he established a Hutchins presence in Oberlin when he was called to the Second Congregational Church, hard by the campus, and he also served the College as a trustee. Of his three sons, only Will followed him into the ministry. His remarkable daughter, Fannie, could not have done so in that day, but she was a pioneer in a field all but closed to women, earning a medical degree and establishing herself in Cleveland as a specialist in neuropsychiatry.

The youngest son, Francis Sessions, became a successful Wall Street lawyer, but only one of the brothers was suspected of having sold out to Mammon. This was Grosvenor junior, who made a fortune in Columbus and went on to become vice president of the Commercial Bank of New York. Honoring Will Hutchins at a testimonial dinner in 1939, Robert said, "My deep distaste for rich, powerful and corrupt people dates from the Christmas on which he received a photograph of one of his rich, powerful and corrupt friends. He put it on the piano and said to us, 'I will put this here to remind us of the things we are fighting against.' " Privately Robert identified the benighted "friend" as his uncle Grosvenor.[10]

Aunt Fannie, the formidable lady physician, shared her brother Grosvenor's outlook. "She looked like a Prussian grenadier," Robert recalled:

> She was certain that our mother was incompetent to bring us up. She descended upon us periodically. We all took to the storm cellars. She thought Father was incompetent because he was not rich like his brothers, who had married well. I remember this conversation: Aunt F: "I am impressed by the things money can do." Father: "I am much more impressed by the things it *can't* do." This was no doubt the origin of my prejudice against doctors.[11]

This dim view of one of his sons on the part of another posed a practical problem for Grosvenor senior when Will elected to move on to Oberlin. In a letter to President Henry Churchill King, he noted that he had strongly urged Will's acceptance of the appointment, so much so that he thought the filial spirit he had invoked made him largely responsible for his son's decision:

> About one thing I have some misgivings. I refer to the salary of $2,000. About this I wish to write to you a word without Will's knowledge, in strictest confidence. It is probably true that $2 in

Oberlin are worth $3 in Brooklyn. But there are some fixed charges, like premiums on life insurance. . . . Thinking not merely of his personal happiness, but of his usefulness to the college and the seminary, I have been led to ask whether some relief from the strain of excessive economy might not be provided.[12]

He thought help might be forthcoming from his eldest son. "I would not on any account have Grosvenor know that I had mentioned his name in this connection," he wrote, "but as a matter of fact he has a large income and could provide such relief without at all missing the money."[13] Although he stressed that he and Will must not be mentioned in any such negotiation, he urged King to call on Grosvenor and suggest that he make $350 a year available to the Seminary to cover Will's insurance.

The president responded with sympathy and deep reservations. If such a gift arrived spontaneously, it would, of course, be welcome. But if he undertook the solicitation, he feared he might appear to be favoring one member of his faculty over the others. He promised to give the proposal further consideration, but there is no indication that anything ever came of it.[14]

However they managed it, the Hutchinses lived reasonably well in Oberlin. They rented, and later bought, a capacious two-story frame house that still stands on tree-shaded grounds at 95 Professor Street, a few blocks from the campus with its broad green and its cluster of Victorian buildings. Donald M. Love, the biographer of President King, recalled everyday life in the village as having the feeling of a Trollope novel: "It was pleasantly intimate, with an old-fashioned neighborliness prevailing among the faculty members and townspeople which expressed itself in small dinners, cozy tea parties, and many casual calls in the afternoon."[15] Robert's impressions of his new hometown were somewhat less glowing:

When my father became a professor at Oberlin in 1907, whatever metropolitan flavor Brooklyn had given us was quickly drained away. We became residents of a Puritan island in the Middle West. Here communication and transportation were even more primitive. Church was, if anything, even more frequent. The town, and our lives in it, were dominated by the college. All the pleasures of the flesh were denied or decried.[16]

Young Robert found the surrounding countryside wholly unprepossessing, "the hottest, coldest, wettest, flattest part of the state of Ohio, so uninteresting and disagreeable that Plum Creek, the arboretum, the reservoir, and even the cemetery seemed like scenic gems set in a dull setting of yellow mud.''[17] But this was part of a conscious, if not divine, design. Love described Oberlin's genesis:

> The pious founders of the colony in 1833 had deliberately chosen a heavily wooded swamp site in order to insure the opportunity of building from the bottom, physically and socially. They had found cheap land, so unattractive that it had not drawn earlier settlers who might perhaps have had divergent social and religious views, and there they had "raised their Ebenezer," confident that Providence would either lift them out of the mud in due season or teach them to live with it.[18]

In response to its straitlaced code of personal conduct, Oberlin became a center of reformist political thought and action. Its founders were uncompromising abolitionists who in pre–Civil War days outraged southern Ohio's "copperhead" gentry by making the town a stop on the underground railway that smuggled refugee slaves north to Canada. Oberlin College was the first in the country to admit black students and, a few years later, women, making it a center of suffragette protest. Late in the century the Anti-Saloon League was founded there. Although rigorous academic standards were maintained, in the years before World War I the institution was characterized by one of its admirers as "more a cause than a college."[19]

Oberlin's motto was "learning and labor," and it applied even to those as young as Robert. At the age of eight he landed a part-time job as an apprentice in the print shop of a local weekly, but when his curiosity was aroused by a form of Greek type all set up to print, he managed to pi it — thereby abruptly terminating a journalistic career that paid him four dollars a week. He mowed lawns, carried a paper route, and tried his hand at door-to-door salesmanship, peddling a patent retractable clothesline without notable success.

With it all he established a scholastic record at the Woodland Avenue public school that enabled him to skip the seventh grade. He maintained his academic pace when he entered secondary school at Oberlin Academy, operated by the College to prepare faculty children and their more fortunate neighbors for higher education. His grades never fell below 4.5 out of a possible 5, except in geometry, algebra, and physics — and only in physics did he dip below 4, to 3.8. Hutchins had an explanation for this comparative lapse when he recalled his school days many years later:

My father happened to remark to me that he never liked mathematics. Since I admired my father very much, it became a point of honor with me not to like mathematics either. I finally squeezed through Solid Geometry. But when, at the age of sixteen, I entered Oberlin College, I found that the authorities felt that one hard course was all anybody ought to be asked to carry. You could take either mathematics or Greek. Of course if you took Greek you were allowed to drop Latin. I did not hesitate a moment. Languages were pie for me. It would have been unfilial to take mathematics. I took Greek, and have never seen a mathematics book since. I have been permitted to glory in the possession of an unmathematical mind.

My scientific attainments were of the same order. I had a course in physics in prep school. Every Oberlin student had to take one course in everything — everything that is except Greek and mathematics. After I had blown up all the retorts in the chemistry laboratory doing the Marsh test for arsenic, the chemistry teacher was glad to give me a passing grade and let me go.[20]

He had, and obviously enjoyed, a full extracurricular career at the Academy. *Etean,* the senior yearbook, listed him as captain and manager of class basketball teams, president of the athletic association, manager of the football team, captain of the debate team, and commencement orator. The yearbook appended this description to his class picture: " 'Bob' is energetic, genial and has been a member of the class of '15 for four years. These taken together made him very popular and, as is evidenced by the honors heaped upon him, he makes an admirable public servant. . . . He is a logical reasoner and persuasive orator. 'Here was a Caesar, when comes there such another?' "

In Robert Hutchins's personal papers there is a neatly typed poem he later titled "An Early Treatise on Education." It was written the year he graduated from Oberlin Academy and entered the College. He satirized this rite of passage in the kind of lighthearted verse he continued to dash off for the private amusement of his friends:

> *In Oberlin, I must not smoke.*
> *I don't.*
> *Nor listen to a naughty joke.*
> *I don't.*
> *To flirt, to dance is very wrong,*
> *Wild youths choose women, wine and song.*

> *I don't.*
> *I kiss no girls, not even one,*
> *Why I don't know how it's done.*
> *You wouldn't think I'd have much fun.*
> *I don't.*[21]

In fact he had a great deal. Most of those who replied to a circular letter sent to Oberlin alumni of the classes of '18 and '19 recalled not only Hutchins's academic prowess and leadership roles but his mischievous spirit.[22] Several were convinced that he was the one who in the dead of night had adorned campus landmarks with the class initials, a crime he confessed to years later when he addressed Oberlin alumni in New York and recalled that he "had climbed the smokestack carrying paint, had agitated against the smoking rule, and had successfully striven to make himself a general nuisance to the dean and faculty."[23]

Margaret Rice Egeland had no doubt that he was responsible for the alarm clocks planted in the chapel balcony and timed to go off in the middle of a speech by the eminent English suffragette Emmeline Pankhurst. Susan B. Taylor recalled that the girls in the soprano section of the Second Congregational Church choir had a clear view of the baritone section: "There good-looking Bob Hutchins often appeared to be 'up to something' other than serious singing — frisky and having a good time." For Thomas E. Rea, his classmate's presumed attraction for coeds was affirmed when he went to his first class reunion in 1920 and saw "a notice in the *Oberlin Review* to the effect that all girls formerly engaged to Bob Hutchins were to meet in Finney Chapel, which has a seating capacity of 1,900."

Then there was the Great Oberlin Auto Heist, as the *Cleveland Plain Dealer* termed it when it published a reminiscence by its editor, Nathaniel Howard, another preacher's son and town boy in the class of '19. The auto, a handsome red Winton touring car, was the pride and joy of Thomas W. Henderson, a Scot with a handlebar mustache and a mighty temper who regularly attended evening prayer meeting at Second Congregational, leaving the Winton nearby with the keys in the ignition.

"Bob Hutchins and the rest of us would jump in and go for a joyride," Howard said, "and of course our joyrides were a well-kept secret known only to the entire student body of Oberlin College." The Winton was always put back in place well before prayer meeting ended, until one fateful night when it ran out of gas on a muddy road outside of town. Howard recalled that placards went up offering a $150 reward for information leading to apprehension of the thieves:

Bob Hutchins came over to me and said he knew a few Oberlin students who would do anything for $150. I agreed and endorsed his suggestion that we make a clean breast of it to Mr. Henderson himself. And we did go to Mr. Henderson's house and Hutchins finally told him why we were there. First Mr. Henderson was hopping mad. Then he was jumping mad. It took him several minutes to get to the point where he could call the mayor over.

The mayor recommended immediate incarceration, but Henderson had cooled down and decided to try prayer. The culprits' manifestation of piety led to forgiveness: "We got down on our knees on Mr. Henderson's oriental rug and prayed with him. Twice. Three of the joyriders moved discreetly to the door. As we tried to sidle out we heard Hutch saying, 'Now Mr. Henderson, don't you agree that we have saved you $150 by confessing? Would it be possible for you to share your savings with us?' " It was no sale, but the Christian spirit prevailed and the sinners were allowed to go unpunished.[24]

As an outstanding member of the graduating class of the Academy and a familiar of the other town boys and girls, who made up a substantial portion of the College's enrollment, Hutchins was elected president of the freshman class virtually by acclamation. If this inspired him to try a career as a political boss, he met his comeuppance in his sophomore year, when he put together a slate of handpicked candidates for student office. Elisabeth Burgess Nielson recalled, "It was a rigged election. They announced the winners as the slate of Bob's henchmen, although they had not won. Mildred Blair knew this and felt it her duty to report it. She did, and the real winner took office. I am sorry to report this."

Walter K. Bailey, who in his eighties was still an active trustee of Oberlin, had no such qualms about confirming the details of the rigged election:

Bob was respected for his abilities by all in our class, but I must say the arrogance he showed in later years was evident even in 1915–16. Therefore he was not loved by all. He was so much smarter than all of us he had to have respect. . . . I know he accomplished a great deal but it always seemed to me that the arrogance of his youth, carried to adulthood, prevented him from full success. He could have been humble part of the time.

Most of the alumni who responded to the circular letter accorded Will Hutchins a full measure of the admiration that some classmates withheld from his son. Bailey wrote, "I am afraid that our great love and affection for his father (who in my opinion was one of the greatest men who ever lived) affected my feelings about Bob. Perhaps I was a bit arrogant myself and I could not compete." Rea recalled that the senior Hutchins made a two-hour Bible class seem like fifteen minutes: "W. J. Hutchins was a man who could have made Ronald Colman seem like a rank amateur. Good-looking, a splendid voice, and an AAA1 communicator."

Oberlin's moral code gave rise to an entrenched prejudice against pomp and ceremony. It rained on the night of a reception in honor of Henry Churchill King, the distinguished dean of the Seminary who had just been elected president of the College. In view of the weather King suggested calling a hack, but Mrs. King said, "No, we have always walked into town, and it would seem sheer ostentation to ride tonight." And there were those at the affair who objected to the presentation of a bouquet of roses to Mrs. King on the ground that cut flowers out of season were an unjustified extravagance. The faculty voted 17 to 15 against wearing caps and gowns in the inaugural parade, and King said approvingly, "We must remember the significance of the ceremony. We must keep it from degenerating into mere show."[25]

But the doctrinal rigors of the Calvinist faith were significantly tempered during King's administration, and the liberating effect on the faculty was profound. In the 1900s the denominational colleges were having their own civil war, Love wrote, "and the *Uncle Tom's Cabin* of that struggle was Charles Darwin's *Origin of the Species*."[26] King, described by F. H. Foster in a 1939 study as "a great theologian, certainly the greatest of the developing Liberal movement," was one of those who found it possible to equate evolution with the biblical version of creation. "He had been the first in the New England succession to put the principle of love, presented in a new phrasing as 'reverence for personality,' into application in well nigh the whole range of theology."[27]

By the time the class of '19 was enrolled, King had developed "a program in the training of youth, not for specific occupations, but for living in a free society and for functioning as serviceable members of that society because they had first developed within themselves the absolute best of which they were capable."[28] This concept made an indelible impression on Robert Hutchins, one that would color his thinking when he embarked upon his own career as an educator.

When Hutchins returned to Oberlin in 1934 to deliver the commencement address, the denominational ties had been loosened and the rules of personal conduct had been relaxed, though they remained stringent by comparison with those of contemporary institutions. Oberlin, he noted, was now more college than cause, but he chose to pay tribute to it as it had been in his undergraduate days. His device for doing so was to assume the role of "The Sentimental Alumnus," as he titled his speech. It was a characteristically ironic touch for one who prided himself on his lack of sentimentality. Like all old grads, he said, he saw his alma mater as a mirage, fixed in time:

> For me the campus still has two little red brick buildings crumbling away on its corners. For me there is no retiring age for members of the staff, nor any new appointments. For me the class of 1919 never went to war and never graduated. This static, beautiful Oberlin wherein my friends and I are forever young and forever friends deprives me of the powers of reason and leaves me the powers of recollection. . . .
>
> I must also admit that there have vanished from my mirage the things I wish to omit from it. With a struggle I can remember aspects of the Oberlin of my time which are no longer part of it to me. . . . I can remember sitting every day in this room on the most uncomfortable of chapel seats trying hard not to hear what the speaker was saying. I can remember the dancing rule, the rule confining ladies to their rooms at earlier and earlier hours in inverse proportion to the time they had spent in college, and the smoking rule, which I abhorred but was not robust enough to violate.
>
> But these items do not disturb me very much. On the contrary they help me preserve my illusions of the uniqueness of the Oberlin of my day. It assists me in this view to believe that my college had the worst climate, the hardest seats, and the silliest rules of any institution in the world. . . .[29]

On reflection Hutchins concluded that the unfavorable items were another manifestation of the uncompromising independence of an institution that cared nothing for money or fame. The spirit of Oberlin set it so far apart from the general run of American colleges that its conventions were unconventional. It was assumed that anyone who did not abide by the rules would leave, voluntarily or otherwise, and he could recall no departure from this attitude. When a professor's son was caught smoking, he was summarily expelled, and the community agreed that the only thing for that boy to do was join the Navy. In a place where students who were working their way through school enjoyed an elevated social standing, the tone of the College was set by those to whom education meant opportunity rather than ritual.[30] Hutchins concluded his commencement address:

> We acquired from Oberlin's independence not only habits of work and respect for work but a love of the true and beautiful. We also absorbed the reforming spirit which is merely another aspect of independence. . . . Today one cannot associate with a group of Oberlin alumni without being struck by the fact that, far from accepting the world, they are trying to improve it. . . .
>
> Any friend of any college should say to it, "The Kingdom of Heaven is within you." Oberlin did not need to have it said. Intent on doing better teaching, it gave us the best teaching I have seen or experienced anywhere. With all allowances for the enthusiasm of youth and the devotion I feel to Oberlin, it seems to me that it had attained at that time that serenity which comes from clarity of purpose and the certainty of its accomplishment. In that scene of turmoil which was American education, it knew where it was going and why.[31]

Robert Hutchins was to spend the rest of his life endeavoring to establish a similar pattern at the institutions he headed.

CHAPTER TWO

———

"Over There,
Over There . . ."

T he Oberlin of Robert Hutchins's undergraduate years was a place where "the outside world existed but it was definitely outside and it could wait. A polite interest was about all that students were required or expected to show in public affairs."[1] In the early years of the First World War, Woodrow Wilson's pledge of neutrality was generally approved of on the campus, but by 1916 President King had concluded, as Wilson himself was soon to do, that the United States had a moral duty to enter the war on the side of the Allies.

There was, of course, some dissent from King's view. A Puritan stronghold was not likely to contain many outright pacifists, but there were some who were not convinced that a collision between European colonial powers constituted a just war. The debate, such as it was, became abstract when the United States declared war on Germany in April 1917. The reality came home to Oberlin with passage of the Selective Service Act, authorizing conscription to fill the ranks of the two-million-man expeditionary force being organized to support the embattled Allies.

There were some among the students for whom the prospect of combat service posed a problem of conscience. Hutchins's bosom friend Thornton Wilder was one of these. He could not bear the thought of killing another human being, he said. In the end he volunteered for the coast artillery, telling Hutchins that at least he probably wouldn't be able to see the people he was shooting at.

None of these issues touched Hutchins. He was one of the innocents, he recalled, who looked upon the war "as a chance to travel, see the world, and vary the monotony of our daily lives, and do it in the aura of patriotism."[2] Conscientious objectors were accommodated, in part at least, by the organization of an Oberlin unit of the US Army Ambulance Corps, which meant that volunteers would not be required to bear arms. But this had no bearing on Hutchins's decision to join it when his eighteenth birthday made him eligible for military service.

Physically he had departed from the mold of the male members of his family, who were of average height or less. In his teens he had grown past six feet and had developed a robust physique to go with his impatient temperament. Will Hutchins regarded him as a biological sport. "Neither your father nor your mother could ever claim the strength which is yours by some gift of some remote ancestor, even back of Isaac Hutchins," he wrote.[3] And this tall young man was ready and anxious to go to war. He assumed, he said, that he would be issued a box lunch and a change of underwear and be dispatched forthwith to the thick of the fighting.

In September Robert and his brother William received word that there were vacancies for them in the Oberlin unit, which was already in training at Allentown, Pennsylvania. They quite reasonably assumed that their decision to volunteer would be approved by their father, who had already enlisted for service befitting a man of his age and calling. When they entrained for Allentown they sent a telegram to Will Hutchins at Camp Sheridan in Alabama, where he was stationed as a field representative of the Young Men's Christian Association. The wire apparently went astray, and by the time he learned from his sons that they had enlisted, Will had already received a message from *his* father, Grosvenor, warning that the boys were too young and naive to be exposed to the sinful temptations of army life.

"When I got your telegram I thought it certain that the boys would wire me before they took final action," Will replied. "They had never failed to consult me in previous emergencies; but this time when it is a question of physical and moral life and death for them they do not even ask my advice. It has been to me incomprehensible." This, however, may have been a case of the junior parent placating the senior, for he also said, "I am not going to give them anything but cheer and courage and hope."[4]

Will dispatched a conciliatory letter addressed to "Bobs," telling him he need not bother about parental feelings of disapproval: "If we have a big fight you will want to be in it."[5] Robert replied in kind:

We certainly would not have enlisted if we had thought that you would not like it. I went because I felt that although I am not 21, I might as well be, as far as appearance and place in school are concerned. I figured that if I did not go in now, next spring I should feel compelled to go in, and in the artillery, more disagreeable work and with a crowd I did not know or like particularly.[6]

The two late arrivals at Allentown had been assigned to a casual unit, along with other new recruits and those being punished or awaiting discharge. They would receive their introductory training there before being transferred to the Oberlin unit. "At present, I am absolutely sore, discontented and mad," Robert told his father. "The officers are doctors and know no soldiering. Hence your son is a drill sergeant." Despite these discontents, however, he firmly rejected the suggestion that Will might write to the camp commandant and urge that his sons be granted deferments so they could continue their education.[7]

In his new assignment Robert, as usual, excelled — so much so his commanding officer offered to promote him to first sergeant if he would stay with the casuals. He was not tempted; these bunkmates hardly inspired in him a desire to establish a closer relationship. He sympathized with his father's effort to spread the gospel among such men. "There isn't much applied religion in this camp," he wrote, reporting an overheard conversation: " 'Hell, you'll go to church this morning and tonight you'll be down at the prophylactic tent.' " But, he asserted, sin arose from ignorance, and these sinners were "as good-hearted and as fine a bunch to work with as you could find."[8]

His letters to his mother in Oberlin were sanitized discussions of camp routine coupled with requests for knitted socks, toilet soap, and the like. But those to his father were replete with reassurances that he was successfully avoiding temptation. After a home leave he told of attending a talk by Sergeant Arthur Guy Empey, an author whose *Over the Top* was used by the Army as a combination morale builder and recruiting manual. The language the sergeant used in soliciting funds for the YMCA appalled Private Hutchins: "I wouldn't have said those things to my mother or sister, much less to a chapel audience." And when young couples paired off for a waltz at an evening entertainment, he primly told his hostess, "I do not dance."[9]

The elder Hutchins's concern for his boy's immortal soul had prompted him to urge Robert to adopt "four standards" — to avoid profanity, liquor, tobacco, and the company of loose women. Robert wrote that his experience with the casuals, who smoked or chewed incessantly and indulged in vile conversation, had served "to disgust me, and not to induce me to do likewise." And now he was among his own kind in the Oberlin unit. Some of these swore occasionally, and about half smoked, but "they do not bother with the numerous women of Allentown, and are about the cleanest crowd I have seen. Therefore, I hereby make the four promises you mentioned."[10]

The Hutchins boys and their Oberlin compatriots were anxious to get overseas, but this was not so much a matter of rampant patriotism as an understandable desire to escape the drudgery and discomfort of their makeshift camp. When he recalled his Allentown experience in later years, Hutchins cast it in terms of burlesque. The miscast officers compounded the inherent inefficiency of a jumped-up citizens' army, and some of them coupled their ineptness with pomposity.

All this was summed up for Robert when he emerged from his tent one morning to gaze upon a mustachioed figure approaching across the muddy parade ground, resplendent in Sam Browne belt, fawn riding breeches, and glistening boots. When he was confronted with a peremptory demand for a salute, Private Hutchins recognized that he was facing none other than Captain Adolphe Menjou, the renowned dude of stage and screen.

There were no ambulances to train with, and not enough vehicles of any kind to permit most trainees to learn to drive, still a rare skill in those days. So their time was taken up with basic infantry training — seemingly endless close-order drill and irrelevant field exercises — and carpentry work on the temporary barracks that converted the bare Allentown Fairgrounds into an army base.

In June 1918 the Oberlin unit embarked for Genoa, where it became Battalion IV, US Ambulance Service, a part of the American expeditionary force assigned to the Italian Army. For another two months the would-be soldiers languished in rear areas, but at least there were sights to see. For Hutchins it provided an opportunity to employ his remarkable facility with foreign languages. His letters home, now usually addressed "Dear Family," were duly purged of the salty observations he included when writing directly to his father.

In July he reported long hikes on the beach, visits to nearby cathedrals, and a birthday dinner for William at an elegant restaurant, where their appetites were not affected by the haughty stares the two enlisted men drew from Italian generals, British naval officers, and their own colonel. Robert was reading the French daily *Le Matin*, "rather easily," had begun translating a story by Pierre Loti, and was a quarter of the way through Pascal's *Reflections*. He was also putting out a unit newspaper "in which will appear two or three risqué rhymes by Hutchins."[11] Unfortunately no specimens of his literary handiwork have survived.

On August 6, in a letter headed "Somewhere else in Italy," he wrote, "We are no longer with the main bunch at Port of Debarkation, but at a temporary base a good many miles from action. Tomorrow will bring us closer to said much-desired action."[12] On the move forward he had parted company with William, who had been assigned to a different unit and would later be transferred to France. His detachment, Section 587, put in at a base camp at Castel Cucco, two and a half miles from the front, and "we are all hoping for a big drive so that everybody can see a little action."[13]

Robert went up to observe Italian army positions on Mount Pallone and Mount Grappa, overlooking the front held by entrenched Austrian troops. All was quiet his first time out, but he came under heavy bombardment on a second trip to the mountain stronghold. "Saw some of the war, which is well worth seeing," he reported, "but it was an awful climb."[14]

In the following weeks the ambulance unit began its active service, shifting from position to position behind the lines, evacuating Italian wounded to base hospitals. This was what he had come to Italy for, and in Hutchins's letters home he treated the experience lightly until October 23, when massed Allied forces attacked on a front extending from Venice to Asiago. In this final campaign on the Italian front, the initial drive across the Piave River required the capture of rugged Mount Spinoncia, across the valley from Mount Tomba. The two-man ambulance crew of Hutchins and Arthur "Stump" Limbach was part of the evacuation unit ordered to Caniezza, where they were stationed a hundred yards behind the lines. He described the scene:

> The return of excellent weather, an interesting change in base, and an increase in work, make almost every prospect pleasing. . . . Stump and I made our fourth trip through the winding, rock-bound trenches up to the first line last night to observe the progress of affairs by moonlight. All the valley was aflame; all along the line we could see the guns firing and the shells bursting. A great many star shells are used here; they are very pretty, but they make you crouch down in the trench, and wonder whether the Austrians saw you.[15]

But the nineteen-year-old Hutchins was beginning to acquire a soldier's appreciation of the significance as well as the beauty of the terrain. What he saw from the forward positions convinced him that he would hate to be an infantryman, and he paid tribute to "the brave Italians who made trip after trip down into the valley to attack Spinoncia, but were driven back each time by concentrated machinegun fire." Some of those who dragged themselves back up Mount Tomba died in Hutchins's ambulance before they reached the foot of the mountain.

It's this lack of desirable flatness that makes the ambulance man's life on the Italian front one of sorrow and weariness. We have to come all the way up this mountain in low, and it takes an hour to do it. The road zigzags, of course, and it's necessary to back and fill a good many times to get around all the angles. Then take too this lightless business, a high wall on one side and a drop into eternity on the other, a rainy night, and a road just right for skidding, and no light because the Austrians might shoot you if the guards don't. As Mr. Cowdery has so often said, "It's a hard life, and few of us get out of it alive."[16]

For Hutchins and Limbach, the driver, the new offensive meant a day-and-night shuttle up and down the mountain, with the road now under heavy Austrian artillery fire. They subsisted on salmon eaten straight from the can, and Hutchins later claimed that the Italian War Cross he was awarded recognized his valor in staying with this diet until it finally poisoned him. "The work on Tomba ruined me," he wrote, "and after four days I went to bed for two."[17]

Reports that the Austrians were pulling back all along the broad front resuscitated him, and he "hopped on Limbach's car and we went still closer to the enemy's retreating rear." They came upon villages and towns that had been literally shot to pieces, and they were put to work evacuating large numbers of wounded Austrians, who, Hutchins reported, were treated very well:

The signs of a hasty exit were evident everywhere. Every retiring Austrian threw his helmet away, and the result was that the unwieldy things were lying around like Old Man Cadmus' celebrated dragon's teeth. Dead Austrians and dead horses lay along the early part of the road in large numbers, but as we went along we could see that only the slightest resistance had been offered and there were no more dead lying along the road.[18]

By now any romantic notions he may have brought with him to Italy had been eroded by his experience under fire. In those closing days of the campaign, his letters were studded with sardonic observations of the kind given immortality in the next world war by cartoonist Bill Mauldin's footslogging dogfaces Joe and Willie.

As the Allied forces closed in on the remnants of the Austrian army, its rear guard began surrendering in droves, and Hutchins noted that these prisoners "looked about the same as Italians. But that's heresy." And he took note of the traffic that began to pass the ambulance on its way to the front: "King Victor Emmanuel sailed past us on our way up there. All the other generals did. By this time the danger was over, so they could come up." A letter announcing that censorship had been lifted in the wake of the armistice was headed, "Base Hospital 102, Vicenza, With the Wop Army."[19]

On November 17 Hutchins wrote from Vicenza, where he was himself a patient. His disillusionment with his military service and his jaundiced view of his Italian comrades now colored all his letters home:

> The weather is rather rotten in these parts now and the doctor won't let me out of bed, even to walk around the hospital, for fear I'll catch cold. I was liking this hospital very well until yesterday. They filled up our half-empty ward with Italians in the recovering stage. They have been hollering around ever since. Individually, the Italians are *the* people I shall avoid most after the war. You have to admire their collective bravery when things are going their way, but as persons they are *rotten,* that's all. They have no sense of decency and they will steal your gold teeth in your sleep.[20]

He did not encounter anything remotely resembling the romance that Ernest Hemingway's fictional hero enjoyed at a similar base hospital. During the five months that dragged by before the Oberlin unit sailed for home, he seems to have found no solace in the opportunity to explore historic surroundings and absorb the first foreign culture he had ever known. There was no longer any trace of the ebullience that had marked his embarkation upon what he thought would be a high adventure, and he would never indulge in such romanticism again.

He even risked offending his revered father by indignantly rejecting what was apparently an effort to arrange a more congenial assignment: "If any more YMCA boobs call up and want my address please tell them I am in Russia, or Africa, or at the North Pole, or anywhere. I don't like

YMCA work and I don't like foreign countries. I wouldn't stay over here another minute if I could beat it."[21]

It was April before the Oberlin unit disembarked at New York, and PFC Robert Hutchins ended his service with an honorable discharge issued at Camp Dix. The first family member to greet the returning hero was Uncle Frank, the New York lawyer, who reported to his brother Will that his son was in splendid shape, adding, "I think Robert rather regrets that he did not get into more active service, and is envious of the boys who were continuously in the trenches."[22]

If Hutchins ever heard of his uncle's unlikely impression, it seems probable that he simply ignored it. Once it was behind him, he rarely talked about his wartime experience, and when he did he treated war in general, and the Italian campaign in particular, as a kind of theater of the absurd.

The net effect of his combat service, he said, was to make him as much of a pacifist as he ever managed to become, but his reaction seemed to be not so much one of moral outrage as one of resentment over the waste, including most particularly that of his own time: "The First World War was probably one of the most futile exercises in history. The United States Army was a laughable affair in any point of view in which I could see it, and the role we played in it was of no importance to anybody."[23]

It was not the horror of the human suffering he had seen that stuck in his memory, but the pointless training at Allentown and the footless wait for a ship to take him home from Italy. Toward the end of World War II, in a speech to the students at the Asheville School, where his brother William served as headmaster, he indulged in bitter irony as he noted that many of the young men in his audience would soon be "entering upon the career of heroes":

Now my brother and I were heroes once. I know we were because on the day we arrived in this country from the Italian front twenty-five years ago, the *New York Times* said, without mentioning our names, that our heroes were returning, and added that we had been burnished in the white heat of sacrifice. This last clause makes me think that perhaps it was a case of mistaken identity after all. Perhaps the *Times* was not talking about me, but only about my brother. I knew that he had committed sacrifices of the burnishing type; but as for me, all I could remember was a white heat of dislike for all officers, commissioned or noncommissioned, and sacrifices of the order required by living with my brother and two other boys in a pen formerly occupied by one prize hog at the fairgrounds in Allentown, Pennsylvania; by being placed under arrest at a time when the rest of the outfit was celebrating my brother's birthday; and by eating a can of salmon for breakfast in Italy when there wasn't anything else. These were sacrifices, all right; but I have never been able to figure out where the burnishing came in, or what polish my mind and character received. . . .

The real horrors of war can never be told, never described, and never adequately felt by anybody to whom they are set forth. How can you describe dreadful, consuming monotony and boredom? The intellectual equipment of our outfit, as I remember it, consisted of several decks of cards and a lot of Gilbert and Sullivan records. Since I had allotted home all my pay, nobody would play cards with me; and after we had been six months overseas I confidently expected to be carried off to the nearest insane asylum because I couldn't make up my mind whether I was the captain of the Pinafore, a wandering minstrel, or three little girls of Japan.[24]

From the beginning of his service the allotment from his monthly pay had been assigned to his mother, with instructions that it was to be held to help meet his expenses at Yale, where, it had been decided, he would join his brother William when they were discharged. Once he was home, his distemper disappeared as he began to contemplate the possibilities of life at New Haven, sensing that at least it would be markedly different from anything he had known before, at home or abroad.

CHAPTER THREE

"Bright College Years, with Pleasure Rife . . ."

When Robert Hutchins enrolled as a junior at Yale in 1919, he had a new home address. His father, Will, was preparing to move on from Oberlin to assume new duties as president of Berea College in Kentucky, a natural enough transition since Berea too was a Puritan island. The New Englanders who in 1855 founded the institution on a Cumberland mountain ridge overlooking the bluegrass country went there with the idea of providing schooling for blacks. When this proved impermissible in a slaveholding commonwealth, they amended their mission to provide a Christian education for the whites of benighted Appalachia. True to their abolitionist faith, when the end of the Civil War brought emancipation, they promptly admitted black students.

From the beginning Berea was a self-help institution, designing its curricula to meet the special needs of children for whom schooling of any kind was usually unavailable. The campus embraced five schools when Will Hutchins took over — the college, with an enrollment of 217; a normal school, with 457; a vocational school, with 487; two secondary academies, with a total of 615; and a "foundation" school, with 638. Relying primarily on northern philanthropy, Berea charged no tuition, and all students were required to earn their keep.

His immediate predecessor, William Goodell Frost, thought that Berea had carried out its historic mission by providing an overlay of book learning while improving the vocational skills of the mountaineers. He said of the foundation school's winter term, which was arranged to attract farm workers during the lay-by season, "One winter is enough for a boy to be converted, buy a Bible and a dictionary, and go home with a new start in culture like that imparted by a trip to Europe!"[1]

The new president set out to reorganize the campus into an upper and lower school, with increased emphasis on liberal arts at the college level. This touched off a faculty protest, with President Emeritus Frost later charging his successor with a lack of interest "in any forms of education except those he has himself been through."[2] Will Hutchins finally succeeded in upgrading Berea's educational offerings, but it could not be said that he failed to honor the tradition of service to the disadvantaged, which he accepted as an obligation of his Christian faith.

After nineteen years of the senior Hutchins's administration, and another twenty-eight years under his son Francis, who succeeded him, the college literature defined Berea's mission as "providing a high-quality liberal arts education at low cost within the context of the Christian faith. . . . Berea also is probably the only college in the U.S. which turns away otherwise qualified students because they don't have financial need."[3] The Calvinist ethos continued to dominate the campus and its environs; in the 1980s the township was still one of the few in Kentucky to scorn the state's pride in its traditional bourbon whiskey and exercise its local option to ban the sale of all alcoholic beverages.

Robert Hutchins saw little of the remote mountain enclave dominated by the college and its adjunct Union Church, where his father often filled the pulpit, having let it be known that he expected to see members of the faculty in the pews. Robert no doubt fully sympathized with the paternal effort at educational reform, which in many ways presaged his own in later years. But he was absorbed in making his way in the sharply contrasting atmosphere of New Haven.

His father's precepts, however, continued to influence him, as they would all his life. "As a man looks through a preacher's eyes at the life of our times, there seems at first much to dishearten him," Will Hutchins said in one of his sermons. "We turn back with envy to the great days of the Puritans, when men actually went to church."[4] At twenty, Robert also saw much to dishearten him, and worldly though he was rapidly becoming, his Puritan heritage survived his ultimate drift away from the formal doctrines of the Presbyterian faith.

Following in his father's footsteps, he became an accomplished public speaker, and though he was never to don a preacher's robes, his style took much from the homiletics that Will Hutchins taught. His father eschewed the bombast and sentimentality that marked so much of the preaching of his day. He once told a gathering of young Calvinist ministers:

> If preaching could have been killed, it would have been killed long ago by the thousands of imbecile sermons that have poured forth from countless pulpits throughout the ages of the church. A keen observer has said that in no country whatever is a genius for public speaking a more useful and commanding endowment than in America. Men do not like to listen to dullards, but men still delight to listen to a man who utters truth through personality.[5]

Will Hutchins taught his students and, by example, his son to "become familiar with the fine brotherhood of men of letters. All truth, wherever learned, used to be, and will once more become 'the property of men of thought throughout the world.' "[6] And he warned against undue solemnity: "The laughter which laughs never at people, but with people, helps to carry a strong man's message to men."[7]

His influence could be seen in the oratory that enabled young Robert to become a big man on campus at Yale. He displayed his usual academic prowess but tempered it with a personal charm that effectively disassociated him from the bookish grinds scorned by those who set the social pace. And he managed this in spite of the fact that he had to maintain himself with jobs as menial and time-consuming as those endured by the students at Berea.

His scholastic record at Oberlin and his father's status as a distinguished alumnus insured his admission to the venerable institution but carried no adequate financial entitlement. At first he made out by washing dishes and working in an ice-cream-spoon factory, while a job as an assistant house steward enabled him to join a social fraternity, Alpha Delta Phi. But this was to be his last experience with physical labor; by the end of his junior year he had established a cooperative tutoring service for backward students, whose fees were enough to keep him afloat.

Robert's abilities as a public speaker were quickly recognized, and he was given ample opportunity to hone them. He was captain of the debating team, and he delighted Will Hutchins by winning the DeForest oratory medal, as his father had done before him. Appropriately, there was a parental salute in the prize speech, titled "Our Contemporary Ancestors," which, without naming Will, praised the missionary work being done at Berea and appealed for its support.

The backward mountaineers of the southern highlands, Robert contended, were not degenerates but survivals — their bloodlines and mores were those of the English and Scotch-Irish pioneers so revered in contemporary America. Now the isolation that had preserved their preindustrial culture was breaking down, and they were in danger of being swept unprepared into the slums of the nation's great cities:

> How will the mountaineers meet this civilization whose forerun ners are now among them? The answer depends on us. Shall we allow them to disappear like the American Indian before the rush of modern life? Four times these mountain people have risen to our aid in wars for liberty. Forgetful of our debt to them, shall we, whose educations have been thrust upon us, give no thought to these Americans struggling to achieve theirs? Our path to learning has been made smooth and easy; theirs is blocked by obstacles we alone can remove. . . . Give them the opportunities they crave, and we shall yet impart to these ancient Americans the ideals of today's America. We shall yet make the mountains "a good place to be born in"; we shall emancipate five million people.[8]

As in all the thousands of public addresses he would deliver over the years, there was implicit in this early effort an affirmation of the Puritan belief that America had been conceived as a shining city on a hill and might yet achieve its lofty ideals if those who enjoyed the benefits of a democratic society also accepted its obligations. And as he would do all his life, Hutchins emphasized that education was the means to that end.

This hortatory address, designed to meet the solemn demands of the DeForest contest, is wholly devoid of the ironic humor that was to become the hallmark of Hutchins's platform manner. That quality, however, was in full flower a few months later when he was dispatched to address New Haven's Yale alumni chapter as a representative of the student body.

Despite the traditional conflict between Town and Gown, he proclaimed, burgeoning cultural interests had brought the two camps together. This was manifest when a lecture by the visiting English author John Galsworthy drew an overflow audience of local matrons and aspiring undergraduates, necessitating a last-minute change of halls:

> Eager students leapfrogged over the heads of their townie rivals to get out of Sprague and into Woolsey. Their townie rivals used hatpins and knitting needles to beat the horrid Yale boys to it. The students were determined that nobody should deprive them of this short (and free) cut to culture; the ladies were positive that nobody should prevent them from saying that they had seen John

Galsworthy. . . . At the end, undaunted by a supremely dull lecture, the undergraduates stormed the platform to beseech the autograph of Mr. Galsworthy. One hour later Mr. Galsworthy was carried from the hall in a half-fainting condition, but what is that to Those Who Wish to Be Literary?[9]

But his primary mission was to refute the charges of moral turpitude brought against the student body by the New Haven Civic League. The allegations of debauchery in the fraternity houses were greatly exaggerated, he said, and such lapses as had occurred had been corrected: "The Prom this year was almost mid-Victorian in its primness; the Sheff fraternities, it would seem, have been undergoing a sort of spiritual regeneration. . . . To the Civic League we might almost say, 'Take first the beam out of thine own eye,' suggesting that before the organization cleans up Yale it clean up New Haven." He illustrated that necessity with an anecdote he was to use repeatedly when addressing other alumni groups:

> I remember my own introduction to your fair city. I wandered in from the untutored and unsophisticated west one bleak September, and followed the crowd from the railroad station to Chapel Street. When I arrived at Malley's Department Store I received a shock from which I have never recovered. There was a large window full of all kinds of lacy, frilled garments. They were garments of which I do not know the names. They were not outer garments; they were not masculine garments. The window was full of them, and there in the center of it all was a huge sign saying, WELCOME, MEN OF YALE! Now I ask you, if that is the attitude of New Haven, what can you expect of the men of Yale?

> > *New Haven is not safe, I'm sure,*
> > *For youth of minds refined and pure.*
> > *How can it be, when such signs greet*
> > *The modest eye on Chapel Street?*[10]

In addition to this lapse into doggerel, he indulged his lifelong weakness for puns. The usual bickering among the undergraduates had subsided, he proclaimed, and the true-blue Yale spirit had been restored with the advent of spring, the triumphant season of the varsity baseball team, and the arrival of a new president: "Dr. Angell has come and conquered. In a single address the president-elect won the confidence and support of every undergraduate. Today at Yale we have enthusiasm instead of criticism. We have almost what Mr. Harding would call 'Apple Blossom Time in Normalcy.' ''[11]

The speech's success was to be attested in the most tangible way. A year and a half later James Rowland Angell brought Robert back to New Haven as secretary of the Yale Corporation, and among his duties was that of maintaining a fruitful liaison with the university's alumni chapters.

In later years Hutchins quoted a line from Yale's alma mater, "Bright college years, with pleasure rife," with an ironic addendum: "— if you could afford it." Impecunious though he was, however, his intelligence, wit, and extraordinary energy made it possible for him to enjoy most of the pleasures that brightened the undergraduate years for his affluent classmates.

His social status was certified by his election to Wolf's Head, a top-drawer senior honor society. "As an undergraduate I was one of the lower orders — a member of the debating team and even of Phi Beta Kappa," he attested in an address to the society when he returned as secretary to the Corporation. "From my position in the social gutter Wolf's Head raised me." But as he did at every opportunity, he went on to remind the brethren that he was an exception that proved the rule:

> As a self-supporting student of Yale College I took more or less trouble to measure the opportunities and the difficulties of those of us who had not been born with anything like a silver spoon in our mouths. . . . We could by special effort in our studies, or by the special interest of our friends, acquire certain scholarships. . . . These, however, had to be supplemented in almost every case by a large amount of unintellectual work which brought us very meager returns and which consumed in my own case six hours a day. . . . By the very fact that we were forced to devote ourselves to the business of earning a living we were compelled to restrict our extracurriculum activities so that nobody knew us or knew what we could do. It is idle for me to tell you that under these circumstances there was developed in my class a group of men variously known as the Arabs, the Chinese and the unwashed, that they were men for whom the ordinary avenues of advancement at Yale were absolutely closed, and yet there were men, many of them I have no doubt, whom the Class of 1921 will delight to honor in not less than ten years' time.[12]

He pointedly reminded the young gentlemen of Wolf's Head that a college true to its professed educational ideals had no place for social distinctions based on financial resources. An honor society, he contended, was hardly worthy of its designation unless it sought to eliminate, rather than enshrine, this invidious stratification.

Although they could hardly be classified as unwashed, some of his talented classmates of limited means were among Robert's closest friends. Three of these were, like him, endowed with fathers who had gone forth from Yale to make their way in respected but ill-paying professions. Within the ten years postulated by Robert in his Wolf's Head admonition, all three had found a place among those whom the class of 1921 was delighted to honor: Henry Luce, son of a Presbyterian missionary to China, had launched *Time* and was on his way to becoming the most influential journalist of his day; William Benton, whose father left the pulpit to become a college professor, had earned a fortune on Madison Avenue and was preparing to sell his successful advertising agency and undertake a career in public service; and Thornton Wilder, sired by a journalist-diplomat whose uncompromising devotion to the Puritan ethic put him at odds with his aesthetic son, was recognized as a leading American novelist and playwright.

Across the years all three maintained a close personal and professional relationship with Hutchins, as did a number of other Yale men who became active members of what came to be called the American Establishment. Robert recognized early that such contacts would provide the principal benefit conferred by the College. In retrospect, he wrote:

> If Oberlin's object was to perfect our moral character, Yale's was to perfect our social character, using *social* in the sense in which it appears in the phrase "high society." We went to Yale to become Yale men. Yale men could pass through portals and scale heights which others could not attain. They could do so not because of what they knew, but simply because of where they had been. . . .
>
> No Yale professor or administrator would have admitted in those days that this was a fair description of the purpose, goals or achievements of Yale University. But I was there. I became a Yale man, and I know how it was done and what the results were. The benefits flowing to me from my acquisition of this title have been considerable, and I do not underrate them. My point is that these benefits had nothing to do with any intellectual development. . . .[13]

Although he graduated with his class and received an A.B. degree summa cum laude, he abandoned the College at the end of his junior year and enrolled in the Law School. There he found the sense of dedication he had missed in an atmosphere where "courses were something you had to get through if you wanted a degree." He later described the experience:

> In that year I did all my work in the Law School, except that I had to obey a regulation of obscure origin and purpose which compelled every Yale College student working in the Law School to take one two-hour course in the College. I took a two-hour course in American Literature which came at twelve o'clock. A special advantage of this course was that the instructor, who was much in demand as a lecturer to popular audiences, often had to leave at 12:20 to make the 12:29 for New York.
>
> I see now that my formal education began in the Law School. My formal education began, that is, at the age of twenty-one. I do not mean to say that I knew then I was getting an education. I am sure the professors did not know they were giving me one. They would have been shocked at such an insinuation. They thought they were teaching me law. They did not teach me any law. But they did something far more important; they introduced me to the liberal arts.
>
> It is sad but true that the only place in an American university where the student is taught to read, write and speak is the law school. The principal, if not the sole merit, of the case method is that the student is compelled to read accurately and carefully, to state accurately and carefully the meaning of what he has read, to criticize the reasoning of opposing cases, and to write very extended examinations in which the same standards of accuracy, care, and criticism are imposed.[14]

The Law School was small and dedicated, a community where faculty and students spent all their waking hours talking about the subjects at hand. But here too there was disillusionment for one who came from a Puritan background:

> The only thing we were sure of was that we had to get high grades; without them we could not hope to enter any of the big law firms in New York. If we had been asked why we wanted to get into a big law firm in New York, we would have had to reply that we wanted to be rich and famous, or at least rich, and the road to these objects lay through a Wall Street firm.[15]

* * *

It can be assumed that Hutchins's stalwart defense of the underdog and his ridicule of the pretensions of Ivy League campus life eased the pangs of his inherited Calvinist conscience; there is nothing in the record, or in the recollections of his contemporaries, to indicate that he was beset by a sense of guilt as he assumed as much of a bon vivant's life-style as his limited means permitted. But the irreverent gaiety that marked his social manner may well have served to conceal a sense of betrayal as he indulged in worldly pleasures proscribed by his upbringing.

"Two years of irrational living in the army gave us all the bad habits we needed to conform to the ways of the world," he wrote. "As for me, after I got out of the service I went to Yale, where the bad habits I had acquired were confirmed, and a few were added."[16] Two of the four "standards" he had promised his father he would uphold had been breached while he was still in uniform; he was smoking and swearing when he arrived in New Haven. Although he generally avoided obscenity and scatology, his speech henceforth would be sprinkled with the mild profanity customary in masculine precincts, and he was never to rid himself of his addiction to tobacco. At Yale, braving the hazards of bathtub gin, he became a connoisseur of the dry martini, showing no sign that he was troubled by the fact that this violated not only his father's injunction but the law of the land.

As to his pledge not to consort with loose women, the evidence is inconclusive. It seems probable that his innate fastidiousness kept him away from the bawds of Allentown. We have his own testimony that he did not succumb to the wiles of the practiced sirens of Italy: "I discovered that there was a world far from Oberlin, Ohio, devoted to wine women and song; but I was too well brought up even to sing."[17] He didn't really escape the Oberlin influence until he got to Yale, he said. There the opportunities for dalliance were surely abundant for one who had grown up collar-ad handsome, with thick, wavy hair, chiseled features, and a cleft chin topping a lean, six-foot-two-and-a-half-inch frame upon which Ivy League clothing draped with careless grace. He was eminently qualified for the role of man about New Haven and the New York exurbs.

Hutchins was no prude, nor was he judgmental in his personal relationships. Among his choice companions were some of Yale's raunchiest undergraduates, and he found their peccadilloes amusing; as his doggerel indicated, he took delight in the comic aspects of the mating game, from flirtation to consummation. But then and later, those who knew him well found it difficult to imagine his joining in the chase or maintaining his decorum by staking out a mistress on some convenient back street.

In any case, his opportunities for playing the field were soon limited.

On a weekend visit to his uncle Frank's home on Long Island he met a tall, impetuous nineteen-year-old whose dark beauty was, in feminine contrast, the equal of his own. The beguiling Maude Phelps McVeigh, just out of finishing school, concluded that she had found Mr. Right, and she made her intentions known. As an impecunious student with a year and a half of college still ahead of him, he may have entertained reservations about the prospect of matrimony, but he didn't have it in him to argue with a lady — most particularly this one.

Early in January of his junior year Robert wrote his parents to tell them he was betrothed. It was hardly the missive of a moonstruck swain. After assuring them that this love affair was the real thing, he covered eight more pages of Biltmore Hotel stationery with a sort of lawyer's brief in which he responded point by point to anticipated objections to his marriage in light of his age and current situation. Shortly thereafter Maude wrote to Will and Anna Hutchins to tell them that she saw no reason to keep such a great love secret and that the engagement was to be announced forthwith.

"Bobs" received a prompt and heartening reply from his father, informing him that Uncle Frank had certified Maude, an orphan living with her aunt in Bay Shore, as a suitable bride; though without material dowry, she was descended from old Long Island stock on her mother's side and a proper Virginia family on her father's. Her Puritan connections included Wolcotts, Warshams, and Allyns and were, at least in her own view, superior to those of the Hutchinses. Will passed on Uncle Frank's views and added his own:

> Of course he speaks with modified enthusiasm because of your youth and lack of immediate prospects. But, as he says, neither his father, your father nor your uncles have a great deal to say on this score. He does, however, intimate at the close of his letter that "it may pass away anyhow." But he says, as far as the girl is concerned, there is nothing to be sorry about.
>
> Now, very frankly, if you have found the girl whom you can love, and who loves you, I don't want this to "pass away." And as there is in all love an element of will, I want you to see that it doesn't pass away, and to show as much to Uncle Frank.[18]

The love affair did not cool during the protracted engagement. Maude visited Berea, and her artist's eye was taken with the mountain landscape. On Will and Anna Hutchins's twenty-fifth wedding anniversary, she wrote them a letter that in retrospect can only be seen as wistful. She wished they were all there together so she could "look out and up at the infinite, then in and around at the finite and at Bob who is such a happy mixture of both — and I'd wonder what I'd wonder twenty-five years hence. . . . People forget so quickly — at least most people seem to. Bob and I will try to be like you two and remember what we dreamed. And we won't play traitors to ourselves and laugh at what we dreamed — because if our more special dreams shouldn't quite materialize and get very solid it is something simply to have dreamed and kept the faith."[19]

Will Hutchins came up from Berea to perform the wedding ceremony on September 10, 1921, at the home of Maude's aunt, Mrs. Samuel Ludlow Thompson. The groom, who had spent the summer desperately seeking a job that would provide an income sufficient to sustain a married couple, may have been wondering why at their recent commencement his Yale classmates had voted him "most likely to succeed."

CHAPTER FOUR

The Genesis of an Educator

In contrast to the enlightenment and inspiration he attributed to his education at Oberlin, Hutchins always wrote off his undergraduate career at Yale as an intellectual dead end. He found no fulfillment in the college classrooms and no effective substitute for it in the extracurricular activities that introduced him to the diversions of the affluent upper class. "The Yale of my day," he recalled, "was a place where you could get excited about girls or liquor or parties or athletic contests, but it wasn't a place where you'd get excited about learning."[1]

It was not, he insisted, a career choice, but rather boredom and frustration that prompted him to enter law school at the end of his junior year; he signed on as a refugee, not as an aspirant to a legal career. Even so, he immediately impressed his professors as a potential ornament of the bar, and after a year of legal studies he was offered a clerkship at a New York firm, Alexander and Green, which would provide a subsistence wage and an opportunity for him to continue working toward a law degree.

But as commencement neared, he found himself already "going stale" on the case studies that made up the law curriculum. Selected to deliver the class oration, he chose as his title "Should Institutions of Learning Be Abolished?" When he took the platform, his own diploma safely at hand, he paraphrased Matthew Arnold, who contended that ideas are rare among the upper classes:

. . . if our college life has been idyllic, haphazard, humoristic, without any infusion of scholarship, it has merely reflected American life. . . . If at college we have never tasted what may be called the sweetness and glory of being rational animals, it is because America does not know or highly esteem that sweetness and that glory. And we are products of America. But we are supposed to be the finest products of America. Where shall our country find its leaders if not among that two percent of her population who have been favored by four years of college?[2]

It was at this juncture that Hutchins backed into the career that was to occupy him all his life. The law clerk's stipend at the Wall Street law firm might have been enough to sustain him, but it could not also support the wife he was about to acquire, so he put out feelers in areas where he thought there might be a possibility of gainful employment.

As far back as October his inquiries had prompted a letter from the Reverend John W. Herring, pastor of the First Congregational Church of Terre Haute, Indiana, to President King of Oberlin: "I have just received a very interesting letter from Bob Hutchins in answer to one of mine, saying that he would consider taking a church here for three years if the church is available for capture."[3] King replied: "I have not had the opportunity to hear him preach, but he certainly ought to know what good preaching is and if he takes at all after his father he certainly would not be likely to fail at that point."[4] Nothing came of that putative bid to enter the Lord's service, and Hutchins turned instead to his father's other vocation, teaching.

Following the example of his brother William, who had graduated from Yale the year before and embarked upon the career he was to follow all his life, Robert wrote to the headmasters of preparatory schools that supplied Yale with students. At one point he thought he had a chance for a post at Lawrenceville, but competition for such jobs was keen in the depression year 1921, and none of the leading institutions made a firm offer.

He had to settle for an appointment at the now-defunct Lake Placid School. The surroundings were pleasant at the upstate New York resort, and in winter the school was relocated to sunny Florida. And he had no complaint about his compensation, which included room, board, and laundry for himself and his wife, plus a two-thousand-dollar stipend, which represented the highest net income above expenses he was to enjoy for some years to come.

The trouble with the Lake Placid School, he discovered, was its students, whom he described as rich juvenile delinquents, and its curriculum, which was designed solely as a drill to equip them to pass the College Board examinations. He taught English and history, taking his students through the standard texts eight pages at a time, emphasizing the points that had turned up in previous exams. "As one who has prepared students for the College Boards, I can testify to the limits they set to education," he said of that experience. "In the school I taught in, I did not dare try to educate my charges. It would have confused their minds."[5] He found this kind of pedagogy barely tolerable in his first year and was appalled at the prospect of repeating the routine for a second.

Deliverance came in the form of a telegram asking him to meet the treasurer of Yale at Utica to discuss a possible opening in New Haven. This turned out to be the post left vacant by the retirement of the Reverend Anson Phelps Stokes, who had been a legendary campus fixture for many years as secretary of the Yale Corporation. After interviewing Hutchins, President Angell wrote to offer him a salary of $5,500, adding, "You will, of course, understand that, should you continue in the office and prove yourself competent to develop its possibilities, this salary may from time to time be increased."[6] The fall term had started, but Angell was able to obtain Hutchins's release from his contract with the Lake Placid School by finding a suitable replacement and recommending him to the headmaster.

Hutchins, who was prepared to seize any opportunity to escape from the classroom, savored the irony but interposed no objection when his benefactor told him that he had obtained approval for the appointment by pointing out to the trustees that the candidate was the only Yale man of his generation who had shown any interest in education.

On January 1, 1923, Hutchins became an officer of the corporation chartered in 1701 "for founding, suitably endowing and ordering a Collegiate School within His Majesty's Colony of Connecticut." The charter had been amended with the evolution of Yale University to provide for a governing body made up of three ex officio members, the governor and the lieutenant governor of Connecticut, and the president of the University, as well as ten life fellows and six graduates, each elected by the alumni for a six-year term.

Subject to the Corporation's final authority, Hutchins quickly discovered, "the president ran, or was supposed to run the place. The Provost was supposed to be in charge of the educational program, and I did the rest."[7] His duties included public relations and fund-raising, which entailed frequent speaking engagements at alumni meetings and class dinners and made him responsible for arrangements at the University's public occasions. He supervised the staff of fifty that produced all Yale publications, sat in on meetings of the Corporation and its committees, and had access to all academic departments as the principal administrative assistant to President Angell.

"The advantage of the position, if I had been interested in university administration, which I was not, was that it was a central position to see every operation of the University," he said. "You could be in a better position than anybody except the president himself to see the way the place operated."[8] So, while performing his multitudinous duties in exemplary fashion, he resolutely refused to consider the career in education for which he was being uniquely equipped, and he again entered the Law School as a refugee.

His sponsor in his baptism into the law, as he put it, was Professor Charles E. Clark, who had been impressed by the precocious youth when he taught him in one of his undergraduate courses. Clark persuaded the dean of the Law School to bend attendance requirements so that Hutchins could put in a full day at his secretarial duties and still keep up with his class. This was made possible by Hutchins's being assigned to assist Clark with the law books he was writing, thereby entitling him to course credit for research and drafting he could undertake at odd hours.

And these hours were odd indeed, for Hutchins's duties as secretary required frequent travel throughout New England and as far south as Washington to keep engagements with the alumni, and there were many evenings in New Haven when he was expected to be on hand to see to it that University-sponsored occasions went off as planned.

Angell had consented to his taking time off to attend courses at the Law School's summer session, a slack period for the general administration, and in August Hutchins wrote to seek approval for his enrollment in classes that met at 8 A.M. and 4 P.M. during the regular term. "Your fears about my health have been shown to be unwarranted," he added, "for at last reports it would appear that the Law School has caused me to gain six pounds this summer."[9]

To meet this schedule he established a routine he was to follow all his life: finding that he could maintain his efficiency with considerably less than the usual eight hours' sleep, he arose before six each morning and used the early hours for undistracted reading and writing. At his office he disciplined himself and, insofar as he could, his visitors to keep all conversations brief and to the point — a practice that saved a great deal of time but also contributed to the reputation for arrogance that had accompanied his precocity ever since his prep-school days at Oberlin.

Out of necessity he became an accomplished speed-reader. One of his New Haven contemporaries, Morris Tyler, recalled seeing Hutchins go through a single-spaced memorandum almost as fast as he could turn the pages. When Tyler's wife expressed doubt that anyone could get anything out of such rapid scanning, he handed her the memo and said, "Try me." Under questioning he demonstrated that he had in fact absorbed the essence of the fairly complicated document and could quote key passages verbatim.[10]

After more than a year and a half in office, Hutchins was clearly meeting his obligations to the satisfaction of all concerned. Still, he suffered an attack of Calvinist remorse, and in September 1924 he wrote to Angell,

> . . . I am unwilling to have any member of the Corporation or of the Faculty think that I am procuring my legal education at the expense of the University. It is true that my classes are outside of the time which I would normally spend in the office, and that my preparation for them has been made and will continue to be made in the evening or at times when I am not engaged in University work. Still, it may be said that the Secretaryship is a full-time position and that I should not take on any other duties. For this reason I beg to indicate formally by this note my desire and willingness to accept a reduction in my salary for the current year in proportion to the amount of time which it may be thought I am taking from the work of the Secretary's office to devote to the study of law.[11]

The offer was dismissed by Angell, and both the salary and the formidable schedule remained in effect. Such a regimen would have been hard on most newlyweds, but Maude was herself enrolled in the Yale School of Fine Arts and was absorbed in perfecting her skills as a sculptor. With it all, the strikingly handsome pair found time to share an active social life with younger members of the university community.

Some of Hutchins's classmates were still around, and Maude had family connections in Connecticut. A cousin in New Haven, George Dudley Seymour, shared her interest in their genealogy and admired one of her proud possessions, a sword that had belonged to their Allyn ancestor and was said to have been made by the first silversmith in the colony. Years later, when Seymour sent him a copy of a pamphlet, "Documentary Life of Nathan Hale," Hutchins replied, "You and your cousin Maude, I must confess, bore me deeply with your air of superiority. I want to assure you that Nicholas Hutchins, who came to Groton, Mass. in 1670, was a whole lot better man than any of your relatives, including Governor Thomas Wells."[12]

Morris Tyler, a native of New Haven who became a partner in the city's leading law firm, had known Hutchins as a fellow member of Wolf's Head. He and his wife spent many pleasant evenings at 139 High Street, where the young couple lived in half of an old house they shared with Philip Jessup, a lifelong friend who became a justice of the International Court of Justice at the Hague. Tyler recalled Maude as a somewhat distracted hostess whose charm complemented her genial husband's proficiency with the martini pitcher.[13]

The scores of speeches Hutchins delivered during his tenure with the Yale Corporation are touched by a sort of sardonic gaiety. He was promptly dubbed a boy wonder by the press, a designation he detested but was never able to escape, even when his graying locks required an amending "former." When he identified himself to the Boston Yale Club as "the youngest college executive in the world," he added, "may God speedily grant me advancing years." He told of arriving at Grand Central Station to find a welcoming delegation complete with a band playing "Hail to the Chief," only to discover that the reception was for an even younger celebrity — the child movie star Jackie Coogan.[14] His self-deprecating prefatory remarks usually included references to his family's residence in rural Kentucky, which enabled him to give a personal touch to the hillbilly and "coon" jokes that in the twenties were still an acceptable part of the public speaker's repertory.

But when he got down to the business that brought him before the alumni groups, an appeal for funds, he always managed to work in a hortatory passage that urged his listeners to use their support to make the University more democratic as well as more solvent. As he had as an undergraduate, he spoke up for those students who, despite their presence on the campus, were not regarded as proper Yale men. In one of his earliest secretarial addresses, to the class agents of the Alumni Fund Association, he said:

> While I was an undergraduate, Yale to us was a group of schools,
> all of them of minor importance except the College and Sheffield.
> A graduate student, especially if he happened to wear a green hat,
> we put beyond the pale of Yale society and permitted him to live
> only because we were too busy with ourselves to exterminate him.
> He appeared to us as an immigrant must appear to a sightseer at
> Ellis Island. We averted our gaze from him, particularly from his
> hat. But, as the Graduate Schools' contributions to the Alumni
> Fund show, a difference in hats makes no difference in loyalty to
> Yale. Nevertheless much progress in this field may be made if

new dormitories can be given at an early date to the graduate departments, for as everybody knows a difference in the quality of rooms may make a difference in the quantity of loyalty which a difference in hats could not affect.[15]

When he was engaged on another of his missions, extolling Yale's glories to prep-school students, he reiterated his reservations about his own undergraduate education. At Hotchkiss he warned the seniors that things were no different at the other Ivy League schools they might be headed for:

> Perhaps the most distressing feature of eastern universities is their uniformity. . . . One student body prides itself that it is more intellectual than another; a second that it is more manly than the first; and a third that it is more polished than either. But in the main it is hard to distinguish the representatives of the three institutions. They are all unmistakably the college type, and upon a man who, by wearing a green hat for instance, varies from that type, they look with disfavor and with some distrust.
>
> With the same disfavor and distrust they look upon a man who varies from the college type of thinking. Of the 236 men in the senior class in Sheff only seven would admit this year they were Democrats. . . . Referendums at New Haven on questions ranging from compulsory chapel and the honor system to prohibition and the world court are significant not so much because of the vote cast as because it is all on one side. Those who grow apprehensive about atheism and bolshevism in the colleges merely betray their ignorance, for the most conservative places in America today, as faculty members know, are the universities.[16]

In these public utterances Hutchins gave free rein to a restless and skeptical intelligence, yet his wit and charm were so disarming that his frequently caustic observations aroused no protest, and he turned out to be an entirely successful public-relations man. At the end of his tenure as secretary, when his relationship with Angell was such that he felt free to address him in the bantering style he used with his intimates, he replied to commendations the president had passed on: "Since the Secretary is now conceded to be the leading University whooper-up and ballyhoo man in America . . . the Secretary gratefully acknowledges receipt of his mark in Yale Publicity and hopes his teacher will announce it with the other honors Commencement Day."[17] In retrospect he concluded that his youth had provided a kind of protective coloration for his iconoclasm; he prospered because no one took his controversial ideas seriously.

The Law School provided a sustaining contrast to the banalities of his secretarial career. The sense of community and common purpose he had found in his first exposure to it was enhanced as he gained more intimate contact with the small but able faculty; his mentor, Professor Clark, soon became a close personal friend. He still chafed under the kind of rote learning entailed by the case studies that made up most of the curriculum, but he recognized that the Socratic method employed by his teachers required a mental discipline that could take a dedicated student well beyond mere analysis of legal statutes as they had been interpreted by the courts. There he found "a dazzling panorama because all the facts of human life get into it, and get into it in concrete terms."[18]

Still, he found much of the routine instruction a waste of time, the result of the conviction, shared by faculty and students alike, that the institution was essentially a trade school. Its success was measured by the percentage of its graduates who passed the bar examinations, and Hutchins thought this had the same stultifying effect he had encountered at the Lake Placid School, where the emphasis was on passing the College Boards. It meant that most of a student's time was devoted to learning technical skills — how to draw up a will, frame a contract, examine a witness, and the like. These were techniques that he believed could be readily mastered during the period of apprenticeship in a law office that was, in any event, going to be required of those who entered practice.

The case-study method, which involved what Hutchins called "homeopathic doses of experience," had been perfected at Harvard and adopted by the other leading law schools. It assumed that the object of studying law was to enable the practitioner to predict what the courts would do. If one accepted the premise that the law was what the judges said it was, then there was little point in paying much attention to jurisprudence, which was concerned with broad legal principles; Yale offered only one such course, and that, Hutchins found, was largely ignored by most of his classmates.

He was clearly devoting much thought to the deficiencies of the Law School, even as, indeed, he was forming adverse opinions on the whole of the education available at Yale. "The University had already upset me a great deal," he recalled. "My legal education upset me still more. The whole organization of the University upset me. The Law School, for example, might just as well have been in Alberta, Canada, as where it was, because it had no connection with the rest of the University. These things upset me a great deal."[19]

Upset though he may have been, Hutchins in later years denied that he had begun by this time to consciously consider devoting his own efforts to improving what his logical mind found to be an incomprehensible educational structure. In his last year in law school he told Angell that he had no intention of going into practice, but he gave no indication of what he might do as an alternative.

There is no evidence that he bothered to look around for a place in a law firm after he turned down the offer from Alexander and Green. But then he may quite reasonably have expected to be offered a wide choice of possibilities if he changed his mind, for once again he was on his way to being graduated at the head of his class. And he confounded the faculty members who had objected that his irregular schedule would cause him to miss essential practical training: he finished second in the state bar examination, topped only by a classmate who had concentrated on the special requirements of Connecticut practice.

The 1925 Yale commencement was a happy occasion for the Hutchinses. Robert was one of only two in a class of eighty-five to receive his law degree magna cum laude. Maude was awarded first place in a competition of the Beaux Arts Institute of Design — the fifty-dollar Lloyd Warren Prize for a draped nude male figure that she titled *Disarmament*. Moreover, a vacancy had opened on the Law School faculty, and the star graduate was drafted to fill it. Whether by accident, as he always insisted, or by predestination, as some of his Calvinist forebears might have concluded, Robert Hutchins had become an educator.

CHAPTER FIVE

The Ebullient Experimentalist

The view of the Yale Law School from the standpoint of a teacher rather than that of a student reinforced Robert Hutchins's conviction that the curriculum was largely irrelevant. As the junior member of the faculty, he inherited those courses his seniors had no interest in teaching. These included criminal law, which aroused little enthusiasm since there was no real money in its practice, except for the elite of the criminal bar, lawyers of questionable repute whose company held slight attraction for a proper Yale man. Hutchins found the course to be largely a survey of crimes that no longer existed:

> We spent a lot of time on mayhem. And it seemed to me that this was a very remarkable way to try to cope with the problem that even then was one of the most important that society had to deal with. It seemed to me that the only way you could sensibly go after criminal law was to go into the whole system, to go into criminology, go into corrections, and for these purposes try to draw on what I assumed to be the vast knowledge of psychologists and psychiatrists, who were then a budding profession in this country, and anybody else who could shed light on what the actual role of the criminal law was, and how it could be made to work to reduce crime and to do justice, rather than to increase crime and increase injustice.[1]

In the two years during which he advanced from instructor to associate professor, Hutchins became an expert on the rules of evidence. And characteristically, he also became an outspoken critic of the manner in which these rules were applied in the courts and taught in the law schools. In December 1926, in a speech to the Association of American Law Schools, he mounted an attack.

He began by asserting that the existing rules, which to a large extent left it to judges to determine the credibility of witnesses, were themselves psychological in character, based on rule-of-thumb assumptions about human behavior that the judges applied introspectively, with no objective basis for their conclusions. After citing instances that demonstrated the fallacy of imputing such omniscience to jurists, he brought into question the theories of John Henry Wigmore, the dean of Northwestern Law School and an accepted authority on evidence, who held that "we may determine the preventive effect of punishment for crime by searching our own hearts; no statistics are necessary."

> With the utmost deference, and nothing less is due his great authority, one may reply to Dean Wigmore's injunction that we have been searching our hearts for centuries; and no one has shown more clearly than he on every page of his work on evidence how utterly we have failed in the hunt. Every page of that masterly treatise discloses the mass of conflicting rules, of metaphysical doctrines, of methods of concealing the truth now sanctioned in our courts.[2]

Hutchins may very well have been sincere in his backhanded tribute, but Wigmore concluded that the honeyed words were freighted with irony. In a letter to President Angell he characterized the speech as "a jaunty and witty but irresponsible dismissal of the recorded experiences of lawyers and judges," one that left the dean "in the classification of fossils." Hutchins, he complained, displayed an extreme devotion to psychological behaviorism, which Wigmore likened to the free-silver craze in economics. Angell sent Hutchins a copy of the letter, along with the comment, "I get the impression that you must have stepped on some of his most sensitive corns."[3]

It is likely that most of the assembled law professors shared Dean Wigmore's reservations, for in his usual hortatory conclusion Hutchins followed up his criticism of the prevailing practice by urging an unorthodox solution to a problem he plainly felt his colleagues had been too obtuse to perceive:

Are we not justified in attempting another tack? May not the objective psychologists help us to extricate the administration of the law from the morass into which our subjective psychology has let it fall? . . . They employ the scientific method, a method psychology now makes available for us. If we cannot grasp this opportunity we shall abdicate our position as specialists in human behavior, reaffirm the traditional conservatism of the profession, and permit the rules of evidence to recede still further from reality.[4]

Even those who rejected his conclusions, however, could not deny Hutchins's mastery of the subject. It was as an acknowledged expert on evidence that he joined the distinguished company of law professors who, following the lead of Felix Frankfurter of Harvard, came forward to protest the conviction of Nicola Sacco and Bartolomeo Vanzetti in the Massachusetts murder trial that became a landmark civil-liberties case when the presiding judge refused to permit consideration of new evidence that cast doubt on the prior verdict. While protest mounted from those who felt that the defendants were victims of ethnic prejudice, compounded by their admitted anarchist ideology, Hutchins approached the matter with calm detachment:

What happened with regard to the Sacco-Vanzetti case was simply that I read the opinion of the Supreme Judicial Court of Massachusetts and I then went to work on what it meant to leave the admissibility of testimony under the Massachusetts rule to the discretion of the trial court when the trial court had displayed its prejudice against the defendants at every turn of the road.[5]

Hutchins was no doubt moved by the human tragedy, but his primary concern seems to have been with using his expertise to call attention to the broader issues involved: "I wanted to make clear that from a strictly technical, legal point of view the trial court had grossly mishandled these prisoners, and if these practices were continued many innocent people would die."[6]

When Hutchins's evidentiary attack on the handling of the Sacco-Vanzetti trial was published as a case note in the *Yale Law Review,* President Angell received a protest from another distinguished legal figure who was also an influential Yale alumnus. Chief Justice William Howard Taft noted that Hutchins was associated with Felix Frankfurter, who seemed to be "closely in touch with every Bolshevik communist movement in this country."[7]

                              *   *   *

In 1927 the obstreperous young professor was appointed dean of the
Law School. In his usual laconic fashion Hutchins wrote off this
extraordinary elevation as another of the accidents that propelled him into
a career as an educational administrator; when the office became vacant,
he said, his colleagues nominated him because they mistakenly thought
his close association with President Angell gave him a measure of
influence that he could use on their behalf.

Hutchins was to maintain this fiction of inadvertent promotion to
account for every step in his phenomenal rise in the nation's educational
hierarchy. It apparently reflected the puritanical conviction that a man's
advancement should be based on recognized worth and that any effort that
might be construed as self-seeking was unseemly if not immoral. Beyond
that he no doubt hoped that his deprecation of his own accomplishments
would temper his elders' resentment of the brash young man who had
passed them by.

Whatever his own role may have been, it is clear that he hardly
became head of the Yale Law School by happenstance. When Guido
Calabresi, who occupied the dean's office in the 1980s, looked into the
relationship between the law faculty and the Yale Corporation, his
research convinced him that Angell had taken an active role in Hutchins's
appointment, personally suggesting him as a compromise when the
faculty could not agree on either of the two candidates proposed to
succeed Dean Thomas W. Swan upon his appointment to the United
States Court of Appeals.[8]

Certainly Angell's staunch support was necessary to secure the
Corporation's approval of a dean who was still a month short of his
twenty-eighth birthday. When the law faculty settled its differences by
agreeing to nominate Hutchins, the president manipulated the bureaucratic machinery with due caution. First he moved for his appointment as
full professor and acting dean. Four months later Hutchins was reappointed acting dean, and after another two months the qualification was
finally removed.

Angell was motivated by something more than a desire to do a favor
for a young friend who had served him well. As the first non–Yale
graduate to head the institution since the American Revolution, he was
determined to impose true university standards upon what he considered
an inbred traditional college with a few graduate and professional schools
appended. "The Yale Law School in the early 1920s was still to all
intents and purposes a Connecticut school with out-of-state students," the
legal historian Robert Stevens wrote, "and it was intellectually overshad-
owed by Harvard and Columbia."[9]

Angell, a psychologist who had studied under John Dewey at the University of Chicago and served as dean of faculties there, was naturally sympathetic to Hutchins's idea of incorporating the social sciences into the study of law. Beyond this he wanted somebody to shake up the Law School, and he had ample reason to believe that he had found his man.

Even as a neophyte instructor Hutchins had begun to press for curricular reform. He had joined his mentor, Charles Clark, who shared his dim view of traditional law courses, in working up a proposal for an Institute of Procedure, which would undertake research in those areas in which the two men specialized. Coupled with this would be an honors course in which top students would be allowed to substitute research projects for case studies, as Hutchins himself had done under Clark's tutelage. Finally, they proposed that the standards of admission be raised and the number of students reduced.

"We stood absolutely alone on all these matters and were opposed at every step more or less actively by the Dean," Hutchins wrote.[10] But they had a powerful ally in the president's office. Angell privately indicated his approval of the proposal and followed up by writing to Dean Swan (sending a copy to Hutchins) to suggest that there ought to be a reply to an article in the *New Republic* that exalted the Harvard Law School by invidious comparison with Yale. The president indicated that he thought this might be something Hutchins, who was still acting as secretary, could handle.

"The Dean suggested that I draw up such a reply to be discussed by the faculty yesterday," Hutchins wrote to Karl N. Llewellyn, another dissident who had recently departed the Yale faculty for Columbia:

> It seemed to me the hour had struck. I therefore prepared a thousand word press release announcing that the Yale School of Law would become the first honors or research law school in America. The document alleged that we would restrict our enrollment to 300, substantially increase our tuition, and attempt to train our men to discover the actual operation of the law rather than to memorize its rules. This was read to the faculty yesterday and created enormous consternation. . . . I am particularly sorry that I was the person to present it. The impression created by having the youngest member of the faculty produce a revolutionary plan was not, I think, satisfactory.[11]

The consternation diminished only after Dean Swan persuaded Angell that the reduction in the number of students would impose a severe financial burden, and after its opponents managed to water down the proposal for an honors course. The faculty came around to provide a lukewarm endorsement for the Institute, and Angell recommended it to the Corporation, but no funding was ever obtained for it.

When Hutchins became dean the situation was reversed: he was still the junior faculty member in age, but he was senior in rank. Those who thought he had been assigned a caretaker's role were quickly disabused of that idea; a week after he took office he named a three-man committee that included himself and Clark and promptly recommended faculty appointments for a psychologist and an anthropologist. Another committee formulated curricular changes similar to those being urged at Columbia, where a group of reformist professors was attempting to launch the movement that came to be called legal realism. In short order the leading advocates of realism were brought to New Haven, and Yale became the center of experimentation in legal education.

Hutchins did not need to mount a raid on the Columbia faculty; some of the would-be reformers resigned in protest when their efforts to create a curriculum based on "sociological jurisprudence" were blocked by President Nicholas Murray Butler's appointment of an unsympathetic dean. When news of the rebellion reached New Haven, Hutchins immediately obtained authorization to hire three of these, the most notable being William O. Douglas, another brash and impecunious young man, who had come east from Washington State to work his way through Columbia Law School. In his autobiography Douglas recalled his first exposure to Hutchins, who had traveled to suburban Pelham to address a men's-club dinner:

> We met in a foul-smelling locker room at the country club, that being the meeting place because only there could bootleg liquor be served. I was with the committee that put Hutchins on a New Haven train very late that night.
>
> The next morning I was awakened by a call from Hutchins, always an early riser. He told me he had summoned the Yale faculty to a nine o'clock meeting and they had elected me to the faculty. My first question to him was almost insulting: "Where is Yale?" I was so ignorant of the East that I actually didn't know where the university was. [12]

Once he found it, New Haven proved to be entirely satisfactory. "Its physical beauty and intellectual grace made it an ideal habitat," he wrote. "People were intimate and friendly." [13] And as he discovered, he now had a dean who cherished iconoclasts. The first test came when he imposed his hard-bitten version of the Socratic method upon his students:

> I tended to treat the class as the lion tamer in the circus treats his wards. Soon the class was in protest, sending a committee to Dean Hutchins to have me fired. Hutchins called me into his office and told me what the committee had said.
>
> I replied that the students were the grandsons of very eminent and at times disreputable characters, and that as a result of the wealth of their ancestors the students had been spoiled all their lives. I said I thought it was time they learned that when they stood before a court or a jury, they would be judged by their perception and fidelity to the law, not by their ancestors.
>
> "It's fine with me if you fire me," I said.
>
> "Don't be silly. I'm merely passing the complaint on to you," Hutchins told me.
>
> "I am inclined to bear down even harder on the spoiled brats."
>
> "That would be revolutionary and wonderful."
>
> And so I stayed on at Yale.[14]

He remained for another five years. "Before leaving for the Securities Exchange Commission and ultimately the Supreme Court," Robert Stevens wrote, "Douglas had joined with others to establish Yale as the *enfant terrible* of legal education."[15]

Hutchins tried, and failed, to bring to New Haven another fractious young member of the Columbia faculty who, like Douglas, was to become a lifelong friend and collaborator. He first heard of Mortimer Adler when C. K. Ogden, editor of the *International Library of Philosophy,* mentioned the work he was doing on a book to be called *The Technique of Controversy*. Hutchins apparently misconstrued this when he wrote to Adler: "Mr. Ogden tells me you are thinking about doing something in evidence. Since that is my field I am, of course, much excited that a psychologist, or a philosopher, or a logician should care about it."[16]

Although Adler actually knew nothing about the subject, he accepted an invitation from Hutchins to come to New Haven for further discussion, and then he promptly repaired to Columbia's law library to read Dean Wigmore's five volumes on the law of evidence. This may have been a waste of time, but it at least demonstrated that he had the energy and speed-reading skills required to keep up with Hutchins.

Adler arrived at the dean's office expecting to be greeted by a secretary, only to be welcomed "by a handsome young man in white sneakers, white ducks and a white T-shirt." At 5:00 P.M. the dean's wife, wheeling their daughter, Franja, in a pram, arrived to fetch the pair home for dinner. "Maude Hutchins was as tall, as lithesome, as impressively handsome as her husband — and, once started, more loquacious," Adler noted in his autobiography.[17]

The visitor was struck by the pungent scent of the plasticene she had been modeling, and when "martinis both strong and numerous loosened my tongue . . . the whiff of the odor produced a state of embarrassed excitement in me, even to the point of my blushing."[18] The olfactory prompting caused him to pour forth the details of his recent love affair with another sculptress. Despite, or perhaps because of, this lapse in reticence, Hutchins offered Adler a Sterling Fellowship at the Law School.

But the young philosopher, unlike the mountain-climbing Douglas, was an unreconstructed New Yorker. "I could not bring myself to leave the big city and live in a sleepy little village like New Haven," he wrote.[19] But even though he remained on the Columbia faculty, he collaborated on a Yale Law School project involving psychological aspects of evidence. An intellectual bond had been forged between the two men, one that made inevitable the merging of their ascending careers.

In addition to the kindred spirits he brought to the law faculty, Hutchins discovered one at the Yale Medical School, where his opposite number, Dean Milton C. Winternitz, also believed that his curriculum should be revised to incorporate the social sciences. Winternitz was another bright, energetic young man, and he had had the president's active support in obtaining grants that made possible Yale's pioneering Institute of Experimental Psychology.

In 1927 Angell and Winternitz sought to expand that base into an Institute of Human Behavior, which would incorporate other appropriate disciplines. They had not yet succeeded in obtaining funding when the new Law School dean proposed that his institution be included in the grand design. The renamed Institute of Human Relations would be located adjacent to the Medical School, and Hutchins wanted to add the Law School to the complex, using the funds already promised for a new building.

The joint proposal written by Winternitz and Hutchins was submitted to the Rockefeller Foundation with a request for a grant of $7.8 million. Angell's summary pictured a collaborative institute that would house psychiatry, psychology, child development, and "the social science group," serving as a connecting link between the Medical School, "studying the applied phases of individual behavior," and the Law School, "studying the applied phases of social behavior."[20]

In January 1929 the Foundation came through with $4.5 million, and the new Institute's building was erected in due course. But the funds that Hutchins was hoping to use for an adjacent law building had been bequeathed by John W. Sterling, a wealthy Wall Street lawyer, and the trustees of his estate were convinced that he would have abhorred anything smacking of "sociological jurisprudence." They firmly rejected the proposal that the contemplated building, already on the drawing board, be erected on the new site. With equal firmness, and a touch of indignation, they turned down Hutchins's suggestion that a more modest design be substituted so that some of the bequest might be used to endow research fellowships. John Sterling's memorial eventually emerged full-blown near the center of the main campus, a gray stone Gothic triptych, complete with tower, that embraces both the library and the Law and Graduate schools.

Hutchins tried nevertheless to establish an organic connection between the Institute and the Law School. He managed to install as executive secretary Donald Slesinger, a psychologist whom he had brought to the law faculty to work with him in his effort to provide a scientific basis for the rules of evidence. Clark, Douglas, another Columbia import, Underhill Moore, and a half dozen other law faculty members undertook pioneering research under the Institute's auspices.

But the compromises required to obtain approval for the interdisciplinary venture left it with a fatal flaw. It was agreed that the Institute would have no faculty as such; those who worked on its projects would be, in effect, volunteers, since they would all have departmental appointments and attendant obligations. This created a centrifugal force that, fueled by faculty politics, was never to be overcome.

"The whole Yale law project gradually faded," Douglas wrote in 1974. "The total effect of the Institute and of all our efforts was zero, because we could not find enough people who were willing to devote effort to such matters. The same problems are still being discussed in the law schools to this day, as well as in the whole profession. Yet almost nothing has been accomplished in all this time."[21]

In a meticulously documented evaluation of "the Yale experiment in legal realism and empirical social science," John Henry Schlegel concluded that it was the colorful, impetuous style of the young Law School dean that made that experiment possible:

> In considering Hutchins' career at the law school one can almost hear him yell, "Do something!" And his style reflects the command. The pace was frenetic as he constantly pushed, jostled and probed both law in general and legal education in particular for ways to make them better, more sensible, more reputably a subject of academic inquiry. At times, as in curriculum reform, toward which he made three starts in little over a year, the style could verge on a kind of educational guerrilla warfare. Then, movement, keeping the enemy — old, tired ways of thinking and teaching — off balance, became more important than the careful planning that may be essential to the success of the endeavor. . . .[22]

Hutchins was fully aware that many of the projects he was launching might well end in failure. In 1928, describing the changes at Yale to a meeting of law professors, he characterized the reforms he had inaugurated as frankly experimental:

> We hope we shall not recklessly abandon anything that is good or recklessly embrace new ventures simply because they are new. But we do not care much whether all our experiments are successful. We shall be satisfied if other law schools can profit by them if only to the extent of avoiding our mistakes. After all, the great thing about a university is that it can afford to experiment; and I use the word *afford* not in its financial connotation, but to remind us that a university is free to cultivate and exhibit the independence of thought, the willingness to depart from tradition, the readiness to take a chance, if you will, that may come from the possession of a life that is nearly immortal.[23]

It was this kind of philosophical detachment that enabled Hutchins to concentrate on issues and avoid personalities; he could hardly escape the charge of arrogance, but he was rarely accused of self-righteousness. These qualities helped him maintain the warm personal relationships that were essential to a scholarly community imbued with a sense of excitement and collective purpose.

Although he doubled the size of the faculty of seventeen he inherited from Dean Swan, he intentionally kept the Law School small. There were 422 students when he became dean; by 1928 he had reduced the total to

318 and expected to achieve his original goal of 300 the next term. The stated purpose of the reduction was to free his interdisciplinary faculty from routine instruction so that the Law School could be converted into a research institution that gave selected students an appreciation of the underlying principles of jurisprudence as well as an understanding of how the law actually worked.

The change also allowed Hutchins to achieve another of his objectives. Dean Swan had resisted the move to limit enrollment on the basis of grades because he felt that it would eliminate applicants of "old American parentage," with the result that the school would have an "inferior student body, ethnically and socially."[24] It followed that "Hendrie Hall, which housed the law school, was populated by young men wearing three-piece suits, silk ties, and gold watch chains."[25] It was hardly surprising that Corby Court, the private dining club for law students, was believed to be a citadel of subtle discrimination. Hutchins made certain that family pedigree was no longer a consideration in the choice of students, and he refuted any lingering suspicion of anti-Semitism by appointing Jews to the faculty and embracing Dean Winternitz not only as a collaborator but as a close personal friend.

In his annual report to the faculty, an ebullient Hutchins claimed that "the conclusion of the year 1928–1929 finds the Yale Law School in the best condition in its history."[26] He cited substantial additions to the endowment, a student body selected from an impressive number of applicants, and a materially strengthened faculty. The end product of his efforts at reorganization would be judged a failure, but that verdict lay some years in the future.

In 1983 Robert Stevens, the historian of legal education, found that legal realism as it had evolved at Yale had passed from the scene by the beginning of World War II, and that Hutchins's anathema, the case-study method, had survived as the standard instructional tool. But he conceded that the realist movement "was a crucial, and probably necessary force in the development of the American legal culture . . . which ultimately did for law what Russell and Wittgenstein did, with appreciably more intellectual elegance, for philosophy."[27] For Hutchins, the uninhibited experimentalist, that was enough to justify giving it a try.

By commencement time in 1929 he also had tangible evidence that despite his youth and his iconoclastic approach to the academic verities, he had been accorded a place in the very front rank of American educators. After being approached more than a year earlier by a search committee seeking a new president for the University of Chicago, Hutchins was summoned for a final inspection by the trustees and the senior faculty, and on April 26 his appointment was announced.

*   *   *

The Hutchinses had a happy time in New Haven. Although Maude was also busy with her sculpture and an infant daughter, the young couple were active participants in the modest but stimulating social life of the university community. There was a playful quality in Hutchins's relations with his contemporaries; though he usually managed to restrain his satirical bent in public, when he was among friends he was an irreverent deflator of the pretensions of New Haven's leading citizens.

Long after he departed Yale, some of his doggerel remained in circulation. In 1985 two companions of his Law School days, Morris Tyler and James Cooper, were able to produce copies of a half dozen of Hutchins's satiric works, along with fond memories of evenings when some of these were set to music and sung by a convivial company.

A parody of "The Tattooed Lady," a popular ditty of the day, portrayed Yale notables, including the president, engaged in unseemly activities on suggestive portions of the subject's anatomy. "The Ballad of a Fast-closed Door" recounted a meeting of the Yale Corporation at which the hostess led a venerable Harkness heiress to the wrong place to wash her hands, unseating a dignified counselor who was saved when "Just in time to avert the crime/ They heard Dean Hutchins roar/ Say, Angel-face, that ain't the place/ MY GOD! DON'T OPEN THAT DOOR!"[28]

Now the halcyon days were ending for the young couple. Bob and Maude would become Mr. and Mrs. Hutchins when they departed their High Street quarters, where tolerant neighbors were not upset by bibulous guests floating a ribald song on the midnight air. They would take up a domestic life ministered by servants in a formal presidential mansion at the heart of another Gothic campus, this one situated in a brawling midwestern metropolis. It would be their home for two turbulent decades, and the burden of decorum would never rest lightly on either of them.

CHAPTER SIX

"A Gamble on Youth and Brilliancy . . ."

Robert Hutchins's summons to the Midwest may well have come from the only first-rank educational institution that would have considered making him president. Chicago had been unconventional from the beginning. When it was created de novo in 1891, it was arguably the only American university, with the possible exceptions of Johns Hopkins and Clark, that truly deserved the title.

Free of the tradition that imposed parochial collegiate obligations upon its elder brothers to the east, and of the political considerations that shaped the more recently founded state institutions, Chicago was modeled on European centers of higher learning that placed primary emphasis on scholarly research. Its declared mission was to advance the frontiers of human knowledge, and only incidentally to educate the children of the gentry.

The creative genius who served as the University's first president was only five years older than Hutchins when he took office, a prodigy who at eighteen had earned a doctorate at Yale. "I have a plan for the organization of the University which will revolutionize College and University work in this country," William Rainey Harper proclaimed. "It is 'bran splinter new,' and yet as solid as the ancient hills."[1]

The grand design was made possible by the openhanded financial support provided by John D. Rockefeller, a devout Baptist who was persuaded to underwrite his denomination's ambition to establish a national institution of higher learning. Harper, a Hebrew scholar, had been a professor at the Baptist Union Theological Seminary in Chicago, where Rockefeller served as a trustee, and the millionaire philanthropist kept in touch with him after he moved on to the faculty at Yale. He was known to be satisfactory to the patron as well as to the national leaders of the church when the American Baptist Education Society presented Rockefeller with its proposal for a new college to be established in the Midwest.

Harper not only converted the proposed institution into a full-fledged university but also managed, without arousing significant opposition, to keep it free of what could have been the stultifying effects of its denominational ties. Its charter originally provided that the president and two thirds of the trustees were to be Baptists, but it also stipulated that "no other religious test or particular religious profession shall ever be held as a requisite for election to said board, or for admission to said University, or to any department belonging thereto . . . or for election to any professorship."[2]

By the time Hutchins came into the ken of Chicago's presidential search committee in 1928, the charter had been amended to remove the requirement of Baptist affiliation for any trustee or officer, and the University had a deserved reputation as a nonsectarian citadel of academic freedom. But as Chairman Harold Swift of the board of trustees put it, "Our president has always been a member of a Protestant church, which we consider very desirable in view of the fact that it is the purpose of the board to insure the continuance of the University forever as a Christian institution."[3]

Hutchins qualified on that score since he had not severed his Presbyterian ties and maintained the habit of regular church attendance that had been ingrained in him in his youth. Still, his advanced ideas and frequently irreverent personal style could be taken to indicate a tendency toward free thinking. He did nothing to dispel that view in his first encounter with Swift and other key members of the board. While he professed to deplore the "boy wonder" image conferred upon him by the press, he had created it himself "with his own tongue, which is brash, witty, pungent — and frequently insolent to those who are strong enough to fight back."[4]

He was in his usual iconoclastic form at a meeting of midwestern legal scholars when he was approached by Frederic ("Fritz") Woodward, a law professor who was then acting president of the University of Chicago. Hutchins assumed that the invitation to lunch with Woodward and five of the University's trustees meant he was being considered for an appointment as dean of Chicago's law school. By way of testing the temper of his hosts, he went out of his way to point out that he had published articles denouncing the Massachusetts courts for condemning Sacco and Vanzetti. No one seemed visibly shocked, but when he learned that it was the presidency that he was being considered for, he went back to New Haven convinced that he had blown his chances.

He was still skeptical when he returned to Chicago a year later for another inspection by the trustees and the senior faculty. His principal interrogators were Swift, who was also his host, and the Reverend Charles W. Gilkey, dean of Rockefeller Chapel, who had both trustee and faculty status. Before the two-day visit was over, he was exposed to twenty-six of the twenty-nine board members, as well as the ranking academics.

"We talked about education and the University of Chicago twenty-four hours a day, but always on the basis of 'getting acquainted,' " he wrote his parents. "Swift, alone with me, asked me questions about my youth, and Gilkey, equally alone, interrogated me for two hours, in a most gentlemanly manner, about my religion, if any. You will be surprised to learn that I was able to give more satisfactory answers to Gilkey than to Swift. There is no answer to the charge of youth. You can lie about your religion."[5]

Gilkey indicated that he would vote for Hutchins, as did Woodward, who was not himself a candidate, and the distinguished political scientist Charles E. Merriam. "On the other hand," Hutchins wrote, "it was perfectly clear that Swift was terrified of my youth. . . ."[6] He had completely misread the chairman. Swift, who had been strongly attracted to him when they first met, had become his indispensable supporter as the search committee winnowed scores of alternative prospects.

A prudent man, Harold Swift had conducted a thorough check on Hutchins before he led his colleagues in undertaking what he called "a gamble on youth and brilliancy."[7] He apparently adapted the phrase from a recommendation that carried particular weight — that of Edwin R. Embree, president of the Julius Rosenwald Fund, which had just made a two-million-dollar matching grant for new dormitories on the Midway. Anticipating reservations because of Hutchins's age and unorthodox style, Embree had concluded, "A conventional leader may continue the University as a respectable institution. A brilliant choice may enable the University to return to its earlier role of a real leader in American education."[8]

But there had been one pointed warning against the appointment, which might well have proved fatal. Hutchins's Yale patron, President

Angell, after reacting negatively in an interview with an emissary from the search committee, took it upon himself to reinforce his views in a personal letter to Swift:

> Of the intellectual keenness of the young man there can be no question, nor of his diligence and personal charm. . . . His shortcomings are such as spring from youth and inexperience, but in connection with the post for which you are considering him these lacks are momentous. He has had no opportunity for wider and intimate contact with general educational problems and in consequence is ignorant of them. . . .
>
> There is no adequate basis upon which to estimate his essential sobriety of judgment, in dealing either with men or measures. He is temperamentally rather impatient of men who disagree with him — and possibly a bit intolerant. These are probably in part defects of youth accentuated by the quickness and acuteness of his mind.
>
> If he develops as he now promises, he should in five or ten years be an extraordinarily able and well trained man. I cannot believe that at present he is mature enough wisely to shoulder so grave and critically important a task as that of your presidency.[9]

Circulated unadorned to the other trustees, this appraisal could have been devastating, coming as it did from one who not only had intimate knowledge of Hutchins's career but, as a former dean at Chicago, could also be presumed to have a special appreciation of the requirements of the presidency. But Swift raised the question of whether Angell could be considered a disinterested party, pointing out that he had compelling reasons for wanting to keep Hutchins at Yale, particularly since the young dean had been instrumental in obtaining a large foundation grant for the Institute of Human Relations, which was still in the process of being organized. He added his own judgment as one who had grown up in the executive suite of a major corporation: "There is no doubt this man is an administrator."[10] The search committee's nomination was approved without dissent.

If the chairman's support was essential to Hutchins's appointment, it was no less so in guaranteeing his survival over the years of controversy that lay ahead. Swift exercised far more influence than normally attends a trustee's role. His identification with the University began virtually at birth — both his and the institution's — and it was to grow closer as the years passed.

The capacious Swift family home was on Ellis Avenue, only a few blocks away from the campus, and he had been educated in the neighborhood, becoming an undergraduate at the University while President Harper's inspiring presence was still setting the tone. After graduating as president of the class of 1907, he was elected a trustee in 1914, the first alumnus to be so honored. He remained a member of the self-perpetuating governing board for forty-one years, serving for twenty-seven of those years as chairman.

Young Harold dutifully followed his father and older brothers into the management of Swift & Company, the family's giant meat-packing business. But at the end of his freshman year at the University he had transferred from the College of Commerce and Administration to the College of Literature, which had eventually awarded him a bachelor's degree in philosophy. In due course his brother Charles would observe that while Harold drew a handsome paycheck from Swift & Company, he really worked for the University of Chicago. Moreover, though he was the youngest in his family, he became the de facto manager of the philanthropies of his ten brothers and sisters, who were counted among America's wealthiest citizens.

His own considerable gifts to the University were made anonymously, as were most of those he solicited from his relatives. These ranged from a major donation for the Divinity School building by his mother, Ann, to a ten-thousand-dollar gift to the library for the purchase of rare Bibles — the latter arranged when Swift, after being informed of the availability of a collection at what he considered a bargain price, told the librarian to go ahead and buy it and to charge the purchase to the R. S. Maguire Fund, a drawing account provided by his sister Ruth.

This kind of flexibility, coupled with his intimate knowledge of the University and its needs, made Swift an exceptionally valuable patron. It also set a pattern for financial support from other board members drawn from Swift's peers among Chicago's wealthy elite. And as Hutchins noted in a posthumous tribute, Swift's unshakable commitment to academic freedom provided an example for conservative trustees who tended to flinch when the University drew fire from their own kind.

The trustees were men of means who no doubt were, as Thorstein Veblen said, "endowed with the retentive grasp." The radical economist offered that characterization about the time Swift became a trustee, dismissing the board as "an aimless survival from the days of clerical rule." Businessmen, Veblen said, were inherently unqualified to serve: "If the higher learning is incompatible with business shrewdness, business enterprise is, by the same token, incompatible with the spirit of higher learning."[11]

Whatever merit this view might have as a generality, Veblen's presence on the faculty was a palpable demonstration of its inapplicability in the case of Chicago. Regarded as the most trenchant contemporary critic of American capitalism, he was inveighing against the conspicuous consumption of the leisure class during the very years when the unprecedented gifts of Rockefeller, the much-maligned oil baron, inspired the rising tycoons of the Midwest to join him in making the University possible. When Rockefeller made his last gift in 1910 and closed out the books, his contributions totaled $34,702,375.28, a benefaction that remains unmatched when measured by its value in a day when a full professor's salary at Chicago — six thousand dollars — was the highest being paid by any university, and more than double the national average. In their formal acknowledgment the trustees declared that Rockefeller also had left an intangible legacy of equal importance:

> Mr. Rockefeller has never permitted the University to bear his name, and consented to be called its founder only at the urgent request of the Board of Trustees. He has never suggested the appointment or removal of any professor. Whatever views may have been expressed by members of the faculty, he has never indicated either assent or dissent. He has never interfered, either directly or indirectly, with that freedom of opinion and expression which is the vital breath of a university, but has adhered without deviation to the principle that, while it is important that their conclusions be correct, it is more important that in their teaching they be free. . . .[12]

This was the tradition Harold Swift was instrumental in maintaining during the years when Hutchins repeatedly put it to the test.

A lifelong bachelor, Swift maintained an elegant, if unostentatious, life-style, and he tended to treat those he favored as an extended family, generously offering them access to the material blessings he enjoyed. On April 25, the day before the public announcement of the new president's appointment, he sent a telegram instructing that his usual Fifth Avenue florist arrange to have delivered to Maude Hutchins in New Haven "two or three dozen very nice roses either long stemmed Pernets or other fine pink or red roses, enclosing my card." He also told his secretary to find out what Maude's favorite candy was.

These courtly gestures were followed up in more tangible ways. Hutchins, who was engaged in turning over the administration of the Yale Law School to his friend and successor, Charles Clark, would not move to Chicago until the fall. Swift, who still lived in the family home on Ellis Avenue and also had a summer and weekend place at Lakeside, Michigan, made both available to the Hutchinses until such time as the president's mansion was prepared to receive them. And he took it upon himself to see to it that their new home not only met the family's needs but suited its new mistress's taste.

The presidential residence, built to face the broad, grassy Midway pleasance between the soaring stone Rockefeller Chapel and one of the college quadrangles, was a solid, if comparatively unimposing, structure. The first floor was made up of a vast drawing room opening off the entry hall, a formal dining room with a table that seated sixteen, a large, paneled library, and the kitchen and serving pantries; the upper floors contained family living quarters, guest suites, and maids' rooms. The interior had been more or less done over three years before, but Swift anticipated that Maude might want to change the draperies and furnishings. On May 1 he wrote to Hutchins in preparation for her first visit: "Undoubtedly, there will need to be some decorating on the upper floor . . . and possibly the bathroom fixtures will need to be modernized." As to furniture, there was a good deal on hand, "and the University will want to provide whatever else is necessary."[13]

On June 21, after Maude had had an opportunity to inspect the premises and consult with Mrs. Quincy Wright, a decorator who had been retained to carry out her instructions, Swift turned to the problem of household servants. He had determined the availability of a cook who had served the preceding presidents, and he also had a suggestion as to the other key members of the staff. Maude had indicated that she preferred maid service, and Swift agreed that a butler might seem "high hat" to some. Still, he thought they should consider Fred and Emma Meyer, who had run the house for Hutchins's predecessor and were presently serving Swift.

"I think extraordinarily well of Fred and Emma, seeing them as I do from the front of the house," he wrote. His high-strung housekeeper, however, did not share his view. "She says he doesn't work well with other servants; he is somewhat domineering; and that the smile which is attractive in the front of the house is conspicuous by its absence *ad rearium.* . . . Probably the proper summary of the situation is that Fred would get on better with his wife and one other maid than with as large a number of servants as we have." The Hutchinses would be doing him a great favor, he said, if they could see fit to relieve a situation that meant that "either through slow design or a quick blow-up, we shall be looking for a new combination butler-valet and a new parlor maid."[14]

Hutchins replied that he thought "it would be a grand thing for Maude to start off in Chicago with trained servants.'' They had seen Fred and Emma in action while staying with Swift, and his only question was whether they "have got above general work of the kind they would have to do for us." Hutchins put an asterisk after this, and handwrote a footnote: "E.g. I have breakfast at 6 A.M.!"[15] Also, Emma would have to look after Franja on the afternoons and evenings when, by contract, her nurse was entitled to relief.

In his reply Hutchins also thanked Swift for arranging to have his company's German, Austrian, and Parisian agents stand by to facilitate the European tour he and Maude would undertake in the interval between their departure from New Haven and their arrival in Chicago. When they returned they found that Swift had overlooked no detail in arranging for a quantum leap upward in their life-style.

In November, at his own request, Hutchins received an accounting of the University's expenditures in making the mansion ready for his family. In addition to the interior refurbishing, a studio had been built for Maude on the upper floor of the old carriage house, and the grounds had been fenced to keep Franja in bounds. The original appropriation of eight thousand dollars was almost exhausted, but the secretary had been instructed to inform the president that "Mr. Swift is prepared to ask the Board for such further appropriation as is necessary to complete the work to the satisfaction of yourself and Mrs. Hutchins."[16]

Nor did the chairman's personal interest end there. In January, when Maude decided that the skylights in the studio were not as high as they should be, Swift took up the problem with the university architect. The matter was pursued at the highest levels until Maude was satisfied that she was getting all the north light available in a gloomy Chicago winter.

In his tactful, self-effacing way Swift thus eased the transition of the young president from a provincial household maintained on an income of less than ten thousand dollars a year to one that required five live-in servants plus a full-time gardener and a chauffeur for the limousine provided by the University. With all this, plus expense allowances for entertainment and travel that left his twenty-five-thousand-dollar salary virtually intact, Hutchins was able to maintain his family in a style his father would have considered unseemly, if not downright sinful.

For Maude, however, this was a return to the kind of milieu she had known in her childhood. Her parents had died in a scarlet-fever epidemic before she was a year old, and she had been reared by her maternal grandparents on a Long Island estate established long before newly moneyed New Yorkers began moving into the neighborhood. Conditioned by a grandfather who considered Commodore Vanderbilt an upstart, she was not overly impressed when, only two months after his inauguration, she and her husband found themselves the houseguests of Mr. and Mrs. John D. Rockefeller, Jr., in New York.

The occasion was an address by Hutchins to the men's Bible class once attended by the University's founder and now looked after by his son. Hutchins could only regard this as a command performance, and he was duly deferential in writing to thank his host. Declining the latter's offer to cover his wife's travel expenses, he felt constrained to add, "Since Mrs. Hutchins was off on a frolic of her own I don't think you or the Bible Class ought to finance her. As you know we were both considerably embarrassed that Mrs. Hutchins should accept so literally your invitation to treat your house like a hotel."[17]

But no offense was taken, and proof that the young couple had passed muster was forthcoming. "Nothing would give Mrs. Rockefeller and me greater pleasure than to have you and Mrs. Hutchins and your little girl spend the summer at Seal Harbor," their host wrote. "Having bought out the Realty Company so as to be in a position to control at least to a degree the type of people who should spend their summers at Seal Harbor, I have two or three houses that it has been a pleasure to have various friends occupy from year to year."[18]

Hutchins promptly accepted, noting that his entourage would include his butler, cook, a maid, and his daughter's nurse. But his chauffeur would not be in attendance, so they would need an automobile they could drive themselves. This ultimately resulted in what Rockefeller saw as a "blot on the honor of Seal Harbor" — a minor accident in which the Hutchinses encountered a policeman whom Maude considered discourteous. That, their host assured them, would never happen again, and he urged that they accept his check to cover the costs: "By so doing, I shall be sure that you have forgiven my exposing your reckless driving so publicly at Mr. Morgenthau's luncheon the other day."[19]

The Hutchinses spent another summer at Seal Harbor after Maude was assured that she could have Mrs. August Belmont's house rather than one that she rejected as being too dark. Although he would continue to profess a puritanical disdain for material goods, Hutchins had no difficulty in adapting to the rarefied surroundings those with unlimited means could provide for themselves and their chosen companions. He might have justified this indulgence as a necessary part of his job. Instead, in his usual sardonic fashion, he described his attitude as that of the man who said he had no desire to become a millionaire — he just wanted to live like one.

CHAPTER SEVEN

The Harper Legacy

I f John D. Rockefeller was the founder of the University of Chicago, William Rainey Harper was its creator. Like Hutchins, he was a bold experimentalist. Physically, Harper and Hutchins had little in common. The first president was an unprepossessing five-foot-seven, plump, bespectacled, with a high, reedy voice. But what he lacked in personal appearance, he made up for in his "remarkable combination of a passionate enthusiasm for scholarship and the expansive salesmanship of a Chautauqua manager."[1] Hutchins shared that enthusiasm and accepted the fact that he too would have to serve as the University's primary salesman.

In a study of the evolution of university public relations, Scott M. Cutlip credited Harper with doing "more than any other educator to harness the power of publicity to the cause of higher education early in this century. . . . In an era when most public relations programs were initiated in response to attacks from the muckraking journalists, and thus were of a negative nature, William Rainey Harper saw public relations as a positive means of gaining the requisite funds, faculty and freshmen to build a university."[2]

The faculty and students were in place when Hutchins arrived on campus, but funds were still needed, and journalists were still raking muck. The generally favorable press he had enjoyed at Yale did not long survive his new prominence, and he came to appreciate the feeling that had caused Harper to write to a friend, "I wish very much that there could be enacted a law in the state of Illinois inflicting the death penalty upon irresponsible reporters for the miserable way in which they misrepresent the truth."[3] But he recognized that as distasteful as the process might be, the projection of a favorable public image would be essential to maintain the backing he must have if his administration was to succeed.

Hutchins also followed Harper's lead in staging grand assemblies featuring visiting academic celebrities whose presence would insure wide publicity and impress the trustees and prospective donors who were invited to mingle with them socially. Harper did not wait to mark the progress of his fledgling institution by the decade; in 1896 he celebrated the anniversary of the founding with a five-day quinquennial, followed by a decennial in 1901 and a sesquidecennial in 1906:

> The quinquennial started with a graduate matutinal, a breakfast given by the president for the candidates for higher degrees, and included a convocation, a luncheon for "associated alumni," a reception in honor of Mr. and Mrs. Rockefeller, seminars, and the laying of cornerstones for three laboratory buildings. This prolonged celebration of Chicago's fifth birthday, a rarity for its day, was, in the words of one guest, "the greatest festival in the educational history of the West."[4]

A member of the Chicago faculty, Daniel Boorstin, coined the term "pseudo-event" to describe such contrived occasions. It was not inapplicable, though Hutchins saw to it that the celebrations of his day included learned colloquies of genuine significance, providing grist for the scholarly journals and books produced by the University of Chicago Press. But he was not unmindful that they also provided him with an appreciative audience for carefully prepared but seemingly spontaneous remarks from the dais and for the graceful, witty introductions of honored guests at which he excelled.

All of this was by way of backdrop for fund-raising, the inescapable obligation of a twentieth-century university president. Harper recognized that a basic purpose of philanthropy was to improve the public image of those who provided the funds; he had no problem with the fact that the Rockefeller beneficence was prompted, in part at least, by the desire of the oil magnate to offset the robber-baron reputation conferred upon him by the muckrakers. Hutchins, acknowledging his debt to Harper, kept in his desk drawer a sign that he produced when someone questioned the source of proffered funding: WE LAUNDER DIRTY MONEY. It is doubtful, however, that he displayed it when he was soliciting the help of the three men he described as the giants who in those days dominated the world of big money — and philanthropy — in Chicago: Samuel Insull, William Wrigley, and Julius Rosenwald.

He was intrigued by the manner in which these three put their bounty to work on behalf of causes they endorsed. "These men were not managers, or, if they were, this was not their primary role," he recalled. "They owned things, or controlled them. They could do what they wanted. They were different in almost every respect; but they were alike in one: They had an aggressive faith in the possibilities of the country and of Chicago in particular."[5]

Wrigley pledged a hundred thousand dollars to Hutchins one afternoon and the next morning at six o'clock called him on the telephone: "Yesterday I gave you a hundred thousand dollars. . . . Here are the names of seven other so-and-so's who ought to do the same thing, and you tell them I said so." The seven others didn't do the same thing, Hutchins found, "but they did a great deal more than they would have done without Mr. Wrigley's message."[6]

The head of the giant Sears, Roebuck mail-order company preferred the carrot to the stick:

> Mr. Rosenwald believed that money existed solely to be given away and dedicated himself to making his fellow millionaires see the light.
>
> He would put on his hat, call on a victim selected at random, and say: "The Rockefeller Foundation has offered to pay half the cost of a building at the University. The donor of the other half can put his name on it. I'll pay a quarter; you pay a quarter, and you can put your name on it."[7]

When Insull, the utilities magnate, was raising funds for the Civic Opera House, "every citizen who did business with his companies, or hoped to do business with them, shuddered when the voice came over the telephone, 'I am calling for Mr. Insull.' It meant a compulsory subscription." With that in mind, Hutchins once tried a little reverse English:

> When we launched a campaign to raise ten million dollars for the University, we started out by asking ten men to give us $100,000 each. We got nine. But where was the tenth? "Well," I said, "it's a cinch. I'll go over and ask Mr. [Al] Capone. I'm sure he'd give us $100,000." But Samuel Insull, the chairman of our campaign, said this would be immoral, that we could not take Mr. Capone's money. Insull later went to jail for some distinctly

immoral practices of his own. Insull was an interesting gentleman. Once, when I was having dinner with him, he mentioned that he couldn't get somewhere on time because of railroad connection problems. I suggested that he fly. "Young man," he said, "if you had the responsibility for $14 billion of other people's money you wouldn't fly." But when the sheriff came for him during his troubles he flew off to Canada.[8]

Harper had gained support for his unconventional educational ideas by equating innovation with excellence, thus appealing to the pride of midwestern millionaires who were scorned as uncultured moneygrubbers by the wealthy aristocrats of the Eastern Seaboard. In Hutchins's day many of Chicago's leaders still suffered from an inferiority complex identified as "the second city syndrome" by A. J. Liebling in a supercilious *New Yorker* series.

Harper had recognized that to unsnap these deep purses it would be necessary to demonstrate that the University ranked with, or possibly ahead of, its Ivy League counterparts. Forty years later the trustees still believed this to be true; Hutchins concluded that they would not have summoned him had he not borne a Yale cachet that could be presumed to impress those who still thought it socially necessary to send their sons and daughters east to college.

Excellence, however, had to be demonstrated. The great Gothic quadrangles that Harper had brought into being might provide an illusion of the antiquity associated with the more notable seats of learning, but the real test turned on what went on inside the monumental buildings. Harper met it by assembling the most distinguished faculty money could buy, and Hutchins was ever mindful of that precedent too.

Rockefeller's beneficence had made it possible for Harper to offer salaries of six thousand dollars for full professors and seven thousand for department heads, which exceeded the going rate at any contemporary university. Still, it was not easy to transplant men of established reputations to a new, untried institution located in what many regarded as an unprepossessing city. So Harper held out additional bait.

His emphasis on graduate work embodied the promise of freeing his recruits from the burden of routine college teaching; their primary obligation would be to conduct research and to train apprentices for careers in their own specialties. "Promotion of younger men in the department will depend more largely upon the results of their work as investigators than upon the efficiency of their teaching, although the latter will by no means be overlooked," he wrote. "In other words it is proposed in this institution to make the work of investigation primary, the work of giving instruction secondary."[9]

He sought out men and women who had trained in the European universities upon which he was modeling Chicago, and he urged the younger recruits to spend as much time abroad as they could before they reported for duty. Thus the original faculty of 120 included fifteen from Clark University, which, along with Johns Hopkins, had been founded on the continental model. He even persuaded the sitting presidents of Brown University and Colby College to join him, along with six former presidents.

Hermann Von Holst, the leading German authority on the American Constitution, came from the University of Freiburg to found the history department. Political economy was organized by J. Laurence Laughlin, who brought along his radical young protégé, Thorstein Veblen. The English department soon included Robert Herrick, the novelist, William Vaughn Moody, a leading poet of the day, and Robert Morss Lovett, who with his colleagues articulated a new socially conscious literary criticism. By 1907 the University had its first Nobel laureate, Albert A. Michelson, a physicist.

This remarkable aggregation was a tribute to the high scholarly reputation Harper had earned as a linguist and student of biblical literature. But if he gave priority to the requirements of investigation at the graduate level, he was also an impassioned teacher. As professor of Semitic languages at Yale he had attracted so many undergraduates to his Hebrew class he had to be assigned the university's largest lecture hall, and he had enjoyed a similar response from the young ladies at Vassar, where he taught a course. In the summers he was a platform star in the pioneering experiments in adult education at Chautauqua, New York.

In assuming his new role at Chicago Harper continued his active concern with the educational structure as a whole. His scientific colleagues' faith in empirical fact-finding, now shared by the new disciplines of social science, represented a departure from the speculative philosophy of nineteenth-century German idealism, but he thought the liberal arts, with their emphasis on human values, still should have a prime place in the educational scheme.

Harper sought to meet the problem by making a clear division between the University, which would be dedicated to specialized inquiry into the unknown, and the College, where the faculty would be concerned with imparting existing knowledge. And while the University was situated at the apex, he held that the institutions below were inextricably linked to it.

Chicago, as he designed it, was intended to embrace all levels of education and experiment with their improvement. Hutchins always insisted that the innovations with which he was credited were simply an effort to implement the organizational structure Harper had set forth in six "Official Bulletins" issued between January 1891 and May 1892. His blueprint combined scores of extant educational notions in one comprehensive program:

> There was the idea of the quarter system, which would keep the institution running throughout the year; a press with its own printing plant to publish scholarly work; an elementary school and academy, and a college level or two as laboratories of the university; coeducation at the university level; extension work (away from the campus and by mail); and, most important, graduate and professional work in many fields.[10]

Harper's most radical innovation involved the undergraduate Colleges of Arts, Literature, and Science, which were organized in two-year segments and designated Academic and University, later to be renamed Junior College and Senior College. "The work of the first two years partakes largely of the Academic character," he explained. "The regulations still must be strict. The scope of election is limited. . . . The close of the second year marks the beginning of a new period. . . . The student begins to specialize and in many cases certainly may to advantage select subjects which will bear directly or indirectly upon the work of his chosen calling. . . . The student gradually changes from the College atmosphere to that of the University."[11]

The general education to be given in the Junior College was essentially a continuation of that which the student received in the last two years of high school. This led Harper to propose that the Senior College be incorporated into the University and the Junior College combined with the last two years of high school to create a new degree-granting institution.

Many secondary schools were capable of undertaking this program, he said, which would make it possible for many people to pursue their education locally, at least to this higher point. Further, "a large number of so-called colleges do not have sufficient endowment to allow them properly to do the work of the junior and senior years. . . . These institutions in many cases would be disposed to limit their work to the lower field, if it were made possible for them to do so. They find it necessary, however, to give a degree."[12]

The scheme was put into effect at Chicago, embracing the upper two classes of the Laboratory School, which had been created by John Dewey as an adjunct to the professional School of Education. But Dewey's academy could supply only a limited number of students, and most of the undergraduates continued to come to Chicago after receiving their secondary education elsewhere. Harper never realized his hope that the first two years of college instruction might be given off campus by affiliated institutions, permitting "the University of Chicago to devote its energies mainly to the University Colleges and to strictly University work."[13]

He contended that an effective program of general education would require a separate faculty in which recognition and promotion would depend upon the quality of teaching rather than upon the research and publication employed by the University as the measure of worth. His failure to achieve such an arrangement on his home ground gave rise to a divisive internal conflict that was still unresolved when Robert Hutchins assumed the presidency.

While some of the senior professors had no objection to teaching undergraduates, and were very good at it, the department heads wanted to shape the undergraduate curriculum to serve their own ends. The basic issue was specialization; most of the chairmen insisted that concentration on specific subject matter ought to begin in the early college years in order to attract likely students to their fields of study and prepare them properly.

The issue came to a head in 1898 as the culmination of a running debate between classicists and scientists over Latin as a mandatory subject. A noted geologist, T. C. Chamberlin, argued that requiring study of the dead language was not only a waste of time but an affront to modern scholarship. Latin, he said, had come to stand for much the same thing in the scholarly world that Romanism had in the ecclesiastical world, and requiring it "commemorates the attitude of the old scholasticism, from whose tyrannies we are not yet escaped."[14]

In an effort to broaden the issue, Harper urged the faculty to accept "as its fundamental principle . . . that an essential element in the education of every man, and especially that of the scientist, is a study of the great heritage we have received from the past." This meant that students should be required to take "a specified number of courses in the study of the history, the institutions, and perhaps the literature of the past."[15]

Harper was not impressed by the objection that this might limit the time a student could devote to the study of science and the cultivation of the techniques of observation his future specialty would require: "If the scientist demands all of the time of the student from an early age, he is demanding what will in the end prove injurious to the cause of science; and with such demands there can be no sympathy on the part of one who is interested in the development of other departments of human knowledge."[16]

After Harper's death in 1906 there was no one in a position of authority to champion the cause of general education. His successor, Harry Pratt Judson, a political scientist, declared in his first presidential report that the curriculum should contain no inflexible limits to a student's election of specialized courses: "It is quite possible to attain general culture in a college course and yet so to plan a good part of the work that it would lead directly toward a profession already chosen."[17] This meant the institution of the elective system developed at Harvard by President Eliot and subsequently adopted by most American colleges. In the seventeen years of Judson's administration it resulted in "the almost total submersion of the college or undergraduate program under the dictates of the graduate schools."[18]

A primary device Harper had used to recruit established scholars was the promise that each full professor would be free to determine his area of investigation. To guarantee this, the University's charter effectively dispensed with the usual layer of administrative responsibility between the departments and the president, and it also vested considerable power in the university senate, made up of professors of full rank.

When Albion Small retired as dean of the Graduate School in 1923 after twenty years of service, he wrote:

The "autonomy of the departments" has not only been our theory but our practice. . . . At present, if one of the deans were to inquire of the officer representing a given department as to the wisdom of a certain schedule of courses, as to the most effective distribution of duties within the staff, as to the quality of work performed by certain members of the staff, and similar subjects, that department would be within its constitutional rights if it regarded the dean as an intruder and interloper.[19]

This inevitably had an adverse effect on Harper's concept of undergraduate education. The division between the Junior and Senior colleges became largely a fiction. The original requirement of an entrance examination was abandoned, with the freshman year being largely devoted to making up deficiencies in the usual secondary schooling. The last three years were then primarily occupied with professional training.

But this departure from the Harper dictum that "special training looking toward a particular profession or line of work is not the province of the College"[20] was not enough to satisfy the department heads. In 1920, when undergraduate enrollment had reached three thousand and was rising, President Judson complained that the College had become a burden: "The inevitable tendency is to siphon off funds from more advanced work to the great embarrassment of this essential part of University activities."[21]

Chauncey Samuel Boucher, who in 1926 became dean of the Colleges of Arts, Literature, and Science, wrote of the post–World War I years:

> Undergraduate work was grossly neglected; even worse, the College came to be regarded by some members of the family as an unwanted, ill-begotten brat that should be disinherited. Nearly all finally agreed that we had reached a situation that necessitated a decision either to abandon the College or to develop it.[22]

By the time Judson retired, in 1923, the College had degenerated into a training ground for graduate students, with a hundred of these teaching elementary courses as part of a faculty with an annual turnover of 40 percent. The trustees attempted to restore the Harper tradition by appointing as president one of his original disciples, Ernest DeWitt Burton, a New Testament scholar who had joined the faculty in 1892. The new president declared that the development of the undergraduate division of the University was "no less obligatory than the development of the work of the Graduate and Professional Schools."[23]

A joint commission of trustees and faculty was established to consider the future development of the Colleges. Its recommendations generally followed Harper's prescriptions, but consideration of them effectively ended with Burton's death only two years after he took office. He was succeeded by the first outsider to head the University, Max Mason, a distinguished mathematical physicist from the University of Wisconsin.

Mason was caught in the middle. Within the faculty and the board of trustees there was substantial support for a new emphasis on undergraduate education. But there was also the position exemplified by Dean Gordon J. Laing of the Graduate School, whose faculty was largely responsible for Chicago's high academic standing. Laing contended that "not even in the best [university] is the graduate work on the scale or of the quality that would be possible if the institution were entirely free from undergraduate entanglements."[24]

Mason, who never really settled into the president's office, resigned at the end of the 1928 term to accept an appointment as head of the Rockefeller Foundation. In his farewell address he said, "I have spoken much before faculty dinners of the undergraduate problem. Most of the *support* has gone to the graduate work; a good many of the *words* have gone to the undergraduate department. I hope it will be treated with the seriousness it deserves."[25]

Thus the dilemma was left on the doorstep to await Mason's successor, Robert Hutchins.

Although the organizational changes adopted in his early years at Chicago were labeled the New Plan, Hutchins always pointed out that he had inherited most of his ideas from Harper, along with most of his administrative problems. After studying the proposals of a faculty committee that had been established by Dean Boucher with Mason's blessing, he concluded that no effective reform of undergraduate education could take place without a drastic reduction of the power Harper had conferred upon the department heads. And that could be done only by Hutchins's demonstrating that he took quite literally the provision in the charter that designated the president as "the executive head of the University in all its departments, exercising such supervision and direction as will promote the efficiency of every department."[26]

Harold Swift had judged him correctly when he assured his fellow trustees that in Hutchins they were getting an administrator. In his years at Yale he had devoted much thought to the possibilities and limitations of the executive role in the corporate setting of a university. He understood that no final authority was vested in the president; he could be thwarted from above by the trustees and from below by the faculty, which by statute and tradition had effective veto power in educational matters. But the lessons he had learned at Yale as Corporation secretary and Law School dean were cautionary; he was determined that he would not administer Chicago in the fashion that prevailed in New Haven and at most contemporary institutions. In retrospect, he said,

Everything I did at Chicago may be regarded as the reverse of what I had been through at Yale. I sat for six years for the Yale Corporation and the president of the university never made a recommendation to the board. Not one. And they would say to him, well Mr. President, what do you think? What is your recommendation? And he would say, very skillfully he would say, on the one hand we have this and on the other we have that, and this is a matter for you to decide. Well, I could see that this was no way to run a university. These people didn't know anything, or insofar as they knew anything, they knew what Yale had been like, therefore they were not prepared to agree to any changes. Therefore, it seemed to me that it was irresponsible on his part.[27]

The role of passive mediator seeking to placate the conflicting interests that exist on every campus was foreign to Hutchins's nature. Yet he always rejected the term "leader" and insisted that "administrator" was the proper designation for one who accepted ordained limits on his authority. But he also assumed responsibility for determining the ends the institution ought to be serving and for advocating means of achieving them. Since no university, in his view, came close to meeting its declared goals, change was the order of the day for an academic administrator.

He recognized that an established institution was bound to be beset by inertia and that any effort to alter the status quo would face opposition. He had made up his mind, however, to act on the assumption that if the ends were acceptable (as they generally were in theory), reasonable men would accept a reasonable plan for achieving them. If his proposals could be shown to have flaws, or did not work in practice, the inveterate experimentalist was always willing to take a new tack or start over.

But he had evolved these operating principles in a law school, where he had dealt face-to-face with a small group of like-minded professionals and could employ the compelling force of his personality to full effect. He had yet to encounter a large faculty whose interests were diverse as well as vested, and defended in the name of academic freedom. When he did, he promptly precipitated what came to be known as the Great Chicago Fight.

CHAPTER EIGHT

"A Hell of
a Good Time . . ."

Ｔhe faculty Robert Hutchins confronted when he set out to reorganize the administration of the University of Chicago was a formidable body — by professional reckoning the best to be found in any institution in the country. In a ranking of twenty graduate departments in American universities, as determined by a poll of scholars in those fields, eight at Chicago placed first: botany, French, geography, geology, mathematics, physics, sociology, and Spanish. The astronomy, education, political science, and zoology departments ranked second; classics, economics, history, philosophy, and psychology third; chemistry and English fourth; and German fifth. The results placed the University well ahead of its Ivy League counterparts and those few state institutions whose departments ranked among the top five.[1]

Chicago's annual register for 1929–1930 listed 868 men and women as "officers of instruction (above the rank of assistant)." These senior faculty members devoted most of their time and energy to the 4,386 graduate students and the 3,169 in the seven professional schools (medicine, law, divinity, education, commerce, social service, and library). The 4,097 undergraduates received the bulk of their instruction from what Hutchins described as a "Coxey's Army" of graduate students. (Another 3,824 part-time students studied under a part-time faculty at the downtown University College.) In the matter of coeducation William Rainey Harper's prescription still held: women were well represented in all departments and were a majority in some.

By 1929 the campus, which had originally embraced only a few acres along the Midway pleasance, had become a sprawl of Gothic quadrangles and less ornate structures that encompassed some fourteen blocks of Chicago's once-fashionable Hyde Park section. Operation of the University required an annual budget nearing the ten-million-dollar mark, and the book value of the endowment topped sixty million, making it the fourth largest in the nation behind those of Harvard, Yale, and Columbia.

Although the University's location in the nation's second-largest city permitted many students to reside at home, the student body had always had a regional character, with some of the more notable departments providing a national, and even international, flavor. The Oxbridge-style quadrangles included student housing, and new dormitories and club facilities were being erected across the Midway.

A number of fraternity houses were also located nearby. One of Hutchins's first stops was at Alpha Delta Phi, where he assured his brethren that he considered fraternities a proper adjunct to collegiate life, making their own contribution to the idea of community he considered essential to a proper educational institution. Believing, as he did, that nurturing of the social graces should not be a concern of the university proper, he was not being sarcastic when he said of the fraternities, "Upon them must depend the development and maintenance of a wholesome, virile social life."[2]

The thirty-year-old president displayed no symptoms of awe, or of humility, as he took over the management of this considerable enterprise. The advent of the striking and gifted Hutchinses made a stir in the city. Carroll Mason Russell, wife of a University trustee and neighbor of Harold Swift, recalled meeting the couple at the Lakeside compound the weekend before they officially took up residence on the campus:

> We came over for dinner from our house next door, and were indeed well impressed. Harold, as usual thinking ahead of his guests' comfort, had arranged for Franja to stay at the Lakeside house with a nurse so that her mother would be free to get the family settled into the president's residence on the Midway. The handsome couple was featured in the city press when they arrived there early in September, and the whole University population was keenly interested. That group found a very tall and finely-built young president and his wife, the former Maude Phelps [*sic*], who was several years younger, quick-witted, a gay and free spirit, and already a respected sculptor.[3]

Maude's free spirit, however, would create problems for Hutchins, and they began early, though for some time they remained beneath the surface. John U. Nef, who as chairman of the innovative Committee on Social Thought was to become a close collaborator with Hutchins in his educational reforms, recalled that his first encounter with the president's vivacious wife was, to put it mildly, startling. He was seated by Maude at a dinner for senior faculty members at the campus Quadrangle Club, and her opening remarks, directed to him but audible to all present, were a tirade against the parochial stuffiness that she had found characteristic of the academic community.[4] Other leading social lights had similar unsettling experiences with the president's outspoken and unpredictable consort.

Hutchins himself was spending much of his time on the public platform. Capacity audiences turned out for the informal speeches he delivered during the weeks preceding the inaugural ceremonies on November 19, 1929 — all marked by the lighthearted self-deprecation he employed to take the sting out of his irony.

In October, making his first appearance at a faculty dinner, he confessed that the combination of his youth and Chicago's retirement age of sixty-five had engendered a horrible thought he was sure his audience would share:

And that thought, gentlemen, is that the University is to have one president for thirty-five years. Think of it. Thirty-five years. It is a generation, an epoch, an era, an eon, an age, the life span of a good, strong horse. It is 140 quarters, 1,820 weeks, 12,775 days, 306,600 hours, 18,396,000 minutes, 1,003,760,000 seconds — but there is one minor consolation; if we can protract this meeting we can go home to our wives and say, "Well, we did one good thing tonight anyway, we got about 100,000 seconds of this administration out of the way."[5]

At a Chicago Yale Club dinner he gently ribbed his fellow honoree, President Angell, and the memory of the revered Old Blue, President Harper. It was as a Chicago dean, he suggested, that Angell had acquired a yen for monumental stone edifices, and it was "that experience in the wrecking, draining, contracting and construction business that has enabled him in a few years to destroy and rebuild New Haven. . . . Any building that wasn't Gothic would be secretly torn down in the night."[6] And he assured the doughty millionaires of the Union League Club that his speech there would include no appeal for funds; at Yale he had learned from their kind that "you couldn't raise money by public address. You have to catch them unawares."[7]

At his inaugural Hutchins got down to business. In his carefully crafted address, delivered without manuscript or notes, he paid the obligatory tribute to Harper and affirmed his own belief that the heart of the University was its faculty. Since the end of the Rockefeller benefactions in 1919, he noted, the University had received fifty-three million dollars in cash and pledges but had been free to use only seven million of that sum for general salary purposes. The massive bluestone buildings the gifts had made possible were important, he conceded, but Chicago would have become a great institution even if the scholars whom Harper assembled had met in a tent.

Having cheered the faculty with these sentiments, Hutchins went on to give pause to many of its most distinguished members. Harper had made research and experimentation paramount, and he pledged that the tradition would continue. But he thought the time had come when narrow departmental lines must give way to a more cooperative interdisciplinary approach. "We are studying and proposing to study problems that do not fit readily into the traditional departmental pattern of a university," he warned.[8]

The program he foresaw would recognize that graduate study must be concerned with the education of teachers as well as with the production of researchers. "Yet the training for the doctorate in this country is almost uniformly training in the acquisition of research technique, terminating in the preparation of a so-called original contribution to knowledge. . . . [But] most Ph.D.'s become teachers and not productive scholars as well. Their productivity ends with the dissertation." Changing this would require reconsideration of the function of the undergraduate Colleges:

The emphasis on productive scholarship that has characterized the University from the beginning and must characterize it to the end has naturally led to repeated question as to the place and future of the colleges. They could not be regarded as training grounds for the graduate schools, for less than 20 percent of their students went on here to graduate work. Nor did the argument that we should contribute good citizens to the Middle West make much impression on distinguished scholars anxious to get ahead with their own researches. . . . At times, therefore, members of the faculty have urged that we withdraw from undergraduate work, or at least from the first two years of it. But we do not propose to abandon or dismember the colleges. . . .

If the University's function is to attempt solutions to difficult educational problems, to try to illuminate dark and dubious fields, it cannot retreat from the field of undergraduate work, so dark and dubious today. . . . If the departments are to experiment with the education of teachers, they must work out their ideas in the colleges here.[9]

On the day after the inaugural Hutchins appeared before a student assembly, using the occasion to address a concern expressed in a *Daily Maroon* editorial suggesting that a university president was "no longer an educator, but a salesman and extortioner *ne plus ultra*. . . . The importance of this mercenary and unsavory function of the administrator is particularly evident here where the grey towers continue to rise on a Gargantuan scale. It is to be hoped that the pressure of this work will not require the whole devotion of President Hutchins."[10]

It was a tender point with Hutchins. In New Haven he had sat with the Corporation during the Gothic building boom he ridiculed in his Yale Club speech, and he had seen the officers and trustees spend most of their time playing with building blocks and neglecting what he deemed to be primary educational concerns. In later years he would deplore the "edifice complex" that affected too many ambitious educators, but on this occasion he dissembled by observing that he had the good fortune to succeed presidents who had already raised funds to meet the University's most pressing building needs.

Obviously, this is a question of emphasis and degree. It is as foolish to say that men should not be emphasized first of all as it is to suggest that no new buildings should be accepted. Men do come first at Chicago. They always have. They always will. We are at the moment subordinating everything to the improvement of the staff. We are again and again directing the attention of the public to the fact that funds for salaries are the one great overshadowing need of the University. Through this process we may educate donors and in time produce a new attitude toward the value of professors as against the value of places to put them in.[11]

In January the seemingly endless round of speaking engagements brought him to the annual trustees' dinner for the faculty, which featured addresses by a board member, the president, and a designated faculty member. This occasion, held off-campus in the main dining room of the South Shore Country Club, was inaugurated by Harold Swift and remained one of his pet projects. Under his direction the board secretary worked out elaborate arrangements to insure congenial contact between trustees and professors. Each trustee was assigned as host to a table, and the assignment of faculty members took into account ''many factors including departmental affiliation, personal unfriendliness, and general suitability for placement at a particular table.'' In a memorandum setting forth these requirements, the secretary noted that ''one factor to be kept in mind is racial prejudice.''

> Working with this volatile mix of opinions and personalities, departmental affiliations and competitions, Swift tried to create an evening of fellowship. ''It isn't 'We Trustees' and 'You Faculty,' '' he advised one man who was to speak on behalf of the Trustees. ''But it is 'We, Us & Company, all together.' '' He counselled caution as well as congeniality. . . . But Swift's efforts to create good feeling were sometimes undercut by Hutchins' using the Trustee-faculty dinner as a platform for provocative remarks.[12]

He demonstrated that proclivity in his maiden address. In his usual ironic fashion, Hutchins began by confessing that he had been guilty of generalization and ambiguity in setting forth his priorities:

> If the faculty is the backbone of the University, the president is its vocal cords, which just now are a trifle frayed. This custom of having the president make a speech on every occasion or even when there is none is just as annoying to me as it is to you, if that is any consolation to you. Yet there is, you will be surprised to learn, some real reason for my addressing you tonight, for I do owe it to you, I suppose, to explain what the inaugural address was about. . . .
>
> When the newspapers inquired why it was that I seemed to understand so little of a speech I had just made, I followed the example of Mary Baker Eddy and Brigham Young, and attributed the composition directly to God — not the God I was brought up to believe in, but the God . . . who is interested in social progress, the family, radioactivity, reality, integration, cooperation and high salaries.
>
> These are great words. As I listened to them in the inaugural address I thought them soothing and sonorous. But I had difficulty

then, as you must have had, in determining just what they meant. What does it mean to integrate a university, for instance, and bring it into touch with reality? We can all agree on one point, I suppose — it means a lot of work for somebody. But where does that work begin?[13]

His answer was that integration would require a degree of cooperation among departments that too often did not exist: "At present, for instance, programs in the general field of human behavior are developing independently in four different divisions of the University. It is certainly not essential and perhaps not desirable that they be organized into one massive unit. It is essential merely that they be organized so as to supplement one another and to proceed economically and in harmony instead of wastefully and in conflict."[14]

Chicago, he said, must become preeminent as a pacemaker in education as well as in research: "Our aim should be to secure men if possible who are both distinguished scholars and creative educators. If this is impossible, and it is on a large scale, let them be one or the other."[15] He even raised the question of whether tenure was an impediment to improving the quality of the faculty, but he conceded that it was impossible to consider altering the practice while current faculty income levels prevailed.

President Harper had assembled an extraordinary faculty by offering salaries above the going rate, but now, forty years later, Chicago's pay scale was still about what it had been at the time of its founding. In his inaugural address Hutchins had predicted that the trustees would raise the salary level when finances permitted. Now he embroidered the implied promise.

"This matter involves more than salaries," he said. "It involves also faculty housing, the education of faculty children, faculty clubs and perhaps even investment facilities for the faculty." But he took a little gloss off the appeal by pointing out that one way to improve the lot of the individual professor was to distribute the available resources among fewer members: "We can derive little satisfaction from the thought that our faculty is getting larger each year. The university with the longest list of courses is not necessarily the greatest."[16]

Trustees and professors alike must have been bemused by his conclusion:

I commend to your imagination the picture of a university with a faculty of one hundred men and women all getting, and deserving, $50,000 a year. In the absence of additional endowments specifically for additional work, suggestions that additional work be done amount to suggestions that the salaries of the present staff remain as nearly constant as possible. If we can restrain our enthusiasm for a larger faculty until we are sure that all the men and women we have are worthy of their compensation, and have compensation worthy of them, we shall secure not perhaps the biggest group of scholars in America, but certainly the best.[17]

Hutchins had a good deal going for him as he began to translate his administrative theories into concrete proposals. The faculty had welcomed him, and the press had generally praised the appointment. The *New York Times* and the *Herald Tribune* devoted editorials to approving comment on his youth, and the Chicago papers followed suit. Only *The Nation* sounded a sour note that would echo among the left-wing intellectual coterie throughout Hutchins's career:

There is good reason . . . to doubt that Mr. Hutchins's future services will be directed toward scholarship. His capacity for high-powered organization, such as the recently founded Institute of Human Relations, his zest for all the academic intrigue and machinations required to put such big ideas across, is so great it seems to outrun his interests in the schemes themselves, whatever be their merit. His ability to raise money and wangle his way through the most intricate academic politics certainly recommends him for his new office.[18]

Hutchins was soon to demonstrate that his youthful impatience, coupled with his Puritan conscience, actually denied him the Machiavellian skills *The Nation* attributed to him. Knowing that he would face adamant faculty opposition once the honeymoon period was over and recognition of what he was intending began to sink in, he sought to bring to Chicago some of the like-minded colleagues who had worked with him at Yale. The attempt promptly rekindled the banked fires of campus politics.

He broke through the existing pay scale by offering an unprecedented salary to William O. Douglas. Although Douglas shook up some of the trustees when he came out for an inspection visit and delivered an address on "Termites of Capitalism," Hutchins managed to secure their approval by assuring them that he was the outstanding professor of law in the nation. In his memoirs Douglas set the proffered salary at twenty-five thousand dollars, but a biographer, James F. Simon,[19] found that it was only twenty thousand. In any case it was sufficient to support the rumor that he was being imported to take over the Law School, then headed by an acting dean.

Although Douglas accepted the appointment, he never reported for duty. Requesting repeated leaves of absence, he stayed on at Yale, where he was named Sterling Professor and given a handsome raise in salary. Employing the badinage that marked all their exchanges, Hutchins wrote to tell him, "You should be flattered to have the name Sterling attached to yours, even if it is only the name of a crooked old lawyer in New York and not an indication of high quality as in silver."[20]

The next year Hutchins was urging Douglas to forward his plans for the coming session to Dean Bigelow of the Law School, who felt he should know who was actually going to be on his faculty before he announced it: "He has a very unadministrative feeling that he should not misrepresent the situation in his catalog."[21] In June 1932 the trustees accepted Douglas's resignation. Hutchins never chided his old friend for his defection; he told Simon, "I never understood why he didn't come to Chicago. He just said he couldn't come. I don't remember his giving a reason."[22]

A less famous but no less prodigious Hutchins comrade-in-arms did arrive on campus at the opening of the fall term in 1930. On the day Hutchins's appointment at Chicago was announced, Mortimer Adler had just finished writing his doctoral dissertation at Columbia. This is usually a traumatic ordeal for a Ph.D. candidate, but Adler noted in his autobiography that he polished his off in "twenty hours at the typewriter, turning out seventy-seven pages between 9:00 A.M. one day and 5:00 A.M. the next."[23] By the time his doctoral credentials were formally conferred, he had another job offer from his friend and admirer in New Haven.

During the summer before his inauguration Hutchins sought Adler's advice on how he should proceed in his new job. In July he urged him to join him on the Midway, in a letter that echoed William Rainey Harper's ebullient prediction upon his own accession: "There's going to be no university in the world like Chicago, and besides we could have a hell of a good time there."[24]

The prediction proved to be correct, but both men soon had doubts about the addendum. "My very first suggestion to him led him to make one of the most disastrous mistakes of the early years of his administration," Adler wrote, "and one from which he — and I — never fully recovered."[25] The suggestion was that Hutchins bring to Chicago, along with Adler, Richard McKeon of the Columbia faculty and Scott Buchanan of the University of Virginia. This was intended to change the direction of the Philosophy Department, which Adler considered to be hopelessly mired in pragmatism.

"It never occurred to me that academic appointments are not made by presidential fiat," Adler wrote.[26] Hutchins, at least, knew better. He followed protocol in suggesting that the Philosophy Department consider Adler, McKeon, and Buchanan in making recommendations to fill an existing vacancy and two other places held by members who had already reached retirement age. In its evaluation the faculty found McKeon's qualifications passable and Buchanan's questionable, and they "entertained grave doubts as to Mr. Adler's competence in the field."[27]

Hutchins backed off on Buchanan and McKeon and sought to placate the philosophers by suggesting that Adler not be given a tenured position but be appointed associate professor for three years and assigned only two philosophy courses, plus two in the Law School and two in psychology. Largely as a courtesy to the new president, the arrangement was approved, effective as of the fall of 1930. But when Hutchins gave Adler, who had been earning $2,400 as an instructor in psychology, a salary of $6,000, J. H. Tufts resigned as department chairman in protest. This was more than was being paid to any professor in the department, including the eminent senior member, George H. Mead.

Hutchins managed to paper over this dispute, and Mead agreed to take over the chairmanship from Tufts, who was due for retirement. But Adler's rambunctious debut on the campus confirmed rumors that he was being imported to organize a new Department of Philosophical Studies. Hutchins agreed to support Adler's effort to sell this proposal to his new colleagues, provided "you adopt the posture of proceeding with naive inquiry and intelligent humility." But, Adler wrote, "no advice could have been more ill-suited to the temperament and style of the person advised."[28]

Adler not only antagonized his fellow philosophers but began sending shock waves through other departments. The psychologists, sociologists, economists, and political scientists were outraged by a speech that began, "The distinction between exact science (the physical sciences) and inexact science (the social sciences) is a distinction between good and bad science, not between two different kinds of science."[29]

Hutchins, while trying without success to restrain his protégé, fueled the controversy by handling complaints from the philosophy faculty in a cavalier fashion that acknowledged the professors' right to a voice in naming their colleagues but clearly indicated his doubt that they were competent to exercise it. By January the matter had reached scandal proportions, with three members of the philosophy faculty — Mead, E. A. Burtt, and Arthur E. Murphy — announcing their resignations in a lengthy statement circulated to the faculty. Citing repeated instances of what they deemed to be bad faith on the president's part, the trio concluded:

> Under these conditions we cannot go on with the responsibilities of a philosophy department at the University of Chicago.
>
> (1) We have been painfully and most reluctantly forced to a position of complete distrust of the president's intent and methods in relation to our department.
>
> (2) Even if his intent and methods in the future should be above reproach or question, he has already created a situation in which it is impossible for us to do work here that a philosophy department should do.
>
> Since we have very favorable openings elsewhere, we are ending our terms of service to this university.[30]

The new opening was indeed favorable for Mead, who went to Columbia at double his Chicago salary of five thousand dollars. Burtt landed at Cornell, and Murphy at Brown.

In February a self-appointed committee from the faculty at large called upon Chairman Swift to discuss "the general situation with the president." On February 6 the *Chicago Tribune* published a restrained report on the resignations, which it attributed to "a difference of opinion between President Hutchins and Dr. Mead and his associates over appointments to fill vacancies in the department of philosophy."[31] The matter came before the faculty senate, but no action was taken and the controversy simmered down.

Although Hutchins had hardly won a famous victory, he had survived his first administrative skirmish without seriously impairing his position, and he was ready to confront the faculty on a broader and far more crucial issue: the evolution and adoption of a plan that would finally implement Harper's design for a new undergraduate college committed exclusively to general education.

CHAPTER NINE

Of Habits
and Morals

I f Robert Hutchins derived his plan for the reorganization of the University from the theories of William Rainey Harper and the shortcomings revealed by the earlier effort to put them into practice, he had his own fixed idea of the obligations that came with the president's office. It fell to him, as he saw it, to determine the ends the institution should be serving, and to employ all legitimate means to see that they were attained. In pursuing his goals he would not be deterred by the prospect of controversy, or indeed by that of defeat.

He described himself as "the classic example of the young man brought up to good habits who could not understand why he or anybody else should have them until his own experience forced him to try to find out."[1] The good habits were the product of his Puritan heritage; he grew up believing it was his bounden duty to respect the individual, beginning with himself, to work hard, to improve his mind, to tell the truth, to avoid the sins of the flesh, and to treat equals equally and the less fortunate with compassion. Duty, as Wordsworth put it, was the "stern daughter of the voice of God!"

But as Hutchins entered his thirties the voice of the Calvinist God, or any other, was no longer clearly audible to him. His continuing effort to find a rational basis for the moral code he believed a civilized community required came to preclude religious faith. But this was a gradual process, in no sense a rebellion against his upbringing. Nor did his skepticism alter his close relationship with his devout father or hinder his professional and personal association with some of the leading theologians of his day, among them the eminent Protestant Reinhold Niebuhr, President John Cavanaugh of Notre Dame, Rabbi Robert Gordis, the eloquent Jesuit John Courtney Murray, and the French Catholic philosopher Jacques Maritain.

He was still a Presbyterian communicant when he came to Chicago, and for some time he regularly attended Sunday services at the Rockefeller Chapel. He described his departure from the fold with his usual irony. It came one Sunday when the Reverend Charles Whitney Gilkey, the chaplain of the University, opened his sermon, "Yesterday I was on the golf course and as I teed off I was reminded that we must follow through in life." It was at that point, Hutchins said, that he "acquired a weekend hideaway and never reappeared in the chapel of the University of Chicago. . . ."

> If you are the son and grandson of ministers and have had to go to church twice on Sunday, to Sunday School and to the Wednesday-evening meeting of the Young People's Society for Christian Endeavor, you are entitled to be spared from the continuation of such formalities when you have anything serious to do. Because these were not serious gatherings. They were social assemblies of one kind or another. And my objection to the truths that were delivered by Mr. Gilkey was not that they were untrue, but that I had heard them over and over again. And frequently or sometimes in a better literary framework.[2]

The good habits of his youth survived the rejection of the faith of his fathers. Hutchins was never to shirk the obligations of any office he held or those he imposed upon himself as a matter of conscience. He continued to act upon his belief that it was possible to maintain "those habits of mind and conduct which are generally defined as Christian without having faith in one God, the Creator, or having faith in the immortality of the soul or any of the other central doctrines of religion."[3]

This meant that he had to be willing to accept the role of dishonored prophet without any hope of divine intervention or future reward. He was sustained, he wrote, by another central conviction inherited from his Calvinist forebears:

> My childhood was nourished by the stories of their independence, and I began to think at an early date that the ideal American was the perpendicular man. These ancestors of mine were all stubborn, and some of them were vain. Their notion of success did not seem

to involve material goods so much as it did holding on to their own convictions in the face of external pressure.[4]

The disdain for conspicuous consumption also endured. He chided his flamboyant friend Mortimer Adler as a sybarite. Adler, who cheerfully admitted that he did not find high living incompatible with high thinking, replied that this only proved that the elegant Hutchins was a closet anchorite. But if he still felt an occasional twinge of guilt, Hutchins had long since sloughed off any Puritan inhibitions as to his personal conduct. Although he would never have to plead guilty to the sins of lust, gluttony, or sloth, his conviction that the good life was also the moral life did not prevent him from relishing creature comforts, good liquor, fine wine, and haute cuisine.

The philosophy that had evolved out of his pre-Chicago experience was a kind of pragmatic idealism — a dichotomy as those terms were employed by the empiricists who had begun to dominate the academic world. Although he had been much taken with the emerging social sciences when he began experimenting with legal education at Yale, he had come to question their professedly value-free approach to the study and analysis of human affairs. At Chicago these reservations provoked an adverse reaction that was bolstered by a proud tradition, for early in the century the University had been the fountainhead of a pragmatic world view hailed by William James as "so simple, massive and positive that . . . it deserves the title of a new system of philosophy." Amy Apfel Kass cited the contrast with the liberal-arts movement espoused by Hutchins:

> The "Chicago School" came to be identified with a certain attitude toward knowledge and the nature of the knowable and, hence, with a certain view of education and the role of a university. The assumptions underlying the view could be found in the new mechanistic biology, in behaviorism, in the new scientific sociology, as well as in writings and ventures in progressive education. . . . The devotion to "progress," scientific and social, required special training in facts, methods and techniques.[5]

Two founders of the Chicago school, George Herbert Mead and James H. Tufts, were principals in Hutchins's showdown with the philosophy faculty over Adler's appointment. Another, James R. Angell, had become the university administrator whom he cited as a reverse role model. The leader, John Dewey, with whom he was to enter into a controversy that would rally opposing schools in academia, had moved on to Columbia, where he became the gray eminence of the progressive education movement that influenced a generation of American school-teachers.

Hutchins had no illusions as to the entrenched opposition he faced on his own campus and elsewhere. In his first year in office, addressing a gathering of southern educators at the University of North Carolina, he referred to the program he was attempting to institute at Chicago as "the organization of the University of Utopia" and predicted,

> None of you will ever adopt it. Perhaps it may serve as the horrible example [of youthful folly] I promised you at the beginning. At least it will give you something to laugh about when, in the great age I hope for all of you, you sit before the fire with your grandchildren on your knee and recall the amusing conference at Chapel Hill back in 1930.[6]

But this was only an outsize dose of the irony with which the brash young man laced all his public speeches. Like W. R. Harper before him, Hutchins regarded Chicago as a laboratory dedicated to experimentation in educational reform, and his own role as that of a missionary charged with pushing the whole of American education toward achievement of its highest ideals. If the objective was utopian, the effort to move toward it was not. The first question any proposal for change posed for the educational administrator, he insisted, was not whether it could, but whether it should be done. If the answer was yes, the administrator's duty was to use the means at hand in a full-bore effort to bring it about.

He was never to significantly temper that view. Twenty-five years after the Chapel Hill speech, summing up what he had learned from his sometimes bitter experience as a university president, he said:

> The minimum qualifications of an administrator in his dealings with the means are four. They are courage, fortitude, justice, and prudence or practical wisdom. I do not include patience, which we are told President Eliot [of Harvard] came to look upon as the chief requirement of an administrator. . . . I regard patience as a delusion and a snare and think that administrators have far too much of it rather than too little. . . .
>
> Nor do I include the theological virtues: faith, hope and charity, though the administrator needs them more than most men. I omit them because they come through divine grace, and I

am talking about what an administrator can accomplish by his own efforts. Since it is not within his power to obtain the theological virtues, I must leave him to work that he may deserve them and pray that he may receive them. . . .

If the administrator is to function at all, he must have prudence or practical wisdom, the habit of selecting the right means to the end. But the administrator's life reveals that, though the virtues may be separated for purposes of analysis, they are one in practice. The administrator cannot exercise prudence without courage, which is the habit of taking responsibility; fortitude, which is the habit of bearing the consequences; and justice, which is the habit of giving equal treatment to equals.[7]

Toward the end of his life Hutchins recalled that he had, as was his custom, found a classic quotation to use in response to fainthearted sympathizers who cautioned that an adamant stand on principle only increased the odds against him: "I would remind you of the words variously attributed to William the Silent and Charles the Bold. I have quoted them over and over: 'It is not necessary to hope in order to undertake, nor to succeed in order to persevere.' "

Hutchins employed all his good habits, and a few bad ones, in advancing what came to be called the New Plan. As a starting point he had a report by Dean Boucher, prepared for President Mason, which made a strong case for guaranteeing a new degree of independence for the undergraduate College and establishing general — that is, liberal-arts — education as its primary objective. And with a grant from the General Education Board, seven outside experts had been brought in to go over the University's administrative structure from top to bottom, with, as Hutchins put it, "a cold and impartial eye."

In October, when the faculty senate reconvened for the 1930–1931 term, Hutchins was ready to present a reorganization plan that carried the endorsement of deans Boucher, Laing, and Henry Gordon Gale of the Graduate School of Science. Characteristically, he reduced the sweeping proposal to a single typewritten page. It called for grouping the academic departments in four divisions — Humanities, Social Sciences, Physical Sciences, and Biological Sciences — and establishing the College as a coequal fifth. Each of these divisions would be headed by a dean charged with preparing a consolidated budget and approving all appointments before they were recommended to the president.

The separation of general and specialized education was made clear in pointed language: "This [College] division would do the work of the

University in general higher education. A student would pass from it on completing his general higher education and would be admitted to one of the other divisions on presenting evidence of his ability to do advanced work. Specialized study in Arts, Literature and Science, whether professional or non-professional, would be carried on in the upper divisions."[8]

The plan was promptly approved by the senate and by the board of trustees. In redrawing the administrative lines and redefining the function of the deans, Hutchins had placed himself in a position to exert the authority of his office through a few men of his choice rather than having it be diluted by the necessity of dealing directly with seventy chairmen presenting separate departmental budgets. But the details of the general education this new dispensation made possible, and the manner in which it would be offered, remained to be determined. Hutchins placed that responsibility on Boucher, whom he appointed dean of the College.

When he arrived at Chicago Hutchins had no firm ideas about the content of undergraduate education, except that it should be different from the miscellaneous elective courses he had endured at Yale. But Mortimer Adler had ideas — a plethora of them — and he had bombarded Hutchins with lengthy memoranda in the year before the president succeeded in bringing him to Chicago.

Adler thought that all the offerings of the University, graduate and undergraduate, ought to be subjected to philosophical scrutiny by a new class of "student professors" who, having spent enough time in a department to sufficiently educate themselves in the subject matter, might achieve "a critical reorganization or approach . . . and give others the benefit of this insight."[9] This, indeed, was the primary purpose of the Department of Philosophical Studies, which he was now trying, with a foreordained lack of success, to sell to colleagues who were making him less than welcome.

Despite the spreading controversy generated by Adler's confrontation with the philosophy department, Hutchins made him his surrogate in dealing with the committee that was working under Dean Boucher to create a new curriculum for the College. And in the critical early negotiations the president had to impose restraint upon his impetuous friend long-distance, after it became necessary to remove Maude Hutchins to Arizona for a rest cure at a desert sanatorium.

Hutchins had survived the travails of his first year in office in good health and spirits, but the pressures had taken their toll of his wife. Maude's reaction to her new role as the consort of a prominent educator was described in the memoir by Carroll Mason Russell, a not unsympa-

thetic neighbor who played a leading role in the social affairs of the
university community:

> She was still in her twenties and I think had no idea at first that
> being the wife of the leader of a university that was in the public
> eye involved actions on her part that were very important to her
> husband's success. Bob Hutchins must have discovered gradually
> that she simply could not, or more accurately would not, organize
> social affairs, make friends with the ''right'' people, or arrange
> for the ''right'' dinner parties. I heard her say that the thought of
> it bored her. Nor could she take much interest in helping her
> husband win approval of the rather unsettling changes in teaching
> methods that he introduced within a year.
>
> Maude had an engaging but fanciful way of carrying on a
> conversation which, if one were inclined to be practical, was
> disconcerting. On the busy, social north side of Chicago the two
> were, of course, much in demand. They dressed properly; they
> were handsome to an extraordinary degree; they were knowledge-
> able, witty, and in the news. How desirable! But for Bob and
> Maude these sallies into the world of the rich was not their
> favorite use of time. He was soon distracted by controversies on
> the other side of town. She was constitutionally disinterested in
> most of mankind. Yet one could easily see that they enjoyed each
> other in those first years. Their mutual intelligence bounced back
> and forth between them and plainly made lively companionship.[10]

By January Maude's physical and mental condition was such that
Hutchins felt it necessary to get treatment for her, and his concern for
shielding their family life from public view dictated that it be undertaken
away from Chicago. On February 2 he wrote to his father from Tucson:
''We have been here two weeks now and like it very much. They are
keeping Maude quiet, though not in bed. . . .'' She would remain under
the doctors' care until April, and he cautioned, ''Nobody knows we are
here.''[11] He dealt with his own situation in a letter to Thornton Wilder:

> The doctors suddenly told us that Maude had to get away and get
> built up if she was going to lead the kind of life she seemed to
> have to lead. . . . I shall have to go back this week or get fired.
> The reports from Chicago are so discouraging that I hate to appear
> there just now. Apparently the faculty has decided that that
> S.O.B. of a President has pushed them far enough and they aren't
> going to be pushed any further. Consequently I appear to be

licked, or about to be licked on my proposed curriculum. . . . All the boys that agreed in taking the lead are welshing, scared to death.[12]

During the president's stay in Arizona, Adler sent him detailed reports from the front by letter and telegram and in turn received brief responses intended to keep attention focused on the limited objectives that Hutchins had specified. As summarized by Adler, these were:

(1) General education instead of specialization in the college; (2) a standard curriculum, required by the standards of an examination . . . ; (3) broader training in the field of a student's special interest than is given by departments. In addition, there are a number of minor objectives in your original plan: (1) the elimination of departmental courses; (2) the elimination of English composition; (3) the qualification of students for small classes and tool courses.[13]

The "tool courses" were those intended to give students the skills required to pursue a specialty in the upper divisions, and some of these survived in the compromises that were necessary to bring the departmental faculties into line. But Hutchins stood firm in insisting that the bulk of the College student's time should be devoted to independent study, as outlined in a syllabus to be prepared for each of the broad survey courses. At his option he could attend lectures by senior professors from the divisions or participate in small seminars in areas of special interest. Counseling would be available, but each student would determine his own pace.

Adler's reports on the interdepartmental negotiations followed the roller coaster of his own emotions. The faculty as a group, he concluded, were not educated men, and what was worse, they didn't want to be. There were a few exceptions — those who generally sided with him — but they were not vehement enough to suit him. When Hutchins attempted to cheer him up, he warned against false optimism:

You have huge mountains of convention, prejudice, laziness, stupidity, vested interest and economic fear against you. . . . It comes from all quarters. The science people are prejudiced because of their conventional notions of how science must be taught; the humanities are trying to save their language courses;

they are all greedily protecting their private diggings and what gets me sorest is that they are doing so under the false banner of educational theory.[14]

But even Adler conceded that the plan the faculty adopted in March was an acceptable compromise. A student's mastery of the general-education courses would be measured by examinations constructed by independent scholars and administered by a newly formed University Board of Examinations. These could be taken at any time and when passed would certify the student as having satisfied the requirements for further study.

The system broke the lockstep that subjected all students to placement according to the number of course hours taken. Examinations were also required for entry to the College; they measured competence as age and grade-point averages could not. Chicago was finally on its way to achieving for its undergraduates the dispensation Harper had prescribed forty years before: "The student will receive his diploma, not because a certain number of years have passed and a certain day in June arrived, but because his work is finished. Whether earlier or later than the ordinary period of college education, it does not matter."[15]

There was widespread reaction to the New Plan, much of it favorable, except for the internal dissent that, while muted, was still very much in evidence. The *New York Times* reported in a lengthy account of the inauguration of the New Plan:

With 250 more applications for admission to the freshman class than last year, but with a conspicuous lack of enthusiasm on the part of the students who will now be sophomores, the University of Chicago is starting on Thursday its first term under its new, much liberalized plan of instruction.

Introduced by the new president, Robert M. Hutchins — amid mixed feelings among the faculty as well as among the new and old students — the arrangement goes the whole way in throwing on the student responsibility for his own education. Where some universities are trying tidbits and spurs in the way of honors systems and house plans, Chicago has begun to treat the under-graduate as though he really desired an education and needed only signposts to help him get it.[16]

It was the insistence that college students should be treated as responsible adults that intrigued, and in some cases appalled, the general public. Hutchins held that the University was not, and should not be, concerned with offering instruction in the moral virtues and the social graces. If a student reached college age without having acquired the self-discipline necessary to maintain good habits, he would not, in any case, be able to benefit from the intellectual offerings that should be the sole province of higher education:

> We have to expect that the family is the source of the beginnings
> at least of such moral virtues as the individual acquires. It is . . .
> ridiculous to attack universities for the conduct of students
> between eighteen and twenty-five years old, an age at which their
> characters — by which I mean the sum of their virtues or lack of
> them — are very largely formed and very difficult to change.[17]

Under the New Plan the dean of the College was charged with seeing to it that the students had a healthy and orderly environment in which to pursue their studies, but beyond that the administration assumed no responsibility for their personal conduct. Although this has long since become standard practice in most American institutions, it was a radical departure at a time when middle-class parents were still imbued with the "finishing-school" concept of undergraduate education.

"Students will be educated in independence," Hutchins proclaimed. "They will be given all the advice they can stand, but their education will be up to them. . . . By breaking down the routine progression of students through the institution we break down the barriers that have separated some of them from an education."[18]

But escaping from the custodial restraints of in loco parentis, and from what Hutchins scornfully referred to as the arithmetical method of determining educational progress, was only a start. The actual courses to be given within the new framework had to be worked out, as did the examinations and syllabi that would be based upon their content. As he turned his attention to these matters, the young president recognized that he really had no clear idea of what a sound general education ought to be. At this point, he later said, his own education began — under the tutelage of the redoubtable Mortimer Adler.

CHAPTER TEN

The Great Conversation

U pon his precipitate elevation to the rank of university president, Robert Hutchins took stock of his own learning and recognized that he had arrived at the age of thirty "with some knowledge of the Bible, of Shakespeare, of *Faust,* of one dialogue of Plato, and of the opinions of many semi-literate and a few literate judges, and that was about all." Mortimer Adler, apprised of this sparse inventory, warned him that he would soon be swamped by administrative detail and that unless he "did something drastic he would close out his educational career a wholly uneducated man." The remedy, Adler suggested, was a crash course in the classics of Western civilization, beginning with the ancient Greeks. This, he promised, could provide "the whole of a liberal education or certainly the core of it."[1]

Adler's own awakening had begun when he took John Erskine's general honors course during his junior and senior years at Columbia. This required reading a classic a week for sixty weeks, with a two-hour seminar on each book. Adler later taught the course at Columbia himself, and from 1926 to 1928 he joined Scott Buchanan, then the assistant director of the People's Institute, in inaugurating the Erskine "great books" course for fifteen adult discussion groups in the five New York boroughs. The discussion leaders included Richard McKeon, Clifton Fadiman, Jacques Barzun, and Mark Van Doren, all of whom became noted scholars and/or literary figures.

As a means of providing a similar education for himself and testing

Adler's proposition that systematic reading and discussion of the classics could provide the core of a liberal-arts curriculum, Hutchins instituted a similar course at Chicago. The 1930 Autumn Quarter Time Schedule carried a terse description of General Honors 100: "By invitation and limited to twenty students . . . the one two-hour class session a week, of a two-year course, will be taught by Adler, Hutchins."

The twenty students were chosen at random by the dean of the College from among the top entering freshmen. The reading list was modeled on Erskine's, and the students were examined orally at the end of each year by Adler's former colleagues McKeon, Van Doren, and Buchanan, and by a new recruit, Stringfellow Barr of the University of Virginia.

Dean Boucher of the College, Adler discovered, "found everything about this venture disturbing." So did many of his colleagues. As a placating gesture, members of the faculty were invited to observe the oral examinations given the first class and to report their impressions. Hutchins noted that one distinguished scholar thought the course was over the heads of the students: "Consequently he is going to be careful to put the General Humanities Course for Freshmen under the heads of his pupils. I assume he will begin by having them recite the alphabet in chorus." But the invitation to the faculty did stir up considerable interest, discussion, and argument, and to Hutchins that was always a good thing. "It is even possible that the course may have some influence on the progress of American education after you and I are dead," he wrote to Adler.[2]

The experiment began to attract outside attention, and a string of visiting celebrities stopped by to watch Adler and Hutchins engage their young confreres in Socratic dialogue. Among them were Katherine Cornell, Gertrude Stein, Orson Welles, Ethel Barrymore, Lillian Gish, and Westbrook Pegler. In summing up the session attended by the acidulous Hearst columnist, Hutchins said, "Metaphysics, then, as the highest science, ordered the thought of the Greek world as theology ordered that of the Middle Ages. One or the other must be called upon to order the thought of modern times." He then asked Pegler what he thought of the evening's discussion. "I don't know," came the reply. "I fell off the sled at the first turn."[3]

After her visit to the class Miss Stein had dinner at the president's house, where she began berating her host for teaching the classics in English translation. This led to a spirited exchange with Adler, which ended when she whacked him on the head and announced, "I am not going to argue any further with you, young man. I can see that you are the kind of young man who is accustomed to winning arguments.'' As they were leaving, her companion, Alice B. Toklas, said, ''This has been a wonderful evening. Gertrude has said things tonight it will take her years to understand.''[4]

Great-books seminars were also offered as extension courses, and a ''Fat Man's'' class led by Adler and Hutchins became an evening fixture at the downtown University Club, enlisting as participants many of the Chicago trustees and other leading local figures. A half century later that seminar was still meeting regularly, and when he was in town it was still led by Mortimer Adler.

For Hutchins it was a strenuous, if enlightening, business. He described his role to students at Saint John's College, where Adler was an occasional visiting lecturer:

> You who receive two hours of instruction from Mr. Adler three or four times a year can scarcely imagine what it is like to sit at his feet five and a half hours a week. We have an hour and a half conference and then spend four hours in the presence of students where I act as Mr. Adler's straight man. And all this and the preparation for it has had to be carried on between board meetings, faculty meetings, committee meetings, conferences, trips, speeches, money-raising efforts, and attempts to abolish football and otherwise wreck the educational system.[5]

The Erskine reading list, revised and augmented over the years with the advice of a number of ranking scholars, was ultimately given a formal title: ''Great Books of the Western World.'' The fifty-three volumes ranged across the ages, from Homer to Freud, including the works of seventy-seven philosophers, theologians, scientists, dramatists, novelists, poets, historians, biographers, and political and social theorists. Most of the books used as texts in higher education prior to the twentieth century were included; contemporary works were omitted on the ground that only the test of time could certify a classic.[6]

The learned examiners found that students could become familiar with this literature in the two-year course of readings and seminars. But even so quick a study as Hutchins often found the going tough. In 1931, vacationing with Maude while preparing for the second year of the seminar, he wrote to Adler: ''I have read all the easy books: *War & Peace, Crime & Punishment,* ho hum, John S. Mill — and then for some damned fool reason I started to read Hume. I don't care for Hume. I can't seem to get interested in the old ass. And yet I think I ought to read him.''[7]

In fact Hutchins was much interested in the eighteenth-century Scots philosopher, but in a negative way. For it was David Hume who pushed John Locke's empiricism to positivism in science and skepticism in philosophy. To Hutchins and his fellow "liberal artists" Hume could be seen as a patron saint of the Chicago school, one who endowed his contemporary disciples with "the kind of positivism that asserts that everything except mathematics and experimental science is sophistry and illusion."[8]

It was precisely for this reason that the "old ass" had a place in the Great Books. His ideas had influenced generations of thinkers, and it was only through the examination of conflicting theories, Hutchins insisted, that one could discern truth. Hume's voice was essential to the continuing dialogue he called the Great Conversation in the preface he wrote for the set of Great Books published by Encyclopaedia Britannica: "It is the task of every generation to reassess the tradition in which it lives, to discard what it cannot use, and to bring into context with the distant and intermediate past the most recent contributions to the Great Conversation which has gone on from age to age in these creative writings."[9]

Prior to this century, he noted, no man could be considered educated until he was acquainted with the masterpieces of Western literature. Hutchins had concluded that this was still the case, and that the proper basis of the higher learning had been lost when the empiricists imposed their demand for narrow specialization upon the colleges and riddled undergraduate curricula with electives.

The educational philosophy that evolved out of Hutchins's collaboration with Adler was grounded in the belief that the study of the classics, in a context that related them to modern scholarship, was essential preparation for the good life. Although this kind of education was, almost by reflex, condemned as elitist, Hutchins from the outset insisted that it should be available to, and expected of, every citizen in a society that deserved to be called democratic. In the area of his immediate influence, he declared it indispensable for those whose formal education ended with the bachelor's degree — and not less so for the influential minority who would go on to graduate school to undertake specialized training for careers as scholarly researchers, teachers, or professional practitioners.

Throughout his tenure at Chicago Hutchins continued to join with Adler as a Great Books discussion leader. These courses were offered in the College and in the Law School, and for the curious citizens who enrolled in the "Fat Man's" course. Those who signed up enjoyed a unique personal exposure to the seemingly aloof president, and it left a profound impression on most of them.

Hutchins and Adler worked at making the seminar a genuinely participatory exercise. The two sat at tables pulled together to form a hollow square so that all those ranged around it were equally placed. If, as he had a tendency to do, Adler threatened to overdo his hectoring mode of cross-examination, Hutchins would bring him up short by engaging him in witty repartee. His own Socratic style led him to deflate the windy and irrelevant with a sardonic jab or two, but the atmosphere was such that no genuinely interested student could take offense.

Edward Shils, a social scientist who became both an admirer and a critic of Hutchins's, looked in on one of these sessions and described

> as harsh a piece of brow-beating of a student as I have ever witnessed, carried out by Mortimer Adler. . . . Hutchins, in contrast with Adler, was indulgent, even affectionate toward the students; he tried to reformulate their stumbling words so that they could discover what they dimly intended and he did it with a remote kindliness. Adler's and Hutchins' procedures, different as they were from each other, made a remarkably effective combination. Those students who survived Adler's harsh schoolmasterly style look back upon the Great Books courses as a glorious moment when it was a joy to be alive.[10]

For many the classroom experience had an enduring effect. Fifteen years after he departed the campus, John Godfrey Morris wrote,

> I tried on [Hutchins] the system that had worked, more or less, in other courses: skimming or even skipping readings and relying on "safe" phrases. The results could hardly have been more painful. First Adler, then Hutchins pounced on me until my brain lay naked on the table, each empty little cell exposed to the view of my classmates. Never, since then, have I felt safe in using a cliché. For a journalist this is a great contribution. . . .
>
> Mr. Hutchins continued to disturb me after my graduation. I was perforce engaged in the great American game of Getting Ahead. But . . . Getting Ahead to What? Why? Right ends, first principles — these kept haunting me. What had they to do with my weekly paycheck? The money came uneasy to my palm. The suspicion grew that I had only begun my education.
>
> I went back to the books, great ones and little ones. I sought the forgotten passages in the works of philosopher, historian, novelist. I found, too, that words which once were wasted on me in the classroom now had a meaning derived from life. . . .[11]

Sidney Hyman, who went on to a career as a writer and teacher, recalled the excitement that touched those whom Hutchins called Great Bookies. It was a combination of the exposure to the wisdom of the classic authors, he thought, and the inspiration engendered by the discussion leaders. And in his case Hutchins provided a lesson of great value to a beginning writer. When Hyman submitted an essay required by the course examination, Hutchins, whose oral and written style was the apotheosis of clarity and brevity, returned it with the notation, "Should be cut by half. Which half doesn't matter."[12]

Bernard Weissbourd took the course while an undergraduate majoring in chemistry. When he came across the platform at commencement to receive his diploma, Hutchins, even more imposing than usual in full academic regalia, leaned down as he handed it to him and said, "You're wasting your time with chemistry." Two days later, while Weissbourd was still pondering this unsettling comment, he received a telegram from the president: "Why don't you come in to see me?" Hutchins pointed out that one who had read the Great Books deserved something more stimulating than employment in a paint factory, and he suggested that Weissbourd try the law. He did, and he went on to become head of Metropolitan Structures, a major urban-development company, and a trustee of his alma mater.[13]

Having demonstrated to Hutchins's satisfaction that the Great Books could provide the core of a liberal-arts curriculum for undergraduate education, Adler served as his closest associate in the early years of the effort to reorganize the University. In his autobiography Adler candidly appraised the strengths and weaknesses he brought to the role:

> I was an objectionable student, in some respects perhaps repulsive
> . . . and emotionally immature I remained for many years
> thereafter — not only during the years that I was a member of the
> faculty of Columbia University, from 1923 to 1930, but also to a
> serious extent during the greater part of the twenty-two years I
> held a professorship at the University of Chicago. That, however,
> indicates a defect in my own makeup rather than in the educational
> theory I gradually developed.[14]

Hutchins, though inescapably aware that he was often the victim of his friend's defects, never deviated from his support of Adler's educational concepts. When the Philosophy Department refused to renew Adler's appointment, the president persuaded the Law School to create the position of associate professor of the philosophy of law. Adler was now known to his legion of critics as "professor of the blue sky."

Hutchins also persisted in his effort to bring to Chicago the other two members of what he called the "holy triune" — McKeon and Buchanan. When Adler first proposed their appointment, he sent Hutchins brief biographical sketches that included the usual professional data plus his own appraisal of their personalities.

Of Buchanan, a Vermonter who had studied at Amherst and Oxford before earning a doctorate at Harvard, he wrote, "Doesn't drink very well; is quite handsome, is married; has a most extraordinary man-child of six; is not a member of Phi Beta Kappa; supports an invalid mother; Presbyterian and Scotch by ancestry; generous and frank by nature."[15]

McKeon, a Columbia graduate who had studied at the Sorbonne before returning to his alma mater to earn a doctorate and receive an appointment as assistant professor of philosophy, was described as "quite a drinker; is a member of Phi Beta Kappa; is single but impecunious; not handsome but has it in some quarters; has no children; Irish and Catholic by ancestry, but just Irish by nature; has a little too much pride and dignity, but can be cured; is always a scholar and sometimes a gentleman."[16]

Hutchins was amused by these descriptions, which turned out to be accurate enough, but, knowing Adler, he no doubt entertained some reservations about the sketch Adler appended to his own vitae: "Easily intoxicated; is married to a beautiful woman; has no children but you never can tell; is not good looking but quite lovable; Jewish and German by ancestry, but anti-semitic and esperanto by nature; dislikes being thought of as a psychologist; is always philosophical, except in water."[17] The last was a reference to Adler's unique distinction as a Ph.D. who did not hold a bachelor's degree, Columbia having denied him one because he refused to take swimming and qualify for a required physical education credit.

Buchanan wanted to work as a philosopher in the Medical School, and Hutchins tried to place him there but was rebuffed. He did manage to obtain financial support from a Chicago philanthropist that enabled Buchanan to spend a year in England doing research tied to his interest in the relationship between mathematics and nonmathematical subject matter, reflected in his book *Poetry and Mathematics*. When the year was up he returned to the University of Virginia, where he worked with Stringfellow Barr on proposals for curricular reform.

Hutchins had better luck with McKeon. In 1934 he came to Chicago as a visiting professor in the Department of History and the next year was made dean of the Division of the Humanities, where he also had professorial appointments in philosophy and Greek. He would play a significant part in Hutchins's continuing effort to restore the priority the liberal arts had once enjoyed in higher education.

Adler, McKeon, and Buchanan were philosophical counselors to Hutchins, who never claimed to be a philosopher himself. Another early import, Thornton Wilder, served a similar role in aesthetics, sharpening and broadening Hutchins's interest in the arts. These were trusted friends as well as professional associates, and the usually embattled president freely unburdened himself to them when dealing with his educational concerns and aspirations, often indulging in the kind of sardonic comment that he rarely made publicly.

But only Wilder became a true confidant. Looking back over more than fifty years of close association with Hutchins, Adler could recall no more than six occasions when there had been any discussion of his friend's intimate personal affairs. Wilder, however, had a prior claim. He was cast in the same New England Puritan mold as Hutchins, had been his classmate at Oberlin and at Yale, and, repelled by the harsh austerity of his own father, had found solace with the more tolerant Hutchins family.

He was summoned from Lawrenceville, an Ivy League prep school where he was teaching English, by the offer of a faculty post at Chicago paying $666.66 a month. He had just published his second novel, *The Bridge of San Luis Rey,* and welcomed the prospect of "a congenial daily routine to occupy me while the dim notions of books shape themselves."[18]

Wilder's appointment, like the others suggested by the new president, was greeted with reservations. He had no graduate degree, and worse still, his novel had enjoyed popular as well as critical success, a condition that raised suspicion among literary academicians. But in his case the chill rapidly wore off; his wit, infectious enthusiasm, and natural eloquence insured his acceptance on campus. Hutchins explained why:

> One reason (the first) the English Department became enthusiastic about you was that you were the most popular teacher in the place and made the Department popular with the undergraduates. The Department thought of you as a great seducer who would lead the lambs into graduate work.[19]

Wilder was equally welcome in the company of the artists and writers who had gravitated to the neighborhood of the University, where they found cheap lodging in decaying Victorian houses and apartment buildings left behind by middle-class migration to the suburbs. In Prohibition days there were wide-open bars on Fifty-fifth Street where gin bucks and quarts of murky beer could be had for twenty-five cents, with every fourth drink on the house. They were convenient to such low-cost havens as Kuditch Castle on Harper and the inhabited storefronts just east of the Illinois Central tracks on Fifty-seventh Street. Here lived people who had known Sherwood Anderson, Floyd Dell, and James T. Farrell in the days when the area began to earn its reputation as a bohemian retreat.[20]

As his celebrity increased Wilder also became a lion in demand at the grand parties of the sophisticated rich on the other side of town. "Chicago in 1930 was a fighter's, jazzman's, writer's town," Gilbert Harrison wrote in describing Wilder's fascination with a milieu that contrasted sharply with his Puritan upbringing. "It was a depression town of workers without work, evicted tenants, race riots. But it boasted a wide handsome boulevard along Lake Michigan from the Blackstone to the Drake Hotels, and it was the home of a bustling university on the south side. . . . Wilder came to Chicago because of Hutchins; he stayed there because his years there, 1930 to 1936, were the happiest of his life."[21]

Wilder retained fond memories of an evening when he pulled Edna St. Vincent Millay in a rickshaw at the World's Fair, and of another when Texas Guinan from atop her piano introduced him to a nightclub audience, saying that she had read his book in jail and had cried and cried. He responded by taking the notorious Miss Guinan to a party for the Chicago elite, given by Harold Swift's sister and her English husband. "But best of all, and enclosing everything," he wrote to Hutchins, "was the *geist* you had infused throughout the Midway, ricocheting from stone to stone and eyes to eyes."[22]

Hutchins no doubt took vicarious pleasure in seeing his vivacious friend circulating among the varied strata of Chicago society in such an uninhibited fashion — an experience denied the young president by his position, his natural fastidiousness, and his family situation. And Wilder, who never quite succeeded in becoming the untrammeled free spirit he sought to be, had a special sympathy for Hutchins's mounting distress over his inability to cope with his wife's eccentricities.

Maude Hutchins accepted Wilder as a fellow artist, and he reciprocated in a way that made him the favorite guest of both husband and wife. But Hutchins later reminded Wilder that even in those early years the two old friends "had to watch every word because we couldn't tell what would set my then wife afire. Those days would have been intolerable without you."[23]

By 1936 the success of his novels and plays had made Wilder economically self-sufficient, and he decided to move on, using a summons from Hollywood as the stated reason. Privately he said he was sick of "hearing people say that Bob Hutchins has good ideas, but was tactless."[24] Hutchins wrote a gallant farewell in his usual ironic style, but the hurt showed through:

> What I want to know is, how can you do this to me? If you were going to do it to write a great masterpiece I should sadly consent. But don't you dare go and make a lot of money in Hollywood at my expense. Here is the University of Chicago just at the point where something might be made of it. Here is your old friend Hutchins at the Crossroads. . . . How can you talk so glibly of California? You might as well run hot (or cold) iron through my heart. . . . You deliver a blow that sends me reeling and are surprised that I do not welcome the chance to sacrifice my institution and myself on the altar of art. Well, boy, make it good art; that's all I have to say.[25]

Since Hutchins was always tied to an institutional base and the peripatetic Wilder was an early convert to what came to be called the international jet set, there was never again to be sustained personal contact. But the intimacy was maintained through the exchange of lengthy handwritten missives that continued throughout their lifetimes. Hutchins never abandoned the effort to persuade Wilder to return to the campus for a year, a semester, or just to deliver a lecture. In 1946, when Maude's obsessive demands for Hutchins's undivided attention were pushing the marriage toward its final disintegration, he added a poignant personal note to the usual entreaty:

> I need you very badly. The situation with which you — and only you — are familiar has grown steadily worse. Sometimes I think I must get out of here because I cannot carry the duties of the office. No time, and too much preoccupied. I can't travel any more and can seldom even get out in the evening. If you were here, we could sit and talk, and that would make me think, as it always did, that I was accomplishing something.[26]

CHAPTER ELEVEN

"DEBONAIR, FLUENT, LOGICAL, PROVOCATIVE . . ."

The compelling persona Robert Hutchins presented to the world virtually precluded a neutral reaction. It was difficult to ignore one who was usually the tallest, best-looking, smartest, and, if he chose to indulge it, wittiest man in any company. But he was always surrounded by controversy, and those who did not share his views often resented the natural gifts his supporters admired.

Although he observed the common courtesies, he considered himself obliged to be candid in dealing with his peers on matters of policy, and he was impatient when they did not reply in kind. In personal contacts the often abrasive effect was tempered by his instinctive good manners and patrician sense of noblesse oblige. Many of those who saw him up close, on social occasions or in the studied informality of his office, would have agreed with the appraisal of T. V. Smith, a young philosophy professor in whom he evoked mixed feelings:

> Why, Hutchins was a gentleman even when he tried to be churlish. . . . He was what I would have willed to be: debonair, fluent, logical, provocative, courageous and handsome. I regarded him as one man in ten million and rejoiced that he had come to head the great University which was my life. My work was my religion, and my profession was my church. Hutchins stood for me, therefore, as a spiritual leader.[1]

Hutchins always disclaimed any such grandiose description of his role, insisting that he was only an academic administrator engaged in an effort to find logical solutions to educational problems, upon which reasonable men could agree. Yet he did pay unyielding fealty to the ideal of the university as a community of scholars free not only of outside interference but of the stultifying restrictions of conventional academic organization and practice. Here he gave no quarter and asked none.

Inevitably, his forthright approach alienated those committed to the status quo. But it could also cost him the support of others who were generally in sympathy with what he was trying to accomplish. Smith, one of his few admirers among the original philosophy faculty, frequently opposed his policies during the two decades they were together at Chicago:

> He often seemed to me off-sided. I never wished to get rid of him as president, and always disassociated myself from any movement which reached that stage of opposition. He was incautious and he was close to arrogant. To have his superb administrative abilities show for what they were worth, he required consciences as stout as his own to oppose him. . . . He took upon himself to try to exercise a function which constitutionally, I thought, belonged to the faculty (or to God); and he did this by methods that often trenched upon the high-handed.[2]

Hutchins's eloquence and self-deprecating wit tended to ease the qualms of those whom he dealt with individually or in small groups. But most of the faculty enjoyed no such proximity. The size of the University, and the inescapable demands upon the president's time, afforded little opportunity for casual contact. When he laid his proposals before the faculty senate, made up of some 150 full professors, he refused to indulge in the calculated ambiguity that might have papered over actual and perceived differences. The senate was never left in any doubt as to what he intended. And whether out of pride or principle, he would not lobby.

Richard McKeon recalled going to Hutchins in advance of a senate session where they were to present a proposal for an interdisciplinary program in the Division of Humanities. " 'I've been sounding opinions,' " McKeon told him. " 'We don't have a chance. We will have our pants taken off.' And he said, 'You still think it's a good idea, don't you?' I said 'Yes — eventually we will do it, but we can't do it now.' He said, 'If it's a good idea, let's go in and have our pants taken off.' "[3] As McKeon had predicted, the faculty voted down the proposal, but five years later it was put into effect. It was Hutchins's conviction that changes he thought essential could not be made without controversy, and the sooner the issues were on the table, the better.

In the beginning he tried to establish a hail-fellow-well-met image on the campus. Although he ridiculed the rah-rah aspects of undergraduate life, he made ritual appearances at traditional student events. Angus MacLean Thuermer, a young neighbor who cut between the president's house and Rockefeller Chapel on his way to Hyde Park High School so regularly the famous presidential Great Dane, Hamlet, stopped barking at him, could never forget the sight of "Hutchins, arm-locked with his Alpha Delta Phi brothers, marching into Hutchinson Court at the Interfraternity Sing and the awarding of 'C' Blankets. Hutchins and C blankets seems unlikely, but I Was There."[4]

Hutchins also manfully turned up at the annual "Revels" of the Quadrangle Club, a Gridiron-style musical burlesque for which he provided a prime target. His statement that Chicago wasn't a very good university, just the best there was, produced this lyric sung by a chorus of professors:

> *It isn't a very good faculty,*
> *It's simply the best there is. . . .*
> *Though each eminent sage*
> *Draws a starvation wage*
> *You can quote us to wit and viz,*
> *It isn't a very good faculty*
> *But it's the best*
> *'Cause it's better than all the rest*
> *It's simply the best there is.*

And after he had abolished intercollegiate football, Hutchins appeared on the stage himself, clad in helmet, shoulder pads, jersey, padded pants, and maroon-and-white-striped socks, and sang "The Rose Bowl Blues."[5]

Throughout Hutchins's career his associates urged him to make greater use of his personal charm to soften opposition to his ideas. Adler, who recognized his own limitations in that regard, pointed to the example of Beardsley Ruml, an old friend from his Yale days Hutchins brought to Chicago as dean of Social Sciences. Ruml, a man of prodigious appetite and girth and a true bon vivant, maintained a suite at a nearby lakefront hotel where he regularly plied his department heads and senior professors with rare wines, fine viands, and Havana cigars.[6] Hutchins, Adler thought, would have been twice as effective had he employed similar tactics.

Hutchins did not reject such an approach on principle. In the case of fund-raising, which he accepted as a prime responsibility of his office, he recognized the value of informal contact in a salubrious setting. "The very rich vary in temperament and outlook," he said, "but they have one thing in common: a short attention span. When you have that kind of money you don't have to listen."[7] So he regularly went downtown to lunch with one or more of the trustees and any prospective donors they might bring along. But as he pointed out, he could not be at both the elegant and exclusive Chicago Club and the campus Quadrangle Club, where the faculty lunched — and where his infrequent attendance was a constant source of criticism.

There were other limiting circumstances. He was in constant demand around the country as a speaker, and as front man for the University he felt obliged to accept the more promising invitations. In the era of train travel an engagement more than a hundred miles from Chicago usually meant at least two days away from the campus. And when he was home, the predilections of his artistic wife virtually precluded routine entertaining at the presidential mansion. In a 1935 cover story on Hutchins, *Time* magazine noted:

> Like nearly all university presidents' wives, Maude Hutchins has been roundly criticized for snobbishness. Mrs. Hutchins, however, is a New Englander with a mind of her own. Scores of faculty folk have sat at her board, but she figured out long ago that if she entertained six faculty folk per night, five nights a week, it would take practically a year to go down the list. Hence she and her husband live quietly with their nine year old daughter Mary Frances (Franja) and their great dane "Hamlet" on the second floor of the big yellow brick president's house overlooking the Midway, entertain intimates there.[8]

"The problem of time, at least in a university, is insoluble," Hutchins concluded early in his tenure. "The administrator should never do anything he does not have to do, because the things he will have to do are so numerous he cannot possibly have time to do them all." As a result, the question of priorities posed a dilemma beyond the reach of public-relations techniques: "A university administrator has at least five constituencies: the faculty, the trustees, the students, the alumni, and the public. He could profitably spend all his time with any one of the five.

What he actually does, of course, is to spend just enough with each of the five to irritate the other four."[9]

Among the constituencies, Hutchins fared best with the trustees. There he had the advantage of sustained personal contact, enhanced by his meticulous attention to keeping the governing body fully informed. He never challenged the board's ultimate authority, and he fully appreciated the trustees' role in interpreting the policies and practices of the University to the community at large. This he recognized as indispensable for a private institution dependent upon voluntary contributions for its financial support.

But perhaps his greatest asset in the early days was the fact that his arrival at Chicago coincided with the onset of the Great Depression. He was inaugurated within a month of the 1929 collapse of the stock market, and over the next four years the precipitous decline in the value of common stocks, bonds, and real estate reduced the University's endowment income by 35 percent. And as he recalled, it was hardly a time when even the most charming and persistent seeker of philanthropic gifts could expect a welcome from the usual sources:

> The sudden shock of the Great Depression came to Chicago in a very dramatic way. Bank after bank exploded. Almost all the principal hotels went bankrupt, some of them spectacularly. The suicide of one or more leading citizens was reported every day. Most of the rest of them seemed to be under indictment, though I cannot recall that any of them went to jail.[10]

On top of all of this, as unemployment spread, a question arose as to how many students would be able to afford Chicago's relatively high tuition fees. Except for endowment and special-purpose foundation grants, which were also being drastically curtailed, these fees were the only source of income for an institution burdened with fixed operating costs.

Hutchins, who was convinced that beyond a certain point size became a detriment to excellence in education, actually welcomed the necessity of cutting the budget to meet the drastic loss of income, insisting only that reduction of faculty salaries be undertaken as a last resort. For reasons that had nothing to do with the fiscal plight of the University, the New Plan resulted in the elimination of some 350 course offerings. This permitted a reduction in faculty, accomplished by attrition under a mandatory retirement age of sixty-five. "We could have parted with ten per cent of our faculty with a light heart," Hutchins reported to the trustees, "if we could have selected the ten per cent."[11]

The line was held on faculty salaries, though the privilege of earning extra income by teaching extension courses or during the fourth quarter was revoked, with the departments required to carry such instruction as part of their regular work — a major factor in paring the catalogue. Administrative salaries, including Hutchins's, were cut, the highest by 20 percent, the lowest by 10. All nonrecurring expenditures, including book purchases and publications, were sharply reduced.

This was the kind of budget-balancing management the business-minded trustees admired, and they were prepared to listen sympathetically when in 1935 the president warned that no further economies were possible without changing the character of the University. The estimated income from student tuitions during 1934–1935 was some 18 percent more than the income from endowment, an unprecedented condition that "inhibits experimentation, tends to decrease the emphasis on research, and to exaggerate the importance of the demands of students and their parents . . .":

> The most serious element in the University's situation, and the only disturbing one, is its financial position. We have been able to preserve all the essential characteristics of a great University — academic freedom, excellent research, and competent teaching — in the face of unprecedented hardships. We may take some pride in the fact that we have in this period improved our organization and made significant contributions to education. Instead of being demoralized the University is now better prepared for its task than it was five years ago.[12]

That was as close to boasting as Hutchins ever allowed himself to come, and it seems to have served its purpose. The trustees rallied to his call, and he never had to temper his frequent assertion that while Chicago was not a very good university, it was still the best there was.

Every public man's personality is to some extent contrived; one cast in the role of advocate, as Hutchins was by choice, shapes his manner to serve the ends he pursues. Hutchins was much too young to assume the solemn dignity that usually attends the office of university president, and he made no effort to repress the mischievous quality that went with the "boy wonder" title the press had conferred upon him. But his exceptional natural endowment was such that he could never pretend to be what in his day was called a regular fellow. The wisecrack, an often irrepressible manifestation of his quick mind and his sense of the absurd, became a device he employed to avoid seeming pretentious.

T. V. Smith recalled his first encounter with the new president, at a banquet session with a business association where Smith was the speaker. Hutchins took a seat at the head table next to a leading local tycoon, identified himself, and inquired, "What's *your* excuse for being here?" After Smith had baited the roomful of potential donors, Hutchins muttered a conventional compliment. "I looked him straight in the eye," Smith wrote, "and said with a slight turn of the dagger, 'I hope you liked it.' He looked me straighter in the eye and said with a more decided turn of the dagger, 'You go straight to hell.' " Smith said he loved Hutchins from that moment forward: "He knew what the score was and did not flinch."[13]

His wisecracks attained wide circulation in their day, and some still endure. While he was at Yale he is said to have encountered a venerable Supreme Court justice who greeted him with, "So this is the boy-wonder law-school dean. I understand you teach your students that the nine old men down in Washington are all senile, ignorant of the law, and indifferent to the public welfare." Hutchins replied, "Oh no, Mr. Justice, we don't teach them anything like that. We let them find it out for themselves."[14]

His oft-repeated claim that when he felt an urge toward physical exercise he lay down until it went away was well suited to the indolent pose he adopted to divert comment from his truly formidable energy. The line, which he had in fact borrowed from the humorist J. P. McEvoy, was one of the many apt quotations filed away by Hutchins in his capacious memory. One of his favorites was from Gibbon's *Decline and Fall of the Roman Empire:* "Twenty-two acknowledged concubines, and a library of sixty-two thousand volumes, attest the variety of his inclinations, and from the productions which he left behind him, it appears that the former, as well as the latter, were designed for use rather than ostentation."[15]

Any gathering of Chicago alumni is bound to produce anecdotes about the striking young man who achieved the status of a mythical figure on campus. There is doubtless much apocrypha in these recollections of the days when Chicago was in ferment, but it should be possible to rely on the trained memory of a distinguished journalist. In an obituary column, David Broder, the Washington political commentator, gave Hutchins credit for conditioning him to endure the tribulations suffered by White House correspondents during the presidency of Richard Nixon.

"No one who had experienced the intellectual and social scorn Hutchins could direct at a student editor was likely to be intimidated by Nixon and his bunch of 'plumbers,' " he wrote. As a sample, he recalled an encounter in the office of the dean of students. When Hutchins walked in unexpectedly, the dean politely identified his visitor: "You know Dave

Broder, the editor of the *Maroon."* Hutchins raised an eyebrow and replied, "Can't you put him to work doing something useful, like washing windows?"[16]

At the end of Hutchins's first five years in office, *Time* wrote of him: "Chicagoans on & off campus agree on two facts about President Hutchins: (1) He is exceedingly smart and able; (2) he is entirely too flip and smart alecky." But the magazine found that after his colleagues had become better acquainted with the young president, his popularity had soared: "Most facultymen who still dislike him fall into three classifications: (1) mossbacks; (2) peanuts; (3) strangers."[17]

Other than on the platform, where he presented a formidable presence, Hutchins had a relaxed and informal manner. At Chicago, as in the Ivy League, "Doctor" was never employed as a form of address for any holder of an advanced degree other than a physician, and "Professor" was reserved for formal use, leaving "Mr.," "Miss," or "Mrs." as the standard courtesy titles. In his day-to-day contacts Hutchins didn't bother with these but instead used first names for the males with whom he had any sustained relationship, indicating that he expected to be called Bob in return.

He became famous, on campus and off, for his abbreviated responses to written correspondence. When Wellington Jones, a professor of geography, wrote to politely question some of his administrative maneuvers, sending a copy to Chairman Swift, Hutchins replied, "You are a dope. Instead of writing Mr. Swift and me long letters that are not on the point and that I haven't time to read, why don't you come in to see me?" Jones replied that being of naturally timid disposition, he preferred to communicate his criticism in writing: "I appreciate your suggesting that I come to see you, and some time I may get up my courage and surprise you, if for no other reason than to find out what you mean by a 'dope.' " So the correspondence continued. A letter in which Jones asked if his conclusions were not right was returned by Hutchins with *right* underlined in red and the notation "You are! RMH." As the exchange progressed, he began addressing Jones as Duke. "I have no objection (to be honest I rather like it) to your calling me 'Duke,' as does nearly everyone I know in the University," Jones wrote. "My inhibitions are few, but . . . I still find it not quite right to salute my University President either as Robert or Bob." The file of correspondence left behind in the geography department archives seems to indicate that the two never got around to exchanging views face-to-face.[18]

Toward the end of Hutchins's tenure at Chicago, when he had assumed the title of chancellor, the distinguished Italian classicist

Giuseppe Borgese complained that his terse style denied "the voluptuous role of the paragraph." The remark became famous in the inner circle of the administration and provided the title for a sampling of Hutchins's correspondence put together by Vice President W. C. Munnecke. This led off with apt quotations from Abraham Lincoln, Defoe, and Rousseau and the work of an unidentified "minor twentieth-century poet":

> *The Academic Mind, among its Works,*
> *Makes Mental Giants out of Mental Jerks. . . .*
> *And yet, Each Coconut provides some Meat:*
> *Within each Mound of Chaff resides some Wheat.*
> *All Candles have a chance to cast a Beam:*
> *All Fish can make a choice — and swim Upstream.*
> *A Zephyr changes Furled Flags to Unfurled:*
> *One Letter makes One Word into One World.*
>
> *Gaze on the Words of Hutchins, and Explore*
> *The Wordy Wisdom of Our Chancellor.*

Following that, in their entirety, were six typical Hutchins letters: "Dear Pomp: I'll be sure to do it"; "Dear Willie: No, if you will spell *accommodations* with two *m*'s"; "Dear Pat: I'll be there"; "Dear Flash: I do"; "Dear Reuben: 1. No"; "Dear the Central Administration: By God I am."[19]

Only with women did Hutchins lapse into the old-fashioned formality he had been trained to accord them in his youth; the few exceptions were contemporaries in age whom he saw socially. Esther Donnelly, who joined him at Chicago and served as his personal secretary for most of his remaining years, was Miss Donnelly until death did them part, and it would never have occurred to her to refer to him, in or out of his presence, as anything other than Mr. Hutchins.

There was more to this than mannerism. While he never blinked at the most disputatious confrontation with his professional peers, he was incapable of sustained argument with the women in his life. He was married twice, and his daughter Clarissa thought he spoiled both her mother and her stepmother. He was never a stern disciplinarian, she said, and he could be playful, but his reserve created a barrier that she and her sisters found it difficult to penetrate.[20]

Most students and faculty considered him aloof, but he was in fact approachable by anyone who had business with him and generally tolerant of those who didn't but came to see him anyway. If he didn't suffer fools gladly, he usually contained his feelings in their presence.

His expression was normally impassive, and unless it was relieved by an occasional smile or the impish grin that accompanied one of his own sallies, this effectively distanced him from anyone who threatened to waste his time. For unduly verbose visitors he kept a sign that he would remove from a drawer and place on his desk: "Don't tell the president what he already knows." He could chill the atmosphere, but he rarely indulged in any comment that could be considered personally insulting, and he made it a rule never to reply in kind to ad hominem attacks by his critics.

His unorthodox personal style also served as a shield for his private feelings. His Puritan heritage had schooled him not to display emotion, and he testily rejected the suggestion that, to some at least, he had become a charismatic figure. An appeal for support that was intended to evoke a sentimental response would have offended him in any circumstance, and he thought it particularly obnoxious in a university setting. His posture was that of a rational man convinced that reason could be made to prevail — and any doubts and fears he may have entertained were revealed only to the very few intimates who were allowed behind the facade he presented, formally or informally, in his role as a public man.

With those whom he knew well Hutchins was likely to employ badinage in the discussion of even the most serious matters. It provided a safeguard against the sentimentality he abhorred, and since it invited a reply in kind, it removed any suspicion of pretentiousness. Milton Mayer, who became adept at emulating Hutchins's ironic style, provided a perhaps embroidered example in recounting how he joined the president's staff.

A Chicago alumnus, Mayer had become disillusioned with his employment as a reporter on William Randolph Hearst's afternoon *American*. Knowing that Hearst had offered Hutchins the editorship of his Chicago newspapers and been turned down, he went to the president's office to seek aid and comfort. He found him leaning back in his swivel chair with his feet propped up on a desk drawer, reading Aristotle's *Metaphysics*. Hutchins recalled that they had had a similar talk once before:

> "You were an Old Plan boy as an undergraduate, and as a result
> you were unemployed. You may remember that on that occasion
> I despaired of anybody's ever being able to do anything for you.
> I was right, as usual. Look at you now. You are a hireling of
> Hearst. You ought to be ashamed. Are you ashamed?"

"Worse than ashamed," I said, "and that's what I have come to talk to you about."

He looked at his watch and said, "Professor Adler and I have to conduct a Great Books class in half an hour. This" — holding up the *Metaphysics* — "is a Great Book, and Professor Adler will be here in twenty minutes. So make it snappy, Son."

"I have come to be saved," I said.

"You have come to the right party," he said. "What do you want to be saved from?"

"William Randolph Hearst," I said. . . . "How did you get saved from him?"

"I didn't," he said. "A few years ago, when I was chairman of the Regional Labor Board, I found for a C.I.O. union and Hearst called me an accomplice of Communists and murderers. When he found he couldn't lick me, he tried to join me; he offered me a job. I turned it down and became an accomplice of Communists and murderers again. But you're wasting my time. What do you want me to do?"

"Save me."

"What will you do to be saved?"

"Anything."

"Anything? How much is Hearst paying you?"

"Ninety. I'm the white-headed boy."

"I'll give you forty-five and you'll be the black-headed boy."

"I can't live on that," I said.

"You didn't say you wanted to live," he said. "You said you wanted to be saved. You cannot be saved any cheaper."

Mousetrapped.

"Your offer is irresistible," I said. "What do I do?"

"Get educated, like me," holding up the *Metaphysics* again. "I will introduce you to Professor Adler, who is educated, and he will introduce you to Aristotle, and you will learn that the cause of all ruin is ignorance, a condition which you exemplify by supposing that Hearst is the cause of your or anybody else's ruin. Hearst is not a cause but an effect. He is the effect of your ignorance. Wise up. . . . Get out of here and think it over."

Think it over, my foot.

Thornton Wilder once said, "Bob Hutchins has the habit of being right." But he wasn't right the day he hired me for forty-five dollars a week. He could have had me at twenty-two fifty.[21]

*   *   *

Mayer signed on for the Great Books course while serving as a public-relations aide to the president, and became a discussion leader himself. Emerging as a sort of philosopher manqué, he went on to become a Quaker convert, antiwar activist, eloquent free-lance writer and lecturer, and sometime college professor. In later years he recorded lengthy discussions with Hutchins in preparation for a biography that remained unfinished at the time of his death in 1986. The transcripts of those sessions, which were more dialogue than interview, demonstrated that the passage of the years had had little effect on the style of either man.

Forty years after that exchange in the president's office, Mayer recounted it in an address at a Shimer College dinner honoring Hutchins, citing it as "an anecdote for those of you who are young and who know the Hutchins words but do not know the Hutchins music." Of his old mentor he said: "I know that he has not succeeded in changing the world, but I know something much more marvelous than that: I know that the world has not succeeded in changing him."[22]

CHAPTER TWELVE

Impolitic
Politics

Robert Hutchins's youth, the high academic office he held, his controversial ideas, and his striking personal style combined to make him a media star a generation before that term was coined. If the generally stodgy newspaper proprietors and editors of the day tended to look askance at the brash young man, their hired hands sought him out. "[He] is too dynamic in action and too ornamental in repose to escape the photographers," J. P. McEvoy wrote, "while the reporters who come to sip at the spring of his wisdom remain to dunk in the sauce of his wit."[1]

The leading literary magazines and some of the popular ones welcomed the trenchant articles he fashioned out of his public addresses, and his comments were frequently featured in *Time,* his classmate Henry Luce's influential newsmagazine. He took naturally to the first network radio talk show, NBC's "Roundtable of the Air," which originated on the Chicago campus.

Although he generally confined his public utterances to educational subjects, his approach was on so broad a front it inevitably touched upon contemporary political issues. His open contempt for pragmatic materialism and laissez-faire government constituted an implicit indictment of the Republican administrations that had been in power since he came of age. As dean of the Yale Law School he had attracted enough attention to prompt Connecticut party leaders to offer him the Democratic nomination for the United States Senate, which he declined. As the deepening depression made Republican failures evident, and privation splintered the traditional constituencies, the outspoken young celebrity again began receiving political overtures.

The economic collapse that ushered in the 1930s had sharpened the skepticism with which Hutchins viewed the received wisdom of market-place economics. As a novitiate university president watching his institution's income decline in tandem with the stock market, he encountered a pervasive unreality when he voiced his concerns among the influential Chicagoans to whom his office gave him entrée. "It does not seem possible that there was another decade like the thirties, distinguished by the air of stupefaction, not to say petrifaction, that hung over us," he wrote in retrospect:

> We were and remained prisoners of our illusions. We rejected the evidence of our senses. We declined to think. When we acted, we did so because we were forced to. . . .
> When the Depression struck, we did not know what hit us or why. The general feeling was that speculation had been excessive and that when the stock market had been shaken out things would settle down again — and then resume their upward course.[2]

Hutchins was employing literary license when he included himself among those whose "received ideas were so deeply and widely held that we could not understand what was happening, and we could not figure out what to do about it." But he was right that dissenting views had made no impression on the collective "we" who "entered the thirties with a free-wheeling and autonomous economy and with no suspicion that there could be anything wrong with such a system or that it could ever come to an end."

> In 1931 I had dinner at the house of Colonel Robert R. McCormick of the *Chicago Tribune* with Winston Churchill and Samuel Insull. The date was unfortunately chosen, for Britain had just gone off gold. Mr. Churchill, who as Chancellor of the Exchequer six years before had pushed his country downhill by putting it back on the gold standard at $4.86, apologized to the three of us for the dishonorable conduct of his Government. Colonel McCormick, after a scholarly allusion to perfidious Albion, wondered whether money would be circulating a week later. And Mr. Insull was moved to a certain shame at having been born in England.[3]

When Hutchins expressed the view that a catastrophe of the magnitude of that affecting the American economy could hardly be explained by the decision of a trading partner to go off the gold standard, the only result was a decline in his dinner invitations: "It was immoral, or at least unpatriotic, to hold a different view; it showed a lack of faith in America. So Samuel Insull, who ruined everybody in Chicago by pyramiding utility companies, justified himself by saying he had believed in the future of our country."[4]

But Hutchins's skepticism had resonance in less rarefied circles, and when the Democrats began preparing for their 1932 national convention in Chicago, he was urged to draw up a "platform for youth" to be presented to the delegates. At the behest of a young Chicago lawyer named Adlai Stevenson, he was invited to address the meeting of the Young Democratic Clubs on the evening before the opening of the quadrennial party gathering. "I will personally indemnify you against loss or damage from cabbages, cocktails and/or Congressmen," Stevenson promised.[5] The executive secretary of the national organization reinforced the invitation with a telegram: "Nationwide hookup of Columbia network secured and prospect is that most prominent Democrats in the country will attend."[6]

In his opening remarks Hutchins noted that his counterpart, Nicholas Murray Butler of Columbia, had addressed the recent Republican National Convention, prompting Will Rogers to voice the suspicion that his real mission was to raise money for his university. If that was so, Hutchins said, he had gone to the right place. The Democrats, who had always prided themselves on being poor but honest, had no such attraction for a university president. He came before them only as a rapidly aging young man who ventured to say a few words on behalf of other young people who were sick of "the mess our predecessors have made of things. . . ."

> Upon what terms may a political party claim our allegiance? I see no present possibility that the Republicans can claim it. We demand an honest party. The Republican party is disingenuous. We demand a party of the people. The Republican party is the party of special privilege. We demand a progressive party. The Republican party is the party of false conservatism. We demand intelligent leadership. The Republican party has provided no leadership at all.[7]

He went on to cite the failures and contradictions of the Harding, Coolidge, and Hoover administrations, and to ridicule the vague and wordy platform the Republicans had adopted. By way of contrast he lauded Democratic history and tradition. If a little more eloquently phrased than usual, this was standard rhetorical fare at a partisan political rally. But Hutchins did not leave it there.

He was disquieted, he said, by the impression that the party's leaders were trying to assure the voters that Democrats were just as safe as Republicans, perhaps a little safer. He found the candidates for the pending presidential nomination "characteristically Republican in their efforts to conceal their ideas and thus secure the maximum number of votes by virtue of their personal charm. In short, the ambiguity that has surrounded the Republicans has begun to enshroud the Democrats."[8]

Warning that the greatest mistake the Democrats could make would be to behave like their political enemies, he challenged the party to set forth a progressive program in unmistakable terms. Then, in five hundred astringent words, he laid his own recommendations before the delegates.

The Democratic platform, he said, must begin by pledging the party to the promotion of peace. This would require the United States to lead the way in disarmament, with or without the cooperation of other nations. Adherence to the World Court and cooperation with the League of Nations were in order, but should not commit the nation to using its military or economic power against any other country. To revive international trade there should be a moratorium on war debts of not less than twenty years' duration. Soviet Russia should be recognized. The tariff should be revised downward.

On the domestic side, the party should deal honestly with government finance. This meant that the cost of government must be distributed in proportion to the capacity to bear it — that is, income and inheritance taxes must be increased to carry increased governmental costs. The public debt must be reduced in times of prosperity and increased, if necessary, in times of depression. Governmental costs could and should be reduced, not by cutting back those activities designed to promote the welfare of the people as a whole but by progressive disarmament and the reduction of military and naval expenses.

Since Prohibition had failed to prohibit, the party should commit itself to seeking the repeal of the Eighteenth Amendment. Special privileges should be ended for all groups. The destitute must be assisted, but veterans should not be singled out because of their service in the late war. Manufacturers must surrender the advantages that tariffs provided them at the expense of the consumer. Monopolies based on the possession of natural resources must submit to government regulation and, if necessary, government operation.

If it was impossible to have a sound banking system as long as bankers were actuated by the desire for personal gain, then steps should be taken to eliminate the motive of private profit from banking. Farmers should receive assistance through the development of an intelligent allotment program and through relief from the tax burden on farmland. The party should work for compulsory state unemployment insurance and old-age pensions, the creation of federal unemployment exchanges, and an adequate program of public works, including elimination of the slums. There should be no doubt that the party was committed to federal relief for the unemployed in any form that might be necessary.

Here, Hutchins said, was "the minimum program demanded by the present emergency. In that sense it is truly conservative, for the true conservative is not interested in conserving chaos. If the Democratic party will issue a clear and decisive challenge in such terms as these, it may command the allegiance of the rising generation."[9]

In that brief compass he managed to gore most of the sacred cows in the nation's political pasture, and he brought the Young Democrats to their feet, cheering. "Hutchins Speech Starts a Boom," the *New York Times* headlined its report. "Proposals by Young Head of Chicago University Inspires Talk of Place on Ticket."

> Taking a stand for repeal of the Eighteenth Amendment and expressing his views on other national and international problems, Dr. Hutchins established himself among Democratic leaders not only as "timber" to be seriously considered in choosing a candidate for the vice-presidential if not the presidential nomination, but also as an orator with spellbinding qualities.

The speech, the *Times* reported, "set candidates' row and the Democratic chieftains in the Congress Hotel and elsewhere talking of Dr. Hutchins."[10] But the boom died there. The chieftains went on to adopt a platform couched in the usual ambiguities. Hutchins said they deserved credit only for being brief and trying to be liberal. And to head the ticket they named Governor Franklin Delano Roosevelt of New York, who was surely among those whom the boy orator of the Midway had condemned for concealing his ideas and relying on his personal charm.

Hutchins was a political animal in Aristotle's sense, but not in that of officeholders who accept the principle that the way to get along is to go along. In later years he identified himself as an Independent who never found it possible to vote for a Republican, and in 1932 his reservations also applied to the Democratic candidate. He declined to join a Chicago faculty delegation in a public endorsement of Roosevelt: "They said his heart was in the right place. I think this was true. But I didn't think having his heart in the right place was enough.'' So though he was never persuaded of the validity of Marxist economic theory, he announced in August that the failure of the major party candidates to face reality constrained him to vote for the Socialist nominee, Norman Thomas: ''Thomas kept the issues alive — like La Follette, he kept the issues alive.''[11]

Nor did his dim view of Roosevelt improve in the heady early days of the New Deal, when the President cast aside the vague balanced-budget platitudes of the campaign and launched a vigorous program of government action that embraced many of the ideas Hutchins had set forth in his speech to the Young Democrats. He saw FDR as the precursor of the type of ''great communicator'' that has come to dominate American politics in the television age — one who ignores the structural flaws in the economic system and instead relies on incantation, as in Roosevelt's famous peroration ''We have nothing to fear but fear itself,'' to restore public confidence in the presumed self-correcting capacity of the free market. In the case of the New Deal, Hutchins thought,

> the psalm-singing was accompanied by a great show of activity. . . . Roosevelt, once he was in office, began a long vaudeville act in which he pulled one rabbit after another out of his hat. Each time a rabbit showed its head the people hoped this one would run. Unfortunately, few of them did. Some of them even proved to be cannibals. But each one, until it was consumed or faded away, served to keep hope alive.
>
> Then there was Roosevelt himself. He was not a very good administrator, and I have some doubts about his claims to statesmanship. But nobody can deny that he was a tremendous showman. The sodden solemnity of Hoover, depressing to the gayest of audiences, was replaced by the lightheartedness of a man who was born to perform in public, who was not hampered by many convictions he could not talk himself out of, and who therefore could — and did — experiment with anything he could get the electorate to approve.[12]

Although Hutchins made no secret of his reservations about the new administration, there were those with considerable influence in the capital who tried to sell him to Roosevelt and actively lobbied on his behalf. Secretary of the Interior Harold Ickes was one of these, and the President's principal aide, Harry Hopkins, became an ardent Hutchins man. Another was T. V. Smith, his admirer/critic on the Chicago faculty, who had been elected to Congress and had found a place among the young intellectuals on the fringe of the White House inner circle.

Hutchins refused to take any of this seriously, but he did respond when Smith set up an interview for him with Colonel E. M. House, Woodrow Wilson's de facto chief of staff, who served as a talent scout at the beginning of the Roosevelt administration. Smith recounted the result:

> [House] later asked me point-blank: "Can your friend Hutchins take advice?" I gave the Colonel an extempore eulogy of Hutchins. He repeated, "Can he take advice?" I gave him a passionate panegyric. The Colonel persisted in his gentle voice, "But can your friend take advice?" "Please don't ask me that again, Colonel. I've told you only half of how great a man I esteem Hutchins to be. But . . . if you insist on an answer to that question, it is no, sadly no!" House shook his head and concluded, "Then I am afraid we cannot use him. He's too young to go it alone."[13]

When Smith asked Hutchins about his interview, he said he had told Colonel House that the only position he would consider was that of secretary of war, which he expected to occupy only long enough to fire all the officers he had served under in World War I. It is not surprising that the only appointment of consequence Hutchins ever received from Roosevelt, or from any President who succeeded him, was a thankless one he accepted out of a sense of duty.

In the surge of emergency measures enacted in the epoch-making first hundred days of the new administration, the National Labor Board was created to deal with tensions between unions and management accentuated by the Depression. The task of mediating these disputes was left to virtually powerless regional bodies made up of unpaid public members serving along with representatives of employers and their workers. Hutchins sat for a year as the impartial chairman of the Chicago Regional Labor Board.

Discussing the experience in a speech to the Industrial Relations Association of Chicago, he pointed out the futility of leaving such matters to those who were either committed partisans of one side or public members who had no background in the issues at hand — and whose only reward was to be chastised as crooks or thugs by those they ruled against:

> I wish to confess to you in the privacy of this gathering that I have never met such rank, complete and utter dishonesty . . . as I have

met with as chairman of the Chicago Regional Labor Board on the part of the industrialists who came before me. My friends whom I meet around the Loop and with whom I have lunch occasionally would come in and lie themselves black in the face and tell me afterward they had.

Now I put it to you that it is impossible to operate any provisions as to collective bargaining as long as that spirit prevails, as it does today in this area; and the various associations of employers and . . . manufacturers are not attempting to alter that attitude. They have at least in certain cases to my knowledge done everything they could to support it. Industrial members of the board have privately, after they have participated in decisions, informed the members of the companies against which we ruled they were under no obligation to pay any attention to the decisions at all.[14]

The privacy Hutchins spoke of was, of course, nonexistent, and his citation of management duplicity obtained wide currency among the leaders of Chicago's business community, including those who sat on the University's board of trustees. These men paid little attention to the fact that he had also characterized the labor leaders who appeared before the Labor Board as hopelessly inept. Nor did they take seriously his prophetic warning that unless management became more cooperative, the country was in for a wave of bitterly divisive labor strife — the kind characterized by the "sit-ins" that disrupted the major industrial centers until the Wagner Act of 1935 established the authoritative government mediation service Hutchins had declared essential.

So long as the controversy he generated was largely confined to the academic community, Hutchins had attracted little outside criticism. The public was not surprised by unorthodox behavior on the part of those characterized by the media as intellectuals, and conservative leaders could accord him the tolerance they reserved for the irritating but often amusing and sometimes useful gadfly, a patronizing appellation Hutchins detested but would never escape. But now his extra-academic activity in the increasingly charged political atmosphere that marked the advent of the New Deal began to be perceived by conservatives as radical. And that tag too would stick with him for the rest of his life.

The Roosevelt reforms activated the dominant Chicago newspapers: the *Tribune,* which reflected the reactionary views of the "Morning Colonel," Robert R. McCormick, and the more moderate but unshakably Republican *Daily News,* headed by the "Afternoon Colonel," Frank

Knox. These two served the middle- and upper-income readership and corralled the most lucrative advertising. The struggling afternoon *Times* was a lonely supporter of the New Deal. That left the mass of low-income, largely ethnic and black readers to William Randolph Hearst's morning *Examiner* and afternoon *American*.

Hutchins's rousing speech before the Young Democrats made head-lines all over the country, but not necessarily in Chicago. The *Tribune* ignored it entirely under an edict from Colonel McCormick that banned any mention of his erstwhile dinner guest by name. It drew a mild scolding from the Afternoon Colonel. The *Times* gave it a front-page spread and a laudatory editorial and published the entire text. The Hearst papers didn't quite know how to handle Hutchins.

The coming of some of the New Deal reforms that Hutchins had called for posed special problems for those metropolitan dailies whose policies were dictated from their owner's castle at San Simeon on the Pacific shore. The Hearst papers had always attracted their readership with unabashed sensationalism and calculated appeal to the prejudices of semiliterate first- and second-generation immigrants. Now these were flocking in unprecedented numbers to the Democratic banner. To attack the Roosevelt administration, as the wealthy Hearst's ideology and self-interest required, a lurid, superpatriotic diversionary tactic was needed. An old standby was trotted out — the Red Terror that had served so well in the aftermath of World War I.

The field commander in this campaign was Victor Watson, sent to Chicago to try to resuscitate the ailing *Examiner*. His primary target was purported radicalism on college campuses, and in February 1935 he zeroed in on Professor Frederick Schuman of the University of Chicago. The young political scientist was grossly misquoted in an editorial that appeared in all the Hearst papers, pillorying educators as "authorized disseminators of Communist propaganda in the U.S. who deliberately and designedly mislead our fine young people and bring them up to be disloyal to our American ideals and institutions and stupidly to favor the brutal and bloody tyranny of Soviet Russia."[15]

The campaign by the Hearst papers and other anti–New Deal journals, including the *Tribune*, was directed against most of the nation's leading educational institutions. But as Milton Mayer wrote, the crème de la Kremlin was the University of Chicago, with Hutchins serving as one of Hearst's leading bêtes rouges.

Hutchins's reaction was foreordained. He had affirmed his position on academic freedom in a 1931 address before the American Association of University Professors: "We have got to make ourselves clear. The only question that can properly be raised about a professor with the institution to which he belongs is his competence in his field. His private life, his political views, his social attitudes, his economic doctrine — these are not the concern of his university."[16]

The faculty was naturally delighted by his uncompromising stand, and the trustees had accepted it with some reluctance. That reluctance grew as Hutchins's political pronouncements created waves in the financial community. The president of the National Association of Manufacturers, C. M. Chester, said one of his Yale classmates in Chicago had informed him that Hutchins was a "parlor red" who had converted the University into "a hot bed of radicalism." The speech to the industrial-relations group was cited as prime evidence.[17]

While stopping short of challenging Hutchins's stand on academic freedom, Harold Swift expressed concern over the effect these attacks were having on financial support for the University among wealthy Chicagoans who were already disposed to send their children east to the Ivy League. So matters stood when the Illinois legislature, egged on by the *Examiner* and the *Tribune,* launched an investigation into allegations that Communism and other heresies were being advocated on the Midway.

The circus that followed in the appropriately named Red Room of the LaSalle Hotel went into civil-liberties annals as the Walgreen Case. It was touched off on April 10, 1935, when Charles R. Walgreen, the wealthy proprietor of a chain of drugstores, notified Hutchins by letter, with copies to the trustees, that he was withdrawing his niece from the University because "I am unwilling to have her exposed to the Communist influences to which she is insidiously exposed."[18]

The letter appeared in the *Examiner* on the same day Hutchins received it, and when the University asked for evidence to support the charges, Walgreen replied that he would provide it only at a meeting of the trustees open to the press. He had plenty of ammunition, the *Examiner* said, and the Illinois state senate promptly voted to provide him with a forum in the guise of an investigation of grounds for rescinding the tax-exempt status provided the University under its state charter.

The "evidence," when it finally surfaced at the hearing, turned out to be unsupported statements by eighteen-year-old Lucille Norton of Seattle, who was living at her uncle's house and at dinnertime regaled him with chatter about her day on the campus. She was being taught Communism out of Communist textbooks, she said, and there were attacks on the family as an institution and talk of free love. It was not until much later that her bemused relative began to consider the possibility that she might have been putting him on.

Through the weeks of the hearing Walgreen sat at the complainant's table, represented by Joseph H. Fleming, who also happened to be the attorney for the *Tribune*. Opposite him sat Hutchins and Swift, flanked by two of Chicago's leading lawyers, Laird Bell and James H. Douglas, both trustees of the University.

Walgreen's case, based entirely on his own testimony and that of Miss Norton, quickly fell apart. The works on Communism she had been exposed to, it turned out, were offered in a course that also included Herbert Hoover's *American Individualism*. The attack on the family consisted of Professor Schuman's response when asked at a student symposium if he believed in free love. Only for himself, he had replied, and it hadn't occurred to Miss Norton that he was being facetious, though she admitted that many of the students had laughed.

Hutchins, Swift, and appropriate members of the faculty offered low-key testimony that effectively refuted the charges. But the circus was only beginning. When the hearing seemed about to run out of steam, two "expert witnesses" appeared beside Walgreen at the complainant's table. Elizabeth Dilling, the author of *Red Network,* a compilation of alleged subversives in high places, was a regular collaborator in Hearst's anti-Communist crusade. Harry A. Jung, to whom Mrs. Dilling had dedicated her catalogue, headed the American Vigilant Intelligence Federation, which enjoyed rent-free office space in the Tribune Tower.

Mrs. Dilling's list of subversives included Chief Justice Charles Evans Hughes, Senator Robert A. Taft, the National Council of Churches, the National Catholic Welfare Conference, and the YWCA. In her nonstop testimony before the committee she offered a number of Chicago faculty members selected from her roster, and then turned to point an accusing finger at Chairman Swift: "There's a cream-puff type that would get its throat cut. Some rich men play with chorus girls, others with booze, and others with Communism. Mr. Swift wouldn't have a nickel left — he wouldn't have that pretty suit he's wearing — if the ideas he's playing with had their way."

But before they self-destructed, Mrs. Dilling, Jung, and an unidentified witness wearing an American Legion cap and testifying from the back of the hall put the finger on a faculty member who was technically vulnerable. Robert Morss Lovett, professor of English at Chicago since 1893, was a Boston Brahmin who blithely spoke out on behalf of underdogs no matter who attacked, or defended, them. In championing Sacco and Vanzetti, the Scottsboro Boys, and the like, he often found himself on the same side as the Communists. The FBI found his name on four hundred letterheads, Milton Mayer reported, and only four of them could safely be said to be free of any possible Communist taint — the

Pulitzer Prize Committee, the National Institute of Arts and Letters, the Harvard Club of New York, and the American Red Cross.

When he appeared before the committee, Lovett produced a worn briefcase full of papers he identified as lecture notes for his course in seventeenth-century literature. "I should like to read them aloud on this occasion," he said. "I am unable to find anything subversive in them, but there may be something of the sort, and I should like to have expert opinion in the matter."

Lovett was the only culprit cited when the hearing finally foundered on its own absurdity. The committee voted four to one to exonerate the University of the charge of subversive teaching and indoctrination. But a majority found that the venerable professor's off-campus activities were not "conducive to effective or helpful service on his part as a member of the faculty of the University of Chicago, and that in view of his long service and scholastic achievements in the field of English literature, he is deserving of honorary retirement, with usual and suitable provisions for emeritus professors."

The *Examiner* proclaimed this dubious edict a triumph for the forces of righteousness and, a week after the hearing closed, produced a front-page streamer: "U OF C TO LET LOVETT GO." The deed would be done on Christmas Day, it was alleged, when Lovett would become eligible for a pension. The story prompted Professor James Weber Linn to confront Hutchins with a promise that "if the trustees fire Lovett you'll receive the resignations of twenty full professors tomorrow morning." "Oh no I won't," Hutchins replied. "My successor will."

The trustees met that afternoon and approved a statement to be delivered to all the local newspapers for immediate release. Signed by Hutchins, it announced that in view of the distinction conferred upon the University by Professor Robert Morss Lovett and his unfaltering capacity to continue his valuable work, the board of trustees had waived the compulsory retirement age of sixty-five and persuaded him to remain on the faculty.

On the way to the hearing room on opening day, Laird Bell had made a proposition to Hutchins: "I'll give the University a hundred dollars for every wisecrack you don't make." Accepting this as the admonition it was intended to be, the young president displayed unaccustomed restraint in the witness chair and in his comments to the press. But as he passed the complainant's table on that first day, he leaned over its occupant, smiled affably, and said, "Mr. Walgreen, this is going to cost you half a million dollars."

Within weeks after the close of the hearings, intermediaries were passing word to Hutchins that the druggist was feeling contrite. A meeting between the two was arranged, and a magnanimous Hutchins came away with $550,000 to establish at the University the Charles R. Walgreen Foundation for the Study of American Institutions. The two regularly lunched together after that, and when Walgreen died two years later, his family asked Hutchins to deliver the eulogy at his memorial service.

There were other dividends. All told, some four million dollars in benefactions came in as a result of the University's stand, which was seen by foundations and concerned individuals as a defense of all educational institutions. There was even a political payoff, or at least the potential for one. Hutchins received a letter marked "Private and Confidential" that began "Dear Bob" and concluded, "You must have had a vile time with that inquisition. I sometimes think that Hearst has done more harm to the cause of democracy and civilization in America than any three other contemporaries together."[19] It was signed Franklin D. Roosevelt.

CHAPTER THIRTEEN

"More Than
Pious Hopes . . ."

Robert Hutchins could claim a famous victory in his skirmish with the red-baiting Chicago newspapers and their legislative fuglemen. At the annual trustee-faculty dinner he noted that the Walgreen Case had demonstrated that "if eternal vigilance is not the price of eternal liberty, certainly eternal patience is." His notable deficiency in that regard had caused him to chafe under the cautionary counsel of his associates, but he now conceded that the restraint urged upon him had been as successful as it was dignified:

> Even in LaSalle Street you can hardly find a person who is willing to repeat the stupidities popular last year. Outside Chicago the University's reputation is greater than ever. Other universities feel that we have fought a battle for them all. The alumni have been aroused to a new interest in their alma mater. The Trustees have borne the burden of our defense with courage, vigor, and even with cheerfulness. . . . Because of our trials of last year the faculty has been united for the first time in this administration and probably in any other. And the students have had the time of their lives.[1]

There was other good news. For the first time since he had arrived at Chicago he could wish his colleagues a happy new year with some expectation that they might have one. Economic recovery had begun to ease the fiscal restraints brought on by the Depression, and the reorganization that had kept the University in turmoil since 1930 was substantially complete.

But on the educational front, the success of the New Plan represented only a limited victory in the bruising campaign that was to occupy Hutchins for the next fifteen years. He had made little progress in securing for the College a faculty wholly devoted to general education. And this Hutchins deemed to be a minimum essential if Chicago was to take the lead in restoring the liberal arts to their once-dominant position in undergraduate education.

The combination of the first two years of college with the last two years of the University's Laboratory School had been approved in 1932 as the second phase of the New Plan. But it was still only a paper consolidation, far short of what would be required to point the way to the wholesale restructuring of American education he had come to believe was necessary to halt the erosion of the traditional values of Western civilization.

If the concept was grandiose, his approach was realistic, at least in the sense that the changes he called for could be made within the capacities and limitations of the institution he headed. Moreover, he had precedent on his side. "The great academic characteristic of suspended judgment, of not doing anything until nobody wants it done, or until it ought not to be done, or until something radically different ought to be done, has not infected this university," Hutchins had proclaimed in announcing the abolition of course credits under the New Plan. "This university has behaved as a pioneer university ought to behave. It has enthusiastically determined that something ought to be done, and it has done it."[2]

As to the second phase, he was trying to carry forward the project William Rainey Harper had initiated when he called for ending secondary education at the second year of high school so that students could then enter a new kind of college devoted wholly to general education. That effort had launched the movement that by the 1930s had brought into being some 450 junior colleges, most of them appended to public school systems. But these, limited to two years and unable to grant degrees of their own, existed as a kind of inferior adjunct to state-supported institutions of higher education.

Hutchins saw in this a new opportunity to spread the Harper gospel beyond his own campus. The addition of the junior college was only one of the structural changes that were now significantly altering a public school system originally based on eleven years of primary and secondary education. Many systems had instituted one or two years of kindergarten, inserted a junior high school incorporating the seventh, eighth, and ninth grades, and added a twelfth grade.

Compulsory attendance laws required every child to attend classes until he had earned a high-school diploma or was certified as incapable of doing so. A substantial majority of Americans now went the distance, and every state had tax-supported institutions that made it possible for an increasing minority to earn a bachelor's degree.

Hutchins's initial criticism of the expanding system was on the grounds of inefficiency. It was this, he charged in a speech to the National Education Association, that was responsible for lagging financial support for education in the face of the increasing demands being made upon it. The movement to create a universal public school system had been launched with religious fervor in the last century, and generations of Americans had sacrificed to support it. But many now felt that their faith had been misplaced:

> The elementary schools are eight years for no better reason than that Horace Mann when he went to Germany to find a school to imitate imitated the wrong one, and imposed upon this country as a preparatory unit a school that was terminal in its native land. The high schools are largely dominated by collegiate requirements that have no application to a majority of their students. The junior colleges are frequently two years more of high school or pale imitations of the first two years at the state university. The colleges of liberal arts sometimes seem to duplicate the high school at one end and the university at the other. The universities are weird mixtures of general education, specialized study, professional training, and college life. If we are ever to alter the public attitude toward education, we must clarify the functions of all these organizations and their relationships to each other.[3]

This was the task Hutchins had intended his own university to initiate when he was authorized to create a new college along the lines Harper had prescribed. He hoped to provide a working model that, if widely adopted, would require the reconstitution of the nation's educational structure from top to bottom. But after five years the College was still without the new curriculum that it needed in order to carry out its mandate under the New Plan: to "do the work of the University in general education."

Some of the opposition was captious, no more compelling than the complaint of professors in the upper divisions that it would be demeaning for them to teach at what had formerly been the high-school level. But other objections were fundamental. Entrenched senior faculty members continued to block the effort to eliminate specialized courses from the College curriculum, for this would also require changes in the courses offered to those who moved on to advanced study. This, of course, was exactly what Hutchins had in mind.

Like Harper before him, he advocated awarding the bachelor's degree upon completion of what was now the second year of college, an action that would entail reconsideration of the requirements for all graduate and professional degrees. Hutchins proposed that after another three years of specialized education the master's degree be awarded as a credential for those who would need it to find a teaching post. And in his inaugural address he had suggested reserving the Ph.D. for those who would become teachers and awarding a D.Sc. degree to those committed to research. This was sacrosanct territory; seven years later he confessed that he had not yet found a single member of the faculty who agreed with him.

The most practical objection to putting the total scheme into effect was that it might deprive the College of its existing source of students and bar its graduates from the educational mainstream. It would not be desirable, even if it were possible, to depend upon the University's Laboratory School as the sole source of entering freshmen. Students might be accepted after two years at any high school if they could pass the entrance examination. But the curriculum would also have to be adapted to accommodate those who had completed the usual high-school course, as most would continue to do pending widespread adoption of the new formulation. And if the accrediting associations did not recognize Chicago's bachelor degree, there would be problems for those who wanted to enter graduate school elsewhere.

At the close of the 1935–1936 academic year Hutchins reported to the trustees that he had found it impossible to obtain faculty agreement for a curriculum that would, while providing a considerable flexibility of approach, take students over common educational ground during their time in the College: "The Curriculum Committee has taken no action modifying or reorganizing the course of study. It has had various proposals before it, all of which would have improved the curriculum, but has so far been unwilling to adopt any of them."[4]

He had, therefore, asked Dean McKeon of the Humanities Division to create a Committee on the Liberal Arts, which would undertake a study of the overlapping curricula of his division and the College, taking into consideration the place of the seven liberal arts in modern education:

The seven liberal arts were grammar, rhetoric, logic, arithmetic, geometry, music and astronomy. They constituted the whole of general or pre-professional education in the Middle Ages. In view of the state into which these disciplines have fallen, the vocational attitude of most students, and the ignorance and hostility of many professors, it is doubtful whether they can be adapted to contemporary conditions. The difficulties of framing a program of general education without some resort to them, however, justify the attempt.[5]

Hutchins had obtained gifts from anonymous donors to fund the Committee for three years, and he hoped this would guarantee its independence from the faculty. To lead the study he had finally assembled the "holy triune." McKeon would be joined by Adler and by Scott Buchanan, who was made a visiting professor. A similar appointment went to Stringfellow Barr, a professor of history at the University of Virginia who had become a dedicated "liberal artist" while working with Buchanan on an aborted program of curricular reform at Charlottesville. Others, handpicked by Hutchins and the triune, were added to the Committee, but these would be the principals.[6]

Adler had been the original prime mover in the effort the Committee would now undertake, but Scott Buchanan became the dominant figure. The ascetic aspect of Buchanan's New England Puritan heritage, unlike that of Hutchins's, remained essentially intact; he had no interest in material goods and little tolerance for the practical concerns of those who administered educational institutions. His interest was in the life of the mind, which he deemed to be the only proper concern of the philosopher; mundane human affairs were only shadows on the wall of the cave.

"He is the only distinguished representative I know of a species practically extinct, or in any case obsolescent — the vagabond intellectual," Clifton Fadiman wrote in dedicating his book *Fantasia Mathematica* to Buchanan. "Though he is a philosopher by training, his real interest is simply in thought, thought in almost any area. Wherever intellectual curiosity has led him, there he has strayed, as reveler or as ponderer."[7]

Buchanan came to Chicago because Hutchins was the first university president he had encountered who shared his conviction that education should be a wholly intellectual enterprise carried on by a community of scholars. He had not found that at Harvard, where he had been a student and something of a protégé of Alfred North Whitehead, nor at Oxford, where he had studied as a Rhodes scholar. After his first meeting with

Hutchins he wrote him from the University of Virginia, where he had reluctantly accepted a conventional faculty appointment at the behest of his Oxford classmate Barr, and entered upon what he described as a period of academic hibernation:

> On account of various incidents in my moderately wide experience with universities I have for some time assumed that very little of importance could be done with them; they should be borne with fortitude and humor. Hence my decision to come here where there is as little of a university as there can well be and still provide a living for its members. Reports of your intentions to do something at first startled me, for after all I had always heard that you were a sensible young man, intelligent and unsentimental. I am now convinced that you are not only all these but also that you are wise. In other words I have a strong hunch that you will do something, perhaps a great deal.[8]

That hope, like most of the others Buchanan entertained when he allowed himself to contemplate the contemporary intellectual scene, was soon to be dashed. Before he arrived he had a letter from Adler informing him that the announcement that visiting professors would be members of the Committee on the Liberal Arts had caused insurrections in the Humanities Division and in the College: "They see that what Bob is up to is a trick of getting men he wants appointed by hook or crook, and so by hook or crook they are going to stop him." When the Committee was convened in October, Buchanan was given the title of director. He was soon complaining to Hutchins:

> The Committee must have an authorization of its status and function fitting to its single-minded end and aim. The possibility of a decision to stay depends on this and this alone. . . . I don't think there is any hope of getting the job done or even underway unless the Committee has orders from you that cannot be countermanded or shaved down, or diverted by other academic powers and authorities.[9]

Barr, with a touch of humor, forwarded a similar request. The trouble, he thought, was overreliance on oral communication. He found this particularly chancy on a campus where he had been disabused of his naive belief "that Virginians could out-gossip any other group of people in America." He urged a presidential mandate in writing: "Your instructions to Professor Buchanan as to how we ought to proceed struck me . . . as wise. But I have not your faith that they will reach the Committee (and I am making no charges against Mr. Buchanan when I say this, except that he is a poet) in their original form."[10]

But this turned out to be the least of the problems besetting the Committee. Its members were all dedicated to the liberal arts, but it quickly developed that the triune was divided by doctrine and by temperament. Buchanan and Adler insisted that the new curriculum should be built around the Great Books, but they disagreed on where their deliberations should begin; Adler urged an initial reading of Aquinas, while Buchanan held out for Aristotle. McKeon thought the Committee should first take a look at the liberal arts as they stood in the present, and he questioned a curriculum based on ancient texts.

Adler had had a presentiment of impending cleavage during a discussion with McKeon the previous summer. "I detect a fundamental difference between Dick and myself," Adler wrote to Hutchins:

> Everything he says these days seems to indicate an avoidance of philosophical questions. . . . Dick is today taking the position I took in *Dialectic* eight years ago, and which I now think is nothing but clever sophistry. One way of avoiding the obligation to take sides, and take the chance of being wrong, is to try to straddle all issues by this approach–method–point of view gag. My own deep private guess is that this is Dick's way of avoiding religion and theology. And that I feel sure is his deepest fear and concern. . . . How much of his queasiness comes from his early training and his adolescent revolts, and how much comes from being a dean at the University of Chicago I don't know. . . .[11]

The ascetic Buchanan, the mercurial Adler, and the temporizing McKeon soon reached a hopeless deadlock, and after three meetings the Committee disintegrated. The "Virginia party," led by Buchanan and Barr, retained the title, but at McKeon's insistence the group was removed from the Humanities Division and made advisory to the president. Adler pulled out altogether. "I was no longer willing to entertain the tenability of positions on opposite sides of any issue," he wrote in his autobiography.[12]

Without even the tenuous connection with the faculty that was provided by identification with the Division of Humanities, the Committee was wide open to attack. The effect was to unleash those who, as Buchanan wrote, had always seen revision of the curriculum as a "power conspiracy on the part of the administration, which was pictured as a 'baby president' aided by Savonarola and Richelieu.''[13]

The Committee was out of business by the end of the academic year. Buchanan provided a bitter epitaph:

> The University of Chicago saw red, and they almost burned our books so that we couldn't read. Our presence [gave] . . . the Dean of the Humanities a great deal of trouble. It was a great relief for everybody but the donors of the money for this project when Saint John's called the members of the Liberal Arts Committee to put its program into operation.[14]

The model Hutchins had tried to create at Chicago came into being at an unlikely site in Annapolis, Maryland. Situated hard by the Naval Academy, Saint John's was the third-oldest college in the nation, with roots going back to 1696. The small, nondenominational men's college, like many of its kind, had fallen on hard times in the Depression and was looking for salvation when one of its trustees, Francis Miller, ran into Buchanan at an educational conference. Miller, a classmate of Buchanan and Barr at Oxford, saw in the aborted curriculum they had drafted the new approach that he and other trustees were convinced was necessary to attract financial support for their failing institution.

In June 1937 the board of visitors appointed Barr president of Saint John's, with Buchanan as dean and head of instruction. Adler was named a visiting lecturer in the liberal arts, and Hutchins joined the board and later became its chairman. The *1937–38 Catalogue of Saint John's College,* largely written by Buchanan, laid out the seminars, formal lectures, tutorials, and laboratory experiments all students would have available as they spent four years making their way through the Great Books. This was followed by Buchanan's concluding injunction:

> The liberal arts are chiefly concerned with the nature of the symbols, written, spoken, and constructed, in terms of which we rational animals find our way around in the material and cultural world in which we live. . . . There are concrete data and artificial products that must be distinguished from the abstract principles and ideas which govern them. There are many connections that these aspects have with one another, and it is the business of the liberal artist to see these apart and put them together. Success in this constitutes intellectual and moral health. Failure is stupidity, intellectual and moral decay and slavery, to escape which the founding fathers set up institutions of liberal education. It is

reassuring to know that they had more than pious hopes in their minds when they made charters for Saint John's College and its sister institutions.

Despite daily assertions to the contrary, there is no educational device for assuring worldly success to the student. To cultivate the rational human powers of the individual so that armed with the intellectual and moral virtues he may hope to meet and withstand the vicissitudes of outrageous fortune — that is education.[15]

Hutchins would continue to propagate that faith, but he would never see it put fully into effect outside the limited confines of the little college on the Chesapeake Bay and the campus Saint John's later established in Santa Fe.

CHAPTER FOURTEEN

"No Friendly Voice"

Throughout the 1930s Robert Hutchins spent a considerable amount of time on the lecture platform expounding his ideas on educational reform. Every formal address was carefully prepared, initially written on a typewriter, if one was handy, or inscribed on a blue-lined yellow legal pad. It was a slow process of ongoing revision; he estimated that his final drafts were produced at the rate of about 250 words an hour. By the time he turned his marked-up copy over to a typist, he had committed it to memory. The absence of a manuscript or notes when he stood on the rostrum became a trademark.

Since he scorned anything that could be construed as an emotional appeal, his platform manner was magisterial. His voice was husky but distinct, his accent cultured and free of any regional imprint. His delivery was described by Milton Mayer as "characteristically wooden . . . with the passionate cadence of a superannuated train caller."[1] Edward Shils thought his voice carried "a slight overtone of the speaker's distaste or distrust of his audience." But Shils found that this "did not distract from the matter which his words treated; it was a perfect vehicle for his lucid, geometrical thoughts. He always spoke in sentences which were short and perfectly formed; he never rambled, and by-lanes did not tempt him from his theme. . . ."[2]

He was as sparing of adjectives as he was of gestures, and any colorful passages were likely to be ironic. Yet his content was inescapably hortatory. If he was appalled by the florid style of his evangelical grandfather, it was apparent that he had been influenced by the more restrained pulpit oratory taught and practiced by his father. Although he thought Will Hutchins tended to be too sentimental and to include too many illustrative stories, he considered him the best serious orator he had ever heard. His first published collection of speeches, *No Friendly Voice,* was dedicated to "The President of Berea College."[3] And the title itself, taken from Milton's *Paradise Lost,* denoted his chosen role as a critical moralist.

"Hutchins, addicted to alliterative triads, usually sought to demonstrate a grievous need, provide an answer to the need, and conclude with a challenge for conversion," Robin D. Lester wrote. "The generalist seemed to be working, albeit he denied it, for an artistic (rhetorical) end, not an intellectual one. . . ."[4] Hutchins would have rejected the implication that he made his case on other than rational grounds, but it was a narrow distinction, for he conceded that he spoke as an advocate, and his evident intention was to persuade.[5]

His commanding presence and spare oratorical style made Hutchins an arresting speaker, and he was accorded rapt attention by his audiences. He received more than a thousand speaking invitations a year and accepted about a hundred. He could have had a handsome side income from his efforts, as did many of the platform stars of the day, but he often spoke without receiving any fee, and when there was one, he turned it in to the University's treasurer.

His reputation as a controversialist enhanced his attraction, and he cultivated it. It came naturally to him to seize the attention of an audience by challenging its preconceptions. But he was no professional gadfly, as patronizing editorialists often termed him. He was never content merely to sting the complacent; he cited shortcomings and specified remedies in the context of what he saw as the moral and cultural deficiencies of contemporary society.

The audiences he selected were for the most part professional — teachers, educational administrators, lawyers, doctors, journalists — and he also appeared on the leading university campuses, acquiring an extensive collection of honorary degrees. A favorite device was to cite the deficiencies in his own undergraduate and professional education by way of pointing out that his listeners had been similarly deprived.

In a typically self-deprecating opening, he began an address to the American Association of University Professors: "I appear simply as an individual who has been hanging around educational institutions in one capacity or another as long as he can remember. . . . Under these circumstances you will understand that if I talk tonight as though I thought I know something about education, it is not from conceit but compulsion. It is not that I know education well; it is simply that I know nothing else at all."[6] In a fashion that quickly refuted his own disclaimer, he went on to offer a detailed indictment to support his charge that the educational establishment, rather than recognizing its sins of omission and commission, was compounding them.

"In the preparation of teachers we are involved in a vicious circle," he said on another occasion, in a passage that he often repeated before audiences of educators. "The teachers are badly educated. They educate their students badly. Some of the badly educated students become badly educated teachers who educate their students badly."[7]

Before the American College of Surgeons, he said of the typical medical-school graduate,

> Without intellectual scope or grasp, with the belief that thought is memory and speculation vanity, with no obvious incentive but the need to make a living, he becomes a proud product of our institutions of higher learning. Now that health has succeeded happiness as the ruling passion of mankind, your profession has an obligation to be intelligible and intelligent surpassing that of any earlier day. To that end I recommend a return to Galen, which is perhaps only another way of saying what Galen said in the title of one of his treatises, "The Best Physician Is Also a Philosopher."[8]

On Founder's Day at the University of Virginia, he denigrated the sainted Thomas Jefferson, whose memory was being honored, as one who had confused the accumulation of facts with education:

> The intellectual life was not [his] concern. . . . What used to be called the "intellectual love of God," what we now call the "pursuit of truth for its own sake," the inculcation of which is the object of human learning, scarcely appeared in his prospectus. He was a practical social reformer anxious to make his people prosperous and civilized. He was correct as far as he went. Our mistake is [in] taking him farther than he meant to go.[9]

At Phillips Academy, a proud exemplar of Ivy League preparatory schooling, he said, "New England invented the horrid machinery composed of course grades, course credits, course examinations, and required residence through which we determined by addition, subtraction, multiplication, division, and a logarithm table the intellectual progress of the young. Of course this machinery has nothing to do with education and constitutes, in fact, one of the prime obstacles in its path.'' And he charged that the Ivy League, by establishing a snobbish model for less venerable institutions, had imposed upon the country the fallacious notion that "athletics, architecture, personality, character, and gentlemanliness are the essence of the intellectual life.''[10]

Citing the devastating effects of the Depression on the public schools in a speech before the Pittsburgh Teachers Association, he called for federal aid on a permanent basis and the elevation of the Commissioner of Education to cabinet rank: "I have been a long time in education, and I have yet to hear a single valid argument against the position that education is a national responsibility.'' But, pursuing a theme he repeated before scores of similar organizations, he warned that as a result, national standards would be imposed, creating new political pressures. Education was particularly vulnerable because it was

> carried on by people grossly underpaid, in political units which have proved the most unreliable in the country, subjected to the gravest social and political hazards. We know, too, that when our people have recovered from their hysteria they will turn to us again and demand that we solve their problems for them. They will insist that we bring up their children for them because they cannot be bothered and frequently cannot be trusted to do it themselves.

And the school system was woefully unprepared to meet the challenge: "It has not withstood the strain already placed upon it. It will not withstand the strain it will meet in the years to come.''[11]

"Of course the greatest aggregation of educational foundations is the press itself,'' he told the American Society of Newspaper Editors:

> We all take our opinions from the newspapers. Indeed I notice that in spite of the frightful lies you have printed about me I still believe everything you print about other people. And if the press is an educational agency, we must inquire, I suppose, whether it is giving a good education or not. . . .
>
> Everything that we call adult education has until recently been entirely in the hands of the newspapers and the public libraries. Sixteen years of formal classroom education is nothing compared to a lifetime of education through the press. And you have this education being administered by a series of organizations [which], since they must operate at a profit, seem condemned to refrain

from exercising all the intelligence they possess and from calling on their readers to exercise any at all.[12]

Although he deplored the unplanned impact of technology on society, he was no Luddite crying out against the forces of change. At Chicago he initiated experiments involving motion pictures in the classroom, and he encouraged the use of radio for adult education. But he insisted that those responsible for creating, operating, and regulating the new means of communication must be held responsible for adapting them to educational purposes. And in those early days of broadcasting he was already citing the failure of stations to meet the public-service obligations implicit in their federal licenses.

In an address to the National Advisory Council on Radio and Education, he rejected the alternative of government ownership, but added,

> Proposals of this sort are presented not because of the virtues of greater public control but because of the vices which have so far attended private management. . . . The charges that can be substantiated are these: the claims of minorities have been disregarded, the best hours have been given to advertising programs, the hours assigned to education have been shifted without notice, censorship has been imposed, experimentation has been almost nonexistent, and the financial support of educational broadcasting has been limited and erratic.[13]

To a gathering of Young Men's Christian Association officials who were disturbed about the future of their institution, he suggested that the American public was, if anything, overexercised and overbathed: "The vast resources of the YMCA should not be directed primarily to aggravating this great evil." The Association's Christian mission required that it deemphasize the gymnasium and shower room and devote its energies to educational pursuits:

> A vague, sentimental desire to do good and be good does not seem to me to constitute religion. Still less does it seem to me to constitute in the present day a challenge to youth. The old methods of emotional appeal have lost their effectiveness. I doubt if they ever had much permanent influence. Certainly they will not bring young men to Christ today. The appeal that must be made to them is the appeal to reason. A process of conversion to be

worthy of that name must be an intellectual process. Faith is an intellectual assent.[14]

He titled his address to the Bond Club of New York "The Professor Is Sometimes Right" and chided the financiers for dismissing the views of intellectuals as irrelevant to their pragmatic concerns. The professor, having no vested interest in the marketplace, might see things in a given situation that had escaped the profit-oriented businessman: "His income is small. He knows it always will be, and he knew it when he decided to become a professor." But the professor was not always right when it came to matters of education, for there he suffered the same handicaps that beset the financier: " . . . he has vested interests, personal ambitions, and ancient habits, all of which he wishes consciously or otherwise to protect. Every great change in American education has been secured over the dead bodies of countless professors."[15]

Hutchins was not alone in citing the deficiencies of the educational system. Many of the country's leading educators agreed that the general education presumed essential for an enlightened citizenry was being undermined by excessive specialization and vocationalism. The sub rosa commercialization of college football was already beginning to produce whiffs of scandal, and many saw this as a symptom of pervasive materialism on the burgeoning campuses. Critics of the public schools pointed to the high dropout rate as evidence of the failure of the system to meet the needs of those it was presumed to serve.

But among intellectuals much of this was mere iconoclasm, and reformers within the system usually offered only patchwork solutions for specific problems. Hutchins was unique in advocating a complete scheme for the reorganization of the nation's educational structure, including a formulation not only of the ends it should be seeking but of the means for achieving them. He was attempting, moreover, with some success, to put his theories into practice at his own institution.

He made no claims to originality. The proposals for combining the last two years of high school with the first two years of college and for employing the liberal arts as the basis for general education were an acknowledged inheritance from William Rainey Harper, as was Hutchins's insistence that specialized research and training be confined to the graduate and professional schools of the University. The notion of basing the undergraduate curriculum on the Great Books was the product of his collaboration with Mortimer Adler, Scott Buchanan, and Stringfellow Barr.

But these were reforms that would take effect only at the culmination of an educational process that was now presumed to be open to all citizens. They were intended to reinstate concepts that had prevailed before the national culture was profoundly altered by a tidal wave of technological and demographic change. And since they dated back to the time when only the children of the upper class had access to any but the most elementary schooling, they were subject to the charge of elitism. If he was to get a hearing from the teachers and administrators of the publicly funded institutions that now provided the bulk of American education, Hutchins would have to address himself to an experience that was significantly different from his own.

He had arrived at Chicago with no personal knowledge of, or interest in, public education, and Dean Charles H. Judd of the School of Education had been warned by a Yale colleague that he had little reason to hope that the new president would understand the issues that concerned him and his colleagues. "Of course Mr. Judd's friend in New Haven was right," Hutchins conceded. "What he did not reckon with was that Mr. Judd was a great teacher. . . . He began to teach me about the organization of education, the relation of private and public education, and the relation of the federal government to education."[16]

Hutchins adopted from Judd the idea that the task of preparing teachers should not be relegated to a specialized school or department, as it usually was, but should be the responsibility of the university as a whole. The venerable dean earned Hutchins's admiration and respect when he recommended abolition of the professional school he headed so that apprentice teachers could work at large in the Division of Social Sciences. Judd's reforms enhanced Chicago's reputation as a leader in teacher education, and his friendship and unstinting support gave Hutchins credentials when he addressed himself to the practical problems of the public schools.

Hutchins would never shake off the elitist label, even though he insisted from the outset that the system he proposed should be available in its entirety to all children: "Education is an act of faith; and it is an article of my faith that no one is ineducable — no one, that is, above the grade of moron."[17] Replying to the reiterated charge that under his aegis the University of Chicago stood for limiting education to the intellectual elite, he pointed out that he had always rejected the practice of sorting out children and placing them on separate educational tracks. He recognized, however, that some students, for lack of interest or out of a need to earn a living, could not be expected to pursue his scheme of institutional general education to its culmination with the award of a bachelor's degree. He enunciated a principle of differentiation, as opposed to the kind of arbitrary, class-based selection that confined higher learning to a privileged few in Britain and Europe.

This differentiation would take effect at age sixteen, when all students had completed six years of elementary and four years of secondary school. All would have been rendered literate and numerate, and should have acquired some familiarity with the culture and institutions of contemporary society. They would then have the option of continuing their schooling, at public expense if necessary. Under Hutchins's formulation they could choose "one of two programs which would occupy four years, more or less. One should be concerned with general education. The other should provide technical or homemaking training of a sub-professional type for those who do not want, or would not profit by, a general cultural education."[18]

While Hutchins did not oppose vocational training, his fervor for the liberal arts convinced many of his critics that he did. He conceded that useful skills could and should be taught, though he contended that in many cases this could best be done on the job. But he insisted that a distinction must be made between education, defined as an intellectual undertaking intended to enhance the rational powers, and training, in which techniques were mastered through experience. He attributed the failure of the American educational system to a misguided effort to combine the two, with results that were detrimental to both.

"Education," he said, "is not a substitute for experience. It is preparation for it. There is no substitute for experience."[19] The mission of the educational institution was to enhance its students' ability to understand and deal rationally with the world in which they lived. If it succeeded in doing so, they would bring to the learning process beyond the classroom the values essential to the good life.

Hutchins appealed to the idealism of his audiences by holding before them "the dazzling vision of millions of young Americans receiving an education adapted to their needs at the hands of teachers who are truly educated themselves."[20] But in these speeches he rarely stepped outside his role as administrator, pointedly addressing the objections of those who accused him of having a cavalier disregard for practical matters of organization and finance. The real issue, he insisted, was one not of means but of priorities.

The demands upon the educational system, he pointed out, were external and had little to do with the theories of educators. In the Depression years of declining employment the schools had become holding pens for youths for whom there was no room in the emaciated workplace. Long before the term came into general usage, Hutchins cited this as structural unemployment, and he warned that much of it was the result of the rapidly changing nature of the job market, which would not end with an upturn in the business cycle.

It was this trend, he suggested, that had led to the American invention of adolescence, the interval when the young were considered no longer children but not yet adult. In previous generations, childhood had ended at puberty, if not before, and then the working life had begun. Only in this country were teenagers consigned to institutions that were presumed not only to educate them but to mold their character. The obligation of moral training of the young still must be the province of the family and the church, he insisted, and the effort to impose it upon the schools had been as wasteful as it was misguided:

> The moral virtues are habits. The environment of education should be favorable to them. But only a diffused sentimentality will result from the attempt to make instruction in the moral virtues the object of education. And, in addition, resources that might go into intellectual training will be lavished on athletics, social life, and student guidance, a kind of coddling, nursing and pampering of students that is quite unknown anywhere else in the world.[21]

Hutchins insisted that his scheme was far from being a blue-sky proposal for a further increase in money for the schools. It could be properly judged only in terms of efficiency: the proportion of national income presently devoted to education would be adequate if educators were freed from the extraneous obligations that threatened to submerge their central intellectual purpose. And there would be funds enough to upgrade teaching at all levels to true professional status if educators would end their needless proliferation and duplication of course offerings.

The introduction of compulsory school attendance in this century had resulted in a rapid increase in high-school students, many of whom were now demanding college education as well. The result might seem commendable in principle, Hutchins said, but in practice it had produced a competition in which universities "started departments simply because the institution next door has them. The present wave of enthusiasm for departments of public administration, forestry, housing, and aeronautics will lead to useless expenditure of the taxpayers' money by spotting competing enterprises all over the map when, from the educational point of view, two or three centers were all the country requires."[22]

At Chicago Hutchins was attempting to practice what he preached. He had used the budget cuts mandated by the Depression to weed out peripheral course offerings, and he continued to urge further internal consolidation. When he happened upon an idea that seemed to offer an unprecedented opportunity to advance that effort on a wholesale basis, he showed no trace of the territorial protectiveness that characterized the usual university administration.

In 1933, on a train coming back from Springfield, where Hutchins and President Walter Dill Scott of Northwestern University had both been testifying in one of the state legislature's investigations of purported Communist influence, the two began comparing notes on the inroads the Depression had made on their institutions. The universities, situated on opposite sides of Chicago, had traditionally competed for endowment money, and their common resources were rapidly shrinking. "I suggested to Walter that instead of competing we should join," Hutchins recalled. "He instantly said, 'Let's do it!' Since he was then in his sixties, I thought this a remarkable example of his youthful imagination and courage."[23]

The Chicago trustees greeted the possibility with interest, and Scott persuaded those at Northwestern to at least pursue the idea. Committees of the two boards met in protracted sessions, and negotiations reached a point where lawyers were called in to frame a merger agreement. Rumors flew, word of the negotiations leaked to the press, and Hutchins found it necessary to make a public statement at a student convocation.

"The single fact which is indisputably true is that the University and Northwestern are considering some form of cooperation, affiliation, or consolidation," he said. This had come about because their reduced endowments had raised fundamental questions about their future:

> Study may show that this area cannot be expected to finance two great endowed institutions of higher learning; that it cannot be expected to finance two great professional schools of law, medicine, business, and education; that it cannot handle two competing systems of adult education; and that two great graduate schools will be one too many for it. If, then, boom times are not soon to return, damaging economies will be necessary, and mediocrity will be visited upon one or both of the universities and upon their competing schools.[24]

Although he treated these as open questions, Hutchins left little doubt that he hoped to see a consolidation that would center all graduate education on the Midway. The Northwestern campus in suburban

Evanston would then become a conventional but high-quality liberal-arts college, and undergraduate teacher training would also be located there. The College at Chicago would continue to serve as a laboratory for further experimentation in improving the curriculum.

The two medical schools would escape the merger because their missions were already sufficiently differentiated; the emphasis at the Midway was on research, and downtown, on teaching and treatment. Hutchins thought the downtown campus might also become the place where all professional training and extension service would be centered.

He made it clear that in his view the financial considerations that motivated the trustees had simply made possible a course of action that ought to be initiated in any case throughout the educational system — and certainly it was an appropriate course for Chicago, since it embodied the principles that Hutchins had adopted from Harper and had been trying to put into effect for the previous three years:

> With emphasis in Evanston on undergraduate education, on the South Side on research and improvements in collegiate education, and downtown on professional education and community service, we might have sometime the three strongest centers in these three areas in the world. We might also perhaps succeed in retaining for the three groups the advantages of membership in a university and at the same time prevent them from hampering the development of one another through the confusion of their aims. It is possible that some such arrangement might give American education the clarification that its future urgently demands.
>
> All these things are possible. None of them is certain. Since no definite plan has yet been proposed, all we can do is preserve an open mind until we see what can be worked out. Open-mindedness under such circumstances is, I am told, one of the principal objects of university training. At any rate it is the attitude that I commend at the moment to the constituency of this university. The whole proposal may prove to be impractical, inexpedient, and impossible. If it does I shall shed some natural tears, for the conception is a grand one, and one that is consonant with the high traditions and glorious past of your alma mater.[25]

Open-mindedness did not prevail on the other campus; in the end the Northwestern trustees balked at any degree of consolidation that would deprive their university of its separate identity. Hutchins had identified his anticipated tears as "natural" because Milton so described those that Adam shed when he was banished from Paradise.

CHAPTER FIFTEEN

Facts vs. Ideas

So long as Robert Hutchins confined his advocacy of educational reform to structural matters, the controversy he engendered was generally limited to the issues customarily debated among educators: course content, scope of curriculum, teacher training, and the like. But as he sharpened his attack and began to couch it in philosophical terms, he broadened the debate and brought into it a variety of aroused intellectuals.

He had begun his tenure with solid faculty support, and a considerable majority stood with him through the reorganization of the departments and the implementation of the Chicago Plan. The more distinguished professors, secure in rank and reputation, tended to admire his unconventional style and to appreciate his uncompromising defense of academic freedom and his commitment to raising the level of faculty pay. The less secure felt threatened by his relentless attack on the status quo, and it was usually these who complained of his arrogance and disregard for faculty prerogatives.

Although many of the natural scientists disagreed with his insistence on banning specialized training in the College, they could not complain about his support of research at the graduate level — to the point of advocating complete autonomy for the graduate schools of the University under the proposed merger with Northwestern. The social scientists, however, were alarmed by what they perceived as Hutchins's innate disdain for their disciplines — and this was enhanced by intemperate criticism on the part of Mortimer Adler, which they assumed reflected the president's own views.

Hutchins had done nothing to allay their fears when he appeared at the first major ceremony he presided over after his inauguration, the dedication of the ornate new Social Science Research Building, which had been made possible by a grant from the Laura Spelman Rockefeller Fund. The Chicago faculty, and the leading American and European social scientists who were assembled for the occasion, could hardly have mistaken the reservations implicit in the brief remarks of the new president:

> If social science has value, it should be revealed under conditions so favorable as these. If the type of organization of the social sciences here is useful, that should be made plain; for no physical difficulties stand in the way of success. If this building does not promote a better understanding of society, we shall know that there is something wrong with the social sciences or something wrong with us. . . .[1]

As it happened, the building featured a description of the kind of quantitative social science Hutchins had seen degenerate into what he contemptuously called counting telephone poles after he introduced it into the curriculum of the Yale Law School. The Gothic structure was festooned with decorative comments on its function in the form of stone carvings, rosters of names, and mottoes. William F. Ogburn, chairman of the faculty's Committee on Symbolism, was responsible for these ornaments:

> Ogburn selected an adding machine, the sign of the Greek *psēphos,* the sphere enclosed in a cube, and representations of a graph. Members of the departments responded with lists of names for the cornices and a sprinkling of relevant quotations for the bay, the most popular of the latter being Aristotle's *Anthropos Zoon Politikon. . . .*
>
> Ogburn's favorite phrase from the beginning had been a quotation from Lord Kelvin much too long for the space available, to say the least, although Ogburn spent page after page of graph paper trying to block it out: ''When you can measure what you are speaking about and express it in numbers, you know something about it; but when you cannot measure it, when you cannot express it in numbers, your knowledge is of a meagre and unsatisfactory kind.'' The terse convenience of Aristotle, even in

translation, threatened to win out — and undoubtedly would have been the "popular" choice, but Ogburn finally managed to carve the cumbrous Kelvin into shape. "When you cannot measure . . . ," it finally read, "your knowledge is . . . meagre . . . and . . . unsatisfactory." An imaginative stonemason marked the lacunae with roses.[2]

If Hutchins was appalled by the quotation, so was the most distinguished occupant of the new building, Charles E. Merriam, the political scientist who had been an effective advocate of Hutchins's appointment when he served on the presidential search committee. His biographer, Barry D. Karl, described his reaction:

> Merriam returned from an extended summer trip to find the commandment engraved, the stones in place. Standing there alone as the sole statement of the building's function, it sent him into a rage. He considered having it removed. Kelvin's "law" clearly would have had a place in whatever decalogue Merriam might have constructed, but not at the top. Measurement, for Merriam, was only one of the essentials of scientific knowledge. It shared with intuition, observation, and experience, a place none of them held alone and all of them competed to maintain. Kelvin's words, therefore, hammered into the building, never ceased to offend Merriam's eye. If there was only one kind of truth in social science, then everything he was trying to do was false.[3]

It could not be said that Merriam and Hutchins ever saw eye to eye on their basic concepts, but there was enough common ground to ensure an amicable working relationship. "While he maintained a strong dislike for many of Hutchins' appointments to the faculty and administration of the University," Karl wrote, "his attitude toward Hutchins himself was that of one political power toward another with whom compromise was always possible and victory could only be Pyrrhic."[4] That was a fair description of the attitude of other senior men on the various faculties.

Hutchins drew the battle lines in speeches he labeled "The Higher Learning." In the first, delivered at a student convocation, he declared, "The gadgeteers and data collectors, masquerading as scientists, have threatened to become the supreme chieftains of the scholarly world."[5] His elaboration of the charge produced a *Daily Maroon* headline — "Hutchins Address Divides Faculty into Two Camps" — and ushered in the incendiary phase of the campus controversy that became a running feature of the student newspaper and eventually spilled over into the general-circulation press. In "The Higher Learning II," delivered at the annual faculty-trustee dinner in January 1934, he provided his indictment with chapter and verse:

> I have affirmed on another occasion that the object of a university is to emphasize, develop, and protect the intellectual powers of mankind. Scholarship and teaching must be tested by their contributions to this intellectual end. I have attempted to show that facts are not science and that the collection of facts will not make a science; that scientific research, therefore, cannot consist of the accumulation of data alone; that the anti-intellectual account of science given by scientists has produced unfortunate effects on the work of other disciplines which wished to be scientific; and that our anti-intellectual scheme of education, resulting in large part from this anti-intellectual account, was misconceived and incapable of accomplishing the objects set for it by its sponsors.
>
> At the same time I have proclaimed the value of observation and experiment. Nor have I suggested that ideas are revealed. All ideas come from experience. Propositions, however, do not. Propositions are relations between ideas, and science consists of propositions.[6]

He offered testimony from leading scholars — Whitehead, Jevons, Poincaré, Claude Bernard, and Bertrand Russell — in support of his contention that the experimental method could not produce abstract ideas, but must be directed by them. He recognized that there was a place for empirical research, as in the case of physics, but here the scientist was bound by the intellectual heritage of such abstract thinkers as Galileo and Newton. This was not true, however, of the law, the humanities, or the social sciences, which had fallen victim to the notion that the scientific method consisted simply of collecting data. And now he included the natural scientists in his bill of particulars:

> You may deny that natural scientists even think or talk as though science were the accumulation of data. For answer I refer you to what they teach. We have in every university in America the interesting spectacle of pure scientists teaching in ways which cannot be reconciled with the way they work. They offend as much, or more than, the rest of us in filling their students full of facts, in putting them through countless little measurements, in

multiplying their courses, in insisting they must have more of the student's time so that they can give him more information, and in dividing up their subjects into smaller and smaller bits. . . .

An anti-intellectual attitude toward education reduces the curriculum to the exposition of detail. There are no principles. The world is a flux of events. We cannot hope to understand it. All we can do is watch it. This is the conclusion of the leading anti-intellectuals of our time. . . . So, to anti-intellectuals, rational values are worthless; they are based on the past. They cannot be valid for the future, because man and his world [are] changing. A curriculum of current events, without reference to the intellectual and artistic tradition that has come down to us from antiquity, is the only possible course of study which anti-intellectualism affords.

Anti-intellectualism dooms pure science; it dooms any kind of education that is more than training in technical skill. . . . But if research is understanding and education is understanding, then education and research are what the world needs. They become at once the most significant of all possible undertakings. They offer the only hope of salvation, the hope held out to us by the intellect of man.[7]

These were fighting words. Moreover, Hutchins apparently interpolated the names of those whom he considered the principal villains of his piece. They are not identified in the text of the speech as it appears in the presidential files, but in Mortimer Adler's autobiography the line in the key passage reads: "This is the conclusion of the leading anti-intellectuals of our time, William James and John Dewey." And this, as Adler noted, was bound to cause an eruption in a "university which, since its inception and certainly in its heyday, had been dominated by the scientific spirit, by empiricism and pragmatism, and by the instrumentalism of John Dewey."[8]

Leading faculty members who had remained on the sidelines now joined in the counterattack. The student editor of the *Maroon,* John Barden, a Great Bookie who dismissed Hutchins's critics as "pundits . . . with vast collections of prejudices,"[9] drew the fire of Harry D. Gideonse, an economics professor. "We are tired of reading the Gospel by Barden out of Adler," he complained in a letter to the editor, the heading of which, "Facts vs. Ideas," provided a shorthand title for the protracted exchange that followed.[10] Harry Kalven, who was to become the leading authority on the First Amendment at Chicago's Law School, then chided Gideonse for a stand that "openly belittles the importance of ideas in education and ridicules rather than refutes a constructive criticism of the educational system.''[11] Frank Knight, the faculty's most distinguished economist, rallied to Gideonse's defense, charging that ''the application of formal logic to social problems . . . is a species of high-pressure salesmanship designed to bulldoze the timorous and confuse the uninformed.''[12]

Hutchins managed to stay above the immediate fray, but Anton J. Carlson, an irascible physiologist nicknamed Ajax, challenged Adler to a debate, and Adler accepted even though both Hutchins and B. Ruml urged him not to. The confrontation drew an overflow audience in the campus's largest auditorium, and Adler thought it ended in a draw. A more detached observer, Edward Shils, agreed, but found it a shabby performance:

> Each was obstinately inattentive to what the other said. Adler was quicker and more syllogistic in his procedure and he seemed to be unaware of what scientists do. Carlson was simply astonished that something so self-evident as his science could be challenged by a person who was not a scientist and understood nothing of it. He was intellectually speechless and in his own rustic plebeian way demagogic. It was a vaudeville show, not an intellectual debate. Yet the audience went for it because it enjoyed a brawl.[13]

Inevitably, the controversy spilled over into the social life of the inbred campus community. A beleaguered hostess, Carroll Russell, recalled a Sunday evening when John U. Nef, chairman of the Committee on Social Thought and a Hutchins supporter, was her dinner guest along with Frank Knight. ''Somehow the conversation got onto the subject of the existence of truth,'' she wrote. ''To my embarrassment, John's defense and Knight's attack became almost a shouting match.''[14]

The wholesale charge of anti-intellectualism brought by Hutchins would have been enough to arouse the antagonism of many of his faculty members, though there were those who agreed with the general thrust of his indictment. But the abiding issue arose over his proposed solution, which invoked ideological ghosts most thought had been laid to rest in the last century, when the scientific method had begun to supersede speculative philosophy as the dominant mode in the higher learning.

Hutchins believed that general education, which he insisted should be the precursor of specialized training, must be rooted in the philosophical concepts of Aristotle, as refined into a system of values by Thomas Aquinas. This required the reinstatement of metaphysics, defined as not only the study of first principles but all that flows from it. In his formulation the theoretical grounding of ethics in metaphysics, as viewed in the practical order, led to philosophical knowledge organized for the sake of action.

It was Hutchins's thesis that there could be no proper education in law without an inquiry into justice, or in medicine without consideration of the metaphysical bent of Galen, or in the social sciences without an investigation into the nature of politics and society. Thus, in the face of the prevailing liberal view that research and teaching should be value-free, he was contending that education without a vision of first principles was meaningless, and quite possibly destructive.

In making his case Hutchins invoked Saint Thomas's explication of natural law, which demonstrated by rational means that a civilized society depended upon acceptance of values rooted in respect for the sanctity of human life and the understanding of nature. But he did not accept the Thomist contention, central to Roman Catholic theology, that Aquinas had also demonstrated the existence of God. To those who were so convinced, he insisted, this was a divinely revealed truth — a matter of faith, not of reason — and it required a faith he did not share.

To Hutchins, metaphysics provided the basis for putting speculative ideas to the test of experience — the essence of science, properly understood as a means not of mastering nature but of understanding it. Yet his persistent use of the term aroused the suspicion that his advocacy of value-oriented education implied a return to a form of scholasticism, the religious dogma that had grievously restricted, and sometimes condemned, the pioneering practitioners of the scientific method.

Adler agreed with Hutchins that Aquinas had not succeeded in providing rational proof of the existence of God, but he thought that it could be adduced and that he might be the one to do it. He had entered upon what he called his Thomist period, proclaiming theology the queen of the sciences. In his autobiography he noted that he became "something of a legend in Catholic circles" and was honored with the Aquinas Medal of the American Catholic Philosophical Association.

In time Adler was satisfied that he had located Aquinas's error and that by correcting it he could provide a logical demonstration of the existence of a divine presence. Hutchins suggested that he try it out on Chicago's Catholic archbishop, Cardinal Mundelein, who invited the two of them to lunch. They were received with episcopal elegance in a dining room where His Eminence sat at the head of a long table flanked by the archdiocese's leading theologians. This distinguished company, Adler recalled, looked with disdain upon the young Jewish upstart who had the temerity to insist that he could prove that one of their ranking saints hadn't known what he was talking about. The cardinal was not convinced, and neither was Hutchins, though he solaced his friend by telling him he thought he had come closer to the mark than Aquinas himself.[15]

The suspicion that Adler had accepted not only Saint Thomas's thinking but also his religion was inevitably extended to include his intellectual fellow traveler: "Rumors of all sorts were rife at the University of Chicago — that Bob Hutchins and I had been secretly baptized, that we had been seen on our knees at the altar rail of the Catholic church near the university campus."[16]

Although Adler, unlike Hutchins, accepted the validity of religious faith as the basis of metaphysics, he did not become a Catholic convert. When asked why not, he replied, "The simple truth of the matter is that I do not wish to live up to being a genuinely religious person."[17] Hutchins, who sought to live up to the Christian ethic without the benefit of divine revelation, never deviated from his insistence that education must proceed on the assumption that it is possible to embrace natural law without an accompanying belief in God.

Hutchins admired and respected many Catholic theologians, and he counted Father John Cavanaugh, the president of Notre Dame, among his closest personal friends, but his Puritan heritage had imbued him with deep reservations about the Church's authoritarian hierarchy. After he left the University, a special audience with Pope Pius XII was arranged for him in Rome, and he invited Adler to join him. Although his fervor had begun to wane and he had ended his Thomist phase, Adler made the grueling overnight flight from New York. "I had always wanted to see Hutchins on his knees," he explained. And he recalled that as they waited in an ornate Vatican anteroom, they were sighted by an even more committed skeptic when Thomas Mann, the great German author, and his wife passed by on their way from a private audience of their own. Recognizing Hutchins and Adler, they stopped to exchange greetings. "It was embarrassing," Mrs. Mann told her daughter Elisabeth, "rather like running into friends in a brothel."[18]

In 1935 Hutchins polished and expanded his disquisitions on the higher learning and delivered them as the Storrs Lectures at his alma mater. He left no doubt as to the grounding of the educational system that he believed to be essential to the survival and improvement of a democratic republic:

> It is in the light of metaphysics that the social sciences, dealing
> with man and man, and the physical sciences, dealing with man
> and nature, take shape and illuminate one another. In metaphysics

we are seeking the causes of the things that are. It is the highest science, the first science, and as first, universal. It considers being as being, both what it is and the attributes that belong to it as being. The aim of higher education is wisdom. Wisdom is knowledge of principles and causes. Metaphysics deals with the highest principles and causes. Therefore metaphysics is the highest wisdom.[19]

When the Yale University Press published the four addresses in a 119-page volume titled *The Higher Learning in America,* the controversy went national. Intentionally or not, Hutchins had baited the defenders of the scientific method by questioning their motives: " . . . the love of money, a misconception of democracy, a false notion of progress, a distorted idea of utility, and the anti-intellectualism to which all of these lead conspire to confirm their conviction that no disturbing change is needed."[20]

The little book sold eighty-five hundred copies, a remarkable circulation for a work of its kind, and the reaction to it in the lay press was generally favorable. The laudatory review in the *New York Herald Tribune* was perhaps foreordained, since it was written by a friend and sometime collaborator of Hutchins's, Mark Van Doren. The proposed formula, the Columbia professor concluded, properly defined what a university could and should do:

It can study first principles, it can concern itself with the permanent truths about "man as man"; it can cultivate the intellectual virtues; it can provide an understanding both of the past and [of] the present in the light of which things absolutely new may be examined, it can tell us whether any given thing is in fact absolutely new, and if it is not can remind us how it has been dealt with before; it can relate the departments of our knowledge to one another, and by discovering the common intellectual basis of all the professions can relate them; it can decide what kinds of research are of permanent importance and then conduct them at leisure; it can, in a word, make itself the only stronghold of wisdom which in the nature of things it is possible for a democracy to have. . . .[21]

The *New York Times* reviewer, Ralph Thompson, agreed: " . . . no one else has, so far as I know, in the space of even a dozen long books, diagnosed so accurately as Dr. Hutchins the evils and confusions of our colleges and universities, and put forward so sound a plan for their rationalization and improvement. Adopted even in part, this plan might very well, as the author suggests, alter the character of American education."[22]

Both reviewers stressed the fact that Hutchins's proposal was in fact modest, in the sense that it required a contraction, not an expansion, of the institutions charged with providing higher education. "Mr. Hutchins asks no more than that we think of the whole thing, and if we agree, that we reorganize a few universities so as to give them the content and the dignity he desires," Van Doren wrote. "I cannot see how any thinking reader would go about it to disagree with him or to desire less."[23]

Whether they were thinking or not, some of the heavy hitters in academia lined up to denounce *The Higher Learning* as a snare and a delusion and, worse still, as ideologically subversive. Most of these charged Hutchins with having an authoritarian bent. On his own campus Harry D. Gideonse brought forth a volume titled *The Higher Learning in a Democracy: A Reply to President Hutchins' Critique of the American University*. He professed to read into Hutchins's lucid prose ambiguities that could signify that his rejection of the president's ideas was based on a misunderstanding of them. He appealed to Hutchins to make it clear that he had not meant what Gideonse thought he meant:

> The dominant emphasis, the detailed criticisms, and the educational suggestions which Mr. Hutchins' books present originate and make sense only within the framework of the traditional metaphysics of rational absolutism. It may well be that their author is changing his emphasis and perhaps to some degree his philosophical position. But . . . the misapprehensions — if misapprehensions they be — are responsible for the idea that the higher education in America is to forsake its path of science and humanistic concern for a democratic society and return to the Ivory Tower of absolutist metaphysics. There are even rumors — incredible as it may appear — that the faculty of the University of Chicago, nourished by Scholasticism, is to take the lead in charting this new course for the higher learning. This essay is contributed to the discussion with the purpose of correcting these misapprehensions and rumors.[24]

No such pious intent diluted the onslaught of Myres S. McDougal, a Yale Law School professor who had become a leading exponent of the "legal realism" espoused by Hutchins when he was dean there. McDougal believed that he and his like-minded colleagues had been sold down the river when Hutchins was converted to Thomism by Mortimer Adler.

"In President Hutchins' higher learning remedies and religion become hopelessly entangled," he wrote in the *Yale Law Journal.* ". . . The obvious danger is that credulous converts may assume that metaphysics is not merely a religion but some esoteric instrument of discovery, independent of and in competition with scientific method."[25]

In two issues of *The Social Frontier,* one of the two men Hutchins had identified as the nation's leading anti-intellectuals picked up the gauntlet. John Dewey, while agreeing that higher education was indeed in a deplorable state, roundly rejected the proposed reforms as a retreat to the Ivory Tower that ignored the realities of contemporary life. And he too denounced Hutchins's concept as authoritarian:

> I would not intimate that the author has any sympathy with fascism. But basically his idea as to the proper course to be taken is akin to the distrust of freedom and the consequent appeal to *some* fixed authority that is now overrunning the world. . . . Doubtless much may be said for selecting Aristotle and Saint Thomas as competent promulgators of first truths. But it took the authority of a powerful ecclesiastical organization to secure their wide recognition. Others may prefer Hegel, or Karl Marx, or even Mussolini as the seers of first truths; and there are those who prefer Nazism. As far as I can see President Hutchins has completely evaded the problem of who is to determine the definite truths that constitute the hierarchy.[26]

Invited by *The Social Frontier* to reply, Hutchins quoted Dewey's principal charges, followed by contradictory quotations from his book. This was intended to demonstrate that he had relied on contemporary authorities as well as on the ancient Greeks and the medieval Aquinas; that he had not dismissed science as merely empirical and in fact had given it a prominent place in his ideal university; that he had not called for "the greatest possible aloofness from contemporary social life," but had recognized that first principles must be put to the test of contemporary experience; that it was Dewey who had described metaphysical truths as "fixed" and "eternal," while he himself had specified that "research in the sense of the development, elaboration and refinement of principles together with the collection and use of empirical materials to aid in these processes is one of the highest activities of a university and one in which all of its professors should be engaged."

Mr. Dewey's dexterous intimation that I am a fascist in result if not intention (made more dexterous by his remark that he is making no such intimation) suggests the desirability of the education I have proposed. A graduate of my hypothetical university writing for his fellow alumni would know that such observations were rhetoric and would be received as such. As a matter of fact fascism is a consequence of the absence of philosophy. It is possible only in the context of the disorganization of analysis and the disruption of the intellectual tradition through the pressure of immediate practical concerns. . . .

Mr. Dewey has suggested that only a defective education can account for some of my views. I am moved to inquire whether the explanation of some of his may not be that he thinks he is still fighting nineteenth-century German philosophy.[27]

Dewey replied in kind in the next issue, but beneath the usual poisonous formality and technical jargon with which academics cloak acrimony, the real issue between the two was made clear by the exchange. Hutchins's book, Dewey wrote, had made it "incumbent upon those who did not accept the classic traditional theory to state an alternative conception upon which their ideas regarding the way out of present educational confusion are founded. I say *an* alternative, but I believe that there is but one ultimate alternative; namely, the primary place of experience, experimental method, and intimate connection with practice in determination of knowledge and the auxiliary role of what is called Reason and Intellect in the classic tradition."[28] Hutchins, of course, reversed the priorities; but he could endorse Dewey's capitalization, for to him Reason and Intellect were primary, all else auxiliary.

CHAPTER SIXTEEN

Inflammable Gases

Throughout the late thirties Hutchins was the storm center of American academic life," Edward A. Purcell, Jr., wrote in *The Crisis of Democratic Theory.* "The breadth of his attacks, the fact that he was himself an apostate [legal] realist, and his acceptance of a medieval philosophy — the prime historical symbol of ignorance and repression to most American intellectuals — helped spur the intense rebuttal." But the quality of the intellectual support he received convinced Purcell that Hutchins had introduced the possibility of "a fundamental reorientation in American thought."[1]

Harold Taylor, the president of Sarah Lawrence College, saw it differently. He dismissed the controversy as a tempest in an intellectual teapot. "To me," he wrote, "the doctrine of general education is an administrative device, not a philosophical principle."[2] The effect of Hutchins's proposals, he charged, would be to institute an undergraduate curriculum conceived by educators who had little knowledge of, or interest in, the real needs and desires of contemporary students:

> Having carried the art of the sweeping statement to one of the highest levels it ever reached in the public discussion of cultural issues in America, Hutchins was able by reason of his gifts in exposition and command of the public media to create what amounted to a national polarity in popular thought between the progressive philosophy and educational theory of John Dewey and

the classical view of the Western tradition. His achievement was to make a kind of rousing public wrestling match between Dewey, the common man's friend and everybody's intellectual, and Aristotle, the all-time heavyweight champion of Western thought.[3]

There were advocates on both sides of the controversy who took the argument well beyond the essential case made by John Dewey for the scientific method, and that for the liberal arts made by Hutchins, as a stand-in for Aristotle. There was in fact a considerable area of agreement between the two. Both saw the contemporary educational system as lacking in unity of aim, material, and method, burdened with an overloaded and congested curriculum, and engaged in vocational training that was both narrow and illiberal.

But Dewey asserted that there was a fundamental conflict between metaphysics, which he equated with religion, and science. His attack on Hutchins and his "theological fellow travelers" rejected the Thomist premise that the nature of man is everywhere and always the same. That, he said, was a provincial notion taught in Sunday School: "The reactionary movement is dangerous . . . because it ignores and in effect denies the principle of experimental inquiry and firsthand observation."[4]

Hutchins insisted that he accorded the scientific method a vital place in the educational scheme. But when Dewey demanded, "Are we compelled to hold that one method obtains in the natural sciences, and another, radically different, in moral questions?,"[5] Hutchins replied, "We are compelled to hold just that, because moral questions are not susceptible of scientific treatment."

> The faith of our fathers makes a place for philosophy and science. The faith of John Dewey leaves no place for philosophy or religion. . . . We do not say you must give up science if you believe in God. Mr. Dewey says you must give up philosophy and religion or you cannot truly believe in science. He requires us not merely to have faith in science, but to have faith in nothing else.[6]

Many years later Mortimer Adler would conclude that the differences between Dewey and Hutchins were not in fact insurmountable, and he dedicated one of his books[7] to both men, citing them as leaders in the effort to attain a unified general education. But in the years when the controversy first erupted, he graphically described its effect on Hutchins's home grounds: "The intellectual atmosphere at the University of Chicago had become overheated and was filled with inflammable gases."[8]

When Adler, vacationing in New England, wrote to tell him that he planned to dedicate his *Art and Prudence* to him, Hutchins felt constrained to reply,

> I am very touched by your suggestion that A & P might be dedicated to me. I have never told you, I think, that I pondered long over the question of dedicating the H. L. in A. [*The Higher Learning in America*] to you. I finally abandoned the notion on the grounds on which I am afraid you should abandon your very flattering intentions. The grounds are political, and worse than that they are stupid, but they are important. Theoretically there is no reason why you and I should not be friends. Everybody knows we are anyway. But this is just the kind of thing that would agitate everybody and convince the bastards who make up the faculty that you and I were going to turn the University's endowments over to the Catholic Church. So I shall content myself with a private dedication if you will do the same.[9]

The volatile Adler had virtually given up on the University of Chicago. He recognized that there was no prospect of gaining faculty acceptance for his proposed Institute of Philosophical Studies, which he envisioned as the central agency for curricular reform. By 1936 he was urging Hutchins to take a year off to raise funds to establish a new, experimental college where their ideas on the liberal arts might be put into effect. He wrote from New York to say that he had turned up a live prospect, Mrs. Henry Ittleson, who was fascinated by Hutchins's *No Friendly Voice* and thought he ought to organize a group of like-minded intellectuals and devote the next ten or fifteen years to clear, dispassionate thinking about basic problems of education, politics, and economics: "A little nutty, but I encourage her anyway. Henry isn't well, and she is going to be the master of millions soon."[10]

That summer the Adlers visited the Mark Van Dorens at their rustic retreat at Cornwall in western Connecticut. This was country that also appealed to Scott Buchanan, and Richard McKeon came up for a weekend visit. It seemed to Adler to provide a proper site and a likely name for a Cornwall College. But Hutchins demurred, pointing out that if Adler was to carry out his grand design, he would need an established institution with a variety of graduate programs.

"The trouble with Cornwall College," Hutchins wrote, "is that there isn't any place for an Institute of Philosophical Studies. So what, Doctor, so what? Why not try to capture Columbia on Nick's retirement?" If he was being ironic, it didn't register with Adler. He couldn't see much possibility of organizing a coup that would install Hutchins as a replacement for Nicholas Murray Butler, but he did think they might take over the rambunctious City College of New York. Hutchins again had reservations: "What would bother me a little, only a little, Doctor, would be the political aspect of the matter: the Tammany politicians, the Board of Education, etc."[11]

Adler continued to urge Hutchins to find a more hospitable environment for the two of them, and Hutchins continued to demur. He invoked the famous World War I cartoon in which a British Tommy, huddled in a shell crater under artillery fire, says to a complaining companion, "If you know a better 'ole, go to it." "We have always known that if we could find a better hole we should go to it," Hutchins wrote. "So far we haven't found one that is better. (All of them are holes.)"[12]

The proposals, and the demurrers, would continue. In the summer of 1937 Adler wrote, ". . . I am devoted to your future, and I cannot conceive of my own programme of work for the years ahead apart from yours. . . . You know that I am ready to do whatever I can to serve you in whatever field your own plan of action takes you. But I do have to have some insight about where you stand on fundamentals, theoretically and practically. . . ."[13]

Hutchins replied, "The trouble, as you see clearly, is my dual role. I am a university president. I have been forced to become, under your pressure and guidance, an educational philosopher. Being an educational philosopher and running an educational institution are often two incompatible occupations."[14]

Hutchins was not immune to a despondency occasioned by the limitations his office imposed upon his ambitions, though there was never a quiver in the stiff upper lip he displayed in public. But his hot seat at the University had its compensations. There was, first of all, his unshaken conviction that education was a high and essential calling, and he could think of few, if any, jobs with a greater potential than the one he had. And he deeply believed that the kind of ferment he had engendered on the campus was a vital part of the educational process.

He used the plural, but he was obviously speaking of his own institution when he told the graduating class of 1935,

> If what you want is a dead level of mediocrity, if what you want is a nation of identical twins, without initiative, intelligence, or ideas, you should fear the universities. From this standpoint universities are subversive. They try to make their students think; they do not intend to manufacture so many imitative automatons.

By helping the students learn to think, the universities tend to make them resistant to pressure, to propaganda, or even to reward. They tend to make them dissatisfied — if there were no dissatisfaction there would be no progress. . . .[15]

There were few neutrals among the faculty and students during the years when Hutchins inspired dissatisfaction at Chicago and encouraged its free expression. If those who lived through the Chicago Fight were sometimes bruised, they were never bored. In a retrospective article in *Chicago Magazine,* Georg Mann recalled the atmosphere:

It was not only satisfying — although anybody there would have denied it under oath — but it was perhaps the most exciting center of education since the University of Paris in the thirteenth century. The excitement was generated by the confrontation of a first-rate faculty, accumulated over the years, with an adventurous breed of undergraduates attracted by Hutchins' "New Plan" of education. . . . In the climate on the Chicago campus, the student chose his ideas a great deal more carefully than he did his necktie. He (or she) would have just as soon have appeared before his contemporaries without his ideas in order as he would have ventured forth with strategic buttons out of place. But the ideas were not chosen, as they often seem to be today, to justify pre-existing emotions. The latter were strictly discounted. Ideas didn't grab an individual, he grabbed ideas. And ideas were all around.[16]

Mann was present in Mandel Hall when Adler debated "Ajax" Carlson. "The debate changed few opinions but solidified many," he wrote. Those who professed to be rigorous logicians responded even to such queries as "How are you?" with "Relative to what?" Upon acceptance of even a single premise,

the Adlerian was prepared to chase any opponent up an alley and pin him until he cried "Uncle!" Carlson's followers, on the other hand, had a standard reply to any flat statement, "What is the evidence?" And unless the data were in order, the propositions of the opposition were distributed in neat little heaps around the premises.[17]

Some of the more musically inclined students reduced their arguments to parodies of familiar hymns suitable for group singing. "Nobody knows what Aristotle meant," one side sang, "Nobody knows but Adler." The other replied: "Wave the flag for Social Sciences, / They stand for facts alone, / Ever shall they be dogmatic, / John Dewey they enthrone."[18] Hutchins, an inveterate punster, was particularly appreciative of "Should auld Aquinas be forgot. . . ."

Some of this was no more than intellectual horseplay. Edward Shils, who deplored the running controversy as a diversion from the serious consideration he thought Hutchins's critique of higher education deserved, disapproved of the arguments used by both sides. He blamed Adler and his followers for a dogmatic reduction of the real issues

> to first principles which were extremely simplified and schematic and far from self-evident; these forced the debate onto questions which no reasonable man could discuss. The debate raged furiously about spurious issues.
>
> President Hutchins did not engage directly in the public debate, as far as I can recall, except through lectures delivered outside the University. His own contributions on these occasions were extremely lucid; they were also very simplistic and exaggerated in their cool and condescending rhetoric. . . . Hutchins did not improve matters much. He too argued by hyperbole, distorted the position he opposed, and was as schematic and unrealistic as Adler. But he always argued like a man reasonably explaining obvious things to the wrongheaded. . . .[19]

Hutchins's personal detachment and innate civility permitted him to maintain amicable relations with faculty members who most vehemently opposed him. Frank Knight was a notable example. As the leader of the "Chicago school," the economist was the mentor of Milton Friedman, who would succeed him as the nation's leading exponent of anti-Keynesian free-market orthodoxy. Friedman cited Knight as the outstanding figure among a faculty that could have included Adam Smith, "who but for the accident of having been born in the wrong century and the wrong country would undoubtedly have been a distinguished-service professor at the University."[20]

Knight and Hutchins maintained their respect for each other's intellectual attributes even though the economist had a leading role in the Facts vs. Ideas controversy, activated by what Shils described as his vehement, old-fashioned anti-Catholic bias:

> . . . the odors of Rome were too much for an unbeliever of Protestant sectarian origins, and he regarded President Hutchins

as in some way a remote agent of the Pope. [He] was a querulous, cranky debater who would fasten on a point and not let it go; he was moreover often injurious to those with whom he disagreed and was equally quick to take offense. In fact one of the best things about Hutchins was his amused and patient affection for Knight.[21]

Hutchins made no direct public reply to his faculty detractors, but in his address at the annual trustee-faculty dinner in 1937, he took note of the sharp divisions in his audience and tempered, though he did not eliminate, his usual irony:

As I have said before, the ideal of a university is an understood diversity. Under present conditions we do not need to worry very much about getting enough diversity. We can afford to concentrate for a while on getting some understanding.

The labors of those great and good men, Charles W. Eliot and John Dewey, who did so much for all of us, have led to consequences they could not have anticipated and for which they could not have wished. Those consequences are nothing less than the disintegration of the universities and indeed of the whole educational system. If we are to perform in our day the function which the community is entitled to expect, . . . we must achieve their reintegration. . . .

At Chicago the divisional organization and the College curriculum and the general examinations are steps toward integration. What more is required? . . . I suppose you understand by now that when I discuss such issues I am merely exercising the academic freedom I insist on for you. I hope to use it to keep your attention focused on the fundamental questions affecting our existence as a university. From my point of view the answers to these questions are not so important as asking them.

To the question how can we achieve the reintegration of the university and the educational system, for example, I give you my own answer. I have no doubt that there are other and better ones. My object is to provoke you to find and state them. Nobody has yet questioned the validity of my criticisms of American education. If the criticisms are valid, some way of meeting them must be found. You are not relieved of the responsibility of finding it by saying that you don't like mine.[22]

The speech did nothing to quell the clamoring of his critics, and it drew a particularly unkind cut from Adler, who complained that "the faculty in general took that address as a retreat, an admission of backsliding, etc." Adler thought Hutchins's terse style was largely to blame. "You can't, and I am sure of this now, ever really satisfy your critics so long as you insist upon writing short books or essays," he wrote him in forwarding a prolix commentary on Gideonse's *The Higher Learning in a Democracy*. "You have to do a large job. You have to correct them all along the line on their bad intellectual history, you have to do a fairly complete analytical job on the relation of philosophy and theology, on the relation of philosophy and science, on the history of modern times in respect to these matters." And he added a postscript: "Gee, I wish you'd go one step further and deal explicitly with religion as well as philosophy. That would be doing the complete job — the modern synthesis as it should be done: religion, philosophy, science."[23]

Hutchins may have agreed that he was getting nowhere with his efforts to demonstrate that he was not a closet Scholastic, but he also felt that the course his friend was proposing hardly offered a solution to that problem. Instead, he began to quietly disassociate himself from Adler's brand of Thomism.

When Malcolm P. Sharp of the Law School joined twenty-four senior professors in deploring an Adlerian pronouncement on religion and philosophy, "in view of the wide assumption that [his] views on education are shared by President Hutchins," Hutchins replied in a personal letter, "I don't know what you are talking about. Mr. Adler's statement was not written by me. You can hardly expect me to repudiate it any more than I would repudiate the statement of any other member of the faculty. I certainly do not admit that Mr. Adler speaks for me."[24] Sharp did not accept this disclaimer, and Hutchins wrote again "to spare you the necessity of toiling through Mr. Adler's works to find the clue to what I laughingly call my mental processes";

. . . we have had some conversations, and from them you could gather, if not what I was talking about at least what I was not talking about. You know that I am not talking about the Catholic Church as a political, economic, social or educational force. As a matter of fact, I have publicly and in print condemned Catholic education. Since you know my attitude toward the Church, and since you imply that it is what it is not, you are in a position analogous to that of some of Mr. Roosevelt's ex-associates who know very well that he does not want to be a dictator, but who, for political effect, keep warning the world that he does. . . . I think it is just as bad to see a Catholic under every bed as to find a Communist there.[25]

Hutchins also had problems with Milton Mayer, who was now working out of his office and fancied himself something of an agent provocateur in the Chicago Fight. Edward Shils found Mayer guilty of "fluent flippancy . . . an ignorant and sentimental zealot who combined cynicism and naïveté."[26] But the closest Hutchins came to disavowing either Mayer or Adler was to point out that neither had any license to speak for him. When John Nef told him that one of his associates at the Committee on Social Thought was worried about an alleged presidential secret agenda, Hutchins said he hoped he "would ask me any questions that he has about my attitude and not take seriously anything he hears from Adler and Mayer, who are both degenerating into frightful academic gossips. Good men, too, in their way."[27]

If Hutchins's aplomb remained unshaken in public, he found it increasingly difficult to maintain it at home. By instinct and training he was a family man, brought up in a household where the traditional roles of husband and wife were cheerfully accepted and where he never heard the voice of either parent raised in anger or complaint. But his own wife observed no such conventions, and he found his private life governed by her unpredictable moods.

The physical attraction still endured, as evidenced by the birth of a second child, Joanna Blessing, in September 1935. And embarrassed by it though he often was, Maude's quirky irreverence amused the ironist in Hutchins. One evening Ellery Sedgwick, the pompous editor of the *Atlantic Monthly,* who was supporting the 1936 Republican nominee for President, Alf Landon, reported that he had urged the candidate to send a "personal" postcard to five hundred thousand young voters with a facsimile signature. "He said, 'I advised him to have on it a picture of Washington, or of Lincoln, or of Theodore Roosevelt,' and Maude said, 'Or of Shirley Temple,' " Hutchins wrote to Thornton Wilder in a letter signed, "Yours for more tactful wives."[28]

Hutchins believed that Maude's more outrageous behavior grew out of frustration with her artistic career, which had been eclipsed by his own prominence as a national figure. He sought to promote recognition of her undoubted talent and quietly enlisted his friends in the effort. Mortimer Adler responded by suggesting that she prepare a slide presentation of her silverpoint anatomical drawings, in which the figures were treated as linear forms without representational content. This would be accompanied by his reading of an essay he had composed to illustrate how language could also be nonnarrative and nonrepresentational — devoid, that is, of conventional meaning.

In its first appearance, before a packed house at Mandel Hall, the Maude and Mortimer act hardly created a stir. Carroll Russell, who was in the audience, wrote, "The sentences he read could not have been provocative, and the drawings of her unsexed figures were as static as arrested movement in a well-choreographed dance. The event, although odd, was as controversial as a spring morning."[29]

The reaction was different when the pair took the presentation downtown to the Friday Club, a hallowed cultural organization composed of Chicago's leading matrons. When Adler concluded his reading, he let the polite applause run on and then announced, "If any of you believe you understand anything I have said you have missed the entire point of this exercise." Thinking they had been deliberately duped, the ladies arose in ruffled indignation like a barnyard full of outraged hens. "Mortimer seemed surprised," Elizabeth Paepcke reported, "but Maude was delighted. This was exactly what she wanted to happen."[30]

Adler had persuaded a friend at Random House to combine the drawings and text in a book titled *Diagrammatics,* to be published in a limited edition of 750 numbered copies and priced at twenty-five dollars a copy. Maude returned the favor by objecting to the quality of the reproduction of her sketches, demanding that the entire edition be destroyed, and ordering a new printing on her own.

During this period her distinctive work adorned the Christmas cards the Hutchinses sent to friends and faculty, and one of these drawings — more detailed than those in *Diagrammatics* — depicted a nude, nubile young girl who was unmistakably their daughter Franja. That Yuletide greeting, Carroll Russell wrote,

> aroused matronly fury that the child should be so exposed to scrutiny. The affair, of course, further separated Maude from conservative faculty wives. The result was a lack of communication that was partly endured by Maude, but also partly intended, I fancy. She made a few friends outside the academic circle, but with a very busy husband who left the house every morning at seven, maids to run household matters, and a nurse for the children . . . she must have felt loneliness. I know she felt frustrated.[31]

When her husband ordered a pastel portrait of her from Maude, the sympathetic Mrs. Russell found that he "had recently been party to a confession from Bob. Life at home was hard on him because Maude was not getting enough commissions to satisfy her."[32] Others rallied around as best they could. For four summers Harold Swift made available a house at his Lakeside retreat for the Hutchins daughters and their nurse. This made it possible for the couple to reduce the tensions by traveling abroad, where Swift & Co. agents would smooth the way for itineraries dictated largely by Maude's whims.

The Russells frequently dined at the presidential residence, and they found that the evenings could be pleasant enough if they helped see to it that the conversation did not stray from topics of interest to Maude. But Adler recalled that when he and his host lapsed into talk of the University matters that preoccupied them, the hostess was capable of interrupting them with a peremptory, "Shut up! Now you are going to talk about me!"[33]

Mrs. Russell noticed that in moments when Hutchins did not feel obligated to take an animated part in the conversation, his face relaxed into an expression of "ineffable sadness."[34]

CHAPTER SEVENTEEN

The Madison Avenue Touch

A bold headline in the *Chicago Daily News* raised the question, "WHO IS TO RULE U. OF C.?," and the following article defined the issue: "Whether President Robert Maynard Hutchins or the faculty of the University of Chicago is to rule the university is a subject which has divided the Midway campus into two warring factions — quiet, perhaps, but determined."

> Ultimately must come a showdown before the university senate and, possibly, the trustees, but it will be a year or two, and, until it does come, the president and his official family in the west wing of Harper Memorial Library insist they will remain silent.
>
> Spokesmen for the two factions are less reticent among the faculty. Basically the division is between those who claim the staff should have a responsible part in appointments, promotion and tenure questions as a safeguard against educational dictatorship, and those who hold that the president must retain power and responsibility in such matters.[1]

Actually, the existing powers were fairly well balanced. While the president had ultimate responsibility for determining the quality of the faculty, he could only recommend an appointment to the appropriate department, whose members could and often did veto his choice. He, in turn, could veto a faculty recommendation or use his budgetary authority to determine salary and terms of appointment. He had specified what use he would make of that authority five years before, when he outlined the means he would employ to meet the Depression's inroads on the University's income:

> Although I am in favor of a congenial faculty, congeniality sometimes suggests appointments which will be restful rather than inspiring. I have no doubt that the desire for friendliness has something to do with the fact that in 1929 52 percent of the entire faculty had received their highest degrees at the University of Chicago. For so young a university that is a very large, perhaps a too-large, proportion.
>
> I am also in favor of a humane administration. Under present conditions I should be opposed to dropping any member of the faculty who had been here more than a year or two unless he had another job or unless he was grossly and admittedly incompetent. But I am not in favor of a sentimental policy which would dictate the promotion of members of the staff merely because they had been in residence a long time. Such a policy must result in the deterioration of the University.
>
> Still less do I favor the view that the eminence of a department depends on the ground it covers. . . . And so I cannot become interested in the restoration of the Divisions and Schools to their pre-Depression numerical strength. I am on the other hand interested in very little else [other] than their restoration to their pre-Depression distinction. This means that as we get the money we should find the men and women who will succeed not to the subjects studied or the courses taught by those who have retired, but to their high rank in the scholarly world.[2]

While Hutchins turned down some proposed appointments, there is no credible evidence that in doing so he ever departed from his announced policy. Those who were not promoted or whose contracts were not renewed usually held the president responsible, even though in many cases the action was based on the recommendation of their colleagues. And since no one likes to admit incompetence, Hutchins was often charged with ideological bias. The suspicion would not down, though it was refuted by the record. Under Hutchins such notably conservative departments as Economics and Social Science, which housed his most vociferous critics, continued to be dominated by professors who did not share his views on matters of educational or public policy.

Perhaps the ultimate test of Hutchins's open-mindedness was provided by the man he brought in to head the Department of Education and who later served as the dean of social sciences. Ralph Tyler, a follower of John Dewey, came to Hutchins's attention when the latter was looking for a replacement for the retiring university examiner. Tyler, a professor of education at Ohio State University, was directing a cooperative study of general education funded by the Progressive Education Association. When he was summoned for an interview, which developed into a day-long discussion, he asked Hutchins why he was considering someone whose educational philosophy seemed to be quite different from his own. "I know that you're the kind of person we want," Hutchins replied. "You have ideas about what should be done both in the examination staff and in the department of education. You're a person who's intelligent, who's known to follow through on whatever he undertakes, and that's what I want."[3]

Hutchins not only accepted Tyler but also found office space for the staff of presumed Deweyites who had been working under his direction at Ohio State. Tyler remained at Chicago throughout the Hutchins years and later testified, "I know of no case in my time in which Hutchins turned down an appointment that was approved by the department and the dean."[4]

The opposition cited by the *Daily News,* however, was not based on what the president was doing, but grew out of a near-paranoid fear on the part of some faculty members about what he might do: "Behind this . . . is Dr. Hutchins' devotion to a spectacular educational philosophy that makes headlines and violent enemies alike. Those who fear the appointing power, fear it may be used to impose the president's theories on the university."[5]

The infighting came into the open when the Chicago chapter of the American Association of University Professors, under the chairmanship of Harry Gideonse, undertook a study of faculty tenure. Its committee found that 60 percent of the 1936–1937 faculty held one-year appointments; only 32 percent had permanent tenure, as against 48 percent ten years before. The report gave no weight to the fact that the reduction in tenured faculty was the result of a Depression measure adopted in 1931, which mandated retirement at age sixty-five. With the increase in limited contracts, the report charged, "there will be a tendency to convert the whole university into an instrument of presidential policy, accompanied by a decline not only in the sense of faculty responsibility, but in freedom of opinion and freeness of speech. If that time comes, although the program may be advanced, the university will decline. It is inherent in the situation."[6]

On the basis of the AAUP report, the university senate approved a parallel investigation by its policy committee. The vote was close; only forty-two of the seventy-six members present supported the motion, and the president would serve as ex officio chairman of the investigating body. But Hutchins recognized that even if he headed off the immediate threat, he would still be left with a serious public-relations problem. While he retained solid trustee support for his personnel policies, the board members were concerned about the publicity generated by the controversy. It was not, as Chairman Swift pointed out, conducive to attracting the offspring of the midwestern elite and enlisting their parents' support for the endowment fund.

When he faced a problem of this complexity, it was Hutchins's practice to seek professional help, preferably from people he knew well. Now he turned to a companion of his youth who also came of Puritan stock but had become prematurely wealthy by mastering the worldly ways of Madison Avenue. William Benton, like Hutchins, had shoe-horned his way into Yale as the impecunious son of an alumnus who had gone west as an ordained minister and had become a college professor. But there the resemblance ended.

Benton's style provided an absolute contrast to that of the elegant Hutchins, who disguised his formidable energy with a pose of indolence, professed disdain for material goods and the competition involved in their acquisition, and proclaimed the intellectual life the only one worth living. The short, sharp-featured Benton was an unabashed hustler who had marked his rapid rise in the business community by proudly displaying the trappings of wealth. His ambition was a kinetic force; he spoke in staccato bursts, with an apparent lack of any restraining sensibility, and, with his eye always on the main chance, attempted to bulldoze every encounter in the direction he wanted it to take.

The association of this odd couple had begun at New Haven, where Benton was a member of the debating team and Hutchins was its captain. Writing to his mother of a debate with Harvard, Benton provided a revealing characterization of the two of them:

> As the number two man, I threw away my prepared manuscript and pitched into Harvard. But Bob, in the number three position, went ahead with his beautifully prepared speech and proved the case beautifully — the very case Harvard had conceded. I wanted to win by making the most of Harvard's weakness. Bob, indifferent to Harvard's weakness, wanted to persuade the audience about truth itself.[7]

While Hutchins was earning top academic honors, Benton used his remarkable mathematical gifts to win money from wealthy classmates at auction bridge and to devise means of promoting the *Yale Record,* the university humor magazine, which in those days featured he-she jokes and flapper drawings in the style of John Held, Jr. As chairman of the *Record,* Benton put it on the newsstands of New York alongside the popular *College Humor,* built its circulation to an unheard-of six thousand copies, and during his year in charge turned in a profit of twenty-five thousand dollars.

Benton fondly recalled the most famous line he contributed to the *Record:* ''In the spring a young man's fancy lightly turns to what the girls have been thinking about all winter.''[8] His literary and personal style was no handicap to his career in advertising, and the leading agencies in New York and Chicago were soon competing for his services as an innovative promoter and salesman. In 1929, the year Hutchins was summoned to Chicago, Benton joined with another youthful Yale alumnus, Chester Bowles, to form a successful agency of their own.

His mother, the formidable headmistress of a fashionable St. Louis girls' school, with whom he maintained an almost daily correspondence, had never approved of her son's employing his talents in the crass business of selling soap and toothpaste. As a result he had an understanding with Bowles that when he had made a million dollars, he would forsake Madison Avenue and turn his talents to more worthwhile endeavors. He had put away that much and more by 1936, when he informed his partner that the time had come for him to sell his interest in Benton & Bowles.

When Hutchins got wind of this he headed for New York with a proposition: if Benton wanted to do something useful, how about becoming secretary of the University of Chicago with responsibility for public relations and fund raising? Benton flatly refused. If he had wanted to continue his career as a promoter and salesman, he would have stayed where he was. But there was another, more compelling reason for his reluctance: Benton's ambition for public service, as his later career would demonstrate, could only be satisfied by political office.

He was then being urged by some influential clients of the advertising agency to become publicity director of the coming Republican campaign to replace Franklin Roosevelt with Alf Landon. Although he had always voted Democratic, Benton agreed to discuss the proposal with leading Landon supporters. One of these was Eugene Meyer, the publisher of the *Washington Post.* The wealthy ex-banker did not persuade Benton to join the GOP, but he did inadvertently kindle his interest in the Chicago proposal, for Meyer was an admirer of Hutchins's educational ideas and had enrolled his daughter Katherine at Chicago.

While Benton was wavering, Hutchins sought to counteract the pressure from his advertising clients by sending three of Chicago's trustees to New York to make the case for the University: Harold Swift, John Stuart, head of Quaker Oats, and Edward L. Ryerson, chairman of Inland Steel. These three certified Republicans assured Benton that the University was more deserving of his services than Alf Landon. They urged him to come out to Chicago and look the place over, and Hutchins finished the selling job, accepting Benton's counterproposal to come on a part-time basis to do a professional survey of the University's public-relations problems and to help implement any remedies he might suggest. Hutchins admonished him:

> I wish you would stop worrying about the Republican party, which is beyond redemption, and concentrate on education, which may yet be saved. The most hopeless element in the GOP is my old pal Frank Knox [who was on the ticket as running mate with Landon]. If you let your wife see him, she'll never want to come to Chicago. And I am very anxious to have her come. . . .
>
> I am eager to have you do the survey which is now in progress, and still more eager to have you come to Chicago for as long a time as you will. When you get here you should stay. It will be a damned sight more interesting and important than trying to make Frank Knox into a statesman. I can promise you that.[9]

Hutchins sweetened the offer, and a year later Benton became one of the University's two vice presidents. He accepted a salary of $10,000, minuscule in comparison to the $250,000 he had been earning at Benton & Bowles, but stipulated that he wanted to have six months of the year free to pursue other interests. And Hutchins assured him that he was expected to be more than a high-toned huckster. The clincher was Hutchins's recognition that Benton's experience with commercial radio, which in those days depended on programming created by the advertising agencies, qualified him to play a major role in developing the University's educational outreach through its extension services.

"If I tend to emphasize my interest in educational broadcasting, and in educational moving pictures, and if I tend to minimize my functions as the Middle-Western King of Money Raisers, I know you will excuse that," he wrote Hutchins after he faced the difficult task of trying to explain to a protesting Chet Bowles why he had decided to give up a fortune and move to Chicago. "I wanted to drop you this note today to tell you that my enthusiasm is mounting rapidly, and, I believe, will continue to mount. . . ."[10]

Enthusiasm was essential to the drive that kept Benton in near-perpetual motion, and Hutchins had guessed correctly that he would sell himself on the proposed job as he carried out his part-time commitment. He was hooked by the time he completed his report, which he delivered to the board in February 1937. Only fifty numbered copies of the 192-page document were printed, and each bore the admonition that its contents were absolutely confidential. When Hutchins received an advance proof for final editing the only change he suggested was the addition of an opening sentence: "A report like this, to my knowledge, has never before been written; surely never before for any university."[11]

Benton was credited with pioneering the development of market research while he was an executive at Lord & Thomas, and he applied those techniques to surveying the Chicago situation. First he had to familiarize himself with the "product" to be sold — in this case, the education provided by the University. As he sailed through interviews with leading faculty members, he appraised what they had to offer in terms that would have meaning to laymen who had to be convinced of the value of the institution.

He was intrigued by what he found in the academic grove, and he reacted to it in characteristically personal terms. When John Howe, the university publicist whom he drafted as his guide, told him that Professor Nathaniel Kleitman was engaged in a study of sleep, Benton got the idea that he hoped to cut two hours off the normal night's rest. "Why, John," he said, "gaining those two hours a day would practically amount to doubling my creative life. Those would be *golden hours*. Most of a man's waking hours are taken up with routines — bathing, eating, answering the phone, etc., etc. Few men have more than two hours a day for creative effort — wholly free hours. If Kleitman can tell me how to get two more, what a gift that would be!"[12] As it turned out, the professor couldn't tell him, but Benton's enthusiasm continued unabated.

He brought in a team of Benton & Bowles market researchers to survey public attitudes toward the University in seven midwestern cities, and on his own interviewed twenty prominent figures in the Chicago area. As a national leader in the advertising world, he found the doors of the most lordly executive suites open to him, and as he inquired as to what these tycoons thought of Bob Hutchins and his university, he also engaged in a preliminary selling job, recognizing that at this level the best way to dispel anti-Hutchins prejudice was to expose these men to his client in person.

On one such visit with the disaffected Charles Walgreen he set up the meeting with Hutchins that led to a half-million-dollar gift. But an even more remarkable result came from Benton's call on Colonel Robert R. McCormick in his eyrie atop the Tribune Tower. For more than five years, by the colonel's edict, Hutchins had been a nonperson, never mentioned by name in the *Tribune*. But Benton persuaded the colonel to meet with the man he had consigned to oblivion, and Hutchins completed the disarming process. In a Yuletide editorial counting Chicago's blessings, the *Tribune* astonished its readers, particularly those on the Midway, by citing the University as the city's most priceless asset and its greatest ornament.

Benton's report and recommendations, accompanied by five fact-filled appendices, made a profound impression on the trustees. He was unflinching in summing up the criticisms his researchers had found in their sampling of public opinion, citing these as a "major cause of sales resistance":

Radicalism: The University teaches subversive doctrines; over-emphasizes communism; is New Dealish to the point of pinkness; fosters social unrest. . . .
   Environment bad for students: There is too much emphasis on book learning; scholastic requirements are too high; social life is neglected and fraternities are being killed off; the University is cold, impersonal toward students. As a result there are too many Jews, too many of the big-browed type, too many neurotics and bookworms. As evidence of much of the foregoing look at the football team (and basketball team).
   Unsound Administration: Mr. Hutchins should fire radical and communistic professors; he actually sympathizes with them and encourages them; is unsympathetic towards outside complaints and criticisms; does not engage in community activities; has too little respect for tradition.[13]

But Benton recognized that there was no way to effectively alter the stance and the style of his classmate. The answer, then, was to appeal to regional pride by presenting the young president as one who had given comeuppance to the Eastern Seaboard snobs who looked down upon the Second City. Excellence was the catchword of the proposed sales pitch; the record would show that Hutchins's controversial activities had enhanced the University's worldwide reputation as an institution ranking alongside, if not ahead of, Harvard and Yale. So he recommended even greater public exposure of the young president: "Mr. Hutchins is unorthodox in personality and in speech. He does not conform to preconceived standards of a university president. 'What Hutchins needs,' as one man put it to me, 'is something like Queen Mary's hat.' "[14]

Not even the inventive Benton, however, could dream up a way to provide a more conventional and soothing persona for a man who dismissed contrived personal publicity as an undignified distraction from the ideas he advocated. While he recommended that Hutchins deliver speeches to such nonintellectual groups as the American Legion, and that he schedule more frequent informal meetings with Chicago's movers and shakers, he recognized that here the president's sharp wit presented a special hazard: "Like any great gift, it is difficult to control. . . . I do not believe Mr. Hutchins can possibly realize how much he is quoted. Stories go around about him as they do about Dorothy Parker or Will Rogers. He should be extremely careful to avoid all criticism of people with whom the University hopes to work. . . ."[15]

But in the main Benton's proposed remedies were positive. The University had a story to tell, and if it was told properly "the tribulations of the University will be better understood and often forgiven; students will come in surfeit; the public will support the institution against the politicians; and those with money will realize that dollar for dollar there is no better philanthropic investment than the University of Chicago."[16] He recommended a seventy-five-thousand-dollar increase in the niggardly public-relations budget, and when Hutchins objected that he could hire ten fine professors for that amount, he replied that this was also an educational investment, one that would enable the institution to meet its obligation to educate its neglected public constituency.

Behind Benton's brash salesman's approach lay a genuine devotion to the University and an almost frenetic concern with exploiting its possibilities. "If I have not had one new idea in twenty-four hours I count it a lost day," he said.[17] He bounced these fermenting notions off anyone he could buttonhole, but it was usually Hutchins who had to judge their merit. Only one in ten might turn out to be worthwhile, and he had to figure out which one it was with no help from Benton, who treated them all with aggressive enthusiasm. His impact upon the more sheltered faculty members was often abrasive. "Indisputably, I lack tact, and this is a serious fault," Benton said in self-appraisal. "I alibi my bluntness by calling it 'candor.' Some of my associates get used to it; at least they know where I stand. But I overdo my tactlessness."[18]

Still, there was a form of flattery in the evident fact that the learned professors aroused his boundless curiosity. He became a welcome, if unsettling, fixture at the Quadrangle Club's luncheon round table, where he reveled in the informal exchange of ideas and gossip. He was taken with the idea of bringing such figures as these into regular contact with the circle of top-ranked businessmen with whom he continued to associate in pursuing his outside interests. Along with Paul Hoffman, a trustee of the University and head of the then-thriving Studebaker Motor Company, he perfected plans for a consortium of educators and business executives that ultimately became the Committee for Economic Development, with a membership drawn from the top drawer of the American establishment.

Hutchins watched his dynamic friend's impact on the staid university community, and the faculty's impact on Benton, with sardonic amusement. He often recited, with particular delight, the story of Benton's first exposure to the faculty senate:

> It was a solemn occasion. Two hundred full professors had assembled to discuss whether the bachelor's degree should be relocated at the end of the sophomore year, giving it and other degrees a meaning they had never had before. The faculty debated this proposition for two hours without ever mentioning education. The whole discourse concerned the effect of the proposed change on public relations and revenue. Mr. Benton, fresh from Madison Avenue, stormed out of the assembly shouting, "This is the most sordid meeting I ever attended in my life!"[19]

Benton made many contributions to the University during the years of his formal association. He was undeviating in his personal devotion to Hutchins and to the educational ideas he espoused, and in his own right he was, and continued to be, an uncompromising defender of academic freedom and free speech. He looked back on his years on the Midway as among the most rewarding of his life. But he never realized one of the hopes that brought him there.

It would have seemed that his decision to abandon the fleshpots of Madison Avenue for a financially unrewarding university post would have pleased his puritanical mother. But Elma Benton, who had earned her advanced degree in education at Columbia Teachers College, never really approved of Bob Hutchins. She was soon urging the forty-year-old son she still called Billy to end the collaboration that meant so much to him: "I fear it is a case of Old Dog Tray getting into bad company. Your mother did not raise you that way. . . . Your will is not your own. Hutchins is marching to a certain doom and you are being dragged along to it by him."[20]

Sidney Hyman, who became Benton's biographer, thought the unsevered silver cord explained the extraordinary drive that produced Benton's overlapping careers in advertising, education, publishing, and politics: "He grew into a man who seemed unafraid of anything, including God's final judgment — unafraid of anything, that is, but his mother's frown, while longing for her approving smile, which he never got."[21]

CHAPTER EIGHTEEN

No Place to Go

As he approached the end of his first decade at Chicago, Hutchins had reached a standoff with his faculty. He had failed in his effort to create a Great Books curriculum for the College, but there was now the beginning of a separate faculty operating on the stated principle that "the end of general education can be achieved best by helping students to master the leading ideas and significant facts in the principal fields of knowledge. . . ."[1] The Laboratory School and other institutions in the area were annually providing more than a hundred students who demonstrated the feasibility of beginning one's college education after two years of high school, and all the undergraduates now followed a unified basic program that limited electives and precluded specialization.

As it developed over the next decade, the Hutchins College, as it came to be called, was destined to be misunderstood by some of its critics and caricatured by others, who portrayed it as consisting of an eccentric faculty playing games with eccentric juveniles. While it admitted students on the basis of entrance examinations, regardless of their age or previous schooling, and graduated them whenever they could demonstrate that they had mastered the required curriculum, it was hardly a playground for free spirits. F. Champion Ward, who joined the faculty in 1945 and in 1947 succeeded Clarence Faust, the founding dean, noted that

> the Hutchins College required attendance at classes in the first two
> years; it housed younger resident students in dormitories whose

life it regulated; and above all it held to the view that quite apart from regulations, intelligent young Americans in their middle teens are more apt to learn to conduct themselves profitably and responsibly in the atmosphere of a college rather than a high school. The College was distinctive in its assumption that the best time in a student's life to acquire a general, higher education was during the four years between ages sixteen and twenty. . . .

The College offered a balanced and prescribed program of studies in the humanities, social sciences and natural sciences (nine courses), mathematics, writing and foreign language (three courses), with culminating efforts to employ history and philosophy as means of integration.[2]

The subject matter of the College's curriculum, then, was not different in kind from that available to undergraduates elsewhere. The difference was in the manner in which it was taught, in the use of original works rather than the rehashed versions found in conventional textbooks, and in the fact that it was required of all students. Theoretically, a student could meet all the requirements for a bachelor's degree by mastering the source material on his own, but to do so would be to miss the shared experience that to the majority was the most exciting and rewarding aspect of their college years:

In half the College's courses there were no lectures at all, and in the others lectures were secondary and, when given, were not conceived as talking textbooks devoted to "laying out" the subject. Instead, teaching and learning occurred in discussion classes of fifteen to twenty-five students, usually meeting three times weekly. In those discussions, students were expected to attempt to answer questions raised in the first instance by their teacher and, as the discussion proceeded, by other students and themselves.[3]

In imposing upon undergraduates a required curriculum instead of the elective system, which allowed them to largely determine their own course of study, the College was accused of being undemocratic, and the program itself was cited as an example of Hutchins's purported efforts to impose scholasticism upon the University. Ward testified that on the contrary, Hutchins encouraged experimentation and never interfered with the design of the curriculum or the choice of faculty. To the dean, another product of Oberlin's Protestant tradition, Aristotle provided no more than a useful guide:

This Aristotelianism was not doctrinal. (The College was never able to digest a Thomist.) . . . The aim was not to equip the student with a single synthesis of human knowledge or to assign a single meaning to human history. Rather it was to enable him to use the disciplines of history and philosophy (particularity and generality in their most inclusive embodiments) in the search for knowledge and wisdom which every civilized man (and woman!) should carry on throughout his (or her) life.[4]

Adler regarded the reconstitution of the College as something less than half a loaf. He continued to urge that Hutchins seek another berth for the two of them, pointing out that Saint John's, with its hundred-proof Great Books curriculum, would welcome them in any capacity, Stringfellow Barr having indicated that he would be happy to remove himself as president in that event.

A meeting with leading members of the Saint John's board was arranged, and Adler and Hutchins, accompanied by Maude, traveled to Annapolis by train. Adler recalled that Maude seemed to be in a receptive mood when Hutchins opened the fitted bag that constituted his traveling bar and served martinis in their Pullman drawing room. But when they arrived and were housed in a handsome old guesthouse, she made it clear that she had no intention of moving to Annapolis by refusing to leave her room to inspect the campus and greet their hosts. Adler recognized that this ended his Saint John's gambit.

In the summer of 1938 Hutchins replied with some asperity to the continued Adlerian insistence that he make a firm decision about the future:

> There is no answer to it. What you say about Chicago is true. What is the alternative? I don't want to go to Saint John's. There isn't any other place I can go. I have thought and thought but I can think of no alternative. I could resign without an alternative. That hardly seems the act of a prudent man.

He added a pointed postscript: "As for you, you dope, you had a pretty good year last year. What more can you ask than all the time you want for writing?"[5]

In response to that admonition Adler subsided. In his autobiography he said he simply decided to "withdraw from the affairs of the university and use my academic tenure and salary to provide myself with the means for carrying on with my own work — writing books and giving lectures."[6] But regular publication and frequent platform appearances were not enough to exhaust his energy or satisfy his ambition.

Will Hays, the head of the Motion Picture Association, enlisted Adler's help in staving off the threat of censorship that mounted as World War II flared in Europe and Hollywood was accused of propagandizing for Britain. He signed on as consultant and ghostwriter, with a retainer that was more than half of his salary at Chicago. "It did not take me long to discover my susceptibility to lavish surroundings and their accompaniments," he wrote.[7]

With Adler in abeyance, Hutchins acquired another, vastly different confidant and advocate. John Ulrich Nef, an economic historian who had joined the faculty the year before Hutchins arrived, was a certified member of the old guard. A close personal relationship developed between the two as Nef sought presidential support for a radically different interdisciplinary program of graduate education. In his memoir, *Search for Meaning,* he described what amounted to a mutual-assistance pact:

> My desire as an individual to introduce a new kind of department offered Hutchins a unique opportunity, not least because of my background. I was not his appointee, as were other, different kinds of reformers, such as Scott Buchanan, Stringfellow Barr and Mortimer Adler. All my family connections were with faculty elements opposed to the proposals attributed to this brilliant and attractive young president. Considerable opposition in the beginning had originated in the scientific faculties, and here was I, the son of the founder of the Chemistry Department. The fiercest opposition came from the Philosophy Department. Most prominent in this opposition at the beginning of Hutchins' term of office was George Mead. . . . He was my guardian. How therefore could Hutchins oppose *my* initiatives? Especially when he agreed with some of them?[8]

At thirteen, when his father died, Nef became a ward of the Meads, joining a household that also included their beautiful niece Elinor Castle, heiress to one of the great Hawaiian fortunes amassed by descendants of the early missionaries. The two were married after Nef's graduation from Harvard, and her wealth made possible some years of residence in Paris, where they were intimates of the avant-garde artists and writers of the day. They were living in England when Nef published *The Rise of the British Coal Industry,* which established his scholarly reputation. This cosmopolitan background enhanced the salon they maintained in their elegant house just off the Chicago campus.

Carroll Russell, who had grown up with John and Elinor, described their life-style:

> Visiting lecturers were usually close friends, and a glittering array they were. Arnold Toynbee, Frederick Hayek [*sic*], T. S. Eliot and R. H. Tawney gave public lectures that I attended. Some stayed for a few days, some for a week, and some for months. Most were guests in the Nefs' house (where the food was memorable). I shall always remember sitting in their living room while Artur Schnabel played Beethoven to a small group; or being seated for lunch next to the frighteningly erudite Jacques Maritain.[9]

This kind of cachet gave Nef a standing among the faculty that he exploited on Hutchins's behalf. When the AAUP-inspired motion to investigate the distribution of tenured appointments was introduced in the faculty senate, he denounced it as an underhanded move to reduce the statutory powers of the president. "The time has come," he said, "when I must speak out against the medieval witch-hunting directed against the most distinguished man my generation of Americans has produced."[10]

Nef was an aesthete whose residence was adorned with the works of Derain, Dufy, Chagall, Signac, Grosz, Sigonzac, Picasso, Matisse, and Rouault, artists he had known during his sojourns in Paris. This made him one of the few faculty members whom Maude found acceptable, and Hutchins encouraged the friendship, urging Nef to do what he could to bolster his wife's faith in her own artistic talent. "As a painter Maude never really rose above the mediocre," Nef said, "'but of course I didn't share that opinion with her.'"[11]

During those years the frustrations of his professional life and his increasingly strained relationship with Maude prompted Hutchins to give serious consideration to leaving the University, even though, as he told Adler, he could think of no satisfactory alternative. Had he been interested solely in money and a change of scene, he apparently could have become the first full-time president of the New York Stock Exchange, charged with restoring that institution's tarnished reputation.

The occasion arose in 1938 when Richard Whitney, a prominent member of the Exchange, was found guilty of embezzling funds to shore up his bankrupt brokerage firm, and the Securities and Exchange Commission, headed by Hutchins's friend William O. Douglas, cast a cold eye on those responsible for regulating stock-market operations.

Hutchins rejected the overture, and the job went to another outsider, William McChesney Martin. Hutchins did accept an appointment as one of three new public members of the board of governors, which had previously been made up wholly of Exchange members. The others were General Robert Wood, president of Sears, Roebuck and a Chicago trustee, and Carl C. Conway of the Continental Can Company.

Hutchins's experience in the upper reaches of the world of finance was brief. He resigned the day the governors convened to consider the disclosure that at least three members of the Exchange had failed to warn them of Whitney's defalcation, though they had known for months that their colleague was desperately trying to cover a shortage of funds in his brokerage accounts. Martin agreed with Hutchins that such conduct was reprehensible, but he held that the board should do nothing about it.

Before they got to the Whitney matter, the governors voted for a stern censure of a small-fry broker whose partner, without his knowledge, had withheld $3,200 from a customer — this in spite of the fact that the money had been paid as soon as a valid legal claim was made. Hutchins thought this a telling contrast to the decision to take no action on the Whitney cover-up, approved by a 27–1 vote in which he was the lone dissenter. In a confidential letter to Douglas, he wrote,

> It is my considered opinion that the real reason for the inaction of the Stock Exchange was that influential and important people were involved in this case. Under the constitution as it was at the time of the incident the persons, among others, who might be disciplined were J. P. Morgan and Junius Morgan, who hold the seats for J. P. Morgan and Company. No member of the Board of Governors was willing to "lay his head on the chopping block." . . . I have no doubt that if Mr. Goldsborough [the censured member], for example, had done what George Whitney, Thomas Lamont, or E. E. Simmons did he would have been expelled from the Exchange. This result seems to me inherent in the situation. No private, voluntary organization can ever discipline the "big men" among its membership. Some outside impartial agency has to do that.[12]

When Hutchins's resignation was announced, Douglas sent him a telegram: "WELCOME TO THE TRENCHES." An item in the *New York Herald Tribune* probably reflected the prevailing view in the business community: "Far from regretting the evident lack of harmony at the Stock Exchange shown by the resignation of Robert M. Hutchins as governor, many in Wall Street were inclined to regard the step as an ultimate benefit.''[13] General Wood told Hutchins he had made a mistake: ''I think the Exchange needs your intellectual ability and honesty. On the other hand, I think you need the contact with men who are in business life.''[14]

The experience reinforced Hutchins's conviction that his conscience would not permit him to adapt to the kind of corner cutting that appeared to be necessary in the business world. A few months later he rejected the invitation of his old friend Henry Luce to join the board of directors of Time, Inc.: ''I can think of nothing that would be more interesting to me than to be associated with you and your publications. Unfortunately, I am afraid I can't do it.''[15] He used as an excuse the purported feeling of some of his trustees that he shouldn't take any more time from the University's business. The real reason, however, may well be reflected in the afterthoughts of Bill Benton, who had urged him to accept Luce's offer:

> I have been thinking about the Time directorate. My hunch is that I gave you a bad steer. I was overinfluenced by the fact that this might be your legitimate opportunity to make some real money.
>
> But I doubt whether your future is as a moneymaker.
>
> Except from the angle of making money, it won't do you any good to be connected with a publishing enterprise. In fact it won't do you any good to be connected with any business enterprise. . . .
>
> Doesn't it seem to you that Harry's magazines are being edited, more and more, with a political bias?[16]

In the end Hutchins concluded that there was only one job that would justify a career change. But this one required the cultivation of politicians — and he had an abiding distaste for most of those who made the compromises that were necessary to gain elective office. Colonel House had read him correctly when, as a New Deal talent scout, he interviewed the derisive Hutchins and concluded that he was too young to go it alone in Washington.

Hutchins was older now, but his temperamental need for a high degree of independence had been reaffirmed by his experience in academia. The only place in the top echelon of government where he could answer only to his own conscience was the Supreme Court of the United States. But a candidate for one of the nine places on the bench could not simply declare his interest, present his credentials, and expect to be judged on merit. Appointment to a seat on the high court required the personal favor of Franklin Roosevelt, a consummate politician who was primarily interested in advancing his program and pleasing his constituency.

By 1934 the party loyalists in Roosevelt's inner circle had forgiven, or forgotten, Hutchins's 1932 apostasy, when he declined to endorse the Democratic ticket and publicly declared that he would cast a protest vote for Norman Thomas. Well-placed friends in Washington kept his name before Roosevelt as key positions opened in the alphabetical agencies that were expanding like amoebas to implement New Deal reforms. Such service, as his friends kept pointing out to the reluctant Hutchins, was necessary to catch the President's attention and earn his gratitude.

Hutchins's name came to the top of the prospect list when Roosevelt found it necessary to get rid of General Hugh Johnson, the hard-nosed "czar" of the price- and wage-fixing National Recovery Administration. At the behest of Secretary of the Interior Harold Ickes, Roosevelt summoned Hutchins to Washington and offered him the chairmanship of the reorganized NRA. It was understood that this would become effective as soon as the President could arrange for the resignation of Clay Williams, who then held the post. Roosevelt volunteered to personally request the University trustees to grant Hutchins a nine-month leave of absence, and Hutchins agreed.

The deal fell apart before it could be consummated. In his published diary Ickes placed the blame on the maneuvering of Donald Richberg, the NRA counsel who eventually succeeded to the chairmanship. Richberg persuaded the agency's board to oppose the Hutchins appointment, and the threat of public resignation by some members was sufficient to stay the President's hand.

The offer to Hutchins was made in early October, but when it was not confirmed by the end of November, he told Ickes he intended to inform the President that he was no longer available. Ickes urged him to delay until they heard from two other active supporters, the "brains trust" adviser Rexford Tugwell and the Chicago political scientist Charles E. Merriam, who were to take up the matter during a visit to the presidential retreat in Warm Springs, Georgia. But they also failed to get an affirmative answer, and Ickes summed up the result in his usual curmudgeonly fashion:

> I am thoroughly convinced that Richberg's connection with NRA can only result in harm to that organization. I believe that he is out to make a place for himself at whatever cost. I do not believe he can be trusted. I am convinced that it was he who inspired the opposition expressed by the NRA Board to Hutchins. In my judgment he will leave no stone unturned to prevent Hutchins

from going to Washington. As matters stand, he has a board that has been carefully handpicked by himself and through which he can control in his devious, indirect way. . . .[17]

Garbled versions of these maneuvers found their way into the newspapers. One that caused much glee among Hutchins's critics at the University had it that he had gone to the White House without an invitation to seek the appointment and had then leaked the story for purposes of self-aggrandizement. Recitation of these alleged facts by one John Healy so outraged Thornton Wilder that he wrote him a tart letter canceling a dinner engagement: "Let's not do ourselves harm through raising each other's bile."[18]

Ickes noted that the President was embarrassed by his failure to carry out his commitment, and so, obviously, was Hutchins. But with his usual stiff upper lip, and not unmindful of future political possibilities, he avoided any indication of resentment. In June 1935, when *Time* revived the story upon the occasion of Richberg's resignation as NRA chairman, Hutchins wrote to Roosevelt:

The current issue of *Time* on page 33 contains an exaggerated account of our discussions last fall in regard to the N.R.A. I have steadily declined to tell anybody anything about those conversations. I took the same attitude when asked about them by the writer of the *Time* article. Apparently this was unwise. If I had told him the facts I might have prevented the publication of a distorted version.[19]

The President replied with a "Dear Bob" note: "Beginning with the first number of *Time,* I discovered that one secret of their financial success is a deliberate policy of either exaggeration or distortion. Pay no attention to them — I don't!"[20]

During Roosevelt's second term Hutchins was as active a candidate for a Supreme Court appointment as it was possible for him to be. This involved the kind of lobbying he despised, and he was never comfortable with it. When Adler was pressing him to move on from Chicago, he testily reminded him that a college president couldn't put a want ad in the paper: "He has Dignity. If somebody doesn't come around and offer him a job, he can't get one." But he added, "I'm doing my damnedest now on . . . the Supreme Court."[21] This involved actively encouraging the Washington insiders who supported him and seeking out others who might have influence with the President.

Ickes, the maverick Bull Moose reformer and a longtime admirer of Hutchins's, brought up his name every time a vacancy occurred on the Court. In 1937 the President indicated some interest in him as a replacement for Justice Van Devanter, but the appointment went to Hugo Black. Upon the retirement of Justice Sutherland, Ickes tried again, only to discover later that the President had already decided on Stanley Reed. He somewhat huffily summarized the conversation in a diary entry for January 18, 1938:

> I urged Hutchins' availability. The President said he had begun to have his doubts about Hutchins and I wondered why. He said he hadn't heard anything from him for a couple of years. I replied that, considering all the circumstances, this was not surprising. I reminded him that Hutchins had expected to come to Washington to head up the NRA after Hugh Johnson had resigned. As a matter of fact, I was authorized to offer this place to Hutchins, who came to Washington and had the President confirm the offer. Then the President never went through with it. . . . The President knew what I was talking about.[22]

Hutchins had other supporters in the little group of insiders who regularly played poker with the President. One of these was Harry Hopkins, the attenuated former social worker who had joined Roosevelt in Albany and was as close to being his alter ego as anyone in the entourage. Another was Bill Douglas, now situated in Washington as chairman of the SEC.

In the letters that were frequently exchanged between the two old friends in those years, Douglas, tongue in cheek, referred to himself as Hutchins's "agent," and Hutchins, replying in kind, promised him a finder's fee. The badinage continued, but the serious purpose was clear enough. In July 1938 the demise of Justice Brandeis prompted a prophetic telegram from Hutchins: "I LAMENT THE DEATH OF MY LEARNED FRIEND BUT AM RELUCTANTLY WILLING TO TAKE HIS JOB IF YOU DON'T BEAT ME TO IT. "[23] At the end of the month, departing for Bermuda for a vacation with Maude, he wrote,

> Let me know if there is anything I can do to help you earn that commission. Your learned friend Mr. Jerome Frank is reported to have said, "If Hutchins' name is being mentioned it must originate at the University of Chicago; they're trying to get rid of him." How right he is; how right he is![24]

In early August, still in Bermuda, he wrote, "I am expecting a long distance telephone call from you any minute telling me to move to Washington. When I come what good times we'll have! You can write my opinions & I'll write your speeches & the whole country, to say nothing of you & me, will gain by it."[25]

At this point Douglas, with a wife and two children to support, was running into debt on his ten-thousand-dollar salary at SEC and had about made up his mind to accept the deanship at Yale Law School, which had been left vacant by Charles Clark's appointment to the federal circuit court of appeals. Hutchins countered this with an offer of his own, a fifteen-thousand-dollar salary as dean of the Chicago Law School:

> Charlie's move ought to be a good thing for everybody, at least for you: it will give you a choice of deanships. In spite of my plans to move myself away I hope you take this one: the salary plus the finder's fee will be bigger.
>
> Do you want me to come to Washington? I can and will come any time you say. When do you think the thing will be decided? If you want an advance payment on the fee let me know and I'll send it by Western Union.[26]

In September he wrote,

> General Robert E. Wood, the guy who runs Sears Roebuck, wants to go to Washington to talk with the President about my [candidacy] for the Supreme Court. He wants to go in October. Can you tell me (1) whether the good General stands well enough to be helpful, and (2) whether October is too late or too early?[27]

Douglas replied,

> I cannot tell from your letter whether General Wood really wants to get rid of you, whether he would like to have me in your place, or whether he is working for his country. Whatever his motives and design, I think he might carry some weight. In any event, he would do no damage and I really do not think October would be too late.[28]

The Brandeis seat remained open well into the following year, and the lobbying continued in full force. On March 12, 1939, Ickes wrote in his diary,

On Tuesday Bill Douglas called me and asked me if I could have lunch with President and Mrs. Hutchins and himself at the Mayflower. When I got there I found Lowell Mellett also. . . . The luncheon turned out to be a sparring match between Hutchins and Douglas with respect to the vacancy on the Supreme Court. They are old and devoted friends and both are nimble-witted. I took the position that we needed both of them in Washington to take part in the last-stand fight that the liberals are making under President Roosevelt's leadership. I suggested that the first thing to agree to was that both would come here and let the jobs be distributed as best they could. If Douglas should go to the Supreme Court, then Hutchins would go in either as chairman of SEC, which Douglas would vacate, or as Chairman of Federal Communications. The two of them were so busy sparring with each other that I had a good deal of difficulty making any serious observations.[29]

The campaign ended with a John Alden denouement. When Douglas went to the White House to submit his resignation from the SEC, the President told him that he had to call upon him to perform one more arduous and unpleasant service before he left Washington. Then, flashing his famous smile, he announced that he was appointing him to the Brandeis seat on the Supreme Court.

Hutchins displayed no resentment against his friend Douglas as he was cast in the Myles Standish role, but he was hurt by Roosevelt's rejection. When at the end of March the President invited him to visit at Warm Springs, Hutchins wrote to reassure John Nef, who was appalled at the thought of his leaving Chicago, "The Warm Springs journey is a purely social call, produced by the President's insistence that I must come to see him. After declining twice, I thought it ungracious to refuse to go. I said that I would go on the understanding that I would not accept any of the positions he had to offer me." After the visit he wired Nef: "HAVE BEEN OFFERED ALL THE INSIGNIFICANT POSTS IN THE GOVERNMENT AND HAVE DECLINED THEM ALL BECAUSE I LOVE YOU SO."[30]

The posts were hardly insignificant. Roosevelt offered him his choice of the chairmanships of the SEC and the FCC, as Douglas and Ickes had recommended. Hutchins recalled that after he declined the SEC appointment, Roosevelt reminded him of their conversation in the wake of his resignation from the Stock Exchange's board of governors: "Roosevelt said: 'Well, I understand, but I'm sorry because it would have been such a wonderful joke on the Exchange.' I said: 'Well, you can play jokes on the Exchange, but not at my expense.' ''[31]

Ickes noted that the President was quite surprised by the rejection and told him that he thought Hutchins was making a mistake: "He suggested that if Hutchins should take the chairmanship of SEC he might be considered along with other young liberals for Vice President on the Democratic ticket next year."[32]

T. V. Smith, the professorial congressman, provided a footnote. He had been assured by Tom Corcoran, a White House insider, that Hutchins would have one of the first three appointments to the Court. When Douglas's name was sent to the Senate for confirmation, Smith asked Corcoran what had happened: "He replied that he remembered his assurance to me and regretted that he had not been able to fulfill his promise. The truth was, he added, that the 'Boss' was not certain that Hutchins was on 'our' side."[33]

When Smith reported this conversation to him, Hutchins said that Roosevelt had indicated that "something worthy of him might be found if Hutchins would get himself in line with the Administration so there wouldn't be a confirmation fight in the Senate. Roosevelt meant appointment to the Court, said Hutchins, and intended it to be so taken."[34] But he went on to say that he no longer trusted Roosevelt's promises after the way he had been treated in the case of the NRA.

There is no doubt that wounded pride, compounded by the grating of his Puritan conscience as he curried favor in order to advance his personal interests, had much to do with Hutchins's reaction. But there was another reason. By the spring of 1939 Roosevelt was obviously committed to the Allied cause in the European war, even though he continued to profess neutrality. And Hutchins was soon to go public with his own reservations about any course that might plunge the United States into the conflict.

CHAPTER NINETEEN

A Not So Happy Birthday

Robert Hutchins's tenth-anniversary address at the annual trustee-faculty dinner was better received than any he had made before. "It was the first time I was ever called upon to rise and take a bow," he wrote to John Nef. "McKeon called me up the next day and said I was just like [Nicholas Murray] Butler; the end of the first decade marked the disappearance of rancor. I replied that I was just like Butler; the end of the first decade marked the disappearance of ideas. You will note that there is none in the speech. It is a nice little administrative pep talk."[1]

If rancor had not entirely disappeared, the faculty, students, trustees, and alumni had united behind Hutchins when he made a move that no other major university president would have dared undertake — the abolition of intercollegiate football, this at an institution whose "Monsters of the Midway" had once dominated the mighty Big Ten Conference. And he had done it on the eve of a critical fiftieth-anniversary drive to raise twelve million dollars to offset the annual deficit, which was running at $1,200,000.

Hutchins advanced a variety of reasons for his opposition to the sport as it had developed under the stress of intercollegiate competition and growing popularity beyond the campus. He refused to indulge in the hypocrisy of his peers, who looked the other way while their coaches violated the rules of amateur competition the athletic conferences had adopted. Everyone knew that winning football in the Big Ten required subsidies and relaxed academic standards for star athletes. In a 1938 article in the *Saturday Evening Post,* "Gate Receipts and Glory," Hutchins charged that money had become the root of the evils of intercollegiate athletics.[2] "Football," he said in 1939, adapting a quotation from Thorstein Veblen, "has the same relation to education that bullfighting has to agriculture."[3]

But he presented the case to the trustees in practical terms when he brought the issue to a head in 1940, pointing out that a private university with a small, select student body could no longer compete on even terms with gigantic state universities that offered scholarships and cash inducements to muscular young men. The record bore him out. In 1939, the last year it participated in intercollegiate competition, Chicago defeated only Oberlin and Wabash, and it lost to Michigan 85–0, Harvard 61–0, Virginia 47–0, and Ohio State 61–0. Hutchins made his recommendation for abolition against a background of groans from frustrated fans:

> Since we cannot hope to win against our present competition and since we cannot profitably change our competition, only two courses are open to us: to subsidize players or to discontinue intercollegiate football. We cannot subsidize players or encourage our alumni to do so without departing from our principles and losing our self-respect. We must therefore discontinue the game.[4]

The decision created a furor on the nation's sports pages, and a half century later it remains the single Hutchins biographical item most often cited by the popular media. When the Chicago Bears won the national professional football championship in 1985, the *Wall Street Journal* recalled Hutchins's sardonic response to the demand of local sports editors that he adopt prevailing Big Ten practices: "We could buy a team, but the Chicago Bears aren't for sale." Instead, the *Journal* noted, "Bears owner George Halas appropriated the oblong *C* that had been designed as the university's varsity letter, and that remains on the Bears' helmet."[5] Hutchins would have savored the irony when the symbol became a centerpiece in the ocean of hype in which the Super Bowl now floats.

In educational circles the decision drew considerable praise, and there was much talk of "deemphasis," though no other university of consequence followed Chicago's lead in discontinuing the sport entirely. One president who had ample reason to condemn football as one of the "worst excrescences of our educational system" wrote to congratulate Hutchins. He was J. William Fulbright, then head of the University of Arkansas, the only non-Texan member of the sky's-the-limit Southwest Conference.[6]

Announcement of the end of football coincided with the kickoff of the

University's fiftieth-anniversary fund drive, and despite the trepidation of some of the trustees, it turned out to have a positive effect. "When the university dropped out of intercollegiate football last year and abandoned big Stagg Field to schoolboys, students and alumni uttered scarcely a whimper," *Time* reported. "Last week Chicago's old grads delivered a verdict on their university: 15,000 of them, a third of all Chicago's alumni, chipped in for a $506,810 birthday gift to meet university deficits."[7]

The need for money was acute. During Hutchins's first ten years in office, $58,750,000 had been received in paid-in gifts, 80 percent more than had been raised in the previous decade. The endowment now ranked fourth in the nation, behind those of Harvard, Yale, and Columbia. But 40 percent of the endowment income had been wiped out by the inroads of the Depression, and the trustees agreed that Hutchins had done all that could be done to cut costs in his effort to hold down the size of the faculty without impairing its quality.

One of the principal sources of funds had been cut off. After John D. Rockefeller snapped his own purse shut, his heirs continued to make funds available; the total Rockefeller benefactions accounted for half of the $142,000,000 value of Chicago's endowment and plant. But now John D. junior made it clear that while he and his siblings were proud of their investment on the Midway, the rising generation of Rockefellers did not intend to add to it.

Hutchins spent a good deal of time on the road seeking replacements for the bountiful Rockefellers. One of his female admirers in the University community took a summer job in the president's office in hope of getting some personal exposure to her hero. After she had been at work for a week or more without catching a glimpse of him, she meekly inquired when she could expect to see the boss. When her query was relayed to Hutchins, he instructed his secretary by phone: "Tell the young lady that if she lived in New York and had a lot of money she would certainly see President Hutchins."[8]

Substantial gifts could not be had without Hutchins's efforts as prime mover. Bill Benton could beat the bushes for prospects, and the trustees could bring their rich friends to lunch, but only the president could make the final sales pitch and close the deal. At the beginning of the fund drive he established an office downtown, and he deftly satirized the role he played during the months preceding the formal birthday convocation:

This is the Fiftieth Anniversary Year, a year of jubilation, tempered by oratory and money-raising. Until recently I had thought it was a year of progress, too. But I . . . ran across a letter from Mr. Harper to Martin Ryerson, then president of the board of trustees. The letter was dated February 28, 1900, and it said, "I have arranged my affairs so that I can be downtown between 9:30 and 4:30 every day." Forty years of progress have made no impression on the schedule or the aim of the president of this university. His schedule still calls for looping the Loop; his aim is still money.

And in terms of the accomplishment of this aim there certainly has been no progress in forty years. Mr. Harper had the Midas touch; everybody he touched turned to gold. I have the Medusa glance; everybody I look at turns to stone. The number of our fellow citizens who have given their entire fortunes to worthy causes just before I call upon them would amaze you. . . . It is as though the wealthy men of Chicago looked out the window and said, "Here comes Robert Medusa Hutchins. I must give all my money to the Salvation Army before he gets here." I have at least the satisfaction of feeling that I have assisted many worthy objects.[9]

At the fiftieth-anniversary convocation in October it was evident that despite the Medusa glance Hutchins had also successfully assisted the University. He could announce that $9,200,000 of new money was in hand, with the remainder of the twelve-million-dollar goal in sight. And *Time*'s report on the convocation fulfilled all the specifications Benton had set forth in his treatise on public relations. It began,

Under a hazy summer sun that lay warm on the Quadrangles and the green Midway, 500 of the world's great scholars met last week to celebrate the 50th birthday of one of the western world's youngest and most vigorous great universities. The University of Chicago could hardly match the ancient names and traditions of learning represented by its guests from Cambridge, Oxford, Aberdeen, Glasgow, Dublin, Edinburgh. But the delegates had come to honor not age but youth. At Chicago they found the civilized spirit still green and hopeful.[10]

This finding did not apply to Hutchins himself. In the atmosphere of personal triumph and congratulations, he displayed his usual aplomb. But to do so he had to subordinate the dark thoughts that had begun to occupy him even while he was looping the Loop in search of funds. A year before, when he had inaugurated the anniversary year at a commemorative service in Rockefeller Chapel, there was a pronounced Cassandra touch in his address, which he titled "What the University Celebrates":

> With the rest of the world in flames and this country confused, bewildered, and disillusioned, we hold this celebration to raise a standard to which all honest and right-thinking men can repair, to which embattled humanity can rally. It is the standard of freedom, truth and justice. . . .
>
> We must agree to large expenditures and the concentration of national attention on the material means of national defense. It is necessary, and that is all that can be said for it. Those who regard war or preparation for it as a splendid spiritual undertaking with elevating moral byproducts must be extremely ignorant or extremely bored. . . . Almost nowhere in the world, except in this country, can the standard of freedom, truth and justice be raised. Even if we enter the war, we can, in a modest way, keep the flag of civilization flying, for our geographical situation will preserve our universities from the fate of those in Great Britain. The American universities are the last resource of a world plunging to destruction.[11]

It was a measure of Hutchins's extraordinary stamina and iron will that he was able to maintain his usual jaunty public persona throughout this exhausting interlude. He accepted the task of fund raising without complaint as an obligation of his office, but his satirical references to it reflected a deep distaste for the mendicant's role. A seat on the Supreme Court would have provided an honorable excuse for putting all this behind him, but the quest had ended in bitter disappointment even though he had, by his own lights, debased himself in seeking it. And he found little comfort in his home life.

In the early years he and his family had made regular use of one of the guesthouses at Harold Swift's Lakeside compound, and the chairman offered to deed one of the places to him, as he had to Pete Russell, a protégé who had become a bank president and fellow trustee of the University. Hutchins declined, and Mrs. Russell noted, "The Hutchins family was not among Harold's steady guests after the thirties. The reason must have been the rift that was developing between Maude and Bob. One did not ask questions and Harold, never given to gossip, was naturally mum about the president of the University."[12]

In the mid-thirties Hutchins acquired a country retreat of his own on the opposite side of Chicago, a place where Maude could, as she increasingly insisted, have him to herself. It was an elaborately rustic lodge on an island in an artificial lake at Mundelein, a few miles inland from the fashionable suburb of Lake Forest and not far from the Libertyville farm of the charming young lawyer Adlai Stevenson, who had become, and would remain, Hutchins's close friend.

The mile-long lake, surrounded by virgin forest, had been created by Samuel Insull, the utilities magnate, and the spacious timbered lodge had been built for his son. Before Samuel junior could occupy it, however, his father's holding company collapsed and the elder Insull fled the country. Forced to liquidate his own holdings, young Insull offered the place to Hutchins at a bargain price.

It was ideally situated for one who had a pressing need to get away from his usual environment. The island could be reached only by boat, of which the lodge's separate boathouse contained twenty-two of assorted sizes when the new owner took over. There was a resident caretaker and housing for other servants on a nearby island. And there were no neighbors within eyesight or earshot. Without risk to his carefully cultivated reputation as a man constitutionally opposed to physical exercise, Hutchins became a fisherman who rowed his own boat. He even took up gardening.

It was, above all, a place for quiet reflection, and he was a troubled man with much to think about. The isolationist sentiments expressed in his anniversary address had emerged at the very beginning of the European war. In September 1939 he wrote to Nef,

> The war has got me down. I wish I could think either that it will be short or that we could stay out of it. I think it will be long, and that though we should stay out of it, we are not likely to. I remember 1914 with horror and 1917 with something worse. I don't see either that, after the war is over, though Hitler will be gone, the actions of the French and English governments will be any more enlightened than they were after the last war.[13]

In the beginning most Americans, including President Roosevelt, expressed similar reservations about American entry into the conflict. But as the months passed and the fortunes of Great Britain and France declined, sentiment began to shift, and Hutchins was drawn into what was to become a great national debate that would create a remarkable collection of strange political bedfellows.

Even before the war Giuseppe Antonio Borgese, the émigré Chicago classicist whose book *Goliath* traced the rise of Italian fascism, had sought to organize a group to rally Americans to protest the authoritarian threat to Western culture. In May 1940, with funding provided by Bill Benton, he called together twelve prominent intellectuals to consider drafting a proclamation warning of the worldwide danger to political freedom. Hutchins was there, along with President William Allan Neilson of Smith College, Reinhold Niebuhr, Lewis Mumford, and Herbert Agar. A group of distinguished refugees headed by Borgese's father-in-law, Thomas Mann, were present to bear witness to the disastrous effects of the spreading tyranny. In his autobiography Mumford recalled the three-day session at Atlantic City:

> Antonio Borgese, with his swarthy Sicilian skin, his beetling brows, his protrusive underlip, quietly dominated. He has a voice that is unusually strong and sonorous, but sometimes caressing, always speaking with eloquence, in the ironic vein of Settembrini in *The Magic Mountain,* but no windbag. At the extreme opposite pole was Robert Hutchins: tall, urbane, boyish looking; keen but supercilious, rational and outwardly reasonable, but shallow; an unawakened isolationist. . . .
>
> At the beginning our minds met in a series of personal affirmations and discussions, superior in moral texture to those of any other group I had ever worked with. The tragic decisions we were all facing, as gravely as if we were the responsible political leaders, lifted our spirits to the highest plane: a plane well above our private egoisms, vanities, or ambitions. At first it even seemed we should achieve a consensus.
>
> But the next day, when we began to discuss Borgese's plan that the Conference make a joint declaration on behalf of democratic principles, it turned out that our financial sponsor, William Benton, an advertising magnate, would perform the classic role of him who held the money bags. Before our morning discussion could approach a point calling for a resolution, Benton intervened to express his opposition to Borgese's half-outlined proposal. He told us we were all insignificant (read *"unpublicized"*) people: he even suggested — in the presence of Thomas Mann! — that none of us was as capable of composing an effective statement as were the advertising writers he hired. This unexpected assault, in the middle of our deliberations, was as Neilson later characterized it to me, exactly like a Nazi dive bomber breaking up a gathering of civilians going about their business. . . .[14]

After the dissidents pulled out, the interventionists salvaged the proposal and Borgese, Mumford, and Agar were appointed to draft a "broad, general declaration, summoning all the latent forces of world democracy to save humanity from a malign totalitarian victory." Written largely by Borgese, it was titled *The City of Man* and was duly published. "But," Mumford wrote, "truth compels me to confess that the Chicago advertising magnate's estimate proved correct. Our little book sold perhaps eight or ten thousand copies, and at best reinforced the convictions of a minute number of the already awakened minds."[15]

As the 1940 election approached, Franklin Roosevelt was privately committed to guaranteeing the defeat of the Axis powers. In order to carry out that commitment, he decided to go against the no-third-term precedent, but he found it expedient to keep secret his intention of seeking renomination. And he continued to insist that he would never send American boys to fight abroad, though the military draft had been reinstated and the armament industry vastly expanded.

This tended to defuse isolationist resistance to the rearmament program. It was, Roosevelt insisted, simply prudent preparation for national defense against the possible threat of an Axis invasion of the Western Hemisphere. And to offset the no-third-term tradition, he contrived the appearance, at least, of a draft at his party's nominating convention. Playing the role of lame duck, he encouraged all the Democratic hopefuls who were seeking a place on the ticket, while refusing to endorse any one of them.

Hutchins had concluded that he was barred from the political circuit so long as Roosevelt dominated it, and he was amused when his name was entered in the presidential sweepstakes. This was done by a man he had known only by reputation, Sinclair Lewis, the iconoclastic novelist, then at the height of his popularity. Lewis, whose only political connection was on the distaff side, through his wife, the syndicated national-affairs columnist Dorothy Thompson, came to visit Hutchins in Chicago and let it be known that he was going to Washington to send up a trial balloon.

"The man needed must have integrity — what we used to call character," Lewis said in a speech at Constitution Hall. "He should have both ideals and ideas, and the two are usually found in inverse ratio. He should have executive ability and executive experience."[16] Hutchins met those specifications, he proclaimed, and he was serious in recommending his election, even though, as he confessed, he had only met his candidate once.

Bill Douglas sent Hutchins a clipping from the *Washington Herald*, headlined "HUTCHINS BOOMED FOR PRESIDENCY." "So you see that at last you not only have a manager, you have a sponsor," he wrote.[17] Hutchins replied, "You are my man for 1940. I am taking the matter up with Sinclair Lewis. His wife (Dorothy Thompson) prefers blondes. This is all on the understanding that your first official act will be to appoint me to the Supreme Court."[18]

In retrospect, it seems unlikely that someone who had openly expressed reservations about the popular President's foreign and defense policies could have been seriously considered as his successor or, as it turned out, his running mate. But the intervention issue had been blurred, and as long as the President indicated that he would not run and at the same time refused to anoint an heir apparent, the field seemed to be wide open. And Hutchins had an advocate with an inside track, Harry Hopkins.

Robert Sherwood, the White House speech writer, noted that there were

> considerable numbers of liberals, many of them in the Roosevelt Administration itself, who opposed the President's unneutral policy. . . . Harry Hopkins would undoubtedly have been included with his friends Senator Robert La Follette and Robert M. Hutchins in this category of liberal isolationists had it not been for his fervent conviction that Roosevelt could not possibly be wrong on any major issue.[19]

Benton, who had accompanied Lewis when he made his nominating speech, made the rounds in Washington to check the political reaction. Douglas told him, "Your friend Hutchins could have had the vice-presidential nomination of the Democratic Party for the asking if he had accepted the chairmanship of the SEC when Roosevelt offered it to him at the time I resigned the chairmanship to go onto the Supreme Court. By turning it down, he forfeited his chance." That may have been the case, Benton said, but it was not the end of the matter:

> Later, while the 1940 Democratic Convention was getting under way in Chicago, Harry Hopkins called on Hutchins at his home on the University of Chicago campus. The oldest Hutchins child, Franja, was then about fifteen. She opened the door of her home, peered up, saw Hopkins standing there and said to him: "Who are you and what do you want?" Hopkins replied: "I am Harry Hopkins and I have come to offer your father the vice-presidential

nomination of the Democratic party.'' Hopkins and Hutchins
were on the telephone that night with Roosevelt. What was said?
I don't know.[20]

Whatever it was, Hutchins took it seriously. He was at the convention
when Hopkins let it be known that while Roosevelt would send the
delegates no direct word, he expected to be drafted by an overwhelming
vote. A ''spontaneous'' groundswell was duly arranged, and the other
contenders withdrew and began trying to line up support for second place
on the ticket.

At this point Hutchins went to see his old friend Harold Ickes, who
was among those interested in the vice presidency. ''What Hutchins
really had come to see me about was to enlist my support for his own
candidacy,'' Ickes wrote in his diary. ''When he discovered what had
been running in our minds, he offered to do anything he could in my
support. I told him I would be perfectly satisfied if he were nominated
and, in the end, we agreed to team up. He volunteered to have some of
his friends send telegrams to the President in my behalf and, personally,
he sent one to Tom Corcoran.''[21]

Ickes reciprocated with a wire to Roosevelt: ''It might appeal to the
imagination of the people to give them a new and attractive person like
Hutchins. . . . I am inclined to think he would be the strongest man we
could name. May I say also that if Hutchins does not appeal to you, I
would be honored to be considered as your running mate.''[22]

But signals had changed in the White House. Hopkins was now
instructed to pass the word that Roosevelt wanted Secretary of Agriculture
Henry Wallace on the ticket. There was bitter opposition to the choice,
but the President had not yet accepted his own nomination, and he let it
be known that he would not do so if Wallace were rejected. That ended
Hutchins's last real prospect for a career in public office.

CHAPTER TWENTY

"Drifting into Suicide . . ."

With his reelection assured, Franklin Roosevelt abandoned any pretense of neutrality. After the fall of France he pledged "all aid short of war" to Great Britain, and turned over to British crews fifty overage American destroyers to serve as escorts for merchant ships carrying arms across the Atlantic. He then moved to replace "cash and carry" with "lend-lease," which permitted American financing for the British war effort. And the Navy was authorized to shoot on sight if its ships encountered German submarines in the shipping lanes.

The contention that all this was being done solely in America's national interest was subordinated to a humanitarian appeal. The President identified the goal as "a world founded on freedom of speech, freedom of worship, freedom from want, and freedom from fear." The commitment to Britain was said to demonstrate the support of the United States for "the supremacy of human rights everywhere."

The concept was given a bipartisan gloss when Wendell Willkie routed the isolationist Old Guard and won the Republican nomination in a coup largely engineered by Henry Luce, who brought a Calvinist fervor to the campaign. The homespun utilities lawyer whom Harold Ickes dubbed the "barefoot boy from Wall Street" held out a vision of a postwar "One World" finally freed from ideological conflict.

Yet both party platforms pledged that American military forces would not be committed abroad, and both candidates reiterated the position in their stump speeches. "And while I am talking to you mothers and fathers, I give you one more assurance," Roosevelt said in a radio address. "I have said this before, and I shall say it again and again: Your boys are not going to be sent into foreign wars."[1]

Hutchins was appalled by the presidential campaign. Both candidates seemed to him to be joined in an exercise in hypocrisy intended to disguise the fact that the country was actually being prepared for direct military intervention in a foreign war. The freedoms being touted by the President had not yet been achieved in his own country, and he could see no rational prospect that they might be instituted in the shattered nations that would be left in the wake of an Allied victory. The disillusionment Hutchins had suffered in World War I, compounded by its aftermath, was evident in all of his 1940 speeches.

"We set out in the last war to make the world safe for democracy," he reminded his students in a convocation address in which he argued that the call for American preparedness was based on expediency rather than on principle. "We had, I think, no very definite idea of what we meant. . . . Though Hitler is infinitely worse than the Kaiser, though the danger to the kind of government we think we believe in is infinitely greater than in 1917, we have less real, defensible conviction about democracy now than we had then."[2]

The test of democracy, as he defined it, was the ability to combine law, equality, and justice. The United States had not fully achieved it, but there was still hope that we might yet create a state that could meet the test. Thus the government was still worthy of support:

> The state is necessary to achieve justice in the community. And a just society is necessary to achieve the terrestrial ends of human life. With this background we can detect the error in the extreme pacifist position. Since the individual cannot exist without the community and the community cannot exist without the adherence of its members, the individual must respond to the call of the community and be prepared to surrender his goods, his temporal interests, and even his life to defend the community and the principles for which and through which it stands.[3]

His Aristotelian metaphysics condoned the right of the government to mobilize its citizens for national defense. But he did not let the matter rest there:

> The first principle in the practical order is that men should do good and avoid evil. The statement, for example, that men should lay down their lives in a just war is true, if the war is just. The

statement that they should wage war to gain power or wealth or to display their virility is false.[4]

Hutchins doubted that any war waged by Americans outside their own hemisphere could be just. And even a wholly defensive war would meet the test only if it was fought to protect the ideal of democracy — an ideal not fully understood by many of those who paid lip service to it. As always, Hutchins fixed the blame for that deficiency on an educational system that did not accept the first principle that the state was an indispensable means but not an end. Democracy required that the end for a political organization must be the moral and intellectual development of its adherents:

> Only democracy has this basis. Only democracy has this end. If we do not believe in this basis or this end, we do not believe in democracy. These are the principles we must defend if we are to defend democracy.
>
> Are we prepared to defend these principles? Of course not. For forty years and more our intellectual leaders have been telling us they are not true. They have been telling us in fact that nothing is true which cannot be subjected to experimental verification. In the whole realm of social thought there can therefore be nothing but opinion. There is no difference between good and bad; there is only the difference between expediency and inexpediency. We cannot even talk about good and bad states or good and bad men. There are no morals; there are only folkways. . . . The aim of human beings and human societies, if there is one, is material comfort. Freedom is simply doing what you please. The only common principle we are urged to have is that there are no principles at all.[5]

True preparedness, as he saw it, called for the preservation and revitalization of an American democracy that had been eroded by pragmatic materialism but that still represented civilization's last, best hope. This would require the country's educational institutions to focus their energies and resources on the contribution that they alone could make to the moral, intellectual, artistic, and spiritual growth of the citizenry.

> In the great struggle that may lie ahead, truth, justice and freedom will conquer only if we know what they are and pay them the homage they deserve. This kind of preparedness has escaped us so

far. It is your duty to your country to do your part to recapture and revitalize those principles which alone make life worth living or death on the field of battle worth facing.[6]

Hutchins was now squarely in the isolationist camp, but he was never comfortable there. He could admire the principled stand taken by conscientious objectors, but he did not share their religious conviction. To many who opposed the course being charted by the administration, Hutchins's moral concerns were a secondary consideration, if they carried any weight at all. In Congress the opposition was led by such conservative Republicans as Senator Robert A. Taft. The noisiest isolationists were flag-waving chauvinists of the kind Hutchins abhorred, and at the fringe there were overt or covert anti-Semites attracted to the Nazi cause and latterday know-nothing nativists who despised all foreigners.

Opposition to intervention, prompted by such a mixture of motives and embodying so many shades of opinion, was widespread but incoherent. Frustrated by the lack of a presidential candidate who could give isolationist sentiment a political focus, a group of graduate and law students at Yale set out in September 1940 to expand what had begun as a student movement into a respectable national organization. They called it America First, and it soon had active chapters in every major city, with a total of eight hundred thousand members.

The organizers were junior members of the American Establishment. Among the four men on the executive committee were a future President of the United States, Gerald Ford, and a future justice of the Supreme Court, Potter Stewart. When the prime mover, R. Douglas Stuart, Jr., went to the Republican National Convention to try to head off the Willkie boom, he was accompanied by Kingman Brewster, the future president of Yale.

But to gain acceptance as something more than a youth movement, the organization needed supporters who had already achieved prominence and prestige. Stuart, whose father and uncles were principal owners of Quaker Oats, established an office in the company's headquarters building in downtown Chicago and began recruiting family friends. Hutchins's patron General Robert E. Wood agreed to serve as national chairman, and the America First letterhead soon listed a remarkable array of leading citizens.[7]

Hutchins never joined the organization. "I am not an isolationist," he declared on the nationally broadcast "Town Meeting of the Air." "I have not joined the America First Committee. I don't like its name. I should like to join a committee for Humanity First."[8] But both Hutchins and Bill Benton became active supporters of the antiwar effort. Elma Benton, berating her son for this isolationist fellow traveling, accused Hutchins of leading him astray, but it was, if anything, the other way around.

As early as September 1939 Benton was touting to Hutchins the text of a radio speech by Charles Lindbergh, one of the first nonpolitical celebrities to speak out against intervention. At Benton's behest, Chicago's "Roundtable of the Air" became a national forum for discussion of the preparedness issue, with the isolationist position well, if not disproportionately, represented.

Benton became a primary public-relations adviser to the group that was attempting to form a national anti-intervention organization. Here he joined forces with his advertising-agency partner, Chester Bowles, one of the few liberal Democrats who defied the party leadership to become a founding member of America First's national committee. In June 1940 Benton wrote Hutchins from New York,

> Chet agrees with your angle on waiting on the Republican Convention, but is not hopeful, thinks it looks like Willkie. Chet is so steamed up over this problem that he'd like to see you take to the radio this week, go on record, address a speech either to the world at large or to Winston Churchill in particular announcing that millions of Americans are against any form of intervention whatsoever — Mr. Churchill, don't fool yourself and don't fool the English.
>
> Chet and I privately agree that if England can and does hold out for one year, the U.S. will drift into this war. There isn't any leadership on the horizon to keep us out of it.[9]

In this instance Hutchins was a reluctant crusader. In October he was still fending off the importunate Benton:

> . . . I don't overestimate the effect of my speeches. I make them largely for the record and to get something off my chest. This is especially true of the few speeches I volunteer to make. I don't really expect to affect the policy of the country. Therefore unless I have something important to say I don't want to say anything. I doubt if I have anything important to say on the details of the kind of world we want or on the specific political organization or economic order the world ought to have. And all the general principles I have already stated.

I am afraid I am a counter-puncher. I never would have said anything about the war if Mr. Roosevelt hadn't pulled the four freedoms. Probably I won't be able to think of anything useful on the kind of world we want unless he or somebody like him, e.g. Churchill, starts to be specific about the kind of world he wants.[10]

Hutchins held out until January 1941, when he accepted an invitation arranged by Benton to speak on "America and the War" on the NBC network. He agreed to make the speech, he wrote Thornton Wilder,

because I thought Mr. Roosevelt and a lot of my other friends were getting awfully lighthearted and even irresponsible about going into battle. . . . I got mad, too, about Mr. Roosevelt's message to Congress, where he appropriated all the idealism in the world for what the *Chicago Tribune* calls the War Party. The disregard of our own shortcomings and the calm assumption that we had done such a wonderful job in the rest of the world seemed to me to border on the hypocritical and to approach the ancient political maxim: when you are in trouble at home, start a foreign war.[11]

Hutchins's radio address pulled no punches, counter- or otherwise. It was virtually free of his usual ironic asides, and its opening was as sensational as any he was ever to employ:

I speak tonight because I believe that the American people are about to commit suicide. We are not planning to. We are drifting into suicide. Deafened by martial music, fine language, and large appropriations, we are drifting into war.

I address you simply as an American citizen. . . . I wish to disassociate myself from all Nazis, Fascists, Communists, and appeasers. I regard the doctrine of all totalitarian regimes as wrong in theory, evil in execution, and incompatible with the rights of man.

I wish to disassociate myself from those who wish to stay out of war to save our own skins or our own property. I believe the people of this country are and should be prepared to make sacrifices for humanity. National selfishness should not determine national policy.

It is impossible to listen to Mr. Roosevelt's recent speeches, to study the lend-lease bill, and to read the testimony of cabinet officers upon it without coming to the conclusion that the

President now requires us to underwrite a British victory, and, apparently, a Chinese and a Greek victory, too. We are going to try to produce the victory by supplying our friends with the materials of war. But what if this is not enough? We are to turn our ports into British naval bases. But what if this is not enough? Then we must send the Navy, the Air Force, and, if Mr. Churchill wants it, the Army. We must guarantee the victory. . . . The conclusion is inescapable that the President is reconciled to active military intervention if such intervention is needed to defeat the Axis in this war.[12]

Hutchins rejected what he termed the presidential call for a holy war to save suffering humanity. As he had done in his convocation address the year before, he contended that the nation was not morally prepared for such a crusade. The freedoms Roosevelt sought to guarantee abroad did not yet exist for many of his own constituents. Here Hutchins pointedly cited the failure of the New Deal to reach its own professed goals before its reforms were suspended in favor of the preparedness effort. Americans might proudly hail the four freedoms, but they would have no meaning unless it could also be shown that those who applauded believed in human dignity:

Human dignity means that every man is an end in himself. No man can be exploited by another. Think of these things and then think of the sharecroppers, the Okies, the Negroes, the slum-dwellers, downtrodden and oppressed for gain. They have neither freedom from want nor freedom from fear. They hardly know whether they are living in a moral order or in a democracy where justice and human rights are supreme.

We have it on the highest authority that one-third of the nation is ill-fed, ill-clothed and ill-housed. . . . More than half our people are living below the minimum level of subsistence. More than half the army which will defend democracy will be drawn from those who have had this experience of the economic benefits of "the American way of life."[13]

Hutchins could see no prospect of renewing the effort to correct the deficiencies of the American way if the nation went to war. The practical as well as the moral course, then, was to continue to aid the Allies and provide refuge for those who were fleeing tyranny, while maintaining behind our ocean moats a bastion where democratic values might be restored and preserved: "If we go to war, we shall not know what we are fighting for. If we stay out of war until we do, we may have the stamina to win and the knowledge to use the victory for the welfare of mankind."[14]

The speech drew predictably mixed reactions in the press. Hutchins suffered a low blow from the Committee to Defend America by Aiding the Allies, the counterorganization to America First, which charged that a shortwave broadcast by the Nazi propaganda ministry showed that Hitler and Dr. Goebbels had known the content of his speech twenty-four hours before he delivered it. The interventionist *New York Herald Tribune* gave this implication of collaboration a large headline, "NAZIS FORETOLD HUTCHINS' TALK," though the editors must have known that this signified nothing since the text of the speech had been distributed to the wire services two days before it was delivered, at 9:30 P.M. on January 23.

A week later, writing to Benton to thank him for his help, Hutchins reported that he had had about three thousand messages in response, all but 3 percent of them favorable. The reaction of the board of trustees was also favorable, though a handwritten note added, "Laird Bell called since dictating the above. Sore as hell."[15] Some 158 faculty members expressed their dissent by signing a petition in support of the lend-lease bill, but Hutchins said he had received at least as many indications of approval for his stand.

But if the division of sentiment at the University was more or less even, it produced some spectacular anomalies. When Hutchins reiterated the points he had made in his radio address at a student convocation, the *Maroon* followed up with a headline, "ADLER OPPOSES HUTCHINS ON WAR," and noted that McKeon also dissented. John Nef wound up in the middle, unwilling to abandon Hutchins and unable to support his isolationist views. And Ajax Carlson's name turned up on the letterhead of America First.

The bedfellows on the interventionist side were at least as strange as those among the isolationists. Identification with the mother country by WASPs brought together descendants of Yankee abolitionists and slave-holding Confederates. International bankers and traders in the Eastern Seaboard cities were allied with anti–Wall Street populists in the hinterland. The promise of large profits for producers of war goods and increased employment for workers provided common cause for the NAM and the AFL and CIO. Out on the fringe Communists and fellow travelers made a U-turn from isolation to intervention when Hitler abrogated the Soviet-Nazi nonaggression pact and invaded Russia.

Intellectuals in general, influenced by their traditional admiration for the high culture of England and France, tended to support Roosevelt. This posed a problem for young Douglas Stuart, who was having difficulty persuading notables from the fields of education and the arts to join the solid citizens on America First's national committee. He approached Hutchins with a project that could be endorsed by those who, like him, sympathized with the effort but declined to allow the use of their names on the letterhead.

"I'm still awfully upset by the Gallup Poll," Stuart wrote Hutchins in May. "I am enclosing a clipping from Henry Luce's jazzy sheet *Life*. I fear that darned question which resulted in 68 percent favoring a war if it were necessary to defeat Germany is going to cause a lot of trouble. As Luce points out, it makes Lindbergh's position somewhat ridiculous."[16]

Hutchins agreed to chair a committee to supervise a public-opinion poll in which more carefully phrased questions would, he was convinced, show a much more widespread antiwar sentiment. Benton lined up Samuel E. Gill of New York, a professional pollster, and the America First Committee put up the funds for a national survey of five thousand respondents.

Upon Hutchins's assurance that they would be free to make an independent judgment of the polling technique and results, two prominent ministers and four college presidents signed on: the Reverend Harry Emerson Fosdick, Raymond Kent of the University of Louisville, Henry Noble McCracken of Vassar, the Reverend Albert W. Palmer of Chicago Theological Seminary, Alan Valentine of the University of Rochester, and Ray Lyman Wilbur of Stanford.

While the poll was in progress Herbert Hoover made a nationwide broadcast from Chicago that impressed Hutchins with its reasoned argument against what the former President called "this notion of an ideological war to impose the four freedoms on other nations by military force and against their will."[17] He told Hoover about the poll and asked him to assist in lining up prominent Americans to offer supporting comment when the results were made public. President Felix Morley of Haverford was designated by Hoover to collaborate with Hutchins in drafting a statement to be signed by him and the others chosen.

The Gill Poll was released July 14. Only 20.3 percent of those surveyed answered yes to the question "Do you believe that the United States should enter the war as an active belligerent at this time?" The percentage rose only to 34.4 percent when a possible British defeat was postulated. "American public opinion is overwhelmingly against participation in the European war," Hutchins declared in the press release that set forth the detailed findings of the poll.[18]

The announcement acknowledged that America First had paid for the survey, but it emphasized the independence of the sponsoring committee of ministers and educators. Hoover's collaboration was evident in the lineup of Republican heavyweights who would be standing by to discuss the poll results with the press. Senator Robert A. Taft had been chosen to address the subject in a nationwide radio address. Available in their home communities would be Hoover and Alf Landon, the 1939 presidential nominee; senators Gerald P. Nye, Bennett Champ Clark, Burton K. Wheeler, A. H. Vandenberg, and D. Worth Clark; former governor Phil F. La Follette; and President John L. Lewis of the United Mine Workers. Only two members of America First were on the list: Charles Lindbergh and General Wood.

Hutchins was not to take an active role in the antiwar effort again, though Stuart and Benton continued to importune him. He had other things on his mind. His wife's antipathy for President Roosevelt had brought the two of them closer together. In November he wrote to Wilder from a friend's working cattle ranch at Rimrock, Arizona, where he and Maude were alone except for the cowboys: "Maude says I can now tell you the big news. SHE IS GOING TO HAVE A BABY IN FEBRUARY."[19]

Benton passed along, without endorsing the idea, the information that an impeachment drive against the President was being discussed by some in America First. Hutchins replied,

> Maude, who has all good ideas long before anybody else, has been demanding the impeachment of Roosevelt for over a year. I have no doubt that the President has supplied ample grounds for impeachment. But I am prejudiced. The question [of] whether as Commander-in-Chief he has invaded the Congressional prerogative of declaring war is one I answer in the affirmative; but his propaganda has been so artful and so successful that many people can honestly take another view. This means that a demand for impeachment would promote hysteria, and that's about all.[20]

In early December Benton wrote Hutchins to urge that he consider an invitation to speak at Yale if network radio time could be arranged, and to tell him that he had a firm commitment for an appearance on "Town Meeting of the Air" in January. Hutchins replied that he wasn't sure he had another speech in him. Before he could decide, the question became moot.

On December 7 the Japanese bombed Pearl Harbor. That evening America First issued a statement pledging its full support for the war effort against Japan. The next day Douglas Stuart sent a letter to his chapter chairmen, telling them the committee would adjourn, "holding itself in readiness to renew activity when the need arises. . . ."[21] The need, or at least the opportunity, never arose.

In January Stuart wrote Hutchins to tell him that he had volunteered for military service and would soon report for duty at the Artillery Officers Training School at Fort Sill, Oklahoma. The crusade the young Yale men had launched eighteen months before was over:

> Without you we could not have made such a strong fight. You made us almost respectable. You gave us our moral cause. In the face of bitter criticism, your willingness to support your deep convictions of what was best for America was an inspiration.
>
> The days ahead look dark but nothing can dim the record of your patriotism. We have a war to win and a nation to rebuild. As the magnitude of this task is gradually understood, this country will count on you increasingly for leadership and guidance.[22]

CHAPTER TWENTY-ONE

"An Instrumentality
of Total War . . ."

After the United States Congress formally declared war on the Axis powers, Robert Hutchins set aside his moral reservations and, in his role as the responsible executive officer of the University, went before the faculty to make his own declaration:

> . . . long-run activities must be sacrificed to the short-run activity of winning the war. Education and research, as we have understood them at the University of Chicago, are long-run activities. We have stood for liberal education and pure research. What the country must have now is vocational training and applied research. What the country must have we must try to supply.[1]

Chicago's most significant contribution would be made in the very area Hutchins was often accused of neglecting: "We are experts in scientific research. We have today the strongest collection of natural scientists at any university in the world." He could not resist pointing out that these uniquely talented scholars were in a position to turn their attention to war work because "the organization of the College and the Divisions has helped us to avoid much of that weird incoherence characteristic of the American curriculum. Research with us is a serious undertaking and not an occupational disease." And he offered a prophecy that would be borne out in spectacular fashion on the Midway: "This war will be won in the laboratories."[2]

This meant that for the duration he would have to bend his basic educational principles, but he did not abandon them entirely. As he had done in the case of the curtailed budgets of the Depression years, he sought to use the new stringency to clear away course offerings that reflected what he regarded as a misapplication of the scientific method:

> If we want to serve our country, we should submit every course, every day of every course, every research project, every appointment and every expenditure to two tests. Every part of our work should meet one or the other of these tests or be instantly abandoned. The two tests are, first, does it help to win the war? And the second, has it an intellectual purpose, has it intellectual content, and does it require intellectual effort?
>
> Vocational training courses that will help win the war are courses that we must invent or foster. Vocational training courses that will not have no place in the University for they are a waste of its resources. The manufacture of gadgets that will help win the war is a necessary and laudable part of the University's work. The manufacture of gadgets that have no military purpose is not a University activity. Neither is that kind of research which is merely aimless wandering through the fields of fact, nor that kind of teaching which is merely transmitting information which the student could get out of a book over the weekend. This is waste.[3]

Efficiency had become a life-and-death matter now that the University was being converted into "an instrumentality of total war." This, he thought, gave special weight to his usual plea: "I go before the trustees every year and swear that every expenditure I am recommending is essential. I am sure I commit less perjury than most university presidents. I solicit the further cooperation of the faculty on behalf of my immortal soul."[4]

Hutchins did not blink at the fact that the course he now proposed negated the stand he had taken for the last three years, when he had said repeatedly that

> the intellectual activities of the University were the symbol of everything we had to defend and that the best service we could render in defense of our country was to see to it that these activities were maintained in full force and vigor. You may well ask

> > "Whither is fled the visionary gleam?
> > Where is it now, the glory and the dream?"

My answer is that our basic function remains the same. Another has been superimposed upon it which will make it hard, perhaps very hard, perhaps impossible to carry on our basic function. . . .[5]

He closed with a quotation he had used before and would have many occasions to use again: "The task is stupendous. But I offer you the words of William the Silent: 'It is not necessary to hope in order to undertake, or to succeed in order to persevere.' "[6]

Efficiency was also the touchstone when Hutchins addressed the students less than two weeks after Pearl Harbor. He reiterated his previous endorsement of universal registration and compulsory military service, but he also called for a prohibition against volunteering. Speaking as a "retired private," he warned against repetition of his and his classmates' experience in the First World War:

It would have been far better for the country if we had stayed in college and taken part-time military training until in the process of an orderly program the government had put us in the places in which we could be most useful. As it was, we were on the payroll nine months too long; and it took painful and costly experience on the Italian front to show which of us were qualified for the duties which first-line service in time of war required.[7]

But he also insisted that the universities should not provide a refuge for those who sought to avoid combat service, or to improve their odds of surviving it by obtaining an officer's commission. The Student Army Training Corps of the First World War, he said, had provided "enough training to destroy the curriculum, but not enough to produce good soldiers."[8] So when the draft was enacted in 1940, the University had established an extracurricular Institute of Military Studies to prepare students for active duty while they continued their studies.

The Institute covered the same ground as the Reserve Officers Training Corps course offered in the land-grant colleges and some private institutions. But "by concentrating on essentials and reducing such trivialities as close-order drill to a minimum it is able to cover the basic course in half-time or less," he pointed out. However, the Institute did not lead to a commission, as ROTC did, and Hutchins thought, as a matter of principle, that it should not:

One of the best ways to build up the morale of a conscript army is to insist that promotions should be made from the ranks and that officers' training camps should be open not to college students without military experience, but to private soldiers and noncommissioned officers selected because of their military ability rather than because of the educational opportunities their parents have been able to give them.[9]

The Institute represented the kind of innovative approach Hutchins encouraged in any field. If the University had to accept the onerous necessity of devoting its educational resources to war work, he could at least see to it that they were used to develop better ways of accomplishing it. In addition to its student program, the Institute began experimenting with training for civilian defense, and by May 1941 it had enrolled sixty men and women from leading industrial enterprises in the area. Hutchins wrote to his old friend Secretary Ickes to suggest that the government fund it:

> It happens that through the Social Science Division and Public Administration Clearing House we have a group of men here interested in [civilian defense] and probably more competent than any that could be assembled anywhere in the country. . . . They have raised with me the question [of] whether the Institute of Military Studies at the University of Chicago might not, with governmental assistance, become the center for the training of leaders in the field of civilian defense. Our people would undertake to teach others how to teach people in their communities to do the job. We are thinking, in short, of a teacher training center.[10]

He also wrote to Secretary of the Navy Frank Knox to suggest that his faculty might be of use to the government in its work on codes and ciphers:

> "Cipher brains" are born, not made, but ancient language scholars in any linguistic field usually have the mental qualifications and a type of specific training essential to cryptographic work. In addition to these specialists in codes and ciphers, the University has on its staff specialists in French, German, Italian, Spanish, Russian, Portuguese, Polish, Chinese, Arabic, Syriac, Persian, Greek, Turkish, Dutch, Swedish, Norwegian, Danish, Modern Hebrew, Aramaic, and other languages. If the University can render service in these or other areas, we are yours to command.[11]

Hutchins was attempting to discharge his duty as a loyal citizen while living up to his responsibility to the University. Still young enough to be classified 3A by his selective-service board, he was acutely aware that the occupation of many of the younger members of his faculty might soon be declared nonessential. This would not be true of the natural scientists, but it would certainly affect those in the social sciences, the arts, and the humanities. But if he could convert a professor of Aramaic into a teacher of cryptography, or a sociologist into a trainer of civilian-defense workers, he might be able to keep them around for a while.

In the summer of 1942 Thornton Wilder passed through Chicago. He was now in uniform, having been commissioned as an intelligence officer in the Army Air Corps, and his old friend Hutchins wrote to congratulate him on "the beautiful picture printed in the *Chicago Daily News*. The cap was very becoming, and at just the right angle." In the handwritten letter he went on to unburden himself of some of the dark thoughts he had concealed from almost everyone else:

> Of course you disturb me very much. The only reasons I don't go and do likewise are bad reasons, viz., domestic and financial. I certainly can't flatter myself that I am doing anything important here. We are now almost entirely a military establishment: 2,500 sailors, 85 research contracts on military secrets, 2,700 students — not counted in our enrollment — being trained for war industries, 1,000 in the Institute of Military Studies. But any vice president could take care of these things. My departure wouldn't affect them at all. And when you realize that all the good young and middle-aged faculty members are leaving, outside of natural science, you can see that there is not much hope of being able to believe that we are keeping the spark of intellectual life burning. We shall have nothing but old men and cripples after a year or two. But I suppose I shall stay on just from inertia unless I am offered something that jolts me into a decision. I am too full of inertia to seek anything. And my relations with the Administration are not such as to make it likely that I shall be offered anything. So I wiggle on my aimless way.[12]

Among the secret military projects he did not feel free to mention even to Wilder was one code-named the Metallurgy Project. Under that euphemism a group of the world's most distinguished scientists, many of them refugees from the Axis powers, had been assembled on the

Midway. This was the team that would split the atom and usher in the age
of nuclear warfare.

The Chicago physicist Arthur Compton was the director of the
Metallurgy Project, but the presiding genius was Enrico Fermi, an Italian
whose pioneering work on the release of radioactive elements by neutron
bombardment had earned him the 1938 Nobel Prize. When he went to
Oslo to collect it he had already decided not to return to Italy and commit
his talents to Mussolini's fascist regime. Finding a haven at Columbia
University, he compared notes with other refugee scientists and learned
that German physicists were attempting to adapt his discoveries to the
production of new weaponry. Seeking someone who could understand
how devastating this could be, he went down to Princeton to consult his
most eminent colleague, Albert Einstein. Fermi, Leo Szilard, and Eugene
Wigner drafted the fateful letter Einstein dispatched to President
Roosevelt to warn him of the potential danger.

Roosevelt appointed an advisory committee, headed by the president
of Harvard, James B. Conant, to consider the possibilities of relevant
experimental projects that were already under way at a number of
universities. In 1941 it was proposed that the work be concentrated at
Chicago, and Hutchins readily agreed. Fermi and his colleagues were
soon at work creating the world's first atomic pile in a converted squash
court under the stands at Stagg Stadium. John Gunther described the
genesis of the project:

> Several industrial organizations and other universities had been
> approached by the government to construct the necessary but
> awesomely hazardous pile. They had refused to accept re-
> sponsibility. Hutchins had long been sympathetic to the isolation-
> ist position. He did not like the war. But he did not want to lose
> it. To decide to accept a mission which would presumably make
> practicable the production of the atomic bomb was surely one of
> the most onerous any man ever had to make, and Hutchins made
> it purely on his own.[13]

On December 2, 1942, the pile produced the first controlled atomic
chain reaction. Fermi, Compton, Szilard, and Harold Urey were standing
by when George Weil pulled a cadmium rod out of the pile and confirmed
the success of the unprecedented experiment. No one had thought to
provide a prearranged code, so Compton was forced to improvise when
he telephoned Conant at Harvard with the literally earthshaking news.
"The Italian navigator has landed in the New World," he reported.

"How were the natives?" Conant asked, and Compton replied, "Very friendly."[14]

What had begun as a fifty-thousand-dollar contract involving a handful of researchers mushroomed into the two-billion-dollar Manhattan Project, which created whole new communities in the hinterlands of Tennessee, Arizona, and Washington State in order to bring the new weaponry into being. Not only was the Chicago campus a military installation; with most of its research facilities engaged in secret military work, much of it was also under armed guard. By the end of 1942 Chicago had lost nine hundred of its regular students to the draft, but it had received more than five thousand who were sent by the government for specialized training. There were 127 government contracts, Hutchins reported to the faculty, with more coming in every month. By the time the war was over, Chicago had handled a greater volume of military projects than any other single institution.

One of Hutchins's maxims, usually offered with a wry grin, held that when one was handed a lemon, one should try to make lemonade. This, in effect, is what he himself did with the burdens the war effort imposed upon the University. The requirements of military security caused him no great problem, for it had always been his administrative practice to compartmentalize the areas for which he had ultimate responsibility, delegating duties to his subordinates in a fashion that kept them fully apprised of what they needed to know but prevented them from becoming involved with matters that were not their immediate concern. His own primary interest was in devising means by which the extraordinary demands being made upon the University's administrative structure might be used to advance his educational goals.

In his address to the faculty setting forth the new direction the University must take, Hutchins renewed his argument for awarding the bachelor's degree at the end of the sophomore year, pointing out that this would permit most students to reach a definite educational objective before being summoned to military service. The faculty senate, after a decade of quibbling, finally capitulated. In 1942 it was decreed that the divisions would no longer award the degree; instead it would be granted "in recognition of the completion of general education, as defined by the College faculty." The only exception was the bachelor of science degree, which would continue within the province of the Physical and Biological Sciences divisions, but only for "the continuation of the national emergency."[15]

The immediate effect was to give the College genuine autonomy and to facilitate the creation of a core faculty primarily concerned with teaching the liberal arts. Clarence Henry Faust, a professor of English who shared Hutchins's views on undergraduate education, had been appointed dean of the College in 1941. Under his leadership the curriculum was finally adapted to an examination system that determined placement and measured progress without regard to the usual course requirements. The entrance standards were set forth in a single paragraph:

> Admission to the College is based upon evidence that the student is intellectually and socially prepared to benefit from the work of the College. Such evidence may be found in the quality of his academic achievement as reported by his high school, the judgments concerning the student to be found in recommendations of his high school principal, teachers or other persons who know him, and scores made on standard scholastic aptitude tests. . . . Each student will be given placement tests to help fit him into the College courses, whatever the amount or kind of high school work he has had.[16]

The war provided a compelling argument for a system that would make it possible for students to qualify for a bachelor's degree before they reached the draft age of eighteen. And the flexibility of the system allowed the College to adapt to the diverse educational backgrounds of the students who were sent to Chicago by the armed services. During the 1943–1944 academic year, 25,583 students — civilian and military — attended courses at the University. Recruits sent by the Air Corps for "premeteorology" training, as well as those in the Army Specialized Training Program, were assigned to the College.

In his study of the development of general education, Reuben Frodin found this to be a critical factor at Chicago, which set the pace for other institutions:

> The experience of a substantial number of the College faculty with the war programs, when coupled with knowledge of the way achievement examinations had worked in the regular curriculum, speeded the consideration of entrance requirements and placement tests for regular students in the College. The desire on the part of the faculty to get the men in uniform adjusted to academic work, regardless of details of their background, and the satisfactory results obtained with various groups, demonstrated better than hours of faculty discussion could have done what was needed in placing students in any collegiate curriculum. The fact that the Office of the University Examiner was constructing tests for all

branches of the armed services, as well as for the Armed Forces Institute, likewise tended to make the entire faculty examination-conscious. . . . By the end of the academic year 1945–46 the College had, in reality, become a four-year program, in which students were placed on the basis of their performance on examinations, irrespective of whether they had spent two, three, four or five years in high school or even a year or two in another college or in an army training course. . . . One of the several noteworthy results which the scheme of placement brought forth was the means to handle the veterans who came to the University in great numbers in 1946 and 1947.[17]

Another Hutchins-supported enterprise came to fruition during the war years, this one the new, interdisciplinary approach to graduate education called for by John Nef. An economic historian, Nef had become convinced that his own discipline was failing in its mission to relate the past to the present. Like Hutchins, he believed that this was due in large part to the specialization that had accompanied the phenomenal growth of the natural sciences and of the technology produced by their application. "A much more comprehensive approach to the civilizing experience of our human past seems to be essential," Nef contended. "The roles played by the search for beauty, for virtue and for the subjective truths derived from imaginative good taste need to be given the actual place which history has hitherto denied them."[18]

The possibilities of such an interdisciplinary approach were explored at regular meetings of Hutchins, Nef, the economic philosopher Frank Knight, and Robert Redfield, an anthropologist who later became dean of social sciences. These developed into a Committee on Civilization, which initially limited itself to discussion of the interdisciplinary relationship of economics, politics, jurisprudence, and ethics. In 1942 Hutchins suggested that the Committee be formally recognized by the Social Science Division so that it could begin to develop a curriculum leading to master's and doctoral degrees.

Nef, who became the chairman of what was to be the first fully integrated, independent interdisciplinary faculty in any American university, has recounted its genesis. Redfield, he recalled, responded in some distress to Hutchins's suggestion that the necessary degree-granting authority should be sought from his division:

> "John, I can never get us set up with that name — the Committee on Civilization. It frightens the executive committee of the Division."

"What would you suggest?"

"How about the Committee on Social Thought?" he said.

"What does it mean?"

"I haven't the faintest notion," he answered, "but I think the chairmen of departments in social science might not object because no group is studying social thought."

In short, we announced another specialty, when my purpose was to transcend specialties.[19]

In its early years the Committee had no faculty of its own. Nef devoted virtually all his time to developing a curriculum outside the divisional and departmental structure and to tutoring candidates for graduate degrees. "My three distinguished colleagues helped in these matters, particularly by personal interviews with students," Nef recalled. "Bob Hutchins once gave two hours to a young woman who wept real tears because she could find no one who could explain to her what Plato meant! We had plenty of students, mostly young women, for it was wartime. Some were no less neurotic than this one."[20]

Things improved when five distinguished faculty members were added to the Committee, among them Wilbur Katz, the dean of the Law School, and Ralph Tyler, the chairman of the Department of Education. Both were willing to find a nominal place on their faculties for young scholars recommended by Nef, with the private understanding that they would in fact devote themselves full-time to the Committee. And the Committee's graduate students were given access to a parade of visiting lecturers for whom Nef provided bountiful hospitality, with his wealthy wife picking up the tab. Among these were such luminaries as T. S. Eliot, Jacques Maritain, Julian Huxley, Paul Tillich, Isaiah Berlin, Marc Chagall, Frank Lloyd Wright, Arnold Schoenberg, and John von Neumann.

At the end of the war, with the active support of Hutchins and Tyler, who had succeeded Redfield as dean of social sciences, the Committee was empowered to recommend professorial appointments, and it became in effect a department of the University. The Committee did not hesitate to grant full professorial status to men and women who did not possess conventional academic credentials. Among the appointees who earned top honors in their disciplines after being turned down by other faculties were the social scientist Edward Shils, the philosopher Yves Simon, the economist Friedrich von Hayek, and Daniel Boorstin, a law professor who decided in midcareer to become a historian. Later additions included the philosopher Hannah Arendt, the art critic Harold Rosenberg, and the novelist Saul Bellow, who became chairman when Nef retired and who continued his active association even after his books began to please both the critics and the public and earned him a Nobel prize.

In due course the Committee began to attract students from all parts of the United States and, after the end of the war, from abroad. Only thirty at a time were accepted, on the basis of a rigorous personal examination. Nef described the highly flexible curriculum:

> We devised new methods of training students, by selected readings, tutorial and seminar meetings — in basic principles of philosophy (including political philosophy), of history (as written by great historians), and of various arts (as demonstrated by masterpieces). The Fundamentals this was called, and all students must pass an examination on them.[21]

Hutchins joined Nef in looking around for talented nonconformists who could be expected to thrive on such a faculty. One of these, David Grene, an Irish classicist, was about to return home in disgust after a year of teaching at Harvard when his discontent was called to Hutchins's attention by a mutual friend. First given a joint appointment to teach in the College and in the Division of Humanities, Grene found himself at odds with both deans, Faust and McKeon, and, being congenitally contentious, was soon fired by both. Hutchins, who had stipulated that Grene could not be removed without his clearance, arranged for his appointment to the Committee, where he became a colorful fixture.

The Committee, as an unconventional, sometimes eccentric experiment in graduate education, conformed to Hutchins's idea of what a university should be about. The notion that students might follow their intellectual curiosity wherever it took them, provided they could master what Nef called the Fundamentals, was akin to the Great Books curriculum Hutchins advocated for undergraduate education. So the Committee enjoyed not only his blessing and his support but also his active participation.

Nef tended to give high priority to aesthetics, and Hutchins welcomed the opportunity to improve his own appreciation of the arts. Grene concluded that Hutchins continued to measure literature in terms of the philosophy of ideas, with no real sense of any other values. But the aesthetes had no complaint about the manner in which Hutchins exercised his ability to intervene more directly in faculty appointments than he could elsewhere in the University. The survivors of the Hutchins years have agreed that the only standard he insisted upon was excellence — and, other things being equal, boldness.[22]

*   *   *

The success of the Committee on Social Thought and the independent status he finally secured for the College provided some satisfaction for Hutchins in the war years. He was pleased too that under his aegis his protégé Ernest Colwell, the dean of Chicago's nondenominational, graduate-level Divinity School, had succeeded in establishing a Federated Theological Faculty to grant University degrees to undergraduate students at the three independent Protestant seminaries in the vicinity of the campus. As a child of the parsonage, Hutchins could appreciate what a truly remarkable ecumenical feat this was in light of the traditional doctrinal divisions among the denominations. And after ten years of negotiation, he had finally managed to sever the University's forty-year-old connection with Rush Medical College and the downtown Presbyterian Hospital, where its students received their clinical training.

In 1898 William Rainey Harper had arranged the affiliation with Rush in order to provide his fledgling university with a medical faculty made up, as most were in that day, of physicians in private practice who taught part-time. But in the 1920s, reflecting the national reform movement in medical education, Chicago had assembled a distinguished full-time faculty devoted primarily to research, and in 1927, with financial support from the Rockefellers, another Gothic quadrangle housing the Medical School and its own Billings Hospital had appeared on the campus.

From the beginning of his tenure Hutchins had backed the medical faculty in its insistence that the downtown hospital should move to the Midway and consolidate with Billings, but the Rush trustees were adamantly opposed. Finally a deal was worked out whereby the University of Illinois would assume the role formerly played by Chicago. To Hutchins this was simply a belated and all too rare triumph of reason over entrenched academic interests. In his sardonic fashion he noted in his address at the 1944 trustee-faculty dinner, "Since any sane man could see that one medical school was enough for any university, we cannot exalt our own intelligence and courage by pointing out that this university, which once had two, now has one."[23]

But these were small gains in comparison with the inroads that the military effort made on what he considered to be the central function of the University. The restoration of Chicago's great tradition in the postwar years, he concluded, would require even more drastic changes in the organization of the University than any that had been effected so far. So he laid before the faculty two proposals that initiated the final round in the Chicago Fight.

CHAPTER TWENTY-TWO

"A Moral, Intellectual and Spiritual Revolution . . ."

In the midst of the pressures and distractions the war effort imposed upon him, and the uncertainties of a global conflict whose outcome was still very much in doubt, Robert Hutchins called upon his fellow educators to consider what their role should be in the postwar world. In the William Douglass White Lectures at Louisiana State University, published in 1943 under the title *Education for Freedom,* he reiterated the themes he had stressed throughout his career and related them to what he conceived to be a radical historical disjuncture:

> The repercussions of the war upon our political and economic life are bound to be severe and may drastically alter the political and economic structure in which we have been brought up. We are under a duty to inquire into the first causes of the catastrophe, into the methods of averting its most serious consequences, and into the foundations of the new order which the survivors should seek to lay.
>
> It will not be enough to examine these questions in terms of the relocation of boundaries and the redistribution of power. We cannot be content with a rearrangement of things in the material order. At the root of the present troubles of the world we must find a pervasive materialism, a devastating desire for material goods, which sweeps everything before it, up to, and perhaps over, the verge of the abyss.[1]

The issue, as Hutchins defined it, superseded the ideological conflict between capitalism and communism that had shaped so much of recent world history and, though it was in abeyance now that the Soviet Union had joined the Allies against the Axis, was fated to become a consuming obsession in the postwar world. Communism, he asserted, was simply the most technically perfect realization of materialism:

> Communism does not reject the mechanization of life; it completes it. It does not deny that economic activity is the principal basis of civilization; it asserts that it is the sole basis. It does not oppose large concentrations of economic power; on the contrary, in order to facilitate and control the work of concentration, it accumulates all capital and concentrates all economic life in the hands of the state. Russian communism is simply the logical prolongation of capitalist materialism.[2]

Hutchins took ironic note of the outcry that had followed the publication of his book *The Higher Learning* six years before. His insistence that education must be measured not by its material contributions to modern technology but by its intellectual content had drawn a rejoinder from the president of the New York State College for Teachers: "Education is not even primarily intellectual, certainly not chiefly intellectual. It is the process by which the emotions are socialized."[3] A Yale professor had said that the trouble with Hutchins was his intense moral idealism; this, he conceded, did appear to be an unusual attribute for a university president. But the greatest hue and cry had arisen over Hutchins's contention that education must be based on metaphysics. He knew it was a long word, he said, but he had assumed that his learned critics would know what it meant — only to discover that many apparently thought it was a technical term for superstition:

> I might as well make a clean breast of it all. I am interested in education, in morals, in intellect, and in metaphysics. I even go so far as to hold that there is a necessary relation among all these things. I am willing to assert that without one we cannot have the others and that without the others we cannot have the one with which I am primarily concerned, namely education.
>
> I insist moreover that everything that is happening in the world today confirms the immediate and pressing necessity of pulling ourselves together and getting ourselves straight on these matters. The world is probably closer to disintegration now than at any

time since the fall of the Roman empire. If there are any forces of clarification and unification left, however slight and ineffectual they may appear, they had better be mobilized instantly, or all that we have known as Western Civilization may vanish.[4]

The blight of "vocational-informational" philosophy had been enhanced, he said, by the necessary response to the demands of the war effort, resulting in what he acidly termed "educational futilitarianism." A materialist, anti-intellectual emphasis was inevitable since the character of education was determined by the character of society. Yet education, if properly conceived, still had the capacity to provide a great, peaceful means of improving society:

> . . . we must not assume a defeatist attitude. The alternative to a spiritual revolution is a political revolution. I rather prefer the former. The only way to secure a spiritual revolution is through education. We must therefore attempt the reconstruction of the educational system, even if the attempt seems unrealistic or almost silly.
>
> We must first determine what ideals we wish for our country. I would remind you that what is honored in a country will be cultivated there. I suggest that the ideal we should propose for the United States is the common good as determined in the light of reason. If we set this ideal before us what are the consequences to the educational system? It is clear that the cultivation of the intellect becomes the first duty of the system. And the question, then, is, How can the system go about its task? The only way in which the ideal proposed could ever be accepted by our fellow citizens and by the educational system would be by the gradual infiltration of this notion throughout the country. This can be accomplished only by beginning. If one college and one university — and only one — are willing to take a position contrary to the prevailing American ideology and suffer the consequences, then conceivably, over a long period of time, the character of our civilization may change.[5]

One university had been willing to take such a position, or at least its president had, and he had already suffered some of the consequences. The decision of the University of Chicago to grant the bachelor's degree on the basis of examinations rather than a computation of courses taken had been deplored by "almost all the academic potentates in sight," including major accrediting associations. "This marks an all-time high in educational deploring," Hutchins noted.[6]

It also reinforced the opposition of those on the Chicago faculty who had resisted the changes Hutchins had wrought. To him this was simply further evidence that the conventional university administration, even as amended by Harper's efforts and his own, was incapable of dealing with the educational needs of the postwar world. In his address at the trustee-faculty dinner in January 1943, he presented the case for a basic reorganization:

> The colleges and universities have entered a new phase in their history, the phase of education by contract. Institutions are supported to solve problems selected by the government and to train men and women chosen by the government, using a staff assembled in terms of requirements laid down by the government. . . .
>
> I see no reason to suppose that education by contract will end with the war. On the contrary, a government which has once discovered that universities can be used to solve immediate problems is likely to intensify the practice as its problems grow more serious. . . . Since the government is establishing in the public mind the doctrine that technical training is the only education for war, the public mind will eventually conclude that technical training is the only education for peace.[7]

Hutchins conceded that, financially, the contractual relationship had proved beneficial. The University had become "an essential part of the American military machine. No plans can now be made for war research or the special training of military personnel which do not include the University of Chicago."[8] Under the impact of war work its income and expenditures had become larger than those of any other university in the world, and its reserves were growing as the suspension of most of its usual activities reduced the expenditure of endowment income. With the cost of the primary activity covered by government payments, the balance sheet of even a nonprofit institution was bound to show a healthy bottom line.

But that, in Hutchins's view, was an essential part of the problem. The government's disposition to maintain the contractual relationship, and the lure of the financial rewards attendant upon it, would create a formidable pressure against the University's returning to its traditional role as an independent center of scholarly research and teaching.

In the spring of 1943 Hutchins addressed a memorandum to the trustees, citing the manner in which defense contracts were handled as illustrative of the need for some basic administrative changes. He offered two alternatives. The diffusion of authority and responsibility made the existing organization both undemocratic and inefficient, Hutchins contended. It could be made democratic by giving the faculty final authority in educational matters, with its chairman replacing the president as executive officer. This he labeled Plan I. If efficiency was the primary objective, it could be achieved under Plan II, which would vest final authority in the president; the faculty would have a consultative role, but it would be able to hold the president accountable, as would the trustees:

> The present organization of the University has broken down and is leading to a presidential dictatorship. The president, without consulting the faculty, and often without consulting the board, is deciding important educational issues himself because the speed and secrecy required make consultation impossible. I do not believe that this situation will be materially altered at the end of the war. . . . Entirely apart from governmental projects, an active and complicated institution like the University of Chicago, with many external contacts, will always be confronting problems with which speed and secrecy are necessary and as to which consultation with the faculty is impossible. . . . The present president of the University is full of good will; but I think that no individual, however benevolent, should be permitted to decide crucial educational questions without such checks and safeguards as proposed in Plan II.[9]

The board referred the proposals to a Committee on Instruction and Research, chaired by Laird Bell. At Hutchins's suggestion the faculty senate appointed a similar committee, and the two groups met frequently over the next twelve months.

By the end of the year it was clear that the trustee and faculty committees, while they had rejected Plan I, were nowhere near reaching an agreement on an organization that would embody the allocation of authority Hutchins had set forth in Plan II. In his address at the trustee-faculty dinner in January 1944, he brought the issue out into the open. He said he had only one little point to make:

> It is that nothing has been done here in the last fifteen years. That is, the University is not excellent enough. I do not deny that there

have been events on campus. But they have been of a low, negative, obvious order. We have been engaged in pushing over pushovers. And since some of them have been large, as well as old, their collapse has caused a good deal of noise, which we have been inclined to mistake for the rushing sound of progress. . . .

But, you may ask, if this is so, whence comes our great reputation for pioneering on the frontiers of education and research? It is partly, of course, the result of our propaganda, to which I do not object, because its success may compel us to live up to it. But we owe our reputation chiefly to the state of American education. The state of American education is not bad; it is terrible. A turtle, if it is in motion at all, will seem to whiz by a stationary object; and if the stationary object ceases to be stationary and starts slowly sagging downhill, the turtle will appear to be climbing at a terrific rate. . . .

The difference between us and the rest of American education does not lie in our intelligence, courage and originality. It is simply a slight difference in tradition. The tradition elsewhere is to agree that something ought to be done, but that nothing can be. The tradition here is to agree that if the consensus of all literate men and women through the ages is that something ought to be done, perhaps we ought to try to do something about it. . . . An institution, like a man, should be measured by the degree to which it realizes its potentialities. Since this institution has, I think, greater potentialities than any in the world, it has the greatest obligations.[10]

Those obligations could not be met, he said, so long as the University, like all its contemporaries, maintained an organization he described as an involved, bewildering, and indefensible hybrid of business and political procedures, with some academic accidents thrown in for good measure. In the administration there was no correlation between responsibility and authority:

. . . we are encumbered by an academic organization appropriate to Amherst in the '90s and altogether unworkable in a university of the size and complexity of this one. This, more than any other single thing, is responsible for the fact that the movement of the University in the last fifteen years has been that of a well-intentioned turtle. Who is in a position to do anything about it? Who can be held accountable if nothing is done? For the matter of that, who wants anything done? Any educational changes are likely to be viewed with suspicion by the faculty, because such changes are by definition changes in their activities. The trustees like to feel that the University is a great place; but they cannot be expected to be enthusiastic at the prospect of alternatives that will cause controversy and may cause expense. From the alumni, whose hearts are full of nostalgia for the good old days, we are fortunate if we have more than reluctant acquiescence as the good old days recede. I have the impression that the students want the University to struggle upward toward the light; but we all know that if we wait long enough the students will graduate. The untutored layman, looking at a university, would conclude that it was a gigantic conspiracy to preserve the status quo. Our organization is based on this conspiracy. It is one in which there can be no sins of omission.[11]

In order to create a true intellectual community, whose members would be wholly dedicated to scholarly research and teaching, fundamental changes would be required:

We are still entangled in the farce of academic rank. It performs no function except to guarantee a certain constant measure of division and disappointment in the faculty. Tenure means something. New members of the faculty are guaranteed permanent tenure after ten years of service. Salary means something. . . . Rank means nothing except trouble. We should get rid of it.

As academic rank divides the academic community, so does our tendency to regard that professor as most successful who has the greatest number of paying interests outside the University. The members of the faculty should be put on a full-time basis; they should be paid decent salaries; and they should be free to engage in any outside activities they like. To make sure that the ones they like are the ones that are good for them, they should be required to turn over all outside earnings to the University.

We should promote the sense of community within the University by reconsidering the whole salary question. The only basis of compensation in a true community is need. The academic community should carefully select its members. When a man has been admitted to it, he should be paid enough to live as a professor should live. This would mean that a young man with three children would have a larger living allowance than a departmental chairman with none. Under the present system the members of the faculty who get any money get it when they need it least and starve and cripple themselves and their scholarly development because they get nothing to live on when they need it most.[12]

Hutchins had no illusion that the faculty was likely to agree to these proposals even if he could demonstrate the need for them. The question of rank involved the ego of senior professors, and the limitation on outside income and the removal of seniority as a basis for compensation threatened the personal interests of the same influential group. This could be overcome only through the relocation of authority he had proposed in Plan II:

> The remedy is as obvious as the disease. All we have to do is to elect the president for a very short term, require him to ask the faculty's advice at every stage, and compel him to decide and take the consequences. If it is felt that giving him authority to decide during even a very short term will endanger the University, there are many ways of protecting the institution, such as an annual review of the administration by a joint trustee-faculty committee or votes of no-confidence which must produce the president's resignation.[13]

The reaction of the university senate was predictable. The 180 full professors who comprised it were those whose personal interests would be most affected by Hutchins's proposals for the abolition of rank and outside income. Its most active members were those who had been at odds with the president for more than a decade, having charged him with seeking the kind of dictatorial power they saw embodied in Plan II. And the most vocal of these were those who professed to believe that Hutchins would use this enhanced authority to impose upon the faculty a Thomist philosophy rooted in scholasticism.

Matters came to a head on May 22, when the senate, with Hutchins in the chair, by a 94–42 vote adopted a motion requesting the president to forward a "Memorial to the Board of Trustees on the State of the University," which had been signed by seventy faculty members. This verbose document mentioned the issues of rank and compensation only in passing, while expressing the signers' "deep concern" over the ideas Hutchins had set forth in *Education for Freedom* and then reiterated in his address at the trustee-faculty dinner. They rejected as improper, if not subversive, his call for a crusade to procure a "moral, intellectual and spiritual revolution throughout the world," which would involve a reversal of "the whole scale of values by which our society lives."

Although its text denied it, the Memorial was clearly intended as a vote of no confidence in the president. The signatories conceded that the University would face new issues in the postwar world, but insisted that Chicago could not maintain its great tradition

> if it is committed to any particular social, moral, philosophical or spiritual ideology or other specific formulation of unity. The senate is convinced, moreover, that if the University is to be safeguarded against the encroachment of dogma, as well as against a progressive lowering of its standards, there must be continued control by its members, organized according to subject matters in departments, divisions and schools, over the appointment and promotion of those who are to give instruction or conduct research in their respective fields. . . . The senate believes that the educational leadership of the president must be leadership achieved through discussion and persuasion, and that the fundamental constitution of the University, therefore, must be such as to secure to the proper faculties and ultimately to the senate, or other central academic ruling body, a decision on all proposals which substantially affect educational ends, policies, and organizations of studies.[14]

In the showdown Hutchins had his defenders, but there were conspicuous defections. Richard McKeon voted for the Memorial, even though all the deans and administrative officers had endorsed the reorganization plan before it was submitted to the board. When Ralph Tyler asked him how he could take such a stand, McKeon replied that most of the professors in his division were for it, and he couldn't afford to go against them.[15]

Strong supporting statements by John Nef and the political scientist Jerome G. Kerwin were featured in the extensive press coverage, but it was the ideological charges that made the headlines, as in the case of the *New York Times* ("GROUP CHARGES THEIR PRESIDENT MENACES ACADEMIC FREEDOM WITH 'ONE-MAN RULE' ") and the *Chicago Daily News* ("FEAR RECENT PROPOSALS TO 'COMMUNIZE' STAFF ARE POWER GRAB").[16] Bill Benton, who had seen a copy of the Memorial when it was first circulated, had warned Hutchins: "I hope you won't minimize the skill with which this is written. It is a most persuasive document. . . . Your rhetoric, lifted from context, has an ominous sound."[17]

Hutchins made no public comment, but in a letter to his father he said he had been subjected to a campaign of character assassination that culminated in the most political faculty meeting he had ever attended. The board had not made up its mind how to answer the Memorial, and unless it could bring itself "to make a few clear and definite statements about the University and its operation I think it may prove impossible to continue the administration."[18]

Since the Memorial stopped short of demanding that the president be fired, the board, under its policy of noninterference in purely educational matters, took the position that it was not required to take any action. Laird Bell was instructed to continue his committee's consideration of possible administrative reorganization. And Hutchins agreed to withdraw both Plan I and Plan II.

In late July he addressed the central issue at a convocation of students and faculty in Rockefeller Chapel, saying that in view of the misconceptions that had been spread around, it seemed desirable as well as proper for him to explain his position. First of all, it was necessary to understand what the university senate was and what it wasn't. Contrary to the implications of the Memorial, no issue of academic freedom was involved in the controversy:

> Academic freedom means that the professor must be protected in his teaching and research from the president, the board, and the public; and here that protection is complete. Academic freedom does not give the professor, or the whole body of professors, control over the destiny of the University. That, according to the constitution, is the responsibility of the board. The voice of the faculty in the management of the University originates in the desire of the board to leave matters within the special competence of the faculty to their decision as far as possible and to obtain their views when it is feasible to do so. . . .[19]

But the university senate was in no sense a consultative body representing the faculty as a whole. It was made up exclusively of full professors; they were not elected but were accorded membership along with their rank. The great majority of the faculty — instructors, assistant professors, and even tenured associate professors — had no voice in senate proceedings. It met only when it had business, and unless something exciting was scheduled, only 10 percent of the members or fewer bothered to show up. "There is, therefore, no way of consulting the senate and no way of consulting the faculty, except by mail."[20]

Hutchins dismissed the charge that he was attempting to impose a particular philosophy on the University. He had always rejected the idea that a university might be unified through the imposition of an official dogma. What he sought was a means, arrived at through discussion and agreement, to achieve unification of the educational effort without suppressing the vagrant intellect or violating the claims of freedom. Without such a goal, "all attempts to jump the barriers between departments, divisions, and schools remain so many admirable but ineffective substitutes for a common purpose."[21]

The opposition was based on the contention that the University could not and should not seek such unity of purpose. This was an arguable proposition, he said, but it was being advanced in some quarters as dogma; the implication was that this was so obviously true and so universally agreed upon that even to question it was to betray the University and the higher learning.

His own philosophical position, as set forth in *Education for Freedom* and viewed with such alarm in the Memorial, was simply a reiteration of what he had been saying ever since he came to Chicago: "The moral, intellectual and spiritual reformation for which the world waits depends, then, upon true and deeply held convictions about the nature of man, the ends of life, the purposes of the state, and the order of goods." It was being suggested not that these views were false, but that they were irrelevant to the purposes of the University:

> To say "Let us gain knowledge and power and our ends will take care of themselves" is not to fashion the intellect of the modern world but to submit to it, for this is what the modern world is saying. Here the university abandons the task of intellectual leadership and mirrors, symbolizes and justifies the great reversal of ends and means which is the underlying disorder of our society. And it does so at a time when all we have to do is look around us to see that the growth of knowledge and power gives us no hint as to how to use them; for the world has reached at one and the same moment the zenith of its information, technology, and power over nature, and the nadir of its moral and political life.[22]

Hutchins was never to retreat from that position. But he had once again fallen short of obtaining the means to advance it at the University of Chicago.

CHAPTER TWENTY-THREE

"The Good News of Damnation"

Robert Hutchins held open the possibility of resigning during the continuing negotiations between the trustee committee chaired by Laird Bell and the representatives of the university senate. "I have decided to let nature take its course in regard to reorganization and resignation," he wrote to a concerned John Nef. "When the reorganization is finally decided on, I can make up my mind whether resignation will help or hurt. You are correct in saying that I do not want to give up the struggle. But on the other hand I do not want to continue unless I have the confidence of the majority of the faculty. (I do not mean the Senate.)"[1]

By the end of the year it was evident that the faculty committee would not agree to reducing the senate's authority by increasing that of the president, and Bell terminated the discussions. On December 28 he recommended to the board a plan for the reorganization of the central administration that recognized the validity of Hutchins's complaint about the existing diffusion of authority and responsibility while rejecting both of his alternative solutions:

> The strength and distinction of the University have been achieved not alone by the eminence of its scholars. The University has been characterized chiefly by its willingness to pioneer. To leave ultimate decisions of educational policy solely to a faculty body is not in our judgment consonant with pioneering. The faculties have

become too large and specialized to warrant us in expecting aggressive progress from them, however much individual scholars may wish to act. They need leadership and stimulus and unified direction. For that we should look to a president. On the other hand, we believe that to give such control solely to a president, for even a brief period and regardless of safeguards, is to lose a large measure of what the scholars can and should contribute.[2]

The committee's solution was to put an end to the senior faculty's control of the senate by increasing its membership to include associate and assistant professors. The primary function of this unwieldy body would be to elect, on the basis of proportional representation, a forty-member council. Members would serve staggered three-year terms, and a seven-member executive committee would consult with the president on a biweekly basis.

The council would be a deliberative body, "authorized and required to take affirmative action on educational matters instead of the present provision for negative action," and it would have veto power over any action proposed by the president. But the president would also have a veto on any action taken by the council. In the event of an impasse, the issue would go to the board of trustees for resolution.

In adopting the committee report the board reaffirmed its commitment to "the principles and practices of academic freedom, which we regard as the settled policy of the University." The statutes were revised to incorporate the new dispensation, and twenty years later Edward Shils could say of it, "A combination of university self-government and presidential authority has in this manner become so firmly established that cleavage between 'administration' and 'faculty,' so common throughout the American university system, has been largely avoided."[3]

That was not entirely true during the remainder of Hutchins's tenure, but his hand was greatly strengthened in dealing with the faculty, and he accepted the board action with good grace, terming it "as remarkable as it is admirable." His ruthlessly logical approach to any controversy tended to strip away ambiguity and to couch the issue in terms that, if accepted, required a drastic solution. But he no doubt anticipated the board's inevitable tendency toward compromise, and he could interpret the wording of its resolution as a mandate for further action. In his annual address at the trustee-faculty dinner in January 1945, he returned to his old charge: "The attitude of the board opens to us new opportunities and lays upon us heavy obligations."[4]

In his role as chief administrator he presented a catalogue of unfinished business that should be on the new council's agenda. There was, first of all, the matter of liberal education. There were still those who approved of it only so long as it was not allowed to reduce the enrollment in a given department, division, or school. And in the College rising admission and graduation requirements tended to limit its reach to students of high intelligence. The College, he said, had demonstrated that it could educate high-school valedictorians for citizenship; "What about citizens of relatively low intelligence? Can they be educated for citizenship, or must we train them to be self-supporting and let it go at that? If they are to be educated for citizenship, where and by what methods shall it be done? . . . We have no answers to those questions."[5]

As for postgraduate education, the additional year beyond the baccalaureate that was required by most universities for the master's degree justified the observation that a graduate student was one who did not know enough to go home when the party was over. Here Chicago had an opportunity to point the way to constructive change:

> The principal reason why I was interested in the relocation of the bachelor's degree was that I thought it would give the divisions a chance to do something that has never been done in an American university, to work out coherent, nonprofessional courses of study to the master's degree. Liberal education in my view is the education every citizen should have. The place to educate the *leadership* the enlightened citizenry should have is the three years which Chicago now has available to the master's degree. Though we have made some encouraging progress in taking advantage of this opportunity, we have a long way to go before we can say we have made the most of it.[6]

Then there was the imprint of excessive materialism on the professional schools, and the consequent lack of emphasis on ethics. And adult education, which would take on crucial importance when the end of the war released a horde of seekers after some form of higher learning, "has exhibited all the worst features of the education of adolescents without acquiring any of its virtues."[7]

These matters directly involved the educational function of the University and should be of immediate concern to its faculty. But concentration on improvement in those areas was not enough. For Hutchins, the unreconstructed metaphysician, these agenda items were only preamble: "Those who in our time have thought most profoundly about universities, from Newman and Arnold to Whitehead and Ortega, have held that a principal function of the university was the transmission, criticism, development, and systematization of that body of ideas which constitutes or underlies the culture of the race." Yet, he charged, the kind of synthetic, generalized scholarship this required had disappeared with the rise of specialization; it was not only nonexistent in American institutions, it wasn't even respectable:

> The task of the universities is the task of integration. The universities must therefore combat the centrifugal forces always at work within them, which are closely analogous to that power which Henry James referred to in the preface of *What Maisie Knew* as the constant force that makes for muddlement. The universities must make sense of themselves before they can make sense of the world. . . .
>
> The resolutions of the board of trustees give us a new chance for integration. The creation of an academic legislature representing the whole academic community; the establishment of new and regular means of communication among all parts of the community; the new methods of obtaining uniformity of policy and uniform quality in the staff; and above all the spirit which the board has shown — these things provide us with the conditions we need to answer the great questions which must be answered if the American universities are to play the role which history has assigned to them.[8]

In action apart from the administrative reorganization, the board had approved Hutchins's recommendation for an increase in salary for those faculty members who agreed to turn in all their outside income to the University. This would be required of future appointees, and a new "4E" contract would be available to present faculty members who voluntarily accepted the terms, as most of the younger professors did.

The intent was to permit professors to concentrate their entire attention and energy on their scholarly pursuits and to help correct what Hutchins regarded as a basic inequity — the low pay for young scholars when their family needs were greatest, with the highest salaries reserved for senior members, who often needed them least.

When he argued that need was the only proper basis for compensation and coupled that with a recommendation that faculty rank be abolished, Hutchins laid himself open to the charge that he was advocating socialism. But he could point out that the precedent for the 4E contract had been established at Chicago some years before he arrived. After Billings Hospital was established on the Midway campus in 1927, the medical faculty had been put on a full-time basis, with the considerable fees they earned from their practices at the teaching hospital and clinics being retained to finance their research. The same principle was now to be applied throughout the University. Moreover, Hutchins did not think that a faculty job could properly be compared with any other:

> A faculty member, and certainly a faculty member with permanent tenure, dismissible only for moral turpitude or gross incompetence, is not an employee of the University in any ordinary sense. He is a member of a community of scholars with great powers in its management, including the determination of educational policy. . . . A faculty member enjoying such status and such rights, including those of absolute academic freedom, can hardly maintain that he is on an eight-hour day, free outside of working hours to engage as he desires in any pursuit for profit.[9]

The furor that accompanied Hutchins's confrontation with the faculty over these issues impressed even his iconoclastic aide Milton Mayer. "All hell has broken loose on the University of Chicago campus again," Mayer wrote in *The Progressive,* "and the heller, as usual, is Mr. Robert Maynard Hutchins."

> . . . I think I can tell you why Mr. Hutchins suddenly, in the midst of a great war, popped his revolution. . . . I think he is bored running a colossal war plant, for a war plant is what the University of Chicago now is. I think that he thinks that the production of signalmen, meteorologists, explosives and poison gases has very little to do with education, and he is interested in education. . . . So, with everybody saying, "We don't need to worry about Hutchins for a while; the war will keep him busy," he decided to stage a one-man commando raid on the unguarded shrine of Let Well Enough Alone.[10]

It is certainly true that Hutchins spent his life assailing the doctrine of Let Well Enough Alone, and his flip self-deprecatory style may have lent support to the notion that boredom was a contributing factor. Many of his critics discounted the seriousness of his purpose as a means of dismissing the seriousness of his indictment. Others achieved the same end by characterizing him as egocentric, as the *New York Herald Tribune* did in commenting on his latest confrontation with the faculty:

> His ideas would evoke keen interest and wide sympathy if he were content to make a better mousetrap and let it speak for itself. . . .

It is the ruthless rectitude that estranges. It is reminiscent of the delighted mother at a Fifth Avenue parade in 1919, who found everyone out of step except Junior. History records that in ancient Troy a royal princess uttered significant prophecies. Psychology suggests that life with Cassandra must have been difficult.[11]

Hutchins's nephew, an intellectual historian who saw him in action on a good many occasions, thought jesting and irony were central to his style. "He saw his role as provocative, and spoke to stimulate, and not as an abstract analyst," Francis Hutchins, Jr. wrote:

> People point out that many of his statements were "absurd," which is true, but misses the point that they were intended to be just that. . . . My central image of him is not as a "worldly Puritan" — however accurate this certainly is — but rather as an "imperious jester"; not a philosopher-king, but a jester-king. . . .
> It was obviously unnerving to have such a puckish character in a position of authority, particularly if you lacked a sense of humor yourself, and this made a great many people in Chicago uncomfortable. Their fear was that humor might translate itself into meanness and perversity and cynicism, but Uncle Bob always tried to be scrupulously fair in the role of authority figure. Jesters aren't supposed to be kings. . . . But his effort to combine roles as jester-king resulted in a unique historical impact. . . .[12]

Whatever may be said about Hutchins's intent and method, the most striking aspect of his wartime speeches is their prescience when they are viewed in the light of more than four decades of postwar experience. He was often charged with operating in the unreal confines of the Ivory Tower, but the issues he so cogently dealt with were those that still dominate the agenda of every educator in the land, and by extension that of every responsible politician. So it was with the broader public issues to which he increasingly addressed himself.

It is difficult to imagine any other university president, then or now, delivering a public address comparable to the one he made on "The New Realism" at a University convocation while the country was still celebrating the victory over Nazi Germany:

> The words *peace, justice, cooperation, community,* and *charity* have fallen out of our vocabulary. They are, in fact, regarded as signs of weakness and as showing that one who uses them is guilty of the capital crime of modern times, lack of realism.

The rise of the new realism was bound to produce confusion in America; for the new realism is nothing but the old *Realpolitik*. It represents the conquest of the United States by Hitler. . . .

This moral confusion is matched by intellectual disintegration. We seem not to see or not to care about the stupidity of following contradictory policies and taking contradictory attitudes. Intellectual integrity is coming to be regarded as a sign of softness, too.

So we call Japanese soldiers fanatics when they die rather than surrender, whereas American soldiers who do the same thing are heroes. We prove that all Germans are murderers and all Japanese apes, and at the same time insist that we are going to have one world in which all men are brothers. We say we are going to reeducate the Germans, and adopt a policy of nonfraternization. We hate slavery and propose forced labor. We want Europe rebuilt, but will have no heavy industry in Germany. We want order in Europe, but not if we have to sacrifice to prevent starvation. We are against dictatorship, but the dictatorship of the proletariat is an exception. And the new day dawns by the light of the burning homes of Tokyo and Yokohama. . . .

The conquest of the United States by Hitler is revealed by our adoption of the Nazi doctrine that certain races or nations are superior and fit to rule, whereas others are vicious and fit only to be exterminated or enslaved. We are now talking about guilty races. We are saying about the Germans and Japanese what Hitler said about the Jews. And we are saying about ourselves — or at least we are strongly hinting it — what Hitler said about the blond teutonic "Aryans." . . .[13]

He foresaw the Nuremberg trials and condemned them in advance. While agreeing that war criminals should be punished, he doubted that the victor was in position to pass judgment on the vanquished, even under the minimum requirement he stipulated — that the criminal act must be shown to be one that a patriotic American would not have committed had he been a patriotic German:

I should feel better about having Americans judge the anti-Semitism and the concentration camps of Germany if I could forget the anti-Semitism and lynchings in the United States. Our religious and racial intolerance is unorganized, and violence is sporadic and illegal. We have not yet gone in for these things on the grand Nazi scale. But we are sufficiently vulnerable to lay ourselves open to some embarrassment if we set ourselves to pass judgment on the domestic conduct of other nations.

Of one crime the German people were certainly guilty, and that is the crime which the new realism sanctifies, the crime of indifference. . . . As for ourselves, it is not unfair to say that the American people, except for a few million of them, are guilty of the crime of indifference in the face of race prejudice, economic exploitation, political corruption, and the degradation of oppressed minorities. This guilt does not assist our claim to judge and punish the German people for theirs.[14]

As he looked forward to the end of the war, Hutchins had a more immediate concern that he could not talk about in public. When the Metallurgy Laboratory mushroomed into the Manhattan Project, its overall administration was assigned to the Army Corps of Engineers, which built the facilities required to produce the materials from which nuclear weapons could be made. But the University of Chicago retained a key consultant role, and its scientists provided essential guidance for all of these projects. Hutchins knew that in the spring of 1945 the group at Los Alamos, New Mexico, headed by J. Robert Oppenheimer, had completed work on the first atomic bomb.

The nightmarish possibility that Germany might make the first nuclear breakthrough was now eliminated, and some of the Chicago physicists were having second thoughts about the actual employment of the devastating weapon they had helped create. Leo Szilard paid another visit to Albert Einstein, taking with him a memorandum in which he argued that with the end of the war in sight, the global situation had changed, and any temporary military advantage that might be gained by using the bomb against Japan would be offset by its adverse political effect. Einstein once again wrote a forwarding letter to President Roosevelt.

There was no reply before Roosevelt's death on April 12, and no indication that his successor, Harry Truman, had seen the memorandum or that he would have understood its implications if he had. In May a group of concerned physicists urged Hutchins to try to arrange an audience with the new president. He called Bill Benton in Washington, told him simply, "We've got it," and asked him to see if he could obtain an appointment with Truman for Szilard, Harold C. Urey, and Walter Bartky.

Benton was unable to deliver, but Matt Connelly, the White House appointments secretary, arranged for the scientists to see James F. Byrnes, who had just ended his assignment as coordinator of war production and was rusticating in South Carolina before taking up his new duties as Truman's secretary of state. He received them in Spartanburg on May 28 but gave them no encouragement. Congress, the veteran politician pointed out, had issued a blank check without knowing what the funds were to be used for. Now more than two billion dollars had been spent to develop the bomb. How, he asked, could they ever explain such an investment if they never used its product? Byrnes's reaction to the Szilard visit and his attitude toward the scientists who had made the bomb possible were attested in his memoir, *All in One Lifetime:*

> [Szilard's] general demeanor and his desire to participate in policy making made an unfavorable impression on me. . . . A few days later when I mentioned to General Groves the scientists' visit to Spartanburg, he told me that he already knew of it; that one of his intelligence agents had been following the three gentlemen, as they followed others connected with the project. The diligence of Groves impressed me then as it had done before.[15]

On July 16, 1945, a test bomb was exploded at Alamogordo, New Mexico. Air crews were already in training for the historic mission that would take them over Hiroshima and Nagasaki in August. The end of World War II was at hand, and the nuclear age had begun.

The mushroom clouds over Japan posed a question for Hutchins that he had never seriously considered before. He had always accepted nationalism as a necessary corollary of the effective organization of human society. When he argued against the entry of the United States into World War II, it was on the assumption that, as a sovereign state, the country could preserve its democratic institutions and serve as an exemplar for nations that would be shattered by the conflict. After Pearl Harbor he never questioned the necessity of using armed force to guarantee national sovereignty. But on the Sunday after the holocaust at Hiroshima, he said on the NBC broadcast of the Chicago "Roundtable of the Air":

> Up to last Monday I must confess that I did not have much hope for a world state. . . . But the alternatives now seem clear. One is world suicide; another is agreement among sovereign states to abstain from using the bomb. This will not be effective. The only hope, therefore, of abolishing war is through the monopoly of atomic force by a world organization.[16]

When one of the other participants objected that the emergence of any such supranational authority was a thousand years off, Hutchins replied,

Remember that Leon Bloy, the French philosopher, referred to the good news of damnation, doubtless on the theory that none of us would be Christians if we were not afraid of perpetual hellfire. It may be that the atomic bomb is the good news of damnation, that it may frighten us into that Christian character and those righteous actions and those positive political steps necessary to the creation of a world society, not a thousand or five hundred years hence, but now.[17]

Hutchins was launched on a crusade that in one form or another would command his attention and efforts for the rest of his life.

CHAPTER TWENTY-FOUR

Looking Toward the Apocalypse

When the reorganization of the University's central administration was complete Robert Hutchins had a new title that left his authority intact but was intended to signify a reduction in his responsibility for administrative routine. On July 1, 1945, he became chancellor, and the title of president was conferred upon Ernest C. Colwell, who had been dean of the Divinity School.

Two new vice presidents were appointed, Reuben G. Gustavson, a chemist who had been acting president of the University of Colorado, and Neil H. Jacoby, an economist at the Business School who had also served as university secretary. At his own request William Benton gave up his title and was designated assistant to the chancellor. A few months later the severance became complete with Benton's appointment as assistant secretary of state.

Although the new delegation of authority had little effect on the final decision-making process, it was welcomed by some of the dissidents who had been overwhelmed by Hutchins's presence. This was the case with chairman William T. Hutchinson of the history department, who complained that Hutchins had often ignored faculty recommendations: "As a rule, the responses to these communications were slow in coming, or absent altogether. The answers sometimes alleged that the department had given excess emphasis to filling vacant 'fields' and too little stress on the distinction possessed by the scholars recommended."[1]

When Hutchinson called a meeting to deal with these matters, the new president sent a note to the new chancellor: "Mr. Hutchinson doesn't want you to attend the first meeting of the Central Administration with the History Department. You are too good at rapid discussion and debate. He doesn't think the rest of us are so good, so that they will have half a chance."[2]

Hutchins needed any additional time he could salvage, for his own responsibilities were still expanding. Although Benton was no longer on the payroll, his association with the University had not ended, nor would it for the rest of his life. In February 1943 he became co-owner, publisher, and chairman of the board of directors of Encyclopaedia Britannica, Incorporated, with the understanding that a major share of its earnings would be consigned to the University. His first act was to appoint Hutchins chairman of *Britannica*'s board of editors.

Benton's interest in the venerable reference work had been triggered in the fall of 1941, when he learned that the Rockefeller Foundation was consulting scholars at Chicago and elsewhere on the advisability of funding a new edition. This reflected general agreement in the educational community that the encyclopedia should be rewritten from A to Z. Benton suggested to Hutchins that they discuss the matter with General Robert Wood, the head of Sears, Roebuck, which now owned the Britannica publishing company.

Sears had taken over the failing enterprise at the behest of the philanthropic founder of the giant mail-order house, Julius Rosenwald, whose primary motive was to insure the continued availability of the reference work. In 1928 he tried to persuade the University of Chicago Press to produce a new fourteenth edition, offering to underwrite the cost himself. Chicago turned him down, and so did Harvard. The editors resorted to what they called continuous revision, updating some of the content with each new printing. The set was peddled door-to-door by commission salesmen, with Sears providing operating funds and collection facilities for the installment payments considered essential since half the purchasers had incomes of $2,500 or less.

Wood reviewed this history at lunch with Hutchins and Benton. It was clear that to Rosenwald's successor the publishing enterprise he had inherited was an unwanted orphan, and on their way back to the campus Benton suggested to Hutchins that Sears be asked to give it outright to the University. Hutchins was interested but thought it would be best to postpone any such request while the possibility of a Rockefeller grant remained open.

Two days after Pearl Harbor, Benton had another matter to discuss with Wood — the liquidation of America First, which the general had chaired and Benton had served as public-relations consultant. They met at the Chicago Club for lunch, and by the time coffee was served their other business was concluded. Benton seized the opportunity to bring up the subject of *Britannica*:

> "General," said he, "don't you think it's rather unsuitable for a mail order house to own the *Encyclopaedia Britannica* — and isn't it even more unsuitable in wartime?"
>
> "Yes," the general snapped. "We should never have acquired it to begin with." He agreed with Benton's intimation that the ownership of the *Britannica* could even be an encumbrance now that the United States was at war.
>
> "Does it make any money?" Benton hesitantly asked.
>
> "Yes," said Wood. "It will turn the corner this year and should earn about $300,000." Though this meant profit before taxes, the figure surprised Benton. Everything he had previously heard about *Britannica* from Wood and other sources led him to assume that the *Britannica* was still a splash of red ink on Sears's ledgers.
>
> "Well, general," Benton said when he rallied from his surprise, "you know that universities don't have any money to buy businesses. Why don't you make a gift of *Britannica* to the University of Chicago?"[3]

Wood made no response, and the stony silence continued as the two men stumped down the stairs and out the front door, where the general's chauffeur-driven car was waiting. Benton's mortification was relieved when Wood rolled down the back window, grinned, and said, "All right, Bill, I'll give you the *Britannica*."

There were strings attached. The University would have to pay $300,000 for inventory, and its financial advisers estimated that another $750,000 in working capital would be required to replace that provided by Sears. When Hutchins presented the proposition to the board, the response was negative. Julius Rosenwald's son Lessing, now a Chicago trustee, argued against it, warning of the possible reinstatement of the government ban on installment selling that had brought the company down in World War I, prompting his father to pick up the pieces.

Benton remained convinced that the deal offered the University the equivalent of a substantial endowment, and he persuaded Hutchins to keep the matter open even though a canvass of Benton's friends in publishing proved equally negative. Henry Luce, Harry Scherman of the Book-of-the-Month Club, the advertising agency head Albert Lasker,

Dewitt Wallace of *Reader's Digest,* the newspaper and magazine publishers John and Gardner Cowles, and George Delacorte of Dell Publishing all advised against it.

The indefatigable Benton continued to negotiate with Wood, and the general sweetened the pot, finally withdrawing his demand for payment for the inventory and agreeing that Sears would continue to provide financing and collection services at cost. Benton calculated that under these terms the venture could be financed with an investment of $250,000 or less, and Hutchins endorsed his memorandum to the board urging acceptance. It opened with a prescient summary of the arguments that would be heard for years to come:

> We are sure to be criticized for our editorial management. If we stick to the "annual revision plan," which I emphatically favor from what I know about it, we'll be criticized by scholars for not bringing out a new edition. If we bring out a new edition [it] will be criticized, as new editions always are. They never can live up to 10,000 expectations. Then again, we shall have some criticisms of our "commercialization" of the University, particularly in respect to the Encyclopaedia's installment selling methods.[4]

Benton conceded that there were financial risks, but he argued that the possibility of earning a substantial profit far outweighed them. General Wood had told him that while the gift was officially being offered to the University, he was really giving it to Hutchins and Benton. Pointing to Benton, he said, "If you'll interest yourself in the *Britannica* and go to work on it, you can build it into a big business. This is a five-million-dollar gift. Please tell that to your trustees." Benton did, individually and collectively, over the next year. In a memorandum to Hutchins he wrote,

> I concede that the teeth in the mouth of this gift horse are not solid gold. On the other hand, the glint that you see in those teeth is gold. The teeth are at least gold-filled. . . . I urge speedy consideration of the gift, and enthusiastic acceptance of it, with the full knowledge that the University is taking on its shoulders a perpetual headache, a headache, however, with the promise of a golden cure which, God knows, is lacking in most of the headaches to which you and I are thoroughly accustomed.[5]

The trustees were still unwilling to commit University funds, and Benton came forward with an offer to put up $100,000 of his own money in return for a stock interest. Encyclopaedia Britannica, Incorporated, would pay the University royalties, estimated by Benton at $100,000 a year, in return for its editorial advice, consultation, and imprimatur. When the deal was consummated, it provided that Benton would have two thirds of the stock, and the University one third. For seventeen months the University would retain the option of reversing the proportion of ownership and taking control of the company.

Washington did not reimpose restrictions on installment sales, but automobiles, refrigerators, and the other durable goods usually purchased in that fashion were not available during the war years. Benton had guessed correctly that this would provide the means for many families to respond to *Britannica*'s sales pitch that a renowned set of reference books was essential to their children's education. By mid-1944 the company was prospering, and Benton expected to become a minority stockholder as the University exercised its option to take control. Instead, the board voted to continue the royalty arrangement, which by then had returned $300,000. All the voting shares were now in Benton's hands, with the University's one-third interest represented by preferred stock.

In February 1943 Hutchins called the faculty together in Mandell Hall and recounted the prodigious selling job that had culminated in the contract with Encyclopaedia Britannica, Incorporated. The University would share in any profits, he noted, but any losses would be borne exclusively by the new owner: "Vice President Benton has become the victim of his own propaganda."[6]

Hutchins saw the production of a new, improved encyclopedia as a fitting part of the University's educational obligation. Before the *Britannica* was relocated to the United States from England, an edition had been compiled under the supervision of the faculties of Oxford and Cambridge, but it had degenerated into a "hunt and find" collection of facts. Hutchins looked forward to something more than "a piece of printed furniture."[7]

Benton agreed, and with his usual hyperbole spun a vision of a "congress of teachers" presenting in print a "world-girdling university, coherent, well organized, but without walls — a meeting place for the brains of the world, an agent to synthesize the knowledge they possessed, to disseminate that knowledge to everyone."[8] Publication would continue in the existing format, but planning for a new edition would be assigned to the board of editors, chaired by Hutchins. The initial appointees were deans Redfield, McKeon, and Tyler, but the list was soon expanded to include intellectuals from outside the University.[9]

Benton retained the experienced management Sears had assembled at the downtown headquarters of the publishing company. But he warned Walter Yust, the veteran editor, "I'll come up with a lot of editorial ideas. I always do that. I get about five hundred ideas a week and if one or two of them work out I feel I've had a successful week."[10] Almost all those ideas were expansionist.

Although he was perilously short of capital, within a year after he made his deal with the University Benton bought on credit another unwanted corporate orphan — a subsidiary of AT&T that was earning no significant profit, even though it had become the nation's largest producer and distributor of educational motion pictures. This became Encyclopaedia Britannica Films, Incorporated, and Hutchins became chairman of still another board, this one made up of distinguished consultants.

In the midst of this frenetic activity Bill and Helen Benton enrolled in the "Fat Man's" Great Books class conducted by Hutchins and Mortimer Adler. Benton found that he had to search the bookstores in order to purchase the volumes he was supposed to read, or had to seek them out in a library. Another publishing project was born out of his frustration over what he considered an intolerable waste of his time.

When Benton suggested that publication of a set of these volumes was a natural for an educational book company, his sales executives were appalled. They estimated a cost of six dollars per volume against less than a dollar for editions in the Modern Library, which included many of the books in question. They could see no prospect of door-to-door sales comparable to those of *Britannica*. Hutchins was also skeptical; even if a handsomely packaged set could be peddled as "colorful furniture," who would read it? To Benton these objections only demonstrated the need for a gimmick, and he suggested one to his Great Books discussion leaders:

> "We need," said he, "some kind of allure that will induce people to take the great books off the shelves and actually read them to find out what they want to know. Why not some kind of index?" Adler . . . pounced on Benton's suggestion and quickly expanded it. "An index of ideas, of great ideas!" he cried. "We can get up an index that will help the average reader learn about topics in which he is specially interested. It will save the student and the scholar unnecessary drudgery before his thinking starts, and it will show that the thinkers of the past had something to say to the present. A man won't have to read through all the books to find what he wants to read about. He can turn right to it in book after book — whether the subject is democracy, or astronomy, or love, or any of the other great ideas."[11]

The Great Books title was officially capitalized and copyrighted, and Hutchins was named the editor, with Adler as associate editor charged with compiling the index of ideas he called the Syntopicon. An editorial council was recruited that included the original "Great Bookies," John Erskine and Mark Van Doren of Columbia and Stringfellow Barr and Scott Buchanan of Saint John's, plus Clarence Faust and Joseph Schwab of the Chicago faculty and Alexander Meiklejohn, who as president of Amherst had originally inspired Buchanan's devotion to liberal education.

Only $60,000 of the initial $500,000 budget was set aside for the Syntopicon project, but Adler later confessed that he was beset by "my passion for outlining and organizing vast amounts of material as well as my passion for very large projects, a touch of megalomania on my part."[12] He had soon filled a building near the campus with fifty indexers and a clerical force of seventy-five, who would devote a total of 400,000 man-hours of reading to arrive at 163,000 references assembled under 3,000 topics. When it was completed seven years later, the Syntopicon had cost more than a million dollars in addition to the million spent on the rest of the Great Books project, and Adler noted that Benton never entirely forgave him for what came to be called in the trade "Benton's folly."

Hutchins's new responsibilities were logical extensions of his obligations as chancellor. The University had a financial stake in *Britannica,* and the Great Books project could be seen as an adjunct to Chicago's adult-education program; except for its commercial overtones, it was no more foreign to usual university practice than the publishing program of the University of Chicago Press.

But he plunged into other activities that more prudent educators would have tried to avoid. These came within the scope of his overarching view of the University as a center of independent thought and criticism. Some were also personal matters of conscience, as in the case of the pressing question of further use of the monstrously destructive nuclear weaponry that had been born out of research carried on under his aegis.

Six weeks after atomic bombs demolished Hiroshima and Nagasaki, the University sponsored an Atomic Energy Control Conference with Hutchins in the chair. Included among the fifty participants were Henry Wallace, the secretary of commerce and former Vice President, and Chairman David Lilienthal of the Tennessee Valley Authority, who was soon to head the Atomic Energy Commission. Also present were scientists who had leading roles in the Manhattan Project and scholars in the field of public policy. Glenn Seaborg, a future Nobel laureate who worked on the Metallurgy Project at Chicago, recalled the atmosphere:

> We met at a time when there were thought to be, at most, two unassembled atomic bombs in the world. Virtually nothing was known publicly about the possibility of thermonuclear weapons. Yet, based on what the participants knew of militarism, of national rivalries, of national and international politics, and of human nature, there was a sense of dire foreboding at this conference.[13]

Leo Szilard opened the session by reporting that it was already possible to increase the destructive force of the bomb at least ten times. The Russians, he predicted, would be able to produce such a bomb in two and a half years, and within six years they could have enough to destroy all American cities. There was no dissent from this estimate.

Szilard thought there could be no effective halt to the development of nuclear weapons without an international agreement backed by inspections — but enforcement would require some form of world government, which he considered a remote prospect. No one came forward with a practical alternative, and the conference turned to the immediate issue of secrecy.

Hutchins had relayed a message from General Groves warning the assembled scientists of the security restrictions still in effect on information acquired from work on the Manhattan Project. Some rejected the restriction, saying that the need for secrecy had ended when the bomb was dropped and that it was time for the public and the Soviets to know everything they knew. There were objections that this would weaken the government's bargaining position in upcoming negotiations with the Russians. This issue, too, remained unresolved when the conference adjourned. Looking back after the passage of thirty years, Seaborg wrote,

> Summoning all the assembled knowledge and reasoning power we could, we had tried to discern some way in which the United States could lead mankind out of its new and seemingly desperate situation. Unencumbered by the details of national bargaining positions, which had not yet emerged, and of the nuclear arms race, which had not yet begun, we were able to raise broad questions that, as the years passed and the political and military landscape became more cluttered, it would prove increasingly difficult to consider.

Yet no clear picture emerged of how we could achieve the objective nearly all of us had in mind — a world without nuclear weapons. It was as though the seeds of a nuclear arms race were embedded in human nature and political institutions.[14]

The conference had provided Hutchins with a preview of the arguments that would be offered in support of the futile effort to preserve the secret of the atomic bomb, and of the successful effort to thwart any effective move toward international inspection and control. As the political drama unfolded in Washington, he wired Bill Benton at the State Department: "The inexcusable tragedy of errors is now being played with General Groves in a leading role. The way to make the country strong is to release atomic energy from military control and stimulate research and development. This fortunately is also the way to allay suspicion and fear."[15]

But the issues of secrecy and civilian control were peripheral to Hutchins's central concern. He was convinced that airborne nuclear weapons had eliminated the possibility that peace could be preserved through any kind of alliance among sovereign nations. In his view the cold-war maneuvering in Europe held no prospect of deterrence through balance of power, but might well be the precursor of World War III. Nor did he share the faith of those who thought the United Nations might be the instrument for creating a peaceful world; without supranational peacekeeping authority, he believed the UN was fated to join the League of Nations as another monument to postwar disillusionment.

Hutchins moved to translate his conclusions into action when his "good news of damnation" endorsement of a world government on the Chicago "Roundtable of the Air" program prompted Dean McKeon of the Humanities Division and his colleague G. A. Borgese to submit a proposal to the chancellor:

We were strongly impressed, as many were, by the warning you broadcast on August 12. We think we understand you correctly if we assume that the sternness of your word was a call to action. We are in agreement with the general principles you have stated through the years on the meaning and purpose of a university in our time. . . .

A world constitution is needed. This is a staggering, yet inescapable assignment — and a most pressing one, the deadline being the day, unpredicted but not remote, when the atomic secret will be in other hands. We do not think a world constitution or a preliminary project will be drafted by bureaucratic or diplomatic bodies. Their motions are inhibited by statutory routines; their initiatives, even in this most open-minded of nations, must stop at the dogmatic wall of national sovereignty.[16]

By November the Committee to Frame a World Constitution had been established under the auspices of the Humanities Division. McKeon was chairman and Borgese secretary, but Hutchins was put out in front with the title of president. Eleven other charter members were drawn from the faculties of Chicago, Harvard, and Columbia, and a small research and support staff was assembled in a building on the Midway. Publicity would be avoided during the first year of the Committee's deliberations, and the final fruit of its labors would not be unveiled until July 1947. But Hutchins knew he was providing additional ammunition for those who accused him of megalomania. When he approved the proposal, he privately dubbed it the Committee to Frame Hutchins.

CHAPTER TWENTY-FIVE

"A Stuffed Shirt on Roller Skates"

Asked by an interviewer if he ever read simply for pleasure, Robert Hutchins confessed that he enjoyed detective novels but added that he selected only those published in German so they would also improve his command of the language. Toward the end of his life, reflecting upon his well-spent youth, he said that his Puritan heritage had endowed him with the conviction that having fun was a form of indolence. This was touched with his usual irony, but the fact was that the responsibilities that he felt obligated to assume and the relentless determination with which he discharged them left little opportunity for self-indulgence.

The reorganization of the central administration of the University did nothing to change this. At the end of the war he assumed the burden of reconverting to its original educational purposes an institution that for almost four years had been primarily devoted to applied research and training. And he had to undertake this formidable task in the face of the University's unprecedented relationship with, and dependence upon, government.

"One old battle we do not have to fight is the battle to give the natural sciences their proper place in the universities and in our lives," he said in his 1946 address at the annual trustee-faculty dinner. "The sciences have won this battle by the simple and effective process of threatening to blow up the world."[1] Given the prospect of a continued flow of government funding, the problem, as he saw it, was to keep scientific

264

research, and the applied technology it made possible, from overwhelming the universities at the expense of the general education he considered to be their primary mission.

Hutchins's answer was to create at Chicago more or less independent institutes to carry out pure research in three related areas. The Institute for Nuclear Study, the Institute for the Study of Metals, and the Institute of Radiobiology and Biophysics channeled financial support for their members' projects and at the same time provided a degree of insulation against their influence on the other faculties of the University.

The Institutes served the immediate purpose of retaining at Chicago a number of the distinguished scientists who had been assembled for the Manhattan Project, so much so that Hutchins came under fire from Vannevar Bush, director of the Office of Scientific Research and Development. Bill Benton dispatched an urgent warning from Washington:

> I ran into Vannevar Bush at lunch the other day. You should know, if you don't, how bitterly he feels about the Institute for Nuclear Physics [*sic*] at the University. He feels that the University betrayed its trust in employing the "professors from Princeton and Columbia who went out, on this joint project, to serve their country during the war." He states that, implicit in setting up the project at the University, was a cooperative spirit on the part of the several universities, which was grossly violated by the "greed" and "overreaching" of the University of Chicago.
>
> Furthermore, he states that the move was stupid. He points out that the University is falling down in its efforts to raise money. He claims that "all inquiries on this subject eventually come back to me," and of course implicit in this comment is the idea that he turns his thumbs down as hard and as far as he can.[2]

Hutchins was already aware of Bush's jaundiced view. He rebutted the unwarranted and damaging "Washington reports" in a letter he wrote to General Groves, sending copies to Bush, Secretary of War Robert P. Patterson, and the leading atomic scientists. He pointed out that except for a *Chicago Tribune* editorial "in harmony with the *Tribune*'s policy of representing the city of Chicago as the leader in all fields of endeavor," there had been almost no publicity on the University's key role in the Manhattan Project. As to the other charge,

> the University is under the impression that it is performing a great public service by holding together a group in this field which

might otherwise disintegrate. Its plan is not to monopolize a scientific area but to promote its development by retaining at a strategic location a combination which is certain to give great impetus to this work on a national scale. Far from seeking a monopoly, the University regards itself as a training ground for the country and particularly for the Middle West.[3]

Groves acknowledged the justice of the case Hutchins made, and the fire was apparently banked, if not extinguished. In fact, the credit given the University posed a threat to Hutchins's cherished principle that while pure scientific research had a place on the campus, development of its technological application did not; it was for that reason Chicago had never established an engineering school. Now the new Atomic Energy Commission was charged with responsibility for developing the potential of the split atom, and the expanded offshoot of the old Metallurgy Laboratory was an obvious candidate for ambitious government programs intended to adapt the new source of energy to civilian as well as military use.

The Commission came forward with a proposal, enthusiastically embraced by Hutchins, to retain the University as operating contractor but to transfer the programs to a facility that would be created sixty miles away, in DuPage County, at a semirural site that would facilitate the rigid security measures imposed to protect the presumed American monopoly on atomic energy. The new Argonne National Laboratory would function under a consortium made up of the major universities and research institutes in the Midwest.

This arm's-length arrangement gave Chicago's nuclear scientists, along with those from the other participating institutions, access to essentially engineering operations being carried out by government agencies in cooperation with such private industries as Westinghouse and DuPont. Among the early projects was the development of reactors as a source of cheap electricity, which would, it was widely believed, free the industrialized societies from their dependence on fossil fuels.

Hutchins had no objection to the University's indirect contribution to efforts to improve the material lot of the citizenry. But he thought its primary obligation was to devote its intellectual resources to consideration of the consequences of such development. Long before the issue became commonplace, he was making the point that the technological revolution was rapidly reducing the demand for manual labor and was bound to transform society in unanticipated ways:

. . . in the atomic age the horrors of peace are likely to be worse than those of war. Increasing mechanization means increasing leisure. Increasing leisure means that we Americans must discover some rational notion of leisure or degenerate into a nation of alcoholics, movie fans, and pulp-magazine consumers, a nation, in short, of morons and lunatics. A people who only a few years ago worked ten hours a day will not easily stand the shock of being reduced to four or five. What are they going to do with themselves?[4]

It had been suggested that if the government were to provide a research fund equivalent to the sum invested in the production of the atomic bomb, the social scientists could come up with answers to such pressing questions. But Hutchins had doubts:

For two billion dollars the social scientists could undoubtedly deliver a vast amount of information; but whether it would be as beneficial as the atomic bomb was destructive is highly questionable. The social sciences and humanities are concerned with ends as well as means. Whether you ought to wipe out the people of Hiroshima and Nagasaki is a much more difficult and complicated question than the question of how you are going to wipe them out after you have decided to do so; and it is not a question on which research, in the ordinary sense of the word, will shed much light. . . . Research in the social sciences and humanities cannot become effective in the same automatic way in which natural science becomes operative in our daily lives.[5]

He was, of course, reiterating his argument that social science could make a useful approach to these problems only when it dealt in first principles. A new appointment in the Social Sciences Division demonstrated how Hutchins was attempting to advance this metaphysical concept, and also exemplified his unorthodox recruiting methods. Hutchins had known Rexford Guy Tugwell for some years and considered him to be the kind of broad-gauged intellectual he would like to have on his faculty, so when he heard he might be available he offered him a post at Chicago and left it up to him to decide what he wanted to do once he got there.

Tugwell had earned a solid academic reputation as an economics professor at Columbia before becoming a "brains-truster" for Franklin Roosevelt in his first presidential campaign and going on to Washington as assistant secretary of agriculture. He later served as chairman of the New York City Planning Commission under Mayor Fiorello La Guardia. Now he was ending his wartime service as the last appointed governor of Puerto Rico, a neglected island colony he described as having been acquired by the United States after the Spanish American War in a fit of absent-mindedness. Out of that varied experience he had conceived the need for what amounted to a new academic discipline.

Although professional planners had begun to achieve some prominence in government and industry, their education was usually a byproduct of departments of architecture and engineering, with an emphasis on physical design or systems engineering. At Chicago the need for a new approach had been recognized as far back as 1945, when a faculty committee working with representatives of the American Society of Planning Officials and the American Institute of Architects had initiated discussion of an interdisciplinary school of planning. This had not been followed up, but it provided the basis for Tugwell's proposal to Hutchins, which called for merging the physical aspects of planning with socioeconomic factors to develop a theoretical framework as a separate activity and subject matter, independent of its field of application.

Like Hutchins, Tugwell rejected laissez-faire economics. Einstein's theory of relativity had convinced him that there was no basis for the self-regulating laws of political economy that were purported to correspond to Newton's laws of physics: "What I was led to in my time was the notion that if there was a continuum within which end and events could be shaped, there must be a discipline of planning."[6] His description of the proper role of the planner coincided with Hutchins's activist instinct and metaphysical bent:

> What the planner thinks of himself as doing is rationalizing and bringing into some sort of prospective order the massive flow of events toward a future time. . . . Events so anticipated may be brought into order, made less destructive or more productive and generally made to accord with a people's estimate of their needs and ambitions. His creation — the plan — may be made the subject of rational dialogue as it is molded and remolded. . . .
>
> The planner works not only with columns of figures but ultimately with maps and designs, displaying for democratic decision what the consequences will be if certain choices are made rather than others. He dares to speak of order and even of beauty in future arrangements. . . .[7]

When Hutchins summoned Tugwell to the Midway there remained the problem of where to put him. He would hardly be welcome in the

Economics Department, where Hutchins had just approved the appointment of young Milton Friedman, who in time would eclipse the dedicated disciples of Adam Smith already in command. In his New Deal days Tugwell had been tagged Rex the Red by the reactionary press, and his appointment brought an inquiry from Hutchins's tolerant father. "Mr. Tugwell might not be a good appointment at a 'radical' university," the chancellor replied. "At the University of Chicago, where we have the most conservative economics department in the world, Mr. Tugwell should do the group some good."[8]

Tugwell, quite appropriately, became a political scientist, having been welcomed into that department by his old friends Charles Merriam and Leonard White. In his 1946 report to the trustees and faculty, Hutchins cited the new venture in the field of planning as an example of the obligations the University must assume as the world entered the atomic era it had helped precipitate. "In addition to knowledge we must have the willingness and capacity to act on it," he said. ". . . We must set about finding ways to promote the application to current problems of such knowledge — or even of such good opinion — as we have about human relationships." He went on,

> Another proposal, which originated in the Humanities Division, suggests the role which scholars outside the natural sciences may play in this crisis. That is the proposal for a committee centered at Chicago which would attempt to draft a constitution for a world state. It is not suggested that the constitution drafted might be instantly adopted; it would probably be a calamity if any constitution now drafted were to be adopted. But since we must work toward world government or perish, we ought at once to begin trying to find out what kind of world government we ought to have. . . .
>
> Although there is a tinge of megalomania about it, this is one kind of work the American scholar must perform today. He must bring his knowledge and his objectivity to bear upon the critical condition of civilization. . . . We are justified in assuming that we cannot look to politicians for the vision, the knowledge, or the detachment which the crisis demands. These are or should be possessed by that much-maligned race, the intellectuals. Now is the time for the intellectuals to show whether they have intellects equal to the task.[9]

In addition to Hutchins, McKeon, and Borgese, Chicago supplied four other charter members of the Committee to Frame a World Constitution: Mortimer Adler, Robert Redfield, Rex Tugwell, and Dean Wilbur G. Katz of the Law School. The other founders were, from Harvard, William E. Hocking, professor of philosophy, Dean James M. Landis of Harvard Law School, and Charles H. McIlwain, professor of government; Reinhold Niebuhr of Union Theological Seminary; and Beardsley Ruml, now the chairman of the Federal Reserve Bank of New York. Four members joined later: Albert Leon Guerard of Stanford, Erich Kahler of the New School for Social Research, Stringfellow Barr of Saint John's, and Harold A. Innis of the University of Toronto.

It was contemplated that members might be added from abroad, including Russians, but it was decided that aside from the practical difficulties posed by unsettled postwar conditions, it would be best to proceed in the initial stages with a working group that shared a common language and tradition. An office housing a small research and support staff was established in a former fraternity house near the campus, charged with preparing pertinent documents and maintaining a record of the proceedings.

Between February 1946 and April 1947 the committee held twelve two- or three-day meetings, alternating between Chicago and New York. These were closed sessions at which the members threshed out draft constitutional provisions after the fashion of the American founding fathers who had convened at Philadelphia 170 years before.

It was planned that when a draft constitution was agreed upon it would, as had been the case with the United States charter, be submitted for public discussion through a periodical modeled after the Federalist Papers, published by James Madison, Alexander Hamilton, and John Jay during the state legislatures' debate on ratification. A monthly called *Common Cause* was launched in 1947 with Borgese as editor, assisted by his talented young wife, Elisabeth, the daughter of the expatriate German author Thomas Mann.

Hutchins somehow found time to actively participate in these protracted deliberations and to contribute to *Common Cause* when it appeared. He was similarly involved with John Nef's Committee on Social Thought, the unorthodox graduate program that continued to create controversy even among its supporters. When Nef, who sought to soothe his colleagues by assembling the committee at his sumptuous luncheon table, complained that this did nothing to reduce the bickering, Hutchins replied,

I greatly sympathize with your account of your labors with the Committee. I think the patience of John should be substituted for that of Job in the proverb. What I object to most is the attitude of your colleagues. They are constantly insinuating that this is some private venture of ours and that their sole function is to eat, drink and be critical. I would welcome some real criticism and some real discussion of important matters. What we get is carping and points of no consequence. My conclusion is the one I have often reported: Robert [Redfield] is indifferent and [Frank] Knight is nuts. But I am for going on just the same, as long as you can take it.[10]

The decision of the Committee on Social Thought to bring forth *Measure,* a magazine patterned after *Partisan Review,* led to a clash of egos so protracted that Hutchins could only resolve it by volunteering to serve as chairman of the editorial board. He indicated that it was his understanding that the projected quarterly "was to be critical, concerned with establishing standards in literature and art, and with clarifying the relations of these standards to moral philosophy." It was further agreed that the contents "should not be written for specialists, but for the general public, but without any concession to the popular."[11] It required Hutchins's close attention to see to it that *Measure* met these exacting standards when it was launched by Henry Regnery, a trade publisher who thought it had prospects of becoming financially self-sustaining.

Hutchins read all the articles considered for publication by the editor, Otto vonSimson, and his negative judgment was apparently decisive. In response to an essay entitled "Class Consciousness and the American Worker," he commented, "These social scientists make me tired. In the first place, they can't write: The use of the word *key* as an adjective, and the use of nouns as adjectives and verbs, for example *structured,* gives me a pain. I also object to the numerous barbarisms, such as *behavioral.*"[12] The article was not published.

He made his own contributions to *Measure,* including an essay on T. S. Eliot's *Notes Toward a Definition of Culture,* in which he found that "Mr. Eliot's confusion appears in highly concentrated form." Eliot wrote him in reply,

I must say at once, that this is the first comment I have seen on my rather scrappy remarks which has any value for myself, and I think some of your criticism may oblige me to develop and correct what I have printed. The chapter is, I admit, no more than a rag-bag of random observations, or shall I say, a disorderly quiver of poisoned arrows of various sizes, perhaps as dangerous to the archer as to his intended victims. This is not to say that I quite accept your views either, but merely to thank you for the first stimulating comments I have received.[13]

Eliot came to Chicago to deliver four lectures on "The Aims of Education," which he described as an answer to "a very distinguished educator who, in effect, called upon me to produce something more coherent or make my apology." The lectures were published in successive issues of *Measure,* and the Regnery promotion manager took advantage of the expatriate poet's celebrity to launch a subscription drive using the slogan "The Chancellor and Mr. Eliot."[14]

"I am determined to get you and your institute and your journal established so that nobody can stop what you are doing or thwart the plans you are making," Hutchins wrote Nef in 1946.[15] He succeeded in the case of the Committee, which is still in existence, but *Measure* went the way of countless other little magazines when he was no longer around to sustain it.

Hutchins's extracurricular activities were, if anything, even more time-consuming. Early in the war his old friend Henry Luce had discussed with him the need for an independent survey of the current state and future prospects of freedom of the press, and had asked for a cost estimate. Hutchins thought it could be done for $60,000 a year and would require up to three years. In 1944 Time, Inc., approved a grant of $200,000 to the University for a Commission on Freedom of the Press to be chaired by Hutchins, who would choose the other thirteen members. As usual he selected distinguished scholars and public men with scholarly backgrounds, several of whom were already serving on other bodies he headed.

The Commission was concerned with policy, not journalistic technique, so persons actively associated with newspapers, magazines, radio, movies, or books were excluded. But these were heard from at the seventeen two- or three-day meetings the commission held in various parts of the country. Testimony was offered by fifty-eight leading media proprietors and practitioners at these sessions, and 225 others were interviewed by the staff. Hutchins was heavily involved in all of this, and in the end he wrote the Commission's report, which touched off another fire storm of controversy when it appeared in 1947.

Another old friend was instrumental in creating still another body chaired by Hutchins. Walter Paepcke and his wife, Elizabeth, became close friends of the Hutchinses soon after their arrival in Chicago. She was the daughter of William A. Nitze, a distinguished member of the Chicago faculty, and her mother was the grande dame of the university community. He was a highly successful businessman who headed the Container Corporation of America and later became a trustee of the University. The affinity between the two men was described by James Sloan Allen in *The Romance of Commerce and Culture:*

> Four years apart in age, both molded by severely moralistic Protestant fathers, and both honor graduates of Yale, Paepcke and Hutchins were both driven by a desire to elevate the common run of mankind to the demanding standards of culture and morality that they themselves possessed. . . . And their every labor to accomplish this elevation, separately or together, demonstrated the stringent self-discipline and passion for work, lightened by beguiling wit and seductive social charm, that distinguished both men.[16]

The Paepckes were avid participants in the "Fat Man's" Great Books course, and Hutchins enlisted Walter's aid when the flood of applications for similar adult-education classes began to overwhelm the downtown University College, which had trained nonprofessional discussion leaders for more than thirty groups in the Chicago area. By 1946 a network of such classes stretched from coast to coast, with more than five thousand participants. The idea of expanding the Great Books program beyond the limited facilities of the University was on Hutchins's mind when he had his friend to lunch in February 1947. Paepcke cited two items in his account of what he considered to be a historic occasion:

> One was a foundation which might more properly run the Great Books courses throughout the United States. Another and very intriguing idea was to think about and plan for a bicentennial Goethe Celebration commemorating his birth in 1749 and having a week's festivities — lectures, plays, opera, etc. — to familiarize more adequately the American public with a great writer, poet, philosopher, scientist, musician of German origin and attempt in some modest way to reestablish a cultural relationship between the Teutonic peoples and the rest of the world, following the natural hatred, misunderstanding, and dislocation caused by the last war.[17]

In July the Great Books Foundation opened its offices at the Container Corporation, with Hutchins as chairman, Lynn Williams, Jr., as president, and Paepcke as vice president. The nonprofit corporation took over the entire University College operation, undertaking to organize new adult groups, train discussion leaders, and publish low-cost editions of the books. At the end of the first year there were ten thousand participants, and in time there would be fifty thousand.

In October the Goethe Bicentennial Foundation was created under the three-man directorate of Hutchins, Paepcke, and Wilbur Munnecke. The decision was taken to stage the great celebration at the abandoned mining town high in the Colorado Rockies where Paepcke had established the Aspen Company to create a resort that would combine recreation with a high-minded cultural environment for refugees from the summer heat and winter visitors to the ski slopes.

Hutchins was launched on another venture in which he was expected to generate ideas, line up talent, and raise money. He would spend much time on the road, describing himself as a "stuffed shirt on roller skates with records on his back,"[18] seeking support for the 1949 Goethe Festival, which launched the Aspen Institute for Humanistic Studies.

CHAPTER TWENTY-SIX

A Proposal
to History

Although there was no crack in the jaunty aplomb Robert Hutchins displayed in public during the postwar years, it was evident to his intimates that the inhuman schedule he imposed upon himself was beginning to take its toll. Urging Thornton Wilder to visit him in Chicago, he wrote, "It will be a kind and Christian act of you to see me. The vital juices are dried up. The spirits are low. I am inventing all kinds of excuses for myself — the faculty, the trustees, the public, the world, etc. — and sinking into an abyss of self-pity. I need the old gleam in your old eye. This is a Macedonian cry."[1]

He was traveling constantly, raising funds for the University's new scientific institutes and for the Goethe Festival; testifying before Congress against universal military service and for the reduction of security restrictions on atomic research; speaking out against the cold-war policies of the Truman administration; and still carrying his crusade for educational reform to audiences across the nation.

Apologizing for his delay in replying to a communication from John Nef, he wrote from Detroit, "As usual I have been on the road, Buffalo, Toronto, New York, Philadelphia, now here. I find this life little adapted to correspondence, or anything else worthwhile."[2] Reporting on a swing through the Middle West, he said, "I made some kind of record in South Bend. I arrived at 5:30, made three speeches, and left at 9:30."[3] From Williamsburg, Virginia, he wrote that he had been "running around from Minneapolis to Spokane to San Francisco to Carmel to New York to

275

Milwaukee on behalf of Goethe & God knows what. . . . The Goethe celebration in its financial aspects came to fall on Paepcke and me alone. We have found ourselves obligated to raise a very large sum of money; I could not leave Walter to do it all by himself."[4]

Public discussion of the issues that concerned Hutchins was affected by the anti-Communist hysteria that was then building to the climax of McCarthyism, and he was already in the lists. "It is now fashionable to call anybody with whom you disagree a Communist or a fellow traveler," he noted when he was once again haled before a commission of the Illinois legislature investigating subversive activities. "So Branch Rickey darkly hinted the other day that the attempt to eliminate the reserve clause in baseball contracts was the work of Communists."[5] When one of the members of the commission suggested that a noted cancer researcher who belonged to left-wing organizations might be guilty of indoctrination, Hutchins routed him with the response, "Indoctrination? Of mice?"[6] This investigation, like the earlier one, foundered on its own absurdity, but it helped fuel the anti-Hutchins crusade that had been resumed with increased fervor by the *Chicago Tribune* and the Hearst papers.

The *Tribune* was ready to pounce when the Committee to Frame a World Constitution circulated a confidential copy of its draft charter to 350 experts on constitutional law, inviting their comment prior to its scheduled publication in March 1948. "WORLD STATE'S SUPER-SECRET CONSTITUTION!" the newspaper blared when a copy fell into its hands; "PLAN SPONSORED BY HUTCHINS BARED":

A highly restricted secret document setting up a constitution and plan of a new world government which would supplant the United Nations, abolish the United States and all other countries as nations, and govern, tax and regulate the world's people, with power to seize and manage private property, has been obtained exclusively by *The Tribune*.

It is the product of a self-styled Committee to Frame a World Constitution, one of a rash of militant globalist organizations which have sprung up in the United States and England since the United Nations has demonstrated its uselessness.

The committee president is Robert M. Hutchins, sometime chancellor of the University of Chicago, who frequently takes off on world-saving jobs not connected with education at the Midway.[7]

The implication of conspiracy was farfetched, since the document was designed to bring into focus the already widespread public discussion of the perceived need for some form of supranational organization to preserve peace in the atomic era. A number of organizations with grass-roots support were advocating the surrender of a degree of national sovereignty to the powerless United Nations. If the Hutchins group took the most advanced position among these world federalists, it could hardly be called militant.

"Their ambition or hope," said a foreword to the constitution, signed by Hutchins and G. A. Borgese, "was and is to do their part in taking down to earth or, so to speak, spelling out, the general movement for World Government that has been growing, not always in definite shape, during these years."

> The problems of World Government are hard and intricate. The Committee felt that these problems can best be clarified in a constitutional design, intended as a concrete picture to show what a Federal Republic of the World, under certain conceivable circumstances, *might* look like. Thus visualized in an exact frame of government and law, the Republic of the World does not look so absurd — "utopian" is the word — as defeatism maintains. Neither does it look so self-evident as frivolous optimism would prefer to believe.
>
> That the "conceivable circumstances" for the rise of a World Government are not at hand, the Committee knows full well. Paramount among those circumstances should be the willingness of Russia, but not of Russia alone, to surrender sovereignty. To create those circumstances is beyond the power of any individual or group, and this Committee is not a guild of miracle makers.[8]

Those who advocated increasing the powers of the United Nations were roughly divided into minimalists and maximalists. The former proposed limiting the supranational role to peace keeping — a system under which the member nations would disarm themselves and endow the UN with the authority to adjudicate international disputes and a military force sufficient to enforce its findings. The maximalists contended that this was unrealistic, that there had to be a full-fledged central government, complete with executive and legislative as well as judicial branches, endowed with the kind of ultimate authority conferred upon the federal government by the United States Constitution.

The Hutchins group argued its case on pragmatic grounds. The

Russian representatives at the UN had already rejected the minimalist concept, branding it an antiproletarian maneuver to preserve and expand capitalist imperialism. Ideology aside, a world organization limited to the prevention of armed conflict, and thereby committed to maintaining the international status quo, could hardly expect endorsement by a working consensus of the world's people, a majority of whom were just emerging from colonial rule:

> If what our western world federalists have in mind is a world federal union with . . . no binding commitment toward the final dismantlement of colonialism, outlawry of racial discrimination, provisions for social security — these three being the acid tests of any world federal thinking — if that is the case, our western world federalists may talk to one another for years and decades to come. Those millions inside our borders, those hundreds of millions abroad who do not care much for liberty without bread, who do not have anything to be secure about, who do not remember any blessings of peace or war, will not listen — or will laugh.[9]

The Committee conceded that there was no prospect of the nation states' consenting "to blot themselves out or to be blotted out of the historical picture overnight." It characterized its approach as "a middle road pointing to a survivial of the extant states, in a framework of local initiatives and authority, while depriving them of functions and powers which are basic to the World Government and which cannot be entrusted to entities driven by nature and tradition to wreck, if they have the opportunity, any world union, as they did wreck the League and have all but wrecked the UN."[10]

The draft constitution was brief and lucid. It made its bow to democracy by vesting the primary power of government in a Federal Convention, which would be made up of delegates elected by popular vote on the basis of one per million in population. The Convention would elect a president to serve a single six-year term, as well as a ninety-nine-member unicameral legislature called the World Council. The president would appoint a cabinet whose members could be removed by a no-confidence vote of the Council majority. Judicial authority would be vested in a Grand Tribunal of sixty justices, appointed by the president and approved by two thirds of the Council; they would divide their membership into appellate courts and establish subordinate jurisdictions. A six-member Chamber of Guardians elected jointly by the Council and the Tribunal would have final authority over employment of the armed forces.

The Convention would also elect an independent Tribune of the People, charged with defending the human rights specified in a Declaration of Duties and Rights, which would include all those guaranteed by the United States Constitution but would go beyond it to provide a generalized economic entitlement:

> The four elements of life — earth, water, air, energy — are the common property of the human race. The management and use of such portions thereof as are vested in or assigned to particular ownership, private or corporate or national or regional, of definite or indefinite tenure, of individualist or collectivist economy, shall be subordinated in each and all cases to the interest of the common good.[11]

It was the hope of the framers that this language was broad enough to provide for equitable implementation through the administrative powers delegated to the nine regional groupings that would constitute the electoral units of the federation, and that it could accommodate the variety of reserved powers that would still be exercised by the nation states. What it did guarantee was a concerted attack on the draft constitution by political conservatives, as well as its rejection by moderates, who generally aligned themselves with the minimalists.

One of the original members of the committee, Reinhold Niebuhr, withdrew in protest against "the myth of world government," and the chairman, Richard McKeon, declared himself unwilling to sign the final draft. But those who viewed the enterprise in its own terms found it worthwhile as a beginning point for a discussion of critical issues worthy of the kind of detailed consideration they had not received in the postwar surge of "One World" sentiment.

"Far from being visionary," George A. Bernstein wrote in *The Nation,* "it is a document well worth reading for anyone who seeks a pragmatic solution to the problem of international peace."[12] McGeorge Bundy, then a professor at Harvard, found it "an ingenious document, written by men who had the advice of experts in political theory. Its every grant of power, its every specification of duty, is aimed at some real-life injustice evident to the framers, and evident even to some who oppose the one worlders." But as was so often the case with the reaction of Eastern Seaboard intellectuals to Hutchins's undertakings, Bundy went on to deplore the fashion in which the cause was argued:

> If this constitution were presented only as an essay in ideas, from which men might learn as men have always learned from Utopias,

it might deserve some of the praise it has received. Unfortunately, this is not the tone of its chief interpreters. . . .

The arguments of Mr. Hutchins, in particular, . . . display the stigmata of the irresponsible idealist. Mr. Hutchins believes with passionate conviction that only his solution will prevent world war. He treats with cavalier and demonstrable unfairness the arguments of those who disagree, and he uses in support of his own case facts and arguments which are, to say the least, debatable. . . . It is a pity that at such a time men as prominent as Mr. Hutchins and Mr. Borgese should be spreading confusion by a misguided insistence upon an undesirable and impossible world republic.[13]

The Committee hoped that continued debate on the provisions of the draft constitution in *Common Cause* would stimulate sufficient discussion in the mass media to prompt a movement within the UN looking to its further refinement at regional meetings around the world. Hutchins never considered this an immediate prospect, but he was convinced that the mutation of extant governments into a world republic was as historically inevitable as had been the merger of city states into nation states, and nation states into empires. The issue was urgent, he felt, for only movement toward world government offered a way out of the cold-war confrontation between East and West. The alternative was another world war, out of which would emerge not one Rome but two Carthages.

"Yet World Government shall come — this is practically the consensus in this generation — whether within five years or fifty, whether without a conflagration or after it," Hutchins and Borgese wrote.[14] The consensus, if it existed, did not last. Interest in *Common Cause* dwindled, and publication was suspended in 1951 when Borgese went home to Italy, where he would finish out his years. The world constitution had been offered by its framers as "a proposal to history." In Hutchins's lifetime it never became more than a footnote.

Hutchins advanced his arguments for world government in rational terms. It was a logical extension of his educational theory. "I am an Aristotelian Platonist or a Platonic Aristotelian," he said. "I have not found it necessary to concern myself on questions of religious faith."[15] But he did recognize that mankind was beset by weaknesses that theologians attributed to original sin. "I therefore assume that the human being, being the kind of being he is, is always going to have difficulties of every kind, particularly moral difficulties, as the word *sin* implies."[16] His own faith was grounded in the conviction that a form of education could be devised that would sharpen men's intellectual capacity so that they would be able to identify the basic issues of their time, think dispassionately about them, and arrive at rational courses of action. Logic dictated that the first priority in the nuclear age must be the prevention of war, which Hutchins believed to be beyond the capacity of any nation state.

But now, with the world having been given a glimpse of the Apocalypse at Hiroshima, Hutchins could no longer envision any circumstances in which reason alone could be expected to prevail. The educational system that might focus the attention of the leadership on first principles was not at hand or even in sight. "Other civilizations were destroyed by barbarians from without. We breed our own," he said.[17] These materialist barbarians could be turned back only by changing men's hearts as well as their minds. To a student convocation he preached a sermon that echoed his Presbyterian father's declaration on the eve of America's entry into World War I: "I do say that any honest obedience to the word of Jesus Christ would have made impossible most of the wars of the world. . . ."[18] His son put it this way: "The brotherhood of man must rest on the fatherhood of God."

> Unless we believe that every man is the child of God, we cannot love our neighbors. . . . Unless we see men as children of God, they appear to us as rivals, or customers, or foreigners, unrelated to us except as means to our ends. . . .
>
> I will admit that if the whole world practiced Aristotle's *Ethics* the whole world would be much better off than it is today. But I doubt if any single man, to say nothing of the whole world, can practice Aristotle's *Ethics* without the support and inspiration of religious faith. . . . The modern critic is inclined to scoff at the Aristotelian phrase that men are rational animals. But Aristotle was saying not merely that men were rational, but that they were also animal. Because men are animals, because the flesh is weak and life is hard, the virtues cannot be consistently practiced without divine aid. . . .[19]

He elaborated on this thesis in the 1948 Bedell Lectures at Kenyon College:

> A perfect theory of democracy can be made out of the metaphysical and ethical writings of Aristotle. But as he himself did not have the fortitude to follow his premises to their conclusion and

admit all men to participate in their own government, so it is improbable that the practice of democracy now or in the future can be achieved merely by the demonstration of its reasonableness. Men, simply because they are men, are unlikely to find within themselves the power that can bring the good life and the good state to pass. As Reinhold Niebuhr pointed out in his Gifford Lectures, all anthropocentric ethical doctrines fail at this point; they overlook the fallen nature of man and assume that without grace he can reach a terrestrial end to which, almost by definition, no being with such a nature can ever attain.[20]

Hutchins and Borgese fared better with another enterprise in which they joined hands — the celebration of Goethe's birthday. The idea of honoring the German literary master had originated with the Modern Language Association, but Borgese, who before his emigration had been the leading Italian scholar of Germanic literature, embroidered the notion into something far more dramatic than a conventional academic event:

> The fiery and politically impassioned Borgese immediately saw in the Goethe Bicentennial an opportunity not only to commemorate the great German author of *Faust* and other literary works but to honor Goethe the cosmopolitan humanist and universal man — poet, philosopher, scientist, administrator, and exponent of the cultural unity of mankind — and thereby to help heal the wounds of war and to promote world government.[21]

Borgese had no difficulty in selling the idea to Hutchins. The latter had been introduced to *Faust* by a professor at Oberlin, and he credited that experience with conferring upon him the gift of thought: "When, a year or so later, I was in the American army in Italy, the only book I had in my barracks bag was the first volume of the Witkowski edition; and I memorized long passages while I was on guard duty, reciting the language of the enemy in the midst of my sleeping companions."[22]

Borgese and Hutchins treated the Bicentennial as an extension of the effort they had launched in connection with the faltering Committee to Frame a World Constitution. The *Chicago Tribune,* in its paranoid fashion, seized upon a pronouncement by the East German propaganda minister, who was claiming the heritage of Goethe for the Communist bloc, to suggest that if the Soviets were exploiting the great German for their own sinister purposes, so was the "Hutchins group" using Goethe "to promote its own scheme of a world state under a world constitution."[23]

It was Hutchins's idea that the massive public-relations campaign required to make the Goethe celebration a national cultural event might also serve to attract attention to the mountain resort his friend Walter Paepcke was attempting to establish in the remote Colorado Rockies. Aspen had blossomed during the silver-mining boom in the last century, acquiring a capacious hotel, an opera house, and a row of handsome Victorian dwellings to house its metallic millionaires. But by 1945, when Paepcke became enamored of its lovely alpine setting, the boom-time population of twelve thousand had dwindled to a few hundred, and most of the buildings had fallen into disrepair. Paepcke said he expected Hutchins to change his mind when he

> described faithfully the tumble-down condition of some of the houses, the charred interior of the Opera House, the somewhat out of the way location, and the relatively small surrounding population. However, it seems that they want, and I think correctly so, a location which people would have to go to some little trouble to get to and which would be in a scenically and climatically attractive spot rather than to have it outside of New York, Chicago, or what not, where people who are about to see ''Abie's Irish Rose'' and couldn't find seats could decide to go to the Goethe Festival instead.[24]

Paepcke employed Herbert Bayer, an Austrian refugee who had been a leading figure in Germany's Bauhaus design center, to supervise the restoration of the buildings acquired by his Aspen Company and the creation of a tented amphitheater that could seat an audience of two thousand. A classical-music buff, he also took the lead in recruiting the talent he hoped would help launch an American equivalent of the Salzburg Festival. He wound up with an impressive array: the Minneapolis Symphony, conducted by Dimitri Mitropoulos, the pianist Artur Rubinstein, the cellist Gregor Piatigorsky, the violinists Nathan Milstein and Erica Morini, and the opera diva Dorothy Maynor.

It was left to Hutchins and Borgese to line up the intellectual talent to be featured in the lectures and symposia that would interlard the concerts. To attract national attention a board of sponsors was created, with former President Herbert Hoover as chairman, and a membership that included Thomas Mann, the German Nobel laureate, who was then living in California, and Heinrich Brüning, the last of the pre-Nazi German leaders, who had found sanctuary on the Harvard faculty. But Hutchins insisted that those who were to actively participate in the program must have something more than the name recognition demanded by the

foundation's high-powered Chicago public-relations firm; their achievements must bear some relationship to Goethe's devotion to the natural
sciences and world literature, to humanity and the crisis of civilization, to
ethics and politics, and to the unity of mankind.

Hutchins rounded up a score of speakers and discussants who fitted
that bill.[25] The visitor with the highest scholarly reputation was José
Ortega y Gasset, the Spanish philosopher whose 1930 book *The Revolt of
the Masses* was considered a major contribution to the consciousness of
the age. But the public-relations men were also provided with a superstar
familiar to the general public.

Albert Schweitzer had become famous at an early age for his books
interpreting the Bible. His biography of Bach and his rendition of the
master's music as an organist made him a leading authority on the
composer. But at thirty he abandoned his flourishing career as a professor
at the University of Strasbourg, where Goethe had studied law, and went
off to the Belgian Congo to establish a hospital ministering to the natives,
many of whom were suffering from leprosy. By 1949 he had spent
thirty-six years at his isolated jungle outpost at Lambaréné, and though he
had never visited America, laudatory articles in *Reader's Digest, Life,*
and other publications had made him a popular hero:

> As is generally true of figures larger than life, Schweitzer's true
> worth was attacked and praised in extravagant terms. At one
> extreme he was called a bad doctor who arbitrarily threw modern
> medicines in the Ogowe River and who ran a hospital so filthy as
> to be unbelievable. It was also claimed that his hard work and
> self-sacrifice were really part of his search for publicity and
> power — or were his form of psychic escape from a Europe which
> disappointed him. At the other extreme, he was canonized as a
> saint or God's vice-regent on earth.[26]

In any case the tall, mustached, pipe-smoking Schweitzer was just
what the public-relations campaign required. To the more than two
thousand persons who came from all over the country for the twenty-day
Goethe Bicentennial, the most important aspect of Schweitzer's presence
was, as Norman Cousins wrote in *Saturday Review,* "the simple,
pragmatic fact that he was *there.*"[27] And the great man, like all the other
intellectual celebrities, mingled freely with the visitors who crowded the
little mountain town, many of them consigned to primitive accommodations in the homes of the natives or spartan quarters in dormitories used
by skiers in the winter season. "More even than his lectures, it was the
personality itself of Schweitzer," Elisabeth Mann Borgese wrote, "his

graspable kindness and goodness, the marks on all his manners, on his language, of his all-human experience, which radiated a spirit of world community."[28]

The program and the setting worked their magic, and Hutchins spoke to a sympathetic audience that filled the big tent on the Aspen Meadows when he delivered the Bicentennial's closing address on July 12, 1949. He ended with a quotation from *Wilhelm Meister,* the utopian work Goethe wrote near the end of his life, in which he envisioned a group of pilgrims establishing in America a community with a new political, social, and economic order:

> In *Wilhelm Meister* there is a speech which, it seems to me, is appropriately addressed to this assembly on this great occasion: "Since we have come together so miraculously, let us not lead a trivial life; let us together become more active in a noble manner! . . . Let us make a league for this. . . ."
>
> It is not too much to hope that the connections formed here in the past weeks by people from all over the world may be continued and strengthened and that through such meetings, correspondence, and publication, communication among men of good will may be established and may spread to other individuals and groups everywhere, perhaps even to those behind the Iron Curtain. Let us take heart in remembering that the Lord promised to save the city of Sodom if ten good men could be found in it.[29]

The connections did endure among some of those who attended the Bicentennial, and out of them grew the Aspen Institute for Humanistic Studies.[30] Although Hutchins presented Paepcke with a petition signed by many of those in attendance, urging that a summer program of concerts, lectures, and discussion groups be continued, he never again had an active association with the enterprise. The intellectual baton was passed to Mortimer Adler, who had no difficulty in persuading Paepcke that the Great Books could provide the core activity.

Adler's opening lecture the following summer, on "The Nature of Man," set the tone for group discussions conducted in the fashion of the Great Books classes. Henry Luce attended one of these two-week sessions and suggested they should be used to educate "the great unwashed" — corporate managers who could improve both their minds and their physiques and probably write it off as a business expense. The Aspen Executive Seminars began in 1951, and Adler became a permanent ornament of what James Sloan Allen labeled the Chicago *Bildungsideal,* the German word coined in the eighteenth century to denote the ideal of a fully developed and whole human being.

Somehow the peripatetic Hutchins had managed to keep up with his editorial duties with *Britannica,* which were now demanding so much of his time that he maintained an office at the company's downtown headquarters. As editor of the forthcoming set of Great Books, he worked with the advisory committee to determine revisions in the list compiled by John Erskine. It had not yet been determined that contemporary works would be excluded, so his reading was extensive and not always pleasurable. During a brief respite from his speaking engagements he wrote to John Nef from Bill Benton's Arizona retreat:

> I have read Joyce's *Portrait of the Artist as a Young Man,* Stendhal's *Armance,* D. H. Lawrence's *The Rainbow,* Lewis's *Pilgrim's Regress,* Nabokov's *The Real Life of Sebastian Knight.* . . . Only the first was worthwhile, though the second has some good lines in it, and the Nabokov book has a certain charm. Lawrencism is one of the things that [are] wrong with the world.[31]

He also exchanged views with Nef on the treatment of the classics to be included in the Great Books series:

> What you say about Montaigne — now that I have read through fifty-six of him — seems to me to be the answer, and a very penetrating one it is. There is an old saying about Robinson Crusoe, who had only himself to please. This is the spirit of post-mediaeval civilization; it is the spirit of Montaigne. Since this is what's wrong with the world, Montaigne is not what the world needs. I think he lends support to the doctrine, too, that all things are equally important; even in the hands of a master of style they are not. There are some great essays, but some are trash. My doctrinaire friends on the Great Books project will insist on printing them all. But if they will publish only one novel of Dostoevsky or Dickens why reproduce all of Montaigne?[32]

In late 1946 Hutchins conceded that he could no longer keep up the pace and asked Chicago's board of trustees for a leave of absence. But it was not only his professional life that had become intolerable. His marriage had reached a dead end, and he would use the sabbatical to establish grounds for divorce.

CHAPTER TWENTY-SEVEN

Chancellor
at Large

One evening in 1946 Robert Hutchins and Ralph Tyler were scheduled to address a group of Chicago alumni at North Park College on the northwest side, and it was arranged that they would drive out there in Tyler's car. When Tyler arrived to pick up the chancellor, a grim Hutchins met him at the door to inform him that he would have to go alone. In the background Tyler could hear Maude Hutchins threatening to call the police if her husband dared set foot outside.[1]

It was not an isolated incident. Maude's bouts of illness had become more frequent, and her mental distress more intense. "Maude is exactly the same, except as to spirits," Hutchins wrote his brother Francis. "In this respect she is very much worse. She has now been in bed for four weeks. I expect her to blow the roof off the house at any moment."[2] Her obsession with keeping her husband at her side had become an acute embarrassment for the meticulous Hutchins, who was likely to be confronted with a window-rattling tantrum any time he attempted to leave home in the evening.

By the end of 1946 his domestic situation had deteriorated to the point where Hutchins told his father he felt that he could no longer meet his responsibilities as chancellor:

I know you are right about what would happen to my public standing if I leave the University. The question is how much pain should I put up with for the sake of my public standing? Another question is, how can I keep my public standing anyway when I can't keep or make public engagements? I can write, I suppose, but that's all.

I agree with you about keeping faith with the public. That is why I have stopped making public engagements. I don't think I will last long if I have to have a nervous breakdown every time I am due to go out in the evening or go out of town — and then usually find I can't go at the last minute. And I don't see what in the world I can do about this situation. I have tried everything in the last ten years.

Perhaps I could make the compromise I suggested — remain as Chancellor and put the major responsibility for administration on the President. My principal objection to that is that I think Maude might do better if she left Chicago and returned to the region she was brought up in. I could do as much for the Britannica in New York as in Chicago.[3]

Hutchins's judgment that a change of scene might help Maude was apparently based on the fact that she had begun to achieve some recognition in avant-garde circles in New York; his feeling was that this might assuage her apparent resentment of his prominence. She was now attracting national attention in her own right. *Newsweek* ran a fetching picture of her discreetly posed to the rear of one of her sculptures. The caption explained the camera angle:

Sensation? Maude Phelps Hutchins, wife of the president of the University of Chicago, peers at her frank, life-size nude of a seventeen-year-old boy, which Chicago art circles confidently expected to create a sensation because of its frank realism. (Unfortunately for sensationalism, it was unveiled on D Day.) The nude is of greenish-blue bronze flecked with gold leaf and was commissioned by William B. Benton, vice-president of the university. It's at the Roullier Art Galleries along with portraits of Benton's two daughters.[4]

She had also begun to write poetry. As far back as 1933 Hutchins had taken note of her new interest in a letter to Mortimer Adler: "Most of these poems can never be printed because of their blasphemous and scandalous character. They seem to cover everybody in the United States from Mayor Cermak to Dr. Gilkey."[5] But publishing conventions were now relaxed, and her literary skills had improved. By the mid-1940s her poems were being published in *The New Yorker* and the distinguished Chicago magazine *Poetry,* and she was placing short stories and essays in the little literary magazines.

The pioneering New Directions Press published three of her novels and a collection of essays and short stories, and other publishers followed suit. Her theme was love, with an emphasis on sexuality that prompted reviewers to compare her work to the erotic writings of D. H. Lawrence and Henry Miller. She, perhaps with tongue in cheek, rejected the classification. When the Chicago police attempted to ban her book *The Diary of Love* in 1950, arousing a protest from civil libertarians that defeated the effort, she wrote, "I can assure you that I have no desire to shock, disrupt the morals or undermine the conventions of the general public. . . . My intention was purely artistic, and the subject matter innocence."[6] But an English magistrate didn't accept her protestation and ordered eight thousand copies of the British edition burned. This was sufficient to insure that the *Diary* went through five hardcover US editions and as many in paperback, as well as being translated into Danish, Italian, and German.

Maude Hutchins's "innocence," Maxwell Geismar wrote, "is highly sophisticated, sometimes ribald, and always entertaining. It is really a devilish kind of innocence." In a laudatory introduction to *The Elevator,* he described the collection of surrealist short stories as projecting a "psychological world that may even startle the conventional Freudians. Just as in the typical logic of dreams, the macabre may suddenly turn into the bawdy and hilarious, the comic into the grotesque or the ominous."[7]

Some of those who knew the Hutchinses attempted to read autobiography into these works and to identify their male characters with the author's husband, but the surreal style frustrated the effort. The books do reveal enough of her temperament and outlook to illustrate how different they were from those of the implacably rational Hutchins. The Freudian influence is evident. The dark father she never knew is idealized, and she contrasts his Cavalier Virginian background with that of the maternal grandparents who dominated her childhood and who, like the Hutchinses, were of New England Puritan stock. "I am afraid she is still resenting our early upbringing," her sister Frances, whose sympathies lay with Hutchins, wrote after the first novel appeared. "She is trying to get even with fate."[8]

In *Georgiana* Maude created a heroine who "became a sort of intellectual with a pathetic belief in the abstract. . . . A queer sort of Oedipus-search developed as she hunted with bandaged eyes, as it were, for a lover in later life who resembled the one she had never seen, which was to confuse her as we have suggested, and create a mistake which wasted a lot of her love-making time."[9] And Geismar said of one of her short stories, "One could pity the husband in this story since his wife is involved so inextricably with the phantom spirit of her true needs."[10]

The permissive doctrines of Freud were anathema to Hutchins, and as he had told Nef, he found the sensual works of Lawrence "one of the things . . . wrong with the world." It was perhaps inevitable that when the bemusement of youthful attraction dissipated, a man committed to ideas would find it impossible to continue to live under the same roof with a woman whose responses were primarily sensory. "My love for her has not survived the awful fights we had," he wrote his father.[11] Hutchins eventually terminated their long-standing differences by simply walking out and refusing ever again to communicate directly with Maude. As the marriage was breaking up she published in *Poetry* a poem entitled "Epigram":

> *Please listen*
> *Lift your head*
> *I am not happy*
> *Did you hear me*
> *I am not happy*
> *Now that I have said it*
> *How does it sound*
> *I am not happy.*[12]

In April 1947 Hutchins departed Chicago to spend a month in England on *Britannica* business. "I do not really see any hope in my domestic situation," he wrote to his mother and father. "I cannot face living with Maude again under any conditions that I can conceive of. I hope that while I am away she will decide to get rid of me. I am sure that she, the children, and I will have a better chance if we are not married."[13]

The hope was vain. "Bob has no case against me and the only way a divorce may be procured is for me to divorce him," she wrote to Will Hutchins.[14] Hutchins concluded that the best ground under the restrictive Illinois statutes was desertion, which either party could charge, and he decided to establish it by staying away from Maude for the required minimum of twelve months. In June he wrote his sympathetic father, who had accepted the inevitability of the divorce but urged him to continue as chancellor,

I have reached the same conclusion — that Maude's presence in the house should not determine the Fate of Higher Education. I have taken a room at the Shoreland [a nearby hotel] and shall operate the University from there and 20 N. Wacker Drive [Britannica headquarters] beginning 7 July. I am doing this on account of you and the entreaties of about twenty professors and trustees. I am also refraining from going to another state for a divorce. I will stay here as long as I can stand it.[15]

Later that month he wrote his father, "I do not believe that Maude has changed or can change. . . . If Maude does not seek a divorce soon I shall be compelled to seek one. I do not refuse to see her because I would break down. I refuse because it would be very painful for everybody and could not change my mind. If we had one conversation, another would be called for, and so on and on."[16] And in July he wrote John Nef, who had been besieged by telephone calls from Maude in her efforts to locate her husband,

I don't know how Maude found out where I was, but she succeeded in reaching me last night for the first time since I was away. She brought up all the guns and used all the ammunition. I simply said no, over and over again. After forty-five minutes of this I hung up. Her position at the end was the same as it was at the beginning. She was never going to make any move; the only thing that could be considered or discussed was my coming back.[17]

He became a moving target, staying out of Chicago as much as he reasonably could, shifting among the University Club and several downtown hotels when he couldn't. Walter Paepcke, who was having trouble keeping in touch with him in the course of their mutual effort to raise funds for the Goethe Bicentennial, was relieved when he accepted an invitation to occupy his Lakeshore Drive apartment while the family was away in Aspen. "THROUGH PINKERTON AGENCY FINALLY FOUND YOUR WHEREABOUTS," he wired Hutchins in October at the Ritz-Carlton Hotel in New York, and he was pleased when the reply revealed his friend to be his old wisecracking self: "PLEASE DO NOT WIRE ME AT THIS HOTEL. MY SOCIAL STANDING HERE IS ONLY A LITTLE LOWER THAN THAT OF A FRENCH COUNT. I WOULD NOT WANT THEM TO KNOW THAT I KNOW YOU."[18] There was something of the same touch in a letter he wrote Nef from England:

I had the [R. H.] Tawneys to dinner at Claridge's. The old man was as grand as ever; but she is as crazy as a bedbug. I think they will come to Chicago, but only in a year from now. . . .

> I have met the Prime Minister, the Lord Chancellor, and the Archbishop of Canterbury. I have talked with the Minister of Education and the Minister of Health. I have discussed the Press with the Provost of Oriel and fought with David Astor, who said, "I do not believe in peace." In short, I want you to know that I am a very big shot and that it is an honor for you to be acquainted with me.[19]

By March 1948 Hutchins had established grounds that would make it possible for him to sue or be sued. In the face of a complaint charging constructive desertion, drawn up by his lawyer and presented to hers, Maude finally agreed to initiate the divorce action. The financial settlement, however, posed problems.

At the end of his leave of absence Hutchins raised with the board the question of his resigning as chancellor or greatly reducing his duties. He took the position that if he continued on a full-time basis, he could not accept compensation from Encyclopaedia Britannica. He had always returned his outside income to the University, and in the three years from 1944 to 1947, when his salary was $26,000, this had totaled $47,930; in 1947 the amount was $16,590, more than ten thousand of that from Britannica. During his leave he had felt entitled to accept a salary of $25,000 as editor of Great Books, and Benton thought it should be continued. To John Nef, who as usual reacted with alarm when he heard that Hutchins might be leaving the University, he explained:

> I would like to go on with the Britannica, because there are some things I can do there which I can't do at the University. . . . (If the Britannica is not "worthy of my mind," the University isn't either, because the trivialities of University administration exceed anything I have met with this year.)
> I suggested to Harold [Swift] and Laird [Bell] that I might go on at the Britannica and re-define the duties of the chancellor as the guy who dealt only with those matters which were to be presented to the Board. Harold said I could discuss that only with a committee, and Laird said that people would say that I wanted to keep a good job at the Britannica and run the University, too. I made no reply to Harold — he took my breath away. To Laird I said that I did not want to run the University, that I had resigned, and that what I wanted to do was resign again. I had made my proposal because it had been represented to me that it would not

be good for the University to have me resign. He said he would think it over.[20]

The board reached another Solomonic judgment. Hutchins would resume his full-time status, the $25,000 annual payment offered him by Britannica would go to the University under the 4E contract, and his salary from the University would be increased to $45,000. "The Board of Trustees at its meeting on Thursday last expressed its sympathy for me in my domestic trials and said that it would 'back me up' if I wanted to sue for divorce in Illinois, even if the suit were contested," Hutchins had written Nef back in March.[21] The trustees had kept their promise in the most tangible way. Without the salary adjustment Hutchins could not possibly have met his wife's demands for alimony and child support.

In July the divorce was granted, giving Maude custody of their two younger daughters. Hutchins wrote to his father, who had expressed concern over his financial plight:

I don't see the financial future very clearly; but my total annual income before taxes is $50,000 — after alimony and child support it is $32,600. That is still a lot of money. For some months, until I have paid the lawyers ($6,000) and Maude's vacation and moving expenses ($5,000), I may have to eat a little less — but that will do me good. I still own the Island and $7,500 worth of stock.

I am planning to move into the house as soon as Maude moves out of it, which I think will be the 24th.[22]

That hope too was dashed. Maude stayed on until her presence posed a problem for the board, which delegated a diplomatic lawyer member, James Douglas, to resolve it. He did so amicably, or at least without public outcry, and Maude and her younger daughters moved to Southport, Connecticut, where they spent fourteen months as houseguests of her friend Helen Benton before she found an acceptable place of her own in that elegant exurb. Many years later Hutchins observed to his old friend that he owed him a debt he could never repay. "For what?" Douglas inquired. "You got Maude out of the house," Hutchins replied.[23]

During his sabbatical Hutchins completed work on the summary report of the Commission on Freedom of the Press, and this produced a strain on another long-standing relationship — that with his Yale classmate Henry Luce. Time, Inc., had funded the three-year study, but, unhappy with Hutchins's final draft of the Commission's findings, Luce refused to put up the money for publication of *A Free and Responsible Press,* which defined the term and its scope in a subtitle: "A General Report on Mass Communication: Newspapers, Radio, Motion Pictures, Magazines and Books." Bill Benton footed the bill, and in the spring of 1947 the little 139-page volume with the big title was issued by the University of Chicago Press.

Luce, who had honored his commitment to keep hands off their work, made no public comment, but he sent a letter to the members of the Commission to indicate his disappointment in the result. Hutchins replied,

> I am very grateful for your generous letter to the Commission and to me. You are the ideal benefactor.
>
> In addition to the regrets which I have already expressed orally, I have only to add that I am sorry that very difficult personal problems in the past three years have prevented me from giving the Commission the kind of leadership it ought to have had and the kind which you were entitled to expect from me.[24]

Although Hutchins presented the report in his usual terse, pointed style, it was actually a reworking of earlier drafts by a member of the Commission, Archibald MacLeish, a former Luce editor and assistant secretary of state and Librarian of Congress, and its staff director, Robert D. Leigh, the president of Bennington College. In its final version the report represented the composite view of the thirteen distinguished scholars who had been assembled by Hutchins from a roster of those he considered particularly knowledgeable about, and concerned with, the issues at hand.[25]

The study focused narrowly on the role of the agencies of mass communication in informing the people about public affairs — the function that had prompted the framers of the Constitution to guarantee them freedom from government interference. "Another study could have been made dealing with the interrelationship between the American press and the American culture," Hutchins wrote. "This would have analyzed the present state of American culture and emphasized the dramatic change by which the agencies of mass communication have become a part of the American environment, affecting the thought and feeling of every citizen in every department of his life."[26]

The Commission deliberately avoided conventional research, and its citation of the shortcomings of the press was familiar enough. The advertising-based commercial character of newspapers, magazines, and radio, and the attendant quest for maximum audiences, left them prone to yielding to the demands of private interests and public pressure groups. The concentration of ownership had effectively removed competition while increasing profits, to the point where the proprietors of the media were now in the upper-income brackets and tended to reflect the views of the privileged classes.

Even within the press it was generally agreed, though not often publicly admitted, that the mass media upon which a great majority of the people depended emphasized the exceptional rather than the representative, the sensational rather than the significant. "The result," Hutchins wrote, "is not a continued story of the life of a people but a series of vignettes, made to seem more significant than they really are."[27] The defenders of the press tended to treat this as inevitable, regrettable but fairly harmless, a deficiency that had to be offset by other agencies, notably educational institutions.

The Commission attacked this proposition head-on. The obligation of the press to fully and fairly inform its readers and listeners about public matters was inherent in the First Amendment, and if it was failing to meet it, the question was raised as to whether its performance could any longer be left to the unregulated initiative of the few who controlled it. The new technology of mass communication and the concentrations of ownership it made possible had created a new phenomenon: "These instruments can spread lies faster and farther than our forefathers dreamed when they enshrined freedom of the press in the First Amendment."[28]

But having raised the specter of government regulation as a warning, the commission declared against it: "We do not believe that the fundamental problems of the press will be solved by more laws or by government action."[29] On the contrary, the report recommended that the constitutional guarantee of freedom of the press be broadened by extending it to cover radio, where it had been limited by federal regulation attendant to allocation of broadcast licenses, and to motion pictures, which had been plagued by censorship imposed by state boards of review. The main function of government should be to keep the channels of communication open and to facilitate the creation of new ones.

The question, then, was what could be done to improve the performance of a diverse group of privately owned agencies that had demonstrated a lack of capacity for self-regulation or even self-criticism. "The public makes itself felt by the press at the present time chiefly through pressure groups," the Commission found. "These groups are quite as likely to have bad influence as good."[30] But it might be possible to bring pressure to bear in the public interest if the people had regular access to an informed, independent appraisal of the performance of the media by an agency with sufficient prestige to command attention and promote widespread discussion.

Hutchins's imprint could be seen in the recommendation for the establishment of a permanent commission, created by philanthropy and independent of the government and the press, which would report annually on the performance of the media. It would investigate instances of press lying, "with particular reference to persistent misrepresentation of the data required for judging public issues."[31] Its continuing effort would be to define reasonable standards by which the performance of the media could be realistically judged by both practitioners and their audiences.

The reaction to publication of the report by what was promptly dubbed the Hutchins Commission demonstrated the validity of one of its key findings — that the press consistently suppressed or distorted criticism of its own performance. "No other institution could have been criticized by so distinguished a group as Chancellor Hutchins' commission without having its indictment land on the front page," observed Louis M. Lyons, curator of Harvard's Nieman Foundation.[32] The most complete report, three and a half columns in the *New York Times,* was buried on page 24. Many newspapers, including those of the Hearst chain, ignored it altogether. Others topped brief extracts from wire-service coverage with misleading headlines.

A few newspapers provided approving editorial comment, generally echoing Walter Lippmann, who endorsed the proposal for continuing outside criticism by citing the traditional claim that the Fourth Estate was the watchdog of the other three, and inquiring, "Who watches the watchman, who inspects the inspector, who polices the policeman?"[33] The great bulk of newspaper and magazine comment was adverse, at its mildest dismissing the Commission's findings as the work of airy-fairy college professors who ignored the reality of the communications marketplace. A few editorial writers thought they detected subversion, and the *Wall Street Journal* even caught a whiff of Communism.[34]

The report, as *Newsweek* noted, raised every one of Colonel Robert R. McCormick's hackles. The *Chicago Tribune's* opening blast appeared under the headline "A FREE PRESS (HITLER STYLE) SOUGHT FOR U.S.; TOTALITARIANS TELL HOW IT CAN BE DONE." Frank Hughes, a hatchet man regularly assigned to traducing the University, was given paid leaves of absence to crank out a book, *Prejudice and the Press: A Restatement of the Principle of Freedom of the Press with Specific Reference to the Hutchins-Luce Commission.*

"If there is a disposition in some important quarters of American opinion today to question freedom of the press, to seek to 're-define' it, and to make it more 'accountable,' these efforts can come only from the apostles of despotism," Hughes declared in the opening chapter of his 640-page work.[35] In inimitable *Tribune* style he went on to explain why this was so:

> The philosophy to which Chancellor Hutchins pretends, containing . . . the basic authoritarianism of the Prussians, with a dash of Plato, and much Aristotle and Aquinas interpreted by Adler, according to Marx, is a curious mixture. . . . It cannot be labeled definitely as Communist or as Nazi, although it contains elements of both.[36]

Couched in less extreme terms, the charge that the Commission advocated an unwarranted and dangerous abrogation of First Amendment rights was echoed by more responsible publications — this despite the fact that the report specifically opposed any form of government intervention. This fallacious notion became imbedded in the mythology that surrounded Hutchins's public image, and his response to it over the years was a major item in what he called his antiabsurdity campaign.

In 1955 he reminded the American Society of Newspaper Editors that its president had said that the members of the Hutchins Commission were left-wing professors without experience in the newspaper business, so that nothing they said could be of any importance, though it might be dangerous. "At the meeting of this society in 1947, to which I expected to be invited to receive your congratulations, the only thing that saved me from condemnation was the expressed unwillingness of your committee to 'dignify' me by such action."

> All over the country you attacked the Report. I hope you will read it sometime. But I fear you won't. I shall quote a passage from it that will give you the main idea: "If modern society requires great agencies of mass communication, if these concentrations become so powerful that they are a threat to democracy, if democracy cannot solve the problem simply by breaking them up — then those agencies must control themselves or be controlled by government. If they are controlled by government, we lose our chief safeguard against totalitarianism — and at the same time take a long step toward it."[37]

The idea of an independent agency created to appraise press performance was never to be realized in the terms the Commission prescribed. But forty years after publication of the report, opinion polls showed that its prophecies were being borne out, and distrust of the media was so pervasive that elected officials of all persuasions, from the President down, were advancing their careers by regularly bashing journalists. In 1988 Richard Harwood, in taking over the duties of in-house ombudsman at the *Washington Post,* wrote what amounted to a reprise of the Hutchins Commission's conclusion:

> . . . the ethics and standards of journalism are a morass of contradictions and hypocrisies. We render each day moral judg-ments on the rest of humankind but insist on divine rights of immunity for ourselves. . . . We — newspapers and other media enterprises — have acquired considerable wealth, influence and perhaps real power in this century. We are ripe for reex-amination.[38]

Robert Hutchins's grandfather, the Reverend Robert Grosvenor Hutchins, established the family's presence at Oberlin in 1886 when he filled the pulpit at the Second Congregational Church and became a trustee of the College. (*The William and Francis Hutchins Library, Berea College*)

Left to right: Francis, William, and Robert Hutchins, when they were enrolled in grade school at Oberlin. (*The William and Francis Hutchins Library, Berea College*)

Left to right: Robert, Will, Anna, and William Hutchins, Jr., on the porch of their house at 95 Professor Street, just off the Oberlin campus. (*The William and Francis Hutchins Library, Berea College*)

William (*left*) and Robert at the Allentown, Pennsylvania, Fairgrounds, where they trained with the Oberlin unit of the US Army Ambulance Corps. (*The William and Francis Hutchins Library, Berea College*)

Robert's Yale graduation picture. The yearbook for the class of '21 gave his nickname as ''Hooch.'' (*Yale University Archives*)

Newspaper photographers were at the railroad station to greet the ''boy wonder'' and Maude when they arrived at the beginning of his tenure as president of the University of Chicago. (*University of Chicago Archives*)

Hutchins is welcomed to the Chicago campus by Acting President Frederick Woodward (*left*) and Board Chairman Harold Swift. (*University of Chicago Archives*)

James Henry Breasted, the noted Egyptologist, introduces the new president to the treasures in the University's Oriental Institute. (*Yale University Archives*)

Hutchins sent his Yale classmate William Benton an autographed copy of this picture taken when he was awarded an honorary degree at Lafayette College in 1936, saying he looked "like a retired second-rate Shakespearean actor gazing into his past." (*University of Chicago Archives*)

Maude Hutchins and Mortimer Adler examine a copy of *Diagrammatics,* a collection of her stylized silverpoint drawings of nudes, for which he contributed the text. (*University of Chicago Archives*)

Hutchins discussed issues of war and peace on the first network radio talk show, NBC's "Round-table of the Air," which originated on the Chicago campus. He is shown here in 1944 with Floyd Reeves (*center*) and John T. McCloy. (*University of Chicago Archives*)

In a commencement speech at the Asheville School in 1944, Hutchins delivered a derisive account of his army career in World War I to a graduating class awaiting the call for service in World War II. He is shown here at lunch with his brother William, the school's headmaster. (*William and Francis Hutchins Library, Berea College*)

Will and Anna Hutchins at the time of Will's retirement as president of Berea College. He was succeeded by his son Francis. (*William and Francis Hutchins Library, Berea College*)

Hutchins's expression presages the end of his marriage to Maud in this photograph taken at a University function in 1946. (*University of Chicago Archives*)

In 1949 Hutchins married
Vesta Orlick, shown here
in the receiving line at
the president's residence
on the Midway. (*Univer-
sity of Chicago Archives*)

Hutchins with the Har-
vard philosopher William
Hocking at the 1949
Goethe Bicentennial,
which launched the As-
pen Institute at the Colorado resort. (*University of
Chicago Archives*)

Hutchins is mobbed by students after his farewell address upon his retirement from Chicago in 1951. (*Stephen Lewellyn*)

Hutchins with Paul Hoffman (*center*), chairman of the Ford Foundation, and William Benton, chairman and publisher of Encyclopaedia Britannica, at the dinner launching the Great Books of the Western World series. (*Encyclopaedia Britannica*)

Hutchins chaired Encyclopaedia Britannica's board of editors from the time of its purchase by William Benton in 1943. By 1965 the initial group of University of Chicago scholars had been expanded to include leading intellectuals from the United States and Great Britain. *Standing, left to right:* Charles Swanson, the president of Encyclopaedia Britannica, Howard Goodkind, Thomas Park, David Owen, Richard McKeon, Philip B. Gove, Warren Preece, Clifton Fadiman, Ralph Tyler. *Seated, left to right:* Sir Geoffrey Crowther, Sir William Haley, editor in chief, Hutchins, Mortimer Adler, and William Benton. (*Encyclopaedia Britannica*)

The estate that housed the Center for the Study of Democratic Institutions in the hills above Santa Barbara. Hutchins called it El Parthenon.

Hutchins with his lifelong friend Justice William O. Douglas, who became chairman of the board of the Center. (*Leinie Schilling*)

The author (*left*) with
Hutchins and Rexford
Guy Tugwell at the Center's conference table.
(*Lon Calamar*)

Hutchins, with Linus
Pauling, holds a bust of
Pauling presented to the
Center by one of his admirers. (*Eric L. Hayes*)

Pickets outside the gates on Eucalyptus Hill. The local chapter of the John Birch Society campaigned to close down the Center through the removal of its tax exemption. (*Lon Calamar*)

Hutchins confers with the author, then the executive vice president of the Center, on the terrace of El Parthenon. (*Eric L. Hayes*)

The Center's series of great international convocations brought together leading intellectuals and important political figures. In 1973, on the eve of his retirement, Hutchins was still the dominant presence when ''Pacem in Terris III'' convened in Washington.

Hutchins with Henry Kissinger. (*Leinie Schilling*)

Norton Ginsburg, the dean of the Center, with Hans Morgenthau. (*Leinie Schilling*)

Hutchins with Morris Levinson, chairman of the board of the Fund for the Republic. (*Leinie Schilling*)

Vesta Hutchins with George McGovern. (*Leinie Schilling*)

Hutchins with Nelson Rockefeller. (*Leinie Schilling*)

Hutchins greets his successor, Malcolm Moos, the former president of the University of Minnesota. After a little more than a year, the board demanded Moos's resignation and drafted Hutchins to resume the office. He was president when he died in May 1977. (*Art Waldinger*)

CHAPTER TWENTY-EIGHT

"A Return to 'Normalcy' "

Robert Hutchins, who had been the youngest major university president when he took office, now found himself the oldest chief executive in terms of tenure. If not yet a gray eminence, he was recognized as the most prominent or, depending upon one's point of view, the most notorious educator in the land. In November 1949, on the twentieth anniversary of his inauguration, the board of trustees, noting that he had kept its members in a "healthy state of irritation," unanimously adopted a resolution praising him for the changes he had wrought on the Midway. Despite Hutchins's differences with Henry Luce, *Time* marked the anniversary with its second cover story on him. And to his embarrassment, the American Tailors Guild placed him third on its annual list of best-dressed men for his "learned look."

The look was captured in the color portrait on *Time*'s cover, which depicted him in a neatly striped gray suit set off by a bow tie. There were lines on the imposingly high brow, and the wavy, middle-parted dark hair was touched by bands of white at the temples. The story recounted the controversies that had left those marks, marveled that he had survived them, and concluded that while he usually marched alone, he had left his imprint on higher education:

> Today, many U.S. colleges now require their students to take a broad general curriculum in their freshman and sophomore years. It is not a curriculum of Great Books, which most educators still

regard as a slightly romantic notion. . . . But at least the idea of a basic and common education had become the fashion. Could Hutchins claim the credit? Says he: "There is nothing new in talking about a liberal education. There are traces of it all over the map of history." What he had done was to give it the sweeping approval of a great university while many another topflight school was only nibbling at the idea.

He had done something more. "The academic administrators of America," he once remarked, "remind one of the French Revolutionist who said, 'The mob is in the streets. I must find out where they are going, for I am their leader.' " Hutchins' idea of an administrator's job was different. Since the days of the great Chicago Fight, Hutchins, as perhaps no other university head of his time, has brought the basic issues of education into the open forum. "The worst kind of troublemaker," says he with vast approval, "is the man who insists upon asking about first principles." It is that sort of trouble Robert Hutchins has been making for the last twenty years.[1]

Hutchins was constitutionally incapable of resting on his laurels, but there was a marked reduction in his work load. When a man arrives at the office early, stays late, and turns up on weekends, he once observed, you may admire his devotion but you are also entitled to wonder about his home life. In his case there had been a sea change; in May he had become a happily married man, so much so he felt guilty about it. "Now that my domestic life is peaceful and happy, I am in danger of degenerating into a vegetable," he wrote John Nef. "And though in this condition I should be less dangerous to others, I should probably be even less satisfactory to myself than I have been hitherto."[2]

The thirty-one-year-old bride, Vesta Orlick, had entered his life as the secretary and editorial assistant assigned to him at the Britannica office. "I think you will like Vesta. She is five feet tall, very pretty, pleasant and smart," he wrote Thornton Wilder, who promoted the marriage even though he was not on hand to play matchmaker. He thanked his old friend for his "generosity in letting me talk with you about my private life. I have been following your instructions, with the greatest benefit to my soul."[3]

They were married at the Chicago home of the bride's mother, with Will Hutchins officiating. In attendance were Anna Hutchins, Franja, and Barbara, Vesta's seven-year-old daughter by a former marriage. The nuptials had been carefully kept secret, but word had leaked to the press. The newlyweds managed to elude the reporters and photographers who were staked out at the railroad stations and airports and to make their way unmolested to White Sulphur Springs. Although they found they were sharing the Homestead with successive conventions of Aluminum Makers, Cast Iron Pipe Manufacturers, and Investment Bankers, Hutchins was in such an amiable state, he confided to Nef, that "these gentry really didn't bother us at all."[4]

Upon their return he found that his internal skirmishes at the University had descended from the rarefied level of academic controversy. During his brief unmarried state he had offered no demurrer when it was suggested that the old residence on the Midway ought to be touched up a bit:

> In the pre-Vesta days of winter it was decided that the Chancellor's House should be cleaned, brightened, etc. this summer, a modest decorating job. Then they thought they would brighten the place up by putting windows in the west wall of the library and remodeling the side entrance. As things went on, they thought of more and more that ought to be done, with the result that the damned place is now uninhabitable. It has always been uninhabitable in a manner of speaking. Now it is literally so. And the side entrance looks like the front of Grauman's Chinese Theatre.[5]

Hutchins had always professed a profound disinterest in matters involving the University's buildings and grounds, but Vesta was a collector of antiques and a natural-born decorator. She dealt with the University's architect and the workmen in a fashion that prompted Walter Paepcke to confer on her Napoleon's title, "the little corporal."

Naturally energetic and gregarious, she regarded the social duties of the chancellor's wife as a pleasure, not a burden. But just before the wedding she learned of an ailment that periodically limited her activities. After she fainted while shopping for her trousseau, her doctor discovered that she had a defective heart valve. In those days this could not be corrected by surgery, and while it was not life-threatening, it frequently required her to curtail her physical activity. Nevertheless, she enjoyed her role as the chancellor's consort and was sorry to leave when Hutchins decided the time had come to move on.

Now that he was able to give some thought to his professional career without the distractions of a failing marriage, Hutchins began to seriously consider the job offers that continued to come his way. His ideas about the critical role of education in a democratic society, and its importance in preserving the peace, had not changed, but he had concluded that he could advance them more effectively outside a university setting.

At first he had been intrigued by the suggestion that he might head the United Nations Educational, Scientific, and Cultural Organization when it was established in Paris. But on closer examination he found UNESCO incapable of living up to the challenges it faced. In 1948, speaking at the University of Frankfurt, where at his behest Chicago had initiated a postwar faculty-and-student exchange, he itemized the polyglot organization's inherent deficiencies:

> UNESCO is now at once too small and too large. It is too small because German, Italian, and Russian cultures are not represented in it. It is too large because it is attempting too many things in too superficial a way. It has placed great emphasis on what are called the mass media of communication; but such emphasis is surely wrong when we do not know what to communicate or do not understand what is communicated. It probably would have been better for the peace of the world if the radio, the telegraph, and the motion picture had never been invented; for they have been used to transmit hatred, vilification, and propaganda, rather than understanding. UNESCO has emphasized the abolition of illiteracy, when the principal need of the world is something to read that is worth reading. Or perhaps I should say that what the world needs is to have its population desire to read and understand its classical heritage.[6]

In late 1949 Bill Benton turned up with a proposition that had the possibility, at least, of meeting Hutchins's requirements. Now a US senator from Connecticut, Benton had been approached by emissaries of the Ford Foundation to serve as a go-between in their efforts to persuade Paul Hoffman to become the head of the suddenly enriched philanthropy.

In order to retain control of the motor company, the Ford family was in the process of turning over vast stock holdings to what had been a modest, essentially charitable operation. Henry Ford II, who was now in charge, considered Hoffman, whom he had known in his role as president of the Studebaker company, the ideal man to supervise the creation of what amounted to an entirely new philanthropy destined to become the nation's richest. Hoffman, who had earned high public regard as administrator of the Marshall Plan to rehabilitate the war-shattered nations of Europe, indicated to Benton that he would be willing to end his government service and take on the Ford assignment — if Hutchins could be persuaded to join him as associate director, and if Henry Ford could be persuaded to accept Hutchins.

Benton was immediately successful in the first part of his mission. The ebullient Hoffman, who took an expansive salesman's approach to the world's problems, was a Chicago trustee, and he and Hutchins had established a warm personal relationship. At the end of December Hutchins forwarded a letter through Benton, responding to Hoffman's request that he offer his thoughts on how the new enterprise should be organized and what its objectives should be. He concluded,

> I keep thinking about you and this Foundation all the time, not merely because I have a deep and abiding interest in and admiration for you, but also because I think that what the Ford Foundation does can decide the fate of the things I have been most concerned about all my life. Don't let me bother you — but, if I can be of any help in any way, please let me know and let me try.[7]

In February Benton wrote Hutchins,

> I spent an hour and a half at breakfast with Henry Ford II this morning, and I'll give you more of the background when I see you. Most urgent now is to tell you that he is expecting you to call him and have lunch with him the next time you are in Detroit. You are recommended to join Paul Hoffman in heading up the Ford Foundation but it was felt that you would bring enemies along with you! I assured Henry Ford that no one would have enemies when he had his hands on half a billion dollars. He doesn't seem to realize the enormous impact himself. My own suggestion is that you don't wait too long on a Detroit visit.[8]

The visit was a success. On December 19, 1950, Hutchins informed his parents by telegraph that he had accepted the Ford Foundation appointment. Will Hutchins was himself now a foundation executive; upon turning over the presidency of Berea to his son Francis, he had joined the Danforth Foundation, which had been established in St. Louis by the founder of Purina Mills. "I don't imagine this relationship will help my reputation," he had written Robert. "I feel sure that with some of the Berea people, the idea will prevail that now at the last of my life I am selling my soul to the devil."[9] Robert, who had urged his father's acceptance, added to the announcement of his own entry into the field, "Hope you can find it in your hearts to forgive me."[10]

On the same day he informed the University Council that he was resigning from his post as chancellor. "There was a profound emotional expression when the announcement was made," President Colwell reported to the board of trustees.[11] One of Hutchins's most tenacious critics, the political scientist Leonard White, said on behalf of the old guard, "Although we didn't all agree with Mr. Hutchins's ideas, we can all agree that he always held us to the highest standards."[12] A resolution urging Hutchins to reconsider was prepared by the Committee of the Council and signed by 636 faculty members. Similar expressions came from the deans and administrative officers and from the students. But the deed was done; the trustees had accepted Hutchins's resignation effective June 30, 1951, and in January they approved an immediate leave of absence.

More than a desire not to speak ill of the departing was evident in the responses of leading campus figures to the request by *The University of Chicago Magazine* for valedictory comments on "The Hutchins Influence." Robert Redfield said he could not describe his feeling through anecdote and detail: "If I were a metaphysical poet I would write a metaphysical poem about it. He made me believe in the effort toward excellence."[13]

Charles B. Huggins of the Medical School, who would later be awarded a Nobel prize for his cancer research, wrote:

Under this great humanist the Sciences flourished as never before in our University. The infant medical school underwent its growing pains and its childhood diseases and grew to sturdy manhood with the passive acquiescence and the magnificent remoteness (as is the habit of so many fond fathers) of the Chancellor. Like Art, Science cannot be directed; the Chancellor assembled a splendid Faculty, provided them with every facility and Nature did then take its course so that many of his projects were eminently successful.[14]

Dean F. Champion Ward of the College also cited the remarkable combination of unstinting support and freedom of action that Hutchins accorded his lieutenants: "It is easier to contend that the present College would not exist had it not been for Mr. Hutchins' support of it than to say whether or not it would have had its exact character if Mr. Hutchins had not also left it alone."[15]

Harrison Brown of the Department of Chemistry and Nuclear Physics noted that "the entire scientific world has gained as a result of Hutchins' leadership. He will be greatly missed by the scientists — even by his most severe critics.'' The venerable Charles E. Merriam paid tribute to the chancellor's record as a foremost champion of academic freedom. Dean Edward H. Levi of the Law School gave Hutchins credit for leading the way toward the kind of fundamental reconstitution of legal education he had advocated at Yale:

> The 1937 program made the *philosophy of law* an essential part of the law curriculum. It inaugurated a bold attempt to integrate economics with the law. It placed renewed emphasis on training in legal craftsmanship through the development of a tutorial system to supplement the case method. Most of the features of the new program since have been adopted and adapted in other major law schools. Significantly, many of the law schools which opposed the rhetoric of the Hutchins leadership have been most active in the new development.[16]

''No one else I have known could arouse so much admiration and loyalty, and willingness to support him to the last ditch,'' wrote Hutchins's successor as chancellor, Lawrence A. Kimpton, who had worked with him in various administrative posts:

> Under Bob Hutchins you got a post-graduate course in adminis- tration, but it was administration of the most inspiring kind. It looked for the answer that was principled and true; it repudiated the expedient and assumed the necessity of moral courage. He alone has the resources which made his particular kind of administrative methods workable. On that level he can not be imitated. But on the higher level of the goals and motivations, all of us can aspire to his kind of leadership.[17]

It appeared from this fulsome tribute that in naming Kimpton the trustees had followed the dictum of Laird Bell, the successor to the retired Harold Swift as chairman, who said that in selecting a new chancellor, the first priority should be to find one who wouldn't ''undo Hutchins.'' Kimpton had been a member of the Philosophy Department and had served in administrative posts at Chicago from 1943 to 1947. In 1951 Hutchins brought him back from Stanford and made him vice president in charge of development, and while he refused to offer any advice on the choice of his successor, he had put him in line for consideration. Dean Ward of the College described how the selection method worked in practice. The Kimpton appointment, he said, was a prime example of a process within search committees that might be called the Reverse High Jump. . . . With the bar set at seven feet, candidates of great distinction are found barely wanting. Months later, a tired and torn committee resignedly unites in support of a far less distinguished aspirant who barely clears five feet. . . .

As a member . . . I found the hunger for normality very strong within the committee. With a few wistful exceptions the members, trustees and faculty alike, were like children released from the regime of a demanding school teacher. Hutchins had made the trustees read and discuss the Great Books and in bad times as well as good had expected them to defend the University's integrity as "a center of independent thought." . . . The trustees found this duty honorable and even at times exhilarating, but also a bit strenuous and lonely. There was too much that was hard to explain at one's club.

In their turn, many members of the research faculties had never wanted to be different and for some years before Hutchins' departure had plied Kimpton, as Dean of Faculties, with their discontents. The two chancellors could hardly have differed more from one another. Hutchins was wont to put first things first but nothing second (for example the need to restore the neighborhood), while Kimpton put second things first, for lack of clear priorities of his own. "Don't make me chancellor," he was rumored to have said while the search was on. "I don't have any convictions."[18]

As had Hutchins in his day, Kimpton inherited an unbalanced budget and a critical need for additional income. "We have led a fine expansive life in recent years, but now we have fallen, if not on evil times, at least on economical ones, while our resources catch up with our ambitions," Bell said.[19] The situation was complicated by the fact that Chicago's vast black ghetto had expanded into areas of Hyde Park that had been left behind by white migration to the suburbs, and now extended to the borders of the campus.

Kimpton held Hutchins personally responsible for both conditions, even though the situation at Chicago was hardly unique. All the major universities found that the postwar demands made upon them outstripped their financial resources, and those located in inner cities, as in the notable case of Columbia, faced comparable environmental problems occasioned by the encroachment of black ghettos. Hutchins, always reluctant to invest educational money in bricks and mortar, may very well have given the matter of redevelopment of the Hyde Park neighborhood a lower priority than it deserved. "Academic housekeeping has ever failed to hold my attention," he said in presenting his successor to an alumni assembly.[20]

But the issue raised by the incursion of blacks posed a moral as well as a financial problem for Hutchins. The first reaction of the University's administration had been to meet the threat by buying up vacant housing and supporting the efforts of neighboring property owners to invoke restrictive real-estate covenants that forbade the sale of residential property to blacks. In 1937 a troubled Hutchins wrote his father,

There is little doubt that if the University does not get behind these agreements, it will become in time an island in the midst of the black race. . . . On the other hand, as the descendant of a long line of Oberlinites, I am temperamentally opposed to these agreements, and opposed to having the University take any part in upholding them. I finally come to the conclusion, however, that since they are upheld by the courts of this state and since the University would probably have to go out of business if it were surrounded by Negroes, there is nothing to do but say that we propose to use all honorable means to protect ourselves from inundation. I should be glad to have the opinion of the president of an abolitionist college.[21]

The occasion of his disagreement with the board on the issue, he later recalled, was the closest he ever came to resigning, and he probably would have done so had the US Supreme Court not made the matter moot by declaring such covenants unconstitutional.[22] But the moral issue arose in another form when the federal government launched its program of public housing and left local authorities free to require racial segregation, as those in Chicago did. Funding for the kind of massive urban-renewal projects that permitted the University under Kimpton to lead the way toward converting Hyde Park's crime-ridden slums into an integrated middle-class neighborhood did not become available until late in Hutchins's tenure.

Kimpton's private criticism of Hutchins, sharply at variance with his public praise, went far beyond holding him guilty of misfeasance in matters of finance and the neighborhood environment. After the restraints of civility had been lifted by his retirement from the University and from the corporate positions he subsequently held, a corrosive bitterness colored his responses to questions put to him in writing in 1976 by George Dell, who was then working on a biography of Hutchins:

> Bob Hutchins had alienated almost everyone in the entire community of Chicago, with a few conspicuous exceptions. He was one of the most thoroughly disliked persons I have ever known, and this dislike carried over to the University. . . . With a very few exceptions on the faculty their morale was at a very low point, and they thoroughly disliked Hutchins and the way he ran the institution.[23]

Kimpton claimed there had been a qualitative decline in all the divisions of the University: "When he placed a high priority on a department, or indeed a division, it seemed to go down in quality." This was also true of the graduate and professional schools: "Medicine was the single exception; it remained strong, but this was because Dr. Coggeshall was a very strong dean and would brook no interference in his administration of the unit." He considered the independent faculty that Hutchins had finally achieved for the College to have been a fundamental mistake; the College, in his view, was "a kind of queer and unusual place. Every queer and unusual student who disliked athletics and the normal outlets of younger people was attracted to the Hutchins College. . . . The Great Books course was a joke, and Hutchins knew it was. When I used to kid him about it, how superficial and shallow it was, he would say, 'Well, it's better than getting drunk,' and I think that's a pretty good summary of it. It certainly made no intellectual contribution." Kimpton concluded his indictment:

> This is rather a harsh criticism of Bob Hutchins, I'll admit, but I have very little respect for him as an academic administrator. He almost ruined the University of Chicago, and would have had he remained a few more years. Nothing that he did at the University had any permanence except for his [divisional–professional school] organization, which he never claimed as one of his contributions. . . . Nothing that he did at the University, I repeat, had any degree of permanence, except for the financial headaches, the neighborhood deterioration, and the faculty embitterment.[24]

There is little support for Kimpton's bill of particulars in the record, and few, if any, of the critics Hutchins left behind at the University went so far in denigrating his academic achievements or his character. Kimpton himself, by design or default, assured the impermanence of his predecessor's reforms. Without Hutchins's rallying presence there was no effective force on the faculty or the board of trustees to resist the "undoing" that Laird Bell had warned against. The principal victim was the College.

Just before Hutchins's departure, when the tests of mastery of subject matter that were widely used for admission to graduate schools indicated that seniors in the College ranked well above students who received specialized instruction under standard curricula, Dean Ward asserted, "In the nation, 'general education' is at last in vogue. Its principles bid fair to become the operative educational theory for the remainder of this century." But he was soon disillusioned:

> Three years later, on the darkling plain of the University's inter-faculty Council, my colleagues and I found ourselves struggling to salvage some part of the University's curriculum of general studies and some degree of authority over what remained. I had not yet understood the peculiar mixture of shallowness and volatility which marks discussion of the practice of education in America. . . .[25]

In May 1953, over the unanimous opposition of the dean and the College faculty members on the council, the College was "normalized." "I had the chancellor's assurance that he would publicly oppose a formula which reduced the College's scope to two years," Ward wrote, "but someone else got to him after I did."[26] The reduction was made, and the independent status of the College faculty was ended. In 1985 Donald Levine, the current dean, summed up the dismantlement that followed:

> One by one, most of the great staff-taught general education courses . . . were dissolved. The independent Board of Examiners was disbanded. The comprehensive examinations as a substitute for course credit disappeared. The custom of carefully constructed course syllabi disappeared. The notion of sequential work in the disciplines faded away. And the linchpin of the Faust-Ward College . . . the awarding of the B.A. degree after a program of general education coextensive with the old junior college, was pulled out.[27]

Other bold experiments initiated in the Hutchins era suffered a similar fate. Like Champ Ward, Rex Tugwell departed when he found that there was no longer support for the pioneering program in planning that in its brief span had produced some of the leading experts in the field.[28] The experimental Committee on Industrial Relations suffered a similar fate, and other innovative interdisciplinary programs were also cut back.

The turnabout was the product of Kimpton's conviction that the only way to repair what he considered to be Chicago's adverse public image was to revamp the University so that it would conform to the patterns then prevailing in contemporary institutions. In doing so he rejected the admonition that Hutchins was surely directing at him when he said in his farewell address at the annual trustee-faculty dinner,

> The most dangerous aspect of public-relations work is its reflex action: we find that the public does not like something about the University; our temptation is to change this so the public will like us. Our duty is to change public opinion so that the public will like what the University does, and if this cannot be immediately accomplished, to hold out against the public until it can be.[29]

Such a policy would have required the convictions Kimpton said he didn't have. He apparently was without inner defenses against the kind of sniping the educational experimentation at Chicago had always drawn, as in the notable case of A. J. Liebling's *New Yorker* series ridiculing the midwestern metropolis as the "Second City." Liebling described the Hutchins College as "the greatest magnet for juvenile delinquents since the Second Crusade," and suggested that "if Dr. Lawrence A. Kimpton, who not long ago succeeded Hutchins as chancellor of the University, decides to accept candidates out of the third grade instead of the tenth, he will probably be hailed on the Midway as an even greater innovator."[30]

Hutchins never replied to any of Kimpton's charges, and he consistently refused to comment even generally on the changes in the University. ". . . After I left I have not thought that it was proper for me to deny even the most absurd reports. And nobody would believe me anyway," he wrote Ward. "My mistake was that I thought I was a successful evangelist, when I was actually the stopper in the bath tub. I thought I had convinced everybody, when all I had done was block a return to 'normalcy.' "[31]

CHAPTER TWENTY-NINE

"How Firm
a Foundation . . ."

obert Hutchins often quoted a favorite line from Walt Whitman: "Solitary, singing in the West, I strike up for a new world." As a tribute to William Rainey Harper, and to denote his own concept of how the first president's vision should be carried forward, he once proposed it, to no avail, as an appropriate motto for the University of Chicago. It was certainly in his mind when he traveled to California early in 1951 to take up his duties as associate director of the Ford Foundation.

Paul Hoffman had stipulated that the reconstituted philanthropy should be headquartered in Pasadena, where he maintained his residence. This small city adjacent to Los Angeles had been created as an elegant suburb by wealthy Easterners seeking a salubrious climate, and its genteel propriety was in sharp contrast to the booming metropolis next door, with its mix of movie moguls, glamorous film stars, faith healers, freebooting promoters, and staid migrants, still streaming in from mid-America to populate the bungalows that sprang up among the orange groves.

Pasadena seemed an incongruous site for a major foundation whose counterparts were domiciled in New York, where they could tap into the cultural mainstream that presumably had its headwaters there. But Hoffman did not have a conventional foundation in mind. "I told Henry [Ford] before I took the job that I'm a militant and maybe he didn't really want me," he said. "I don't want to be just a banker, watching over a tightly guarded repository from which dollars could be cautiously withdrawn from time to time to meet the needs of well-established and 'safe' charities."[1]

Hoffman was first and last a salesman, one who had risen from automobile dealer to become sales manager and ultimately chief executive of a major motor company. The selling job he had done on Henry Ford II and the Foundation's board[2] produced an agreement that present employees of the Foundation would be left behind in Detroit. It would be up to the new director to organize a staff to dispose of more than a hundred million dollars already on hand, and an income that would soon provide half that amount each year.

Knowing his friend's freewheeling proclivities and recognizing the potential of the drawing account at his disposal, Hutchins had reason to believe that even if he was not quite alone, he was at last in position to strike up for a new world. There were three other associate directors, but as the officer responsible for education and peace, Hutchins would recommend the allocation of a major share of the Foundation's resources. His colleagues were H. Rowan Gaither, Jr., a young San Francisco attorney who had served as a consultant to the Foundation; Chester C. Davis, a St. Louis banker who had headed the Agricultural Adjustment Administration during the New Deal; and Milton Katz, a Harvard Law School professor who had been Hoffman's deputy at the Economic Cooperation Administration, established under the Marshall Plan.

Katz and Gaither had not yet relocated to Pasadena when the officers assembled in January to begin blocking out the new program. For some weeks Hoffman, Hutchins, and Davis worked out of a one-room office at the ornate old Huntington Hotel, with one telephone among them. "I think it was the high point of the Ford Foundation," Hutchins recalled, "because we had maximum communication. . . ."[3] The heady formative days were described by Dwight Macdonald in a *New Yorker* series that was later collected in a book, *The Ford Foundation*:

> . . . It was an atmosphere reminiscent of Franklin Roosevelt's "hundred days" in 1933 — one of crisis and opportunity, doom and enthusiasm. Both the international situation and the Foundation's own tax problems called for large spending quickly. No one knew when, or if, the Korean war would explode into a world war; reforms had to be swift and expensive if they were to make any difference. "We all felt the world had to be saved by next Tuesday," a Foundation veteran of that expansive era has recalled, adding professionally, "We had a crisis orientation." There was no lack of confidence that the crisis could be dealt with.[4]

The architects of the new Ford Foundation were provided guidelines in a 125-page "Study Report" that had been commissioned by Henry

Ford in 1948. Prepared by Gaither, it was a distillation of the advice received from consultation with more than a thousand experts from a wide range of disciplines. Ford called it "one of the most thorough, painstaking, and significant inquiries ever made into the whole broad question of public welfare and human needs."[5] And it delighted Hutchins because it called for *no* spending on medicine, health, welfare agencies, or the natural sciences — the favorite beneficiaries of the conventional foundations — and warned against the "scatteration" that had diluted the impact of other foundations' grant-making as they dribbled out small sums to a wide variety of supplicants.

Five "areas of action" were recommended: "The Establishment of Peace," "The Strengthening of Democracy," "The Strengthening of the Economy," "Education in a Democratic Society," and "Individual Behavior and Human Relations." In his foreword to the Foundation's 1951 annual report, Ford could have been echoing Hutchins when he noted that "these areas are all concerned with men's relationships with one another. It is apparent that the prime threat to human welfare today is the danger of war and the attendant sense of strain throughout the world. Society needs to find ways of reducing such tensions and of deepening the understanding among men everywhere."[6]

The urgency with which Hoffman and his associates approached the implementation of the guidelines was not dictated solely by their sense of the parlous condition of the postwar world. The Foundation's tax-exempt status required that it expeditiously spend the income from its capital, in this case Ford Motor Company stock, which had a market value of more than half a billion dollars. Hutchins came up with a device for getting rid of the accumulated money in a hurry while decentralizing the bureaucracy that would be required for the disbursement of such a huge sum. He described it in a memorandum to Gaither:

> . . . It is likely that the Trustees of the Ford Foundation can function best as the directors of a holding company. When a field is clearly defined, when it is large, and when the Foundation has decided to remain in it for a long time, consideration should be given to creating an independent corporation to deal with it. This arrangement brings to the assistance of the Officers and the Board the strength of persons specially interested and qualified in the field. The greater the independence of such groups, the greater their sense of responsibility is likely to be. In the long run better people can be recruited for the boards of operating companies than for advisory committees. . . .

The Trustees should approve the general programs and policies of the independent corporations. They should review the work of these corporations often enough to know whether or not it is in harmony with the policies and program of the Foundation. If it is, they should leave methods of execution largely to the boards of directors of these corporations.[7]

The Hutchins scheme was the basis for the operating principle announced in the Foundation's 1951 annual report: "When the officers have decided, with the approval of the Board, to embark upon a program, they have looked for the agency to carry out the program and have given it the money with which to do the work. When they have been unable to find such an agency, they have created one."[8] During the first year of the new regime, three independent corporations were established: the Fund for the Advancement of Education, to deal with institutional education at all levels; the Fund for Adult Education, to operate in all other educational areas; and the East European Fund, to foster programs aimed at easing tensions created by the Iron Curtain that now divided the continent. Others would follow.

From 1951 to 1954, by which time both Hoffman and Hutchins had departed from the Foundation, Ford grants totaled $186,000,000, with $89,000,000 going for education, Hutchins's area of action, and $54,000,000 for the international programs, in which Hoffman was primarily interested. Hutchins's influence could be seen in the selection of the trustees and officers of the operating Funds. He saw to it that their boards were made up of men and women from the very top drawer of the American establishment and that the officers shared his commitment to the liberal arts.

Clarence H. Faust, who had been dean of the College at Chicago, was summoned from Stanford to head the Fund for the Advancement of Education, and the trustees included two of Hutchins's closest friends from the University of Chicago board, James H. Douglas, Jr., and Walter Paepcke, as well as Barry Bingham, the president of the *Louisville Courier-Journal* and a trustee of Berea, which was now headed by Francis Hutchins; Roy E. Larsen, the president of Time, Inc.; Paul Mellon, the president of the Old Dominion Foundation; and Walter Lippmann, the influential Washington columnist. C. Scott Fletcher, the president of the Fund for Adult Education, had been Paul Hoffman's sales manager at Studebaker and later headed Encyclopaedia Britannica films; one of the first beneficiaries under his regime was the Great Books Foundation, which received grants totaling $826,000.[9]

* * *

Hutchins's proposal for the establishment of separate Funds was intended to prevent the Foundation from developing a massive bureaucracy of its own, and to a large extent it served that purpose. Nevertheless the central staff continued to expand; an administrative headquarters was located in a modest building on Green Street, and the executives were provided with offices in the converted bedrooms of Tuerck House, an elegant beige mansion surrounded by palm-lined grounds complete with swimming pool. When Sam Goldwyn, the motion-picture magnate, gazed upon this splendor, he said, "If you have to give away money, this is a wonderful place to do it."[10] Hutchins, who described the Ford Foundation as a large body of money surrounded by people who wanted some of it, dubbed the headquarters Itching Palms.

The Hutchins family found an equally elegant, if somewhat less commodious, abode in nearby San Marino, a WASP enclave with one of the highest per capita incomes in the nation. The arrangement he made with Paul Hoffman allowed Hutchins to feel at home there; the Foundation agreed to pay him the same salary — $45,000 — that he had been receiving at the University, with an increase to $60,000 to cover the loss of his living-expense allowance when his resignation from Chicago became effective on June 30. And he then became free to receive the $25,000 Britannica stipend that he had previously assigned to the University.

Vesta and Barbara delighted in their new home, and the older Hutchins daughters came for long visits. He had many old friends in southern California and made new ones among the considerable colony of artists and intellectuals. These included Aldous Huxley, whom he met at Ethel Barrymore's house. When the University of Southern California put on "an evening in honor of Aldous Huxley," the chosen speakers were Hutchins, the film director George Cukor, and Christopher Isherwood, the poet. Perhaps the most remarkable of Hutchins's new companions was Henry Miller, the uninhibited author of works so sexually explicit they were frequently banned. Hutchins had only mild reservations when a magazine writer asked for an appraisal of his unconventional friend:

> The things that have always struck me about Henry Miller are his innocence and his faith. The first of these qualities leads him to gaze in open-eyed wonder at the world and tell you exactly how it looks to him and what he thinks about it. The second means that he does not concern himself about things that worry ordinary people. . . .
> The word for Henry as a friend is *endearing*. His faith has

been justified. I'm afraid that no general conclusions can be drawn from this fact; anybody who knows Henry Miller would do anything in the world for him. I cannot recommend his faith to anybody else, because there is nobody else like him.[11]

The peripatetic Hoffman was away from Pasadena much of the time, and Hutchins's irreverent humor more or less set the tone at Tuerck House. He found a companion in jest in Martin Quigley, who came over from Earl Newsom and Company, the New York public-relations firm retained by Henry Ford, to take charge of the Foundation's information office. Quigley's talent for satiric verse matched Hutchins's, and his work on the annual report for 1952 prompted the creation of "Philanthropic Stew," a poem that cited most of the Foundation's major projects in the jargon the newly fledged "philanthropoids" seemed unable to avoid:

> *Take a dozen Quakers — be sure they are sweet and pink —*
> *Add one discussion program to make the people think;*
> *Brown a liberal education in television grease*
> *And roll in economics, seasoned well with peace.*
> *Crush a juvenile delinquent (or any wayward kid)*
> *And blend it with the roots of an Asiatic's id;*
> *Draw the aromatic juices that brains of pedants yield*
> *And generously pour into a mediocre field.*
> *To realize an impact, continuing and broad,*
> *Mold a public servant from a bureaucratic clod.*
> *Keep an eye upon the press! Give it now and then a stir*
> *But gently, bless you, lest you bruise the publisher!*
> *Dice teachers' education, and in a separate pan*
> *Mix a sauce of brown technicians from India-Pakistan*
> *And pour it over seed corn in a pilot demonstration,*
> *One that has been flavored with peel-off implication.*
> *Take a board of good conservatives, the nicest you can buy,*
> *And mix them with the white of a beaten liberal's eye;*
> *Now render the conditions of a peace that's just and free*
> *And mix them with insistence on national sovereignty;*
> *Skin the newest talent, and when you've scrubbed it clean*
> *Smother in the leaves of a high-brow magazine;*
> *Grind up a scholar's study of the diverse creeds of men*
> *In a mass communicator until it's mush. And then*
> *Mix everything together; and when the fire's hot*
> *Pour a little Russian exile into the steaming pot.*

Sweeten with publicity all the serving bowls —
(By the way, this recipe serves two billion souls) —
Garnish with compassion — just a touch will do —
And serve in deep humility your philanthropic stew![12]

Hutchins came forth with a Christmas carol set to the tune of "Adeste Fideles":

How firm a Foundation, we saints of the Lord,
We've built on the faith of our excellent Ford.
We've laundered and lighted the Trustees' Report
And left for California,
And left for California,
And left for California,
The place to resort.

How fine the Foundation has been for E.C.A.
And for Hutchins, for Davis, what those boys get ain't hay.
What more can we do than for them we have done?
Way out in Pasadena [three times]
They bask in the sun.

How firm a Foundation; we've Funds by the score.
Have you an idea? We'll establish one more.
We smile through the smog; (some might say that we smirk);
Out here in Pasadena [three times]
The Funds do the work.

How fine a Foundation; we are for peace:
We live peaceful lives, and we hope wars will cease.
We've heard mankind cry, and we've answered the call:
We're out in Pasadena [three times]
Away from it all.

How firm a Foundation; we've three times the dough
And ten times the brains that any other can show.
The hell with Rockefeller and Carnegie, too.
We've left for California [three times]
The hell with you.[13]

When Quigley petitioned for more space for his information office, Hutchins replied with a handwritten note:

> *In my Father's house are many mansions.*
> *Yes, but are there enough to provide for necessary*
>   *expansions?*
> *Besides, I want to make sure that my mansion is every bit as*
>   *good as yours and if possible a lot more spacious.*
> *This is the reason why when the space problem comes up*
>   *you'll find me just a little bit tenacious — not to*
>   *say loquacious.*[14]

These works were intended only for the amusement of the Foundation staff, but the first two were excerpted by Macdonald. Contrasting the mood of the Pasadena operation with that prevailing after the Foundation relocated to New York, he wrote, "It is, for instance, quite impossible to imagine any of the high officers of the Foundation today — or for that matter, any of the sober professionals who run the other big foundations — dashing off the sort of verses with which the amateurs of the Hoffman-Hutchins era relieved their souls on occasion."[15]

Despite the fun and games, a great deal was accomplished. It was a busy time for Hutchins; the Foundation received some 25,000 grant applications in 1951 and by the end of September had managed to dispense more than $23,000,000. Some of these requests were obviously from crackpots, and a majority of the others could be summarily disposed of under guidelines intended to preclude most traditional philanthropic activity. Almost all of the thirty-five grants made in the first year met that test.

Most were related to the Foundation's international concerns — providing for agricultural extension service programs in India and Pakistan, giving assistance to refugee agencies in Europe and to those handling Russian immigrants in the United States, supporting relief agencies in war-battered Germany, and the like. These programs were the responsibility of the other associate directors, but there was an obvious overlap with Area I, "The Establishment of Peace," and with Area IV, "Education in a Democratic Society," both of which had been assigned to Hutchins.

He justified his sometimes resented involvement in overseas activities in a memorandum circulated to the other associate directors:

> My responsibilities in this area have been non-economic and non-political. Perhaps the most comprehensive name for them would be cultural.
>
>   We have taken the view that misunderstanding is usually

involved in disputes between nations and have assumed that, if peoples of different traditions could understand one another better, war would be less likely. Hence Intercultural Publications, Inc., the Redfield project, the support of the American Friends Service Committee, the exchanges with [the Universities of] Frankfurt and Berlin, and a variety of relatively minor expenditures of the same kind.[16]

He pointed out that in keeping with Quaker tradition, the American Friends Service Committee was engaged in a peace program, pure and simple. International Publications was incorporated under Area I because it had been created by the Foundation to facilitate the exchange of ideas and artistic and literary productions as a means of improving international understanding. This was also true of Robert Redfield's program to develop conceptual frameworks for the characterization and comparison of the world's five great cultures:

> If it is admitted that these are important undertakings, the next question is whether it is likely that Redfield can carry them out.
> I have never heard it suggested that he was incompetent. I have heard it said that he was dangerous, which turns out to mean that he has been interested in World Government. I have heard the charge that he was a friend of mine, which should debar Messrs. Faust, Fletcher, Laughlin, Tyler, Shils, Levi and Berelson, who are as close, or closer friends of mine, from further support.[17]

The list could have included another old friend. When he was preparing to leave Chicago, Hutchins assured Hoffman that he was not going to be seeking berths for former colleagues who would be disaffected by his departure: "The only person who is going to insist on leaving is Mortimer Adler. We have been associated so long — even before we came to Chicago — that he cannot imagine any other situation. Since I like him and admire him tremendously, I feel the same way. But certainly there is no way in which he can be connected with the Foundation. . . ."[18] Adler did come to Pasadena to conduct a protracted seminar for the Foundation trustees on the meaning of freedom, but Hoffman summed up their reaction by gently telling Hutchins, "I think you overestimate the appetite of the board for Mr. Adler's messages."[19] A way was found to take care of him at one remove, however, through the Fund for the Advancement of Education.

The Fund made a three-year grant of $640,000 to Adler's new Institute for Philosophical Research, which he established in San Francisco. Clarence Faust explained that a necessary objective of the Fund was to "achieve clarity about the functions of education. This involved us in a consideration of the nature of man and society. The grant was given to work out the basic problems." To Adler this meant a "dialectical examination of Western humanistic thought," looking to a *"Summa Dialectica"* comparable to Thomas Aquinas's *Summa Theologica* of medieval thought.[20] He set the year 2002 as the deadline for its completion, but the Fund's grant ran out after the production of a mimeographed *Research on Freedom: Report of Dialectical Discoveries and Constructions* and an accompanying volume of bibliography. The grant was not renewed.

Although there were inevitable tensions among strong-willed men working on a more or less coequal basis, Hutchins thought his relationship with his associates remained reasonably good. But with Paul Hoffman frequently absent, and with Hutchins directly responsible for by far the largest initial grants — $7,154,000 for the Fund for the Advancement of Education and $4,800,000 for the Fund for Adult Education — there was no doubt that he was the dominant figure at Tuerck House.

His primary interest was in the two education Funds, both of which were initially established in Pasadena. This was reflected in the Fund for Adult Education's emphasis on liberal education in all its discussion programs, as well as in those devoted to the Great Books. Included was "the problem of peace, or international relations, as one of those through which the American people can learn to free their minds and come to more enlightened conclusions about the urgent issues that confront them."[21]

Just as at Chicago he had encouraged experimentation with the educational possibilities of the developing broadcast media, he now supported a grant of $1,200,000 as start-up money for a Television-Radio Workshop. In the hands of talented refugees from the commercial networks, the Workshop went on to pioneer in educational programming for children and to develop the first significant cultural venture in commercial TV — the honors-laden "Omnibus," which lit up the "Sunday afternoon ghetto" where the networks dumped starveling public-service programs on the assumption that the potential audience was too small to be saleable to mass-market advertisers. With the suave Alistair Cooke as the master of ceremonies, "Omnibus" used this more or less abandoned network airtime to present handsomely produced artistic, musical, and dramatic offerings that were a long cut above standard TV fare, generally aimed at the lowest common denominator of audience taste.

The Television-Radio Workshop was the creation of an experienced broadcaster, James Webb Young, who served as a consultant to the Foundation. When, with the creation of the Fund, it was included among Hutchins's responsibilities, he profoundly shocked the executive producer of "Omnibus." Robert Saudek, who came over from the American Broadcasting Company, had a distinct sense of déjà vu in his first exposure to Hutchins. He expected a high-minded, "onward and up-ward" injunction to hold to the highest artistic and intellectual standards. Instead Hutchins bluntly told him he would judge the program solely on the basis of its success in attracting advertisers.

It took Saudek a while to understand that Hutchins was reminding him that the program was intended as a demonstration project to prove to skeptical network executives that high-quality programming could attract enough advertising support to pay for its production costs and turn a profit. If "Omnibus" could survive only with a continuing subsidy, then it was a failure on its own terms.[22] This in fact turned out to be the case, and after Hutchins's departure the Foundation ended its support. But before it went off the air, "Omnibus" pioneered production techniques and set artistic standards that still serve those TV producers who occupy the little high ground left in what came to be called a great artistic wasteland.

The major project of the Fund for the Advancement of Education reflected Hutchins's grand design for restructuring American education. He had long deplored the training in classroom technique that dominated the curricula of most teacher-training institutions, at the expense of courses in the subject matter the graduates would teach. The salvation of Western civilization, he believed, required that potential teachers, whether at the primary, secondary, or college level, master the liberal arts before undertaking specialized training. Faust, who shared that view, initiated a bold new program in teacher education when he took over as president of the Fund.

Financial support was provided for a broad sample of teachers' colleges that agreed to initiate a four-year liberal-arts curriculum for their students, plus a fifth year in which they would receive vocational training through part-time teaching under faculty supervision. To demonstrate that this type of internship could meet the requirements of the agencies that issued credentials for public-school teachers, a statewide experiment was conducted in Arkansas, where all of the state's fifteen teacher-training institutions agreed to participate. To broaden the test, similar programs were initiated in the teachers' colleges at Wayne State, Temple, Goucher, Yale, and Harvard.

The program turned out to be as controversial as any that bore the

Ford imprimatur. "The close-knit hierarchy of professional educators has welcomed this easy access to the mysteries of teaching about as enthusiastically as the Roman augurs would have welcomed a proposal to simplify the interpretation of entrails," Dwight Macdonald wrote. "The American Association of Colleges for Teacher Education at first denounced the Program as 'an eighteenth-century model,' and other educators have seen in it 'a return to the middle ages.' "[23] Alvin Eurich, the executive vice president of the Fund, was hanged in effigy when he went to spread the gospel to an Indiana teachers' college.[24]

The Fund also moved to further Hutchins's idea of combining the last two years of high school with the first two years of college to provide a liberal-arts education that would culminate in a bachelor's degree. A study of the possibilities was funded, and by way of demonstrating its feasibility, a multimillion-dollar "pre-induction" scholarship program was provided to enable gifted students to skip the last two years of high school and enter college. This gained fairly widespread support, since it relieved the pressure on overcrowded schools caused by the postwar baby boom and also permitted students to complete their education before they were drafted for service in the Korean war.

The skeptical Macdonald seemed to agree that "Hutchins' whole career, from one rather jaundiced point of view, can be described as that of a bright young sophomore who becomes a college president without ever ceasing to be a sophomore."[25] But in summing up the activities of the Fund for the Advancement of Education under Hutchins's influence, he wrote,

> When the Fund was first started, someone sourly observed that "Hutchins is trying to buy what he couldn't sell." The witticism seems strained. For one thing, some of Hutchins' main ideas — such as his advocacy of more humanistic and fewer "service-station" or vocational college courses and his conservative counter-revolution against the extremes to which some progressive educators have carried John Dewey's theories — were by no means his alone, although he expressed them more provocatively than others did.[26]

But as the controversy that always attended Hutchins's activities in the field of education began to mount, the merits of his proposals made little impression on the public relations–oriented trustees of the Ford Foundation. When Henry Ford II began to share their apprehensions, Hutchins's days were numbered.

CHAPTER THIRTY

Trouble
in Paradise

With the demise of old Henry Ford in 1947 and of his widow in 1950, the Ford Foundation acquired nonvoting stock in the motor company with a market value far greater than that of the endowment of any other philanthropy. To maintain family control, the shares of voting stock were distributed among the children of Edsel, the Fords' only child — Henry II, Benson, William Clay, and Josephine.

Upon the death of his father in 1943 young Henry had been summoned home from wartime service in the Navy and put to work at Ford headquarters. But at twenty-five he seemed an unlikely candidate to head the giant company. He had enjoyed the pampered upbringing usually accorded the children of the very rich — attendance at select private schools, including Hotchkiss, and a playboy interlude at Yale, where he failed to receive a degree. "In adult life," observed Robert Lacey, a biographer of the Ford family, "Henry Ford II was to display a happy aptitude, when not working, to enjoy himself 200 percent."[1]

But the happy-go-lucky fellow dubbed "lard ass" by his prep-school classmates acquired a strong-willed wife who took a dim view of his wayward life-style. Anne McDonnell, a handsome New York debutante whose family money was old as well as plentiful, was a devout Catholic who attended six-o'clock mass every morning. To win her hand Henry had to abandon his Protestant heritage, and she saw to it that he took seriously the instruction he received from the redoubtable Monsignor

Fulton Sheen. Back home in Grosse Point, Henry knelt beside her each Sunday at Saint Paul's.

By 1945 Henry II had shouldered aside the hired managers who expected to run the company after Edsel's death and persuaded his reluctant grandfather that he was now ready to take over. He had his work cut out for him. Although the company had piled up substantial earnings through wartime government contracts, it had fallen far behind General Motors and Chrysler in the passenger-car market it had once dominated.

Young Henry recognized that the company badly needed an infusion of design and production talent, but recruiting was made difficult by a public image tarnished by the reactionary personnel policies old Henry had encouraged in order to keep the auto workers' unions in check. "It is time management realized," Walter Reuther of the United Auto Workers said in 1945, "that human engineering is just as important as mechanical engineering."[2]

Henry II took this seriously, and Earl Newsom, the company's public-relations counsel, adopted "human engineering" as a slogan to signify the changes being wrought by Ford's twenty-eight-year-old chief executive. The Newsom firm prepared no fewer than eighteen drafts of the speech that marked Henry's first public appearance in his new role. "Labor unions are here to stay," he told four thousand members and guests of the Society of Automotive Engineers. "We of the Ford Motor Company have no desire to 'break the unions,' to turn back the clock."[3]

At first, Newsom and his associates saw the Ford Foundation as a prime asset in their campaign to refurbish the company's image. The announcement of Paul Hoffman's appointment as head of the newly enriched philanthropy had been met with general approbation in the media, as had the Foundation's initial programs of overseas aid and its bold new approach to education. But the McCarthy era was dawning, and the Foundation also had a commitment to support work in the field of civil liberties and civil rights. It was not long before a covey of right-wing commentators began charging that using the fruits of capitalism to further such a cause was un-American.

"Un-Americanism" also served as a device in the campaign by the Republican Old Guard to head off the internationalists who were pushing for the nomination of the World War II hero Dwight Eisenhower. Since it was difficult to challenge the patriotism of the smiling general, the right-wing press unleashed its hatchetmen on his leading supporters — and Paul Hoffman was one of the most conspicuous of these. As Eisenhower headed for election, the Hearst columnist Westbrook Pegler "exposed" a plot he claimed had denied the Old Guard's champion,

Senator Robert A. Taft, the vice-presidential spot on the ticket. The alleged conspiracy centered on the activities of the Ford Foundation under Hoffman and Hutchins, but it branched out to include "the Time-Life propaganda empire under Henry Luce; and the political and propaganda works of William Benton, Senator from Connecticut."[4]

Hoffman, according to Pegler, only pretended loyalty to the GOP, as he had demonstrated by insulting Taft supporters so as to estrange them from the Republican ticket and improve the chances of the Democratic candidate, Adlai Stevenson. This was a prelude to the cabal's machinations in Connecticut:

> The senatorial "contest" in Connecticut between the mock-Republican Luces and their crony, Bill Benton, left the natives puzzled but faintly aroused at last. Luce planted Benton in the State Department under the Roosevelt reign and his wife had waged a regular campaign by dining with Senator Arthur Vandenburg when he was still a true American, which resulted in his conversion to her husband's so-called bipartisan foreign policy. Vandenburg fell as other well-known men have fallen for Mrs. Luce's baby stare.
>
> In this year's queer developments, Luce took up Eisenhower and the Connecticut Republican machine delivered the delegation to him at Chicago. . . .[5]

No matter how farfetched, this kind of derogatory mention of the Ford Foundation was perceived by nervous salesmen of the motor company's products as being bad for business, and their concerns were communicated to the home office. W. H. Ferry, the Newsom vice president whose responsibilities included both the Ford family and the Foundation, soon found himself functioning as a damage-control officer.

Ferry was as much a product of Detroit's automobile aristocracy as Henry II. His father, Hugh, the president of the Packard Motor Company, was one of Detroit's reigning tycoons. He had been a brilliant student at Dartmouth, a Latin teacher and football coach at Choate, and a cub reporter in Detroit before he shocked Grosse Point by joining the CIO Political Action Committee as its public-relations director.

As in the case of Robert Hutchins, the persona that Ferry presented to the public tended to vary according to the eye of the beholder. Dwight Macdonald described him as genial, the sort of hail-fellow who was known by his nickname, Ping, to "old friends of at least thirty minutes' standing."[6] Victor Navasky titled a laudatory *Atlantic Monthly* article on Ferry "The Happy Heretic."[7] To Thomas C. Reeves, who dealt with his career in his book *Freedom and the Foundation,* he was "mordant, iconoclastic, quarrelsomely outspoken."[8] He was to display all of those qualities in the years of association with Hutchins that followed his first exposure to him in Pasadena.

Ferry's initial problem was to allay Henry II's apprehensions about the Foundation's freewheeling operations, and the only practicable means of doing so was to try to put a respectable gloss on the positions taken by Hoffman and Hutchins, so as to minimize public controversy. Protecting and improving the Ford family and corporate image, after all, was what the Newsom Company was paid to do.

Henry II always insisted that his concerns were with the Foundation's management style, not with the ideology of its most conspicuous executives. He complained about Hoffman's protracted absences from Pasadena and about the influence this conferred on Hutchins, whose two education-oriented Funds were now receiving more than half of the allocated money. "We felt that that was too big a proportion to be spent on a very special kind of education and that we were in danger of having the bulk of our income committed in advance," Ford said. "I guess we gave it to him because he was the fastest talker. But I didn't like the idea of being a rubber stamp for his ideas."[9]

It was perhaps inevitable that the sheer force of Hutchins's commanding personality would bruise the ego of an insecure board chairman who couldn't face him without being reminded of his own youth and limited education. "I think Henry was appalled at the speed with which the Foundation was sliding out from under him," one observer said. "He was willing to retire to the sidelines after it got well launched, as Carnegie and Rockefeller had done, but he wasn't prepared to become emeritus in two years."[10]

But a great deal more than a clash of personalities was involved in the tensions that began to surface in the second year of the Pasadena operation. Hutchins's long battle for educational reform had endowed him with enemies who had influence with members of the Foundation board and their retainers. Although he was soon to be converted, Ferry acknowledged that he "came on him too with a great deal of suspicion and hostility."[11]

Ferry said he had acquired his jaundiced view from a Briarcliff neighbor, Harold Taylor, the president of Sarah Lawrence College and one of the educators who wound up in the Dewey camp in the great debate over curricular reform. He recalled that when he told him of his new assignment, Taylor responded, "This is a great opportunity. Tell Paul Hoffman that the best thing he could possibly do for the welfare of this nation is to give Hutchins a million dollars on condition that he live in Afghanistan the rest of his life, and get him the hell out of here.''[12]

Ferry found another Hutchins adversary in a key position on the Foundation board, this one motivated by self-interest as well as philosophical differences. Clarence Faust encountered an even more pointed reaction from the same recalcitrant trustee when he took over as head of the Fund for the Advancement of Education:

A person who'd been most unhappy about the appointment of Bob Hutchins was Don [Donald K.] David of the Graduate School of Business at Harvard. I think Don, who had long been a member of that small original board of the Foundation and a great friend of the Fords, had a feeling that this was going to be just a great Harvard resource, a kind of Harvard endowment, and he knew full well that if Hutchins were in charge of it it wouldn't be turned over to Harvard. When I came into the Foundation he called me and said he hoped that I would never do anything that Bob Hutchins favored, and I told him I couldn't make any such promise and that I thought Bob's ideas were very good. But he made it perfectly clear that he didn't think anything the man did was good and this was one of, I'm sure, the deep tensions in that earlier period and I'm certain that it gave Paul some unhappiness.[13]

Ferry thought trouble also arose from a source even closer to Henry Ford II. Traveling to Pasadena with the Fords for one of their first state visits, he found that Anne was being taken in by the anti-Hutchins propaganda that was then appearing in the right-wing press. He assured her that when she got to know him she would be satisfied that the suggestion that he held pro-Communist views was absurd. The first meeting between the two came at a dinner party at Hoffman's house. Robert Lacey used Ferry's version of the encounter as the sole example cited in his book *Ford: The Men and the Machine* to explain the rift between Henry II and Hutchins:

"How nice," she said, flashing her brightest smile, "to meet someone who knows something about education. Henry certainly doesn't."

She was very hopeful, she said, that thanks to the presence of Hutchins at the Foundation, "we'll get some attention to the thing that I'm interested in . . . the problems of Catholic education, mainly in the city of Detroit."

Ping Ferry had tried to warn Hutchins before the Fords' arrival that the young couple had taken public criticism of the family foundation greatly to heart, and how it would be important for Hutchins to make an effort to charm Anne. But the Hutchins way was not the way of compromise. The former chancellor of the University of Chicago knew what he thought about education, and he launched into a lecture on all the failings of the Catholic school system, and how it was not the job of the Ford Foundation to bail it out. Anne Ford was rich. If she was worried, she could take care of that sort of thing herself.

"I told her . . . ," Hutchins would later recount with glee, "to hell with it — no business of ours." And for good measure he treated the young Catholic mother to a lecture on birth control.

"It was the kiss of death for Bob and Paul," remembered Ferry.[14]

In the oral-history interview for the Ford Foundation Archives from which Lacey embroidered this account, Ferry, who did not hear any of the purported exchange, indicated that he thought that whatever Hutchins said had been in the bantering mode that he usually employed on social occasions. But if so, he added, the irony escaped Anne, who came away with the impression that he hated Catholics and Catholic education and resented her because she was rich.

Vesta Hutchins, who was present, recalled nothing that could have justified such a conclusion. A deliberate insult to an apparently well-meaning lady would have been out of character for the courtly Hutchins, and a man who had often been pilloried as a neo-Thomist was hardly prone to deliver a blanket denunciation of Catholicism. But whatever had caused it, Martin Quigley, the public-information officer, soon recognized that Anne Ford's hostility toward Hutchins and her powerful influence over her husband would be a major source of trouble for the Foundation staff.[15]

Even if it had been possible to avoid such wounded sensibilities, it is difficult to see how the outcome could have been significantly different. The program of reform to which the Fund for the Advancement of Education was committed was inherently controversial, and the Foundation's announced intention to seek ways to protect and advance civil liberties and civil rights was inflammatory in the era that took its name from Senator Joseph McCarthy.

In a more usual political climate, a charge of subversion leveled against the eminent capitalists who made up the Ford Foundation board would have been ludicrous. But this was the season when McCarthy could dominate the news media with an unsupported assertion that the State Department was "thoroughly infested by Communists."[16] A previously unchallenged reputation for probity and devotion to duty provided no protection for General George C. Marshall, the architect of American victory in World War II. He was, McCarthy charged, part of a "conspiracy so immense, an infamy so black, as to dwarf any in the history of man."[17]

A cowed Congress overrode President Truman's veto to pass the McCarran Bill, which established the star-chamber Subversive Activities Control Board. Conservative southern Democrats, employing the tactic of guilt by association to discredit critics of racial segregation, took over the House Un-American Activities Committee. And in 1952 a seven-man select committee of the House was created to investigate possible un-American activities by tax-exempt foundations, with the Ford Foundation as its primary target.

Henry Ford II, Hoffman, and Hutchins were summoned by Chairman Eugene "Goober" Cox of Georgia to explain why the Foundation should not be considered subversive. Ford and Hoffman came off quite well, and Hutchins scored his only triumph before a congressional forum. Ferry, who accompanied him to the hearing, had urged that he avoid quibbling over specific allegations and "take them up the mountain, let them see the big view . . .":

He did take them up the mountain, so much so that Murray Marder of the *Washington Post* was in tears when he finished. It was that effective. And Cox came down afterward and invited Hutchins to go on a turkey shoot with him. He said, "Ah really don't like anything Ah've ever heard about you, Doctor Hutchins, but you're a marvelous man. Ah tell you, that's one of the most wonderful things Ah ever heard and it would be a great honor for me, sir, if you would come down some time in the autumn and go on a turkey shoot at my place." I was standing right there.[18]

Cox's committee gave the Foundation a clean bill of health, but that was before it began to develop the program called for under the Study Report's Area II to support action directed toward "the elimination of restrictions on freedom of thought, inquiry and expression in the United States, and the development of policies and procedures best adapted to protect these rights in the face of persistent international tension." Included in a list of matters of specific concern were "certain aspects of 'un-American activities' investigations, and the conditions imposed on Government employment and Government-financed fellowships.''[19]

Under the circumstances it was not surprising that the board displayed a pronounced reluctance to move ahead with the program the Study Report blandly labeled "The Strengthening of Democracy." In August 1951 Hutchins had managed to get Area II onto the agenda with a memorandum proposing the creation of a "Fund for Democratic Freedoms," which would be empowered to "institute or otherwise support efforts aimed at the elimination of inequalities in the treatment of individuals or minorities." He conceded that "the Fund would deal almost wholly in unpalatable causes,''[20] and suggested means by which its operations could be distanced from the Foundation.

Ferry, who professed little interest in the Foundation's educational and overseas activities, had a reflexive sympathy for mistreated minorities that made him an enthusiastic supporter of the proposal. In an unsolicited memorandum obviously aimed at Henry II, he argued that controversy could still be good public relations:

> Such a policy is not in conflict with the real interest of the Ford Motor Company, although it may sometimes prove irritating to some of its officials, and may embarrass, temporarily, members of the Ford family. In the long run it will bring more credit to the Ford name than the easy and innocuous course of making impressive contributions to established activities or undertaking programs that cannot arouse criticism or opposition. Here it should be remembered that the reputation of the Ford Motor Company largely centers around Henry Ford's lifelong preoccupation with experimentation and pioneering ventures.[21]

In October Hoffman presented the proposal to the board and obtained approval for an initial grant of one million dollars to establish a corporation to be called the Fund for the Republic. Recognizing that the concept for the new venture had been left vague, Hutchins drafted a memorandum that zeroed in on the abuses being perpetrated in the name of anti-Communism, along with some that predated the rise of McCarthyism:

> The Fund should feel free to attack the problem of the freedom of the press; of migrant workers; of the immigration laws and the McCarran Act; of loyalty investigations; [of] the House Un-American Activities Committee; of conscientious objectors; of academic freedom and teachers' oaths; of racial and religious

discrimination in all its manifestations, from lynching to inequality of educational opportunity; of disfranchisement; of dishonesty in government; of the liberties guaranteed by the First and Fourteenth amendments; of the administration of justice, etc.[22]

This ultimately provided the guidelines for the new Fund, as well as a slogan, "Feel Free," which Hutchins displayed on his office wall, embroidered in an old-fashioned sampler. But Hoffman prudently decided not to forward the memo to the trustees, and he agreed with Henry II that the Fund should not be fully activated until a governing board and "preferably a chairman and president" could be found. Hoffman's first choice to head the Fund was a fellow motor magnate, Charles E. Wilson, the former president of General Motors and a member of the Foundation's board, whose conservative credentials were presumed to render him virtually impervious to attack by the McCarthyites. Wilson kept the offer open for six months before declining, effectively freezing any further activity in that period.

During the hiatus, Hoffman and Hutchins compiled a list of some two hundred possible candidates for membership on the Fund's board of directors. The criteria were the same ones used in the case of Wilson; the trustees were to be eminently respectable and socially and financially secure enough to indulge their presumed interest in civil liberties and civil rights. It followed that most of these were listed on the rolls of the Republican party.

Wilson's withdrawal from consideration in May 1952 came when Hoffman was on leave to work for the Eisenhower presidential nomination. Henry II wrote Hutchins that the Foundation board felt that no further action should be taken on the Fund for the Republic until after the fall elections, adding, "I hope you will agree."[23] Hutchins didn't agree, and when Henry and Benson Ford and Charles Wilson came to Pasadena in June for four days of conferences, he steered the discussion around to the possibility of creating a special status for the Fund to insulate the Foundation against any opprobrium it might incur. He recommended that unlike the others, which remained attached to the Foundation by a financial umbilical cord and thus expected further nourishment, the new corporation be given a one-time grant of between ten and fifteen million dollars, and be totally separated administratively from the Foundation. To insure that the Ford money would be spent for legitimate purposes, each Foundation trustee would have a veto on any proposed member of the board of the Fund.

In July the Ford trustees adopted Hutchins's proposal, with the further reservation that no additional money would be transferred until the

Fund's board and program had been approved. The original list of prospective board members had been pared to fifty, and Hoffman and Hutchins now set out to process these names through the obstacle course posed by the blackball accorded each Foundation trustee. In Hoffman's absence this chore fell largely to Hutchins, and its difficulty was indicated by an exchange of telegrams with Henry II.

Ford wired Hutchins on October 1, 1952, "Have no recollection of approving names in Weekly Report of September 22. How could they be elected? Never heard of most of them." Hutchins replied on the same day, "Names mentioned in Weekly Report sent to you in Detroit September 8th have been approved by all members of the Board. Fifteen people have been selected. They cannot be said to be elected until the corporation is formed. If you want further investigation of any individual, please let me know together with how you wish investigation made."[24]

On October 2 Ford cabled Hutchins from abroad, "Only names I agree to with Hoffman are O.K. as far as I'm concerned. I vote negative on all others until I can check on return. Send list of names I previously agreed to." On October 3 Hutchins responded, "You approved of [James F.] Brownlee, [Charles W.] Cole, [Erwin N.] Griswold, [Meyer] Kestnbaum, [Jubal R.] Parten, [Elmo] Roper, [George N.] Shuster, Mrs. [Eleanor B.] Stevenson, and [James D.] Zellerbach. It is my understanding that on the telephone with Hoffman you also approved Malcolm Bryan, president of the Federal Reserve Bank of Atlanta."[25]

These survivors, plus four from the list that was cleared two weeks later by Henry II, made up the original board of the Fund for the Republic. But before they could get organized, the man who had been primarily responsible for their nomination was summarily removed from office. In February Hutchins wrote to Thornton Wilder, "Paul Hoffman has just resigned as president of the Foundation. I came to the Foundation because of him and have been protected by him. I have no idea what will happen now."[26]

CHAPTER THIRTY-ONE

"A Herculean
Effort . . ."

The ostensible reason for Paul Hoffman's resignation as president of
the Ford Foundation was the unanimous decision of the board to
relocate the executive offices to New York, coupled with Hoffman's
desire to maintain his residence in Pasadena, which, it was suggested,
was necessary because of his wife's frail health. The announcement by
Henry Ford II on February 4, 1953, was designed to save face all around,
but it had a palpably hollow ring.

From his inside view, Clarence Faust had seen the ouster coming, and
he noted that Donald David had been urging the relocation for months:
"If he could persuade the board that it ought to be operating in New York
City . . . Hoffman would have no other choice but to resign, which is just
what happened. And as Paul and others watched this development, I think
Paul's own enthusiasm, which was kind of a bright and innocent
morning-light enthusiasm, began to be dimmed. . . ."[1]

Hoffman accepted his abrupt dismissal with his usual impervious
civility, and no reporter or historian was ever able to pry a word of
recrimination out of him. "Paul was a very, very discreet man,"
Hutchins said, "and although I'd been an avid friend of his for many
years, he would almost never confide in me about his relations with the
trustees or anything else, and I didn't know what was happening."[2] But
he had no reason to doubt that the device employed to force Hoffman's
resignation had been designed to eliminate him as well.

He too had a compelling personal reason to remain in Pasadena. "No domestic troubles now except that Vesta's heart was badly damaged by rheumatic fever about [the] age of eight," he wrote Thorton Wilder. "She ought not to live anywhere but California."[3] When he declined to join the migration to New York, Hutchins reminded Rowan Gaither, the predictable successor to Hoffman, that he had relocated his family on the understanding that in the event the Pasadena operation was discontinued, he would remain on the payroll until he found another appointment that he considered suitable.

So Hutchins continued to occupy his office in the emptying Tuerck House, becoming, as he said, an associate director with no one to direct, and with whom no one would associate. Before they too were transferred to New York, the headquarters of the two educational Funds remained in Pasadena, and this provided something of a rationalization for Hutchins's being there. He indicated his willingness to accept a reasonable severance settlement, but since he had been isolated and had no effective voice in Foundation affairs, there was no compulsion for the board to act.

It was an increasingly lonely time for him. His witty friend Martin Quigley had also been placed in limbo after he took issue with what he considered to be improper tactics by his former boss, Earl Newsom, whom he charged with attempting to influence the trustees to use Foundation grants to further the interests of the Ford Motor Company. When he learned that Newsom had not recommended that he continue in his present job under the new administration, he wrote to Gaither,

> My understanding . . . is that the function of the Information Office is to report Foundation actions accurately, as soon and in as much detail as is consistent with the operation of programs and with good taste. . . . The Information Office does not attempt to influence programs or choice of personnel by pointing out what effect they might have on the Foundation's reputation among various groups. I mention this because Earl used the terms "public information function" and "public opinion function" synonymously in his explanation to me.[4]

By June Quigley was on his way back to his native Midwest to accept a partnership in a St. Louis public-relations firm. In a farewell note to "Bold Robert," he noted that the reaction to his most recent communications to Gaither had been "frigid silence."[5]

Hutchins, with a touch of bitterness he never displayed publicly, wrote Wilder that the Ford Foundation had "turned out to be nothing but the public relations arm of the Ford Motor Company."[6] If that unfairly denigrated the motivation of the board, it was soon evident that ridding the Foundation of its controversial reputation had become a dominant concern under the new regime. By 1956 the independent Funds were being phased out, and the original guidelines had gone by the boards. The Foundation now made massive grants for the most conventional purposes: $20,000,000 for National Merit Scholarships, $50,000,000 to raise the salaries of college teachers, $15,000,000 for research on mental illness. With income still piling up, it was then announced that the trustees had voted to parcel out $500,000,000 to privately supported colleges, medical schools, and hospitals. Dwight Macdonald commented:

> . . . The philanthropoids at Ford are reasonably intelligent and knowledgeable men and it is unlikely that it didn't occur to them that a more productive use could have been made of half a billion dollars than just giving it out, pro rata, to everybody. They were scared, or more accurately, Henry Ford II, Donald David and the other trustees were scared, and the fear communicated itself, through channels, to the philanthropoids who run the Foundation for them. Large foundations, like large corporations, are timid beasts, and when they are frightened by some small but vocal minority they envelop themselves in clouds of public relations.[7]

Ironically, the principal means employed by right-wing partisans to intimidate the Foundation trustees was a sustained attack on the Fund for the Republic, which was quite accurately described by Hutchins as not only wholly independent but wholly disowned. This did not deter reactionary propagandists from continuing to link the Ford name to the Fund in their charges of pro-Communist subversion — a task made easier by the fact that two weeks after he was eased out of office at the Foundation, Paul Hoffman was elected chairman of the Fund by the trustees he had recruited.

Ten days later Hoffman led a delegation of the most prestigious of these to Pasadena to determine whether the civil-rights organization, which so far had received only $200,000 of its initial million-dollar grant, was to be strangled in its cradle. A program outline that included all the pertinent provisions earlier set forth by Hutchins was submitted to the Foundation board, along with a request for a closed-end appropriation of $15,000,000. The grant was approved on the motion of Chairman Ford.

In this instance public-relations considerations were working in the Fund's favor. Ford and his colleagues could hardly repudiate their earlier agreement to support the civil-rights organization since its chairman was to be the man they had ostentatiously praised for setting the Foundation on the right course. Hoffman could hope that the action would minimize the widespread impression that he had received a vote of no-confidence from his peers. And while he didn't need a job — the chairmanship of the Studebaker Corporation had been kept open for him — he did need a post that would keep green his reputation as a high-minded public servant.

Hutchins had little to do with the initial operations of the Fund, but there was, as always, much else to occupy him. During his years in Pasadena he elaborated his theories on the relationship between education and democratic governance in the Gottesman Lectures at Uppsala University in Sweden; the Sir George Watson Lectures at Oxford, the universities of Edinburgh, Manchester, and Birmingham, and the University College of North Staffordshire; the Marfleet Lectures at the University of Toronto; and the Walgreen Lectures at the University of Chicago.[8] He also lent his prestige to support causes he favored, discussing the pending Supreme Court decision on school segregation at a meeting of the Urban League in St. Louis and at United Jewish Appeal dinners in Newark, Los Angeles, Cleveland, St. Louis, and Chicago. At one point he even took on a booking agent.

His obligations to the Britannica company were, if anything, increasing. The Great Books project was threatened with extinction when expenditures for Adler's Syntopicon project passed $750,000 and a new president, Robert Preble, ordered it shut down. Hutchins persuaded Bill Benton to grant a reprieve, but when the editors finally declared their work complete, Preble refused to approve expenditures for production. To demonstrate the set's sales potential and pay for an initial printing, Hutchins and Adler took the lead in signing up five hundred founding subscribers at five hundred dollars each.

The subscribers were presented with numbered editions at a star-studded dinner at the Waldorf-Astoria in New York. Jacques Maritain and Clifton Fadiman were the speakers, and among those gracing the head table were Alfred Vanderbilt, Nelson and David Rockefeller, Thomas Watson, Jr., Conrad Hilton, John Mott, Walter Paepcke, Raymond Rubicam, John Cowles, John S. Knight, and Alicia Patterson. Hutchins, in his evangelical mode, proclaimed,

> This is more than a set of great books, and more than a liberal education. Great Books of the Western World is an act of piety. Here are the sources of our being. Here is our heritage. Here is the West. This is its meaning for mankind. Here is the faith of the West, for here before everybody willing to look at it is that

dialogue by way of which Western man has believed that he can approach the truth.[9]

The press response to the launching of the Great Books was generally favorable, but there was one particularly acidulous dissent. In *The New Yorker* Dwight Macdonald's ingrained distaste for Hutchins and his works was reflected in an article titled "The Book-of-the-Millennium Club." His specific complaints about the content of what he described as the "densely printed, poorly edited, over-priced and over-syntopicanized collection" were within the bounds of serious literary criticism. But he went on to resurrect the Deweyite suspicion of a Thomist plot: "Its aim is hieratic rather than practical — not to make the books accessible to the public (which they mostly already were) but to fix the canon of the Sacred Texts by printing them in a special edition. . . . The Syntopicon is partly a concordance to the Sacred Texts, partly the sort of commentary and interpretation of them the Church Fathers made for the Bible."[10]

In an addendum to a reprint of the article in *Against the American Grain,* Macdonald gloated over the set's poor sales in its early years: "I like to think the above review was partly responsible."[11] It seems unlikely that he deserved such credit, since Preble was unimpressed by the publicity, good or bad. He refused to give the set effective sales support, and in 1953 only 138 sets were sold. James E. Colvin, then Britannica's public-relations director, contended that the set was demonstrably promotable, but Preble was adamant.

"Once more," Colvin recalled, "here was a Preble-Hutchins contest of wills: 'I said it was foredoomed to failure, and by God it will be!' was Preble's attitude. Poor Bob; he couldn't prevail with Benton against Preble because Preble had by now made Britannica highly profitable."[12] In the end Hutchins did prevail. Three years later a separate Great Books sales force was formed, with a new manager, and annual sales soon passed fifty thousand, with a gross return of $22,000,000. But the experience was certainly one of the reasons Benton's standing offer of full-time employment at the publishing company was not among the possibilities Hutchins considered when it became clear that he had no future with the Ford Foundation.

The Fund for the Republic, meanwhile, was getting off to a slow start. David Freeman, a Foundation staff member, was designated the Fund's acting president, and he set up headquarters in New York while Hoffman and key members of the board began an active search for a chief executive. A number of persons with the requisite conservative credentials, including Governor Earl Warren of California and Erwin Canham, the editor of the *Christian Science Monitor,* were approached, but there were no takers until Hoffman came up with the name of Clifford Case. The personable forty-nine-year-old congressman from New Jersey had been an ardent supporter of President Eisenhower and, like many other Eastern Seaboard Republicans, had a solid civil-liberties record. His political career had stalled after he dropped out of the race for the Republican gubernatorial nomination in early 1953, and he found the Fund offer attractive. His appointment was effective upon his resignation from Congress in September.

The mainstream media, increasingly concerned over the wild charges emanating from the far right, had welcomed the creation of a civil-liberties organization with a prestigious board of directors. "A group of the most responsible, respectable and successful business and professional men in the country have banded together in a Herculean effort to roll back the creeping tide of what is called, for want of a better word, McCarthyism," Eric Sevareid told his CBS audience. "These are disturbed and alarmed individuals, these men who have taken over the Fund."[13] But there was an inevitable counter-refrain, and Case's Republican identification afforded him no immunity to it.

Westbrook Pegler let fly with one of his nonstop sentences, placing the Fund's new president in the anti-anti-Communist conspiracy as "one of a mysterious group in President-elect Eisenhower's headquarters last fall who secretly got Ike's signature on a 'testimonial' for Arthur J. Goldsmith who tried to win control of Congress for undisclosed eastern financial backers by sending money into states of small population to defeat anti-Communists and all who stand against unrestricted immigration."[14] And before Case departed Congress, his colleagues gave their approval for a new investigation of tax-exempt foundations, to be headed by Representative Brazilla Carroll Reece of Tennessee, who pointedly ignored Case when he proclaimed,

> There can be no question that Hutchins is behind this new Ford
> Foundation project, for he has consistently expressed his concern
> for the civil liberties of Communists. Since we know Hutchins'
> attitude toward Communism and we know that his conception of
> civil liberties is similar to that of Communists, we can be sure that
> the new Ford Foundation project will aid the Communist conspir-
> acy and will try to discredit all those who fight it.[15]

The familiar din on the opposite coast may have had something to do with Hutchins's brief flirtation with a number of influential Californians who urged him to seize an opportunity to take on his congressional traducers on their own ground. The elevation of Richard Nixon to the vice presidency made the Democratic nomination for his former Senate seat particularly attractive, and Hutchins was a man in need of a job. In the early months of 1954 he wrote numerous guarded notes such as this one to Thomas P. Lantos, a Bank of America economist: "Many thanks for your kind wishes. . . . I shall take them into account on reaching a conclusion to the interesting and important subject to which you refer."[16] But in February he wired Alan Cranston, the head of the California Democratic Clubs, who would eventually claim a Senate seat of his own,

> I am sorry that my circumstances are such that I cannot consider this suggestion at this time. In case the matter is raised at the Fresno meeting I hope you will express my deep appreciation of the kindness that has been shown me, and my regret that I cannot accept the invitation.[17]

Back in New Jersey, Case had a similar proposition from a most influential Republican. In March, after less than six months in office, he resigned as president of the Fund to undertake, with President Eisenhower's blessing, a successful race for the United States Senate. On April 15, 1954, the trustees of the Fund unanimously elected as his successor the man who they agreed had been the right choice all along: Robert Hutchins.

In the Fund's sixteen months of existence, its main emphasis had been on commissioning studies by reputable scholars. That prudent approach had not changed with Case's advent. "When we present points of view," he said, "the public must believe we are fairly presenting both sides." One of his aides said that Case saw the Fund's ideological role as providing "a net in the center of the court, no matter who is serving."[18]

The members of the board, who had accepted their appointments out of conviction that the onslaught on civil liberties constituted a national crisis, found this frustrating. When at the end of its first year the Fund had issued no printed matter and its operating expenses nearly equaled its grant total, Elmo Roper wrote to Hutchins:

> Frankly, I can't tell you how the Fund for the Republic is getting on. I think it is probably fair to state that progress is being made, but frankly, it is being made at what to me is a discouraging rate. But I think it is fair to add that no judgment ought to be passed for another three months period. After that . . . ?[19]

Three months was all that was left of Clifford Case's tenure, and the situation had not changed perceptibly by the time he departed.

There were those, some with malice aforethought, who said that the Fund chairmanship represented Paul Hoffman's severance pay. In a literal sense this was absurd, since the post was unsalaried, providing only a modest director's honorarium. The conclusion was more applicable in Hutchins's case; his acceptance of the presidency at the salary he was already receiving resolved the impasse that had kept him on the Foundation's payroll.

He agreed that the Fund's headquarters should continue to be in New York, but he stipulated that he would maintain his residence in Pasadena. To make this arrangement work he had to have a deputy to run the day-to-day operation at the main office, one who shared his views and had the moral stamina to take the heat that was bound to come. His choice was Ping Ferry, who had become a wholehearted convert to the cause and had openly sided with Hutchins in his standoff with the Foundation, with the result that he, like Quigley, was at odds with Earl Newsom.

Ferry had no illusions as to what he was getting into. In New York he would be the point man when the Fund began taking on those he identified as its natural enemies: "The American Legion, the House Un-American Activities Committee and McCarthy, the Hearst papers, and [Westbrook] Pegler and Fulton Lewis, Jr. . . . they were all ranged up there on the horizon, waiting for us to come out."[20] His combative nature, along with his deep devotion to civil liberties and civil rights, led him to accept the post of vice president at half the $75,000 salary he was receiving at Newsom.

On July 1 Ferry reported for duty at the New York headquarters at 1 East Fifty-fourth Street. David Freeman stayed on as secretary-treasurer, but the gaggle of consultants who had been hired during the Case interlude were terminated. In Pasadena Hutchins moved out of Tuerck House and set up shop in modest quarters at the Huntington Hotel, with Paul Hoffman's son Hallock, then the regional director of the American Friends Service Committee, as his part-time assistant. By the time the board met again, the decks had been cleared for action:

> . . . When [the directors] sat down across from President Hutchins to discuss and vote upon the recommendations and proposals sent to each of them in advance, it was as though a whirlwind had suddenly swept away the slow, argumentative, routine ways to which the participants had become accustomed. No figure had ever so clearly dominated a board meeting. The President's

presence appears in virtually every paragraph of the minutes. Past programs were re-examined, new ideas scrutinized, and future possibilities explored at length.[21]

Although he was reluctant to use the Fund's limited resources for conventional academic research, Hutchins agreed that some commitments left over from the Case regime should be honored — most notably a multivolume study of the extent of Communist penetration of American institutions, which was to be undertaken under the direction of Clinton L. Rossiter, a respected Cornell political scientist. This would clearly be useful in factually countering the wild claims of subversion that now filled the air, but it would take years for such an enterprise to produce results, and Hutchins — along with the most influential members of the board — had no patience with the cautious approach that had kept the Fund dormant since its inception. "We were determined to see how far we could go to help people and at the same time maintain our tax exemption," he said. "That was the major difference."[22]

Hutchins would soon be pushing the Fund's tax-exempt status to its limit and, as some of the trustees came to fear, beyond it. The issue was critical, since the Ford Foundation had withheld funds until the exemption was obtained and had stipulated that if it was subsequently lifted, any unspent balance would have to be returned. The test imposed by the Internal Revenue Service to determine what constituted acceptable philanthropic activity was vague; influencing government action through education was permissible, but not if it crossed an undefined line and became propaganda aimed at influencing the outcome of elections. If the congressional inquisitors and their journalistic fuglemen could convince the IRS that the programs devised under Hutchins's administration violated the ban, the Fund would be out of business.

The people whom Hutchins wanted to use tax-exempt funds to help were those whose civil liberties were being violated and those whose civil rights were being denied. In both cases the federal government was culpable. The constitutional guarantees of free speech, free assembly, and due process were being ignored in the case of citizens who were suspected of violating vague standards of "Americanism" asserted by congressional committees and imposed by intimidation upon public and private agencies. The failure to enforce the Constitution's civil-rights amendments meant that black citizens were being denied access to the ballot, education, housing, and employment — by legal segregation in the South and by custom everywhere in the nation.

These violations of the spirit and letter of the Constitution were not new. But the ideological confrontation between the United States and the

Soviet Union in Europe and Asia had given new force to demagogic appeals to the chauvinism that was already ingrained in the American psyche. And Earl Warren, the mild-mannered politician who had been the board's first choice to head the Fund for the Republic, was now the chief justice of the Supreme Court and, to the consternation of President Eisenhower, had led his brethren to outlaw segregation in public schools, thereby unleashing a passionate resistance movement in states that had seceded from the Union once before.

When the Fund under Robert Hutchins finally moved to meet the challenge, its formidable task was to rally to the standard of traditional democratic values a citizenry beset by "a vast impatience, a turbulent bitterness, a rancor akin to revolt . . . a strange rebelliousness, quite without parallel in the history of the United States."[23]

CHAPTER THIRTY-TWO

Attack and Counterattack

Robert Hutchins displayed no surprise when Elmo Roper and William Joyce came to notify him that their fellow directors were prepared to elect him president of the Fund for the Republic. He sent back word that he would accept with willingness and pleasure, and there was a touch of unseemly glee in the letter he wrote to Thornton Wilder to announce this welcome change in his fortunes:

> . . . I've got a new job. It's spending $15 million stolen from the Ford Foundation on civil liberties & racial & religious indiscrimination, if you know what I mean. It's not bad. It's better than the Ford Foundation. . . . It's better than the last years at U. of C., when I got so I couldn't bear the sight of Quincy Wright, Ronald Crane, Harold Swift & Co. I expect to spend all the money and retire in three or four years.[1]

Hutchins could hardly have been serious about that projection, and there was surely irony in his subsequent claim that he made two mistakes when he took the job — overestimating, first, the public understanding of foundations and the way they worked and, second, the public knowledge of, and interest in, the Bill of Rights:

> My only excuse, in the first instance, is that nothing in my experience had prepared me for the public effects of the campaign

of misrepresentation that began as soon as the program of the Fund became known. . . . For [the second] mistake I have no excuse at all. The Chief Justice of the United States was not giving the results of any secret research when he expressed doubt as to whether the Bill of Rights could be adopted today. He was saying what everybody knows and what I forgot or chose to ignore when I began work on the program of the Fund.[2]

His ignorance could only have been chosen. Few Americans had had greater exposure to the unfounded charges of pro-Communism that were employed to undermine the credibility of those who insisted that every citizen had a right to espouse unpopular views. If the current leader of the cacophony, Joe McCarthy, was beginning to self-destruct, Hutchins had every reason to know that there were plenty of replacements available.

It was a poor choice of targets, not adverse public reaction, that brought on McCarthy's decline. Senators who had applauded when his onslaught on the State Department served their partisan interests found it expedient to support his censure when he launched a vendetta against the Army, something that could not be tolerated by a President with a five-star military rank. But this reaction was negative and muted. In 1953, while the Fund was still lying fallow, the Washington pamphleteer I. F. Stone, an indefatigable civil-liberties watchdog, lamented: "The premises of free society and of liberalism find no one to voice them, yet McCarthyism will not be ended until someone has the nerve to make this kind of a fundamental attack upon it."[3]

Hutchins had the nerve, as well as a Puritan conscience that would not permit him to sit out a contest that involved the values he lived by. Since he had already been cited by right-wing commentators as the evil genius who invented the Fund, his appointment as its president signaled an increase in the propaganda barrage by a factor of five. There was good reason for this, for it immediately became clear that he was moving the Fund away from the kind of low-key academic research that had characterized its earlier efforts. The projects he launched were intended not only to gather facts but to make judgments and broadly publicize recommendations for reform, and they were aimed directly at the public and private agencies that were trampling on the rights of citizens in the name of national security.

Grants were made to Samuel Stouffer of Harvard for an analysis of the effect of the Army-McCarthy hearings on public opinion and to Paul Lazarsfeld of Columbia for a study of the fear induced in education by McCarthyism. Funding was provided to the Association of the Bar of the City of New York for an examination of loyalty-security programs that employed dubious standards of un-Americanism to deny government employment. Staff members of the Fund initiated an investigation that would demonstrate how the same system also worked at one remove to foster widespread blacklisting in the entertainment industry. And a bright young Washington lawyer, Adam Yarmolinsky, began compiling revealing histories of government loyalty-security cases.

Hutchins received due warning of the reaction from Walter Millis, a military historian and editorial writer for the *New York Herald Tribune* whom he retained as a consultant on loyalty-security matters. Millis pointed out that the apparent decline of support for McCarthyism would only increase the resentment of those who felt their cause to be imperiled:

> Politicians, publicists, the FBI, ex-Communists, the security bureaucracy, the ruling group in the American Legion, many elements of the Catholic church, have combined to make an enormous emotional and political investment in anti-Communism. The anti-Communists have given themselves the label, and have arrogated to themselves a monopoly in the combat against Communism. It is now apparent . . . that an organization which, like the Fund for the Republic, sets out to examine the methods of this monopoly, to question what seemed to be the excesses of its methods and to ask just what was the real menace which formed the basis of its power and authority, was bound to meet it in head-on and damaging collision.[4]

Thomas Reeves, viewing the collision at a further remove, noted another underlying cause. Hutchins's strategy was to draw support from his natural allies in the Establishment, as exemplified by the membership of the Fund's board and the associates he assembled for his projects. (Millis, for example, was a Yale classmate.) The McCarthyites drew their support from a populist base, and populism, whether of the right or left, is generally fueled by a resentment of the elite. Reeves referred to the extensive scholarly study of the "phantasmagorical fears and hatreds of recent American 'pseudo-conservatism' ":

> It is important to note here that in large part the attack was against the effects of urbanization and the power structure commonly associated with it. At the vortex of this deep reactionary resentment against "liberalism" were men like Paul G. Hoffman, Clifford Case, Henry Ford II, and the editors of *The New York Times:* widely quoted, socially prominent, upper-middle-class citizens who had no basic quarrels with the New and Fair Deals,

who respected academic credentials, who liked Ike (and Adlai), who contributed to *Harper's,* subscribed to *Foreign Affairs,* and read *Time* and *Newsweek,* who professed belief in racial equality, who supported foreign aid and the United Nations, who played prominent (the Far Right frequently used "conspiratorial") roles in national political conventions, and who were often appointed to positions of authority by victorious candidates of both parties. When such men sought to "defend" civil liberties and civil rights with $15,000,000 the reaction was bound to be noticeable.[5]

At its home base in New York, and in the other major American cities, the Fund had no difficulty in lining up respectable support for its efforts to secure and protect the civil rights of racial and religious minorities — an activity that Dwight Macdonald characterized as "politically safe."[6] When Hutchins launched a Commission on Race and Housing to investigate the restrictive practices of landlords and lending agencies that maintained rigid patterns of residential segregation, he was able to recruit a board of directors from the upper crust of urban society.[7]

But the reverse was true in the South, where the majority of the nation's blacks still lived as second-class citizens. It was here that the Supreme Court's 1954 *Brown* decision would have an immediate impact as it struck down the legal basis for the segregated public schools that existed de facto elsewhere. Many white southerners privately agreed with the major religious denominations when they declared the Court's findings morally correct, but few shared the enthusiasm of those who were not affected by them.

Recognizing the lack of popular support for the orders mandated by its ruling, the Court postponed implementation for a full year and called for further briefs on methods of dealing with the social and economic problems local school boards would face in effecting desegregation. During the interval the Deep South's political leaders openly plotted "massive resistance" in response to the reflexive reaction rooted in their constituents' heritage from a lost war.

By 1955, when the Court ordered desegregation to proceed "with all deliberate speed," White Citizens Councils had appeared across the region, charged with the mission of intimidating blacks who tried to exercise the constitutional rights newly certified by the Court, as well as any southern whites who dared to support them. Moderates who argued that the Supreme Court ruling was the law of the land were answered with a rebel yell emblazoned on billboards along the major highways: "The South Says Never! Impeach Earl Warren!"

Even before Hutchins's advent, the Fund had recognized the need to prop up the indigenous organizations that were attempting to bring whites and blacks together to insure an orderly transition from the traditionally segregated society. Popular reaction against the court orders in the school cases was so widespread and deep that local sources of funding for these organizations had virtually dried up. Under Case, the Fund stepped in with grants to the Southern Regional Council, the only significant secular interracial organization, and to Catholic and Protestant church agencies active in the field. The policy was continued under Hutchins, and the funding was increased when it became evident that these programs could not be maintained without it.

While the Fund's financing kept alive the effort to hold in check the incipient violence that was building across the South, it contributed to dampening the ardor of philanthropies that had lent their support to educational and social programs aimed at improving the lot of the black minority. This had been a respectable charitable activity so long as it posed no direct threat to segregation. Now the national propagandists of the far right cited the Fund's action as proof of their equation of desegregation with Communism, and foundation trustees with financial interests in the South were given an object lesson by the White Citizens Councils, which began calling for a boycott of local Ford dealers.

It was at this juncture that I began my association with Robert Hutchins. On November 18, 1954, the directors of the Fund elected three new members of the board: Chester Bowles, Bill Benton's advertising-agency partner, who had gone on to serve as director of the wartime Office of Price Administration, governor of Connecticut, and ambassador to India; Robert E. Sherwood, the four-time Pulitzer prize–winning playwright and historian; and me. I could not match their prestige, but I had other credentials. The board had been without a director with a Deep Southern background since Malcolm Bryan, the Atlanta banker, had discovered that the Fund was committed to bold action on the racial front and resigned after attending only one meeting.

Endowed with the full complement of two Confederate grandfathers, I had grown up in South Carolina, the state that was first to secede in the Civil War and, many felt, had never really rejoined the Union. My college was Clemson, founded by the militant segregationist "Pitchfork" Ben Tillman, at Fort Hill, the up-country plantation where John C. Calhoun had declared slavery not a necessary evil but a positive good. But when I began to practice journalism in my hometown, Greenville, and went on to cover the legislative and the state political campaigns during the Depression years, I came to believe that I was witnessing the end of an era.

That conviction was reinforced by a stint at Harvard as a Nieman Fellow and a wartime tour of duty in the European theater and, after V-E Day, on the Army general staff in the Pentagon. When I came home to settle in North Carolina as editor of the *Charlotte News,* it seemed to me that my first obligation was to try to prepare my readers to cope with a reality most of them refused to recognize — the great, impersonal forces of change that were bringing the region to the day when white southerners, not yet willing to accept blacks as equals, would be confronted by black southerners who were no longer willing to accept anything less.

I had moved on to the western reaches of the old Confederacy as the executive editor of the *Arkansas Gazette* when I came to Hutchins's notice through the good offices of his colleague at the Ford Foundation, Clarence Faust, the president of the Fund for the Advancement of Education. Arkansas had been selected as a laboratory for the Fund's experiment in teacher training, and Faust and his vice president, Alvin Eurich, were frequent visitors. Since I was then serving as a trustee of Arkansas State Teachers College, I saw a good deal of both of them.

In 1953, when the cases that resulted in the *Brown* decision were pending before the Supreme Court, Faust concluded that the ruling, when it finally came down, was bound to subject the South's dual educational system to great pressures, whether it required that the grossly unequal black schools be brought up to par with those of whites or that they be merged with them. There was an obvious need for an accurate estimate of what would be required, but there was no ready source of reliable information, since for fifty years the records maintained by local school boards and state departments of education had been doctored to maintain the fiction of equality.

Faust and Eurich made a tour of the public and private universities in the region, offering a blank check to cover the cost of assembling and interpreting the pertinent data for use by the local and state school officials who would have to devise plans to meet the new dispensation. Individual faculty members were willing to participate, but no university administration was prepared to face the political heat an impartial appraisal of the disparities in the dual school system was bound to engender.

In the spring of 1953 Faust asked me to head the undertaking. In response to my objection that I had no academic qualifications, he replied that this might be an asset because time was short and I was used to working against a deadline; the staff of the Fund would sign up the academic experts, assemble a working group in Atlanta, and administer the budget. I felt as though I was volunteering for hazardous duty, not by stepping forward one pace but by standing still while everybody else stepped back one; nevertheless, my principals at the *Gazette* urged me on.

When I pointed out that my participation would entail some risk for the newspaper since we were already under fire from the Citizens Councils, J. N. Heiskell, the venerable editor and principal owner, said dryly that this was a financial matter and he would leave it to the publisher. Hugh Patterson replied, "Of course it is. It would be an act of fiscal imprudence if we didn't insist that Ashmore accept. When that Supreme Court decision comes down every newspaper in the South is going to have to deal with the consequences, and we'll have the best-informed editor available — at Ford Foundation expense."

Under forced draft forty men and women were recruited on southern campuses to sift through the available statistics and extract corrective data drawn from those who processed the public records or might otherwise have insight into actual conditions. I compressed the voluminous reports into a summary volume, *The Negro and the Schools,* which was published by the University of North Carolina Press on May 17, 1954, the day before the Supreme Court handed down *Brown.* Retired Supreme Court Justice Owen J. Roberts, the Fund's chairman, passed along advance proof copies to his former brethren, and Chief Justice Earl Warren told me later that the so-called Ashmore Report had been one of the sources he and his colleagues had relied upon in fashioning *Brown II,* the implementing decree issued in May 1955.[8]

When I arrived for my first board meeting at the Fund for the Republic's elegant suite atop an office building at 60 East Forty-second Street, Hutchins took me aside for a personal greeting, saying he hoped I realized that service on the board of the Fund would automatically qualify me as a pariah. I told him I was sure I would fit right in, and recounted a recent conversation with an old Arkansas politician. He had asked me what I was up to, and when I told him I was about to publish a book called *The Negro and the Schools,* he said, "Son, it sounds to me like you have got yourself in the position of a man running for son of a bitch without opposition." Hutchins assured me I would now become eligible for election by a much larger constituency.

When I came aboard Hutchins still had things pretty much his own way. "Almost from May 1954," Reeves wrote, "the Fund for the Republic and Robert Hutchins were one. It was unthinkable to lay praise or blame on one and ignore the other."[9] By the end of his first year more than $1,500,000 had been appropriated, and he had replaced two of Clifford Case's three consultants and added nine more.

These veterans of the civil-liberties and civil-rights fronts met regularly to advise Hutchins on how the Fund might most efficiently proceed in the areas of its concern.[10] In addition to reviewing grant applications and recommending individuals and organizations competent to undertake projects, several became full-time employees in charge of programs for which no suitable outside agency could be found.

Hutchins was also concerned with devising effective ways to communicate the product of these efforts to the general public. The Fund published handsomely designed bulletins and occasional papers for distribution to the mailing lists of presumed opinion leaders, and it also made available without cost pertinent publications from other sources. Frequent press releases on Fund activities went to the mass media, but they had little effect on hostile newspapers or those that were, like the radio and TV news operations, largely indifferent. An effort was made to break through the barrier by sponsoring prize contests for essays and broadcast scripts dealing with civil liberties and civil rights, and by creating an audio-tape and film-clip service to provide free coverage of significant events, which would augment the broadcasters' limited resources.

Hutchins, of course, could always make news on his own, as he did in January 1955, when he went down to Washington to address the National Press Club. Some of the capital's leading celebrities turned out to hear him, including his old friends from the Supreme Court, Felix Frankfurter and William O. Douglas. Five chairs away at the head table sat Representative Carroll Reece, whose investigating committee had just issued a 432-page report charging major foundations, such as Ford, Rockefeller, and Carnegie, with promoting socialism, subversion, and "moral relativity" — that era's name for what a generation later would be called secular humanism. Hutchins used the occasion for a response the *Washington Post* termed a "classic roasting":

The Reece Committee achieves some of its gaudiest effects by the simple process of giving old words new definitions and then pinning the old words on the foundations. This is the way that empiricism becomes subversion. Subversion now means, the Committee says, a promotion of tendencies that may lead to results that the Committee will not like. Hence support for the New Deal could be subversion. Social engineering, planning, world government, the United Nations, William James, John Dewey, the American Friends Service Committee, Dr. Kinsey and reform are all subversive in the bright new lexicon of the

Reece Committee. And of course all these things are socialistic, if not communistic, too. . . .

I cannot regard the Reece Committee as having more than symbolic or symptomatic importance. Its wild and squalid presentation affords a picture of the state of our culture that is most depressing. Its aims and methods are another example of the exploitation of public concern about Communism and subversion to further political ambition and to work off political grudges.

We may as well state it plainly: the Reece investigation in its inception and execution was a fraud. . . .[11]

As was usually the case with one of Hutchins's bold forays, there were those who applauded the broadside as an entirely fitting reply to the boorish politicians who were riding roughshod in Washington. Others complained that the speech was an impolitic manifestation of elitist arrogance. To Hutchins it was a calculated move to draw battle lines; as a tactical matter, he did not believe that a softer answer was likely to turn away the wrathful fulminations of Reece and his kind, while a bravura counterattack on behalf of the foundations might rally Establishment support. He was too secure in his own convictions to be moved to anger by personal abuse. His ego had not been wounded, but his intelligence had been insulted. To him the Fund for the Republic was

a kind of anti-absurdity fund, a fund to remind us that we can't have things both ways. We can't brag about the Bill of Rights and talk about Fifth Amendment Communists. We can't say that every man has a right to face his accusers and go on using what the *Denver Post* has called "faceless informers." We can't proclaim our devotion to the process of law and then deny it to people we don't like.

The Fund for the Republic is a sort of Fund for the American Dream. I do not think the Fund can make the American dream come true; but perhaps it can keep it alive and clear. Perhaps it can show where we are forgetting the dream as it once was dreamt and can point out those places, and they are numerous, where the progress toward the realization of the dream has surpassed our most expansive expectations.[12]

Reece shook Hutchins's hand on his way out of the hall, but that was the last manifestation of civility from the Fund's entrenched political opposition. Chairman Walter of the HUAC picked up the gauntlet and demanded access to the Fund's files. The Hearst columnists were soon in full cry, often making use of material leaked by the HUAC.

The bellwether was Fulton Lewis, who in addition to his newspaper column claimed an audience of sixteen million for his nightly radio broadcasts and also appeared on more than fifty TV stations. He laid down the party line: "Every act of the Fund for the Republic has been aimed directly at stopping all investigations of Communism and its agents, at undermining the Government's personnel security program. . . ."[13]

The evidence is that Lewis and the others were largely preaching to the already converted, but the orchestrated campaign also served to intimidate those who might be persuaded that the real un-Americans were those who waved the banners of anti-Communism. The drumfire against the Fund was intended as a warning to members of the Establishment that they could expect similar treatment if they displayed sympathy for Hutchins and his works.

The Fund's board members were directly in the line of fire, and it became evident that the campaign was having its effect on some of them. When the directors gathered for their quarterly meeting in September, Reeves noted that "these distinguished businessmen, educators and authors were troubled, cautious, even a bit frightened." They were men and women of principle, but they were also jealous of their reputations, and until now their elevated positions had given them immunity against scurrilous personal abuse. Skins thickened by exposure were rare: "Of the eleven, only Paul Hoffman and Harry Ashmore had been previous targets of the smears and insinuations of the Far Right. . . ."[14]

The board had before it a docket that included requests for appropriations totaling $1,412,200, but it was soon apparent that, for the first time, the president wasn't going to get all he asked for. The directors backed away from Hutchins's request for a grant to establish a watchdog commission to appraise the performance of the mass media — a version of the project he had first proposed a decade before — and cut back the appropriations for TV programming and the distribution of publications. There was evident relief when the president announced, without explanation, that Professor Goldman had abruptly decided not to go through with the investigation of the American Legion that had been enthusiastically outlined in the docket.

The board's palpable uneasiness and the erosion of the blank-check support he had previously enjoyed were not yet sufficient to be of serious concern to Hutchins, but they were a portent. They were enough, certainly, to remind him of his father's admonition when he decided to join the Ford Foundation. When Will Hutchins asked why he was making the change, he had replied that he could no longer face an endless procession of Chicago Club luncheons devoted to easing nervous University trustees' trepidation over adverse publicity. The elder Hutchins, then in charge of the ebullient Mr. Danforth's philanthropy, gently inquired, "Bob, why do you think foundation trustees are any different?"[15]

CHAPTER THIRTY-THREE

"Too Intellectually Arrogant . . ."

Robert Hutchins always tried to make a distinction between public education and public relations. The first, as he conceived it, involved the use of mass media to make available to the widest possible audience facts and arguments relevant to the basic issues confronting society. The object of public relations was much narrower: manipulation of popular opinion to improve the perceived image of individuals and institutions.

Ideally, the two concepts were complementary; a properly educated public would cherish and support those who made edification possible. But if Hutchins was dedicated to the ideal, he never deluded himself that he had attained it. In order to continue educating the public on the meaning of civil liberties and civil rights, it became necessary to employ the applied techniques of public relations to counter those who were seeking to destroy the Fund for the Republic.

By mid-1955 an increasingly restive board of directors was complaining that the Fund was not doing very well on either front. Bold new ventures proposed by Hutchins were rejected, and some existing programs were scrapped or cut back. A pilot film for a projected TV series in which Al Capp, the "Li'l Abner" comic-strip artist, satirized civil-rights issues was declared a failure. The board voted not to renew the appropriation for a series of TV chalk talks by Herblock, the *Washington Post*'s editorial cartoonist. And the publications program was suspended pending a review by the board at its annual meeting.

The trustees were reacting to a series of public-relations disasters. The most damaging of these was precipitated when Ping Ferry hired a part-time public-relations assistant, Amos Landman, who had pleaded the Fifth Amendment when he was called before the Senate Internal Security Committee to answer to a charge of Communist party membership. Landman was fired forthwith from his job as a press agent for the National Municipal League. Ferry, who knew him to be a competent publicist, thought it eminently suitable for the Fund to fill a vacancy with a qualified man who had been made otherwise unemployable by an arbitrary suspension of the due process guaranteed by the Bill of Rights.

The predictable furor in the right-wing press was compounded when it was revealed that Clinton Rossiter had retained Earl Browder, the head of the Communist Party USA, as a consultant for the Fund-sponsored studies of Communist infiltration into American institutions. Since Browder could provide otherwise unavailable records and testify as to his participation in events that were pertinent to the investigation, this, as Rossiter pointed out, represented no departure from usual scholarly practice.

Both Ferry and Rossiter had logic on their side, and it was preposterous to assume that these minimal connections could provide either Landman or Browder with influence on Fund policy. But even those directors who conceded the logic of Hutchins's defense of what he considered to be entirely justified actions still complained about the poor judgment that had resulted in a propaganda bonanza for the Fund's adversaries.

If Hutchins, Ferry, and Rossiter could be held culpable in the case of Landman and Browder, the board had no such out when an action by its own members provided a cause célèbre for the HUAC. Chairman Walter responded with alacrity when the board's Committee on Special Awards presented a five-thousand-dollar check to a Quaker body because it refused to fire a Fifth Amendment librarian.

Mary Knowles ran the William Jeanes Memorial Library in exurban Philadelphia, an institution that was open to the public but maintained by the Plymouth Monthly Meeting. Her employers were aware when they hired her that she had once worked for a Boston school listed as suspect by the Attorney General, and that she had been fired by a Massachusetts library when she took the Fifth before the Senate Internal Security Committee. She told the Meeting, as she had the Committee, that her refusal to testify or to sign a loyalty oath required by the state was a matter of conscience:

. . . At no time have my professional qualifications as a librarian been questioned; nor, I might add, my integrity as an individual. The issue seems to be whether or not an individual can maintain a means of livelihood and his conscience at the same time. . . .

I believe firmly in the United States of America and in the documents upon which it is founded — the Declaration of Independence and the Constitution of the United States, and I do support, obey and defend them. I do also support the Constitution of the State of Pennsylvania.[1]

She provided the Meeting with the oath she had refused to take when it was demanded by the federal and state governments: "Mary Knowles, being duly sworn according to law, deposes and says that she is not a Communist or a member of any subversive organization."[2]

Nevertheless, the Knowles appointment brought down on the Quakers the wrath of the local township's commissioners, the Daughters of the American Revolution, and something called the Alerted Americans Group, which charged that even if it footed the bill, the Meeting had no right to employ such a person in a post of honor and esteem:

. . . Mrs. Knowles, proven Security Risk, is in such a position. Her controversial beliefs and unpatriotic behavior have already disturbed the peace, set a bad example for our young people and caused widespread suspicion and criticism of the whole Friends Meeting. Her presence in the Library poses a possible future threat to our security.[3]

The Knowles case seemed to provide an ideal opportunity for the Fund to attract public attention to a demonstrable civil-liberties outrage and at the same time use a grant to buck up beleaguered private citizens who were standing firm against organized calumny. The board's Committee on Special Awards was made up of Eleanor Bumstead Stevenson, the vivacious wife of the president of Oberlin; Albert Linton, a Philadelphia insurance executive; and Robert E. Sherwood, the playwright. In presenting the award Mrs. Stevenson said,

I would like to make it very clear that this $5,000 award is being given because the Fund for the Republic wishes to pay tribute to the Friends for their realization that whatever Mrs. Knowles' past associations may or may not have been, she is a loyal American and a highly qualified librarian; that she has every right to earn a living and to be treated with the respect accorded a human being in these United States.

American democracy is in serious jeopardy when one group would stigmatize an individual not in terms of the present situation but in terms of the past, often based on careless assumptions and irrational thinking, and thus deprive him of his basic human rights.[4]

Walter's response was to subpoena the chairman of Plymouth Meeting's library committee and demand to see his records. The HUAC, he said, "wishes to know more about the factors which prompted the Fund for the Republic to consider the retention of a Communist a defense of 'democratic principles' worth $5,000 of tax-exempt money." Communists and their dupes would try to portray this as an interference with religion, he added, but "our sole concern is with the seemingly dubious ventures of the Fund for the Republic."[5]

Walter refused Mrs. Stevenson's demand that she be allowed to testify and rejected the protests of the Fund's attorney, Bethuel Webster, telling him, "You have no rights here, no rights at all."[6] Neither did Mary Knowles. She continued to defy the Committee and was convicted of fifty-two counts of contempt of Congress and sentenced to 120 days in jail and a five-hundred-dollar fine. She was finally accorded due legal process in the circuit court of appeals, which reversed the conviction.

The public controversy over these incidents resulted in the resignation of the Fund's newest director, Arthur H. Dean, a Wall Street lawyer and sometime diplomat who had been elected in May to replace the deceased Richard J. Finnegan. When the Landman, Browder, and Knowles cases began to reverberate on the right, Dean expressed his concerns to Hutchins, but he refused to attend an executive committee meeting where they could be aired. In October he formally resigned, leaving his old friend Paul Hoffman to make a lame public statement: "I don't know the reasons for his resignation, and it would be presumptuous of me to speak for him. . . ."[7]

Another result of the furor was a renewal of pressure on the Internal Revenue Service to lift the Fund's tax-exempt status. At the meeting of the executive committee that Dean declined to attend, Hutchins was instructed to draft a detailed memorandum exploring the past and current activities of the Fund in relation to the requirements of the IRS code. His stiff-necked response conceded nothing to his critics:

I have been unable to think of anything worth doing, to say nothing of anything the Fund has done, that might not lead to pressure on the Commissioner of Internal Revenue. . . . The essential concern of the Fund is justice. If powerful persons or groups were not profiting by injustice, if they did not have a vested interest in it, it would not exist. . . . This is the first time that an organization dedicated to civil liberties has had any money. That fact alone, as soon as it appeared that the organization meant business, would account for almost all the clamor we hear today.[8]

In every case at issue, he insisted, officers and grantees had acted under policies laid down by the board. If the wisdom of those policies was now being called into question, the answer would depend "on the importance that the Board attaches to the principle that loyal and qualified persons should be allowed to earn a living, even if they have resorted to the Fifth Amendment, and their employers should not be intimidated." He concluded:

The objects of the Fund require it to expose injustice, encourage justice, and speak the truth. No lesser mission would be worthy of such a Board as this. We can have no illusions about the consequences to every one of us of persisting in the performance of this task. But we did not promise one another an easy time. We promised one another an important enterprise.[9]

The board was not mollified. At the annual meeting in November, Erwin Griswold, the Harvard Law School dean, centered his complaints on Ferry. There was irony in this, since, as Ferry contended, the Landman case was a textbook example of the kind of abuse the dean had cited in his *The Fifth Amendment Today,* and the board had approved an expenditure of fifteen thousand dollars to provide widespread distribution of the paperback version of the book. But Ferry was vulnerable on other counts. Since Hutchins was still living in Pasadena, it usually fell to Ferry to receive visitors at headquarters and to respond to the increasingly hostile queries from the news media, and he was not one to suffer critics gladly. Fulton Lewis complained on the air that when he called on him, Ferry never bothered to take his feet off his desk.

When Griswold indicated that he thought Ferry ought to be fired, I warned him that this could only be construed as a vote of no-confidence in Hutchins — and in such a showdown Griswold wouldn't have my vote, or very many others'. The bylaws required the annual reelection of officers, and in executive session Griswold cast his vote against Ferry and abstained in the case of Hutchins.

It was the last board meeting I would attend for a year. Resistance to school desegregation had been mounting in the South as President Eisenhower continued to refuse to lend his moral support to the Supreme Court's decision, and I had concluded that the best hope for heading off a disastrous racial collision was to replace him with the moderate Democrat he had defeated in 1952, Adlai Stevenson. I had been urging the Illinois governor to enter the coming presidential contest, and in September he agreed and asked me to take a year's leave from the *Gazette* to serve as his personal assistant through the primary campaigns. It didn't seem to be in either the Fund's or Stevenson's interest for me to continue as a director while I was on a political candidate's payroll.

As it turned out, Hutchins was able to survive without my vote, but it was a near thing. Griswold was a formidable adversary. He had been the principal spokesman when the original directors went before the Ford Foundation board to obtain the fifteen-million-dollar grant that launched the Fund, and his probity and impeccable reputation weighed heavily with Henry Ford II. He was one of those who had complained of inaction during the Case interval, and he had strongly supported Hutchins's appointment.

But Griswold also was an Oberlin graduate with an unyielding Puritan conscience, and he had become convinced that the board had a duty to prevent what he regarded as imprudent actions and expenditures by the officers. "We were responsible for charitable money, not Hutchins money," he said, "and I was considerably concerned." He had concluded that the basic interest of the president was to "promote himself and to advance his own projects — often, but not always, very good projects, but always centered on Hutchins."[10]

Griswold was not alone in that view, and though he refused to concede the justice of the complaint, Hutchins recognized that he was in trouble. At the urging of sympathetic board members, he decided to go directly to the media to make an affirmative case for the Fund's actions, which in the public eye were indistinguishable from his own. He was received respectfully by editorial boards in California and elsewhere, but not at the crucial press conference his aides arranged for him in New York, the media capital.

Among the twenty reporters he faced under the glare of television lights were several Hearst hatchet men, a representative of Fulton Lewis, and the left-wing skeptic Dwight Macdonald. Most of the others were affected by the reductionism of their trade and sought to boil down Hutchins's running controversy with the congressional investigators to a difference of opinion over whether a loyal American would hire a Communist. They gave him no chance to indulge in the reasonable discussion of the Fund's activities he had prepared.

The question that would not down was whether or not Hutchins himself would hire a Communist. Hectored by interrogators who offended his sense of intellectual propriety, he made no real effort to meet the issue by pointing out, as he had many times before, that there could be no pat answer for one who believed in the Bill of Rights; Communism was not illegal in the United States, the Communist party was recognized as a legitimate political organization, and, so long as this was so, its members were entitled to the Constitution's guarantees and immunities. Instead he made the terse response that would be featured unadorned in the news accounts: "I wouldn't hesitate to hire a Communist for a job he was qualified to do provided I was in a position to see he did it."

"Bob was just too intellectually arrogant to submit to the pounding they gave him," said the experienced Walter Millis, who attended the press conference. "We all thought, including Bob, that the whole thing was a dreadful show."[11] And there was worse to come.

In early December Hutchins faced four Washington correspondents on the national TV broadcast "Meet the Press." Frederick Woltman of the *New York World Telegram and Sun* was openly hostile; the waspish May Craig of the *Portland Press Herald* made a career of bear baiting; the professedly neutral chairman, Lawrence Spivak, encouraged controversy; and James McConaughy, Jr., of *Time* was indifferent. Under the compression of the half-hour program, Hutchins was never able to get far away from the matter of hiring Communists.

The negative implications of most of the questions "caused Hutchins to bristle with anger and become evasive, cold and spiritless. . . . The insolent character of the interrogation shattered his usual imperturbability and incapacitated his celebrated rhetorical brilliance."[12] I had joined the Stevenson campaign in Chicago by that time, and though I missed the broadcast, I heard variations of that verdict on all sides later that afternoon at a cocktail party hosted by a University of Chicago professor. Some of the Hutchins loyalists were in tears, and even his critics had been astonished by his faltering performance.

The effect of all this was to further arm the dissident Fund directors. Paul Hoffman, trying to explain his loyalty to Hutchins, wrote to the wife of the wavering Roger Lapham, a longtime San Francisco friend who had recently joined the board,

> . . . I share your disappointment that Mr. Hutchins did not give an unqualified "no" to the question of whether he would employ

a communist. If I had been asked the question, I would have so answered and would have explained that I believe that anyone who is a communist today is either a conspirator or a fool. I would have made this reply despite the fact that there are probably some intelligent people who are intellectually committed to communism and who might conceivably be employable. Whether this is what Mr. Hutchins had in mind, I do not know. I do know that he is a *totally* honest person and a purist. There are times that I wish he were a weak-kneed compromiser like myself.[13]

Chairman Walter of the HUAC announced a full-dress hearing on the affairs of the Fund, to begin early in 1956, but an even more ominous note was sounded by Henry Ford II in a letter to Hoffman expressing his personal objections to some of the Fund's actions. Acutely aware that condemnation by the chairman of the Ford Foundation would greatly strengthen the demands for revocation of the Fund's tax exemption, Hoffman sent Ford a conciliatory reply and urged him to meet informally with the Fund's directors before making any public statement. It didn't work. On December 6 Fulton Lewis gleefully made public a letter from Ford to a New York American Legion Post, in which he said:

> Despite the fact that I have no legal right to intervene in the affairs of the Fund for the Republic, I have exercised my right as a private citizen to question the manner in which the Fund has attempted to achieve its stated objectives. Some of its actions, I feel, have been dubious in character and inevitably have led to charges of poor judgment.[14]

Ford was responding to an orchestrated campaign directed against him from the right. For months the chorus led by Lewis had been demanding that he issue a statement clarifying his position on the Fund, and the coup de grace was delivered in an open letter to Ford from William F. Buckley, Jr., reproduced on a full page of his *National Review:*

> What is your own judgment on those activities of the Fund for the Republic that are at public issue? Do you believe that the present management of the Fund is faithfully and effectively carrying out the intentions of the Foundation in establishing the Fund? . . . A statement from you on these matters is of crucial public importance.[15]

Legend has it that Hutchins responded to the Ford statement, "I'm sure I have been guilty of bad judgment, but I didn't build the Edsel." The comment has to be placed among the apocrypha, however, for years later, when I asked him if he had thus salted the wound left by the spectacular failure of Henry II's pet project, he grinned and claimed he couldn't remember. It was certainly no time for wisecracks, for he was now under fire on all sides.

Some of the most savage attacks came from the left, where a group of born-again Marxists dominated the intellectual coterie that called itself the American Committee for Cultural Freedom. Many of these had been Communists in the days before the locomotive of history made the U-turn occasioned by Stalin's pact with Hitler. Their inside experience with the Communist Party USA and its offshoots, they claimed, made them experts on the true extent of the Communist menace and led them to support the McCarthyite effort to root out subversives. In *The New Leader,* identified by the CCF as "the foremost weekly of the anti-Communist left," they argued that the civil-liberties issue was overblown and that such violations as did occur could be condoned in the face of the need for uninhibited loyalty-security programs to protect the government against a masked and insidious conspiracy.

Their charge against Hutchins, who could hardly be indicted for having Communist sympathies, was one of willful ignorance. His most vociferous CCF critic was the philosopher Sidney Hook, a disciple of John Dewey's who had been denouncing Hutchins since he first engaged his mentor on educational issues. Hook charged extremism, irresponsible judgment, a misplaced sense of methodological nicety, a lack of common sense, and "total political innocence." Hutchins, he wrote, was the prince of "soapy-minded ritualistic liberals."[16]

In December, trying to mend fences anywhere he could, Hutchins journeyed to Morningside Heights to meet with a CCF delegation at Columbia University, taking along as an ideological interpreter Paul Jacobs, a one-time Trotskyite who worked on the blacklisting project. It was a fairly civilized exchange, but Hutchins was puzzled by the author Diana Trilling, who insisted that he seemed to believe that there was something idealistic about the Communist party. On their way back downtown, Jacobs recalled, Hutchins asked how anyone could have so misinterpreted the views of one who had spent his life denouncing totalitarianism: "I tried to explain why the CCF people reacted so passionately about the Communists, but I don't think I was very successful, for Hutchins kept looking at me as if to say, 'I will never understand your friends.' "[17] Nor would they understand him; the attacks in *The New Leader* continued.

*   *   *

As the year wound down, Erwin Griswold's patience ran out. He sent a letter dated December 19 to Paul Hoffman to demand Hutchins's ouster, with copies to all board members. Hallock Hoffman recalled that when Hutchins received his copy in Pasadena, he handed it to him and asked, "How do you like this for a touch of Christmas spirit?"[18] Noting that he did so with great pain and difficulty, Griswold said he had concluded that the president's inflexible views on civil liberties and his seemingly unquenchable taste for controversy had disqualified him:

> He does not primarily seek to explain, to lead, to guide, to speak softly and persuasively, to inculcate wisdom and understanding. On the contrary, his approach tends to be combative, belligerent, provocative, dramatic. Rather than leading to better understanding, this approach evokes strong reactions, and often leads to increased opposition and to misunderstanding. This, I think, is poor human relations.[19]

On the eve of the January board meeting, three of Hutchins's strongest partisans, Elmo Roper, J. R. Parten, and Eleanor Stevenson, met with Griswold and William Joyce, who, along with James Zellerbach, Albert Linton, and John Lord O'Brian, was supporting the demand for Hutchins's resignation. As Roper recalled the meeting,

> Griswold and Joyce honestly believed that Hutchins was searching for people to aggravate, that he was using unnecessarily inflammatory methods to defend principles we all believed in. If Parten or Stevenson or I had ever wavered at any time in our belief in Hutchins, he would have been gone. We had no intention of wavering. You could say he came that close to being removed as president.[20]

On January 6 and 7 the board met for a total of thirteen hours. The directors had before them a twenty-two-page memorandum from Hutchins, which had been vetted by Hoffman and Roper. Although he still did not concede that he had erred, he promised to use an affirmative approach in the future to rally support from the ideological center. "The audience we have to aim at," he said, "consists of those who would be favorable to the Fund if they understood it."

> . . . The problem of the Fund is education, rather than public relations in the usual sense. That is, the process is relatively slow

and long; the Fund cannot be operated in terms of tomorrow's headlines. One thing seems fairly clear: if we operate in terms of tomorrow's headlines, we shall be permitting the enemies of the Fund to manage it. They can write more headlines than we can.[21]

He did not abandon his contention that the decisions in the Landman, Browder, and Knowles cases had been proper and should not have been surprising to the board, since they were consistent with the position he had taken as far back as 1934. But on the practical matters of administration that had been raised by Griswold and others, his capitulation was complete. He pledged that the "Feel Free" era was over; the responsibilities of the officers would be defined so that there could be no question of the final authority of the board.

To that end he proposed to give up his cherished residence in Pasadena and move to New York; to limit Ferry's responsibilities to program and planning; to appoint the diplomatic David Freeman vice president in charge of administration, which meant that he would receive visitors and maintain contact with the grantees; to appoint a new vice president to take charge of public information; and to make all three of these directly answerable to the president.

At the end of the grueling session the board voted to accept Hutchins's reorganization scheme "on a trial basis," subject to approval of a detailed plan to be submitted at the next meeting. In the selection of the new vice president Hutchins would be required to work with the board's Temporary Information Committee. And from that time forward no Communist would be hired for any purpose, and no former Communist or person taking the Fifth Amendment would be retained or given a grant without the board's prior approval.

Two days later, in response to a query, a Fund spokesman acknowledged that at the annual board meeting on November 17, Hutchins had been reelected president. When a reporter asked why the story hadn't been released at that time, Hutchins replied, "It hardly seemed of sufficient importance to take note of." But Chairman Walter took note. The president would be called before the HUAC when it resumed its hearings after the year-end break. "We're not going into the Fund for the Republic," he said, "we're going into Dr. Hutchins."[22]

CHAPTER THIRTY-FOUR

Innocence
by Association

When the board's Temporary Committee on Information[1] began making inquiries about a suitable new public-relations vice president, it found the man it was looking for at the small, well-regarded Stephen Fitzgerald Agency. Aside from his professional qualifications, Frank K. Kelly provided a total contrast to the officers who had been dealing with the media on behalf of the beleaguered Fund for the Republic.

Hutchins treated journalists with a cool detachment relieved by flashes of mordant wit, which alienated as many as it charmed, and Ferry often became truculent when crossed. Kelly, a rotund, effusive, sentimental Irishman, enveloped reporters and editors in a bubble-bath of flattering attention. His approach was intensely personal; believing himself to be on the Lord's side, he proceeded on the assumption that any right-thinking journalist was a natural ally. He was genuinely hurt by rebuffs, and he showed it. When I commented to one of the editors at the *New York Times* on the remarkable success Kelly enjoyed in its august precincts, he explained, "Most of us can't bear to see a grown man cry."

He had the proper background for the job and, as he demonstrated, the skills and contacts the Fund needed. He had begun his career in his hometown as a reporter for the *Kansas City Star,* had graduated to the Associated Press bureau in New York, and had been one of the early Nieman Fellows at Harvard. Before joining the Fitzgerald Agency he had served a stint in Washington as an aide to Scott Lucas, the Democratic leader of the Senate, and had written speeches for President Harry Truman.

While it was up to Hutchins to recommend Kelly's appointment, there was no doubt that he was the board's man. The new vice president acknowledged that he "had been brought into the picture because there were some members of the board who wanted a public information officer who could keep Hutchins and Ferry from engaging in imprudent actions."[2] In a memoir, *Court of Reason,* he wrote of his first session with the full board,

> After the meeting several of the directors asked me to send frequent communications to the board. Griswold told me that he would expect to hear from me on all major issues that arose.
>
> I promised the directors that I would keep in close contact with all of them. I did not agree to make private communications to any of them. I did not regard myself as an agent for members of the board who sought to remove Hutchins and Ferry.[3]

Even one who certainly had no such intention, however, tried to enlist Kelly in the effort to change the president's ways. Paul Hoffman privately told him that he was expected to persuade Hutchins to recant his statement that there were circumstances under which he would hire a Communist. When the nervous Kelly informed him of the chairman's assignment, Hutchins grinned, took him to dinner at the Yale Club, and invited him to have at it. Kelly recalled how he attempted to carry out Hoffman's instructions:

> When we had finished dinner, I said, "At the request of our chairman, I ask you to recant your statement about hiring a Communist."
>
> "I won't recant," Hutchins said.
>
> In spite of my determination to look frustrated, I was really happy. Hutchins knew it. If he had recanted, he wouldn't have been the man I admired so much.[4]

Hutchins accepted the fact that Kelly's presence was a manifestation of the board's concern over his proclivity for bold, direct action. In any case, the policy restrictions imposed in the wake of the effort to unseat him provided an effective restraint on any new programs that might generate additional controversy, leaving Kelly free to concentrate on restoring the diminished respectability that agitated members of the board.

A primary instrument in his campaign was a four-page *Bulletin* portraying the activities of the Fund and its grantees in ingratiating terms. Kelly's forte was name dropping, thus invoking innocence by association to refute the charge that the Fund was a nest of subversives. The hundred-thousand-person mailing list for the handsomely designed periodical included business executives, clergymen, educators, leaders of civic clubs, and anyone else Kelly thought might have some influence in shaping the views of middle-class Americans.

He backed up the *Bulletin* with a deluge of letters to journalists and politicians he or the well-connected members of the board knew personally, and he was soon reaping a harvest of clippings that demonstrated that the Fund still enjoyed the support of a number of leading newspapers and was generally ignored by most of the rest. Kelly extended the name-dropping technique to television by persuading a reluctant Hutchins, and a hesitant Elmo Roper, to approve a deal with the American Broadcasting Company for a thirteen-week series to be called "Survival and Freedom."

The format was simple, a one-on-one half-hour interview with a celebrity to be provided by the Fund. The interrogator was young Mike Wallace, who had made his big-time debut with a program called "Night Beat," in which he employed the tough, prosecutorial style that was to make him famous. No restrictions were placed on Wallace, but the intellectual capacity and acknowledged accomplishments of the guests supplied by the Fund lifted the program a cut above the show-business level of "Night Beat."

The thirteen guests for the most part were drawn from the galaxy of Hutchins's past associates who had achieved name recognition and were likely to respond to any request made on his behalf. Along with such old friends as Mortimer Adler, Reinhold Niebuhr, William O. Douglas, Aldous Huxley, and Adlai Stevenson, the list included the future secretary of state Henry Kissinger; Erich Fromm, the psychiatrist; Sylvester "Pat" Weaver, the former president of NBC; and the better-known directors of the Fund.[5]

Kelly proudly reported to the board that the Wallace series had attracted eighteen thousand letters, 99 percent of them favorable to the Fund, including a few containing financial contributions. Edited transcripts of the interviews were distributed to the Fund's extensive mailing list.

The Fund for the Republic's last and in many ways most sensational confrontation with the HUAC resulted from a program that predated the effort to pull in Hutchins's horns. John Cogley's study of blacklisting in the movie and TV industries had been approved by the board without demur in 1954, but when he submitted a draft of his report in early 1956, Elmo Roper's advisory committee could see trouble coming.

Frank Kelly had not yet taken office, and Roper asked Ferry to solicit the advice of his former associate Earl Newsom. In forwarding the seven-hundred-page manuscript, Ferry apologized for the imposition, adding, "But such is my respect and Elmo's for your judgment on such touchy matters that we agreed nothing would be done until we had some expression from you."[6] This was something more than a call upon an old friend for a favor; Newsom was still Henry Ford's public-relations counsel, and Roper still had hopes that the Fund might regain access to the Ford Foundation treasury.

Newsom found Cogley's report "thorough, objective, and perceptive in delineating a deplorable situation." But he also recommended that it not be made public:

> It seems to me that such fears as we are dealing with here are overcome only by normal evolutionary processes in the kind of democratic society we are committed to develop in this country. It is possible to give these evolutionary processes direction in some cases, but attempts to accelerate them usually result in setting back progress.[7]

This, of course, was the same rationale the dissident board members had used to justify their retreat from the action-oriented programs initiated under Hutchins. But there had been a public announcement that a report on the blacklisting study would be issued, and the media were obviously anticipating it. "To retreat from the public release of this report would invite the denigration of the Fund's very purpose," Thomas Reeves wrote.[8]

The directors temporized by directing Cogley to cut the lengthy manuscript and submit it for review to representatives of the entertainment industry. Cogley complied, and when the board met in March, it had before it a six-hundred-page version that had been vetted by concerned parties and by the Fund's counsel. He now forced the issue by declaring that he intended to have his work published — if not by the Fund, then by a trade publisher. An appropriation of twenty thousand dollars to cover the cost of the final editing and the publication of ten thousand copies was reluctantly approved in a split vote.

The report covered the development of blacklisting in the entertainment industry from its beginning in 1947, when the HUAC, then chaired by J. Parnell Thomas, embarked upon a headline-grabbing investigation of Hollywood figures who were suspected of being soft on Communism. The first, outraged reaction of the industry was reflected by the Association of Motion Picture Producers, which publicly rejected "irresponsible charges made again and again and again and not sustained."[9]

Although some leading Hollywood stars formed a Committee for the First Amendment, they were countered by the Motion Picture Alliance for the Preservation of American Ideals, which provided Chairman Thomas with a few prominent actors and studio executives who testified that there had indeed been Communists among the workers in the Hollywood vineyards. Their leading spokesman, Adolphe Menjou, the dapper actor who had berated Robert Hutchins on the muddy parade ground at Allentown thirty years before, claimed that his organization had kept "an enormous amount of sly, subtle, un-American class-struggle propaganda from going into pictures."[10]

This, of course, was the real issue. Among the creative talents in the film industry there were many who held liberal views that were at odds with those espoused by the Alliance, and they were often frustrated by the self-censorship imposed by the studios to insure that their pictures would not offend any significant portion of the moviegoing public. Some certainly tried to make their work reflect their convictions, and a few of these had Marxist sympathies. But the studios' bland end-product demonstrated how futile any such effort had been. The ironic fact was that the only Communist propaganda that could be identified in movies made in Hollywood was to be found in wartime films idealizing the Soviet Union, produced at the behest of official Washington when Russia became an American ally.

But the initial resolve of the industry's leaders dissipated under the flood of adverse publicity generated by the Washington witch-hunters. The studios abandoned artists with impressive screen credits who invoked the Fifth Amendment to justify their refusal to testify, giving them a place in the dark history of that era as the Hollywood Ten.[11] By 1954, Cogley found, the studios were "unanimous in their refusal to hire persons identified as Communist Party members who have not subsequently testified in full before the House Un-American Activities Committee. The studios are equally adamant about not hiring witnesses who have relied upon the Fifth Amendment before Congressional Committees."[12]

Cogley and his ten-man staff had put together a devastating case history of the manner in which the HUAC had intimidated the movie and television industries to the point where they had institutionalized a blacklist that made a mockery of the Bill of Rights. At its May 16 meeting the board heard from its counsel, Bethuel Webster, that the HUAC had demanded an advance copy of the report, both in draft form as first submitted to the officers and in galley sheets reflecting the final version. This crude effort to intimidate them galvanized the directors. For the first time they voted unanimously to go ahead with publication, and Webster was instructed to delay compliance until after the paperback *Report on Blacklisting* was printed and released to the public.

The HUAC, in turn, was galvanized by the publication of the Cogley report. The Committee was smarting after losing a round to the Fund. In early June Chairman Walter had announced that a number of handpicked witnesses would testify as to whether the Fund's "extensive and diverse activities [are] strengthening or weakening our security structure in the Communist cold war. . . ." He mentioned Henry Ford's description of some Fund activities as "dubious," but H. Rowan Gaither, providing tangible evidence of a shift of public opinion, expressed, on behalf of the Ford Foundation, "full confidence in the integrity and patriotism" of the Fund's directors.[13]

When the HUAC's staff director, Richard Arens, indicated that the hearings would adjourn after the Committee's witnesses were heard, Hutchins wrote a letter to Walter stating that he and the Fund's directors would be present at the hearings each day and would demand equal time "to present witnesses of our selection, including members of our board and representatives of our grantees."[14]

Kelly arranged a dinner for thirty-five leading Washington correspondents, at which Paul Hoffman discussed a recently released report summarizing three years of Fund activities and answered questions about the latest HUAC foray. Behind the scenes, Hutchins spoke to J. R. Parten, who spoke to his old Texas friend Speaker Sam Rayburn, who in turn spoke to Chairman Walter. On June 20 the HUAC announced that the hearings had been postponed indefinitely.

Then, on June 24, the two-volume paperback *Report on Blacklisting* was released to the press. Four days later Cogley was subpoenaed to appear before the HUAC. From the Committee's standpoint, Cogley was hardly an ideal witness; as executive editor of the weekly *Commonweal,* he had earned a solid reputation among Catholic intellectuals, and there was nothing in his record to indicate that he had ever been guilty of Communism or any other heresy. When he walked into the hearing room on July 10, he was accompanied by one of the most conspicuous of those intellectuals, Representative Eugene McCarthy of Minnesota, who had an arm around his shoulders.

A short, tousled man with a soft voice and a diffident manner, Cogley sat alone at the witness table. He had rejected the Fund's offer of counsel, and he opened his testimony by saying that while he thought his summons raised a free-press issue, he would not invoke either the First or the Fifth Amendment and would answer any questions the Committee cared to ask, except those related to sources of information he had received in confidence.

Arens, the staff director, made much of the fact that Cogley's assistant, the brilliant young journalist Michael Harrington, was an active member of the Socialist party, and that one of his reporters, Paul Jacobs, had been a Trotskyite while a student at CCNY. Cogley pointed out that Harrington, like his mentor, Norman Thomas, was an outspoken anti-Communist, as was Jacobs, a labor organizer who had been denounced by the most radical of American labor leaders, Harry Bridges of the Longshoremen's Union.

The interrogators got nowhere with the unflappable Cogley, and when Walter ended the session by asking him if he wished to make a final statement, he said, "I would like to know why I was called here." Walter responded, "We called you for the purpose of ascertaining what your sources were in order to determine whether or not your conclusions were the conclusions we would have reached if we had embarked on this sort of project."[15]

This was exactly what the Fund's strategists had hoped for. The issue was now clearly one of freedom of the press and was certain to rally the support of the journalistic community. This became apparent as the hearing dragged on, with Arens guiding the Committee's witnesses through a familiar litany of denunciations of the Fund, and Walter continuing to reject Hutchins's demands that he and his board members be heard. The *New York Times* commented:

> If the House Committee on Un-American Activities were really interested in examining un-American activities it might long ago have used its great powers as an investigative arm of Congress to look into the thoroughly un-American art of blacklisting in the entertainment industry. Instead, it left that thankless job to the Fund for the Republic, but it has now suddenly raised its hackles because it didn't like what the Fund's independent inquiry produced.[16]

Almost a year later, in what amounted to its last stand in its long campaign against the Fund, the HUAC demanded that members of its staff be provided office space and be allowed "to review documents relating to the Fund's activities since December, 1952." The office space was denied, but the requested matter from the files was mailed to

Chairman Walter, except for materials compiled in the blacklisting study. Cogley then received another subpoena to appear before the Committee. He informed Chairman Walter that under no circumstances would he deliver records of interviews he and his staff had conducted:

> I do not believe that you want to investigate me personally. I have never belonged to any group that might be deemed subversive, even by the most elastic standards of the day. There is nothing in my record, nothing whatsoever, to justify suspicion. However I will report to your Committee on May 15 and answer any questions your Committee may want to ask about my life, my actions or my affiliations. I will do so willingly.
>
> But I will answer no more questions about anything I have written and published. I will not supply you with the documents you demand. In stating this, I know that I may be asking for a great deal of trouble. There may be a high price to pay. Please God, I will be willing to pay it.[17]

Without explanation, the Committee's hearings on the blacklisting report were postponed, and in the face of a rising chorus of condemnation in the press that even included an admonitory editorial in the *Wall Street Journal,* it soon became evident that they would never be resumed.

In February Frank Kelly arranged a name-dropping extravaganza to celebrate the Fund's refurbished public image. "I thought the Fund should demonstrate publicly in Washington that it did have friends in many places," he wrote. "Invitations were sent to members of Congress, to businessmen and labor leaders, to clergymen of all faiths, and to the Washington offices of many national organizations. Five hundred correspondents from newspapers all over the country were included."[18]

When the black-tie audience assembled in the ballroom of the Shoreham Hotel, it was sprinkled with members of Congress, Supreme Court justices, and other Washington notables; Speaker Sam Rayburn's bald head gleamed conspicuously at J. R. Parten's table. Elmo Roper, who had been elected chairman to succeed Paul Hoffman, introduced three eminently reputable new directors drawn from the Protestant, Catholic, and Jewish faiths: President Henry Pitney Van Dusen of the Union Theological Seminary; Monsignor Francis J. Lally, the editor of *The Pilot,* the weekly newspaper of the Boston archdiocese of Cardinal Cushing; and Herbert Lehman, a former governor of and senator from New York. The speaker for the evening was Bruce Catton, a recent addition to the board who could qualify as a secular humanist. The popular Civil War historian and editor of *American Heritage* delivered a resounding address that draped the Fund in red, white, and blue.

This new respectability withstood its ultimate test when, in the spring of 1958, Fulton Lewis cited a leaked HUAC staff report that he said verified that "everything that was ever charged against the Fund — by me, the American Legion or hosts of other critics — was all true and a lot more."[19] It would, he proclaimed, certainly cause the IRS to revoke the Fund's tax exemption, as Chairman Walter demanded when he forwarded a copy of the report to Treasury Secretary Robert Anderson with a covering letter insisting that the Fund was providing aid and comfort to the nation's Communist enemies.

But Secretary Anderson was another old Texas friend of J. R. Parten's, and Parten paid a call on him along with Paul Hoffman, who had been publicly anointed by President Eisenhower as a delegate to the United Nations. The Fund now had, as Kelly said, friends in many places — more of them, and better-placed, as it turned out, than did Chairman Walter. The tax exemption remained in force until the corporation was dissolved in 1979.

CHAPTER THIRTY-FIVE

Back to Basics

E ven before the House Un-American Affairs Committee backed down and its outriders in the media began to lose credibility, Robert Hutchins had begun plotting a withdrawal from the civil-rights and civil-liberties fronts. There were still battles to be fought, but he was convinced that the tide had turned. With its immediate obligations discharged, he concluded, the Fund's remaining millions could be best spent by concentrating on the unresolved basic issues underlying the spasmodic surface reactions that had distorted the nation's political process.

The Senate had recovered from its rout by Joe McCarthy, and in December 1954 it formally censured the maverick senator, consigning him to the political scrapheap where he passed his sodden final days. In May of that year the Supreme Court's landmark *Brown* decision had outlawed segregation in the public schools and opened the way for the civil-rights crusade that would ultimately remove racial barriers in housing, public accommodations, and employment. Under Chief Justice Earl Warren, the Court found the most opprobrious of the government loyalty-security procedures unconstitutional. The McCarthy era had not ended, but it was clearly winding down, and by 1957 public opinion had shifted to the point where the front-line defenders of the Bill of Rights were no longer dependent upon Fund grants for their survival.

The Fund's role in effecting this sea change has always been a matter of dispute. Commentators on the right still regard it as an un-American activity, and the appraisal of those on the far left was colored by their distaste for Hutchins's style. Generally approving of what he set out to do and conceding the courage that his bold actions required, they nonetheless deplored the way he went about it. Dwight Macdonald complained that Hutchins had displayed the same traits that, in his admittedly jaundiced view, had marred his career at Chicago and the Ford Foundation:

> great nerve and courage in pushing unorthodox and generally sensible ideas, combined with superficiality, arrogance, poor judgment about people, and a congenital lack of maturity both in understanding specific situations and in effectively dealing with them. In short, the classic sophomore type, with all his vivid potentialities and his muted actualities — but a sixty-year-old sophomore.[1]

In the pre-Hutchins era the Fund's efforts had been largely concentrated on scholarly research, and despite his reservations, some of this had continued, at the insistence of the board. Some critics thought this kind of conventional grant-making cast, in Macdonald's phrase, an "academic pallor" over the Fund's reputation as an activist defender of the Bill of Rights.

But those scholarly works, even if their lengthy gestation and their balanced style meant that they had little influence on contemporary events, surely had and still have considerable value, and most of them would not have found support elsewhere in the atmosphere of that time. The most ambitious and expensive of these ventures were the studies of American Communism edited by Clinton Rossiter. Thomas Reeves wrote of these and related works:

> Though buried in libraries, away from the flow of daily events, as Dwight Macdonald and other journalists have been eager to note, these volumes, together with the bibliography, the digest, the Stouffer public opinion study, the Lazarsfeld-Thielens study of academic freedom, and Herbert Packer's brilliant analysis of ex-Communist witnesses . . . remain unprecedented and permanent reference works for thoughtful citizens seeking genuine scholarship on the history and effects of the "enemy within our midst."[2]

Some of the Fund's publications — notably Cogley's blacklisting report, Yarmolinsky's case histories of loyalty-security proceedings, and the findings and recommendations of the Commission on Race and

Housing — had a direct impact on current developments. Others were used in discussion programs conducted by a wide variety of civic, religious, and veterans' organizations — even including, until it was brought up short by the national commander, the Illinois department of the American Legion.

The Fund's public-relations program produced newspaper reports and commentary that helped counterbalance the virulent anti-Communist propaganda campaign being waged in the right-wing press. And in its three years of operation, the news-film program produced 155 film clips from the civil-rights front, most of them depicting aspects of the racial upheaval that contrasted with the defiant acts of white resistance groups. Supplementing the limited coverage available in those dawning days of television, these clips were widely used by the networks and local stations, reaching an estimated audience of more than fifty-five million viewers.

The largest total of grants made to a single agency, seven hundred thousand dollars, went to the Southern Regional Council, keeping the interracial organization in the field at a time when it was virtually impossible for it to obtain financial support in its own region or from conventional national foundations. The grants made it possible for the Council to establish local chapters in all of the former Confederate states, and the Fund also provided critical support for interracial programs maintained by the major religious denominations. These activities were indispensable in rallying moderate white support for the black-led civil-rights movement launched by Martin Luther King in the mid-1950s.

Reeves found that some of the Fund's activities were less effective than they might have been because of "Hutchins' unwillingness to soften his language and his occasional inability to clarify publicly the Fund's intentions." He thought the board was right in rejecting his more incendiary proposals and in insisting on tighter management of staff operations. By and large, he concluded, the interaction was constructive: "The often abrasive encounters between the concerned, business-minded men of reputation on the board and the far-seeing, intensely intellectual president enabled the Fund for the Republic to combine achievement with survival."[3] He summarized his findings in his book *Freedom and the Foundation:*

> No corporate body during the years of the Fund's first phase even approached its efforts in what Hutchins accurately called "uncharted and dangerous territory." Fear was the great preventative. The most opulent foundations chose to ignore what were, in many ways, the most serious domestic problems of the fifties. No

organization went beyond its [professed] belief in equal opportunities to pour hundreds of thousands of dollars into channels promoting racial equality. None tried as hard as the Fund to keep serious conversation alive. Dr. Hutchins is guilty of a rare understatement by asserting simply that the Fund for the Republic "did as much as any organization in those years to expand civil liberties." The exact degree of that understatement cannot be known.[4]

No one ever accused Robert Hutchins of running away from a fight. He "dreads controversy as Br'er Rabbit dreaded the briarpatch," Dwight Macdonald wrote.[5] But he did not, as this implied and as many of his supporters believed, deliberately seek trouble. Although he was always willing to ignore personal risk when principles were at stake, he was a dispassionate tactician who rarely allowed his personal feelings to influence his judgment. Thus his decision to change the Fund's direction had nothing to do with any resentment he may have felt over the loss of support from his more timorous directors. Rather, it reflected his recognition that he could not carry the day on the civil-liberties front without them.

This was the reason he swallowed his distaste for the kind of fulsome public-relations campaign Frank Kelly launched to restore the Fund's respectability. He recognized the truth propounded by Harry Kalven of the University of Chicago Law School in appraising the Fund's activities: "For an institution to speak with a powerful voice in a crisis, it must carry a pre-existing reputation and prestige with it into the forum."[6] The Fund had had those, but its reputation had been abraded, and a significant number of the directors who had provided it were now unwilling to mount the barricades. Nevertheless, the Fund still needed their blessing or, failing that, their ostensible neutrality.

Those who found his new direction unacceptable could quietly decline reelection without erecting a public monument to their lack of confidence in the president. This was the course Erwin Griswold followed, but he was never to withdraw his complaints. Thirty years later, after conceding that Hutchins was "a great figure in our time, with more innovative ideas than any other person I can recall in the field of education," he went on to say,

But, in my view, his basic interest was not education, nor freedom. It was Bob Hutchins, and looking out for Bob Hutchins seriously affected his judgment. He was, perhaps, one of the several authentic geniuses I have known — and all of them had serious flaws, in one respect or another. It seems to go with the genre.[7]

But accepting the presidency of the Fund for the Republic and conducting it in the fashion he did were hardly the acts of a man primarily concerned with looking out for himself. It did resolve the sticky issue of compensation that had arisen in connection with his impending severance from the Ford Foundation. But money was never an active concern of Hutchins's, and he would have had no problem in finding a berth that would provide adequate income and status. There was Bill Benton's standing offer of any position he might desire at Encyclopaedia Britannica, Incorporated. Or if he wanted to be rid of administrative responsibilities, he could have had a professorial chair at a university, with plenty of time for the writing and lecturing he had always employed to keep his ideas before the public.

I joined the board shortly after Hutchins took over, and I never had any reason to doubt that he had accepted the presidency out of a sense of duty. His commitment to civil liberties and his willingness to confront those who sought to undermine them were a matter of record. So was his ego, which led him to agree with the board majority that in both background and temperament he was the best, if not the only, person to carry out the mission that had been assigned, largely at his instance, to the Fund.

It is evident, however, that Hutchins looked upon the Fund for the Republic as a temporary diversion from his main purposes. The ideas that had been evolving since he embarked upon an academic career more than thirty years before were now irrevocably fixed. He could never be sure, he once said, whether he clung to them out of conviction or out of stubbornness. In any case, he returned to them as soon as conditions at the Fund for the Republic permitted, but this time he displayed a quality that he had previously disdained: patience.

In 1955, when he began encountering resistance among the directors of the Fund, he delivered an address before the organization that had heard him define the administrative role ten years before. Calling the talk "The Administrator Reconsidered," he confessed that though his circumstances were not effectively different now that he was employed by a philanthropy, his views had changed in at least one respect:

I now think that my lack of patience was one of my principal disqualifications as an administrator. I did not want to be an officeholder; I wanted, as the saying goes, "to get things done." This led me to push matters to a decision, sometimes by very close votes. . . . It is one thing to get things done. It is another to make them last.[8]

Then, having indulged in this uncharacteristic display of contrition, he proceeded to qualify it. Had he been more patient, he said, he would have gotten fewer things done, but they might have lasted longer:

> Of course, I might not have lasted as long as I have — I might have died long since. . . . The pressure of time is so great, the number of people who have to be convinced is so large, interminable discussion of the same subject with the same people is so boring, that the amount of patience a university administrator must have passes the bounds of my imagination, to say nothing of those of my temperament.[9]

"I was interested in effecting permanent improvements in American education, not in keeping the University of Chicago in an uproar," he said.[10] Now, as he renewed that interest, he managed to muster sufficient patience to persuade his new, smaller constituency to go along.

At the conclusion of the May 1956 meeting of the board, which authorized the publication of Cogley's report, Hutchins placed before the directors a memorandum suggesting that a committee be selected "to advise the Board of Directors on the desirability, feasibility, program, organization, financing, location, and personnel of an institute or council for the study of the theory and practice of freedom."[11]

Although he indicated that the cost of such an undertaking might be as much as seven million dollars — which was just about what the Fund had left from its Ford grant — he made no request for an appropriation, asking only for authority to appoint qualified scholars to study the matter and to report on it in September. With the cautionary provision that such a body must act with the advice of board members to be appointed by the chairman, the request was approved. Erwin Griswold voted no.

The new committee was Hutchins's first move in an effort to revive a proposal for a Center for Contemporary Thought he had initiated during the early days of the Ford Foundation. Shortly after the Fund for the Advancement of Education was organized in 1952, four of its board members — Barry Bingham, Walter Lippmann, Paul Mellon, and Owen J. Roberts — were appointed as a committee to explore the feasibility of a Hutchins plan "to form a group of the best minds of our time to attack together the underlying problems, theoretical and practical, of our civilization." He pointed out that there was no such group anywhere:

> There are individuals studying these problems; there are conferences about them. But nowhere is there a continuing organization of first-rate men who are committed to work together for a substantial part of their time to formulate, state, clarify, and advance the ideas basic to the continuation of Western Civilization.[12]

The idea was elaborated at two extended conferences chaired by Hutchins in the spring of 1953. In sessions at Princeton and London the board committee met with twenty leading American and European intellectuals who could certainly be counted among the best minds of the era.[13] They were asked whether they thought it would be possible to establish an institution composed of leading thinkers "in all fields — they need not all be professors — that could advance knowledge and perform the task of illumination by joint consideration of the most important problems, speculative and practical." The reaction at both conferences was favorable, and Hutchins began to sketch in the details of how such an academy might work in practice:

> There is no thought of duplicating the Institute of Advanced Study at Princeton or All Souls College at Oxford. These are places where men pursue their individual interests, free from the demands of their colleagues or of students. The conception that we have is exactly the opposite. The men in the Academy would be committed to devote part of their time to work on a common problem. The group would be free to choose the problems on which it would work; but the essence of the enterprise would be intellectual cooperation.
>
> We have tentatively concluded that the way to begin is to bring together a relatively small group of senior men who are interested and qualified, have them decide on the problem with which they want to start, assign writing jobs to each of them, and circulate the results among them. When the correspondence reached the stage at which another meeting would be useful, it would be held. The problem would be clarified at that meeting and the process repeated until the group was satisfied that the maximum of clarification and agreement had been reached. The results would then be published.[14]

The greatest disappointment of Hutchins's tenure at the Ford Foundation was his failure to obtain the ten-million-dollar grant he considered necessary to launch the proposed academy. Throughout his career he had insisted that in addition to its teaching and research functions, the university should serve as a center of independent thought and criticism. After twenty years of trying to achieve this at Chicago, he had despaired of establishing the necessary community of scholars in a university setting, but he thought it should be possible to do so in a small, freestanding institution where the participants would not be distracted by teaching or hampered by conventional university organization. His and Paul Hoffman's estrangement from Henry Ford had doomed the proposal, but no one would ever convince Hutchins that it wasn't worth a try.

The idea of the academy had originally been couched in terms of its immediate benefit to higher education. "It has become increasingly evident to the Fund for the Advancement of Education that the institutions and practices of contemporary education do not present a set of clear and consistent ideas relative to the practical objects of education," Clarence Faust wrote. "The existence of such an institution should provide a new point of reference for humanists in the universities and elsewhere."[15] But now Hutchins had to sell the concept to a board of directors who thought their mission was to defend and advance civil liberties. If it seemed to some of them a welcome respite from the running battle with anti-Communist zealots, it struck others as the abandonment of the Fund's proper role.

Hutchins insisted that his proposal was well within the limits of the Fund's charter. The concern was still with the Bill of Rights; only the approach was different. At the outset there had been no choice but to deal with the symptoms of the fever that inflamed the body politic, but now the time had come to consider the underlying causes — what Hutchins called, in the catch phrase that came to identify the new program, the basic issues. The problem was no longer one of public relations but one of public education; the trouble was not that Americans did not understand the Fund, but that they did not understand how the Bill of Rights applied to their own lives.

He saw to it that the advisory group authorized by the board supported that proposition; it consisted of three of his old companions in arms, Richard McKeon and Robert Redfield of Chicago and John Courtney Murray, S.J., of Woodstock College, plus two current associates, Eric Goldman of Princeton and Clinton Rossiter of Cornell. Paul Hoffman obliged by appointing Hutchins partisans as the board representatives: George Shuster, Meyer Kestnbaum, and Howard Marshall. "Logical positivism,'' Thomas Reeves noted, ''was somewhat poorly re-presented.''[16]

Hutchins presented the advisory group's recommendations in a carefully crafted, fourteen-page memorandum. It called for a complete reconstitution of the Fund. The sole gesture to the past was the assertion that the Fund would continue to provide reports on ''the operations of American institutions connected with freedom and justice.'' The program would be ''directed and conducted by a group of men of the highest distinction, aided by assistants and consultants, who will devote full time over a period of years to examining the state of the free man in the United States and ideas and institutions associated with the terms 'liberty' and 'justice.' '' A few anchors were thrown to windward:

> . . . We are not suggesting the establishment of an ideological center. It should not get bogged down in metaphysical or theological superstition. The American idea is directed to action — the functioning of a free society — and the effort we propose would have to limit its concern to ideas which relate directly to action in the political and social orders.
>
> We have faith that once the issues are clarified, the good sense of the American people will be brought into play, with highly beneficial results. We believe that issues now fogged in useless controversy will be satisfactorily resolved according to time-tested principles of justice and freedom, once the people see clearly what the issues are.[17]

In a further elaboration prompted by the negative reaction of some of the directors, Hutchins appealed to the businessmen on the board with a promise of greater efficiency: ''I was compelled to admit that the criteria used to arrive at the recommendation or rejection of grants and projects were not altogether clear and consistent. It seemed to me to follow that if more intelligible standards of action could be developed the Fund would be better understood. . . . The first effect of the plan would be to take the Fund off the defensive.''[18]

The details of the new program would be determined by a group of qualified individuals of diverse backgrounds, selected by the president. They would be full-time employees with income and perquisites equiv-alent to those of a professor at a first-rank university. This ''faculty'' would be chaired by Hutchins and would be given the authority, subject to ultimate approval by the board, to plan and carry out all future activities of the Fund.

Anticipating objections to such a delegation of the board's powers,

Hutchins flattered the members by asserting that his recommendation would "not be necessary if the Directors, who are the kind of people who would be sought for the group proposed, could drop everything and devote themselves to the Fund."[19] The board's relationship to the program would be analogous to that of university trustees to their institution, with the officers and staff filling the role of a university administration.

The flattery was not sufficient. The memorandum made it clear that under Hutchins's proposal the Fund would no longer be a short-lived grant-making body but would be reconstituted as a permanent, self-sustaining institution. The mere suggestion of such a change prompted the retirement of three directors — John Lord O'Brian, Chester Bowles, and James D. Zellerbach — even before the proposal was presented to the board. And open rebellion broke out among the officers.

I had rejoined the board after my stint with the Stevenson campaign, and when I arrived for the annual meeting in November I was immediately waylaid by David Freeman and Adam Yarmolinsky, who had been appointed vice president and secretary in the reorganization that followed Griswold's effort to oust Hutchins. They had prepared a seventeen-page counterproposal, which they were attempting to take directly to the board, without reference to the president.

The memorandum urged the rejection of Hutchins's proposal and the continuation of the grant-making program, setting forth a schedule of appropriations that would cause the Fund to be liquidated in five years. But this plan was not, as its authors professed, merely an effort to present an alternate method of procedure to "our employers — the directors." It was an attack on the basic philosophy of their superior officer, and it echoed the authoritarian charge that was so often leveled at Hutchins. Freeman and Yarmolinsky declared their belief that "no individual or group of individuals can find *the* answer to the problem [of civil rights] but that many groups, with different approaches, will help to work out common-sense solutions. We believe that the Fund, for practical as well as public relations reasons, should eschew the position that it knows best how to solve the major problem in its field."[20]

The insurrection died aborning. The most determined anti-Hutchins directors were leaving the board, or planning to do so, and those who had reservations about the new program nonetheless resented the end run being attempted by the disaffected officers. But Hutchins had not yet won effective support for his Basic Issues proposal. The best he could get was a twenty-thousand-dollar appropriation to hire consultants to assist in identifying the major areas to be considered; these were to work with an ad hoc committee of the board and report at the next meeting, in

February. Negative votes were cast by Griswold and Lapham, and the latter grumped to Paul Hoffman:

> Perhaps I'm not educated enough to deal in the abstract along the lines Bob seems to enjoy. . . . I've been trained in the school of getting down to brass tacks. Maybe Bob will find it hard to adjust himself to a school where you have to watch the cash till instead of appropriating cash which flows from contributions not accumulated by personal effort. . . .
>
> Aside from any changes in the board it will be very much of a new picture if Bob's proposal is adopted. Frankly, I hope it won't be.[21]

When it met in February 1957, the board was not yet prepared to go all the way with Hutchins. He got another hundred thousand dollars to employ consultants on the Basic Issues program, but the board still had serious reservations. Chairman Roper summed up: the board was not voting on the president's recommendation to devote the balance of the Fund's uncommitted assets to the new program, but it did recognize that certain grant-making activities were no longer bearing fruit. Hutchins went to work on further revisions designed to convert the doubters.

In May he unveiled the chosen members of the central group of consultants, and by any definition they were a distinguished and diverse lot. There were familiars from the past — Henry Luce, Scott Buchanan, John Courtney Murray, Reinhold Niebuhr, Robert Redfield, and Eric Goldman — plus A. A. Berle, a professor of law at Columbia and a former New Deal brains-truster; Eugene Burdick, a professor of political science at Berkeley; Clark Kerr, then the chancellor of the University of California; and Isidor Rabi, a Columbia physicist and Nobel laureate.

All of these men had endorsed the Basic Issues program by agreeing to devote their time and energy to the project with only minimal compensation, and Hutchins could cite the favorable reactions of more than a hundred leading intellectuals whom he had consulted. Moreover, each director was assured of a more active participation in the Fund's program than he had ever before enjoyed. In areas of their special interest, the members would serve as "liaison directors between the central group and the Board and between the various sub-groups and the Board."[22]

Sixteen of the eighteen directors present, with Griswold and Lapham dissenting, voted to concentrate the Fund's effort on the Basic Issues program for one year, approving the requested appropriations. It was stipulated that this was to be the main, but not the exclusive, effort. But the course was set, and there would be no turning back. Freeman and Yarmolinsky submitted their resignations, and the remaining staff members were assigned to support the consultants on the Basic Issues program.

Hutchins had some more persuading to do before he obtained approval for all the studies he had in mind and for the final phasing-out of the Fund's grant-making operation. But he was once again in command, and the Fund's renewed respectability was attested to by applause for the new program in the mainline press. The *New York Times* said,

> The Fund has been spending its money by and large in some exceedingly useful directions despite ill-informed and often irresponsible criticism that has been directed against it. In so doing, the Fund has helped strengthen American democracy, and the new study . . . gives every indication of being a major contribution to this end.[23]

The Hearst columnist George Sokolsky provided a swan song for the opposition: "Too bad that Voltaire is not alive to investigate the investigators, or Marx to curse them for the poverty of their ideas, or Joe McCarthy to haul them before his committee to discover their foibles."[24]

CHAPTER THIRTY-SIX

"On the Mountain Eucalyptic . . ."

Although he had envisioned a permanent "faculty" in his prospectus, Robert Hutchins launched the Basic Issues program with a group of part-time consultants supported by staff members who had been chosen for other purposes. One reason for this patchwork procedure was that he did not yet have his board's approval for a permanent commitment. The other was that he wanted to be sure he had found the right members before he moved on to establish what he believed the concept required — a residential facility well removed from the madding crowds of the metropolis.

Back in 1953, when he was developing the idea of the academy as a project for the Fund for the Advancement of Education, he had stipulated that those first chosen

> would be obligated to spend not less than a fourth of their time in the work. They would have research and clerical assistance. They would have to travel to meetings. These meetings might last a month or more; but the members would not be required to give up their present posts or move to a common center.
>
> The reason for beginning in this way is that it will be hard to tell which men are qualified until they go into action. As the organization develops, we should decide which members we want to join a residential group. I think that ultimately they should be together for at least six months of the year. I am certain that

face-to-face discussion is necessary for complete understanding and real progress. The only question is, which men do we want in residence, and how soon can we be certain of this?[1]

Although he did not stress this design, he followed the procedure in launching six Basic Issues studies, presenting them as experiments intended to develop their assigned themes. These had been approved in outline, and in some cases modified, by the board. Each was to be assigned to one of the new consultants, along with the appropriate "liaison directors" and a staff administrator. It was also contemplated that each consultant would be free to bring in such outside participants as he thought the project warranted — thus casting a net for possible future members of the central group.

A. A. Berle took over "The Corporation"; Clark Kerr, "The Individual and the Labor Union"; Isidore Rabi, "The Individual and the Common Defense"; Eric Goldman, "The Mass Media"; and Eugene Burdick, "Political Parties, Pressure Groups, and Professional Associations." The reservations of board members over there being too narrow an institutional focus had resulted in a stress on the individual in some titles and the elaboration of others. There was also concern that any approach to religious institutions would founder in sectarian controversy, with the result that Pastor Niebuhr and Father Murray were paired for "Religion in a Free Society." Henry Luce and Scott Buchanan were not assigned to specific themes, but would join with the others in the joint sessions, in which these studies were to be appraised and others considered. Death claimed Robert Redfield before he could assume an active role.

Progress on these fronts was uneven. The most ambitious undertaking was that of Clark Kerr, whose background was in labor economics. He put together an ad hoc staff to assist in his consideration of the internal governing structure of labor unions. With Paul Jacobs as administrator and Hoffman, Kestnbaum, and a new board member, the Broadway lyricist Oscar Hammerstein II, as liaison directors, the project enlisted four social scientists from Kerr's faculty at Berkeley and arranged consultations with twenty-seven top union leaders and management labor experts. The end product was a notable Fund publication, "Unions and Union Leaders of Their Own Choosing."

Other consultants elected to work pretty much on their own, with only cursory reference to their assigned associates. I was a liaison director for Eric Goldman's mass-media project, along with Bruce Catton and another new board member, Alicia Patterson, the publisher of the Long Island newspaper *Newsday*. My contributions were virtually nil, since the

Central High School desegregation crisis had erupted on my doorstep at the *Arkansas Gazette* and I was in no position to fulfill any outside obligations. But I had the impression that my colleagues, including Goldman himself, were not much more diligent. The only publication credited to the project was arranged by Frank Kelly, who as staff administrator commissioned an occasional paper, "Freedom to See," by Herbert Mitgang, a *New York Times* editor, which dealt with the application of the First Amendment to television.

The papers produced in this hit-or-miss fashion constituted the most significant aspect of the Basic Issues program during its first two years. The Fund had on its staff a gifted editor, Edward Reed, who worked the products of the consultants and their advisers into fifty-four pamphlets, shorter occasional papers, and reports, some of which incorporated excerpts from the consultants' discussions. A million and a quarter copies of these handsomely designed publications were distributed. "A great many of the highly popular pamphlets were of superior quality, generating overwhelmingly favorable responses from the press and intellectual circles, and no doubt evoking much public discussion," Thomas Reeves wrote. "Adult education classes, colleges, high schools, and seminaries all over the country were eager to secure copies."[2]

No such encomium could be applied to the Basic Issues program as a whole. The concept of the central group of consultants as a community of scholars engaged in a continuing dialogue proved to be inapplicable to a group of intellectuals who considered their primary commitments to be elsewhere. After a five-day inaugural gathering in a bosky retreat at White Sulphur Springs, two-day meetings were scheduled at six-week intervals, to be held at the Fund's handsome conference room atop the Lincoln Building. These were increasingly desultory affairs, and Hutchins began to receive complaints from within and without.

As early as July 1957 Elmo Roper indicated skepticism after reading transcripts of the disjointed dialogue conducted among the consultants. As he had at Chicago in an earlier day, Scott Buchanan expressed dismay at the discursive exchanges and urged Hutchins to take charge and order the dialogue with a firm hand. Even Ping Ferry, who had been enthusiastic about the new departure and had worked effectively with Berle in the production of a paper on the corporation, had serious misgivings.

The transcripts of the consultants' discussions elicited from Mortimer Adler a thirteen-page denunciation, which echoed the dim view he had taken when Hutchins first proposed the academy idea to the Fund for the Advancement of Education: "I learned from the London conference how undisciplined are even the very best minds in the world when they turn from the solitary tasks of thinking and writing to the collaborative task of discussion."[3] He said of his old friend's current effort, "Collectively, the result is almost zero. There is almost no evidence that any member of the group learned anything from anything said by anyone else or was even stimulated to say something important and new by something said by anyone else."[4]

Hutchins, as usual, was undeterred. At the May 1958 meeting of the board he blithely recommended an extension of the program:

> We have a good deal yet to learn about the methods of making the most of the intellectual resources at our command. The procedure for the conduct of meetings relating the work of the projects to that of the central group, and of using outside experts can, and I hope will be improved. . . .
>
> I believe that the effectiveness of the group would be enhanced if its members knew that the Board of Directors was committed to the program for a longer period than one year. I think we are now entitled to say that the program, in spite of the imperfections and uncertainties in it, is soundly conceived and will be successfully carried out.[5]

The board concurred. The members were impressed by the flow of publications, which reflected progress within the several studies, and by the favorable publicity the industrious Kelly had generated from the name-dropping opportunities the studies provided. The directors were sent transcripts of the consultants' deliberations, and if they actually read these ponderous documents, none, with the exception of Roper, reacted negatively. Without a dissenting vote, they appropriated four million dollars for a three-year continuation of the Basic Issues program. (Erwin Griswold resigned in November, saying that he "had wanted to do so only in such a way and at such a time that his resignation could not be subject to unfavorable inference by persons outside the Fund."[6] He was replaced by the supportive Arthur Goldberg, the general counsel of the AFL-CIO, who would serve as secretary of labor, Supreme Court justice, and UN delegate when the Democrats returned to power.)

During the next year Hutchins phased out the remaining extraneous projects with terminal grants and had the decks cleared for full concentration on Basic Issues. But the cherished dialogue among the consultants never materialized. They met twelve times, for a total of thirty days, but attendance became more and more erratic. Hutchins added his old friend Justice Douglas to the roster, but he, like the other prominent members, was unable or unwilling to attend regularly. In March 1959 only five consultants showed up for a much-postponed session. At the May board meeting Hutchins admitted the failure:

> On the basis of our experience it is clear that though part-time men can be effective critics they cannot be relied on to develop and guide a program in this vast and complicated field. They are under too many different pressures. The more famous they are, the greater the pressure.[7]

This, of course, was no surprise to Hutchins. The inadequacy of the program on a part-time basis, as far as he was concerned, only proved the necessity of what he had wanted all along — a residential center where he could assemble a group of the best minds available and set them to clarifying the issues the consultants had begun to identify. He assumed, correctly, that a solid board majority was committed to the concept and would go along with him when he was prepared to present a concrete proposal.

Hutchins had been dragooned into moving to New York and had remained there under sufferance. The Fund's aerie on the fifty-fifth floor of the Lincoln Building, across from Grand Central, was fine, he said, if one's business was throwing money out of windows, but it was no place for a serious intellectual enterprise. What was needed was comfortable surroundings where the participants would be out of touch with, or at least beyond the easy reach of, importunate competitors for their time and attention.

Vesta Hutchins did not share her husband's distaste for the metropolis. Her heart condition had eased to the point where with reasonable care she could cope with the rigors of life in the city, and she found much there to fascinate her. She had been delighted with the amenities of Darien, where they had first settled among the Connecticut commuters. When the lease on their country house there ran out, they moved into New York, and the discouragement engendered by a dismal flat on Park Avenue had given way to pleasure at the apartment they found at Gramercy Park.

Theater and concerts provided a bonanza they both enjoyed, and Hutchins was as much of a social lion as he chose to be. The couple spurned the kind of charity galas that constituted much of the entertainment for affluent New Yorkers, but there were always invitations for evenings and weekends with people who interested them. Vesta particularly cherished the verbal pyrotechnics that were set off when Hutchins encountered his fellow lions, as he did at an informal dinner at Alicia

Patterson's town house, where the other guests were Frank Lloyd Wright and Carl Sandburg.[8] Any one of the three might have replied as Wright was said to have done to a request for a comment on his reputation for arrogance: "It was inescapable; when I recognized the extent of my talent I realized it was either that or false humility."

But if Vesta enjoyed New York, she had enjoyed San Marino more. Like so many of those who grew up in the Midwest, she and her husband had both been beguiled by the physical beauty and benign climate of California — so much so that they had begun to make active plans for relocating there upon his retirement, which was no longer a remote prospect now that he had turned sixty.

They had found what they were looking for on weekend visits to Santa Barbara, the mission town a hundred miles up the coast from Los Angeles where mountains come close enough to the sea to provide a Mediterranean ambience. They bought a secluded twenty-six-acre tract in the hills looking out to the Pacific across the great estates that dapple the leafy Montecito Valley. There was a small dwelling on the place they could occupy while they built the dream house Vesta was already sketching in her mind.

When the board of the Fund indicated its support for locating what Hutchins now called the Center for the Study of Democratic Institutions outside New York, Vesta joined him in scouting for an appropriate site along the Eastern Seaboard, pointing out drawbacks to pastoral communities in New England and the mid-Atlantic states. A degree of rusticity was desirable, but transportation and communications needs dictated an exurban rather than a rural location. That being the case, Vesta suggested, Santa Barbara neatly filled the bill. The town was within easy reach of Los Angeles and San Francisco and was large enough to provide suitable housing for the staff and resident scholars. Hutchins doubted that the board would agree, but he finally capitulated to her insistence that he had nothing to lose by giving it a try.

He carefully prepared his case. A June meeting of the consultants was canceled, and they were invited instead to spend five days in August at the Santa Barbara Biltmore, an elegant seaside resort. Certain that the contrast with New York's late-summer steam bath had gained the support of most of them, he turned his attention to the board, for which he would need more tangible inducements.

With the assistance of an old friend, Mrs. Horace Gray, one of a number of wealthy Chicagoans who had settled in Montecito, he found an estate with a mansion capacious enough to provide adequate office and conference facilities. Having been held in trust by a bank after the death of the owner, it was available at a bargain price of $250,000, and John B.

Elliot, Jr., a former San Marino neighbor, agreed to contribute $100,000 to pay for the necessary remodeling.

Hutchins then went to another of his admirers, Cyrus Eaton, to see if he could present the Center's proposed new home to the board free and clear. Frank Kelly was with him in Cleveland when he asked the imperious old tycoon to donate the funds or, failing that, buy the estate as an investment and give the new Center a free lease. Kelly described the result when Hutchins spread out the plat of the forty-two-acre property and made his pitch:

> Eaton clapped his hands together. Staff members appeared. Eaton asked for atlases and reports on Santa Barbara and the whole area around the city. When his staff assistants brought them in, Eaton studied them for a while, and then he gave a wintry smile: "I think I'll take a flier with you boys."[9]

The flier was the lease deal; Eaton would take title, but the Center could use the main building for as long as it was needed. The assistant who communicated the good news to Kelly added, "He says that when your board hears what Cyrus Eaton is willing to do, they'll buy it themselves." He was right. Albert Linton, the tight-fisted insurance executive who had been designated comptroller by his fellow board members to husband the Fund's remaining assets, said, "If it's such a good investment, why don't we buy it ourselves?"[10]

With two thirds of its members present and voting, the board unanimously approved the purchase of the Hale estate and the establishment of the Center for the Study of Democratic Institutions as the sole activity of the Fund for the Republic. The Center opened for business on September 1, 1959.

The decaying mansion atop Eucalyptus Hill provided a fitting home for such an undertaking. Like Hutchins, it had an air of old-fashioned elegance, and the long-neglected formal gardens, stables, and tennis court would remain that way, reflecting his disdain for spending money to improve his physical surroundings. The unaccented one-story stucco facade, with curved marble steps leading up to a recessed entrance, contrasted with the ostentatious dwellings maintained by many wealthy Montecitans. Hutchins, taking note of the local Hispanic heritage and the suspicion that he was bent on creating a Platonic academy, called the building El Parthenon.

Inside there was a marble-floored entry hall giving onto a tree-shaded inner courtyard. Marble also paved the flanking colonnaded walks, which led to a large drawing room with curved French doors that opened onto a red-tiled terrace with views of the mountains and the sweep of the coastline all the way to the Santa Barbara yacht basin. Holding that it would be too expensive to fill the Olympic-size swimming pool below the terrace with either water or dirt, Hutchins ordered it covered with wire netting on which vines were trained. In time it would, as a sardonic visitor said, become a handy snakepit.

The sitting rooms, bedrooms, and dressing rooms flanking the inner courtyard were readily converted to offices. The drawing room was refurnished with a hollow, oblong conference table for the daily dialogue. At one end of it there was a wood-paneled library, and at the other a dining room, where a buffet lunch would be laid out for the participants. The rooms on the main floor, as well as those located in the former servants' quarters and storage areas downstairs and in a nearby guesthouse, were outfitted with inexpensive, utilitarian office furniture.

The Hale estate did indeed turn out to be a bargain. As Hutchins patiently explained to those who assumed that such idyllic surroundings must be expensive, he could not have obtained comparable office space and conference facilities for $350,000 if he had bought a building in a warehouse district. Moreover, the acreage was increasing in value at a higher rate than almost any other prudent investment the Fund could have made. In the event the Center experiment failed, the sale of the property would cover severance pay and other costs of liquidating the Fund, which remained the corporate entity.

Functional though they obviously were, the building and its environs would always be cited by Hutchins's critics as evidence that he had retreated to an ivory tower far removed from the real world. At the end of a visit to the Center, the British economist Kenneth Boulding suggested an anthem to be sung to the tune of "Men of Harlech":

> *In a time Apocalyptic*
> *On the mountain Eucalyptic*
> *Full of thought Acropolyptic*
> *Stands the Hutchins Hutch.*

> *In this intellectual Attic*
> *Institutions Democratic*
> *Are studied by the Mode Socratic*
> *With the Midas Touch.*

The Midas touch, unfortunately, was mythic. Hutchins estimated that the four million dollars remaining from the Ford fund would maintain the

Center for only three years. In the absence of a guarantee of permanence, only one of the consultants proved to be available full-time. Scott Buchanan, who had chafed even under the institutional limitations of the college he had been instrumental in creating at Saint John's, was again footloose. The others would continue as before, without any fixed commitment as to the time they would devote to the Basic Issues program. Nor did Hutchins have any success with the leading intellectuals he had sounded out in the course of developing the academy idea.

His own criteria limited the search. He was looking for scholars with a certain cast of mind, and he was not particularly impressed by towering reputations, as he indicated in an exchange of letters with Thornton Wilder, the world-traveling friend he had enlisted as a scout:

> I don't think Heidegger is the greatest living philosopher; but I must admit I don't know who is. Maybe all I mean is that I don't think there is any great living philosopher. Think of Russell, Sartre, Jaspers, etc. They and all the others are journalists. Niebuhr and Schweitzer and Barth have some points as theologians; but are they systematic theologians?[11]

As he had done so often in the past, Wilder turned down repeated invitations to join Hutchins in the new venture: "I came to see that general ideas are not my province. Just as in the shower I am a better tenor than Caruso, so on a long solitary walk I'm the best social philosopher since Ortega; but dammit I dry up in public."[12] But Wilder thought Hutchins was on the right track, as did others who declined to make an immediate commitment but held open the possibility that they might be available in the future.

With the exception of Hutchins and Buchanan, the only Center personnel who took up residence in Santa Barbara upon its founding were those classified as senior and support staff. The Fund vice presidents, Ferry and Kelly, had elected to make the move, as had Hallock Hoffman, John Cogley, and Edward Reed. Paul Jacobs established an office in Berkeley to continue his work with Kerr's trade-union project. Walter Millis would continue with the common-defense study but would work out of the small New York office that had been established for George Shuster, who had retired from the presidency of Hunter College and agreed to spend a year seeking financial support for the new enterprise. Madeline Marina, the office manager, and a few venturesome secretaries had also joined the migration.

Hutchins was determined to keep the administration of the Center as small and unobtrusive as possible and to avoid the kind of stratification that divided scholars and university administrators. In addition to their routine duties, the senior staff, including James Brady, a local real-estate man Hutchins had hired as presidential assistant, were expected to participate in the Basic Issues program, at least as observers.

Ferry had argued against thus involving the Fund personnel. "Bob made a great mistake, in my judgment, in not getting rid of virtually all of the staff, all of us who were with the Fund for the Republic," he said. "We had all been hired for different reasons or different expertness. . . . He suddenly tried to reform us into eggheads, into experts on trade unions, or the mass media, or whatever." Ferry thought only Cogley and Millis were qualified for the new undertaking, but Hutchins rejected his suggestion:

> Bob said he wouldn't think of it for two reasons; first, he owed loyalty to people, and he regarded most of us as semi-unemployable; but second and most important, he said that nobody really knew how to get at the basic issues. And that he didn't believe in eggheads anyway, and to take me as an example, he would much rather have me handling the study of the corporation than anybody else. I responded by saying that he was wrong about this. . . . I wasn't being self-sacrificing. I thought the idea of the academy was good. I also thought, after all, Bob was making a fresh start, why not really do the Center with the best people he could get?[13]

Hutchins later said in defense of his decision that his experience at Chicago had taught him that academicians always tended toward specialization, and that he thought the new members he was seeking for the Center would be well served by a salting of generalists. Ferry recalled that Hutchins responded to his plea of unfitness by declaring him eligible for the august new company "between the thirty-fifth and thirty-fourth floors of the Lincoln Building. 'As former Chancellor of a great university, I declare you henceforth an intellectual,' Hutchins said, putting a hand on my shoulder and startling passengers on the elevator. Others were similarly raised in rank."[14]

Hutchins was convinced that all that was needed to overcome the reservations of the great minds he sought was a demonstration of how the new residential center could work in practice. He counted on the prospect of a respite from the rigors of the weather in their usual habitat to persuade the consultants to participate in more protracted sessions than had been possible before. These began in the fall, and most of the heavyweights were in attendance for sessions that extended over two weeks or more.

A new campus of the University of California at Santa Barbara was becoming a stop on the academic flyway extending from Berkeley and Palo Alto in the north to Claremont in the south, and this enabled the Center to tap into a concentration of talent that rivaled that of the Cambridge-Washington axis in the east. The CalTech geophysicist Harrison Brown was added to the roster of consultants, and other possible recruits were invited to participate in the dialogues and the ongoing Basic Issues studies.

The skeptical Ferry was soon converted. In October he wrote to his friend Stuart Chase,

> Our schedule is already heavy and getting heavier. Last week three days were devoted to discussions of the theory of democratic institutions. There was a seminar last night on the preamble to the Constitution. At noon today Gerard Piel (*Scientific American*) comes to lunch and spends the rest of the day with us on Technology and Law. We expect Aldous Huxley and others from the University of California also to be on hand. On Friday we begin discussions of the Trade Union based on a paper prepared by Jacobs. . . . Walter Gellhorn will spend the day with us the following week, and we hope to persuade him to enlarge on the idea that non-action by the State is official action in a different form. We have additional discussions coming up on Millis's memorandum on Abolition of the War System, and so on and on. [15]

If the Center was not yet a community of scholars, it was attracting transients who could attest to its serious purpose and unique promise. I assumed that I would be one of these when I accepted Hutchins's invitation to spend what I thought would be a sabbatical year at El Parthenon.

CHAPTER THIRTY-SEVEN

Raising the
Encyclopaedic Roof

In July 1959, as he was preparing for the Fund's relocation to Santa Barbara, Hutchins called to tell me that Bill Benton, who had never lost interest in the recommendations of the old Commission on Freedom of the Press, had offered a grant to explore the possibility of establishing a permanent body to appraise the performance of the media. In his offhand fashion he asked me to join him in California and to undertake the assignment as a continuation of, or a replacement for, the mass-media project.

The Little Rock schools had reopened, an orderly process of desegregation had begun, and the *Gazette* was on the way to restoring the circulation and income it had lost to the boycott that followed its opposition to Governor Faubus and the White Citizens Councils. Hutchins knew I now felt free to move on, and he assumed, correctly, that I would be attracted by the prospect of taking an active part in the founding of the new Center. But, I told him, I already had a commitment to the *New York Herald Tribune* for a series on the growing black population outside the South, and to W. W. Norton for a book on the subject. In what I came to learn was his standard hiring technique, he made an instant calculation and came up with an offer he figured I couldn't refuse: a half-time appointment at a salary of twenty-five thousand dollars.

I made the move with my family in late October and was assigned an office in a former bedroom of the old mansion atop Eucalyptus Hill. In addition to pursuing the media project, I was expected to function as a

sort of brevet consultant on the Basic Issues studies. This meant that
along with the members of the senior staff, I would sit in on a daily
dialogue session. We gathered around the rectangular conference table in
the drawing room at 11:00 A.M. and broke up at 12:30 for a buffet
luncheon set out in the adjoining dining room. If the discussion was going
well, it usually continued informally as participants took their plates back
to the conference table or gathered in small groups on the terrace outside.

The procedure called for a discussion paper to be circulated in
advance and to remain on the agenda until Hutchins concluded that the
subject had been exhausted. The author, who might be a resident or a
visitor, was seated at the head of the table with Hutchins on his left. He
was given twenty minutes for his opening remarks, after which discussion
was free-for-all. Participants spoke as the spirit moved them, without
recognition by the chair, and the entire session was tape-recorded for
future reference.

Hutchins's concept of dialogue made this an intimate proceeding. He
believed that the exploration of an issue in this fashion required twelve to
sixteen regular participants, with visiting specialists added as might be
appropriate. A larger gathering inhibited unstructured interchange; once
beyond the upper limit, the assemblage became an audience and the
participants tended to make speeches, talking past each other. Continuity
was essential; as they met together day after day, members of the core
group would come to know each other's viewpoints and styles and would
adapt their own to accommodate them. Although there were sometimes
dull and irrelevant passages, the routine proved to be effectively
self-regulating, with interventions by the chairman required only rarely to
put the discussion back on course, and it was never to be significantly
altered.

The summons to the daily dialogue was the sound of an ancient
monastery bell tolled by Hutchins as he passed down the passageway
from his office to the conference room. On the wall beside it was a
framed injunction from Saint Benedict, which, if it could not be taken
literally, reflected the spirit that Hutchins, the putative abbot, imparted to
El Parthenon:

> If any pilgrim monk . . . will be content with the customs which
> he finds in this place . . . he shall be received, for as long a time
> as he desires. If, indeed, he find fault with anything, or expose it,
> reasonably, and with the humility of charity, the Abbot shall
> discuss it prudently, lest perchance God had sent him for this very
> thing. But, if he have been found gossipy and contumacious in the
> time of his sojourn as guest, not only ought he not to be joined to

the body of the monastery, but also it shall be said to him, honestly, that he must depart. If he does not go, let two stout monks, in the name of God, explain the matter to him.[1]

Participation in the dialogue was the only fixed requirement for those who came under the loose designation of senior staff, but new arrivals quickly discovered, as I did, that it was far more demanding than it seemed. Identifying and defining Basic Issues involved consideration of a wide range of topics, and dealing with them required more than simply reading the discussion papers. Moreover, most of the participants were also responsible for administrative duties or, as in my case, special Center projects.

The relaxed, imperturbable Hutchins set a pace those who were less endowed could only marvel at. He arrived at around eight in the morning, and when he was not engaged in the dialogue, he would sit behind his big desk in his corner office, turning out enough written matter to keep two typists busy, taking phone calls, and receiving visitors, all the while adding incoming correspondence, papers, and publications to a mounting pile on the floor beside his chair that would go home with him in the evening and be returned the next morning duly processed by that remarkable mind.

Like most of those who came to El Parthenon, I was beguiled by the Center's pastoral surroundings. Situated at the end of a curving drive an eighth of a mile from the stone pillars that marked the entry from Eucalyptus Hill Road, surrounded by magnificent live oaks and stately eucalyptus trees, the old mansion was an oasis of tranquillity. On the ocean side the hill dropped away to the shoreline, with the Channel Islands, on the horizon, setting off a spectacular waterscape. Inland, the tawny mountains of the coastal range rose beyond the green Montecito Valley, where many of the staff found attractive dwellings on land carved out of citrus groves and pastures that were considered surplus by those who now occupied the great estates.

It seemed an idyllic setting for the first months of my emancipation from the rigors of daily journalism and the hazards of the civil-rights movement, but I found little time to enjoy it. For most of the winter I occupied an apartment in New York, spending my time in such unprepossessing precincts as Harlem and Bedford-Stuyvesant. The *Herald Tribune* series, syndicated to twenty-five major dailies, appeared in April, and by then I was at work on the book version, which was published under the title *The Other Side of Jordan*.

When I turned to considering the press-commission proposal, it seemed to me evident that the predominantly adverse reaction of the media to the recommendations that Hutchins and his colleagues had set forth in *A Free and Responsible Press* precluded the possibility of an effective hearing for a permanent body appended to so unconventional an institution as the Center. Hutchins agreed: "Such a group is bound to look a good deal like the commission that that man Hutchins proposed. . . . The Fund's public relations are now such that I think we could get pretty good results operating through it. But of course That Man is president of it."[2]

I thought Harvard's well-established Nieman Foundation might provide a respectable base, but a visit with Louis Lyons, the curator of the Foundation, and McGeorge Bundy, then the university provost, disabused me of that notion. I had a more sympathetic hearing from President Whitney Griswold at Yale, who agreed that such an undertaking was very much in order. But he said that Yale had enough public-relations problems without inciting the wrath of hypersensitive media moguls, and he thought I would meet with the same reaction elsewhere. He was right, and that was about as far as I got before I found that this Bentonian notion had been superseded by a far more comprehensive one.

After I had settled in at Santa Barbara I learned that the board of editors of *Encyclopaedia Britannica* was well along with plans for a basic reorganization of the massive reference work. Hutchins and Benton had concluded that they could not rely on the University of Chicago to provide the intellectual underpinning such an ambitious undertaking would require. In 1959 Benton warned the University's trustees that they could not count on increased revenue from their Britannica stock since the new venture would require the company to invest millions of dollars in the creation of what amounted to a faculty of its own. He spelled this out in a letter to Paul Hoffman, who served on the boards of both the publishing company and the University:

> Our Board of Editors will want to develop our research facilities all over the world. We shall want to set up seminars throughout the world, possibly even establish institutes of learning. At any rate, we are going to dedicate ourselves to the editorial improvement of the *Britannica*. The great goal that this could be done through the faculties of the University of Chicago has not worked out. We must look otherwheres.[3]

At Benton's request, Hutchins provided Hoffman with a description of *Britannica*'s "past, present, and future from the educational and editorial point of view":

Today the royalty contract has to be justified in terms of the unknown value of the imprimatur. The faculty of the University proved to be incapable or uncooperative in several fields, such as philosophy, history and literature, with the result that the London office and I made arrangements to have these classifications handled in England. . . . The number of advisors supplied by the University, or the proportion of the total number required, has steadily declined until it does not now exceed 25 percent of the whole group. . . .

As a result, Britannica is developing as an educational institution on its own. . . . The plans of the Board, which will be enormously expensive, should make the Board one of the great intellectual centers of the Western World, with Britannica as its project. . . .

This obviously requires a fresh look at the organization of the whole world of knowledge. At the very least it means contacts with the institutions of learning all over the world, conferences, seminars, and perhaps the creation of new institutions.[4]

By the time he discussed these plans with me, Hutchins had eliminated the "perhaps" from that prospectus. So far as he was concerned, the Center was the new institution that was required to produce what Benton referred to as "the perfect encyclopaedia." Early in 1960 he addressed a memorandum to the board of editors that defined its mission under REP, the Revised Editorial Program, in the same terms he had used in outlining the objectives of the Center's Basic Issues project:

I think it will not be denied that the leading characteristic of our age is confusion. We cannot understand anything any more in terms of the principles, ideas or slogans on which we were brought up. Our situation has changed too fast for us. Meanwhile the institutions that ought to enlighten us have in the United States taken on so many other responsibilities that they have merely added to the confusion. The advance of vocationalization and specialization has cut off most of the light that might come from the educational system. . . .

I suggest that the object of *Britannica* should be to help its readers understand the world they live in and the one that is opening before them. I think this would mean that *Britannica* would set out to re-examine our ideas in the light of our situation. It would seek to advance the dialogue by getting the important issues clear.[5]

After two years of discussion deadlines were set. In Phase I of REP, the editorial staffs in Chicago and London would revise the content of the set in the course of its annual printings so that the entire thirty-six million words could be brought up to date. "Concurrently," Hutchins wrote to Paul Hoffman, "the Board of Editors is planning for Phase II, in which we shall not be restricted to the limitations of the present set but shall be free to ask ourselves what an ideal encyclopaedia should be."[6] It was Benton's desire that the end-product of Phase II be published to coincide with the two-hundredth anniversary of *Britannica,* in 1968.

In the early summer of 1960, Hutchins proposed that I become involved in the undertaking as the editor in chief of *Britannica.* Before approaching me he had discussed the possibility with the board of editors and had overcome the reservations of those who objected to my lack of scholarly qualifications by pointing out that the editors traditionally had been journalists. William Smellie, who brought forth the first edition in Edinburgh in 1768, was described as a "brilliant and bibulous" free-lance writer. Across the centuries it had been recognized that while it was up to scholars and specialists to provide the content of the encyclopedia, rendering it intelligible to lay readers was essentially a journalistic task.

As Hutchins outlined it, this was another offer I found it difficult to refuse. I would not have to be concerned with the tedious Phase I task of updating the present set, which would be done under the direction of John Dodge, the veteran executive editor in Chicago, and John Armitage, the London editor. My responsibility would be to work with Hutchins and the board of editors in developing the format and content for the Phase II encyclopedia, while looking ahead to the editorial requirements of adapting the present set to it. Not the least attractive aspect was that it would permit me to remain in residence in Santa Barbara.

That, at least, was my understanding, and Hutchins's, when it was arranged that I meet with Benton in Los Angeles, where he was attending the 1960 Democratic National Convention, at which I was present as a correspondent for the *Herald Tribune.* I had gotten to know Benton during my service in the Stevenson campaign four years before, and my awareness of his eccentricities, as well as my reluctance to abandon a promising free-lance writing career and resume administrative burdens, prompted me to set my salary demand at seventy-five thousand dollars, a figure I thought he would probably refuse to meet. But Benton had made up his mind that I was the man for the job, and he seemed to admire my temerity in demanding a salary that, he boasted to his friends, made him the employer of the highest-paid editor in the land — no doubt an exaggeration, but probably not much of one in that preinflation era.

The handshake that closed the deal was followed by pro forma visits in Chicago with Harry Houghton, the president of the publishing company, and in London with Sir Geoffrey (later Lord) Crowther, the vice chairman of the board of editors. The rotund chairman of the London-based *Economist* launched me on my new career with a sardonic query: "Has it occurred to you that you are about to become editor of a work you won't live long enough to read?"

It was characteristic of both of these two old friends that there was nothing in writing when Hutchins subsumed the Britannica Phase II project under the Center program on the assumption that Benton would approve the necessary expenditures. There was never a contract or letter of understanding, and the closest thing there was to a budget was a loose-leaf document drawn up by Carl Stover, a young political scientist who had just arrived in Santa Barbara to work as assistant to the chairman of the board of editors. Stover recalled that he put this together primarily to explain the charges that were already being billed to Britannica by Hallock Hoffman as secretary-treasurer of the Center. Paul Armstrong, then the company treasurer, remembered being sent out to California by Houghton to see if he could determine what the financial requirements were expected to be. He and Hutchins arrived at an estimate of $750,000 a year, and Armstrong assumed that this would continue at least until Phase II was completed in 1968.[7]

The Britannica arrangement was accorded minimum publicity, for the company's sales executives feared that if word leaked out that an entirely new encyclopedia was in the works, demand for the existing set would dry up, along with the cash flow required to underwrite Phase II. The public announcement of my appointment as editor in chief simply noted that the Center had contracted to "take part in planning future revisions of *Encyclopaedia Britannica.*"[8] Hutchins assured the Fund's board that this would be compatible with the Basic Issues project:

> The officers of the Fund agreed, subject to approval of the board, to look at the fields of the Center's interests from the standpoint of the *Britannica*. They felt justified in doing so because it appeared that the *Britannica* would endeavor in 1968 to clarify the basic issues in much the same way the Center is trying to do.[9]

The lengthy discussions by the board of editors that preceded Phase II had turned on whether the modern encyclopedist should be limited, as his predecessors had been, to reflecting on the arts and sciences practiced and made by others, or whether he should engage in such practices himself.

It was inevitable that Hutchins should support the latter view. He saw the lack of philosophical unity and the absence of intellectual synthesis in contemporary encyclopedias, including *Britannica,* as corresponding to the condition he had been inveighing against in the academic community for the past thirty years. He saw in Phase II a focus for organizing the deliberations of the same great minds he sought for the Center. And it was his hope that publication of the result in *Britannica* might lead to a breakthrough in the specialization and compartmentalization of knowledge that had come to characterize the higher learning.

That concept aroused opposition among members of the board of editors and the scholars they consulted, as it had among Hutchins's contemporaries in his years as a university president. There were echoes of John Dewey in the insistence of Jacques Barzun, the Columbia cultural historian, that the encyclopedia must be treated first and foremost as a work of reference:

> Its chief use is bound to be as a set of answers to questions about matters of history or scientific fact . . . presented in the briefest form compatible with clarity. No surer way could be found to render the work at once tedious and suspect than to obtrude a didactic intention beyond that of supplying answers to questions of fact and meaning.[10]

A Canadian scholar, George P. Grant of McMaster University, took issue with Barzun:

> What is implied by "obtruding a didactic intention" is that any attempt to make scholarship meaningful by philosophic thought is always suspect as being a kind of propaganda put over by somebody with an axe to grind. . . . As a *reductio ad absurdum* . . . we have before us certain parts of the Soviet encyclopaedia. . . .
> But the problem remains whether the Western world can be content with facing ideologies by excluding questions of meaning, and whether it should do this in so central a document of its intellectual tradition as the *Encyclopaedia Britannica.* . . . The Board of Editors in deciding for or against Mr. Barzun's vision are deciding not only about their particular problem but about issues of magnitude concerning the present intellectual state of the Western world.[11]

Stanley Morison, a distinguished English typographer and Catholic antiquarian, agreed, but he held that the reason the Western intellectual tradition was in disarray was that many of its leading figures had been seduced by Marxism, and that most of the others had been emasculated. *Britannica,* he urged, should launch an ideological counterattack against the

> present illimitable drift of the power-political, the industrial and the intellectual. . . . There is overmuch shyness, timidity and reluctance on the part of the West to commit itself to more than a minimum of faith, belief or conviction. The breakdown of institutional Christianity is one cause, and an undue separation of philosophy and science is the result.[12]

The historian Arnold Toynbee sought to dismiss the controversy as irrelevant to the long view he thought *Britannica* should take. Three hundred years ago, he pointed out, the disputation between Catholicism and Protestantism would have produced "a strong temptation to give the encyclopaedia the form of a polemical work of episcopalian Protestant apologetics."

> Yet an encyclopaedia based on religious propaganda and published in 1668 would have been obsolete, and indeed almost unintelligible, within the next twenty-five years. Before the end of the seventeenth century the long-sustained Western interest in religious controversy suddenly slumped. . . . I should be surprised if the fate of our present-day ideological controversies was not the same. Within the next twenty-five years they may already have come to seem irrelevant and boring. Present passion is no guarantee of future durability.[13]

Scott Buchanan took his stand on the highest philosophical ground, contending that to deal with contemporary phenomena it would be necessary to search out an adequate leading idea, a single theme that would be comprehensive enough to draw out and make explicit the essential and genuine themes of all "the systems, arts, and sciences that labor and clash in our inchoate pluralistic culture." Until the thirteenth century the idea of God had shaped the pursuit of knowledge, only to be replaced from the Renaissance through the first half of the twentieth century by the compelling new concept of the dignity of man. "God was still the light," he wrote, "but the object illumined was man, and man was the proper study of man."

> As both these ideas were accepted by thought, and thought in turn was overwhelmed by them, so now in the twentieth century there

begins to appear another idea to inherit their roles, the idea of the world. It is not, of course that the world did not exist or was not thought of before . . . but in the twentieth century the idea of the world has been moving in on us inexorably and incredibly.[14]

At the level of my immediate concern, the format of the new encyclopedia, the issue boiled down to the practicality of a topical organization of the contents of *Britannica*. Crowther, himself a veteran editor, never let go of the point that any significant departure from the empirical organizing principle would require a reconsideration of what he called the "grand architecture" of *Britannica*'s system of classification — a design that employed, as did most encyclopedias, a rigid alphabetical arrangement as the means of reference. This, while it necessarily fragmented bodies of knowledge, had always been considered necessary for the hunt-and-find user. But, philosophical considerations aside, Toynbee pointed out another reason for a basic change in format:

No doubt the sum of what we know is, and always will be, infinitesimal by comparison with the amount of what there is to be known; but the amount of what is now known has already become overwhelming if we think of it, in a practical way, as something that a single mind has to try to master within a single lifetime. The present situation forces the reader, and therefore the editor, to be deliberately selective in his approach to knowledge. Being selective means being systematic. My own guess would be that . . . the Eleventh Edition of the *Encyclopaedia Britannica* [1910] was probably the last in which it was practically possible for the editors to work on dictionary lines.[15]

It was decided to test out the topical approach by assigning an experimental set of lengthy essays dealing with the "orders" of contemporary society, as opposed to the academic disciplines that provided the structure of even the most ambitious of the current encyclopedia's leading articles. The intent was to treat scientific, social, political, educational, economic, and cultural institutions and processes as they affected the daily lives of ordinary men and women everywhere, rather than in terms of the organizing principles employed by natural scientists, sociologists, political scientists, pedagogues, economists, and artists.

Sir Geoffrey, noting that these works would likely run to book length and would be undertaken at a level of generality well above that of any articles in the present set, employed his architectural analogy to suggest that they be termed "roof articles." The name stuck, and by the end of 1962 thirteen "orders" had been identified as requiring roof-article treatment.[16] Their scope would be defined in consultations and conferences here and abroad and in the course of the continuing dialogue at the Center, which itself was, in substantial part, adapted to the project.

CHAPTER THIRTY-EIGHT

New Faces and New Issues

hile the merger of the Center's Basic Issues program with *Britannica*'s REP Phase II was never a perfect fit, the additional income enabled Hutchins to break out of the limitations imposed by the carryover staff from the Fund for the Republic and by the desultory participation of the consultants. He began recruiting additional participants for the dialogue, designating them "fellows," and while he could hardly guarantee them permanence, the appointments were open-ended and presumably would continue as long as the Center survived and the budget permitted.

Among the first to arrive were William Gorman, a philosopher at Mortimer Adler's Institute for Philosophical Research who had served as general editor for the Syntopicon, and Stanley Sheinbaum, an economist at Michigan State University. There was also the beginning of what was to become a continuous procession of visiting fellows who would remain for extended periods of up to a year. These included three of the consultants, Reinhold Niebuhr, Father John Courtney Murray, and Rabbi Robert Gordis; Yosal Rogat, who was on leave from the political-science department of the University of California, Berkeley; William Lee Miller, a professor of religious studies at Yale; and William V. Shannon, the Washington correspondent for the *New York Post*.

Hutchins had hoped to add other distinguished names to the Center roster. The month before the opening, he wrote to John B. Elliot on the prospects for the new institution he had helped make possible, indicating that Jacques Maritain, "the most distinguished Thomist philosopher in the world," and Charles Cole, the retiring president of Amherst College, were expected to move to Santa Barbara. He also thought that Niebuhr and Gordis would become permanent residents, and that Eric Goldman of Princeton and John Kenneth Galbraith of Harvard would be on hand for at least six months.[1] None of these expectations materialized.

While the salaries of some of these fellows could be charged against the *Britannica* project, most had to be compensated from the Center's dwindling resources. George Shuster and Joseph Lyford, another hold-over from the Fund who was assigned to the New York office, were receiving little encouragement as they made the rounds of the foundations. In the hope of attracting individual donors, creation of the new institution in Santa Barbara was used as the basis of an appeal for "founding members" who would pledge at least a thousand dollars a year for five years.

The Center program, as had the payroll, became an amalgam. Sessions devoted to considering the organization and presentation of bodies of knowledge in the *Britannica* were salted among continuing discussions of the Basic Issues. A published *President's Report for 1959–60* announced that the studies on religious institutions and trade unions were considered complete, and that the others were beginning to wind down. But before the Basic Issues program was finally closed out, the discussion papers and taped dialogue it had generated provided the basis for some of the Center's most notable pamphlets and occasional papers.[2]

The level of generality of the roof articles was such that Hutchins did not have to strain the Phase II rationale unduly to accord relevance to a study of the American character, proposed by John Cogley as a successor to the religion project. Cogley had been on leave to serve in John F. Kennedy's presidential campaign and had played a key role in fashioning the address he made before a Houston gathering of Protestant ministers, which was generally credited with defusing the church-state issue raised by the candidate's Catholicism. In November 1960 Cogley outlined a three-part project that would include "a general analysis of the behavior and distinguishing qualities of Americans; a series of case histories of contemporary Americans involved in significant ethical dilemmas; and a study of juvenile delinquency in urban, suburban and rural areas."[3]

In announcing the new study, Hutchins noted that it would focus on two broad questions: "What, in the view of modern Americans, constitutes the good life? How are our new institutions, or radically changed old ones, affecting the moral and ethical standards of the nation?'' As he always did in defining the focus he sought for Center projects, he emphasized the treatment of abstract issues as they related to the reality of contemporary American life:

> We are dealing not only with changes in thought, but also with changes in the structure of democratic institutions. Anyone studying the American character has to consider the interaction between the two. For example, it might be argued that the TV screen reflects the dominance of certain values, or lack of values, in American life — but how much influence does television have in creating the very values it later reflects? In one way or another, the same question might be asked about publishing, the corporate enterprise, labor unions, education, the military establishment, the political process, and even the administration of legal justice.[4]

Cogley, who tended to run his own show with minimal reference to the Center dialogue, enlisted as his associates Paul Jacobs, who had been otherwise stranded in his Berkeley outpost by the termination of the trade-union project, and another alumnus of the blacklisting study, Michael Harrington. A fellow Catholic journalist, Donald McDonald, dean of the journalism school at Marquette University, was retained to conduct interviews with American leaders on the ethical questions they faced in the course of their careers. These were published as a pamphlet series, and in due course McDonald found a place on the Center staff.

The highlight of the Cogley project was a four-day conference in Washington on the American character. The assemblage of well-known intellectuals[5] provided Frank Kelly with another opportunity for a name-dropping extravaganza in the nation's capital, and he used his old guest list to turn out an audience of five hundred for a black-tie dinner featuring addresses by Justice Hugo Black, Reinhold Niebuhr, and Hutchins. While the primary activity was divorced from the Center dialogue, the project did produce a number of Center publications, and at Cogley's suggestion Michael Harrington used his research on the slum environment as the basis for his best-selling *The Other America,* which focused national attention on neglected problems of poverty.

Serendipity launched another enterprise at the Center that had no connection with the Phase II project and that only by a considerable stretch of the imagination could be identified with the Basic Issues studies. It was, however, financially self-sustaining and bore the promise of generous funding to come. This bounty was provided by the wealthy proprietor of a Los Angeles hotel-supply business, Albert B. Parvin, who was profoundly impressed by the views set forth in a book by Justice William O. Douglas, who contended that an international rule of law was urgently needed in a world fragmented by the demise of colonialism. Parvin approached the justice, whom he had never met, with an offer to create a foundation, with no strings attached, to advance his ideas, and Douglas in turn approached his old friend Hutchins.

The Parvin Foundation was duly established, with a board of trustees made up of Douglas, Hutchins, President Robert Goheen of Princeton, Chancellor Jaime Benitez of the University of Puerto Rico, Judge William O. Campbell of the Chicago federal district court, and Parvin. Douglas decided to focus on the special problems of Third World countries, particularly those in Latin America. Upon incorporation of the philanthropy he became its president, with an annual stipend of ten thousand dollars to cover his travel expenses, on the understanding that he would accept no other compensation — an arrangement that in time would come back to haunt all those concerned.

Douglas could hardly run the foundation out of his Supreme Court chambers or his remote summer retreat in the Cascades, at Goose Prairie, Washington. So it was arranged that the Center would provide staff support, and this was assigned to Hutchins's administrative assistant, Jim Brady, an earnest, engaging Irishman who had settled in Santa Barbara and worked as a real-estate broker after his World War II service in the Navy.

The initial Parvin program looked to providing visits by American experts to Latin American institutions, and Brady made an arrangement with the International Center for Advanced Studies in the Field of Journalism at the University of Ecuador in Quito. The two Nieman Fellows at the Center, Frank Kelly and I, seemed to be logical choices as participants in a regional seminar, and we each paid a two-week visit to the Ecuadoran capital in the fall of 1961. By way of exchange, the Parvin Foundation provided a grant of twenty-five thousand dollars to bring Latin American leaders to Santa Barbara to participate in the Center dialogue.

Hutchins also succumbed to the blandishments of Christopher Janus, a Greek-American stockbroker in Chicago who was seized with the notion of presenting a Basic Issues dialogue in the Greek parliament building in Athens. Janus promised to fill a chartered airliner with affluent Chicagoans, who would finance the expedition and also be live prospects as founding members. It was more of a junket than a serious intellectual enterprise, but with Hutchins looking perfectly at home presiding in the shadow of the Parthenon, Justice Douglas, Representative John Brademas (the first Greek-American member of Congress), Richard

McKeon, Walter Millis, John Cogley, Harvey Wheeler, and I manfully undertook a dialogue on democratic values before an audience that consisted almost entirely of those who had accompanied us from Chicago.

These diverse activities attracted a good deal of publicity, most of it favorable, but the prominence given such an unconventional enterprise had an unsettling effect on some of the encrusted conservatives who inhabited the great estates in Montecito. When Ping Ferry wrote a letter to the editor of the *Santa Barbara News-Press* advocating unilateral disarmament, saying that he would rather see Russian soldiers in Santa Barbara than run the risk of nuclear war, the balloon went up. The local John Birch chapter took up where Fulton Lewis, Jr., and company had left off, renewing the campaign to remove the Fund's tax exemption.

Kelly, who saw himself as the custodian of the Center's good name, was deeply distressed by this new threat to the fledgling institution's hard-won respectability. A singularly uxorious man who hated to spend time away from the bosom of his family and was terrified by air travel, he found himself largely cut off from the personal contacts in New York and Washington that had accounted for his initial success in public relations. Now, except for an occasional day trip to Los Angeles to woo acquaintances among the editors of the then conservative *Los Angeles Times,* he was reduced to concentrating his glad-handing on the executives of a small afternoon newspaper and a TV station with a rudimentary news operation. He did this to good effect, retaining the support of T. M. Storke, the patriarchal owner of the *News-Press,* whose political influence had been demonstrated upon the advent of the Center, when he summoned the appropriate officials to his office and disposed of any zoning problems that might have arisen in the conversion of a one-family residence into a conference center.

The *News-Press* published a letter from Kelly disavowing Ferry's views and stressing the fact that his fellow vice president spoke only for himself. He then arranged a public debate with Ferry, presided over by John Wilkinson, a maverick mathematician-philosopher at the University of California at Santa Barbara who would soon become a Center fellow. Playing on Storke's outrage at the John Birch Society's attacks on the loyalty of the publisher's dear friend Chief Justice Earl Warren, Kelly encouraged a campaign against the Society that won the *News-Press* a Pulitzer Prize.

This largely quelled public protest, but it did nothing to allay the anxiety that Ferry's iconoclasm aroused among conservative Montecitans. A few of these, attracted by Hutchins's patrician persona, had indicated interest in the Center, and two had signed on as founding members. A. B. Ruddock, considered a prime prospect for a major donation, wrote to express his concern over the Kelly-Ferry debate and another public session at which Hallock Hoffman, a Quaker pacifist, had joined Ferry in defending the unilateralist position:

> Is it the role of the Center members to indulge in public controversial debate on a very touchy subject? . . . Is it consistent with the general position of the Center for an individual member of the staff to issue publicly his private opinions on national issues of prime importance and in opposition to Government policy? . . . Individual freedom of expression can, it seems to me, be carried to extremes that can result only in harm to the reputation of an individual and the usefulness to and of the Center itself.[6]

Hutchins's reply was civil but pointed:

> There is no question that the unilateral disarmament controversy has set some teeth on edge and made some good friends of the Center uneasy. It may have been injudicious of Mr. Ferry to raise the question in the first place. But I cannot see the machinery that might be set up to judge whether he ought to do so. No one would seriously advocate testing ideas by whether their expression might result in diminished financial support. This would lead in short order, or so it seems to me, to looking for ideas that would result in increased support.[7]

But there were a good many who did advocate such testing. I was treated to an elegant luncheon at a Montecito mansion where the host and several of his neighbors suggested that the Center would benefit handsomely if I could persuade Hutchins to fire Ferry and see to it that no such heresy was committed in the future. My response was that the issue was one of free speech and that Hutchins could no more be expected to yield than I could be expected to support the notion that he should.

It was, of course, preposterous to think that Hutchins would or could muzzle the kind of strong-minded people he was seeking for the Center. And an institution whose announced intention was to conduct a dialogue embracing the full range of opinion on public issues was bound to include participants whose views would offend conservatives and outrage reactionaries.

The unilateral-disarmament flap was followed by the publication of *Fail-Safe*, a best-selling novel coauthored by Center consultant Eugene

Burdick and Center fellow Harvey Wheeler. The movie treatment ridiculed the Pentagon's nuclear-armament program and added Dr. Strangelove to the galaxy of durable American caricatures. This was no doubt even more alarming to Ruddock, a trustee of the California Institute of Technology, who in a postscript to his letter to Hutchins had cited the antinuclear protest led by one of CalTech's faculty members, Linus Pauling, as an example of the damage such an activity could do: ". . . It has caused us much anxiety and loss of financial support."[8] Pauling, a Nobel laureate, subsequently resigned from CalTech, and Hutchins promptly welcomed him as a Center fellow.

The Center was never to acquire a significant number of major financial supporters in Santa Barbara or its environs. Ideology aside, this was virtually assured by Hutchins's insistence that it should be regarded as a national or international institution and could not be considered a part of the local community.

The only Santa Barbara connection he sought proved elusive. Clark Kerr, now the president of the expanding University of California system, had encouraged the idea of the Center's having an adjunct association with the new campus being created on the grounds of a World War II Marine base at the opposite end of the city. Samuel Gould, the first chancellor of UCSB after a former state teachers' college was upgraded to university status, seemed receptive, and Hutchins thought he had an agreement for joint faculty appointments that would not involve either institution in the other's internal policies. But Gould soon departed, to be succeeded by Vernon Cheadle, a cautious academic administrator who could see nothing but possible trouble in such a joint venture.

Hutchins made himself available to address appropriate civic gatherings, and he hosted occasional receptions and dinners at the Center at which local guests could mingle with distinguished visitors. But he was insistent on maintaining the institutional detachment that would be breached if, as he pointed out to Ruddock, the Center felt constrained to shape its program in response to the concerns and demands of donors, a possibility that would be enhanced if they were close at hand.

The policy frustrated Kelly, who wanted to invite leading citizens to observe dialogue sessions to offset the rumors of subversion, which fed on the suspicion that the Center deliberately conducted its affairs in deepest secrecy. Hutchins considered the presence of outsiders distracting, and the few extra chairs placed against the wall of the conference room were reserved for the wives of fellows and visiting participants.

To Kelly's chagrin, Hutchins even imposed a partial ban on journalists. They would be given a place among the auditors if they agreed to remain through an entire dialogue session, and they were always free to interview the Center fellows or the visiting celebrities who usually attracted their attention. But reporters would no longer be allowed to sit in on only part of the dialogue and then quote bits and pieces of it out of context.

Hutchins, however, was never unmindful of the need for effective communication, which was important in its own right and essential to fund raising. The Center's primary means of addressing the public was through its publications, and these continued to enjoy considerable success; by the end of 1961 three million copies of the pamphlets, occasional papers, transcripts, and reports had been distributed, and sixty books derived from Center deliberations by individual participants had been issued by trade publishers. Since the institution's influence on public affairs was exercised in this eminently public fashion, the suspicion of subversion was absurd on its face. Still, there remained a real difficulty in explaining what the Center was about, not only to its critics but to those whose support it needed. After a year and a half of experience with the daily dialogue, I wrote in an article for *Esquire:*

> This sort of discussion, conceived as having no end and producing no immediate agreement, is marked by inevitable frustrations. Since its range is virtually limitless, and it admits of no certainties, the continuing dialogue at the Center casts up a variety of subjects whose very mention is bound to be offensive to True Believers. Santa Barbara now has an active cell of the John Birch Society, whose members are bent on drumming the Center out of town. Dead cats are hurled with equal fervor from the far Left, which considers the Center's disdain for political action evidence of hothouse decadence. Somewhat more serious is the view of some men of affairs that the Center is a sort of intellectual Disneyland without practical utility, for it is these who must provide the philanthropy upon which the Center depends.[9]

I noted that nationally forty-one founding members had pledged a thousand dollars a year or more, and that additional income was being received under the contract with Britannica. But my conclusion reflected Hutchins's increasing concern over finances:

> Collectively, however, these assorted angels have made no more than a modest dent in the annual budget of $1,000,000 required to maintain the Center in its present style. As things now stand the Center has a firm lease on life for another three years or so; after

that the future is as misty as the lovely offshore islands that loom vaguely in the Pacific reaches beyond Eucalyptus Hill.[10]

Hutchins's concern became acute when he began to recognize that the volatile Benton's enthusiasm for the Phase II *Britannica* project was diminishing, and with it the prospect of continued major financing from that source. This was evidenced in Benton's increasing testiness when he came out to Santa Barbara to attend meetings of the board of editors. Although the San Ysidro Ranch where we put him up was elegant enough to attract leading Hollywood stars and the honeymooning Jack and Jackie Kennedy, he complained that no hotel could be considered civilized that could not provide the *New York Times* at breakfast. This, as far as he was concerned, demonstrated that California was hopelessly cut off from the nation's intellectual mainstream.

It was Benton's practice never to confront his old friend Hutchins directly, and so he communicated his displeasure with Phase II through subordinates. By the end of 1962 he was contending to Carl Stover that all the advance editorial planning should be relocated to company headquarters in Chicago, and he was insisting to me that *Britannica*'s editor in chief must maintain his residence there as well. He made these points even more forcefully to Maurice Mitchell when he came over from Britannica Films to succeed Harry Houghton as president of the parent company. But he added, ''We've got to take care of Bob Hutchins,'' and that, along with Mitchell's personal support, gave the Phase II project a tenuous lease on life for another two years.[11]

CHAPTER THIRTY-NINE

In Search of
Survival

The greatest single problem he faced at the Center, Robert Hutchins used to say, was keeping it small. The notion was rooted in his conviction that the dialogue, which was limited to no more than sixteen participants, was the central business of the institution. All other activity was peripheral and should be confined to those tasks necessary to disseminate the dialogue's product. If the Center had adopted the practice of the "think tanks" that were then coming into fashion, it would have begun taking on projects simply because funds were available and would have found its efforts diffused and its independence threatened.

Yet Hutchins's own proclivities militated against his prescription. As he had in his days as a university administrator, he gave the pursuit of worthy ideas priority over budgetary considerations; if the necessary funding was not in hand, it was his duty to persuade the board that it could and must be found. And a lifetime of dealing with tenured faculty, compounded by his own sensibilities, had conditioned him against firing anyone he had hired. If an appointment turned out to be a mistake, it was as a result of his own misjudgment, and noblesse oblige required that anyone who had placed his financial well-being in his hands should not suffer the penalty.

There were holdovers from the Fund for the Republic who, though they rarely joined the fellows at the Center, remained on the payroll. Joe Lyford in New York, who had been a public-relations assistant, found a place under the umbrella of John Cogley's project on the American character, as did Paul Jacobs in Berkeley. James Real, a Los Angeles graphic designer who had been hired for a Fund advertising project that never materialized, became an associate of Walter Millis, who continued to maintain his base on the opposite coast. And the payroll had to be expanded to accommodate those who were reluctant to depart at the end of their tenure as visiting fellows; Richard Lichtman, a neo-Marxist philosopher, came on a one-year appointment and stayed for four.

If this kind of relaxed administration was in keeping with the "Feel Free" motto that still adorned Hutchins's office wall, it also contributed to a need for additional funding that became inescapable given the prospective withdrawal of the *Britannica* project. Elmo Roper thought there was a chance that the Ford Foundation might renew its original grant now that the reconstituted Fund was no longer making waves in Washington. The board agreed to try again, and Hutchins drafted a request for an endowment of $16,400,000, which was presented to the Ford trustees by Roper and J. R. Parten.

To provide additional weight, he asked Justice Douglas to submit a supporting memorandum that in effect amended the original proposal to stress the international concerns of the Center and to raise the possibility of establishing companion institutions in Asia and Africa. In March 1962 Douglas was invited to a dinner with the Ford trustees and given an opportunity to elaborate on his suggestions. His unencouraging report to Hutchins was lightened by the badinage that had characterized the exchanges between the two since their salad days in New Haven:

> In my oral presentation I elaborated on (a) what the Center has done and (b) what the Santa Barbara, Asia and Africa Centers could do in the years ahead.
>
> There was some discussion, but no one said a thing *pro* or *con* about the Center. Only one question was asked . . . and that was whether the African and Asian Centers would be manned solely by Americans or by Americans and Africans and Asians. I said my idea was the latter.
>
> I am sure I did your cause no harm. Whether I did it good I have no idea. If you have real friends on the Board, my memo will serve as a rallying point . . .
>
> I came away rather despondent, not about the reception to your idea but generally. I felt that before long all of us would be witnesses at an inquest — the inquest on a Free Society. I do not know what the alternative is. It is not liquor. And it may possibly not be women. Perhaps Harry Ashmore will know.[1]

Hutchins assured Douglas that he had done as well for the Center as anyone could have:

> I believe that the reason why they do not discuss their decision with regard to us is that the basis for it is personal animosity. If you would resign from the bench and devote yourself to the combined presidency of the Parvin Foundation and the Fund for the Republic, I believe their attitude would change overnight.
>
> I need not say that I agree with you about the inquest on the free society. The American establishment, as typified by the Ford Foundation, is so insensitive to what is going on in the world that it does not deserve to survive.
>
> I have taken up with Harry Ashmore your question of an alternative: he still believes in liquor and women.[2]

The formal answer from the Ford Foundation was not long in coming, and it was, as Hutchins had anticipated, negative. If the Center was to survive, there would have to be a national campaign to seek out new sources of major funding. And that meant that Hutchins would have to resume the mendicant's role he thought he had finally put aside when he left the University of Chicago to work the other side of the street as a hired philanthropist.

He accepted the necessity with his usual stoicism and set about seeking advice from knowledgeable friends as to how best to proceed. Aldous Huxley, who saw a good deal of him while he was a visiting professor at UCSB, sensed his deep disappointment:

> I thought you were depressed by the prospect of having to make forays into the world of the post-prostate rich, by the spectacle of education in particular, and, in general, of the immense, organized insanity within which we must all live and move and have our being, and from which there seems to be no escape except subjectively, in stoicism, mysticism, or alcohol.[3]

Harold Oram, a veteran New York fund-raising consultant who had made his reputation by rounding up support for controversial organizations and causes, was retained to draft a program for the Center. His proposal, approved by the board in September, told Hutchins what he already knew and hated to hear — that he, with the support of the directors, would have to make personal appeals to individual prospects for major gifts and arrange for public gatherings to generate a wider appreciation of the Center and its worth.

Elmo Roper, along with some of the other original board members, had little enthusiasm for this kind of fund raising. He had indicated his desire to step aside after the Ford Foundation rebuff, but agreed to stay on when Hutchins persuaded Justice Douglas to accept an appointment as cochairman. The bylaws were amended to increase the board's membership from twenty-one to twenty-seven, and the vacancies were promptly filled.

The composition and the character of the board were changing significantly.[4] One of the first of the additions after the move west had been Seniel Ostrow, a wealthy Los Angeles mattress manufacturer whose generous spirit and commitment to civil liberties had made him an influential figure in Los Angeles's affluent Jewish community. He was instrumental in opening up southern California as a primary source of funding for the Center. One of his recruits was Harold Willens, a single-minded young businessman who thought he had made all the money he needed and found himself, as he said, psychologically unemployed. Willens became the chairman of a drive that within less than two years signed up two hundred new founding members — representing an annual income of two hundred thousand dollars for five years if the pledges held.

But while diligent scouts could locate prospects, donors of what the professional fund raisers classified as major gifts could not be signed up without personal exposure to Hutchins. With the resignation of a man taking up a familiar and onerous duty, he began to devote a substantial share of his time and energy to private "parlor meetings" where support could be solicited at retail, and to public gatherings where select groups of prospects could be assembled.

Hutchins insisted that these meetings should have genuine intellectual substance, and he developed a formula for them that provided a semblance of the Center dialogue. But, recognizing the attraction of celebrity, he added to the list of Center participants well-known public figures recruited from his stable of personal friends and former associates. The presence of these "fan dancers," as he called them, was necessary to insure the attendance of men and women whose reputation for supporting worthy causes subjected them to a surfeit of invitations to fund-raising affairs.

The prototype meeting in December 1962, dubbed a symposium, was a weekend gathering featuring morning and afternoon sessions and a catered luncheon at El Parthenon, followed by dinner at the oceanfront

Biltmore Hotel, where out-of-town participants were generally quartered. Ostrow and Irving Warner, a Los Angeles fund raiser associated with Oram, rounded up eighty affluent Angelenos, and ten Montecitans joined the group. The speakers and discussants included Justice Douglas, Paul Hoffman, Aldous Huxley, Jonas Salk, Harrison Brown, Walter Millis, Eugene Burdick, and Sir Robert Watson-Watt, an English scientist sojourning in Santa Barbara. The affair was a marked success, producing $338,000 in cash and pledges.

The symposium's title, "Prospects for Democracy," was adapted for a much larger gathering in New York in January 1963. Fifteen hundred people drawn from mailing lists provided by Oram accepted an invitation to spend two days in the ballroom of the Americana Hotel attending a convocation that had two announced purposes: "To bring together world and American leaders to consider how democratic man can meet problems affecting the survival of freedom with justice in the world. To call upon concerned Americans to assume leadership in marshalling financial support to carry forward the work of the Center for the Study of Democratic Institutions over the next decade."[5]

Hutchins's unimpaired standing among his peers was attested to by the quality of those who responded to his invitation to take part in the program. In addition to Center trustees, consultants, and fellows, the participants included Admiral Hyman Rickover, the creator of the nuclear submarine fleet; Adlai Stevenson, now ambassador to the UN; Attorney General Robert Kennedy; Secretary of Labor W. Willard Wirtz; Arthur Burns, a future chairman of the Federal Reserve Board; FCC Chairman Newton Minow; senators Clifford P. Case, Joseph S. Clark, and J. William Fulbright; Lewis Mumford, president of the American Academy of Arts and Letters; Sylvester L. Weaver, former president of the National Broadcasting Company; Rosemary Park, president of Hunter College; Walter Reuther, president of the United Auto Workers; Lord Hailsham, British minister of science and technology; Lord Francis-Williams, a critic and journalist; Lord James of Rusholme, vice chancellor of the University of York; Pierre Mendès-France, former premier of France; José Figueres, former president of Costa Rica; and Gunnar Myrdal, the Swedish economist who headed the definitive race-relations study summarized in *An American Dilemma*.

Except for speeches given at the luncheon and dinner sessions, each presentation was followed by discussion among a panel of four or five participants, many of whom were only slightly less celebrated than the principals, and when time permitted there were questions and comments from the floor. If there was a show-business aspect to all of this, the program was designed around a coherent theme that reflected the Center's concerns and methods, and the quality of the participants made it intellectually respectable.

The media took the convocation seriously, and the coverage was generally favorable. But the critical success was not matched at the box office; while many of the pledge cards placed beside the plates at the closing dinner were filled in, they totaled only about $400,000, on a per capita basis a fraction of that produced by the Biltmore symposium. The impersonal shotgun approach resulted in modest pledges from those who might have been signed up as founding members in a more intimate setting. For Hutchins the grim lesson was that there was no substitute for personal contact in the pursuit of substantial donations.

Despite these disappointing results, the symposium/convocation became a permanent adjunct to the Center program. It did serve to disseminate, if in diluted form, some of the ideas being generated by the Center dialogue, and it was indispensable as the backdrop for a continuous fund-raising campaign. The ultimate goal was to attract the attention of wealthy individuals who might make the Center a primary object of their philanthropy. This did not seem to be a vain hope, since tax-exempt family foundations had become commonplace among those with large earned incomes.

One of these was the enigmatic, deliberately obscure Joseph W. Drown, owner of the sumptuous Bel Air Hotel in west Los Angeles and, Hutchins claimed, all the land between there and the sea. This was an exaggeration, but Drown did own enough real estate to give him an income of at least a million dollars a year, upon which, through a mastery of the tax laws that awed his peers, he usually managed to pay no taxes at all. He gave away much of the money he salvaged from the Internal Revenue Service, but he disdained recognition for his good works. After serving a term on the Center's board, he agreed to remain on the letterhead but no longer participated in the deliberations. "The greatest advantage of being rich," he explained, "is that you don't have to attend meetings." The Center continued to receive substantial gifts from the Drown Foundation when the spirit moved him. Another board member in the same income bracket, the actor Paul Newman, channeled his contributions through his Nonesuch Foundation.

This kind of sporadic support, however, did not permit the accumulation of funds for an endowment that could insure steady income from invested capital. Such a guarantee of permanence was necessary for the Center to establish the institutional character Hutchins had sought for it from the outset — only to be set back by a campaign for operating funds that was almost wholly dependent upon his own reputation and personal contacts. The Center could be sure of survival, he insisted, only when it made no difference who its president happened to be.

Three years would pass before the Center finally came within sight of that goal, and this would result from a happenstance that Hutchins was to describe as the most serendipitous of his career. A train of fortuitous events was set in motion when in October 1963 Linus Pauling, already a Nobel laureate for his scientific achievements, was awarded the Nobel peace prize. The news was greeted with something less than unrestrained enthusiasm by the CalTech administration, and the *Los Angeles Times* denigrated Pauling in an editorial that included a quotation by Hutchins taken from a Center publication:

> I do not know much about science, but I know a lot about scientists. Though I do not know much about professional politics, I know a lot about academic politics — and that is the worst kind. Woodrow Wilson said that Washington was a snap after Princeton. Not only is academic politics the worst kind of politics, but scientists are the worst kind of academic politicians. . . .
>
> A scientist has a limited education. He labors on the topic of his dissertation, wins the Nobel prize by the time he is thirty-five, and suddenly has nothing to do. He has no general ideas and while he is pursuing his specialization science has gone past him. He has no alternative but to spend the rest of his life making a nuisance of himself.[6]

The quotation of his gibe out of context prompted Hutchins to dispatch an indignant letter to the editor, with a copy to Pauling:

> Linus Pauling is an exception to all rules, and especially to the one that professors are worse than most other people and scientists are worse than most other professors.
>
> I have known Linus Pauling intimately for many years and admire him as a scholar, a citizen and a man. He is chiefly remarkable for his courage and his passion for justice, two moral virtues now generally in short supply.[7]

Pauling telephoned him to express his gratitude for his support. In the course of the conversation he told Hutchins that he had decided to resign from CalTech and inquired if the Center might have a place for him. "He went on to explain," Hutchins said, "that we could have the only

two-time Nobel Prize winner without cost. I found it difficult to refuse."[8]
One of Pauling's former students, sympathizing with his plight at
CalTech, had offered to underwrite his salary and maintenance at any
institution he cared to join. The angel was Chester F. Carlson, the
inventor of Xerox, the patent rights for which had made him one of the
nation's wealthiest men. His interest in Pauling introduced Carlson to the
Center, and in time he became its major benefactor.

A gentle, thoughtful man, Chet Carlson seemed largely unimpressed
and wholly unchanged by the fortune that had suddenly descended upon
him when the Xerox duplicating machine proved to be just what the
ink-stained, carbon-smeared office workers of the world had been waiting
for. He had studied physics at CalTech and worked for a while in
experimental laboratories before earning a law degree and setting up a
practice as a patent attorney. This made him one of the few inventors
fully equipped to safeguard his rights, and he did so after he perfected the
Xerography process in his basement workshop. Thus he became a major
stockholder in a major corporation without acquiring the ambitions and
apprehensions of those who arrive at that estate by the usual route.

Carlson was another benefactor who avoided drawing attention to his
philanthropies or to himself. He retained no consultants to assist him in
disposing of a fortune that far exceeded the needs of a childless couple
still living modestly in Rochester, New York, where the giant Xerox
Corporation had been formed. He made his own investigations of
enterprises he thought worthy of his support, and he no doubt kept an eye
out when he came to Santa Barbara to make the financial arrangements
for Pauling's affiliation with the Center. He looked around, listened
politely, said little, and departed without giving any indication as to
whether his interest extended beyond seeing to it that his old teacher had
a congenial place to work. Two years would go by before he began to
make his intentions known.

The development strategy was proved out when Carlson made his first
major gift in support of the convocation program, which many of the
Center fellows regarded as a distraction from the institution's main
purpose. There was an element of serendipity in this, too. In trying to
make lemonade out of the lemon represented by the fund-raising
campaign, Hutchins began seeking a theme that would give the next
full-dress convocation a sharper focus than the loose-leaf "Prospects for
Democracy." The time, energy, and money that had to be invested in
such a massive public-relations effort could be justified if it could be
shown to serve a purpose other than advertising the Center and its needs.

Hutchins found what he was looking for in an idea put forward by

Fred Warner Neal, a professor of international relations at the University Graduate School of the Claremont Colleges. Neal, a former Washington newspaperman, had served as a naval attaché in the Soviet Union during World War II and as a foreign-service officer in Yugoslavia in the postwar years. He was convinced that the cold war could only be resolved by American-Soviet détente, based on mutual acceptance of extranational spheres of influence. President Kennedy's resounding inaugural address had pointed in the opposite direction, but Neal thought he saw a possible breakthrough in the "Pacem in Terris" encyclical of Pope John XXIII, which departed from the Church's previous unyielding anti-Communism to call for peaceful coexistence between East and West.

Neal enlisted Frank Kelly, who had been a Nieman Fellow with him at Harvard, in presenting to Hutchins a proposal for using the papal encyclical as the centerpiece of an international convocation that would bring together intellectuals from both sides of the Iron Curtain. It turned out to be an easy sale. Hutchins was prepared to consider anything that promised to temper the surge of chauvinism that had shaped the recent presidential election. The year before, shortly after Kennedy's nomination, he had written to Adlai Stevenson to report a conversaton with Arthur Goldberg, "who is apparently right in the middle of the Kennedy camp":

> . . . I attach some importance to Goldberg's remark that you may be too "Europe-oriented" to be Secretary of State. . . . This sounded as though Goldberg was giving me the official line. He says he expects you to be offered the post of Ambassador to the U.N.
>
> Benton, Ashmore and I think that Kennedy is a cool calculator and that he will calculate that he will gain strength by saying that you will be Secretary of State. My only qualification is that he will not want you if he insists on being the Strong Man, towering over all the members of his administration.[9]

Stevenson responded to this prescient evaluation after a visit to Hyannisport, which he described as agreeable but fatuous: "We talked of cabbages, not kings — or their advisors. The orientation is neither Europe nor Asia; just Washington!"[10] He had committed himself, however, to delivering a dozen stump speeches for the ticket during the fall general-election campaign, and he asked for advice on a variety of issues. After forwarding his suggestions, Hutchins followed up with a brief admonitory letter:

All I was trying to say . . . was that I wouldn't bother to defend Kennedy or attack Nixon. That can be left to others. Stevenson talks sense to the American people.

Harrison Brown is not hopeless because he believes on the basis of his personal experiences that it is possible to negotiate with the Russians and that they want to negotiate.

Don't you think that in some way or other the Democratic Party should try to present itself as the party of peace?[11]

Stevenson agreed, but he had no success in moving the campaign in that direction, and his effort to do so may have cost him the office he sought. As Goldberg had predicted, he wound up in the outfield as ambassador to the UN, while those whom the Washington press corps designated as nationalist "hawks" — as opposed to internationalist "doves" — dominated the inner circle of the White House and the cabinet. It would require a public-relations campaign on behalf of peace to change the political climate, and Hutchins saw in "Pacem in Terris" a possible means of launching one on a grand scale. He rationalized his decision as a natural and proper extension of the Center's mission:

Since the Center for the Study of Democratic Institutions was founded to clarify the basic issues and widen the circles of discussion about them, the Center has had to devote much of its attention to the paramount issue of our time, that of peace or war.

A French commentator, Monsignor Bernard Lalande, has said that the encyclical *Pacem in Terris* entered history like "*un coup de tonnerre.*" So it entered the studies of the Center. To the Center the encyclical has appeared as one of the most profound and significant documents of our age. In it a great man states the issues and calls for action.[12]

The clap of thunder signaled a change of direction for the Center. The planning and organization required for the "Pacem in Terris" convocation would occupy much of Hutchins's attention for the next year and a half. The monthlong gatherings of the consultants were abandoned. The project on the American character wound down while John Cogley, who often asserted that he had a low threshold for boredom, took leave to attend the Vatican Council in Rome as correspondent for the Religious News Service. Carl Stover's last contribution was to arrange a 1962 Britannica conference of scientists and technologists to consider the social effects of the dawning age of computers. Shortly thereafter he decided that the increasing evidence of Bill Benton's disaffection with

Phase II made it prudent for him to accept an appointment as a senior political scientist at the Stanford Research Institute.

There was little enthusiasm for "Pacem in Terris" among the Center fellows, and some active resentment. Among the officers, Frank Kelly was an ardent supporter of the convocation, and the pacifist Hallock Hoffman approved, but neither had any capacity for organizing such an undertaking. The only other administrative officer, Ping Ferry, was engrossed in promoting the findings of a radical ad hoc committee that thought it had identified an impending "triple revolution," manifested in the changes produced in weaponry by the nuclear bomb, in manufacturing by computer technology, and in race relations by the civil-rights movement.

I had been devoting most of my time and attention to the *Britannica* project and was not actively involved in the planning and organization of the "Prospects for Democracy" convocation. Now, with the end of the road for the Center's involvement with Phase II in sight, Hutchins asked me to serve as coordinator for the new project. Assembling influential, usually temperamental personages from all over the world to take part in such an unprecedented venture, I soon discovered, required the thick skin and iron constitution of a theatrical impresario. Hutchins began referring to me as the Sol Hurok of the peace game.

CHAPTER FORTY

"An Extraordinary Gathering . . ."

The matter of canceling the *Britannica* project at the Center was never directly discussed at meetings of the board of editors or the company directors, nor was I ever informed of a private confrontation between Hutchins and Benton. But I could only read the publisher's increasingly vehement insistence that I establish my residence in Chicago as a clear indication that Phase II no longer had his support — and that was all that counted, since Benton was still the sole owner of the company's voting stock.

I compromised by taking a bachelor apartment in Chicago and commuting there to consult with Jack Dodge and his editors on the problems we would face in adapting the present content to a new format. I also installed a new graphics department in anticipation of changes in *Britannica*'s limited use of illustrations. But until we knew what the new format would be, this was largely a finger exercise, and my presence in the editorial rooms only increased the anxiety of a staff long set in its ways and unnerved by the prospect of change.

My primary effort was still devoted to reducing the conflicting views within the board of editors to an acceptable prospectus for the roof articles, seeking advice in determining who the best authors for these would be, and obtaining their agreement to take on their assignments. To that end, more than a hundred scholars or other qualified experts participated in meetings at Santa Barbara or were consulted elsewhere. To assist in locating European talent, we retained Hutchins's onetime associate on the Committee to Frame a World Constitution, Elisabeth Mann Borgese, who had maintained her residence in Italy after her husband's death. She was instrumental in organizing a 1964 scientific conference in Florence, a gathering that helped to refine concepts and produced leads to several roof-article authors.

The imprint of Hutchins's concept of dialogue, as well as the reservations of some members of the board of editors, was reflected in the prospectus I finally presented to the authors. Scott Buchanan's soaring idea of the world was neither prescribed nor proscribed. The articles would provide twelve different ways of looking at and organizing intelligence about the world as a whole; the lens would change, but not the object of the view:

> A degree of repetition and overlap has to be assumed, since issues of enduring human concern can only be understood when their interconnections and interactions have been seen and understood. Indeed, a primary justification of the new approach is that it would finally make possible consideration of emerging patterns of relationship well before they could be accommodated by the compartmentalized structures and vested interests of the academic community.
>
> . . . Since the issues are still open, the roof articles must give consideration to all responsible positions. These articles must be dialectical. Authors may be encouraged to develop their own theses, but not at the expense of ignoring all others.[1]

Twelve roof articles were finally assigned. Three of the authors were in-house at the Center: Hutchins was to tackle "Education: The Learning Society"; Harvey Wheeler, "The Political Order: Democracy in a Revolutionary Era"; and John Cogley, "Religion: The Search for Final Meaning." Two others, Stringfellow Barr and Lord Ritchie-Calder, ultimately became Center fellows. Since there was no agreement on how to handle history as an "order," Hutchins turned to his companion in the Great Books crusade to provide a historical overview in an "Epilogue." Calder, the leading British science writer, accepted a permanent Center appointment after spending a year in Santa Barbara working on "Nature: Man and the Cosmos."

The other authors were René Dubos of Rockefeller University, who wrote "Human Nature: Man and His Environment"; R. J. Forbes, of the University of Amsterdam, "The Technological Order: The Conquest of Nature and Its Consequences"; Lon L. Fuller of Harvard, "The Legal Order: The Law — Its Ways and Byways"; Mark Kac of Rockefeller

University and Stanislaw M. Ulam of the University of Colorado, "Mathematics and Logic: Retrospect and Prospects"; Raymond Aron, the French sociologist, "The Social Order: The Promethean Dream — Society in Search of Itself"; Sir Eric Roll, a British economist, "The Economic Order: The World after Keynes"; and Roy McMullen, an American critic living in Paris, "The Fine Arts: Modern Situations in the Arts."

The Phase II experiment was suspended in 1964 on the ground that it would not be possible to produce a new encyclopedia by the 1968 anniversary year. The real reason was fear that any effective move toward a topical arrangement of the set's contents would make it difficult, if not impossible, to sell it to nonacademic users as a reference work. The sales force, opposed to the idea from the beginning, picked up a potent ally in Mortimer Adler, who, though he was not then a member of the board of editors, had continued editorial work on projects related to the Great Books. He had favored the Phase II concept in principle, but he now declared it impossible in practice. Hutchins, he told Maurice Mitchell, was trying to create an encyclopedia that could not be sold. Benton dispatched Mitchell to Santa Barbara to make arrangements to phase out the Center operation.

The roof articles had all been commissioned, and it was decided that they would be issued as a three-volume set, *Britannica Perspectives,* to commemorate the two-hundredth anniversary. I agreed to continue at half pay to complete the editing job. Benton's biographer, Sidney Hyman, noted that I had become known at Britannica headquarters as the phantom editor, while "Benton called him many more pointed things." In public, however, the publisher attempted to make lemonade out of what he regarded as a three-million-dollar lemon:

> *"Britannica,"* Benton was fond of saying as he quoted Lord Crowther, "tells you what you need to know. *Perspectives* tells you what you ought to be thinking about." Judged from a commercial standpoint as a publishing venture, despite good critical reception for the set and lavish praise for some of the essays, *Perspectives* could only lose money. Benton, however, characteristically pointed to the educational benefit of the venture. It was, said he, the kind of thing a privately held firm could offer, free of stockholder pressures for profit for profit's sake. Moreover, it was his hope that the most significant value of the essays would prove to be the influence they would have on the newly launched,

long-range, $25 million program to improve the *Britannica* further.[2]

This program was "Plan B," under which a new in-house development committee was established in Chicago to undertake a revision that would retain the basic alphabetical arrangement. Adler, who was given a lifetime contract by the company, relocated his philosophical institute to Chicago and took over as committee chairman, and Warren Preece returned to the home office as editor of the extensively revised thirty-volume encyclopedia published in 1974.

The scuttling of Phase II was a grievous personal disappointment to Hutchins. He was not one to ignore the practical demands of the publishing market; an encyclopedia that could not be sold would be of no use to the average curious layman who had always been at the center of Hutchins's grand educational design. The format we had begun to develop was based on the assumption that it should be possible to achieve the synthesis he sought without sacrificing the set's utility.

I had advanced the idea of segregating in separate volumes the statistical matter that would require regular updating, along with the shorter, purely factual entries that were of particular use for ready reference. This would minimize, in the main body of the set, the need for alphabetical arrangement that fragmented the existing content. The scheme was adopted for the Plan B revision, but the more comprehensive treatment of major articles that it made possible fell far short of the goal Hutchins was striving for. As chairman of the board of editors, he continued to be consulted as the new format took shape, but Preece found that he gave the matter no more than perfunctory attention.[3]

As always, Hutchins indulged in no recriminations, public or private. But Norman Cousins, who had joined the board of editors, recalled an ironic touch in Hutchins's tribute at a birthday dinner for Benton some years later. When the publisher paid his first visit to the Center, Hutchins recalled, he had responded with fulsome praise for the salubrious setting, the gathering of learned fellows, and the stimulating routine of the dialogue. "It's what you've always wanted, Bob," he said. "You've finally landed the best job in the world." "Not quite," Hutchins replied, "you've got a better one." "How can you say I'm better off than you are?" Benton asked. "Because," Hutchins replied, "you don't have to work for Bill Benton."[4]

With the decline of the Center's involvement in the *Britannica* project, the "Pacem in Terris" convocation became a consuming interest for Hutchins. The object was to bring together persons of influence from both sides of the Iron Curtain who would express their views as individuals, not as representatives of their national governments. This meant that the organization and funding of the conference had to remain private, but it was also essential that we have the approval of official Washington to assure foreign participants that their attendance would not cause diplomatic complications.

Justice Douglas, without reference to "Pacem in Terris," had been seeking a White House declaration for an International Rule of Law Year along the lines of the successful International Geophysical Year, which had brought together Soviet and Western scientists to discuss the problems and opportunities arising from the penetration of outer space. President Kennedy had been interested, and after his tragic death in Dallas, Douglas continued the campaign with his successor, Lyndon Johnson. The "rule of law" concept fitted nicely with the design we were working out for "Pacem in Terris," and Douglas took me with him to the White House to invite the President to deliver the opening address at the convocation. The big Texan received us in the Oval Office and listened sympathetically, and while he made no commitment, he left open the possibility of his acceptance.

This touched off what amounted to a lobbying effort in the year before the convocation. It depended, as all such campaigns do, on personal contacts. On February 28 I wrote to Douglas,

Your follow-up note to Johnson through [Justice] Abe Fortas is fine. We all like the idea of tossing in your International Rule of Law proposal as an added starter — and we are enthusiastic about the idea in general.

As you will see from the attached, I have tried to touch three bases in the White House — Eric Goldman [now a presidential assistant for cultural affairs], Pierre Salinger [held over as press secretary from the Kennedy regime], and Elizabeth Carpenter [the principal aide to the First Lady and a former Washington correspondent for the *Arkansas Gazette*]. Brooks Hays [a former Arkansas congressman and another Kennedy staff holdover] is already enlisted, but I will write him again. We will also ask Jubal Parten, who has a long-standing personal association, to put in a strong plug. I will write [Senate Foreign Relations Committee Chairman] Bill Fulbright and ask for his active endorsement. [Senators] Gene McCarthy, Claiborne Pell, and George McGovern are all familiar with the proposal and enthusiastic about it, so we will ask them to speak up on our behalf.[5]

At the same time Fred Neal was using his contacts with the State Department and the Soviet-bloc embassies to arouse interest in that quarter. When we called a conference in May to perfect final plans, the effort had begun to pay off. The meeting was held at Wingspread, the conference center in Racine, Wisconsin, that housed the Johnson Foundation, a philanthropy maintained by the founders of the Johnson Wax Company. The potent names we were able to drop had much to do with the Foundation's offer to make its staff and resources available to provide logistical support.

The turnout for the three-day meeting was impressive. Fred Neal produced Georgi Kornienko, the minister counselor of the Soviet embassy; Marion Dobrosielski, the minister counselor of the Polish embassy; and Josip Presburger, the counselor of the Yugoslav embassy. We had acquired the blessing of the United Nations, and C. V. Narasimhan, a deputy to Secretary General U Thant, was on hand, along with Sir Zafrullah Khan, a Pakistani judge of the International Court of Justice. The American participants included representatives of major church and other organizations seeking peaceful solutions to international disputes.[6]

The Center's directors met at Wingspread during the conference and were duly impressed. Four new members[7] were elected, including Harold Willens, who saw in "Pacem in Terris" a significant opportunity to expand the founding-members campaign. "Tickets for this history-making convocation in February 1965 will be in great demand and in very limited supply," he warned in a letter to existing members and prospects. "Founding members of the Center naturally will be given first consideration."[8]

Hutchins had even more impressive news when the board met again in November. Although he had expressed to Henry Luce his deep reservations about Luce's declaration of an "American Century" in *Life,* saying that he found it imbued with Calvinist triumphalism, Time, Inc., came forward with a contribution of $75,000 for "Pacem in Terris." And Chester Carlson made his first significant grant — $200,000 to match gifts of $1,000 or more to Willens's founding-members campaign.

When the impressive array of guests gathered in the great assembly hall of the United Nations for the opening ceremonies of "Pacem in Terris," we did not have the President as opening speaker, but we did have Vice President Hubert Humphrey. The quality of the participants and the intense interest of the audience were maintained throughout the three days of speeches and panel discussions that followed at the New York Hilton.[9] John K. Jessup wrote in *Life:*

An extraordinary gathering of the world's movers and shakers converged on New York City to grapple with a staggeringly ambitious project: solutions to the eternal human problem of war. They borrowed as their working title "Pacem in Terris" — Peace on Earth — from Pope John XXIII's great encyclical of Easter Week 1963, which had injected a dynamic new Catholic viewpoint into a dozen crucial issues: disarmament, nuclear weapons, the UN, coexistence, racial equality, human rights, and human freedom. . . .

The guest list would have done credit to a UN Charter meeting or a state funeral: the Secretary-General of the UN; the president of the Assembly and two former presidents; the Vice-President and the Chief Justice of the U.S.; an associate justice and four U.S. senators; Belgium's foreign minister Paul-Henri Spaak; the Italian Vice-Premier, Pietro Nenni; leading officials from Russia, Poland and Yugoslavia; two Justices of the World Court; Historian Arnold Toynbee and Theologian Paul Tillich; all told more than two thousand delegates from twenty nations of the Communist, neutralist and free worlds.[10]

The carefully crafted program began with "The Nature of the Problem" and moved on to a consideration of the main issues cited under four headings: "A European Settlement"; "The Institutional Structure"; "The Non-Nuclear Powers"; and "The Terms of Coexistence." This left ample opportunity to take the discussion beyond the great power confrontation and to consider the usually neglected issues raised by the economic and social disparities between the advanced industrial nations and the underdeveloped nations that were just emerging from colonialism.

The participants in each grouping presented brief opening remarks and then engaged in a free exchange of views. Those who appeared before the overflow audience in the hotel ballroom were drawn from the several establishments represented — figures who were well known for their present or former positions or their scholarly expertise. But each day's proceedings were followed by an informal evening roundtable arranged by Ping Ferry, in which the discussants included representatives of the political left.[11]

If all of the items on the agenda were familiar to the diplomats who had been wrestling with them since the end of World War II, they had never before been presented publicly without the inhibitions attendant upon an official exchange of views. It was an unprecedented experience for the representatives of the Soviet bloc — N. N. Inozemtsev, the deputy chief editor of *Pravda;* Yevgenyi Zhukov, the director of the Institute of

History of the Soviet Academy of Sciences; and Adam Schaff, a member
of the central committee of the Polish Communist party.

Although all those present could agree with Pope John's delineation
of the requirements of peaceful coexistence, there were bound to be
differences over how these might be met. The underlying ideological
conflict between East and West inevitably intruded, but never to the point
of rancor, and there was at least an implied recognition that both sides
were beset by delusions about the motives of the other.

The harshest criticism of the official US position came from George
F. Kennan, the former ambassador and State Department policy planner
who had been the architect of the postwar containment of the Soviet
Union through a Western alliance. Now he insisted that the passage of
time had demonstrated that the post-Stalin Soviet regimes were without
territorial ambition, and he called for ending the division of Germany and
lifting the "Iron Curtain" across Central Europe. But he took issue with
Adam Schaff's assertion, "If a man has his ideals embodied in an
ideology it is a point of honor to go on fighting for it by peaceful
means. . . . Coexistence is a fight, a competition, a noble competition for
the hearts and minds of people."[12]

That meant, Kennan responded, that competition as the Communists
saw it did not "respect what is in men's minds because it does not fully
recognize the organized expression of the popular will."

> . . . It is this which lies at the heart of our disagreement with you.
> We feel that until there exists on the Communist side a disposition
> to accept expressions of the popular will, however imperfect, as
> the ultimate basis of political action and of the determination of
> political authority, there will remain a contradiction between the
> concept of ideological competition that you have put forward and
> the concept of coexistence of which we are speaking.[13]

Flights of impassioned rhetoric were rare as the participants followed
the injunction Hutchins had set forth in his opening remarks:

> This is not an ecumenical council assembled to debate religious
> topics. This is a political meeting. The question is, How can we
> make peace, not peace through the medium of war, not peace
> through the dreadful mechanism of terror, but peace, pure,
> simple and durable. If the principles of "Pacem in Terris" are
> sound, how can they be carried out in the world as it is? If
> they are unsound, what principles are sound, and how can

they be realized? What does it mean to "coexist," and how can we do it?[14]

"Pacem in Terris" was convened against a background of crisis in the United Nations. "There are times, and this is one of them, when the world, in the absence of some tremendous and immediate threat, seems to wallow helplessly in a morass of dispute and discord," Secretary General U Thant said in his closing remarks. The crippling stalemate in the body charged with international peace keeping was produced by the unresolved question of "whether the big powers in unison, through the agency of the Security Council, should take exclusive responsibility for maintaining international peace and security while the General Assembly functions as a glorified debating society in political matters. . . ."[15]

The structural and procedural matters that troubled Thant were discussed at length, and there was widespread sympathy with his complaint that the proliferation of new nations had invalidated the distribution of power under the UN's original charter. But if it could be said that there was a consensus, it was that no amendment of the charter could produce effective peacekeeping machinery until the nation states, great and small, were willing to yield an effective degree of sovereignty to a supranational authority.

Another, more urgent crisis was building, which received scant attention at the convocation. In August President Johnson had ordered air strikes against North Vietnam in retaliation for an alleged attack on American warships in the Bay of Tonkin. Thereafter our White House sources began to indicate that the once bright prospects of the President's addressing the "Pacem in Terris" participants were steadily dimming. The reason was evident when, three days before the convocation opened, "Operation Rolling Thunder" initiated systematic bombing raids against North Vietnam. In the face of this unilateral act of aggression, the President could hardly speak out in support of the International Cooperation Year that he had proclaimed. The Vice President's address was limited to vague generalities, and even so, Hubert Humphrey later confided, he had been under tremendous pressure to cancel.[16]

In the main sessions only Linus Pauling spoke out in condemnation of the United States' intervention in Vietnam, which, he charged, carried with it "the horrible danger of escalation to the catastrophe of a civilization-destroying nuclear war."[17] Although some of those assembled by Ferry for the evening roundtables would soon become vociferous opponents of the "dirty little war" in Southeast Asia, it was now cited merely as an illustration of the need for the kind of peacekeeping machinery that could only be provided by world government. Even

Herman Kahn of the Hudson Institute, who was generally regarded as a superhawk, agreed, conceding that in the nuclear age, "a rather bad world government might be better than no world government."[18]

Hutchins had made it clear that the convocation was not expected to reach agreement on any specific proposal. What was achieved was the general recognition that there could be no effective movement to meet the minimum requirements of coexistence without a thaw in the cold war between East and West. The unprecedented interaction of the participants in "Pacem in Terris" and the public reaction to it were widely praised as a significant step in that direction.

In terms of the Center's immediate self-interest, "Pacem in Terris" was a resounding success. The institution's public image was enhanced by wide and generally favorable reporting and analysis in the media, augmented by gavel-to-gavel coverage by the ninety TV and hundred and twenty-five radio stations of the public network, as well as by the publication of the proceedings in a Pocket Books paperback. The Center's financial supporters, viewing the proceedings in person or on television, were assured in a most tangible way that their money was being used for a worthwhile purpose.

Hutchins had said that the most difficult question he faced when soliciting funds for the Center was, But what does it actually *do?* Proof that "Pacem in Terris" had provided an effective, if incomplete, answer was demonstrated at the closing dinner in Hutchins's honor, when the guests turned in pledge cards totaling $1,400,000. A month later Chester Carlson spent several days in Santa Barbara and told a local reporter, "I am tremendously impressed with the Center. It is a necessity. I don't see how the country can do without it."[19] Before the year was out, he had put up another $750,000 in matching funds.

CHAPTER FORTY-ONE

Conflicting Priorities

To Robert Hutchins, concerned always with the structures and processes of governance, the most striking item on the "Pacem in Terris" agenda had been provided by Kenzo Takayanagi, chairman of the Japanese Cabinet Commission on the Constitution. The charter adopted by Japan in 1946 included a provision that renounced its sovereign right to make war and banned the creation of an armed force in any form. It had been generally assumed that this was a condition imposed on the defeated nation by its conquerors, but Takayanagi said, "This apparently fantastic provision originated not in Washington but in Tokyo."

It became part of the Constitution as a result of a proposal made by Japanese Prime Minister Shidehara and sponsored with much enthusiasm by General MacArthur, who in his letter of December 5, 1957, addressed to me, says, "It will stand everlastingly as a monument to the foresight, the statesmanship, and the wisdom of Prime Minister Shidehara." Shidehara and MacArthur were thinking in terms of the shape of things to come in the atomic era. They entertained a vision that Article IX should serve as a model for the future constitutions of all nations. . . .[1]

The Japanese constitution had since been interpreted to permit the creation of a lightly armed Japanese self-defense force. But Takayanagi reported that his commission had still found strong support for Article IX among the people. In his closing remarks Hutchins announced that he would spend the rest of his life lobbying for a similar amendment to the United States Constitution.

He did not intend for this pledge to be taken literally, but it did represent his renewed commitment to the quest for a workable international order that could insure the peaceful settlement of differences among the nation states. Although he had little faith in their ability to rally majority public opinion, he had always endorsed the peace movements that grew out of emotional reactions to the threat of nuclear destruction, and several of these were soon to acquire a new momentum from the mounting protest against the United States' escalation of the Vietnam war.

One such movement found a home, or at least office space, at the Center. This was provided for Irving Laucks, a retired chemist who had settled in Santa Barbara after making a fortune from his invention of the adhesive used to bond plywood. He had served with Ping Ferry on the ad hoc committee on the "triple revolution" and been much taken with its radical approach to the problems of peace, poverty, and race relations. Laucks made a grant of a hundred thousand dollars to the Center to be used to advance these causes, but it soon became clear that his consuming interest was in the peace movement.

Laucks was a major financial supporter of Women Strike for Peace, a feminist antiwar movement founded by Dagmar Wilson. At one of the "Pacem in Terris" roundtables she offered what she conceded was "probably a preposterous suggestion from the point of view of those who are discussing practical and technical methods of arriving at peaceful solutions to the world's problems." Why not, she asked, simply proceed on the assumption that "each of us needs the other; we need to protect each other from self-annihilation. This should be the factor to bring us together and make it possible to resolve some of our minor differences."[2]

This reflected Laucks's view. His grants to the Center were earmarked for funding the operations of two Women Strike for Peace organizers, Marjory Collins in New York and Eleanor Garst, who joined him in Santa Barbara and was given an office at El Parthenon. Hutchins, whose interest was in what Dagmar Wilson dismissed as the practical and technical means of reducing reliance on armed conflict, was wholly uninterested in this enterprise, which seemed to him to endorse unilateral disarmament and to invoke Lysistrata's sex strike against the warring males of ancient Greece.

Laucks, who was given a seat at the conference table and usually occupied it, was in his turn uninterested in aspects of the Center dialogue that did not deal directly with his own concerns. To Hutchins's distress this also proved to be the case with Linus Pauling, who participated only intermittently and devoted most of his time to his own scientific research.

Everyone associated with the Center shared, to some degree, Hutchins's concern with the overriding issues of war and peace. But the fellows were a heterogeneous group, and they had never really coalesced into the community of scholars that Hutchins so fondly spoke of. Most of them regarded convocations on the order of "Pacem in Terris" as diversions of the Center's resources, the most valuable of which, from their standpoint, was Hutchins's personal interest in their individual projects. Some of the academic purists reflexively opposed anything that smacked of public relations and considered fund raising to be inherently corrupting. And there was the inevitable, all-too-human resentment of any enterprise that drew most of its featured participants from outside the Center.

But the divisions went deeper than that. They seemed to me more temperamental than ideological. Hutchins had always attracted iconoclasts; he was himself a lifelong dissenter from conventional wisdom, and his ideal for the Center, as it had been for the university, was that it serve to promote independent thought and criticism. He welcomed radicals of all persuasions, but those who regarded themselves as revolutionary activists sensed, rightly, that he was not one of them. They were motivated by an anger rooted in alienation, while Hutchins never felt that the flawed democratic institutions he criticized were beyond redemption.

This accounted for fundamental differences between Hutchins and Scott Buchanan, despite the admiration each had for the other. Hutchins looked upon Buchanan as a model teacher who constantly challenged the assumptions of all those he dealt with, but he found him incurably naive in his views about the problems of the real world. When he had approached him with an invitation to join the Committee on Social Thought at the University of Chicago, he had been appalled to find that Buchanan, whose disdain for politics was such that he had never even voted before, had joined the foredoomed Progressive party, created by Henry Wallace in 1948 to oppose Harry Truman's election. Hutchins wrote to John Nef:

He informed me that neither philosophy nor education had any importance today, that the only thing that could be significant was practical politics, that he had joined the PCA and was going to support Wallace. I tried all kinds of appeals, but failed to move him. I think he has everything backwards, but he is not within the realm of argument.[3]

At the end of a dialogue session at the Center in which Hutchins and Buchanan seemed to be far apart in their conception of human freedom, Carl Stover asked Buchanan to characterize their differences:

> He said it was as if they were both aboard the same ship, which had held a single direction for a very long time, guided by fixed stars measured by orthodox principles and instruments. Hutchins, believing this to be the only true course, would strive mightily to maintain it and the systems serving it, while he, Buchanan, was willing to see the ship find a new route, pursuing the movements of the stars through some other mode of navigation. . . . Hutchins found it most important to preserve and perfect the American way to freedom; Buchanan, to pursue the vision of freedom that had inspired America and that held the possibility of still better visions.[4]

By whatever stars it was being navigated, the American ship of state encountered stormy seas in the mid-1960s. The civil-rights movement had spread from the South to the black ghettos of the major cities and had taken on an edge of violence. An inchoate but noisy youth movement centered on the college campuses was proclaiming a generational revolution. And the nation's foreign relations had fallen into disarray in the face of virtually unanimous disapproval abroad for the belligerent course that President Johnson had adopted in support of the shaky puppet government of South Vietnam.

In June 1965 the three under-secretaries of the UN — Ralph Bunche, C. V. Narasimhan, and José Rolz-Bennett — brought veteran diplomats from half a dozen foreign countries to Santa Barbara to evaluate the results of the New York convocation. "The mood of the gathering was dark," I later wrote. "Escalation of the war in Vietnam, they reported, was already imperiling the fragile East-West détente which had made possible 'Pacem in Terris.' Unanimously they urged that the Center try again, with the main effort this time on bringing in the mainland Chinese."[5]

Hutchins agreed with the diagnosis and took the proposal under advisement. My advice pointed up the fact that a convocation aimed at opening contacts with China could not be held in the United States, which had no diplomatic relations with the People's Republic. Mounting

"Pacem in Terris II" in a foreign country would involve financial and logistical requirements far greater than any we had encountered so far.

With my editorial work on *Britannica Perspectives* nearing completion, Hutchins had asked me to assume responsibility for the Center's nonacademic administration, and I found that even exploring the possibilities of such a venture was beyond the Center's staff resources. Convinced that Hutchins, as usual, would ignore the odds and that we would soon be plunging ahead, I brought in John Perry, a journalist-turned-publicist who had extensive promotional experience. He had served as executive secretary to Governor LeRoy Collins of Florida and as vice president of the National Association of Broadcasters when Collins moved to Washington to head the organization.

I had enlisted Perry's help in 1963 when Justice Douglas asked me to go to the Dominican Republic on behalf of the Parvin Foundation to see what might be done to prop up the shaky reformist regime of Juan Bosch, who was elected president after a popular uprising deposed the Trujillo dictatorship. Governor Collins had agreed to line up support from NAB members to provide battery-powered radio receivers to be used in primitive Dominican villages for a crash literacy program that would be broadcast by the state-owned station. Perry was in Santo Domingo making final arrangements when resurgent conservative forces, backed by Washington, forced Bosch into exile.

In addition to Hutchins's conviction that the pursuit of world order must be the Center's first priority, there were practical reasons for undertaking "Pacem in Terris II." The first convocation had been a successful demonstration of the fact that the Center was concerned not only with studying issues that were basic to any democratic society, but also with widening the circles of discussion about them. In his gentle, unassuming way, Chester Carlson appended to each of his gifts a reminder that he was primarily interested in the second aspect of the mission, particularly as it might be employed to advance the cause of peace.

Hutchins's personal contribution to expanding the Center's outreach was a weekly column, "What Kind of World?," which was distributed by the Los Angeles Times Syndicate.[6] "I liked very much your column in this morning's paper entitled 'Why Not Withdraw from Vietnam?' " Carlson wrote Hutchins in February 1966. "This certainly makes very good sense. It should have been done a year and a half ago when we were presumably merely military advisors." He went on to announce that in addition to his earlier commitment of matching funds, he was donating, with no strings, a million dollars' worth of Xerox stock in the hope that it would "increase the effectiveness of the Center in these very trying times."[7]

While the institution was still a long way from being self-sustaining, Carlson's gift eliminated the annual deficit that had been eating into the residue of the Ford grant. In the fiscal year ending September 30, 1966, income was $3,305,057, leaving a surplus of $1,849,904 after expenses of $1,455,153. With those cheerful figures before it, the board raised no question of prudence when in April 1968 Hutchins assembled a group of advisers at the Palais des Nations in Geneva to plan the agenda for "Pacem in Terris II."

The advisers were drawn from the United Nations, the United States, the Soviet Union, France, Great Britain, Japan, the United Arab Republic, Poland, Cambodia, and Mexico; all had taken part in the first convocation or were familiar with the undertaking. I summarized the meeting:

> Hutchins put two questions to them: How could we persuade Peking to participate in "Pacem in Terris II"? If we could not, was there any point in going ahead?
>
> The first question drew a variety of suggestions, all admittedly doubtful. The answer to the second was yes. And the participants on their own motion added an item to the agenda that was to determine the character of the second convocation — and set in motion a train of events that would twice take [me] behind the lines in Vietnam.
>
> The senior Russian at Geneva, N. N. Inozemtsev, observed that while those present might agree among themselves that Vietnam was only one among urgent issues of coexistence, the world no longer thought so; the fighting in Southeast Asia was bound to dominate any program we might devise for "Pacem in Terris II." This suggested a concerted effort to bring Hanoi into the convocation, and thereby to initiate direct American contact that conceivably could open the way for diplomats to make a formal move toward peace negotiations.
>
> The three Frenchmen responded with enthusiasm, and they bore impressive credentials. Pierre Mendès-France headed the French government at the time of the defeat at Dien Bien Phu and the subsequent Geneva Accords; Ambassador [Jean] Chauvel is an old China hand who had recently returned from Peking via Hanoi; and Xavier Deniau had served in then French Indochina as a foreign service officer. They agreed to arrange with the North

Vietnamese legation in Paris to transmit to Hanoi a letter suggesting a meeting with representatives of the Center.[8]

We were now committed to mount "Pacem in Terris II" in Geneva, though the means of organizing and funding it remained to be found.

The Center's fund-raising needs militated against a protracted delay between major convocations, and Hutchins used another of his enduring concerns as the focus for an examination of "The University in America" at a three-day gathering in Los Angeles in March 1966. University and college presidents, as well as trustees and others concerned with "the condition of university education," were in the audience at the Beverly Hilton as an array of leading administrators and scholars responded with considerable spirit to Hutchins's charge: "The university could fashion the mind of the age. Now it is the other way around: the demands of the age are fashioning the mind of the university."[9]

But foreign-policy considerations intruded even here. The most arresting address was that of a former university president, J. William Fulbright, chairman of the Senate Foreign Relations Committee. Now that they had joined together in the development of new military technology, he said, the universities and the government seemed "to have accepted the idea that the avoidance of nuclear war is merely a matter of skillful crisis management." If that attitude persisted, he warned, all-out nuclear war would be all but inevitable.[10]

There was also a whiff of the spreading ferment on the nation's campuses when student leaders were invited to exchange views with a panel of university administrators and trustees. Their abrasive challenge to vested authority and their demand that students be given a dominant role in university governance did not impress Hutchins. He said of the Free Speech movement at Berkeley, which touched off angry campus demonstrations across the country, "They'll all be wearing three-piece suits to the office in a few years."[11]

Hutchins was to be proved right, but as Ping Ferry observed in retrospect, "These were the 1960s, and the Center's agenda was dominated by the decade's stormy issues, from Vietnam to black/white eruptions. It was not Hutchins' preferred agenda. He was discomfited by the presence of blacks and other minorities at the green baize table. . . . The jangle and commotion of the time wore Hutchins down, so that by the mid-1960s he had perceptibly lost interest."[12]

It was not, it seemed to me, so much a matter of discomfiture as one of Hutchins's deep-seated skepticism toward any movement that seemed to be fueled by emotion at the expense of reason. In his own youth this had kept him aloof from the Marxist movements that attracted many of his intellectual peers and had caused him to disdain the Freudian doctrines that bemused others. Now a kind of half-baked Marxism provided slogans for the professed student revolutionaries of the New Left, who were striving, without success, to make common cause with the militant wing of the black protest movement. And an aura of Freudian permissiveness surrounded the youthful hippies who preached a doctrine of love as they dropped out of society to seek self-fulfillment through self-gratification.

Hutchins sympathized with the demands of students for the authority to control their own living arrangements, and with their rebellion against required course attendance and the use of grades to determine progress. He had anticipated those demands and that rebellion thirty years before at Chicago, when he insisted that the University had no responsibility for the moral training or personal behavior of undergraduates, and that academic progress should be measured only by independent examinations. But he had no sympathy for students' attempts to use force to radically politicize the education offered by the universities. He had always encouraged students to challenge their professors and to inveigh against the stultifying educational bureaucracy that existed on every campus. But he could not be convinced that those who were not yet educated were capable of determining what a university education should be — and he certainly did not agree that it was the mission of the university to turn out graduates who were equipped and inspired to impose socioeconomic dogma on society at large.

The idea that those who had nothing in common except immaturity constituted an oppressed class struck Hutchins as an absurdity; youth, he pointed out, was an inescapably transient condition. He thought the angry militants and the passive flower children, while following different paths, were simply retreating from reality. He satirized both movements, and their adult sympathizers, in an address at Brandeis University in which, with a straight face, he claimed to have discovered the most successful disciple of Sigmund Freud, Alexander Zuckerkandl, in the Austrian village of Adl, whose citizens were called Adlescents:

Other men had built systems. Others had told their fellows how they ought to live. They had all failed for one simple reason. They had wanted to change mankind. Zuckerkandlism proceeds from a quite different and far sounder premise. It supplies mankind with the reasons for doing what it is already doing. It does not, like Milton's doctrine, seek to justify the ways of God to man. It justifies the ways of man to God.

At one stroke, Zuckerkandl rids us of those guilt feelings and complexes which, as we all know, are at the bottom of our private and public troubles. It adjusts us. It does this by showing us that we are right. We have been right all along.[13]

In passing, Hutchins ridiculed Transcendental Meditation and the other forms of consciousness raising that were in vogue in the sixties. He characterized these as the oriental counterparts of Zuckerkandlism — "Sen-Sen Buddhism, the Creed That Sweetens Your Breath As It Empties Your Mind." All were based on Freud's massive underlying error, which Zuckerkandl had identified and corrected:

In his last major work Freud says that psychoanalysis is built on the attempt to make people conscious of their unconscious. Zuckerkandl shows that Freud had it just backward. The task is not to make people conscious of their unconscious but to make them unconscious of their conscious. This is the path to the unentangled life, to happiness. . . .

Dr. Zuckerkandl's answer is found carved on one of the foundation stones of his system. It is the theory of Vicarious Experience, which is, in turn, the basis of his theory of the Mass Arts. . . . The Zuckerkandl injunction is, "Let all your experiences be vicarious."

This is the purpose of the mass arts, and particularly of that greatest of all artistic instruments, television. Through television we are exposed to an endless parade of horrors, so dreadful, so continuous, so intense, so varied, that only a few hours a day with this machine will make us totally indifferent to any shock and oblivious of any crime.[14]

Freud, for all his pretended sophistication, was still a victim of the Judeo-Christian mythology. The Superego, which he had identified as a restraint on base human impulses, Hutchins wrote, turned out to be a "nineteenth-century University of Vienna name for the doctrine of original sin. The super-ego turns out to be nothing but Adam and Eve in costumes from *Die Fledermaus*."

Most of those in the audience at Brandeis, which no doubt contained an above-average share of student and faculty supporters of the New Left, failed to detect the satire. This was almost impossible for readers of the elaborated text of the address that Hutchins prepared for publication in *Center Magazine*. He adorned it with numerous footnotes in the most pretentious academic style and added passages in which he indulged his fondness for ribald puns. The goal of mankind, he has Herr Doctor Zuckerkandl proclaim, has been to regain the unconsciousness that was lost with man's emergence from the primeval ooze:

> It seems pretty clear now that our most remote ancestors suffered from the sin of excessive curiosity, or hubris, and that they should have stayed where they were. As the eminent theologian Professor Rameses MacIntosh of the University of Aberdeen has shown in his great work *Whose Ooze?* this original move was the Original Sin; for from the lamentable lack of self-control of our prime progenitors all our troubles have remorselessly followed. . . .
>
> Scientific evidence is supplied by the researches of the psychoanalysts, who have established that our overwhelming ambition is to return to the womb.
>
> The pictures in the anatomy books do not disclose anything particularly attractive about this location. Why, then, should we want to return there? It is because we look back upon our nine months' vacation there as the least unhappy period of our lives; it was one time when we were totally unconscious. We may dismiss as inaccurate, as well as vulgar, the remark of Cyril Connolly that we are all our lives seeking a womb with a view. A womb yes; a view, no.[15]

The Hollywood cartoonists John and Faith Hubley produced an art film based on the text, and their drawings were used as illustrations for an abbreviated version published by Grove Press. The little book did not make the best-seller lists, but it did elicit high praise from a major, though hardly unprejudiced, literary figure. Hutchins's old friend Thornton Wilder wrote,

> The first time I read it here it was very funny, especially the footnotes. Then four days later I read it again . . . and found it the most chilling exercise in nihilism I had come across since reading Céline. You've done it! You've gotten away with it! Not since *Candide* and the last chapter of *Gulliver's* has irony been able to carry so heavy a load of pessimism as though it were just "fun and games."[16]

Despite — or perhaps because of — Hutchins's disdain for the youth movement, the New Left had its adherents at the Center. The more venerable fellows, notably Buchanan and Stringfellow Barr, were put off

by the strident anti-intellectualism that characterized the movement.
Harvey Wheeler, however, took seriously the insistence that children of
the affluent middle class were victims of oppression. "My years in
college, in university, were years of terror," he said, "and my years of
teaching were unrelieved catastrophe. I don't think that the university for
a student or a teacher has changed."[17] But Wheeler was a congenital
loner who would have found it impossible to join any mass movement.

Ferry, a member of the post-thirties generation who could more
properly be identified with the Old Left, shared the students' anger at the
self-centered insensitivity of their elders and applauded their unbridled
verbal assault on middle-class beliefs and practices. But his sympathy
was primarily with the militant blacks, who scorned the efforts of white
college students to join their movement.

Ferry's ingrained pessimism led him to share the view of the black
polemicist James Baldwin that the civil-rights movement was only
another failed slave revolt, and to take seriously the demand by the Black
Muslim Malcolm X for a separate black nation. White Americans, Ferry
declared, would never accept any effective degree of integration:

> My proposition, in short, smashes the liberal dream. It eliminates
> the democratic optimistic claim that we are finding our way to a
> harmonious blending of the races. It changes the words of the
> marching song to "We Shall *Not* Overcome," for what was
> eventually to be overcome was hostility and non-fraternity be-
> tween black and white. My proposition dynamites the foundations
> of the NAACP, the Urban League and similar organizations. It
> asserts that blacktown USA and whitetown USA, for all practical
> purposes and with unimportant exceptions, will remain separate
> social communities for as long as one can see ahead. I am not
> sure, but it may also mean that blacktown will become a separate
> political community.[18]

Seeking to propagate his view, Ferry wrote and made public a letter
to the regents of the University of California importuning them to
establish an all-black undergraduate college and to endow it with
complete autonomy:

> A good deal of the problem rests in the clash between what we
> whites think the blacks should want, and what blacks do want. I
> believe we must pay strict attention to what the blacks say they
> want — even though contradiction and muzziness may sometimes
> be discerned — and go the long mile to helping them achieve it.[19]

When, predictably, he failed to prevail in Berkeley, he began pressing for the Center to reconstitute itself to take on the mission. This came too close to home for the fellows, and Ferry had no visible support except from Paul Jacobs, who was still on the payroll but was now spending most of his time in the urban ghettos that were being put to the arsonist's torch while black teenagers ran through the streets chanting "Burn, Baby, Burn." Jacobs's 1967 book, *Prelude to Riot,* was subtitled "A View of Urban America from the Bottom," but it seemed to be more a celebration than a description of the conflagration that gutted the Watts section of Los Angeles.[20]

Among the original fellows only Hallock Hoffman seemed to be wholly in sympathy with the hippies. Abhorring violence, he embraced the notion that the flower children could raise the nation's consciousness by demonstrating their own liberation from inhibiting social conventions. At one point he brought the founders of Esalen, Michael Murphy and Dick Price, to meet with me to discuss the possibility of merging the Center with the avant-garde retreat at Big Sur, where mixed groups sought spiritual liberation through nude encounters in hot tubs. I suggested that there seemed to be a certain incompatibility between their approach to dialogue and ours, and I said I thought it would be a waste of time for them to pursue the matter further with Hutchins.

But the Center did acquire an eloquent and gently persistent advocate of the hippie creed when John Seeley, a former chairman of the sociology department at Brandeis, became a fellow in 1966. Seeley believed the flower children might offer the only alternative to "the two mass armies of reaction and revolution."

> . . . They protest what is common to the revolutionary and Establishment models. They believe that the one scarcely more than the other has the answer to the most urgent question: What is a viable and human life for man? They also address themselves, simultaneously rather than successively, to the twin problems of good institutions and good persons, believing that the development of neither can be abandoned while the other is being sought. . . .[21]

Seeley saw in the movement the possibility of bringing down "the managed, exploitative, imperialist society by withdrawal of what it depends upon: brains, bodies, and the willingness to manipulate things and people." At least, he thought, there should be reserved "a special place (like the medieval monasteries) for the hippies — a special place, not just geographic but honorific."[22]

Hutchins continued to resist, in his passive way, the conversion of El Parthenon into a hippie retreat or a black-studies center. The civil-rights movement, which had provided the initial incentive and the nonviolent method for the student protest, was now being subsumed by a broader rebellion against the military draft as it expanded to provide troops for the Vietnam war. Hutchins's priority — which by extension became mine — lay in addressing the root causes of that conflict through "Pacem in Terris II."

CHAPTER FORTY-TWO

Public Relations for Peace

Robert Hutchins described the persons to be invited to "Pacem in Terris II" as citizens of the world and friends of mankind. With his customary disregard for the constraints of time and money, he insisted that all the major nations and a representative sampling of the others should be represented. So with the advice of some key participants in the first convocation, we compiled a list of appropriate invitees, and at the end of May 1967 three hundred of these, drawn from seventy nations, convened in Geneva.

In a departure from "Pacem in Terris I," all these were to be active participants. There would be no formal speeches; panel discussions would open each session, and floor microphones would be available to the others in the small, closed ballroom at the Hotel Intercontinental, where the convocation was to meet for two and half days following the opening ceremonies at the Palais des Nations. Everyone would be housed at the hotel, and it was expected that an informal give-and-take among the participants would be a primary device for elaborating the ideas to be presented and debated. The daily sessions would begin at 9:30 A.M. and run as late as 7:00 P.M., and as a reminder that this was not a social gathering, luncheon and dinner would consist of buffet meals accompanied by nonalcoholic beverages — surely a rarity in that gastronomic capital.

The reach now extended far beyond the circle of Hutchins's personal acquaintances upon which he usually relied, and the kind of people we were seeking could hardly be expected to respond to invitations received in the mail. The trick was to first sign up participants of such prominence their names would encourage others to follow suit. Before the formal invitations went out, personal contact had to be made to insure acceptance by those who would be listed on the program as discussants.

A key scout was Fred Warner Neal, who had influential friends in most European capitals and could count on support from his former foreign-service colleagues in the American embassies. "When the uses of charm and his wide variety of personal contacts are exhausted," I wrote, "Mr. Neal takes on the abrasive persistence of a dentist's drill."[1] We were also able to call on Justice Douglas and other members of the Center's board of directors, including, most notably, Bill Baggs. As editor of the staunchly Democratic *Miami News* and an intimate of many of those who went to Washington with President Kennedy, he was of great assistance in our own capital.

The cost of travel for those engaged in rounding up participants on four continents was already formidable, and still ahead was the enormous tab for bringing the hundreds of invitees to Geneva. We were, by conservative estimate, looking for funding of at least three quarters of a million dollars. We did not find it until three months before "Pacem in Terris II" convened — and by that time the invitations had already gone out.

One of the New York directors, Morris Levinson, noted that James Roosevelt, the late President's son, had been appointed vice president of Investors Overseas Services, an enormously successful mutual-investment fund with headquarters in Geneva. He also headed the IOS Foundation, which received a percentage of the company's profits, and Levinson thought it would be useful for me to meet with him in New York.

Roosevelt in turn arranged for me to make my sales pitch to Bernard J. Cornfeld, the one-time encyclopedia salesman who seven years before had launched the enterprise, which was now approaching a billion dollars in assets. The youthful entrepreneur had a reputation for making quick, unconventional decisions, and he simply nodded yes when I pointed out that his company's somewhat dubious reputation could be helped by its sponsoring a peace conference that would bring to Geneva prominent citizens from countries where his salesmen operated. The IOS Foundation, he said, would provide a staff to handle the local arrangements, pay the hotel bills, and send round-trip airline tickets to all those who accepted the invitations the Center had sent out. He didn't even ask to see the guest list.

* * *

In October Ambassador Luis Quintanilla, whose Mexican citizenship allowed him to visit Peking when no American could, presented our invitation to the Chinese foreign minister. He got no encouragement there, but he returned by way of Hanoi, where Ho Chi Minh expressed interest in discussing the details of possible North Vietnamese participation with American representatives of the Center.

This promised a significant opening, and Hutchins decided that Baggs and I should go to Hanoi as soon as possible. We immediately informed the State Department of the invitation, and our passports were cleared for travel into forbidden territory. The understanding was that we would travel secretly and report back on the possibilities of the negotiated settlement the Johnson administration professed to be seeking.

In Hanoi we were received by Ho for an extended conversation, and we came away convinced that he wanted to use us to convey to Washington his genuine desire to initiate secret talks at an official level. He would stand by his previous refusal to negotiate until the United States halted the bombing of North Vietnam, but he indicated his willingness to suspend aggressive military action on his side while any such talks were in progress.

At the State Department we gave a full briefing to Under-Secretary Nicholas Katzenbach, Assistant Secretary for Southeast Asia William Bundy, and Ambassador Averell Harriman. "It seemed to us," I wrote, "that the metaphorical telephone of [Secretary of State] Dean Rusk's standard Vietnam speech, which he claimed always went dead when he tried to make a connection with Hanoi, was ringing loud and clear."[2]

We worked with Bundy in drafting a letter to be sent to Ho over my signature. As it was finally approved, this presented the response of "appropriate officials of the United States government" to our report on our conversation with him. The key passage dealt with the previous sticking point:

> They expressed particular interest in your suggestion to us that private talks could begin provided the U.S. stopped bombing your country, and ceased introducing additional U.S. troops into Vietnam. They expressed the opinion that some reciprocal restraint to indicate that neither side intended to use the occasion of talks for military advantage would provide tangible evidence of the good faith of all parties in the prospects for a negotiated settlement.[3]

The letter noted that we were without authority to negotiate on behalf of the government and that we expected to bow out once the formal talks began. After the *New York Times* reported that we had been in Hanoi, we had no choice but to go public with a description of what we had seen behind the lines in Vietnam, but as we had agreed, we avoided any indication of our involvement with the State Department.

As weeks went by, we were puzzled by the lack of response from Hanoi. We found out why when Ho released the text of a hard-line message that had been signed by President Johnson and transmitted through Moscow at the same time we were preparing our conciliatory letter over at the State Department. The conditions set by the President clearly made it impossible for Ho to take the purported overture seriously.

> . . . As we read the rough-textured Johnson letter we could well imagine the reaction of the addressee. In his wry way, we thought, Ho Chi Minh doubtless would be amused by the President's fatuous argument that he couldn't stop the bombing because this would arouse suspicion that negotiations were under way and thereby impair their secrecy and subject the participants to the temptation to indulge in propaganda — this from a man who a year before had celebrated Christmas by dispatching coveys of senior diplomats to the capitals of the world as "salesmen of peace," and would follow up this Madison Avenue gesture a year later by making a personal Yuletide foray to the Vatican to pray with the Pope.[4]

The irony did not amuse Hutchins. He proposed that Baggs and I make public a detailed account of our experience. The episode had demonstrated that prospects for a negotiated settlement were so dim they could hardly be harmed and might in fact be improved by documentation of the kind of double-dealing we had encountered. My only reservation was that the adverse reaction that would no doubt be engendered in Washington by such whistle-blowing could harm our chances of getting the top-drawer US representation we had been seeking for "Pacem in Terris II."

We had, as always, aimed high. Justice Douglas had discussed with President Johnson the possibility of his appearing in person to present the case for his Southeast Asian policy before a high-level international audience. That did not seem to be a real likelihood, but privately Vice President Humphrey had indicated that he would like to give it a try. And when Baggs and I had a gloomy private conference with Defense Secretary Robert McNamara after our return from Hanoi, he expressed his concern over what he regarded as a far more perilous development than Vietnam — the growing conviction of our senior military officers and their Soviet counterparts that nuclear weapons might be used not merely as a deterrent, but to win a global war. He seemed to be impressed with our argument that the convocation would provide him with an ideal forum in which to go public with those views.

Hutchins, as I expected, damned the torpedoes and urged full speed ahead. We were engaged in a public-relations effort on behalf of peace, he pointed out, and we had an opportunity to advance the cause on the front pages and the evening TV broadcasts. I prepared a documented account of our dealings with the State Department and timed it for release on a Monday morning, when it would have little competition for news play. Headlines were insured by the charge that "this conciliatory feeler was effectively and brutally canceled before there was any chance to determine what response Hanoi might have made":

> Any appraisal I can offer of what actually went on in the ultimate reaches of the Administration during this period is necessarily subjective. From beginning to end of our dealings with the State Department there was an almost total absence of candor on the official side. . . .
>
> The theory that seems to me to fit about as well as any is that the President has taken a ping-pong approach to the problems he inherited in Vietnam. The extent of his personal ambition, so far as I can divine it, is to find a compromise that will permit him to get out of Southeast Asia without appearing to have suffered a major military and political defeat. The technique is to throw his weight behind the advocates of negotiation until do-it-now pressure from the generals and admirals becomes unbearable. Then he cuts the military loose for another turn of the screw, only to clamp down again when the opinion polls remind him how unpopular the Vietnam war really is. The double-dealing to which William Baggs and I were subjected seems to indicate that we passed through both phases.[5]

The State Department responded with a white paper and a press conference with Secretary Bundy. Since I had disavowed the charge that President Johnson was trying to impose an imperialist Pax Americana on the region, we could hardly be dismissed with the usual countercharge that we were wittingly or unwittingly serving Communist interests. Instead, we were written off as amateur diplomats whose egos had given us an inflated view of the importance of our contact with Ho Chi Minh, causing us to react out of pique when we discovered that the President had

chosen to use one of the other channels available to him. Secretary Rusk
described us as frustrated seekers of the Nobel peace prize.

The furor in the press burned out within a week, and it was not until
the eve of "Pacem in Terris II" that counteraction by the grudge-bearing
Lyndon Johnson could be finally confirmed. We were still receiving
expressions of interest from most of those whom we approached as
proponents of official US policy. But we began to wonder if the fact that
we could get no final commitments was merely a result of the usual slow
grinding of the bureaucratic mills. Baggs reported that Vice President
Humphrey was still enthusiastic about making an appearance in Geneva
but doubted that the President would approve it:

> I spent the evening, until midnight, with Katzenbach. It was his
> personal and confidential view that Lyndon was not about to let
> Hubert Humphrey make a speech in Geneva before our group.
> Nick suggested that we should get persons who are lately out of
> government, such as [McGeorge] Bundy, or [George] Ball, or
> Bill Moyers and they would be acceptable to the administration.[6]

The invitations to Bundy, the former national security adviser, and
Moyers, the President's former press secretary, were politely declined,
and Ball, a former under-secretary of state, took his under advisement.
Humphrey had pointed out that the senators who had accepted our
invitation were all opposed to the Vietnam policy, and he provided a list
of five who backed the President. All of these declined except Edward
Brooke of Massachusetts, a moderate Republican whose support for
Johnson was lukewarm at best. In the end we obtained only one firm
acceptance from anyone associated with the administration — Arthur
Goldberg, the former director of the Fund, now the US ambassador to the
United Nations, who obviously was motivated by a personal loyalty to
Hutchins.

In mid-March, when I went to Geneva to join James Roosevelt in a
press-conference announcement that the IOS Foundation would sponsor
the convocation, I began to pick up indications that word was being
passed to American embassies in Europe to quietly discourage participation in "Pacem in Terris II." John Perry, who was sent to Geneva to
coordinate arrangements, soon confirmed this, as did Fred Neal and
Elisabeth Borgese, who was working with us from her base in Florence.

In Washington it became clear that none of those our administration
contacts had urged us to invite was going to be permitted to accept. "We
had been neatly set up for a self-fulfilling prophecy," I wrote, "and the

Administration's many-sided public relations apparatus began pumping out the word that 'Pacem in Terris II' was being deliberately loaded against the United States . . .'':

Once Administration strategists had decided to undermine the convocation they could count on a number of standard reflexes from the news media. . . . Among the certainties we could anticipate was that the *Chicago Tribune* would label it ''Dumb and Disgraceful''; the *New York Daily News* would complain that pacifists had ''snitched'' the ''Pacem in Terris'' title from the late Pope John and applied it to a ''hate-the-U.S.-on-account-of-the-Vietnam-War talkathon''; the *Indianapolis Star* would demand that the convocation's sponsors be jailed under the Logan Act for illegally practicing diplomacy; and William F. Buckley would characterize the Geneva meeting as the ''Hutchins International Conference to Hate America.''[7]

The administration's campaign was covert, which effectively prevented our counteracting it. It was not until May 23, five days before the convocation's opening, that the State Department conceded to the Associated Press that a ''hands off'' attitude had been decreed. By that time a covey of CIA disinformation experts were on the ground in Geneva to see that we were mousetrapped at every opportunity.

The most effective gambit employed Foreign Minister Tran Van Do of South Vietnam, who had been suggested by the State Department as a participant when Ho Chi Minh indicated that Hanoi might be represented. We had then invited leaders from the affected Southeast Asian nations — Laos, Cambodia, Thailand, and Malaysia — all of whom accepted on the understanding that if either of the two Vietnam combatants withdrew, the invitation to the other would be canceled.

On May 19 we received Hanoi's cancellation by cable: ''The USA talks 'peace and negotiation,' only to camouflage new extremely serious escalation steps going even to the length of bombing Hanoi and Haiphong.''[8] We promptly cabled a withdrawal of the invitation to South Vietnam, only to be told that Tran Van Do had departed for Geneva a week early and couldn't be reached in transit. He arrived in due course and demanded to be seated.

Hutchins had arrived in Geneva and accompanied me when I went to meet with Tran, who politely told us that he did not expect to be given a place on the platform in the absence of his opposite number from Hanoi. All he asked, he said, was the right to speak from the floor — a request that Hutchins was forced to refuse, thereby creating the kind of free-speech issue that was guaranteed to draw a glandular response from the American press.

The ironic upshot was that this provided an excuse for the withdrawal of the Soviet delegation, some of whom had already arrived in Geneva. The cable from Moscow concluded with a propaganda flourish: "We also bear in mind that from the very beginning we were placed in difficult position as Convocation sponsors had planned to invite representatives of Saigon regime, which having lost the support of its people is a mere extension of external forces. . . ."[9]

"Pacem in Terris II" was also overtaken by events in the Middle East, where rising tensions between Israel and Egypt were building toward the Six Day War, which broke out three days after the convocation's adjournment. Emergency sessions at the UN prevented Secretary General U Thant from attending the opening ceremonies, and we had to make last-minute arrangements for TV transmission from New York via satellite so that his flickering image could appear on a giant screen in the assembly hall. The crisis caused our only administration spokesman, Ambassador Goldberg, to cancel, along with most of the participants from the Middle East.

On the day before the opening Baggs and I took time out from our hectic damage-control operations to join Hutchins at the hotel's rooftop restaurant, where he was lunching with Senator Fulbright. I had just been with Senator Claiborne Pell, and I reported that he was under tremendous pressure from Washington and thought he might have to pull out. "Let him go," the glum Fulbright said. Well, I said, I can understand why he would be nervous. "A nervous man," Fulbright replied, "shouldn't be here in the first place." Baggs had this sound observation stitched on a sampler, and I hung it on the wall of my Center office as a fitting adjunct to the "Feel Free" motto that adorned Hutchins's.

Despite the defections, the convocation proceeded in an orderly and constructive fashion. The agenda provided as close an approximation of a Center dialogue as it was possible to achieve in such a sizable gathering. In sessions that added up to twenty-two hours of intensive discussion, more than a hundred and twenty of the participants expressed their views. Forty were members of panels; more than seventy-five gave five-minute interventions from the floor; others reported the consensus of groups of scientists and theologians who met in after-hours sessions.

This was serious talk. The participants represented a remarkable range of backgrounds and accomplishments, and those who spoke from the floor were as impressive as the designated discussants.[10] Among the former were US senators, European cabinet ministers, distinguished churchmen, and a Nobel laureate who had attracted the world's attention with his civil-rights crusade. It must have been, I noted, "the first occasion since the Montgomery bus strike when Martin Luther King spent three days in a public place without delivering a sermon, receiving an award, or leading a protest."[11] Through it all Hutchins sat impassively in the front row, puffing his pipe and making an occasional note on a yellow legal pad. He could, in his closing remarks, cite at least two singular developments.

When the Russians pulled out, their Communist colleagues from East Germany, Poland, Romania, and Czechoslovakia did not follow suit. Olof Palme, a cabinet officer and future prime minister of Sweden, opened a session on "Confrontation: The Case of Germany," by observing, "So far as I know, this is the first time that both parts of Germany are represented at an international gathering of this scope."[12]

While Hanoi and Saigon were not represented at the session on "Intervention: The Case of Vietnam," it did bring together representatives of the neighboring Southeast Asian nations, along with Europeans who had taken part in the effort to end the conflict through a previous set of Geneva Accords. The participants from Thailand, Cambodia, Laos, and Malaysia met separately with Brigadier General Said Uddin Khan of Pakistan, the former chief of a UN peacekeeping force in Indonesia, and presented a request that the Center set up a conference in Southeast Asia to continue their efforts to promote a regional settlement.

The war in Vietnam produced spirited exchanges among panelists on the platform and speakers on the floor, but these were by no means one-sided. If there was all but universal condemnation of the bombing of North Vietnam, there was also substantial support for the use of American troops to buttress the South Vietnamese government against invading DRV forces. The dominant concern was that full-scale warfare between these client states of the US and the USSR would further escalate the cold-war confrontation between the superpowers, and in this regard the Soviets fared no better than the Americans.

To Hutchins the unresolved differences on most issues demonstrated that "no national solutions are adequate for the present day." But "Pacem in Terris II," he said in his closing remarks, had produced a consensus: "The cold war must be ended. It poisons every well, and this means that the great myth of Communist conspiracy on which I was brought up, and the great myth of capitalist conspiracy on which our socialist colleagues were brought up, must be seriously modified, if not abandoned."[13]

He endorsed the admonition of Senator Joseph Clark of Pennsylvania, who had urged, ''Ladies and gentlemen, do not despair of the United States of America.'' Hutchins continued,

> . . . You should not despair of the United States of America because it produces men like Joe Clark.
>
> And on the same basis we can say, do not despair of the world when it produces people like you.
>
> But, of course, the problem is not the absence of men and women like you. The problem is that the world consists of structures of power. And the question is how to reform and re-direct these structures. This is the task ''Pacem in Terris'' set for ''all men of good will.''[14]

The immediate influence of the great convocation on the flow of events was probably not great. Although we fared fairly well in the foreign press, the public-relations impact in the United States was badly skewed by the administration's disinformation campaign. The result was indifferent treatment in news reports and broadcasts, and predominantly unfavorable commentary.

At the opening of the convocation Bernard Cornfeld was asked what his mutual-fund companies had gotten out of the IOS Foundation's sponsorship of the event. ''Well, so far,'' he replied, ''only a large stack of unfavorable newspaper clippings.'' If this had some bearing on the Securities and Exchange Commission investigation that ultimately brought down his financial empire, he never complained. In our experience he was a model patron who paid the bills without protest and made no attempt to influence any aspect of the program. And when it was over he said, ''If the cause of peace has been advanced at all the convocation has been worth the effort. If it hasn't, the effort still had to be made.''[15]

CHAPTER FORTY-THREE

". . . Like Peevish Children"

When he reached the usual retirement age of sixty-five Robert Hutchins pointed out to the directors of the Center that as an actuarial matter, they should begin looking for his successor. He repeated these intimations of mortality at every board meeting thereafter, with no perceptible result. The board could not — or at least did not want to — envision the Center without Hutchins.

Had he been willing to recommend a successor, the election would have been pro forma, but Hutchins steadfastly refused to do so on the ground that this would lay the dead hand of the past on a still-evolving enterprise. The unspoken reason was his recognition — and the directors' — that the institution had been created in his image and that it would be practically impossible for him to remain there and turn over the final responsibility for running the place to someone else.

So far he had been so preoccupied with securing a financial base that he had not been able to devote himself to carrying forward his concept of a self-governing community of scholars with himself as first among equals. "As always," he wrote Thornton Wilder in the fall of 1966, "I spend most of my time raising money." But the ideal had not been abandoned:

> I have an idea that I am founding here the Oxford or the model university of the future. All that dreadful business of imparting facts to semi-comatose students will be done by computers. What

will be left is the good old Socratic business that can be conducted only face to face. That's what I am trying to "institutionalize" — dreadful word — here. There is every chance that institutionalization will kill it. I gather it didn't last when Plato tried it in the Academy, and I'm afraid he's a better man than I am.[1]

Wilder replied,

I'm happily excited about your true new vision of a university above universities. . . . Give it a new name. Call it Athena! You can shake off the "subversive" opprobrium. Great centers of learning are above the labels of the marketplace. The social sciences glide so easily into rancorous polemics or into inflated cant when they are not companioned — at the right and left — by philosophy and the humanities. A school for public administrators and thoughtful citizen-politicians is good, but it's not good enough. . . .[2]

That was a trifle grandiloquent for Hutchins, but after "Pacem in Terris II" he felt he was in a position to begin moving in that general direction. Despite the bad reviews in the American press, the convocation had been a box-office success: the Center's extant donors, and some new ones, shared Bernard Cornfeld's view that whatever the immediate result, the intransigence of the Johnson administration justified the effort. Among these was Chester Carlson, now a member of the Center's board, who had chaired the panel on development at Geneva. Although he made no specific pledge, Carlson indicated that he expected to continue the support that had given the institution its first taste of solvency.

That prospect enabled Hutchins to make his first move toward recasting the highly personalized administration that had existed at the Center since its founding. The fellows, he thought, should have collective responsibility for what came to be called the "academic program" — the projects that each of them initiated and the daily dialogue to which they were presumed to contribute. But Hutchins bore too much scar tissue from his years as a university administrator to be under the delusion that this kind of collegial decision making could be extended to budgeting and housekeeping, or to the "communications program," which included publications and the public gatherings associated with fund raising.

He would continue as chairman of the fellows, but in order to promote a collegial spirit, which his own dominant personality tended to inhibit, and to free himself from responsibility for the details of the dialogue sessions, he appointed John Seeley dean and director of academic studies.

At the same time he made a clear demarcation by appointing me executive vice president and naming John Perry secretary-treasurer.

The new dispensation received a mixed reception among the fellows. Scott Buchanan had no reservations on the academic side since he had been responsible for bringing Seeley to the Center, and he had no interest in administration, which he regarded as a necessary evil. Stringfellow Barr and Rex Tugwell told their colleagues they should be delighted to be relieved of having anything to do with what went on in the countinghouse. But Harvey Wheeler, who had a following among the younger fellows, indicated that he would ignore the new arrangement; he regarded his relationship to Hutchins as that of liege lord to monarch, and he would continue to answer only to him. The division was papered over, but it would endure for the life of the Center.

In his conversations with Hutchins, and with me, Carlson made it clear that he wanted his money to be used to insure the continuation and expansion of the communications program. He agreed that the Center's continued independence would best be served by a guaranteed source of income, but he thought that a full endowment would remove the practical compulsion to disseminate the ideas generated by the dialogue. The ideal arrangement, in his view, would be an endowment that provided half the annual income, with the other half to be derived from Center supporters.

The existing program could not meet that requirement. Hutchins had always found drumming up contributions at luncheons and parlor meetings distasteful, and none of the rest of us was particularly good at it. It also appeared that Harold Willens's campaign had skimmed the cream off the pool of potential founding members; recruits were increasingly hard to come by, and some of the old ones did not renew their five-year pledges. We needed a new, broader approach, and my experience at Britannica had convinced me that direct mail might be worth a try.

The enormously successful National Geographic Society seemed to provide a model for the publications program. Its members did not subscribe to its popular *National Geographic* magazine; instead, their tax-exempt dues entitled them to receive a magazine that recounted the activities of the nonprofit educational organization. The present Center publications, which were distributed free, were a major source of red ink in the annual budget. Their replacement, even by a periodical that did no more than pay its own way, would provide the equivalent of some four hundred thousand dollars in new revenue annually — and at the same time give donors some evidence that they were supporting a worthwhile endeavor.

Hutchins was not enthusiastic about my proposal for a Center magazine. Conditioned by his experience with *Measure* at the University of Chicago, he doubted that any essentially intellectual publication could turn a profit. But Chester Carlson liked the idea and indicated that he would guarantee against any loss we might suffer if the initial investment in direct-mail solicitation did not pay off. That clinched the matter, and Hutchins told me to go ahead.

The decision posed an immediate test for the division of authority under the reorganization scheme. No magazine could be edited by a committee, but I recognized the fellows' right to an effective degree of policy control over a publication issued in their name. The solution was to provide that the periodical's content must be derived from the dialogue, which the fellows controlled, while the editor was left free to select and style the material as he saw fit. This worked out quite well in practice, though it never ceased to arouse complaints on both sides.

I tried to persuade Edward Reed, the able editor of the Center's publications, to take on the new job, but he was unwilling to accept responsibility for meeting a fixed publication schedule. I then turned to John Cogley, who had experience as the executive editor of *Commonweal* and had left the Center to become the religious-news correspondent of the *New York Times.*

Hutchins had reservations, not about his competence but about his temperament. Cogley's moody sensitivity to real or fancied slights was so pronounced that he had provided Hutchins with a desk drawer's worth of proffered resignations during his previous tenure. It was, indeed, his thin skin that made him available when I went to New York to discuss the projected magazine with him. I found him brooding because Harrison Salisbury, his immediate superior at the *Times,* had sent a message across the vast city room asking him to stop by his desk. Cogley considered this an insufferable affront: if Salisbury needed to talk with him, he should have walked over to his desk. Hutchins had never sent for him, he said, and I refrained from pointing out that Hutchins always went to see his minions because it enabled him to keep the conversation short.

Center Magazine made its initial appearance as a bimonthly periodical in the fall of 1967. Cogley brought with him to Santa Barbara as managing editor Edward Engberg, a friend who had held editorial positions at *Fortune* and *Look,* and he insisted on making his own arrangements for artwork and design. I assumed that Engberg was competent to put the magazine together, but the first edition was a hopeless mishmash, the format so embarrassingly bad that he and Cogley disappeared for three days after the first copies were delivered by the printer. Cogley offered no resistance when I exercised my prerogative as de facto publisher and insisted that he install Ed Reed as executive editor.

The resignations again piled up in Hutchins's desk drawer, but with Reed and later Donald McDonald backing him up, Cogley made the *Magazine* a distinguished publication. He served as editor until illness forced his retirement in 1974.

Despite the alarums and excursions at the Center, there was an even tenor to the private life that Hutchins always kept at one remove from his professional career. Santa Barbara provided an ideal habitat for one with his essentially reclusive temperament. He appreciated its natural beauty, and the relaxed social life made no more demands than he cared to accept. In the early years Vesta was happily occupied with the creation of the beautiful house that arose at the foot of an alpine meadow high above Montecito Valley. They acquired additional acreage on the mountainside, guaranteeing him a splendid isolation when he repaired there from El Parthenon. And as he reported to Wilder, his relations with his children were better than they had ever been:

> Franja appears to have found contentment and stability at last. Clarissa and Roddy impress me. After going as far as the graduate school in history, he decided to become a vet! Joanna Blessing worries me. She is very unhappy and nothing anybody can do or say makes any impression. She is a marvelous painter. Maybe success at this will cheer her up. Vesta has been a grandmother for three years. The son-in-law is going into the Foreign Service. The daughter graduates from the University of California at Santa Barbara this year.[3]

Although Vesta's heart condition still caused her problems, her ebullience was such that once the housing project was in hand, she opened a gallery in Montecito Village and became a partner in the restaurant next door. Then, in 1964, a dry Santa Ana wind sent flames roaring through Romero Canyon and destroyed her handiwork. My wife and I managed to get through the police lines, and we reached the Hutchins house just ahead of the fire. She evacuated Vesta and the household pets while I stayed behind with Hutchins to see if there was anything to be done to save the dwelling.

Flames were flaring in the canyon below us when the fire-fighting crew urgently recommended that we leave. Hutchins made a last trip into the house. I expected him to return bearing a rare manuscript or a family heirloom, but instead he came out with four bottles of fine French wine Walter Paepcke had given him. We repaired to my house in the valley and opened a bottle. "I must have heard my father and grandfather preach a score or more times urging that we not become attached to earthly things," he said. "At last I know what they meant."[4]

Vesta rebounded from the total loss of the house and its contents with renewed vigor. The fire, devastating though it had been, provided an opportunity for her to correct the things she had decided she didn't like about the first design, and so a new and even more distinctive edifice began rising upon the building pad. Hutchins, situated reasonably comfortably in a rented house in Montecito, offered his blessing and kept his distance. When I asked when he expected the new house to be completed, he said, "You don't understand Vesta. This is not a building project, it's a career."

The Center dialogue was developing in a fashion that provided ample fodder for the magazine, which met with an encouraging reception when the first test mailings were made. But the program still lacked focus. Hutchins had hoped to give it that when he persuaded Rex Tugwell to locate permanently in Santa Barbara, where he would devote the remainder of his life to drafting a model constitution addressing the basic problems of governance he had encountered as a presidential adviser, cabinet officer, city planner, and territorial governor. It had seemed to Hutchins that this would be an ideal project on which to enlist the joint effort of the fellows, but it remained essentially a one-man show.

There was increasing pressure to involve the Center more directly in the clamorous affairs of the outside world. John Seeley urged Hutchins to appoint undergraduate or graduate students as junior fellows so they could infuse the place with the revolutionary spirit abroad on the nation's campuses. Hutchins reluctantly acceded, stipulating that each such appointee be recommended by a senior fellow who would take responsibility for involving him as an apprentice in his own studies. The requirement was never met. Apprenticeship was not for this generation of students; they arrived demanding the right of full participation in the dialogue and in the governance of the institution.

The climax of the Center's involvement in the youth movement came when the resident junior fellows summoned eighteen student leaders from across the country for a three-day conference. Included were student-body presidents from Stanford, Indiana, Howard, and Washington University, a Saltonstall from Yale, an editor of the *Harvard Crimson,* and representatives of the activist student organizations SDS and SNCC. It was doubtful that they represented the views of the mass of college students, but they did reflect the rebellious spirit infecting many children of the affluent upper classes.

Ping Ferry, who had obtained special funding for the meeting from a radical friend, accurately described the mood as "hammering discontent, combined with impatience for action. The participants look on the United States and find it abounding in hopeless contradictions, hypocrisy, and wrongdoing." [5] Devereaux Kennedy, student-body president of staid Washington University in St. Louis, produced headlines in the *Santa Barbara News-Press* and brought on another call by Congressman Charles Teague for an end to the Center's tax-exempt status.

"What I mean by revolution," Kennedy said, "is overthrowing the American government and American imperialism. . . ." The initial role of the students would be to encourage violence in the black ghettos: "They can give these people guns, which I think they should do. They can engage in acts of terrorism and sabotage outside the ghetto." He looked forward to "completely demoralizing and castrating America."[6]

Most of the others were more restrained, and some were, by comparison, downright moderate. With the exception of Seeley, Ferry, and Hallock Hoffman, the senior fellows dismissed the revolutionary rhetoric as unrealistic and deplored the emphasis on power. But Devereaux Kennedy no doubt bespoke the sentiment of all the student participants when he responded to that criticism:

> . . . When I came here I thought it'd be a lot like going into my grandfather's house. I expected to meet a lot of nice old people who are very interested in what the young are doing and I expected them to tell us that we have a lot of youthful enthusiasm and that is good, but there ain't going to be no revolution. . . .
>
> You people really are far, far out of it — so far that every one of us had to go on to points in the discussions we had five years ago, just to bring you people up to where we are today. You've been sitting in this really groovy place called the Center for the Study of Democratic Institutions and you don't know what's going on in the world. I don't think you'll ever understand.[7]

If Hutchins was appalled by the unbridled anti-intellectualism displayed by the students, he made no apology for having sponsored the conference. The 75,000-word digest of the proceedings — published as an occasional paper, *Students and Society* — was an example of the Center's "early warning" function, a term he would use thereafter in describing the work of the institution. A year later the concept received the endorsement of the *Wall Street Journal*. In the aftermath of student rioting at Columbia University, its editor, Vermont Royster, wrote of the report:

Re-reading it today, anyone gifted with hindsight will have a better insight into what happened at Columbia. . . . The conversation here recorded shows that the gap is not just generational, though it often wears that guise. Rather, it reveals a deep philosophic cleavage about society and what it ought to be, in which the rebel young are not so much striking out on their own as reflecting another set of old ideas taught by a different set of elders. You will find the conversation interesting, and you may find it foreshadowing other things to come.[8]

As the decade came to a close, a diverse group of twenty-five persons were listed as fellows of the Center. Elisabeth Mann Borgese, who had been a frequent visitor, established residence in Santa Barbara, as did Bishop James A. Pike after he was relieved of his duties as head of the Episcopal diocese of San Francisco. Another bishop without a diocese, Edward Crowther, who had been barred from returning to his seat in South Africa after his denunciation of apartheid at "Pacem in Terris II," was a visiting fellow, as was Peter Marin, a fractious young high-school teacher. The retired dean of the UCLA Graduate School of Business, Neil H. Jacoby, was commuting from Los Angeles and was expected to make the connection permanent.

No one had departed to make room for these new arrivals. The senior members of the administrative staff were still designated as fellows and were expected to participate in the dialogue and in the ongoing effort to constitutionalize the Center by consensus. There were now regular, usually protracted sessions at the conference table seeking agreement on the proper distribution of authority and responsibility, and Dean Seeley thought the process was proceeding apace. In a report to the board of directors on the academic program, he wrote,

It has also served to draw together and strengthen the Fellowship, while at the same time better, more readily and more surely coordinating the Center as a whole. It marks a true, a good and important advance into Collegiality — something upon which the Center will have to come more and more to rely. (By "Collegiality" I mean nothing more or less than what is meant by the term in the renewal of the Church: the effective and mutually enhancing interdependence of Head and Members.)[9]

But Frank Kelly noted that there was no mention of any role for him in the impressive list of possible projects that Seeley enumerated in his report. "I took part in most of the dialogues at the Center," he wrote, "but I was not expected to be responsible for any of the academic studies."[10] And an embittered Ferry, also not mentioned in the dean's disquisition, wrote in retrospect:

> Disintegration set in. The unspoken question was at last spoken: "Who will succeed Hutchins, and how?" Cracks widened in the Center's collegial structure. Cliques formed and we sometimes seemed like peevish children. Hutchins' taste for adulation ripened into a taste for toadies, of which there was an adequate supply. Even the discussion of a new U.S. Constitution was not enough to hold together the scattering parties. The irony of such a discussion was plain to all of us, for we could not begin to agree on a constitution for the Center itself.
>
> Some such instrument was needed to provide for the succession when Hutchins resigned or died. He was the only thing we had in common: We all admired his mind and accomplishments and — until the breakup in the late spring of 1969 — his principles.[11]

The only way to resolve the impasse was to clean house — and that meant firing some of the fellows, a prospect Hutchins could not bring himself to face. But after more than a year of maundering disputation, his patience ran out. In April 1969 he punctuated the interminable wrangling by scribbling a note and passing it to Seeley, who was sitting beside him at the conference table:

> I am gradually coming to the conclusion that, much to my regret, self-government of this group as it is at present is impossible. 1. Members of the present group are not by mere membership — in many cases accidental — qualified to "be" the Center. 2. Members are not actuated (in all cases) by a desire to achieve the common good. They are expressing their "individuality" or individual prejudices often without regard to the topic under discussion.[12]

The stricken Seeley scribbled a reply: "But I do not know how this is remedied. . . ." Hutchins wrote back: "Fire some or start over." Seeley countered: "But I count upon (half truth, half dogma) that a long slow process will turn all further to the common good. Patience and guidance and strength." Hutchins terminated the exchange: "You are a young man. . . ."[13] But Hutchins wasn't. He had turned seventy, and he recognized that the matter of succession could no longer be postponed. If it was to be tempered by the institutionalizing of a community of scholars, he would have to contrive a new beginning.

He first sought to avoid having to personally fire anyone by creating a committee on reorganization, composed of Seeley, Cogley, Wheeler, Jacoby, and me. Cogley, predictably, declined to serve, but he suggested as the ultimate means of diffusing responsibility a scheme borrowed from monastic practice. Hutchins, as the first senior fellow, would name a second, and thereafter the fellowship would be expanded by the unanimous agreement of those already chosen, until there was none left who could be named without a dissenting vote.

On May 7 Hutchins presented this reorganization scheme to the fellows, noting that the new body would be chosen from those present and from the outside. "If members of the group would like to argue me out of this position, I am open to it," he said.[14] A disgruntled comment by Peter Marin elicited no endorsement, and two days later Hutchins reported to an executive session of the board of directors that the proposal had the unanimous approval of all the fellows except Ferry, who was on vacation in England and had not been apprised of it.

When asked how many of the present fellows could expect reappointment, Hutchins estimated that "six or seven, at the most, would be named senior fellows under any objective procedure based on demonstrated qualifications and past performances. . . . Another four or five probably could be continued on a full-time basis to carry out editorial or administrative duties in which they were already engaged, since there would be no lessening of the publication, development and public relations requirements under the new program."[15]

He received the unanimous approval of the board to proceed with what he called "refounding," along with authority to make generous severance arrangements to provide those dismissed with up to two years' protection against any loss of income. It appeared that Hutchins had managed to arrange for a smooth transition, but that prospect vanished when he made Harvey Wheeler his first choice under the new dispensation. Wheeler recognized that he now had veto power over any subsequent appointment, and he proceeded to exercise it.

CHAPTER FORTY-FOUR

The Center Refounded

The weeks before he initiated the refounding were a kind of Gethsemane for Robert Hutchins. His Puritan conscience would not permit him to simply turn the mess over to a successor and walk away, and his ego would not allow him to abandon the concept he had cherished throughout his career, that of a self-governing intellectual community. I was not much comfort to him.

I had taken the position from the beginning that I would not be a party to any constitutional scheme that would breach the existing line of demarcation between the academic and communications programs, and this had made me the bête noire of the faction seeking to place control of the entire Center operation in the hands of the fellows. When Hutchins raised the possibility that I might succeed him, I sent him a memorandum pointing out that this was a practical impossibility:

> If I read the temper of the present congregation correctly no one except you is going to be acceptable until and unless something fundamental is done to alter the composition of the fellowship. . . . A reasonable constitutionalization along the lines suggested by Neil Jacoby is not only possible but in my view highly desirable — an ultimate necessity for continuity of the Center unless there is somebody in sight who could bring to the position the personal prestige and authority that has enabled you

to operate under the Benedictine Rule. I do not qualify, and I cannot think of one who does.[1]

The Benedictine Rule vested in the head of a monastery full authority to determine its membership and to control its affairs under policies approved by the Vatican — and substituting its board of directors for the Holy See, this was how the Center had operated. Jacoby's proposal would give the fellows the right to collectively determine who should join their company and what the academic program should be. The method Cogley had suggested for naming a new set of fellows would work, I thought, but only if Hutchins retained his final authority and made it clear that the procedure was expected to result in the appointment of

> such of those presently in residence as are clearly qualified; that this group, and others similarly qualified to be added from the outside, would be charged with establishing a constitution for the Center; that a considerable number of those now asserting the right to participate in the constitutionalization process would not be appointed and would be given a choice of remaining if they can be absorbed into the support staff, or of departing with generous severance if they so choose. I do not believe the break can be glossed over, or that it is possible to make it without some wounded feelings and painful recriminations. But we've got those already, on a continuing basis.[2]

This, in essence, was the proposal approved by the fellows, most of whom no doubt acted on the assumption that they would be included among the elect. It certainly represented the understanding of the board of directors. But Harvey Wheeler, once he was anointed by Hutchins, simply ignored it. His position was that no one else at the Center was worthy of appointment. He insisted that nothing further be done until new fellows had been chosen from among the most eminent scholars in the Western world.

Hutchins was hoist on his own utopianism. Since he had always insisted that the Center should be made up of the best minds that could be found, he could hardly object to such a canvass. But as he knew they would, telephone calls to possible candidates in this country and abroad only confirmed the evident fact that such recruiting could only succeed over an extended period.

In the meantime, the impasse created by Wheeler had to be resolved. Twenty-one fellows were left in suspense, each nervously awaiting the verdict that would determine his immediate future. Wheeler told John Seeley that he regarded himself and Hutchins as coequal sovereigns, but this did not seem to carry with it any sense of responsibility for the well-being of the institution and those dependent upon it. When Wheeler finally yielded to Hutchins's insistence that some resident fellows must be named, Seeley recalled his saying that "my whole world has fallen apart, the university has fallen apart."[3]

Rex Tugwell, whose scholarly standing could hardly be faulted, became the third fellow. When Hutchins told me that he intended to propose me next, I suggested that if the matter of academic credentials was at issue, the head of the communications program and the editor of the magazine could serve ex officio. Cogley initially agreed, but as usual, he changed his mind. The two of us were then given full standing, and Elisabeth Borgese and John Wilkinson were added. No one else could muster a unanimous vote.

All but two of the displaced persons accepted the new dispensation with good grace. Seeley claimed that Hutchins had guaranteed him lifetime tenure and accused him of bad faith when he denied that any such arrangement existed, but in the end he accepted the severance settlement. Ferry returned from England, understandably outraged at having been informed of his termination by mail, and filed a lawsuit that challenged the right of the Fund to discharge him after seventeen years of service. He finally settled his severance claims out of court after the attorneys had compiled voluminous depositions documenting the unraveling of the fellowship. He felt he had been personally betrayed by Hutchins, and his bitterness was not to be tempered by the passage of time. The lawsuit was a divorce action, one of the lawyers observed, not a dispute over money.

When Martin Quigley wrote to commiserate with him over the difficulties he must be facing in ending his long association with Ferry, Hutchins replied, "You're right about my sentiments about our friend. He didn't leave me much choice; he wasn't doing anything to speak of himself; most of his time was devoted to attacking other people because they did not do more and better work."[4]

Kelly retained his vice-presidential title, and the key publications and administrative personnel stayed in place, except for John Perry, who resigned for personal reasons. These would participate in the dialogue as before but would have no voice in determining the academic program. Stringfellow Barr elected not to be considered as a senior fellow and moved back to Princeton; he had found Santa Barbara a lonely place after the death of Scott Buchanan the year before. Linus Pauling, who had been on leave to continue his research at Stanford, would not have served in any case. "I have been appalled to read about the changes in the Center," he wrote Hutchins. "I have the impression that you have dropped your good men and kept the dull ones — and the dull projects."[5]

Aside from my insistence and Hutchins's acquiescence, the separation of the academic and communications programs had also become a condition for continuation of the funding that made possible the refounding. As a director, Chester Carlson had been fully apprised of the issues that divided the fellows. His reaction was to propose a means by which businesslike management of the communications program could be insured.

By 1968 the direct-mail campaign had produced more than sixty thousand dues-paying members, and within a year the total would reach a hundred thousand. The income provided a small profit after covering the full cost of the Center's publications, the audiotapes distributed to radio stations and libraries, promotion, and outside meetings. Pleased with this result, Carlson indicated that he was prepared to finance a subsidiary corporation to provide for further expansion.

This was similar to the arrangement Hutchins had helped work out for the University of Chicago and the Britannica company, and it could be set up so that full policy control would be retained by the board of directors. It had the virtue of insuring the communications program against the stultifying intrusion that would likely result from management by a self-governing academic body. Of equal importance, it would keep the fellowship at one remove from pressures to trivialize the dialogue, which might arise from the effort to broaden the audience for Center materials.

With the assistance of John Perry, I had worked up a proposal to accomplish these ends and to meet Carlson's insistence that he wanted to make an investment, albeit one on which he expected no cash return. When I spent the better part of a day going over the details with him at his home outside Rochester, he expressed his general approval and indicated that he had earmarked five million dollars to provide working capital. I summarized his views in a memorandum:

Aside from [increasing] dues-paying members, he seems to have an equal concern with our effort to broaden the audience for Center materials — and he expressed a special interest in having us experiment with means of using television. [When] I made the point that this could run into comparatively heavy investment with dubious chances of ever getting essentially educational programs on a paying basis, he seemed to see the corporation as the best device for such experimentation. . . . He seems to want to turn his money over to some going concern, but not the conventional university or other usual recipient of large benefactions.[6]

On August 13, 1968, Carlson wrote a letter of confirmation to Hutchins: "As an example of good business planning, I think it rates pretty high."[7] Arnold Grant, acting as attorney for the Center, responded to the legal questions he raised, and Carlson instructed his own attorney to work with Grant in drafting an agreement that would result in the creation of a subsidiary Center Communications Corporation. It was stipulated that the Center proper would immediately begin to receive substantial annual royalty payments in return for assigning to the new corporation the rights to produce and merchandize its publications and audiovisual material.

A month later, while the lawyers were still working on the arrangement, a fatal heart attack felled Carlson on a New York street. As a result, the corporation never materialized, but it turned out that the Center's primary benefactor had bequeathed it a sum equivalent to his proposed investment. When probate of his will was completed, the block of Xerox stock left to the Center had a cash value of $4,621,401.96. That brought his contributions to a total of more than $8,700,000, and Hutchins accepted a moral obligation to carry out his wishes within the framework of any constitution the Center might adopt.

The board of directors responded by creating a Committee on Endowment, chaired by Grant, to seek fifteen million dollars in invested capital to provide income to supplement that expected to be derived from the communications program. If it succeeded, this would meet the goal Carlson had suggested at the outset — a guaranteed income sufficient to insure independence and continuity for the academic program, coupled with reliance on a broad base of membership to insure that the Center would not neglect its mission to widen the circles of discussion based on the dialogue.

In the summer following the refounding, Hutchins cast a net for new fellows. A group of scholars of unquestioned standing met at the Center for six days in July to consider how the program should be formulated and to make suggestions as to likely participants in it. Five of these accepted appointments as associate fellows, an arrangement similar to that provided for the original consultants, who were expected to contribute to the program on a less-than-full-time basis.

The new recruits were Alexander Comfort, a British medical biologist, novelist, and philosophical anarchist; Bertrand de Jouvenel, president of the Société d'Etudes et de Documentations Economiques,

Industrielles et Sociales in Paris; Mircea Eliade, a historian of religion at the University of Chicago; Alexander King, president of the Federation of Institutes of Advanced Study at Stockholm; and Sir Arthur Lewis, vice chancellor of the University of the West Indies.[8]

Four who had been active in the Center program accepted the new designation: Neil Jacoby, Stanley Sheinbaum, Fred Warner Neal, and Lord Ritchie-Calder, now a professor of international relations at the University of Edinburgh. The others named were Richard Bellman, a mathematician from the University of Southern California; Paul Ehrlich, a Stanford biologist; and Karl Pribham, a professor of psychiatry at the Stanford Medical Center.

In September, writing to James H. Douglas to urge him to rejoin the board of directors, Hutchins summarized the changes:

> I think the Center is working better than it ever did. The removal of a good deal of deadweight has made our meetings more effective, and we seem on the whole to be more "productive." The list of part-time Associates we have accumulated since July is brilliant; if we can make them work we shall be able to raise the level of our performance still further. We ought to find one or two more full-time Senior people and then concentrate on lowering the average age of the group.[9]

The refounding marked the Center's tenth anniversary, and when he reviewed the decade in a report to the board of directors, Hutchins noted significant changes in its emphasis, if not in its direction. The times were such that the Center had to pay attention to "burning" as well as basic issues — those cast up by the severe dislocations that were having a marked effect on the polity. And the cause and effect of international relations were such that the approach could no longer be limited to the American experience.

The composition of the associates emphasized the new international outlook, and the two British members — Ritchie-Calder and Alexander Comfort — would be given full status as senior fellows upon establishing residence in Santa Barbara. A number of distinguished visiting fellows would be imported from abroad, and most of these would continue as associates after spending a sabbatical year in residence.[10]

The studies undertaken by the senior fellows continued to emphasize constitutional issues. Rex Tugwell presented successive drafts of a proposed national charter, making revisions that took into account the criticism and analysis provided by the dialogue. Hutchins's ongoing project was called "The Constitutionalization of Education," Harvey

Wheeler's "The Constitutionalization of Science"; both dealt with the central question of how to apply the standard of common good to undertakings that by their nature should be immune to government control. John Wilkinson's study emphasized cultural concepts and was called "Civilization of the Dialogue." My work on the electoral process was an offshoot of Tugwell's project, prompted by the burning issue raised by the impact of television — and by the resulting increase of special-interest funding — on the nomination and election of public officials.

In his approach to these studies Hutchins emphasized his own view that they could not be dealt with in terms of national sovereignty, which he believed to have been outmoded by the interdependence required for survival in the nuclear age. This view was not shared by Tugwell, and Hutchins, in his turn, was obviously not impressed by the conventional political scientists whom Tugwell called in to vet his draft constitution. A project nearer to Hutchins's heart was that launched by Elisabeth Borgese, who set out to devise a charter governing those vast areas of the earth's surface where no claim for sovereignty had ever been made — the seabeds, which were now coming within reach of commercial operations made possible by advances in technology, and were promising to yield abundant new food and mineral resources that might be treated as the common property of mankind.

Borgese was a woman of unbounded energy and unquenchable enthusiasm. Her formal education had ended at a Swiss music conservatory, from which she had emerged as an accomplished pianist, but her exposure to the intellectual circles in which her expatriate father and husband moved had made her an extraordinary polymath. She had published novels, poetry, and plays and engaged in research into the possibility that animals could learn to communicate in human language.

In earlier visits to the Center she had brought along a dog she was teaching to spell out words by pressing oversize typewriter keys with his nose. She also shared her household with a chimpanzee she considered potentially literate. Named Bob after Hutchins, he unfortunately lost interest in his lessons when he reached puberty. Although he remained essentially good-natured, he playfully wrecked a house she was renting and had to be sent off to the primate research center at Emory University. Hutchins said he thought Bob should find a university setting congenial.

After planning sessions in Santa Barbara, Borgese launched a continuing series of international meetings to which she gave the title "Pacem in Maribus." These used the dialogue format of the "Pacem in Terris" convocations, and the first, at Malta in June 1970, brought together some two hundred participants from scores of nations, with a heavy representation from the Third World. The continuing "PIM" project became a significant adjunct to the effort on the part of the United Nations to promulgate an international seabeds treaty to regulate commercial activity in the depths beneath what traditionally had been treated as international waters.

The spinoff from the "Pacem in Terris" convocations continued to involve the Center in a variety of undertakings intended to open up dialogue on issues that were banned from official consideration. In the 1970s the most pressing case of this kind involved the United States' lack of recognition of China, a policy we had also imposed on the Japanese. Seeking a break in the impasse, Tokuma Utsunomiya, a member of the Japanese House of Representatives, brought a number of his colleagues to Santa Barbara to discuss the issue with their opposite numbers in America.[11]

Utsunomiya, a wealthy pharmaceuticals manufacturer, continued to enlist the Center's cooperation in Asian projects for which he provided funding. At his behest I made a trip to Seoul to bolster an effort led by the former US ambassador to Japan, Edwin O. Reischauer, to obtain clemency for Kim Dae Jung, the opposition political leader who was being held under house arrest by Korea's military dictatorship. And we worked with Utsunomiya to set up an unofficial meeting in Japan between American political leaders and representatives of mainland China, a meeting that was aborted when President Nixon's surprise visit to Peking signaled the restoration of diplomatic relations with the People's Republic.

A meeting funded by the Parvin Foundation, the goal of which was to consider a greater role for the Latin American nations in the economic development of the hemisphere, brought another group of American political leaders and their opposite numbers to Mexico City for a session chaired by Justice Douglas. The meeting was held there to permit the participation of representatives from Castro's Cuba — but like the Russians at Geneva, they pulled out at the last minute.

Activities of this kind, along with daylong symposia for Center members in major cities and the greatly increased production of discussion papers and transcriptions from the more sharply focused dialogue, provided the basis for expansion of the communications program. In 1970 Mary Harvey, a veteran editor with experience on *Saturday Review* and *McCall's,* was appointed editor of *Center Report,* a bimonthly digest of Center activities that alternated with *Center Magazine.*

A report on the Japanese-American conference, *Asian Dilemma: United States, Japan and China,* inaugurated a paperback book-publishing program. Florence Mischel, a talented audiotape editor, was given new facilities to step up the production of cassettes. These, added to the books produced under the Center's imprimatur or in collaboration with trade publishers, were used in a kind of book-club operation that offered the publications and tapes to the expanding membership list. "I do really believe that the place is in pretty good shape and that it is accomplishing something," Hutchins wrote Thornton Wilder in May 1971.[12]

Except for the illness that had felled him during his military service in Italy fifty years before, Hutchins had never spent a night in a hospital. Then, late in 1969, he circulated a memorandum to the Center's staff that took ironic note of a change in his fortunes. Characteristically, it was intended not only to explain his absence but to fend off those who might seek to commiserate with him:

> The medical profession, eager to discover causes for my peculiar vitality, are holding a seminar "Pacem in Corporibus" beginning Sunday, October 12, at Cottage Hospital in Santa Barbara.
>
> I shall not be allowed to receive callers, messages, flowers, books, candy, liquor, or anything else that will interfere with the general sterility of the performance.[13]

His medical problems thereafter were progressive. In May 1971 he wrote apologetically to Thornton Wilder:

> I have been in such deplorable condition in the last couple of years that I haven't been very communicative. Nothing is more repulsive than an account of other people's symptoms. Most of mine have been of a specially repulsive kind, tumors of the bladder, swelling of the prostate, things you can't mention in mixed company, at least you couldn't when you and I were boys in Oberlin.
>
> Then I had one final — I hope it's final — experience at the hands of the Lebanese wizard in Houston, Dr. De Bakey, an operation for an aneurysm of the aorta.[14]

Although the operation laid him open from sternum to pelvis, it was a complete success and he healed rapidly. The most appalling aspect of his confinement, he said, was the exposure to television while he was helplessly recumbent and trussed up to his tubes. "Houston," he later wrote Bill Douglas, "has what I suppose it deserves, the worst television in the world." And when he turned off his own TV set, "injury was added to insult" as football games permeated the airwaves:

> . . . The entire staff, doctors and nurses, gathered around various television sets and remained totally deaf to the demands of patients. We could have all died and nobody would have known until after the game. Then word got around that I had abolished football at the University of Chicago. Thereafter I got little attention except when people came in to look at me as a curiosity in a museum. They were all indignant.[15]

Unfortunately, that was not to be his last visit to Houston's body works, as he called them. On July 1 he wrote Wilder, "Now I am setting off on the fourth for the Anderson Tumor Institute in Houston to get my cancer of the bladder looked at. I don't know what they will do or recommend; but I hope to get back to Santa Barbara in a week."[16] He did get back, but it was only a brief reprieve. On July 20 he wrote Wilder:

> Those characters told me I must come back and spend a month having "radical" surgery — the kind appropriate to radicals — in my case the removal of the bladder and the prostate. So I'm going to be operated on 5 August. . . .
> Well, to hell with it. My mother had a worse operation and lived sixteen years thereafter. And if I can't equal her record, I can't complain. As I keep saying, I had perfect health until I was 70.[17]

On August 27 he wrote thanking Wilder for his letters. "The only trouble with your bulletins is that they make me laugh and that hurts." But they had the happy effect of transforming "the environment, present and future. I forgot the pain and indignity of becoming a bladderskate, with outdoor plumbing, and began to feel that all was not lost: I might become human again."[18] On September 23 Wilder heard from Vesta:

> This is a happy report I send — Robert dared to go to the Center today for an hour or two to try his wings. It was all so bad these past few months, one shock after another to the system that, happily for everyone, I cannot talk about it. It is behind us! And remembering what happened to Lot's wife, I shall not look there.[19]

Although he had some difficulty mastering the "outdoor plumbing" he was condemned to wear, Hutchins soon returned to his usual schedule. But there was now a new distraction. His illnesses had given the matter of his succession even greater actuarial urgency. While he still refused to make any personal endorsement, he began actively seeking suggestions for prospects to be considered by the board and the fellowship. He wrote Wilder:

> The only thing that worries me about the Center is the choice of my successor. When I was thirty I knew everybody. Now I don't know anybody younger than I, and there's nobody older. In your wanderings have you ever met anybody you could recommend? When I ask the question the usual answer I get is Whitehead. I always say, "Yes, but how do I get in touch with him?"[20]

Finding someone acceptable to both the directors and the senior fellows would prove to be only slightly less difficult than resurrecting the deceased Harvard philosopher.

CHAPTER FORTY-FIVE

The Search
for a Successor

Throughout the 1960s, in sloughs of despond over the state of the union and the state of his personal life, Bill Douglas had talked of resigning from the Supreme Court and settling down at the Center, where Robert Hutchins assured him he could make any arrangement that suited him. In 1964, after he had succumbed to second thoughts, as he always did, I wrote him,

> Bob Hutchins probably has called you by now to express our mutual regret that you won't be joining us soon on this small mountain. But I'm afraid I have to agree that your decision is the correct one. The Center is important, but the Court does retain a certain utility.[1]

The possibility of his relocating to Santa Barbara remained alive because of the Parvin Foundation, which Douglas served as nominal president and Hutchins and I as board members. Albert Parvin, the founder, had made it clear that its assets — some $3,600,000, with more presumably to come — could be used for any philanthropic projects Douglas might care to initiate when he retired from the Court. Joint undertakings with the Foundation had become a significant part of the Center program, and Douglas had always been Hutchins's first choice as his possible successor.

The financial affairs of the Foundation were administered by Albert

Parvin from his Los Angeles office. In the mid-1960s this arrangement was targeted by the Internal Revenue Service for a tax-fraud investigation. The ostensible basis for the IRS action was the suspicion that Parvin had used the Foundation as a front to avoid paying taxes on earnings from his hotel-furnishing business. The real reason was that the company had furnished most of the leading hotel/casinos in Las Vegas and had been paid off with stock in these gambling establishments. Parvin had set up the Foundation with proceeds from the sale of his interest in the Flamingo Hotel.

The Foundation's connection with a Supreme Court justice on one hand and with Las Vegas gambling interests on the other was enough to produce a synthetic scandal when word of the IRS probe was leaked to the press. Although the investigation into Parvin's handling of the Foundation's finances went on for some three years, no violation, or even any impropriety, was ever charged. But in 1969, with Richard Nixon and his plumbers in the White House, the mere fact of the IRS investigation provided the basis for an effort to impeach Justice Douglas.

Douglas was, of course, a tempting target. He was the Court's most consistent defender of civil liberties and other unpopular causes, and his unconventional life-style compounded the outrage of his conservative critics. When Gerald Ford, then the Republican leader of the House of Representatives, began moving toward initiating the impeachment process, the *New York Times* noted that this was the third attempt to unseat Douglas. The *Times* quoted a lawyer friend's description of the justice as "an existentialist figure, really, his own man, fearful of neither people, forces nor establishments. . . . When the heat is on — and it's on now — the only guy on the Court I'd bet on to stand up is Bill Douglas."

> His enemies, political and social conservatives ranging from distinguished Harvard law graduates to rural Southern segregationists, would not disagree with that estimate. Indeed, for many of them his penchant for "standing up" is enough reason to impeach him, an effort that was made in 1953 in the House of Representatives after he issued a stay of execution to Julius and Ethel Rosenberg, the convicted atom spies.
>
> A less serious but perhaps just as heartfelt attempt to impeach him came in the summer of 1966 when Justice Douglas married his fourth wife, the then twenty-three-year-old Cathleen Heffernan, less than a month after his third wife, twenty-six-year-old Joan Martin, had divorced him and remarried.[2]

For many months before Gerald Ford moved for articles of impeachment, the campaign to exploit the Douglas-Parvin association had been waged in the newspapers. Taken out of context, Parvin's Las Vegas associations were used to intimate a possible connection between the Foundation and organized crime. "I know lots of gamblers, and I have points in almost every Las Vegas hotel," Parvin said, "but I don't break the law, and I never would. . . ."[3] A national accounting firm, retained by the Parvin Foundation's directors to conduct an independent audit in addition to the regular outside examination of the Foundation's books, found no irregularity of any kind.

I cited these findings in a lengthy letter to newspaper editors I knew, pointing out that "we are being systematically frustrated in our effort to deal with the IRS head on and satisfy any legitimate questions, while at the same time, on the basis of leaks that can only come from the IRS, Albert Parvin, the Foundation, and Justice Douglas (who obviously cannot reply) are taking a beating in the newspapers." I concluded:

> I apologize for belaboring this at such length, but I think you ought to have all the facts. The Center has only a minor financial interest in this matter, and I have none.
>
> My concern is personal: I am convinced that we are up against an outrageous act of persecution by a federal agency.[4]

The letter was written in 1967, but no part of it appeared in print until May 1969, when the *New York Times* published extensive excerpts after Douglas announced that he was resigning from the Parvin Foundation to spare it further harassment. At the same time, he made it clear that this was the only resignation he was contemplating. "The strategy is to get me off the Court," he said. "I do not propose to bend to any such pressure."[5]

By the end of 1969 it was evident that the impeachment move would go forward in the 1970 session of Congress. President Nixon saw the removal of Douglas as sweet revenge for the Senate's rejection of two of his Supreme Court nominations, and Gerald Ford was a willing errand boy. When he presented his case to the House, Ford relied on material supplied by the White House, which by innuendo attempted to link Douglas with "the international gambling fraternity . . . the pornographic publishing trade . . . intellectual incubators for the New Left and the SDS, and others of the same ilk."[6]

Hutchins was away from Santa Barbara, recuperating from his recent surgery, and Douglas wrote to me, "I wish you'd talk with Bob when he returns. If this is in any way embarrassing to the Center, I could easily and quietly withdraw just on a hint."[7] I replied:

Bob Hutchins won't be back until around January 15, but I am sure his answer is the same as mine:

Under no circumstances would we agree to having you resign from the Board because of the idiocy in the House.

One of the reasons we were so insistent on nominating you as chairman of the executive committee was to lay to rest any suspicion that this kind of blackguarding would affect your association with the Center.

Anyway, I can't think of anybody I'd rather be impeached with.[8]

At the annual meeting in November board titles had been shuffled. Hutchins had succeeded Douglas as chairman, I had succeeded Hutchins as president, and Douglas had succeeded me as chairman of the executive committee, but the changes were only titular. I had accepted on the understanding that Hutchins would continue to be responsible for the academic program as chairman of the fellows. The board certified the arrangement by designating Hutchins chief executive officer and me chief operating officer. Douglas had never been concerned with the administration of the Center and had treated the office of chairman as largely ornamental.

The impeachment proceeding fizzled out after hearings before the House Judiciary Committee demonstrated that there was nothing of substance to sustain the blatantly partisan attack on Douglas. But the affair effectively ended any prospect of his leaving the Court; if he stepped down, his detractors would claim vindication, and the vacancy would give Richard Nixon an opportunity to pick his successor. He managed to outlast Nixon by hanging on to his seat for a year after he suffered a massive stroke, but his incapacity finally forced his retirement in November 1975. There was a double irony in the fact that Gerald Ford got to name his successor, while John Paul Stevens turned out to be a moderate whose views were closer to Douglas's own than to those of the men who had tried to depose him.

With Bill Douglas removed as a possible successor, Hutchins began looking to other possibilities. He still steadfastly refused to designate a personal choice, but he indicated that he would present any likely prospect for consideration by the nominating committee of the board and by the fellows. In the meantime, as he had promised to do, he reopened discussion of constitutionalizing the Center.

On March 4, 1970, he circulated a memorandum inviting recommendations to a special Committee on Organization, which had been created by the board when it authorized the refounding. He set forth the principle he had followed in his effort to reallocate authority and responsibility at the University of Chicago:

> Ideally, an academic community should have control of those aspects of administration which affect the academic program in significant ways. It should be relieved of burdens that it is not qualified to carry and that are more diversionary than rewarding.[9]

My response supported the division of authority implied by Hutchins, and Rex Tugwell also endorsed it. But Harvey Wheeler, who was still pressing for a fully self-governing "Platonic academy," ignored the distinction and insisted that "no important decisions regarding personnel, facilities or finances — as well as substantive and programmatic matters — would be taken without some participation by the senior members of the academy."[10] His proposal would have denied any degree of autonomy to the administration and would have significantly reduced the authority of the board. John Cogley, without being specific, also called for a charter that would "distribute power as widely as possible, and so far as feasible turn the Center into a collegial organization."[11]

These memoranda were appended to the summary report of the Committee on Organization, submitted to the board at its May meeting. The directors rejected Wheeler's and Cogley's proposals, turned down the Committee recommendation that the fellows be given authority to set salaries and determine tenure, and specified that delegation of authority to determine the content of the academic program would remain "subject to budgetary and administrative controls to be adopted by the board."[12] The board's only concession was to agree that the fellows would be consulted on the appointment of a new chief executive officer — and that, of course, was the really urgent business at hand.

To ease his administrative burdens Hutchins created a program committee intended to assume the functions he had delegated to John Seeley as dean. He tried to bridge the chasm that divided the fellows by appointing Wheeler chairman, with Cogley and me as members. But Wheeler resumed his position as liege lord answerable only to the sovereign; he never convened the committee after its initial meeting and instead simply took over on his own the scheduling of dialogue sessions and the invitation of outside participants. In response to mounting protests from the fellows, Hutchins restored the office of dean and filled it with Norton Ginsburg, a professor of geography from the University of Chicago, who was in residence as a visiting fellow.

Ginsburg, an urbane, soft-voiced product of the Hutchins College at

Chicago, was a veteran of academic politics. When he took an extended leave from the University to accept the Center appointment, he was department chairman and had served as associate dean of the Division of Social Sciences and of the College. As a widely traveled geographer, he was a natural ally of Elisabeth Borgese in her "Pacem in Maribus" program. Under his gentle but persistent prodding the academic program entered upon one of its most productive periods.

One of the most notable products of the Center dialogue was Rex Tugwell's model constitution. By 1970 he had worked his way through thirty-seven revisions of his initial draft, in the process writing elegant essays explicating the theoretical grounding for each of the key sections. Taking their tone and style from the original Federalist Papers, these dealt with constitutional fundamentals and served as background for "Version XXXVII of a Model Constitution for a United Republics of America," which was published initially in *Center Magazine*.

Tugwell labeled his work "A Model for Discussion," and when it was used as the basis for "PIT"-style convocations in New York and Philadelphia, it produced widespread reaction. *Time* headlined its full-page treatment "Heresy in Santa Barbara,"[13] and the *New York Times* noted that "like redecorating a cathedral, putting together a new Constitution for the United States is no job for a timid soul."[14] Although Hutchins pointed out that those who participated in the drafting had no notion that the model was likely to be adopted, the Center's critics, joined by a chorus left over from Tugwell's New Deal days, saw a plot to subvert the republic. The *Chicago Tribune* reacted as though Hutchins was still on the Midway, and its sister publication, the *New York Daily News,* as though Franklin Roosevelt had been reincarnated. The *News* described the model as a "hatchet job":

> Old New Deal idea man Tugwell had produced an horrendous hodgepodge culled and cribbed from every source of political quackery from Karl Marx to Benito Mussolini. It is a blueprint for destroying the political and economic system that has made Americans the freest and most prosperous people in the world. . . .
>
> Tugwell serves up his hash as something new. That's so much malarkey. Many of the ideas are straight hand-me-downs from the New Deal with far-out alterations aimed at an even greater concentration of power in the hands of know-it-all, do-it-all central authority run by theorists, technocrats and self-styled experts like Rex himself.[15]

The charges of Marxist or fascist influences were preposterous, but they echoed those leveled against "Rex the Red" when he became a principal architect of the early New Deal reforms. The Tugwell constitution raised the issue of centralized government, which had divided the New Dealers just as it had the political theorists and practitioners who founded the republic. The basic thrust of this call for reform in the division of powers was to provide for governmental planning to develop the economic resources of the nation.

Tugwell was a classic product of one skein of the American political tradition; he had been "country reared" in upstate New York and conditioned in his youth by the progressive tradition exemplified by Franklin Roosevelt's uncle Ted, the rambunctious "Bull Moose." "Even so," I wrote in an introduction to the model constitution, "Tugwell was early convinced that the laissez-faire doctrines bequeathed by the American founding fathers had become inoperable in the transition from the agrarian society of the eighteenth century to the predominantly urban cultures in which he now identified the locus of power. . . ."

Here he parted company with the trust-busters and money theorists who claimed the progressive cachet, particularly those on the Democratic side. The solution to the country's cyclical economic ills, he insisted, lay not in atomization through induced competition and the curbing of malefactors of great wealth, but in government action to produce a concert of interests; the government should not abhor industrial and commercial combines because they might be monopolistic, but should encourage them under controls that would guarantee that the public shared fully in the benefits of increased efficiency.[16]

The divisions still endured. Bill Douglas, in his New Deal days a disciple of the faction led by Justice Brandeis, which opposed Tugwell's advocacy of central planning, was outraged by the proposed constitution and refused to participate in the convocations devoted to discussing the issues it raised. Most lawyers, including particularly the more liberal ones, feared that any opening of the Constitution to revision would destroy the protection it provided for individual liberties. Hutchins, though noting disagreement with some provisions of Tugwell's draft, rejected this argument. The nation was getting a new constitution anyway, he said, through judicial review: "The present system is neither national, nor a republic, nor democratic. Bureaucracy is impenetrable, money too potent in politics, and the existing states an obstruction to the solution of urban problems."[17]

At the New York convocation a rousing rebuttal to both Tugwell and Hutchins was provided by a lawyer who shared most of their traditional enemies — Ramsey Clark, the uncompromisingly liberal former US Attorney General. The *Washington Post* reported,

> While agreeing that the present system is far from perfect, Clark rejected nearly all of Tugwell's ideas. He called for extreme care in changing the country's basic charter — and the audience, about 1,400 persons gathered in the New York Hilton's grand ballroom, responded with a standing ovation.[18]

If Tugwell and Hutchins lost the argument, the convocation was a triumph for the Center. The *New York Times* gave it a multicolumn spread, and there was solid coverage in most of the other major newspapers as well. The capacity audience was made up of Center members who bought tickets that covered the cost of the affair. The membership could now be relied on to fill a hotel ballroom and pay the freight in any major city where the Center chose to display its wares.

But while the communications program had become self-sustaining, the Center was still faced with a substantial annual deficit. Gary Cadenhead, the UCLA professor of accounting who succeeded John Perry as secretary-treasurer, could report substantial surpluses, but this was a temporary condition resulting from the distribution of the bequest from Chester Carlson. In 1969 the board had agreed to initiate an endowment campaign under the chairmanship of Arnold Grant to bring in major gifts and thus prevent the need to invade the funds received from the Carlson estate. But the campaign never got off the ground:

> It was the view of Arnold Grant and the other board members most immediately concerned that it would not be possible to approach individual philanthropists or foundations for major endowment gifts unless they had some clear-cut indication of what the future program of the Center would be — and in practical terms this meant they would have to know and be exposed to the man who would be in charge after Hutchins stepped down.[19]

I had taken myself out of consideration for the obvious reason that Hutchins cited when he wrote to Thornton Wilder in early 1972:

> The Center rocks along pretty well. But I have to find a successor to myself. I think Harry Ashmore would do well, but he is not

acceptable to the academic types among us. Ken Galbraith, John Gardner, etc. have been proposed; they are tied down elsewhere. Have you run across anybody you would recommend?[20]

There were other prominent names among those Hutchins submitted to the board's nominating committee, and some of these were invited to the Center to be looked over by the fellows. Among the academics were President Kingman Brewster of Yale; President Harland Cleveland of the University of Hawaii; President Robben Fleming of the University of Michigan; Ronald Dworkin, a Yale law professor; and Richard Gardner, a professor of international law at Columbia. When Wilder urged him to consider a woman, Hutchins made inquiries about Barbara Ward, the British economist, who proved to be unavailable because of declining health. Two politicians made the list: Russell Peterson, the former governor of Delaware, and the iconoclastic Eugene McCarthy.

"Senator McCarthy has come and gone," Hutchins wrote Wilder. "He is charming, witty and intelligent. But he should have gone to Oberlin. He does not work. Your father and mine would have reminded him of the parable of the talents."[21]

Hutchins was assiduous in pursuing any name suggested to him, but he seemed reluctant to make a real sales pitch to any of those whom he interviewed. In part this was the product of the self-deprecating manner in which he described his own role, and it may also have reflected his unwillingness to cast himself as an advocate on behalf of any of those on the list. Norman Cousins, who had recently retired as editor of *Saturday Review,* told me that he was left in doubt about whether Hutchins was really ready to turn over the final responsibility to a successor.[22] I was with Hutchins when he met with John Gardner, the former Kennedy cabinet member, and it seems likely that he may have received a similar impression.

In his letters to Wilder, Hutchins repeatedly spoke of his frustration that none of those interviewed aroused any enthusiasm on the part of the board or the fellows: "The trouble is I haven't a candidate I want to push, and nobody else has either."

I am not looking, as my successor, for a guy like me. (What kind of grammatical construction is that sentence?) I don't care whether my ideas or policies are continued. I expect the Center to be quite different (and better) ten years from now. All I am looking for is somebody who is capable of helping to make the place one where important subjects are seriously discussed. There aren't many such places now — if any. There must be somebody.

I don't care whether he comes out of education, business, or government. I'd even take him out of the army if I could find anyone there who had a mind.[23]

He did find one — James M. Gavin, the distinguished Army general who had served President Kennedy as ambassador to France and after his retirement chaired the Arthur D. Little management-consulting firm in Boston. General Gavin visited the Center, and Hutchins arranged for him to meet with J. R. Parten, the chairman of the board's search committee. But nothing came of it, and it turned out, after three years of searching, that there was no satisfactory solution to the problem of Hutchins's succession.

CHAPTER FORTY-SIX

"As Well Settled As Could Be Expected . . ."

While the search for his successor went on, Robert Hutchins began to give thought to how he would spend his time when he finally managed to hand over the Center and for the first time in his adult life was free of administrative burdens. These were already diminishing. He continued to chair the daily dialogue sessions, but the details of programming had been taken over by Norton Ginsburg, whose soothing presence submerged, if it did not eliminate, the tensions among the fellows.

The demands of the communications program for public appearances by him were not excessive, and he had, as he reported to Thornton Wilder, mastered his hydraulic engineering to the point where he no longer worried over "whether or not I'm going to turn into a human fountain. . . . I passed my anniversary examination (bladder, prostate, etc.) on 8 August. I am the only person you know who is 'within normal limits.' No mental tests were given."[1]

No longer concerned about his own health, he now worried about Vesta's. While her physicians continued to experiment with medication, there was increasing talk of surgery to repair her damaged heart valve, and Hutchins, who treated his own bouts with the surgeons with sardonic amusement, could not bear the thought of having Vesta go under the knife. While he now felt free to take time off for vacation travel, her frequent lapses made these ventures problematic.

Vesta continued to ignore her condition when it was less than acute.

The new house escaped a second fire that swept the mountainside, but wooded areas of the property and in the adjoining national forest were heavily damaged, and the mudslides that followed ravaged the denuded slopes. Hutchins reported to Wilder on the "Little Corporal's" response:

> . . . Vesta coped with the Army Corps of Engineers, County Flood Control, the U.S. Forest Service, and a swarm of painters, carpenters and contractors, all equipped with bulldozers. They all wanted to restore our property the way the madman restored the *Pietà* the other day. She beat them off.[2]

He continued to recount her confrontations with the invading hordes: "The Corps cowers." As for himself, his primary complaint was ennui. He recognized that his letters to Wilder were becoming a litany of self-pity, and he apologized for it. His old friend, though suffering from maladies of his own, sought to cheer him up by sending along chapters of his work in progress, the semi-autobiographical novel *Theophilus North*, which wryly invoked scenes of their lost youth:

> He had set out to write a droll story to amuse an ailing Bob Hutchins, to whom he sent a copy of each chapter as it was finished, a book that would "hurt your sides — endanger your stitches and all that," but the "old Wilder-Niven inheritance" had taken over. He ended up with a book about Theophilus-the-fixer, the mender of rips and tears in the human fabric, and he had qualms about its reception, fearing that it might be ridiculed and thus embarrass Hutchins, to whom it was dedicated.[3]

The fears were groundless; the critics, for the most part, were as delighted with the novel as Hutchins had been when he read it a chapter at a time. But even his expressions of gratitude became an occasion for bemoaning his own futility:

> What a worker you are! I am filled with admiration. The more so because I am merely putting in my time, hoping to bore myself into activity. But at the office from 9 to 5 there is always enough paperwork to enable me to fritter the hours away with a clear conscience — then, too, remember, Robert, you are not well. I am, of course, perfectly well. I am tired at night, but that's from sitting, not working.[4]

He contrasted Wilder's facile literary style with that of the papers produced for the dialogue, complaining that while the ideas presented in the latter were estimable, the prose was pedestrian, and he seemed to have heard it all before. Reading this stuff, he complained,

is a dispiriting experience, and one fatal to my literary style. The authors are mostly social scientists and you know what that means. The authors have never read any books, or have read nothing but bad ones. I suspect that most of them started with a deep contempt for the English language. Then, under the influence of Publish or Perish, they have proceeded to grind out endless pages of contemptible prose. And of course none of their "peer group" can criticize them because they were all brought up the same way.[5]

Wilder replied to one of his mordant missives,

What a droll fellow you are. Ever since I have known you, you carry a jesting form, a pilgrim's pack of self-deprecation. It comes out several times in your letter. . . . But on closer reading I am struck by a very real buoyancy about these self-flagellations that wasn't there in the previous years. Your tribulations have lightened your pilgrim's pack. Your famous self-belittling has become a sort of feather in your cap that you wear lightly, airily — you never could bear homage or admiration and took refuge in contradicting it — now you merely thumb your nose at it. Oh yes, you are on the mend.[6]

As his vitality began to return, Hutchins renewed his interest in his first love, the law, occupying himself with the United States Supreme Court reports and the leading law reviews. Brief commentaries by him on current cases occasionally served as background papers for dialogue sessions. These reflected his dim view of what he had always considered to be the besetting problem of judicial review, even when the Warren Court was coming down on his side. He commented on the new Burger Court in a letter to Wilder dated "Bastille Day, 1972":

For the last month I have read all the opinions of the Supreme Court handed down since Mr. Nixon's four appointees took their seats. The opinions are worse than the papers of my colleagues. But, boy, are these fellows industrious — or perhaps *garrulous* is the better word. Such long opinions and so many. In the case where they decided 5–4 that capital punishment was unconstitutional, each Justice wrote an opinion — 50,000 words (I'm guessing) right there. The Nixonites wanted to throw the book at every suspect in the name of law and order; the Warren leftovers believe in the Bill of Rights. All very quarrelsome, and it would be interesting if they were not so long-winded.

I can't get it out of my head that law and learning are not what these judges need. A little humanity would go a long way. As Chief Justice Hughes has said, "The Constitution is what the Justices say it is." This means, I suppose, that you can find in the Constitution support for what you want to do. Therefore what is important is what the Justices want to do. The chief aspiration of some of the new ones seems to be to get tough with those who run afoul of the criminal law. Bill Douglas is no philosopher, but he knows what's going on in the world and has a pretty good idea of what ought to go on in it.[7]

He took a prominent part in a two-day meeting of leading broadcasters and First Amendment specialists convened in the wake of the 1972 election, in which Richard Nixon and his running mate, Spiro Agnew, singled out the leading network TV commentators in a sustained campaign against the media's "nattering nabobs of negativism." This had passed beyond mere rhetoric, and the broadcasters saw a real threat of the use of the FCC's licensing power to retaliate against journalists the hypersensitive Nixon considered to be his mortal enemies. Richard Salant, then president of CBS News, asked me to organize a Center conference to consider whether licensed broadcasters were entitled to the same First Amendment immunity from government intervention as the print media.

The participants included news executives of the three networks as well as some of their commentators, two former FCC chairmen, several leading constitutional experts, and an uncompromising and highly articulate spokesman for the administration — Antonin Scalia, who had served as general counsel for the White House Office of Telecommunications Policy and would ultimately occupy a seat on the Supreme Court.[8] There was no consensus at the conference, but most of those present could agree that the subtitle I chose for the summary report, *Fear in the Air,* was not an exaggeration: "Broadcasting and the First Amendment: The Anatomy of a Constitutional Crisis."

The book, which consisted primarily of excerpts from the dialogue covering the principal arguments on both sides of the controversy, concluded by restating the findings of Hutchins's Commission on Freedom of the Press. The National News Council, a much more limited version of the unofficial monitoring agency the commission had recommended, had just been established by the Twentieth Century Fund, and its chairman, Roger Traynor, a retired chief justice of the California Supreme Court, attended the conference. If the News Council was to succeed, I predicted, the media would have to demonstrate that they were capable of self-regulation to achieve responsibility commensurate with the freedom they claimed under the First Amendment:

> [The Council] is intended to provide a place where any outraged private citizen can bring his complaints against the media in expectation of an impartial hearing and a public finding; and it also will be a place where the media themselves can seek a comparable hearing in the face of attacks from their critics, inside and outside the government. . . .
>
> This may seem a frail defense against the enormous pressures generated by the power centers of government on the one hand and the temptations of the marketplace on the other, but at least it breathes the spirit of civility Alexander Hamilton proclaimed as the only solid basis for all our rights. And, after all, an effective forum for those who insist that robust debate on public affairs justifies the protection of the First Amendment was all the Founding Fathers promised when they erected their great monument to individualism. . . .[9]

Stanley Sheinbaum, a Center fellow who had become a man of considerable means after marrying the heiress to a motion-picture fortune, had been so impressed by Hutchins's legal studies that he proposed erecting a separate building to house a law library for his use and commissioned a San Francisco architect to design an appropriate structure on the Center's grounds. Hutchins encouraged the idea, and Sheinbaum sought other donors for the project. But he had no success, and when he was not among the surviving fellows after the refounding, his own interest in the Center waned.

Hutchins would continue his perusal of the law reports and his occasional commentary, but as the Center's reserves dwindled, his attention was again diverted to more mundane matters. He found himself, he wrote Wilder, "trying to keep this place alive until I can find a successor. This involves trips, money raising, and all the old baloney that drove me from the University of Chicago into the Ford Foundation. (I was right to leave; but I went to the wrong place.)"[10]

The communications program, which included "continuing educa-tion" projects of a nonpromotional character, for which Frank Kelly had nominal responsibility, was still self-sustaining, but there was no effective increase in other funding, even though a number of new directors had been added to the board in the hope of bolstering the flagging endowment campaign. It was concluded that another major "Pacem in Terris"–style convocation was needed.

To help obtain maximum TV exposure, Sander Vanocur, a veteran network correspondent, was retained as a consultant in Washington. He had covered the White House for NBC during the Kennedy years and later served the network as national political correspondent. He had transferred to PBS to experiment with new forms of coverage during the 1972 election campaign, only to fall victim to the political pressures cited in *Fear in the Air*. He was, Vanocur said, "pushed out of broadcasting by Richard Nixon's white-collar brownshirts."[11]

In addition to helping to line up participants and TV coverage for a major foreign-policy convocation in the capital, Vanocur would be involved in the effort to find a way to extend the Center's outreach through visual broadcasting. We had done fairly well with radio, where half-hour programs edited out of regular dialogue sessions were regularly broadcast by educational stations. But efforts to add a visual dimension had so far failed.

There had been a number of approaches by Los Angeles TV producers, but all of these foundered on our insistence that the policy that applied to our publications must also be followed if the cameras were brought in — that is, the programming must be derived from the dialogue as it was presently conducted. The Hollywood types lost interest when we refused to yield to their demand that we select celebrity participants who would go after each other in the confrontational style that was usually employed to lend drama to network talk shows.

Technical limitations also caused problems. Production outside a studio was still cumbersome and expensive. A special grant from the Drown Foundation enabled us to experiment with filming sessions at El Parthenon, but the lights and camera crews were a distraction, and the producers insisted on retakes to smooth out the continuity. New, more flexible videotape technology was beginning to be adopted, however, and there was a prospect of more selective programming with the spread of cable systems. Vanocur was able to obtain a grant from IBM to cover the cost of videotaping the three days of "PIT III" from gavel to gavel, and he later edited the material into a series of one-hour programs broadcast over the PBS network.

*   *   *

"Pacem in Terris III" was convened on October 8, 1973, billed as "A National Convocation to Consider New Opportunities for United States Foreign Policy." The three day-long sessions attracted more than five thousand persons to the great hall of the Sheraton-Park Hotel, among them hundreds of Center members who came from all over the country. Fred Warner Neal was called back into service to help line up the stellar array of participants who addressed the proposition that the winding-down of the war in Vietnam represented a watershed break in American foreign policy.

"The need for a dialogue about national purpose has never been more urgent, and no assembly is better suited for such a discussion than those gathered here this week," Secretary of State Henry Kissinger said in his opening address. Later, when five youthful hecklers attempted to interrupt him, he remarked, "The prerequisite for a fruitful national debate is that the policymakers and critics appreciate each others' perspectives and respect each others' purposes."[12]

That spirit prevailed, though there were sharply dissenting views on how the United States should approach the central question of détente with the Soviet Union. Kissinger's version was challenged by Chairman Fulbright of the Senate Foreign Relations Committee and by former Defense Secretary Clark Clifford, among others. The array of prominent participants[13] attracted widespread media coverage, and by any measure — including the financial one — the convocation was a success. Special contributions and gate receipts covered the expenses, and when the board of directors met just before the opening session, one of the new members, W. Price Laughlin, was so impressed that he pledged fifty thousand dollars to finance "PIT IV."

Hutchins had looked forward to the convocation as the ideal time to announce his successor, and he had been pressing the board's search committee to make a choice among three candidates who had indicated interest in the job. Wilder's industry, he wrote to his old friend in July 1973, had inspired him to begin clearing the decks for work on a book of his own, which would not be the autobiography that Wilder and others were urging upon him but might summarize his thoughts on the Constitution as it should apply to public education. He confided,

> The president of the University of Hawaii, the president of the University of Minnesota, and the ex-governor of Delaware are all interested in my job. . . . Out of the lot we might get somebody. I'd love to get a successor elected in October.
>
> I have resigned from Britannica effective Sept. 30. All I ever

did for the company was to try to protect it from the whims of my classmate. Now that he is gone, there is no reason for all these trips to Chicago.[14]

But in August he was complaining that "I cannot get the committee to make up its mind about which candidate for my job it wants. One of them is certain to escape, perhaps all of them, if we wait too long."[15] By September his plaint had a touch of desperation: "I am trying like hell to get the committee to make up its mind about my successor. But as the days slip by they keep stalling. As I was saying, the administrative life is a sad one."[16] Four days before the board was due to meet he was still decrying

the inability or unwillingness of that damned board of mine to make up its mind about my successor. They think one man wants too much money. Another won't be able to raise money. A third has no Ph.D. (Neither have I.) The Board meets in Washington on Monday. I'm afraid no change will be made.[17]

But the board had made up its mind, or at least J. R. Parten, the chairman of the search committee, had. He had dispatched his Texas friend and fellow board member Bernard Rapoport to Minneapolis to conduct final negotiations with Malcolm Moos, the president of the University of Minnesota, and when the board convened in executive session, he announced that Moos was available and that the committee was recommending his election. The only problem was that Moos would need financial assistance to obtain housing in Santa Barbara to replace that provided for him by the University of Minnesota, but Parten indicated that he would try to make an arrangement to take care of that. The board minutes recorded the result:

There was general discussion of the three candidates, with strong support for Mr. Moos indicated by several board members who had previous personal association with him. The consensus was that Mr. Parten should resume negotiations with Mr. Moos by telephone with the view of announcing his appointment and presenting him to the audience then assembling in Washington for the Center's "Pacem in Terris III" convocation.[18]

Parten made his phone call and returned to announce that Moos had accepted his personal offer of twenty-five thousand dollars to assist him in buying a house. He would be available to take office on July 1, 1974, and would come to Washington in time for Hutchins to present him to the convocation audience:

> There followed a discussion of the possible reorganization of the administration of the Center. Mr. Hutchins insisted that the appointment of Mr. Moos must carry with it all the responsibility and authority presently vested in him. Mr. Hutchins would function as chief executive officer until June 30, 1974, and thereafter would be available for any services the Board might call upon him to perform. But after his retirement as chief executive officer, he would not participate actively in the administration, or in the formulation of policy for the academic program.
>
> He hoped to continue and enlarge upon the studies and projects in which he had been engaged as a Fellow of the Center, but he would insist that he not be called upon to function in a fashion that would "lay the dead hand of the past upon the new Chairman." The Board reluctantly accepted this dispensation, but voted unanimously to reaffirm the title of Life Fellow conferred upon Mr. Hutchins at the time of the reorganization of the Center.[19]

I reported to the board that Gary Cadenhead was resigning as secretary-treasurer effective June 30 to accept an appointment at UCLA, and that I did not recommend his being replaced since between them Norton Ginsburg and Peter Tagger could take over his functions. This, I informed the directors, would leave the way open for a reorganization of the administration when the new chairman took office, and I noted that I assumed this would include the abolition of the presidency. I had considered Moos, whom I knew casually, to be the most likely of the three candidates under consideration, and I shared Hutchins's relief that the search for his successor was finally over.

But the relief was short-lived. There had been an intimation of trouble ahead when, before the executive session, Cadenhead handed me a note informing me that Moos wanted him to continue as secretary-treasurer. It seemed odd to me that the new chairman was attempting to take such action before he had even been elected himself, and I told Cadenhead that I would let his resignation stand, though Moos would, of course, be free to reappoint him once he assumed office. But this, it turned out, was only one of the new conditions being presented on Moos's behalf by Harvey Wheeler, who was with him in Minneapolis. When Wheeler arrived in Washington, he informed Hutchins that Moos could not accept the appointment unless there was a guarantee of tenure, the outright purchase of a residence in Santa Barbara, and the designation of Wheeler as head of the Center's academic program.

Wheeler's intervention was not surprising. He and Moos had been young instructors together at Johns Hopkins at the beginning of their careers and had remained in touch, and it was Wheeler who had first advocated his selection to Hutchins. What was surprising was that so experienced an administrator as Moos would have authorized Wheeler to make ex post facto demands that would plainly be unacceptable to the board. When Frank Kelly sought approval for a press release announcing Moos's appointment, Hutchins frowned and told him, "Don't send this out to anybody until I have told you to do so. This thing may still fall through." Rapoport was enlisted by Parten to deal with the impasse:

> Rapoport met with Moos and Wheeler at the Jefferson Hotel. He told Moos that if Moos insisted on a provision for a "whole house" in Santa Barbara instead of the financial assistance Parten had offered — and if Moos was determined to make Wheeler the officer in charge of the academic program — Moos's election was in jeopardy. Moos finally accepted the financial arrangements Rapoport suggested, and he withdrew his requirement for Wheeler's designation as the academic officer.[20]

The next morning Moos and Rapoport met with Hutchins for breakfast. "He's calmed down." Rapoport reported. "He just took my advice and was very amiable and compliant. There was no real discussion. It was just like everything was falling into place."[21]

That afternoon Hutchins introduced Moos to the throng that had gathered for the closing session of the convocation. The retiring president of the University of Minnesota, he said, was uniquely qualified to become his successor as chairman of the Center. Moos responded that he was proud to have been chosen and pledged that the two would work together to make the Center's future brighter than ever.

But their desultory talk at breakfast that morning was to be the last substantive discussion of the Center's affairs Hutchins would ever have with Moos. In November he wrote Wilder to tell him that after their return from Washington, Vesta had been hospitalized for heart failure and anemia. She had recovered and was up and around, but Hutchins felt that "it all has to be blamed on 'Pacem in Terris' ":

> One of the troubles was all the hullabaloo about my successor, marked by several political maneuvers of the worst academic kind. They all failed, and everything was as well settled as could

be expected under the circumstances. I don't know whether the new chairman will be much good. I think the chances are he will. But I am not much concerned. The great thing is to have it settled. He will be moving in 1 July. We are trying to decide whether to stay or leave. I suppose we'll stay, simply to avoid the trouble of moving.[22]

CHAPTER FORTY-SEVEN

An Unsuccessful
Succession

When Malcolm Moos was elected chairman of the Center, only two of the original members were still on its board of directors: J. R. Parten and Eleanor B. Stevenson.[1] Parten, the tall Texas oil millionaire, was a commanding figure in his own right, and his seniority gave added weight to his recommendation that Moos was the best qualified of the three finalists under consideration to succeed Hutchins. The other three members of the search committee were content to follow his lead.

Moos was a slender, personable man who had all the proper credentials. During the years when he taught political science at Johns Hopkins, he was also an editorial writer for the *Baltimore Sun* and a consultant to CBS. From 1957 to 1961 he served in the White House as a speech writer for President Eisenhower, moving on at the end of the term to become an adviser to the Rockefeller brothers. From 1964 until 1967, when he was chosen as president of the University of Minnesota, he held executive positions at the Ford Foundation.

Parten was aware that Moos was in serious trouble with both the regents and the faculty at Minnesota. When his resignation was announced, the *Minneapolis Tribune* reported that eleven of the twelve regents had asked him to leave "because of continuing defections of high-ranking faculty and university administration officials, and growing complaints that Moos was allowing problems to fester."[2]

When Hutchins was informed of these charges, he told Parten that in his experience they could be read either way — to indicate that a university president was at fault or that he was doing a good job. Parten accepted Hutchins's sardonic reaction as an endorsement of the choice, a belief that would influence his actions in the controversies that lay ahead. Frank Kelly wrote in an authorized account of Parten's role:

> The difficulties that would face any successor to Hutchins had been anticipated by Parten. That was why Parten had refused for years to engage in a vigorous search for a successor. Through those years, in letters and telephone calls, Hutchins had pleaded for relief from his burdens. . . . When Moos had been tapped as the man for the job, Parten had telephoned Hutchins to get his approval. "That's fine," Hutchins said, "I'm satisfied."
>   . . . Moos was the man Hutchins had approved, and the fellows would have to accept that. The directors had ratified the choice. . . . As long as Hutchins stood behind Moos — and Hutchins had always fulfilled his commitments during the years Parten had known him — Moos could ride through any turbulence he would encounter.[3]

Parten had been irritated by Harvey Wheeler's attempt to revise the conditions under which Moos had agreed to accept the Center appointment, but Kelly reported that he "felt confident that Moos could control Wheeler."[4] There is no evidence that Moos ever attempted to do so. And Wheeler immediately undertook to complete the housecleaning he had tried to initiate in the course of the refounding.

Parten thought Moos would be well served if Hutchins removed himself from the Center for a protracted period after the new chairman took over, and Hutchins agreed. A month after the Washington board meeting, he wrote Parten to accept his offer to provide the funding to cover a year's leave of absence with pay:

> Perhaps it would be best for the Center if I were officially on vacation during Moos's first year. He will certainly want to propose some changes. It might be painful for him to have the feeling that I was looking over his shoulder. . . . During the year I would be on call from Moos and would try to get ahead with the writing on education and the Fourteenth Amendment I mentioned.[5]

Hutchins assumed his leave would begin seven months hence, on July 1, 1974, when Moos was scheduled to take office. He also assumed, as did I, that the incoming chairman would use the interregnum to consult with Hutchins and the other Center principals in order to familiarize himself with the prospects and problems he would face. As it turned out, he consulted only the impetuous Wheeler, with the result that on November 23 I received a handwritten letter in which Moos cited an agreement with Hutchins that "no long range commitments concerning either staff or programs would be made pending my arrival without my approval."

> The resources of the Center, contrary to my original perception of being adequate to fund us for the next three years, are at the moment hardly likely to carry us beyond the next two years. The compelling need, therefore, is a careful, selective retrenchment and reallocation of programs as we catch our breath and move ahead with new intellectual directions and a muscular, long-range funding program.
>
> This leads me to say that I do not want any commitment to a fourth "Pacem in Terris" program or supporting consultants made at this time. It is my intention to present my own plans to the full Board meeting in January.[6]

I replied that Hutchins and I were in complete agreement in regard to long-range commitments and the need for retrenchment:

> However, Bob points out that in the case of the Washington convocation now scheduled for the fall of 1974 there is no long-range commitment, since the obligation to continue Sander Vanocur as a consultant is specifically limited to the calendar year 1974; the proposal for continuing the successful convocation series was presented to the Board of Directors and approved prior to Bob's conversation with you at the Hay-Adams; and that no allocation or diversion of funds otherwise available to the Center is contemplated.[7]

Hutchins followed up with a brief note in which he diplomatically noted that "you may not have had a chance to look at the minutes of the board meeting before you and I met in Washington. Plans were outlined, commitments were authorized, and a large pledge was made for a convocation in Washington next year. I want to make sure you know how the record stands."[8]

I wrote a lengthy memorandum addressed to Hutchins and Moos, which reviewed the history of the communications program and concluded:

> The issue, it seems to me, is not the isolated question of whether or not we should have another convocation on the scale and in the style of "PIT III." I would be happy to be relieved of the responsibility for organizing such an extravaganza. The larger questions deal with the communications program as a whole, and its relationship with the academic activities of the Center.[9]

I received no reply, nor was I ever to receive a response to any of the communications I addressed to Moos during his tenure. Meanwhile, Wheeler was spreading consternation in Moos's name. When Norton Ginsburg wrote to offer his pro forma resignation as dean and to request an opportunity to discuss his future at the Center, Moos, at Wheeler's urging, construed this as also constituting his resignation as a senior fellow, and he bade him a cordial farewell. "Ginsburg was startled by the speed with which Moos had replied," Kelly wrote, "and dismayed by Moos' statement that he would rely on Harvey Wheeler to aid him in 'projecting new directions.' " Kelly found himself next on the list:

> . . . Wheeler had begun to speak as though he had administrative authority. He told me that Moos wanted all the officers to submit their resignations as soon as possible, as "a necessary formality." It seemed to me that this request should have come directly from Moos.
>
> In a telephone conversation, Parten assured me that Wheeler had not been authorized to make such a statement. "Don't resign," Parten said. He told me he knew Moos wanted me to stay on. . . . Ashmore and [Blair] Clark also urged me to ignore what Wheeler had said. . . . Parten chided Moos for permitting Wheeler to claim such authority, and Moos telephoned me and told me he was not under Wheeler's domination and he hadn't intended to have Wheeler bring up the question of resignations.[10]

In late January my efforts to arrange a conference with Moos finally yielded an invitation to spend a weekend with him in the presidential mansion at the University of Minnesota. When I got to the airport in Santa Barbara I discovered that Wheeler was to accompany me. He was at Moos's elbow throughout the day and a half I spent in Minneapolis, and he stayed behind when I departed. Wheeler aptly described the session to Kelly as "a rather intensive week-end encounter session."[11]

Hutchins had effectively spiked the move to cancel the convocation project and fire Vanocur, but the continuation of the communications program was now treated as part of a package deal. I would be allowed to continue to run it if I agreed to stand aside while Moos put Wheeler in charge of the academic program and purged all of the senior fellows except John Wilkinson and the new arrival Alex Comfort, whose Center compensation, under an arrangement initiated by Wheeler, was covered by the assigned royalties from his sensational *Joy of Sex*.

I rejected the proposal as unconscionable and pointed out that it was also impractical. Moos was adopting Wheeler's recommendation to fire senior fellows before he himself consulted any of them, and under the board policy adopted in the course of the refounding there was some question as to whether he would have the authority to do so even *after* he took office. The fact that Wheeler had enlisted him in this premature coup attempt was certain to bring a protest, not only from the fellows but from board members as well.

I sent Moos a letter summarizing our discussions in Minneapolis and appended the minutes and other pertinent documents that recorded Wheeler's previous effort to purge the fellowship, along with the board's reaction to it. I concluded,

> My status as president is, of course, no longer at issue, since I do not expect to continue in the office as presently constituted. However, if I am to continue to administer and further develop the Communications/Membership program I would want to be assured that the line of policy responsibility runs directly to the Chairman as at present.
>
> If there are any points at issue between us on the continuation of the Communications/Membership program over the next twelve months I am available for further discussion.[12]

There was no further discussion, and when the board convened in February for its postponed meeting, I told Hutchins I had no option but to submit my resignation and explain why.

The cavalier treatment of Ginsburg prompted six of the senior fellows to address a memorandum to Hutchins asking to be reassured that no changes in academic program and personnel would be made without their being consulted. I signed along with Ritchie-Calder, Cogley, Tugwell, Borgese, and Ginsburg. Wheeler and Wilkinson protested that the request might "unduly limit the freedom of the Chairman-Elect." Comfort, writing "as a new boy," said he was disconcerted to find the place being "run like a cross between a Committee to De-elect Someone and the court of Byzantium."[13]

Hutchins wrote to Wilder that "my successor is making noises about firing people here, etc. that upset all the occupants of this castle, who then come to weep on my frail and sagging shoulder. I go home every night soaking wet. I have vowed that I will not interfere. But it seems rude not to listen."[14]

Hutchins clung to his vow as best he could when the directors convened in Santa Barbara, but some of the board members were alarmed by Moos's unquestioning support of Wheeler's heavy-handed maneuvers and by his evident intention to put him in charge of the academic program. Even Parten, Moos's most stalwart supporter, warned him against allowing Wheeler to act on his behalf:

> Harvey Wheeler is a brilliant man without a doubt. He is a real scholar; however, he has shown monumental deficiency in administration and in working with people. Harvey has a reputation at the Center as a pusher for power which is a fact that should concern you.[15]

The effort to force Ginsburg's resignation had outraged some of the Chicago-based directors, particularly Weissbourd, his close personal friend. Others were disturbed by the move to cancel the convocation. An effort was being made to avoid a showdown, and Hutchins had asked me to withhold my resignation until he had a chance to talk to key members. In a subsequent memorandum to Parten, I described the result:

> On the eve of the Board meeting I was informed by Hutchins and James Douglas that an acceptable compromise on the Ginsburg matter had been worked out, that Moos had assured them that Wheeler would be given no responsibility for administering the academic program, and that Moos had agreed to recommend to the Board my election as Executive Vice-President to take effect upon his becoming President and chief executive officer. You then asked me privately if I was willing to accept the executive vice-presidency, and I replied that I would serve in any capacity that you, as incoming Chairman of the Board, believed would serve the best interests of the Center.[16]

Under questioning, Moos assured the board that "he did not intend to have Wheeler acting as an administrator; he would run the academic program himself and he did not wish to have a 'dean.' "[17] My appointment was seen by the dissident directors as a guarantee that Moos would live up to that commitment, and he was pressed by Blair Clark to specify that I would function as *the* chief administrative officer.

Hutchins wrote Wilder in March to tell him that Moos's arrival had been moved up to June 1, and that shortly thereafter he would attend his last meeting as chairman of the board of editors of *Britannica*. His health was good, he said, and he and Vesta were making plans for extended travel:

> My principal reason for wanting to get away is that I don't care much for my successor — nobody ever does, I suppose. But this one seems to have done an unusual job of getting off on the wrong foot, alienating the Senior Fellows, the Board, and the officers. We have been through a very rough board meeting in which one member after another told him he had made a series of unforgivable mistakes. He sure must want the job. Anybody who didn't want it to the point of infatuation would have resigned on the spot.
>
> So far he has not moved to correct any of the mistakes, as he promised to do. Hence everything is in a state of suspended animation — except the gossip. That is very lively indeed.[18]

A board meeting in St. Paul in May accentuated the divisions. There was a parliamentary skirmish over the election of the three new directors chosen by Moos and presented by Parten,[19] and they were finally named only by a split vote — the first time any directors had ever challenged the recommendations of the nominating-committee chairman, a fact that visibly rankled Parten.

At the February meeting Moos had presented a vaguely worded proposal for converting the Center into a "communiversity," which he described as "something like a Rockefeller University for the humanities."[20] Now the board had before it a statement by Blair Clark that pointedly challenged any such departure from the Center's original concept:

> The Center propagates the knowledge and ideas of its Fellows, and of the wide range of thinkers it brings to Santa Barbara, through public meetings and convocations which it organizes around the country and, occasionally, abroad. . . .
>
> The Board believes it has worked remarkably well for fifteen years in this fashion and that the forms that have evolved have proven their value. Therefore any substantial changes in the aims and methods described here will be subject to full consideration

by the Board, upon recommendation of such committees as it may establish to consider, in full consultation with the officers and Fellows, new forms of organization and activity for the Center.[21]

Clark's statement, which was obviously intended, as he said privately, to put Moos "on a short leash," was adopted without dissent and included in the minutes. Moos said he did not interpret it as conflicting with his own statement of the Center's goals, but the polarization of the board was now beyond face-saving.

Parten's pride was wounded, and he convinced himself that Moos was faced with a cabal that had been plotting his overthrow ever since he was nominated. He identified his primary adversaries as Blair Clark, Frances McAllister, and me, rationalizing my opposition to Wheeler's attempted takeover as an outgrowth of frustrated ambition to succeed Hutchins. He dug in to protect Moos and enlisted Kelly and Cadenhead in his cause.

My relationship with Wheeler had always been civil. It could hardly have been otherwise, since he did not respond to those who disagreed with his views, but simply ignored them. Even when they got in his way, as in my case, such dissenters were never addressed directly as he went about trying to remove them by whatever means came to hand. Saturnine and humorless, he seemed to have an infinite capacity for unreality. Describing his wartime experience as an enlisted man in a military government detachment in Europe, he said that he had made no effort to avoid service and had indeed thought the cause was just, but he cited as his own principal accomplishment his successful effort to "goldbrick it out as painlessly as possible":

> . . . I tried to isolate myself from the Army. My name is John Harvey Wheeler, but I'd always been known as Harvey. When I went into the Army they asked me what my first name was, my middle initial, and so on, so I said John, and I always insisted on being known as John, instead of the real me who was Harvey. Nobody in the Army ever called me by my real name; the real me was never in the war, in a way.[22]

The same sort of impervious disregard characterized his view of Center activities that did not accord with his apocalyptic utopianism. The scientific revolution, he believed, had produced a new class "where the relationship between the man of ideas and the man of practical knowledge is changed. In the past the practitioner was on top and the theoretician was subservient."[23] He acted on the assumption that these roles not only should be, but had been, reversed.

He never accepted the fact that most of the Center's income had been generated by the communications program, either through direct return from membership dues or through major gifts from those — as in the notable case of Chester Carlson — who were attracted by the convocations and other public affairs and wanted to see them continued. He therefore rejected the argument that eliminating these activities could only increase the center's deficit and reduce its ability to attract new funding. Nor did he acknowledge the directors' hostility to the proposal that the Center be converted into a degree-granting "communiversity" in which he himself would play a primary role.

Despite his two stormy sessions with the board, Moos apparently accepted all of Wheeler's basic premises. When he took office in June, he ignored his previous assurance to the directors that he would not give his old friend a key role in the academic administration, increased his salary to five thousand dollars more than was being paid to any other fellow, and charged him with designing the new program and recruiting participants:

> I want to move with all deliberate speed to prepare an educational program at the Center to be developed along the lines of the Rockefeller-type university for the social sciences and humanities that is described in my address to the Board.
>
> I am asking you to accept appointment as Coordinator of this program. I hope you will take it on, for I am convinced that your guidance in seeing it through its initial stages to maturity is essential to its success.[24]

Neither the grand design nor the "muscular campaign" to provide the greatly increased funding that such an enterprise would require ever materialized, and the internecine war at the Center continued, with Moos away from Santa Barbara much of the time. With the exception of Parten, Moos had by this time alienated all of the major contributors among the directors.

Drastic financial measures were obviously required, but even if the board approved the Wheelerian scheme to remove six of the senior fellows, there would be no immediate relief, for all would be due substantial severance payments under the guarantee that applied to all staff providing for a month's pay for each year of service. This led to an effort, conceived by Cadenhead and tentatively supported by Parten, to rescind the severance policy.

The board refused to go along, and the next move was an effort to salvage at least the considerable sum due me by having me fired for my alleged disloyalty to Moos. This grew out of negotiations for a possible merger with the Fund for Peace, proposed more than two years before by its founder, the aged multimillionaire Randolph Compton. A committee of the Center board had found that such a merger would be impractical, but Compton came back with an offer to put money into a joint communications program that would serve both organizations.

Since this seemed to offer the possibility of both substantially reducing the Center's deficit and protecting the program against the threat from inside to dismantle it, it seemed to me worth pursuing, and I did so with Moos's full knowledge and, I assumed, approval. But it was soon evident that my involvement precluded any serious consideration of the proposal.

In my last meeting with Compton I told him he would have to pursue the matter directly with Moos. Through Stewart Mott, a director of both the Center and the Fund for Peace, Compton was aware that Moos was in trouble with his board, and he indicated that he saw no point in talking with him. I told him he had no other option, and I declined any further discussion.

A garbled version of this exchange, which reversed the position I had taken and had me urging Compton *not* to meet with Moos, was relayed to the Center by an officer of the Fund for Peace. This was passed on to Moos in Palm Beach, where he was visiting Arthur Burck, one of the new board members he had recommended. Burck proposed an investigation of this presumptive "treason," to be conducted by a University of California law professor, and Parten agreed to retain him on behalf of the board.

Hutchins had remained aloof from the internecine warfare as best he could. Officially on leave, he had hoped to spend most of his time away from Santa Barbara, but consultations with heart specialists were forcing the conclusion that Vesta would have to undergo surgery. Except for a cruise to Mexico, they had to forgo extensive travel. He no longer went to the new, isolated office that had been established for him in the old guest cottage on the Center grounds. In December he wrote Wilder,

I am very depressed about the Center. I do not interfere and speak only when I am spoken to. But the alienation of staff and supporters proceeds apace. Unfortunately the supporters are not replaced. I'm afraid the place will soon run out of money.
Well, it was a great idea.[25]

Arthur Burck's proposal to investigate my presumed treason forced Hutchins's hand. It was, he wrote Parten, an obvious effort to "get Ashmore," and he could have no part in such a project:

Ashmore has been a board member for twenty years. He has been an officer as well since 1964. . . . Mr. Burck is off on a wild goose chase.

I have been hoping we could hold the board together so that they could come to know Mac Moos and he might have time to develop his program and make it clear to them. Mr. Burck's activities will not advance the realization of this hope. On the contrary it will split the board still further.[26]

Parten replied that he would accept Hutchins's advice and call off the outside investigation, but he said he could not accept his reasoning and would present his own findings to the board. But Hutchins's assessment of the split in the board was borne out at the February meeting, when Parten's efforts on Moos's behalf failed every critical test.

The first came when Frances McAllister was not included among those board members recommended for reelection, only to be reinstated by a vote of 12–10, with Hutchins supporting her. When Parten brought his charges against me before the board, a substantial majority voted to drop the matter and to expunge the allegations from the record. And the effort to amend the severance-pay policy failed, leaving the Center with an obligation far in excess of its liquid assets.

It was now clear that the deteriorating financial situation was going to force a drastic reorganization. Bernard Weissbourd proposed transferring the dialogue to Chicago, where part-time personnel would be available at the universities in the area, and promised to provide quarters and raise funds to support the operation. Without the "Chicago plan," Hutchins conceded, "the institution here is not going to survive. . . ." But he also noted that the proposal "deeply offended the directors who want to keep Moos, who number five or six out of twenty-six. But one of them is very rich. We have had two or three public fights and are certain to have at least one more."[27] And Hutchins's Puritan conscience no longer permitted him to remove himself from the fray. "The Center is collapsing at a fairly rapid rate," he wrote to Wilder at the end of March,

And whenever I get paranoid and blame others, I have to remind myself that everybody connected with the place, trustees, staff, janitors, etc., was appointed by me — or at least none of them could have been appointed without my approval. This goes for my successor. I didn't select him, but the Board would not have selected him if I had objected. I know I should pay no attention, but I have been here twenty-one years, and have friends here who are suffering from my carelessness.[28]

The impasse was resolved by the inescapable fact that the Chicago proposal was the only prospect in sight for additional funding when the board convened in May to consider the fate of the bankrupt institution. Parten negotiated a severance arrangement for Moos that guaranteed him seventy-five thousand dollars over three years, and the wispy Minnesotan, who had never been more than a sort of disembodied presence at the Center, departed with a few graceful farewell remarks. The directors voted to initiate the Chicago plan while maintaining a severely pared-down operation at Santa Barbara, where the Center property would be mortgaged to meet the severance obligations to twenty-five employees.

The board approved the termination of all the officers and fellows except Hutchins and Comfort, who was exempted because he had a special contractual arrangement involving the transfer of royalty payments from *The Joy of Sex* and was threatening a lawsuit. A reluctant Hutchins responded to the board's insistence that he resume the presidency, and Ralph Tyler was elected vice president to initiate the Chicago program.

The skeletal holding operation that remained on Eucalyptus Hill bore little resemblance to the community of scholars Hutchins had originally conceived, but he put the best face he could on it. "I believe we can make this work," he told a *Los Angeles Times* reporter. "We may have found a way to operate on a high intellectual level at minimal cost. If that can be done, it's probably more needed now than it ever has been in the past."[29]

CHAPTER FORTY-EIGHT

"Huddled in Dirt
the Reasoning Engine
Lies . . ."

I suspect you are indulging in a great deal of self-reproach," Thornton Wilder wrote to Hutchins when he learned of the Moos debacle. "That is inevitable from the ethos from which we both derive — that ethos was emotional not philosophical. When our fathers, yours and mine, were so religio-emotional there was no room left to think — in fact they thought themselves intellectual giants and they shrank from thinking, and their religion was Jewish. . . ."

> You did splendidly when you were creating — then circumstances — this age we live in — exceeded your control. You had long been the universal donor. (I was one of your signal beneficiaries.) You gathered many under your umbrella. You have the donor complex and the father complex. Then the weather got gusty and the umbrella broke.[1]

"I probably should have walked away from the Center when I 'retired,' " Hutchins replied. "I stayed on the board because I was told that if I didn't the board would fall apart." But the board fell apart anyway, and when the Chicago plan was adopted, he was dragooned back into the presidency:

> I protested but did not think I could decline. I was probably wrong again. I am now nothing but an administrator with a much reduced

staff and all the responsibility of raising money and planning and operating the academic program. Fortunately I feel pretty well, and Vesta is in fair shape. Tugwell, Ashmore and Elisabeth Borgese will be reappointed on a part-time basis. The editors of the publications will stay in Santa Barbara. So I have somebody to talk to. . . .[2]

To Wilder this was simply another manifestation of Hutchins's Puritan conscience: "As I see it you returned to the presidency for two reasons — to save what you could for those whom you had welcomed under your umbrella, and to safeguard what you could of the mission of the institute."[3] He was no doubt right on both counts, though there was nothing much Hutchins could provide in any material way for the surviving senior fellows.

Elisabeth Borgese, Tugwell, and I received no compensation other than the use of our old offices and limited secretarial services. William Gorman, Joseph J. Schwab, and Wendell Mordy, who had been in residence as associates, elected to stay on the same basis. Five other local associates indicated that they would be available for dialogue sessions: Hutchins's old friend the editor and author Clifton Fadiman; Bernard Haber, the retired director of research and engineering at North American Rockwell; and three new recruits from the faculty of the University of California at Santa Barbara: Otis Graham, a historian; Donald Cressey, a sociologist, and Walter Capps, the director of its Institute for Religious Studies.

We were all listed without distinction among the forty associates and consultants whose names were on the masthead of *Center Magazine*. The "senior fellow" designation had disappeared, and the office of secretary-treasurer was filled as an additional duty by Peter Tagger, the director of the membership/publications program. Aside from the greatly reduced support staff, the only other paid employees were the editors of *Center Magazine* and *Center Report,* Donald McDonald and Mary Harvey.

In Chicago, Norton Ginsburg, who had resumed his faculty post at the University, set up a conference room and supporting facilities in Bernard Weissbourd's downtown Illinois Center building. Ralph Tyler, commuting from his home near San Francisco, rounded up a steering committee made up of scholars from the universities in the Chicago area and initiated a series of dialogue sessions.

"The program of expansion and development adopted by the Board of Directors on May 10th is proceeding apace," Hutchins wrote in the July–August 1975 issue of *Center Magazine.* "In recent weeks I have visited with directors and friends of the Center in New York, Chicago and Los Angeles. Their expressions of interest in and support of the Center's program have been mostly encouraging. It seems to me that the Center's most important work may lie ahead."[4]

Hutchins had simply taken up where he left off when he stepped aside to make way for Malcolm Moos. The Center, he noted, had maintained an informal association with the Fund for Peace and would join with that institution in sponsoring a convocation in Washington in the fall. "The convocation — comparable in scale to 'Pacem in Terris III' in 1973 — would deal with American responsibility in world affairs after Watergate, after Nixon, and after Vietnam."[5]

Hutchins was following his own first rule of public relations: having been handed a lemon, he professed to be making lemonade. But if there was a touch of bravado in his pronouncements, he matched his words with action. Under his leadership the volunteer participants in the dialogue began producing papers and transcripts that provided a more consistent flow of high-quality material for the Center's publications than they had enjoyed for more than two years. The membership, still numbering about sixty thousand, continued to provide an income that was sufficient to cover the pared-down budget.

"I must say I find the administrative grind a little wearing after fifty years of it," Hutchins wrote to Wilder. "The Center is a great idea. Running it is a pain." But in fact the challenge of salvaging his brainchild had reinvigorated him. He went on to discount his own complaint about the burdens of office:

> Perhaps my trouble is just that I have a bad case of poison oak, acquired from seven goats we have on the place. They eat poison oak like candy and then come around to be petted. I have to get a shot of cortisone after each meeting.
>
> Also one of our outside cats gave birth to four kittens and then abandoned them. I am keeping them alive by artificial respiration. . . .
>
> Never mind. Vesta is doing well. You have written a Great Book. You are engaged on another. Nixon is falling. Billy Phelps made me hate Browning, but I must say, "All's right with the world."[6]

Fred Neal and I were called back into service to put together the program for the convocation, scheduled for December 2–4, 1975. We subtitled it "American Foreign Policy at Home and Abroad in the Bicentennial Year" and organized the sessions around three overlapping themes: American-Soviet détente and national security; American foreign policy and the Third World; and foreign policy and the American democratic system.

The adverse publicity had not reduced the Center's drawing power; with the assistance of Nicholas Nyary and his associates at the Fund for Peace, we managed to round up an all-star cast, and an audience of more than two thousand turned out to hear the speakers and panelists. "I greet you with enthusiasm," Hutchins said in his opening remarks, "because this must be the largest group of nonlobbying, nonpartisan citizens Washington has seen in a long time."[7]

"Pacem in Terris IV" enjoyed the usual success at the box office and in the press, and Hutchins could report a year of substantial progress when the board convened in April 1976: "The Center has maintained its program in Santa Barbara, started a new one in Chicago, covered its severance obligations, reduced its expenditures by approximately two-thirds and begun to rebuild the board of directors."[8]

Although most of the Moos partisans had departed, J. R. Parten had initially stayed on as chairman of the board to maintain a show of unity. But his suspicions of those who had opposed him seemed near-paranoid, and they now extended to his old friend Hutchins. Although he had challenged the long-standing severance policy, which he professed to believe was an invention of mine, he complained that Hutchins was unduly delaying the creation of a trust secured by the Center property, which would guarantee payment to those who had been terminated. In September he charged that the plan conceived by Hutchins and the executive committee to mortgage the property constituted a breach of trust, and he submitted his resignation.

"You appear to believe that I want to mortgage the property in order to pay the operating expenses of the Center," Hutchins replied. "Nothing could be further from the truth. We don't *need* mortgage money to pay current expenses. We are in the black." He went on to assure Parten that the severance claims were being fully protected while the executive committee worked out the most economical way of establishing the trust. "You served so long and with such distinction that I hate to have you resign on the basis of actions that I think you have misinterpreted," he wrote. Parten replied, "Frankly, I can see no misunderstanding," and let the resignation stand.[9] Although there was another exchange of letters asserting their mutual esteem, the two were never to meet again.

Morris Levinson succeeded Parten as chairman, and seven new

members were named.[10] Hutchins presented the reconstituted board with an upbeat report when it gathered in April:

> Seniel Ostrow's gift of $100,000, which was matched by other contributions, enabled the Center to survive the year. Barney Weissbourd and Joe Antonow have accepted responsibility for the Chicago program up to $100,000 a year for two years. . . .
>
> The Santa Barbara program has been managed on the most parsimonious lines. Very important dialogue sessions and conferences have been held at minimal cost. The most that is paid for a paper is $250. Participants who do not write papers receive only their expenses. Few of them come from any distance. . . .
>
> We of course have to face the possibility that we cannot indefinitely beg, borrow, or steal our program and hope to maintain its quality. . . . Nevertheless, as the *Magazine* and the *Report* show, the Center has been able to carry out its mission of identifying and clarifying the basic issues and widening the circles of discussion about them. The constitutional questions raised by the Campaign Practices Act and the revision of the federal criminal code; the moral and legal problems inherent in the effort to provide decent housing for all our people and at the same time preserve the environment; the necessity of innovation in world organization to meet threats to survival; new issues concerning the freedom and responsibility of the press; the possibilities of liberal education in the United States; full employment; planning; equality — these are among the topics being debated in Santa Barbara.
>
> I think there will not be any argument about the desirability, even the necessity, of the work the Center is doing. That the Center has been able to withstand the trials of the last two years is a tribute to the powers of the ideas on which it is founded and a reflection of the dedication of the board.[11]

Hutchins had managed to create a limited but effective administration to carry out the policy decisions for which he was once again responsible. Otis Graham, the UCSB historian, became the part-time program director and maintained an office on Eucalyptus Hill. Peter Tagger turned out to be an energetic administrator of the Center's nonacademic activities.

There was one damaging holdover from the Moos regime to be disposed of — the lawsuit brought by Alex Comfort to recover the royalty payments for *The Joy of Sex,* which he had assigned to the Center. He based his claim on the contention that the Center had been abolished in the course of the reorganization that followed Moos's departure. But in order to make that claim, he had to expose the fact that he had sought the royalty arrangement in order to avoid paying the high taxes the British government would have exacted had he not been able to establish residence in the United States and channel payments through a tax-exempt institution. To support that assertion, he had to make the false claim that he had actually written the book in the United States while he was an associate of the Center.

The arrangement with Comfort had been worked out by Harvey Wheeler and presented to Hutchins as a means by which the Center might add a distinguished academician to the roster of senior fellows without cost. No one anticipated that his sex manual would earn much more than the twenty-eight-thousand-dollar salary the Center guaranteed him. When Hutchins indicated his approval and turned the matter over to me, I instructed the Center's counsel, Stanley Hatch, to negotiate an agreement with Comfort if he could find a legal means of doing so. He worked out a letter of understanding based on the version of the arrangement provided him by Comfort and Wheeler.

The Joy of Sex had turned out to be a runaway best-seller, however, and Comfort brought forth a sequel that also did well, so the bone of contention involved a sum that might potentially run into hundreds of thousands of dollars. The lengthy pretrial depositions and the testimony called for in Los Angeles federal district court provided an occasion for Comfort and Wheeler, with supporting testimony by Parten, to reiterate the charges of a conspiracy to remove Moos, bolstering the claim that the Center no longer existed.

Judge David W. Williams was not impressed by Comfort's claims or by the Center's. He ordered the return of all royalty payments received after Comfort walked out, but he relieved the Center of severance liability and dismissed the claim for punitive damages. Then he condemned both parties: "The shabby pact was one in which Comfort untruthfully represented that he had written *Joy* in the United States and under the auspices of the Center while using its facilities; the Center winked at the fraud."[12] Neither side felt disposed to appeal.

Hutchins freely conceded the failure of the Center to achieve the goal he had set for it, and he assumed more than his share of the blame. But if he entertained any doubts about the soundness — or indeed the necessity — of the concept, he never admitted it, not even in his most intimate communications to his confidant Wilder.

Shortly after Hutchins resumed the presidency, Clifton Fadiman conducted an interview with him for publication in *Center Report*. Quoting Ralph Waldo Emerson's dictum that a man was what he thought about all day, Fadiman asked Hutchins if he "could detect what Henry James once called 'the figure in the carpet,' any single unifying driving force behind your varied accomplishments." Hutchins replied,

> I think such central intellectual drive as I have had originated in the reflections that were induced by my experiences as dean of a very good and very active law school. It was also at the Yale Law School that I first got an idea which could have been regarded as new and important only by a very ignorant young man. It was the idea that the ideal educational institution was an intellectual community, and the object of anybody who had any responsibility for or even any participation in the educational institution was to try and make it an intellectual community.[13]

By the time he became president of Chicago, that notion had "developed into what has amounted to a lifelong obsession." Fadiman pointed out that his concept had never enjoyed widespread support and that now it was being undermined by the presumed demand for educational specialization in a technological age. "And you are still working at the same problem of the construction of an intellectual community?" Hutchins responded,

> Yes, I am still working at the old stand and I think if we could do it it would be great. . . . I believe in the dissemination of good ideas, even if it gets a little boring from time to time, in the expectation that since man is a rational animal, but not forgetting that he is an animal, eventually the futility or falsity of his prejudices will become clear to him.[14]

He could have had no illusion, at seventy-seven, that he was likely to be around to see that expectation fulfilled. He regarded his mission as overseeing a holding operation that might keep the Center viable until some younger man of a similar persuasion could be found to take it over. Since none such was in sight, he explored the possibility of joint ventures that might hook the remains of the Center onto an institution with better financial prospects. The Potomac Institute, headed by one of the new trustees, Harold Fleming, cosponsored conferences on housing and planning, and to encourage the publishing venture with the Fund for Peace, which had been sabotaged under the Moos regime, *Center Report*

changed its title to *World Issues*. There were also extended discussions of
a possible merger with the Aspen Institute.

Nothing came of any of these moves, and in the absence of funds for
direct-mail promotion, normal attrition steadily reduced the membership
and the income it provided. Peter Tagger found himself scrambling to
meet the expenses of the Santa Barbara operation, and efforts to bring in
additional funding for the Chicago dialogue produced only minimal
results. Hutchins had always been the main attraction for the Center's
major donors, and there was no way to project that attraction into the
future.

Whether as a matter of conviction or of expediency, or both, Hutchins
never expressed, publicly or privately, any doubt that the Center would
somehow survive. But there was a valedictory and sometimes elegiac
note in his now-infrequent public addresses, in which he returned to the
themes that had occupied him throughout his career.

Reminding a Santa Barbara audience that when he had first appeared
before it seventeen years earlier his theme had been "Preconditions of
World Organization," he recounted the brief history of the Committee to
Frame a World Constitution and conceded that "it was a most unacceptable proposal and it was buried almost instantly by the cold war." His
and Justice Douglas's campaign for world law had enjoyed no greater
success. "We have to hang on to the United Nations because it's all we
have,"[15] he said, but it would continue to be an exercise in futility so
long as it remained a league of sovereign states. He asserted, as he always
had, that the survival of civilization would require a new world order, but
this was no call for action. He closed with a somber quotation from
Matthew Arnold's "Dover Beach":

> *And we are here as on a darkling plain,*
> *Swept with confused alarms of struggle and flight,*
> *Where ignorant armies clash by night.*

Education was another recurring theme. Back in 1972 the unprecedented attack on the public schools from both the left and the right had
prompted him to write a lengthy essay, "The Great Anti-School
Campaign," for *The Great Ideas Today*, the yearbook distributed by
Britannica. He wrote to Wilder:

> . . . I found myself blockaded by (1) the sense that I had said it
> all before, a presumption that you rightly condemn, and (2) the
> realization that I had thought very little about public schools and

the reason for having them; this in spite of the fact that Plato, Aristotle, Rousseau and J. S. Mill, all of whom I had looked at, contain rather extensive discussions of the subject. The combination of knowing too little and too much is highly obstructive.[16]

"I had begun to wonder whether any case could be made for them or for any period of compulsory attendance," he wrote Wilder when he had completed the article. "It was hard work because I had never thought about the subject before. I had taken compulsory public schools for granted."[17] After systematically examining the philosophical underpinning of mandatory schooling and the arguments currently being made against it, he concluded that the public system was indispensable in a self-governing society. But his article concluded,

> . . . I have proposed to solve the problems of public education by means of education. Give us educated citizens and the public school will become what it ought to be. This is probably true, but in the meantime the school is far from what it ought to be, and, to paraphrase Keynes, in the meantime we may all be dead. Immediate steps have got to be taken to make the schools more adequate to their task. These steps must be taken within the boundaries set by the Constitution and, unfortunately . . . we cannot always be sure what those boundaries are.[18]

Hutchins was never content to simply state a problem and raise an issue. In his last years he combined his continuing analysis of the opinions of the United States Supreme Court with his concern for evolving a constitutional theory to buttress the public-school system — an evident necessity, as he saw it, since the Constitution made no specific mention of education. He addressed the confusion resulting from this omission in papers prepared for the Center dialogue and sometimes published in *Center Magazine*. In these his concerns for education and for civil rights merged.

He cited "two fateful decisions" as demonstrating the manner in which the Supreme Court had begun to evade the clear mandate of its own unanimous *Brown* decision outlawing school segregation. In *Brown* the justices had declared public education "the very foundation of good citizenship . . . at the very apex of the function of a state" and had held that the opportunity to obtain it "where the state had undertaken to provide it must be made available to all on equal terms."

Yet when a federal judge attempted to end segregation by ordering the predominantly black Detroit school district to be consolidated with the surrounding white districts, a majority of the justices ruled against him. And in a Texas case the Court refused to provide relief for Hispanic parents who complained of the unequal schooling caused by wide disparities in per pupil expenditures between poor school districts and those with a higher property-tax base. The Court, while conceding that the result in both cases might be to perpetuate inequality of educational opportunity, held that under the federal system the states could not be required to eliminate such discrimination.

In rejecting the Court's line of reasoning, Hutchins attacked the fundamental issue raised by the "states' rights" argument, which had been used against the abolition of slavery and presumably had been invalidated by the civil-rights amendments that followed the Civil War. It was this "reserved powers" doctrine that had become the principal reliance of those who opposed affirmative federal action to eliminate discrimination against minorities:

> Unless we take the view that education is of no importance, a view repudiated by the Court, or unless we argue that money is of no importance to the quality of educational opportunity, a view contrary to common sense, we must concede that under the prevailing American scheme the children of poor districts are subject to the kind of invidious discrimination the equal protection clause of the Fourteenth Amendment was designed to prevent.
>
> To remit them to the state legislature for relief is not likely to console them. The lower federal courts in Texas waited two years to give the legislature a chance to act. That body did not care to avail itself of the opportunity. . . .
>
> The practical difficulties of devising an equitable scheme of school financing in Texas and of mapping a metropolitan area in and around Detroit are no doubt considerable. But the legislatures should not be permitted to evade their responsibilities on such grounds. To do so is to deny the constitutional rights of children because legislatures are timid, unimaginative, and indifferent to the formation, maintenance and improvement of the political community — and the Supreme Court is, too.[19]

Hutchins's prescience was demonstrated thirteen years later, when the Court, now dominated by the conservative majority provided by the appointments of President Ronald Reagan, went the last mile and held that children had no constitutional right to an education. In rejecting the plea of a poverty-level North Dakota family that a newly imposed school busing fee would deny their children access to a public school, the Court struck down the controlling doctrine of *Brown* in a 5–4 decision written by Justice Sandra Day O'Connor:

> Statutes having different effects on the wealthy and the poor are not on that account alone subject to strict equal protection scrutiny. Nor is education a "fundamental right" that triggers strict scrutiny when government interferes with an individual's access to it.[20]

Hutchins would continue to work on what amounted to his last testament as long as he could hold a pen and see the lined yellow sheets of the legal pad he always kept at hand. But he was visibly slowing down. During his first consignment to the hospital he had replied to a note of sympathy, "Do you remember what the Earl of Rochester said about the end of the Philosopher? 'Huddled in dirt the reasoning engine lies, who was so proud, so witty and so wise.' "[21] He often expressed to me his worry that he might not be aware of it if his mind began to fail under the inroads of age. That was never to happen, but it became evident that he was maintaining his upright bearing and steady gait only with great effort.

He was relieved of one enduring concern when he finally overcame his and his wife's profound distrust of the medical profession and won her agreement to let the surgeons at Stanford University Hospital repair her damaged heart valves. Her daughter, Barbara, recalled his pacing the corridors during their long vigil and his near-collapse when word came that the open-heart surgery had been a complete success.

Then came word that Thornton Wilder had succumbed to the illnesses he had played down in the letters he wrote to cheer Hutchins during his bouts with the surgeons. In January 1976 Hutchins made the long journey to New Haven to pay his last respects to his oldest and dearest friend. At the memorial service in Yale's Battell Chapel, he said:

> Thornton used to say that he and I were brought up in the "late foam-rubber period of American Protestantism." And the worst of that, he said, was that we didn't have the courage to think what he called "window-breaking thoughts." He quoted Karl Marx as saying, "Tell me in what neighborhood you live and I'll tell you what you think." Thornton thought we had lived too long in the wrong neighborhood. In fact, in his view, I had lived in two of the wrong neighborhoods: the neighborhood of late foam-rubber

Protestantism and, as a semiprofessional money raiser, in the neighborhood of the very rich. "The rich," he said, "need to be lapped in soothing words." What was required was window-breaking thoughts. The enemy was philistinism, parochialism, narrow specialization. The object of education — indeed of the whole of life — was the expansion of the imagination. This could lead to window-breaking thoughts. . . .

Thornton's ultimate word of condemnation was "cruel." Cruelty was a failure of the imagination. . . .

For sixty years he was my teacher. His pedagogical methods were irresistible. They were deep personal concern and laughter. . . . He was the best of teachers and the kindest of friends.[22]

Hutchins was also concerned in the last months of his life with a memorial for another old friend, William O. Douglas. When Douglas, crippled by a stroke and confined to a wheelchair, was forced to resign from the Supreme Court, Hutchins noted the effect his absence was having on the Court's consideration of civil liberties and civil rights. In proposing a "William O. Douglas Inquiry into the State of Individual Freedom," he wrote:

The positions he took on religion, speech, the press, assembly, searches and seizures, double jeopardy, self-incrimination, a fair trial and cruel and unusual punishment have for many years been central in the argument on these cases.

Although Douglas' voice is now missing, the argument has continued since his retirement. The results reached, the reasoning processes used, the opinions written suggest that his departure deprives the Court of an approach to protection of the individual that may weaken the Bill of Rights in important particulars. . . . If changes are impending it is essential that the American people be reminded of the importance of the initial amendments to the Constitution, of the contribution Justice Douglas made to advancing the proposition that liberty is indivisible, and of the great debt all of us owe him.[23]

The Douglas Inquiry was to be "a continuing program of inquiry and public education dealing with fundamental trends in contemporary society that affect the status of the individual citizen"[24] — in effect, a continuation of the appraisal of the rulings of the high court that Hutchins had undertaken. I was called back into service to organize a supporting organization and a Center convocation in Washington to launch the undertaking, but before plans could be completed Hutchins was struck down by his final illness.

In April, though he continued his daily attendance at the Center, he was plagued by a recurring low fever. When a sudden rise in temperature prompted Vesta Hutchins to take him to Cottage Hospital, an acute kidney infection was diagnosed and he was placed in intensive care. He remained there, comatose, for almost a month before his extraordinary life force finally ebbed. He died on May 14, 1977.

CHAPTER FORTY-NINE

Post Mortem

The day after Robert Hutchins's death, Mortimer Adler paid a flying visit to Santa Barbara[1] to inform his widow that a proper memorial service would be arranged at the University of Chicago three weeks hence. But there was also a need for some sort of funeral ceremony to assuage the grief of the little band of survivors at the Center, and it fell to me to arrange it.

Vesta Hutchins agreed that a religious service would be inappropriate, but in the end she decided on a brief benediction by our former associate Bishop Edward Crowther, who was still endowed with clerical authority although he had been relieved of his episcopal duties. Henri Temianka brought his string quartet from Los Angeles and brilliantly performed his old friend's favorite selections from Mozart. But there had to be more than this.

The usual procession of eulogists would have risked a lapse into the sentimentality Hutchins abhorred. I concluded that the best way to explicate the philosophy he lived by, and to insure the brevity and clarity he counted as paramount rhetorical virtues, was to read, without comment, a selection from his own works. He would have been amused, and I think pleased, to find himself delivering his own funeral oration by proxy to the mourners who gathered in the faded elegance of El Parthenon's interior courtyard.

A similar ambiguity was evident in Chicago when three distinguished colleagues delivered memorial addresses in the great Gothic chapel dedicated to the glory of God and the memory of John D. Rockefeller, which also happened to be the place where Hutchins had finally decided to end his fealty to the organized religion in which he had been reared.

His old friend James H. Douglas, the senior trustee of the University, employed extensive Hutchins quotations to demonstrate why he found him "the most exciting leader in education in our generation." Mortimer Adler described his educational role in evangelical terms:

> Resolutely concerned, as Bob Hutchins was, with bringing about a moral, intellectual, and spiritual revolution, he never tired of preaching the gospel of the moral and intellectual virtues, of teaching the doctrine which underlies that preachment, and of assiduously cultivating these virtues in his own life.[2]

Yet in all of this there was no mention of God. Only in the quotation chosen by Edward Levi for his closing remarks was there an intimation of a possible divine purpose in what Hutchins had been about all those years. Levi, his appointee as dean of Chicago's Law School and one of his successors as president, recalled a passage from the address Hutchins gave at his inauguration:

> In 1968 at this university, at an occasion of considerable sentiment to me and I believe to him, he said, "The line that keeps running through my head is 'Reclothe us in our rightful mind.' " He said, "I think it is not blasphemous to direct it now to the university. A child of the parsonage may perhaps be permitted to say that the university is the terrestrial instrument which the author of our being has placed at our disposal for the purpose of getting us clothed and, when necessary, reclothed in our rightful mind."[3]

Hutchins's religious faith, or lack of it, posed problems for all those who tried to appraise his life and works. In an obituary editorial the *Washington Post* portrayed him as "the Thomist who relished the contemplative beauty of reasoned thinking" but noted that he was at the same time "the American pragmatist who asked, How can we use that idea?"[4] Hutchins would never have classified himself as a Thomist; while he did indeed relish the reasoned thought of the sainted Aquinas, he parted company with him in his own effort to discern how natural law might work without God. Nor did he consider himself a pragmatist. "I don't know exactly what practical idealism is," he told Henry Luce, who professed to practice it, "but I don't think I am for it. Being a practical idealist is a little like being a round square; I should think you would have to be one or the other."[5] He pleaded guilty to idealism and often identified himself as utopian, but that didn't quite fit either — not in the sense that practical men use the term to describe those who have retreated from the real world.

I have described him as a worldly Puritan, which seems accurate enough as far as it goes. He was certainly conditioned by the Calvinist faith of his fathers, and all his life he followed the habits of industry and probity ingrained in him by that stern religion. Yet he enjoyed earthly pleasures and saw no need to apologize for his patrician tastes. He was the least judgmental of men, tolerating the sybarites among his companions so long as they stopped short of outright hedonism. He was not being entirely facetious when he responded to the charge of the cosmopolitan Thornton Wilder that his view of the world was limited by his upbringing:

> You have sometimes commented on my Oberlinesque ignorance of reality. I have always resented these remarks because I regard myself as the complete man of the world. (Am I not, after all, a member of the Yale Club?) I have always known, in a vague sort of way, that there was a lot of sin out there. I have even learned to tolerate it, and to practice some of it.[6]

Certainly he rejected quite early the idea of a God of vengeance, as, I think, his father managed to do without abandoning the tenets of the Presbyterian faith his son found unacceptable. In a less histrionic way he was, as Wilder described himself in a letter written a few days before his own death, "temperamentally undiscourageable." Wilder may have accepted a God of love, but he inveighed against the stark religion he believed had blighted their youth, and against the mores rooted in it. Hutchins, spared the trauma of his friend's repressed homosexuality,[7] did not share his passion and must have had reservations about the views Wilder expressed toward the end of his life. These were summed up by Gilbert Harrison in the biography that he aptly entitled *The Enthusiast:*

> People said, "God is dead." Well, "what a dreadful God it was." People viewed with alarm sexual promiscuity at sixteen. Well, "after some decades of adjustment (woeful adjustment), we shall be freed of this omnipresent prurience." People complained of labor unrest, of strikes. "The sacred character of property will be unmasked for what it is: atavistic domination by the strong and guileful." Nations threw their weight around, distrusted each

other, fought; it was only "the last spitting of parochial self-sufficiency as Other Worlds hove into view."[8]

Wilder's responses assumed that historical forces were at work and would bring, if not salvation in a Christian sense, deliverance from the tyranny imposed by parochial society upon incipient free spirits. Hutchins made no such assumption. He did not believe in predestination and found no secular equivalent for it. He did believe in original sin, which he construed as the animal element in human nature that made man morally fallible. But he could not be convinced that mere mortals could be born again by accepting Jesus Christ, converted into New Men by developing a Marxist society, or liberated by Freudian psychoanalysis or the consciousness-raising techniques that were proclaimed as substitutes for it.

His understanding of the human condition led him to conclude that if men and women were to break out of the limitations imposed by their animal nature, it would require the combined effort of individuals committed to the rule of reason. Properly educated, they would be able to apply the wisdom distilled from the experience of past generations to the rapidly changing environment in which they were fated to live. His Puritan conscience imposed upon him an obligation to do what he could to bring that about, and so he became the most celebrated, and contentious, educator of his generation.

Mortimer Adler was credited by Hutchins with launching him on the educational crusade that in one form or another was to occupy both men for the rest of their lives. In the beginning Adler, then in his Thomist phase, urged that God must be included in their grand design. He protested that Hutchins's use of metaphysics as a neutral, if primary, component of liberal education was not enough, and he urged him to include religion along with science, philosophy, and the humanities. Hutchins steadfastly refused, insisting instead on presenting his case in purely rational terms. Adler remained convinced that this was a tactical error. In his memorial address he said:

Reasoning was so suited to the natural bent of Bob Hutchins' mind that it was second nature to him. This led him into the mistake of thinking that the proposition — man is by nature rational — was a self-evident truth. He did not need to have that proved, for he was directly acquainted with the truth about himself.[9]

He may have made that mistake when as a youthful president with "the heart of a swashbuckler, the head of a scholar," he "hit the Chicago campus like a one-man renaissance."[10] But I never saw any indication that he continued to suffer from the illusion that reason alone could carry the day. By the time I had the opportunity to watch him in action, he had become a seasoned campaigner in the marketplace of ideas, and he was a skilled practitioner of the arts of persuasion.

Central to his thinking was the proposition that human beings were not likely to act rationally until and unless they had been educated, or had educated themselves, in a fashion that enhanced their intellectual powers and opened their minds to ideas that might run counter to their instincts or conflict with those they had accepted as articles of faith. His concern was with the institutional means by which this might be accomplished.

At Chicago he was soon reconciled to the fact that the most he was likely to achieve was a laboratory in which the classic concepts of liberal education could be tested and revised under modern conditions, and where the techniques of teaching the arts and sciences could be brought up to date. If his ideas proved out in practice, as he was confident they would, they might begin to spread throughout the educational system.

Hutchins insisted that the only functions appropriate to the university were intellectual ones. The end of a liberal education was the good life, which was also the moral life, but it was not the mission of the educator to inculcate in his students the theological virtues of faith, hope, and charity. These, he said, were the products of divine grace, and though he might need them more than most, they were beyond the educator's reach.

He was never to yield on that central point, but he did come to recognize that time might have run out on the possibility of propagating the rule of reason over the span of generations his education scheme would require. The advent of the nuclear age, and his own not inconsiderable role in bringing it about, gave him a glimpse of the Apocalypse. At the end of World War II he told his students at Chicago, "Many people think, and I am one of them, that we cannot have world peace without world government. But if world government is to last, it must rest upon a world community." Such a community would arise if men were persuaded by reason to practice Aristotle's *Ethics*. "But," he added, "I doubt if any single man, to say nothing of the whole world, can practice Aristotle's *Ethics* without the support and inspiration of religious faith." Therefore, he concluded, it was not possible to speak of the brotherhood of man, as proponents of world government were wont to do, without conceding the fatherhood of God.[11]

But that was as far as he was willing to go. He continued to insist that religion, as doctrine, had no place in education or in public policy. He had occasion to make the point to Henry Luce, another child of the parsonage, whose Calvinist precepts seem to have survived both his worldly success and the best efforts of his wife, Clare Booth Luce, and her confessors to convert him to the Catholic faith.[12] It seemed to Hutchins that his classmate was attempting to transform religious dogma into a triumphalist foreign policy when he used his magazines to declare an "American Century." Asked by Luce to comment on a draft memorandum by one of his editors, Hutchins responded,

> [The editor's] proposition two, in which is implicit the proposition that God exists, cannot and should not be the basis of policy in a world in which policy must command the allegiance of millions who, even in our own country, have not been persuaded of the truth of the proposition. If we cannot persuade them, or ignore them, or suppress them, or kill them, we shall have to get along with them. . . .
>
> There is a public philosophy in the United States. If there were not, the country would not hold together. . . . It is that we do not have to agree with anybody about any propositions in speculative philosophy or religion; we are resolved to live at peace with one another and to settle our differences, when we cannot ignore them, by constitutional means.[13]

Appraising Hutchins in an essay entitled "The Educator as Moralist," Arthur Cohen said of his faith in dialogue based on metaphysics, "It is here, perhaps here alone, that Hutchins is a dogmatist."[14] He began with the conviction that dialogue was the necessary means of opening the minds and enhancing the intellectual powers of students. In the end he came to see it as indispensable to civilization itself:

> The civilization of the dialogue is the only civilization worth having and the only civilization in which the world can unite. It is, therefore, the only civilization we can hope for, because the world must unite or be blown to bits. The civilization of the dialogue requires communication. It requires a common language and a common stock of ideas. It assumes that every man has reason and every man can use it. It preserves to every man his independent judgment and since it does so, it deprives any man or group of men of the privilege of forcing their judgment upon any other. . . . The civilization of the dialogue is the negation of force.[15]

That faith was never to flag. His essay "The Intellectual Community," published in *Center Magazine* three months before his death, reiterated Hutchins's belief in the efficacy of the intellectual community even as he sat among the ruins of the one he had tried to create in Santa Barbara. He concluded:

> The Greek idea was that the city educated the man. And the greatest Greeks thought of themselves as participating in that educational function. . . . The interpenetration of the political community and the intellectual community gave the Greeks that mastery of the whole, that grasp of principles, those critical standards, that comprehension, in short, which has extended their influence through thousands of years. Unless our political and intellectual communities can achieve similar vitality we cannot hope to approach a similar educational ideal.[16]

In rebuttal, Clifton Fadiman argued that the rise of the "techno-state" was producing a society in which "the rowelling spur of principle is replaced by the soft blanket of gratification":

> If we are so conditioned as to believe that life will be complete if enough goods, sensate pleasure, and entertainment are supplied, and if a system is fashioned that actually supplies these goods, then for the first time in human history it may no longer be necessary to understand anything. . . .
>
> The stunning fact is that a perfect techno-state actually does away with the painful necessity of "distinguishing between good and bad acts," as it does away with the necessity for most of us "to understand anything."[17]

Hutchins replied with what must stand as his last testament:

> . . . It may be that what you seem to perceive as an irresistible force — "a new culture dominated by technology" — I see as one of the circumstances of contemporary life which must be and can be tamed in the service of man. . . .
>
> The techno-culture may threaten to sweep all before it. But if that is true, all the more reason to rally human resources, summon the best in man, and try to create those intellectual communities which will subordinate technology to higher purposes.[18]

*　　*　　*

Hutchins's passing rated obituary notices in most newspapers, which generally echoed the view expressed by the *Providence Journal:* "Few men have had so great an impact on American education and American thought. . . ."[19] But most of the commentators prudently declined to speculate on whether this had been a good or a bad thing, falling back on the assertion that in any case the kind of discussion he had provoked was always useful. This tack enabled his inveterate antagonist the *Chicago Tribune* to avoid speaking ill of the recently dead: "However one felt about his various causes, Dr. Hutchins was a man who by his very nature stimulated controversy and discussion. And this, after all, is an important function of the academic man."[20]

A gloomier and, in the short haul at least, more accurate verdict was handed down by the acerbic syndicated columnist Nicholas von Hoffman, who saw Hutchins as "the last of the great and greatly individualistic American university presidents."

> Hutchins' work at the University of Chicago has been totally dismantled. Its years of distinction are long behind it now so that it's another Ivy-League-type training academy for the managerial classes of business and government as well as being a normal school for university professors. . . .
>
> Where Hutchins spoke of the life of the mind, and the perfection thereof, today we have the vacuous sensitivities of self-realization psychologists. A remarkable man, Robert Hutchins, perhaps a great one. Unhappily, he won't be missed, he won't even be remembered.[21]

With the exception of the first, Lawrence Kimpton, none of Hutchins's successors at Chicago appears to have consciously set out to denigrate his educational theories, some of which continued to receive lip service throughout academia. But support for the institutional means through which he sought to put these theories into practice quickly eroded when he departed from the scene. This was also true at Yale, where he began his experimentation, and at the Ford Foundation, where two of the boldly experimental independent agencies he was instrumental in creating, the Fund for the Advancement of Education and the Fund for Adult Education, were brought back under the control of a cautiously conventional board of directors, and a third, the Fund for the Republic, was disinherited.

But the Hutchins reforms did not simply wither away through neglect. In some cases he inadvertently furthered movements that turned out to be a leading cause of the failure of his effort to reinstate a classical liberal-arts education. In 1974, reflecting on the social scientists he had worked with over the years, he wrote to Wilder,

> Sometime I am going to trace my association with these people over the last fifty years and make a record of all the money that has been spent on them and by them, all the trust I had in them, or some of them, and all the disappointments they inflicted on me. I started working on psychology and law when I was teaching at Yale. I received gobs of money for psychiatry at Chicago. (I didn't even have to ask for it.) Same with the social sciences. The foundations decided to make Chicago a Center. It's astonishing how little has come out of it all.[22]

What did come out of it was ironic proof of the absurdity of the widespread belief that a dictatorial Hutchins was attempting to impose his own ideological imprint on higher education. His undeviating commitment to academic freedom permitted the growth at Chicago of schools of economics and social science that are acknowledged to be the most conservative in any of the major universities. And as a result of his pioneering effort to broaden the Law School's curriculum by crossbreeding it with courses in economics, psychology, and sociology, Chicago became the incubator of the ultraconservative legal scholars who provided the philosophical gloss for Ronald Reagan's crusade to reverse the progressive direction long followed by the federal judiciary. Two of its products, Robert H. Bork and Douglas H. Ginsburg, were so far outside the mainstream they were opposed even by conservative Republicans when the President tried, and failed, to win Senate approval for their appointment to the Supreme Court.

The final monument to Hutchins's concept of the dialogue, the Center for the Study of Democratic Institutions, also proved unable to survive his passing. I was called back as acting president and agreed to serve while Ralph Tyler and I sought a successor. When I went to seek advice from Maurice Mitchell, who had been Hutchins's associate as head of Britannica Films and then later of the parent publishing company, I found that he was contemplating retirement from his current post as chancellor of the University of Denver and was willing to test out the possibility of finding renewed financial support for the Center.

Mitchell took office in March 1978, but after spending a little more than a year unsuccessfully importuning foundations and individuals, he informed the board that he saw no possibility of maintaining the Center as a freestanding institution. In June 1979 the directors voted to terminate the last of the employees, dissolve the corporate Fund for the Republic, and turn the remaining assets over to the University of California at Santa Barbara, which agreed to maintain a Robert M. Hutchins Center for the Study of Democratic Institutions.

The assets were not inconsiderable. Although most of the acreage had been sold off to meet severance payments, equity in the main building and the remaining five acres would yield more than a million dollars after all debts were satisfied. And *Center Magazine,* though its circulation had declined, was still a going concern. But UCSB's chancellor, Robert Huttenback, apparently lost interest in the institution once he had acquired it and moved it to the campus. The board he named to supervise the new Center seemed to regard it as a public-relations gimmick that suffered from its association with the Hutchins name. Under a series of inept directors who disapproved of Hutchins's concepts if they understood them at all, the Center degenerated into a conventional campus think tank, and at the end of 1987 a new chancellor terminated its financial support altogether. All that was left was a small line of type beneath the masthead of *New Perspectives Quarterly,* a Los Angeles intellectual journal published by onetime Center fellow Stanley Sheinbaum, which took over the magazine's mailing list.

Hutchins would not have been surprised by the manner in which Nicholas von Hoffman's predictions were borne out. He spoke often of the shrinking of the public attention span under the impact of the new communications technology, and of the resulting lack of historical perspective. This was true not only of the general public but of the academy as well — as was demonstrated in 1987 by the publication of Allan Bloom's *The Closing of the American Mind,* a work on education that astonished the book trade by becoming a best-seller.

As Hutchins had done, Professor Bloom deplored the materialism and narrow specialization that had blighted the higher learning in America, and he called for the reinstatement of classical liberal-arts education. And like Hutchins, he insisted that this would require an undergraduate curriculum based on the Great Books:

> . . . The crisis in liberal education is a reflection of a crisis at the peaks of learning, an incoherence and incompatibility among the first principles with which we interpret the world, an intellectual crisis of greatest magnitude, which constitutes a crisis for our civilization. . . .

Of course, the only serious solution is the one that is almost

universally rejected: the good old Great Books approach, in which
a liberal education means reading certain generally recognized
classic texts. . . .[23]

It was surprising that any serious scholar could mount such an attack,
and offer such a prescription, without even a passing reference to Robert
Hutchins. It was doubly so since Bloom had been an undergraduate at
Chicago when Hutchins was chancellor, as a graduate student had led a
Great Books seminar at the downtown campus in a program arranged by
Mortimer Adler, and at the time of writing the book occupied a chair at
the University's Committee on Social Thought, which had been founded
under Hutchins's aegis.

But the fact was that Bloom's assessment of the causes of the failure
of higher education had little in common with the case Hutchins had
made, and the ends he hoped to achieve as a result of the reinstatement
of the classics in the undergraduate curriculum were directly contrary to
the goals Hutchins had set for the university.

Bloom became a cult figure for neoconservative intellectuals because
of his polemical treatment of the civil- and human-rights movements of
the sixties; he condemned not only the radical activists who campaigned
on behalf of blacks and women but all those who supported the effort to
open higher education to the underprivileged. This, he said, was the end
result of the "cultural relativism" imported into the United States by
refugee German scholars conditioned by Nietzsche, whose critique of
bourgeois values had been appropriated by the political left and, on the
other flank, by Heidegger, the philosopher who supported Nazism.[24]

This was enough to insure the endorsement of the popular right-wing
commentators who gained new prominence during the Reagan years, thus
making the obscure professor an instant celebrity and an overnight
millionaire. He did not fare as well with his scholarly contemporaries,
many of whom savaged his philosophical thesis. He was a victim of
professional tunnel vision, wrote Russell Jacoby, and his obsession with
his fancied "German connection" led him to imagine that "history
proceeded uneventfully from Plato to Eisenhower, after which it went
into a tailspin. Americans, who once revered the Founding Fathers, were
bewitched by value relativism exported by the Krauts."[25]

By any reading, Bloom's work was unmistakably elitist. Equality was
"a democratic prejudice" in his definition. "The real community of
man," he wrote, "is the community of those who seek the truth, of the
potential knowers, that is, in principle, of all men to the extent that they
desire to know."[26] But such as these, he found, were few in number.

While Bloom professed to seek the restoration of classic scholarly and moral values in an age of relativism, Jacoby charged, "he really represents conservatism in an age of cynicism."[27]

Mortimer Adler arose to point out that Bloom's thesis was exactly the opposite of the one that motivated those who had been waging the good fight on behalf of the classics for half a century. He and Hutchins had always argued that any child of normal intelligence was capable of learning and, if properly taught, could be equipped to master the kind of education required of citizens charged with governing themselves. Schooling of this sort was not only the right of every child as a means of self-improvement, but a necessity in the democratic republic envisioned by the American Constitution.

Bloom did not deign to reply to a letter Adler wrote him challenging the omissions in *The Closing of the American Mind*, but in an interview in which he dismissed Adler's complaints as an angry personal attack, he had high praise for Hutchins. Asked why he had not mentioned him in the book, Bloom replied:

> There are not many changes I would make in the book in response to the criticisms I have received but that's one. The University of Chicago was my inspiration, and Hutchins was the University of Chicago. I've always regarded myself as a student of Hutchins, a figure I look up to with the greatest admiration. He was a gem, a genius of an educational administrator.[28]

At eighty-six, Adler was still in the lists, pushing his "Paideia Proposal," which called for the reorganization of the first twelve grades of school to provide a single track for all children. He had formed a national committee made up of prominent educators committed to the principle enunciated by Hutchins — "The best education for the best is the best education for all."[29] The system he envisioned would include the beginning of a liberal education in the last nine grades of elementary and secondary school. This would provide the means to improve the intellectual skills of those who would go on to college and to encourage the others to recognize that learning should be a lifelong process and was not limited to an institutional setting.

The future of the Paideia Proposal was problematic, but then so was that of the public-school system, recognized on all sides to be in grave disarray. Adler, fostering demonstration projects in a number of school districts across the nation, could argue that the project should be seen not as a radical reform but as a rescue mission — which indeed had been the character of all the educational enterprises he and Robert Hutchins had launched.

If Hutchins had lapsed into obscurity, his basic ideas had not. Any serious contemporary discussion of education, of the judicial system, of the inadequacy of mass communications, or of the drastically changed character of international relations began with the questions he raised over the years. If the answers he proposed were still not widely accepted, they could no longer be ignored, and if the discussion fell far short of the dialogue he espoused, at least it was kept open.

He never expected to be honored as a prophet; it was enough that he managed to be heard. His imposing presence made that possible by deflecting the sustained efforts to discredit him as a turncoat revolutionary bent on subverting his country's God-given heritage. It could be seen in retrospect that it simply was never possible to portray Hutchins as un-American. He was the modern embodiment of those Founding Fathers who were democratic enough to open the way for universal suffrage and "aristocratic enough to believe that men less educated than themselves might misuse their right."[30]

His unblinking realism never degenerated into cynicism. In thanking Clifton Fadiman for the critique of his last testament, he said, "I had not realized how optimistic I am."[31] When Eric Sevareid interviewed him in the last year of his life, he asked if he still had faith in the country's future. Hutchins replied:

Yes. I think there is something here that doesn't exist anywhere else. This may be just because I was brought up as a lawyer but I think the Constitution of the United States is just what Gladstone thought of it — the most wonderful work ever struck off at a given time by the brain and purpose of man. There is a Constitution that works fairly well; there is a form of government that we don't really understand but it seems to be working fairly well; and there are the history and spirit of the people. And in all this I would include the educational system which I have always attacked. The whole idea of education is a wonderful exhibition of faith in democracy on one hand and intellectual development on the other.[32]

In that interview Sevareid reminded him of his opposition to America's entry into World War II and of the apocalyptic vision of a nuclear holocaust that had shaken him in its aftermath. Since none of the dread consequences he had foreseen had ensued, did he now concede that he might have been wrong?

The reply was classic Hutchins, a quotation steeped in irony — and I suspect it was one he had often used to remind himself that optimism might be blurring his vision: "Do you know what a Chicago historian said fifty years ago when he was asked what he thought about the French Revolution? He said, 'It's too early to tell.' "[33]

Notes

Preface

1. The comment was made by Keith Tuma, a member of the faculty of Miami University of Ohio, who served as my research assistant while completing his doctoral thesis at the University of Chicago.
2. Hutchins to his father, William J. Hutchins, undated letter, probably 1947. (B)
3. Hutchins to Storer Lunt, May 9, 1973.
4. Hutchins to Frank L. Keegan, September 17, 1968.
5. *Louisville Courier-Journal*, November 23, 1948.
6. Hutchins, *Freedom, Education and the Fund: Essays and Addresses*, 1946–1956 (New York: Meridian, 1956), 51–52.

Chapter One

1. Hutchins, "The Intellectual Community," *The Center Magazine*, January/February 1977.
2. Hutchins to Charles H. Percy, April 1, 1960.
3. Thornton Wilder to Hutchins, July 25, 1971.
4. *Brooklyn Eagle*, Undated newspaper clipping, W. H. Hutchins collection. (B)
5. Ibid.
6. Ibid.
7. Ibid.
8. Hutchins to Wilder, January 21, 1975. (Y)
9. The recollections of his grandfathers were related by Francis Hutchins in an interview with the author.
10. The address was delivered by Hutchins on May 18, 1939, in Louisville, Kentucky; the private conversation was with the author.
11. Hutchins to Wilder, July 8, 1974. (Y)
12. Grosvenor Hutchins to Henry Churchill King, May 15, 1907. Henry Churchill King collection. (O)
13. Ibid.
14. King to Grosvenor Hutchins, May 17, 1907. Henry Churchill King collection. (O)
15. Donald M. Love, *Henry Churchill King of Oberlin* (New Haven: Yale University Press, 1956), 97.
16. Hutchins., "The Intellectual Community."
17. Ibid.
18. Love, *King of Oberlin*, 95.
19. Kemper Fullerton, quoted in Hutchins, "The Intellectual Community."
20. Hutchins, "Autobiography of an Uneducated Man," in *Education for Freedom* (Baton Rouge: Louisiana State University Press, 1943), 3.

21. The poem was found among Hutchins's personal papers by his wife Vesta and made available to the author. The title was added by Hutchins after his nephew Francis Hutchins, Jr., found a copy among his grandfather's papers and forwarded it to him.

22. At the author's request, the Oberlin Communications Office circulated a letter to the 159 surviving members of the classes of 1918 and 1919 asking them for recollections of Hutchins, favorable or otherwise. The responses were sent directly to the author, and unless otherwise identified they are the source of the quotations on this and following pages.

23. Hutchins, "Oberlin Be Yourself," address, the Greater New York Chapter of the Oberlin Alumni Association, January 14, 1927. (O)

24. "Further Particulars of the Great Oberlin Auto Heist," *Cleveland Plain Dealer*, August 4, 1977. (O)

25. Quoted in Love, *King of Oberlin*, 104.

26. Ibid., 23.

27. F. H. Foster, *The Modern Movement in American Theology* (New York: Revell, 1939), quoted in Love, *King of Oberlin*, 101.

28. Love, *King of Oberlin*, 153.

29. Hutchins, "The Sentimental Alumnus," commencement address delivered at Oberlin in June 1934. Reprinted in Hutchins, *No Friendly Voice* (Chicago: University of Chicago Press, 1936).

30. Hutchins, unpublished interview with Milton Mayer at the Center for the Study of Democratic Institutions, October 3, 1973. (USCB)

31. See note 29 above.

CHAPTER TWO

1. Love, *Henry Churchill King*, 191.

2. Hutchins, convocation address, University of Chicago, June 19, 1942.

3. Will Hutchins to Hutchins, May 12, 1945. (B)

4. Will Hutchins to Grosvenor Hutchins, September 14, 1917. (B)

5. Will Hutchins to Hutchins, September 21, 1917. (B)

6. Undated reply by Hutchins to Will Hutchins's letter of September 21, 1917. (B)

7. Ibid.

8. Hutchins to Will Hutchins, October 11, 1917. (B)

9. Hutchins to Will Hutchins, undated, September 1917. (B)

10. Hutchins to Will Hutchins, September 21, 1917. (B)

11. Hutchins to "Dear Family," describing life in the rear area, July 22, 1918. (B)

12. Hutchins to "Dear Family," describing move forward, August 6, 1918. (B)

13. Hutchins to "Dear Family," August 11, 1918. (B)

14. Hutchins to "Dear Family," August 22, 1918. (B)

15. Hutchins to "Dear Family," on combat experience, October 26, 1918. (B)

16. Hutchins to "Dear Family," October 25, 1918. (B)

17. Hutchins to "Dear Family," November 14, 1918. (B)

18. Hutchins to "Dear Family," November 3, 1918. (B)

19. See note 17 above.

20. Hutchins to "Dear Father and Mother and Francis," November 17, 1918. (B)

21. Hutchins to "Dear Father and Mother and Francis," undated, probably February 1919. (B)

22. Francis S. Hutchins to Will Hutchins, April 28, 1919. (B)

23. Hutchins, unpublished interview with George Dell, May 30, 1973.

24. Hutchins, commencement address, the Asheville School, May 18, 1944.

CHAPTER THREE

1. William Goodell Frost to Hutchins, undated.

2. Ibid. President Frost set forth his complaints against Will Hutchins in this

undated letter to Hutchins, then president of the University of Chicago, urging that he "persuade him to 'take thought,' or show us that we are in some way mistaken." Unfortunately there is no copy of Hutchins's reply. (B)

3. "Where Service Meets a Need," brochure, Berea College, Kentucky, 1985.

4. William J. Hutchins, *The President's Ideals and Inspirations* (New York: Revell, 1917), 13.

5. Ibid., 31.

6. Ibid., 14.

7. Ibid., 138.

8. Hutchins, DeForest Lecture, Yale University, November 1920.

9. Hutchins, address, Yale Alumni, New Haven chapter, undated, spring 1921.

10. Ibid.

11. Ibid.

12. Hutchins, address, Wolf's Head, undated, 1923.

13. Hutchins, "The Intellectual Community."

14. Hutchins, *Education for Freedom*, 6–7.

15. Ibid.

16. Hutchins, "The Intellectual Community."

17. Hutchins-Dell interview, May 30, 1973.

18. Will Hutchins to Hutchins, January 8, 1920. (B)

19. Maude McVeigh to Will and Anna Hutchins, August 3, 1921. (B)

CHAPTER FOUR

1. Hutchins-Dell interview, May 29, 1973.

2. Hutchins, class oration, Yale Commencement, 1921.

3. and 4. Both the letter from Herring to King and King's reply (dated October 9 and October 18, 1920, respectively) are in the Henry Churchill King papers. (O)

5. Hutchins, "The Educational Function of New England," Stearns Lecture, Phillips Academy, April 7, 1934.

6. James R. Angell to Hutchins, October 17, 1922.

7. Hutchins-Mayer interview, October 4, 1973. (UCSB)

8. Hutchins-Dell interview, January 6, 1975.

9. Hutchins to Angell, August 27, 1923. (Y)

10. Morris Tyler, interview with the author, December 12, 1985.

11. Hutchins to Angell, September 30, 1924. (Y)

12. Hutchins to George Dudley Seymour, June 28, 1941.

13. See note 10 above.

14. Hutchins, address, Yale Club of Boston, February 14, 1923.

15. Hutchins, address, class agents' dinner, New Haven, January 25, 1923.

16. Hutchins, address, Hotchkiss Academy, May 2, 1926.

17. Hutchins to Angell, February 3, 1926. (Y)

18. Hutchins-Dell interview, May 30, 1973.

19. Hutchins-Mayer interview, October 4, 1973. (UCSB)

CHAPTER FIVE

1. Hutchins-Mayer interview, October 4, 1973. (UCSB)

2. Hutchins, "Evidence and the Scientific Method," address, Association of American Law Schools, December 3, 1926.

3. Quoted in John Henry Schlegel, "American Legal Realism and Empirical Social Science: From the Yale Experience," *Buffalo Law Review* 28, no. 459 (1980): 474–475. Wigmore voiced these views in protesting Hutchins's appointment as dean, which he termed "preposterous."

4. Hutchins, "Evidence and the Scientific Method."

5. Hutchins-Mayer interview, October 2, 1973. (USCB)

6. Ibid.

7. Taft to Angell, May 1, 1927. Quoted in Schlegel, "American Legal Realism," 480.

8. Guido Calabresi, interview with the author, December 13, 1985.

9. Robert Stevens, *Law School: Legal Education in America from the 1850s to the 1980s* (Chapel Hill: University of North Carolina Press, 1983), 136.

10. Hutchins to Samuel H. Fisher, February 24, 1927, quoted in Schlegel, "American Legal Realism," 469.

11. Hutchins to Karl N. Llewellyn, May 7, 1926.

12. William O. Douglas, *Go East Young Man: The Early Years* (New York: Random House, 1974), 163.

13. Ibid.

14. Ibid., 164–165.

15. Stevens, *Law School,* 140.

16. Quoted in Mortimer Adler, *Philosopher at Large* (New York: Macmillan, 1977), 109–111.

17. Ibid., 110–111.

18. Ibid., 111.

19. Ibid.

20. Schlegel, "American Legal Realism," 488.

21. Douglas, *Go East Young Man,* 170.

22. Schlegel, "American Legal Realism," 489.

23. Hutchins, "Experiments in Legal Education at Yale," address, Association of American Law Schools, 1928.

24. Yale Law School minutes, December 23, 1923. Quoted in Schlegel, "American Legal Realism," 472.

25. James F. Simon, *Independent Journey: The Life of William O. Douglas* (New York: Harper & Row, 1980).

26. Hutchins, Report to the Faculty, Yale Law School, 1928–1929.

27. Stevens, *Law School,* 156.

28. Tyler, interview with the author.

CHAPTER SIX

1. Quoted in Albert M. Trammler, *One in Spirit: A Retrospective View of the University of Chicago* (Chicago: The Joseph Regenstein Library, 1973), 18–19.

2. Ibid., 17.

3. Quoted in Dorothy V. Jones, *Harold Swift and the Higher Learning* (Chicago: The University of Chicago Library, 1985), 22.

4. John Chamberlain described Hutchins's encounter with Woodward and his first meeting with the Chicago trustees in an article, "The University of Chicago," *Fortune,* July 1937.

5. Hutchins to Anna and Will Hutchins, April 1929.

6. Ibid.

7. Quoted in Jones, *Harold Swift,* 27.

8. Quoted in Barry D. Karl, *Charles E. Merriam and the Study of Politics* (Chicago: University of Chicago Press, 1974), 161.

9. Angell to Harold Swift, April 16, 1929.

10. Swift to T. E. Donnelley, a trustee who was away during Hutchins's visit, April 9, 1929.

11. Quoted in Jones, *Harold Swift,* 17–18.

12. Quoted in Thomas Wakefield Goodspeed, *A History of the University of*

Chicago: The First Quarter Century (Chicago: University of Chicago Press, 1972), 293.

13. Swift to Hutchins, May 1, 1929.
14. Swift to Hutchins, June 11, 1929.
15. Hutchins to Swift, June 14, 1929.
16. John F. Moulds to Hutchins, November 5, 1929.
17. Hutchins to John D. Rockefeller, Jr., January 29, 1930.
18. Rockefeller to Hutchins, December 16, 1929.
19. Rockefeller to Hutchins, September 8, 1930.

CHAPTER SEVEN

1. Laird Bell, address, trustees' dinner, January 7, 1953.
2. Scott M. Cutlip, " 'Advertising' Higher Education: The Early Years of College Public Relations — Part II," *College and University Journal* 10, January 1971: 28.
3. Ibid., 26.
4. See note 2 above.
5. Hutchins, *Chicago Daily News*, March 1, 1951.
6. Ibid.
7. Ibid.
8. This version of the anecdote is taken from an extended CBS interview of Hutchins by Eric Sevareid, published in *Conversations with Eric Sevareid* (Washington: Public Affairs Press, 1976), 127.
9. Quoted in Trammler, *One in Spirit,* 20.
10. Reuben Frodin, "Very Simple But Thoroughgoing," in *The Idea and Practice of General Education*, F. Champion Ward, ed. (University of Chicago Press, 1950), 26.
11. Quoted in Trammler, *One in Spirit,* 39.
12. Frodin, "Very Simple But Thoroughgoing," 29.
13. See note 11 above.
14. Ibid., 40.
15. Quoted in Frodin, "Very Simple But Thoroughgoing," 30.
16. Ibid.
17. Ibid., 32.
18. Ibid.
19. Ibid., 34.
20. Ibid., 35.
21. Ibid., 35–36.
22. Ibid., 38.
23. Ibid., 40.
24. Ibid., 45.
25. Ibid., 47.
26. Ibid., 49.
27. Hutchins-Dell interview, May 30, 1973.

CHAPTER EIGHT

1. R. M. Hughes, *A Study of the Graduate Schools of America* (University of Miami Press, 1925).
2. Hutchins, address, Chicago chapter, Alpha Delta Phi, October 4, 1929.
3. Carroll Mason Russell, *The University of Chicago and Me*. This memoir by Mrs. Russell, who grew up in the University community and attended the Laboratory School and the College, was privately printed in 1982 and circulated to her family and friends. A copy was provided the author by Arthur Schulz, a trustee of the University. The author also had the benefit of an interview with Mrs. Russell's daughter, Mrs. Albert W. Sherer.
4. John U. Nef, interview with the author, September 20, 1986.

5. Hutchins, address, faculty dinner, October 7, 1929.

6. Hutchins, address, Yale Club of Chicago, Blackstone Hotel, October 18, 1929.

7. Hutchins, address, Union League of Chicago, October 29, 1929.

8. Hutchins, inaugural address, November 19, 1929. The address was circulated to all Chicago alumni with a covering letter from Hutchins, "not because it is an epoch-making document, but because it sets forth briefly some of the plans we have in mind for the development of the University of Chicago."

9. Ibid.

10. *Daily Maroon*, November 19, 1929.

11. Hutchins, address to the student assembly, November 20, 1929.

12. Jones, *Harold Swift*, 47–48.

13. Hutchins, address, trustee-faculty dinner, January 8, 1930.

14. Ibid.

15. Ibid.

16. Ibid.

17. Ibid.

18. *The Nation*, May 8, 1929.

19. Simon, *Independent Journey*, 109.

20. Hutchins to Douglas, June 25, 1931. (LC)

21. Hutchins to Douglas, April 4, 1932. (LC)

22. Simon, *Independent Journey*, 111.

23. Adler, *Philosopher at Large*, 124.

24. Hutchins to Adler, July 6, 1929.

25. Adler, *Philosopher at Large*, 127.

26. Ibid.

27. "A Statement from the Department of Philosophy," University of Chicago, Presidential Papers 1925–1945.

28. Adler, *Philosopher at Large*, 133.

29. Ibid., 135–136.

30. Hutchins, Memorandum to the Members of the University Senate, October 22, 1930.

31. *Chicago Tribune*, February 6, 1931.

CHAPTER NINE

1. Hutchins, *Freedom, Education and the Fund*, 19.

2. Hutchins-Mayer interview, October 2, 1973.

3. Ibid.

4. Hutchins, *Freedom, Education and the Fund*, 13–14.

5. Amy Apfel Kass, "The Liberal Arts Movement from Ideas to Practice," *The College*, Saint John's College Magazine, October 1973.

6. Hutchins, address, University of North Carolina, October 30, 1930.

7. Hutchins, "The Administrator," *Journal of Higher Education*, November 1946. A slightly revised version is included in Hutchins, *Freedom, Education and the Fund*, 169.

8. Hutchins, Memorandum to the Members of the University Senate, October 22, 1930.

9. Kass, "The Liberal Arts Movement."

10. Russell, *The University of Chicago and Me*, 46–47.

11. Hutchins to Will Hutchins, February 2, 1931. (B)

12. Hutchins to Wilder, February 2, 1931. (Y)

13 and 14. These two letters from Adler to Hutchins on the reorganization plan are from Adler's personal files.

15. Quoted in Goodspeed, *A History of the University of Chicago*, 144.

16. Alline M. Ballard, "Chicago Puts New Burden on Student," *New York Times*, September 27, 1931.

17. Hutchins-Mayer interview, October 3, 1973.

18. Quoted in *University of Chicago Magazine*, April 1951.

CHAPTER TEN

1. Adler, *Philosopher at Large*, 129. The conversation took place at the New York Yale Club early in the summer before Hutchins assumed his new duties at Chicago.

2. Hutchins to Adler, undated, 1930.

3. Quoted in J. P. McEvoy, "Young Man Looking Backward," *American Mercury*, December 1938.

4. Quoted in Adler, *Philosopher at Large*, 139.

5. Hutchins, "Autobiography of a Student Who Did Not Go to Saint John's," address, Saint John's College, undated, probably 1939.

6. Hutchins served as editor in chief of Britannica's Great Books series, with Adler as associate editor. The advisory board included John Erskine, Buchanan, Barr, and Van Doren. English, Canadian, and Australian scholars were listed as consultants. The fifty-four-volume set included the introductory *Great Conversation* and a two-volume compilation, *The Great Ideas: A Syntopicon*, which was prepared under Adler's supervision and had cross references to the texts: 4. Homer; 5. Aeschylus, Sophocles, Euripides, and Aristophanes; 6. Herodotus and Thucydides; 7. Plato; 8. Aristotle I; 9. Aristotle II; 10. Hippocrates and Galen; 11. Euclid, Archimedes, Apollonius, and Nicomachus; 12. Lucretius, Epictetus, and Marcus Aurelius; 13. Virgil; 14. Plutarch; 15. Tacitus; 16. Ptolemy, Copernicus, and Kepler; 17. Plotinus; 18. Augustine; 19. Thomas Aquinas I; 20. Thomas Aquinas II; 21. Dante; 22. Chaucer; 23. Machiavelli and Hobbes; 24. Rabelais; 25. Montaigne; 26. Shakespeare I; 27. Shakespeare II; 28. Gilbert, Galileo, and Harvey; 29. Cervantes; 30. Francis Bacon; 31. Descartes and Spinoza; 32. Milton; 33. Pascal; 34. Newton and Huygens; 35. Locke, Berkeley, and Hume; 36. Swift and Sterne; 37. Fielding; 38. Montesquieu and Rousseau; 39. Adam Smith; 40. Gibbon I; 41. Gibbon II; 42. Kant; 43. American State Papers, The Federalist, and J. S. Mill; 44. Boswell; 45. Lavoisier, Fourier, and Faraday; 46. Hegel; 47. Goethe; 48. Melville; 49. Darwin; 50. Marx and Engels; 51. Tolstoy; 52. Dostoevsky; 53. William James; 54. Freud.

7. Hutchins to Adler, July 2, 1931.

8. Hutchins, *The Great Conversation*, prefatory volume to the Great Books of the Western World series (Chicago: Encyclopaedia Britannica, 1959), 24.

9. Ibid., 9–10.

10. "Robert Maynard Hutchins," by Edward Shils, Distinguished University Professor, University of Chicago, unpublished essay made available to the author.

11. John Godfrey Morris, *University of Chicago Magazine*, April 1951.

12. Sidney Hyman, conversation with the author.

13. Bernard Weissbourd, conversation with the author.

14. Adler, *Philosopher at Large*, 7.

15. Adler to Hutchins, June 5, 1929.

16. Ibid.

17. Ibid.

18. Quoted in Gilbert A. Harrison, *The Enthusiast: A Life of Thornton Wilder* (New York: Ticknor & Fields, 1983), 122.

19. Hutchins to Wilder, June 17, 1974. (Y)

20. The neighborhood as it existed in Wilder's time is described in Georg Mann, "The University That Told Us So," *Chicago Magazine*, March–April 1973.

21. Harrison, *The Enthusiast*, 125.

22. Wilder to Hutchins, April 5, 1965.

23. Hutchins to Wilder, September 23, 1966. (Y)

24. Quoted in Harrison, *The Enthusiast*, 141.
25. Hutchins to Wilder, August 7, 1936. (Y)
26. Hutchins to Wilder, May 11, 1946. (Y)

CHAPTER ELEVEN

1. T. V. Smith, *A Non-Existent Man: An Autobiography* (Austin: University of Texas Press, 1962), 230.
2. Ibid., 232.
3. Richard McKeon, interview with George Dell, June 3, 1975.
4. Angus MacLean Thuermer, letter to the author, June 12, 1987.
5. Russell, *The University of Chicago and Me*, 88–89.
6. Beardsley Ruml, who conceived the federal income tax withholding scheme, left the University to accept appointment as vice president of R. H. Macy & Co., the New York department store, prompting Maude Hutchins to remark: "Poor Bee, he's traded ideas for notions." In an obituary written for the Century Club annual in 1960, Hutchins wrote: "In addition to his joviality, the principal thing about him was his objectivity. And he was probably the most original man about ways of getting things done I have ever seen. As is well known, he could absorb enormous quantities of food and drink. I am afraid they got him in the end."
7. Hutchins, conversation with the author.
8. "Hutchins of the Midway," *Time*, June 24, 1935.
9. Hutchins, "The Administrator," *Journal of Higher Education*, November 1946.
10. Hutchins, *Chicago Daily News*, March 10, 1951.
11. Hutchins, Report of the President, 1930–1934, submitted February 1, 1935.
12. Ibid.
13. Smith, *A Non-Existent Man*, 231.
14. Milton Mayer published a version of this exchange in "Rapidly Aging Young Man," an article in *Forum and Century*, November 1933. The version used here was related to the author by James H. Douglas, a Chicago trustee and close friend of Hutchins.
15. Hutchins included the Gibbon quotation in a letter to Thornton Wilder and repeated it for the amusement of his father, adding that he doubted that it would be appropriate for one of his sermons.
16. Quoted in David Broder, AB '47, AM '51, *University of Chicago Magazine*, June 1980.
17. "Hutchins of the Midway."
18. The Wellington Jones file was made available to the author by Norton Ginsburg, a colleague of Jones's who became chairman of the Geography Department.
19. Vesta Hutchins recalled that Will Munnecke, a University vice president, was a dinner guest the night Borgese amused Hutchins with his remark about the voluptuous paragraph. He was the prime mover in putting together a printed pamphlet dated June 30, 1948, and subtitled, in the academic style, "A Critical Study of the Correspondence of Robert M. Hutchins." The byline on the cover is "by an admirer." Others were no doubt involved.
20. Clarissa Hutchins Bronson, conversation with the author.
21. Milton Mayer, "An Undemoralized Man," address, Shimer College trustees' dinner, University Club of Chicago, October 10, 1972.
22. Ibid.

CHAPTER TWELVE

1. McEvoy, "Young Man Looking Backward."

2. Hutchins, "In the Thirties, We Were the Prisoners of Our Illusions; Are We Prisoners in the Sixties?," *New York Times Magazine*, September 8, 1968.

3. Ibid.

4. Ibid.

5. Adlai Stevenson to Hutchins, June 21, 1932.

6. Mayne Albright to Hutchins, telegram, June 27, 1932.

7. Hutchins, address, Young Democratic Clubs, Chicago, June 27, 1932.

8. Ibid.

9. Ibid.

10. *New York Times*, June 28, 1932.

11. Hutchins-Dell interview, January 6, 1975.

12. Hutchins, "In the Thirties."

13. Smith, *A Non-Existent Man*, 235.

14. Hutchins, address, Industrial Relations Society of Chicago, October 19, 1934.

15. Quoted in Milton Mayer, "The Red Room," *Massachusetts Review*, Summer 1975.

16. Hutchins, "The Professor Pays," address, American Association of University Professors, November 27, 1931.

17. C. M. Chester to William Benton, October 20, 1936.

18. Unless otherwise indicated, the quotations in the account of the Walgreen hearing are from Mayer, "The Red Room."

19. Franklin D. Roosevelt to Hutchins, July 1, 1935.

Chapter Thirteen

1. Hutchins, address, trustee-faculty dinner, January 9, 1936.

2. Hutchins, address, student convocation, December 20, 1931.

3. Hutchins, "Education and the Public Mind," address, National Education Association, July 6, 1933.

4. Hutchins, Report of the President, 1935–1936.

5. Ibid.

6. Arthur Rubin, Clarence Faust, R. S. Crane, Henry Prescott, and Norman MacLean were selected from the Chicago faculty. Buchanan brought along from Virginia two of his graduate students, Catesby Taliaferro and Charles Wallis, and three of McKeon's graduate students from Columbia, Paul Goodman, Kimball Plochman, and William Barrett, were also added. William Gorman and James Martin, who assisted Hutchins and Adler in their Great Books courses, were invited to attend meetings of the Committee but were not made members.

7. Quoted in Harris Wofford, ed., *Embers of the World: Conversations with Scott Buchanan* (Center for the Study of Democratic Institutions, 1970), v.

8. Scott Buchanan to Hutchins, March 22, 1930.

9. Unless otherwise credited, the quotations in this account of the activities of the Committee on the Liberal Arts are from Kass, "The Liberal Arts Movement."

10. Stringfellow Barr to Hutchins, October 21, 1936.

11. Adler to Hutchins, August 13, 1936.

12. Adler, *Philosopher at Large*, 175.

13. Scott Buchanan, "The Crisis in Liberal Education," *Amherst Graduate Quarterly*, February 1938.

14. Ibid.

15. Scott Buchanan, "The New Program at Saint John's College," *The 1937–38 Catalogue of Saint John's College*, Appendix II, *Embers of the World*, 227.

Chapter Fourteen

1. Mayer, "The Red Room."

2. Shils, unpublished essay on Hutchins.

3. Hutchins, *No Friendly Voice* (Chicago: University of Chicago Press, 1936).

4. Robin D. Lester, "The Rise, Decline and Fall of Intercollegiate Football at the University of Chicago, 1890–1940," unpublished dissertation, University of Chicago, 1974.

5. In a November 24, 1958, unpublished interview with George W. Dell, a professor of speech at San Francisco State University, Hutchins discussed his rhetorical techniques in detail. He said he thought he had overdone irony, and that he had been guilty of overstating ideas and facts for emphasis: "Any presentation of any material has to be selected. I have no doubt I select the material that I think would be most effective. In doing this I undoubtedly omit materials that are less effective or even contrary to the position I am trying to set forth. I would also concede that my speeches are the speeches of an advocate and not those of a judge and that, like all advocates, I have exaggerated from time to time."

6. Hutchins, "The Professor Pays."

7. Hutchins, "The Sheep Look Up," address, the Modern Forum, Los Angeles, November 25, 1935. The title is from Milton, "The sheep look up and are not fed," and the allusion is to students and their teachers.

8. Hutchins, "Back to Galen," address, American College of Surgeons, October 13, 1933.

9. Hutchins, "Thomas Jefferson and the Intellectual Love of God," address, Founder's Day, University of Virginia, April 13, 1934.

10. Hutchins, "The Educational Function of New England."

11. Hutchins, "The Outlook for Public Education," address, Pittsburgh Teachers Association, April 29, 1935.

12. Hutchins, "The Press and Education," address, American Society of Newspaper Editors, April 18, 1930.

13. Hutchins, "Radio and Public Policy," address, National Advisory Council on Radio in Education, October 8, 1934.

14. Hutchins, "The YMCA," address, Employed YMCA Officers Association, June 9, 1933.

15. Hutchins, "The Professor Is Sometimes Right," address, Bond Club of New York, December 20, 1931.

16. Hutchins, remarks on the dedication of the Graduate Education Building as Judd Hall, April 15, 1948. Hutchins described Judd as "one of my dearest friends who guided my infant footsteps, whom I never repaid for his kindness to me, and whose loss I will continue to mourn as long as I live."

17. Hutchins, "The Sheep Look Up."

18. Hutchins, "The Outlook for Public Education."

19. Hutchins, "The Sheep Look Up."

20. Ibid.

21. Ibid.

22. Ibid.

23. Hutchins to Justin Dart, January 26, 1970. Dart, a son-in-law of Charles R. Walgreen and an alumnus of Northwestern, joined in the effort to persuade his alma mater to accept the merger proposal.

24. Hutchins, address, student convocation. December 12, 1933.

25. Ibid.

Chapter Fifteen

1. Hutchins, "Remarks: Dedication of Social Science Building," December 16, 1929.

2. Karl, *Charles E. Merriam and the Study of Politics*, 154, 155.

3. Ibid., 155.

4. Ibid., 165.
5. Quoted in Adler, *Philosopher at Large*, 162.
6. Hutchins, address, trustee-faculty dinner, January 11, 1934.
7. Ibid.
8. Adler, *Philosopher at Large*, 163.
9. Quoted in Adler, *Philosopher at Large*, 161.
10. Ibid.
11. *Daily Maroon*, February 6, 1934.
12. *Daily Maroon*, February 12, 1934.
13. Shils, unpublished essay on Hutchins.
14. Russell, *The University of Chicago and Me*, 56.
15. Adler recalled the luncheon with the cardinal in a conversation with the author. In his autobiography he identified the philosophical books and essays he wrote between 1935 and 1945 as the work of his Thomist period. He continued to consider dogmatic theology and theoretical physics the two most attractive subjects for anyone who enjoyed intellectual exercise for its own sake. In 1985, at the age of eighty-three, he joined the Episcopal Church.
16. Adler, *Philosopher at Large*, 315.
17. Ibid.
18. The encounter with the Manns was described in interviews by the author with Adler and Elisabeth Mann Borgese.
19. Hutchins, *The Higher Learning in America* (New Haven: Yale University Press, 1936), 87.
20. Ibid., 95.
21. Mark Van Doren, *New York Tribune*, November 8, 1936.
22. Ralph Thompson, *New York Times*, December 22, 1936.
23. See note 21 above.
24. Harry D. Gideonse, *The Higher Learning in a Democracy* (New York: Farrar & Rinehart, 1937), 10. Gideonse's attack on Hutchins did nothing to harm his professional career, and may indeed have advanced it; he moved on from Chicago, where he held the rank of associate professor, to become president of Brooklyn College.
25. Myres S. McDougal, *Yale Law Journal* 46 (1937): 1436. McDougal dismissed Hutchins's contribution to the legal realism movement as "an incomprehensible screen behind which the 'realists' may be able, if they are astute, to put their aspirations into practice. He has taken the advice of the 'neo-realists' to capture the weapons of the enemy and attack in the name of what you would reform." In an interview with the author, McDougal attributed Hutchins's defection to his conversion to Adler's Thomism.
26. John Dewey, "President Hutchins' Proposals to Remake Higher Education," *The Social Frontier*, January 1937.
27. Hutchins, "Grammar, Rhetoric and Mr. Dewey," *The Social Frontier*, February 1937.
28. John Dewey, "The Higher Learning in America," *The Social Frontier*, March 1937.

CHAPTER SIXTEEN

1. Edward A. Purcell, Jr., *The Crisis of Democratic Theory* (Lexington: University of Kentucky Press, 1973), 152.
2. Harold Taylor, *Students Without Teachers* (New York: McGraw-Hill, 1969), 131.
3. Ibid., 144.
4. John Dewey, "Challenge to Liberal Thought," *Fortune*, August 1944.
5. Ibid.

6. Hutchins, address, University of Dubuque, October 17, 1944.

7. Mortimer Adler, *The Paideia Proposal: An Educational Manifesto* (New York: Macmillan, 1982). The dedication is to "Horace Mann, John Dewey and Robert Hutchins, who would have been our leaders were they alive today."

8. Adler, *Philosopher at Large*, 177.

9. Hutchins to Adler, August 16, 1936.

10. Adler to Hutchins, August 13, 1936. The "nutty idea" was quite similar to the concept Hutchins incorporated into the Center for the Study of Democratic Institutions, which he established in California twenty years later.

11. Hutchins to Adler, undated, August 1936.

12. Ibid.

13. Adler to Hutchins, August 11, 1937.

14. Hutchins to Adler, September 5, 1937.

15. Hutchins, "To the Graduating Class, 1935," address, University of Chicago, June 1935.

16. Mann, "The University That Told Us So."

17. Ibid.

18. Quoted in Jones, *Harold Swift*, 44.

19. Shils, unpublished essay on Hutchins.

20. Milton Friedman, "Schools at Chicago," address to the board of trustees, January 1974, excerpted in the *Chicago Times*, November–December 1987.

21. See note 19 above.

22. Hutchins, "Reintegration of the University," address, trustee-faculty dinner, April 9, 1937.

23. Adler to Hutchins, June 25, 1937.

24. Hutchins to Malcolm P. Sharp, November 12, 1940.

25. Hutchins to Sharp, November 16, 1940.

26. See note 19 above.

27. Hutchins to Nef, undated handwritten note, 1940.

28. Hutchins to Wilder, August 11, 1936. (Y)

29. Russell, *The University of Chicago and Me*, 53.

30. Elizabeth Paepcke, conversation with the author.

31. Russell, *The University of Chicago and Me*, 53–54.

32. Ibid.

33. Adler, conversation with the author.

34. Russell, *The University of Chicago and Me*, 54.

CHAPTER SEVENTEEN

1. *Chicago Daily News*, June 16, 1938.

2. Hutchins, "The Future of the University," address, trustee-faculty dinner, January 10, 1935.

3. Ralph Tyler, interview with the author.

4. Ibid.

5. See note 1.

6. See note 1.

7. Sidney Hyman, *The Lives of William Benton* (Chicago: University of Chicago Press, 1969), 69–70.

8. Ibid., 71.

9. Ibid., 164–165.

10. Ibid., 179–180.

11. Ibid., 174.

12. Ibid., 171.

13. William Benton, *The University of Chicago's Public Relations* (privately printed, 1937, in an edition of only fifty numbered copies). Because of its many direct quotations from confidential interviews, the report was strictly embargoed for twenty-five years. In 1962 the *Journal* of the American College Public Relations Association published extensive excerpts, with the comment, "This book — the first comprehensive public relations program ever developed for an American university — is not simply an historical curiosity. It is an amazingly accurate primer of college public relations in 1962." In a conversation with the author in 1986, a leading advertising executive, Arthur Schultz, the retired president of Foote, Cone and Belding and a trustee of the University, said it was still regarded as unsurpassed.

14. Ibid.
15. Ibid.
16. Ibid.
17. Quoted in Russell, *The University of Chicago and Me*, 64.
18. Quoted in Hyman, *The Lives of William Benton*, 195.
19. Ibid., 194–195.
20. Ibid., 239.
21. Ibid.

Chapter Eighteen

1. Quoted in F. Champion Ward, ed., *The Idea and Practice of General Education* (Chicago: University of Chicago Press, 1950), 85.
2. F. Champion Ward, "Requiem for the Hutchins College: Recollections and Reflections," unpublished memoir made available in draft form to the author.
3. Ibid.
4. Ibid.
5. Hutchins to Adler, July 17, 1938.
6. Adler, *Philosopher at Large*, 185.
7. Ibid., 193.
8. John U. Nef, *Search for Meaning: The Autobiography of a Nonconformist* (New York: Public Affairs Press, 1973), 182.
9. Russell, *The University of Chicago and Me*, 81.
10. Nef, draft of a speech forwarded to Hutchins, May 25, 1938.
11. Nef, conversation with the author, September 20, 1986.
12. Hutchins to Douglas, January 26, 1939. (LC)
13. *New York Herald Tribune*, December 18, 1939.
14. General Robert Wood to Hutchins, December 17, 1939.
15. Hutchins to Henry Luce, March 1, 1939. (T-L)
16. William Benton to Hutchins, March 18, 1939.
17. Harold Ickes, *The First Thousand Days*, vol. 1 of *The Secret Diary of Harold Ickes* (New York: Simon & Schuster, 1953), 210.
18. Wilder sent an undated copy of the letter to a mutual friend, Gladys Campbell, who still lives near the University campus. Ms. Campbell made the letter available to the author.
19. Hutchins to Roosevelt, June 24, 1935.
20. Roosevelt to Hutchins, June 29, 1935.
21. Hutchins to Adler, July 27, 1938.
22. Harold Ickes, *The Inside Struggle*, vol. 2 of *The Secret Diary of Harold Ickes* (New York: Simon & Schuster, 1954), 298.
23. Hutchins to Douglas, telegram, July 11, 1938. The exchange between the two that follows is taken from Douglas papers in the Library of Congress.
24. Hutchins to Douglas, July 27, 1936. (LC)
25. Hutchins to Douglas, August 6, 1938. (LC)

26. Hutchins to Douglas, September 7, 1938. (LC)
27. Hutchins to Douglas, September 23, 1938. (LC)
28. Douglas to Hutchins, September 26, 1938. (LC)
29. Ickes, *The Inside Struggle*, 588–589.
30. Hutchins to Nef, telegram, March 25, 1939.
31. Quoted in Sevareid, *Conversations with Eric Sevareid*, 131.
32. Ickes, *The Inside Struggle*, 600.
33. Smith, *A Non-Existent Man*, 235–236.
34. Ibid.

CHAPTER NINETEEN

1. Hutchins to Nef, January 15, 1940.
2. Hutchins, "Gate Receipts and Glory," *Saturday Evening Post,*, December 3, 1938.
3. Quoted in Lester, "The Rise, Decline and Fall of Intercollegiate Football," 266.
4. Ibid.
5. *Wall Street Journal*, January 14, 1986.
6. J. William Fulbright to Hutchins, quoted in Lester, "The Rise, Decline and Fall of Intercollegiate Football." In 1987 the National Collegiate Athletic Association placed seven of the eight Texas Southwest Conference members on probation for violation of NCAA rules limiting subsidization of athletes. The most severe penalty in the Association's history was imposed on Southern Methodist University, which was barred from participating in intercollegiate football for two years after its board of governors kept players on the payroll despite NCAA admonitions that the practice must be ended. Leroy Howe, the president of the SMU faculty senate, charged that SMU's board of trustees, made up of members drawn from Dallas's business elite, had forgotten "the purpose of the university, replacing it with a win-at-any-cost attitude that had been the cornerstone of their own successes. . . . You had a situation here where might makes right. The university community has been betrayed." *Los Angeles Times*, March 11, 1987.
7. *Time*, October 6, 1941.
8. Quoted by Angus MacLean Thuermer, who grew up in the neighborhood of the president's house at Chicago, in a letter to the author, June 12, 1987.
9. Hutchins, address, trustee-faculty dinner, January 8, 1941.
10. See note 7 above.
11. Hutchins, "What the University Celebrates," address, commemorative chapel service, October 8, 1940.
12. Russell, *The University of Chicago and Me*, 93–94.
13. Hutchins to Nef, September 7, 1939.
14. Lewis Mumford, *My Works and Days: A Personal Chronicle* (New York and London: Harcourt Brace Jovanovich, 1979), 391–393.
15. Ibid., 393–394.
16. Sinclair Lewis, address, Constitution Hall, Washington, quoted at length in Douglas to Hutchins, February 26, 1938.
17. Ibid.
18. Hutchins to Douglas, March 1, 1938. (LC)
19. Robert E. Sherwood, *Roosevelt and Hopkins*, vol. 1 (New York: Bantam Books, 1948), 159.
20. Hyman, *The Lives of William Benton*, 231.
21. Ickes, *The Inside Struggle*, 257.
22. Ibid.

CHAPTER TWENTY

1. Quoted in Eugene Lyons, *Herbert Hoover: A Biography* (New York: Doubleday, 1964), 263.

2. Hutchins, convocation address, June 11, 1940.
3. Ibid.
4. Ibid.
5. Ibid.
6. Ibid.
7. America First's national committee listed as its members, along with General Wood, Samuel Hopkins Adams, Chester Bowles, Dr. A. J. Carlson, Otto A. Case, William R. Castle, Mrs. Bennett Champ Clark, Irvin S. Cobb, Janet Ayer Fairbank, Ellen French Vanderbilt Simmons, John T. Flynn, Bishop Wilbur E. Hammaker, General Thomas Hammond, Jay C. Hormel, William L. Hutcheson, General Hugh S. Johnson, Clay Judson, Charles A. Lindbergh, Alice Roosevelt Longworth, Frank O. Lowden, Hanford MacNider, Clarence Manion, Mrs. John P. Marquand, Gregory Mason, Ray McKaig, Sterling Morton, William H. Murray, Kathleen Norris, the Reverend John A. O'Brien, George N. Peek, Isaac A. Pennypacker, Amos R. E. Pinchot, William H. Regnery, Ruth Hanna McCormick Simms, Harry L. Stuart, Louis J. Taber, Edwin S. Webster, Jr., Mrs. Burton K. Wheeler, and Dr. George H. Whipple.
8. Hutchins, "Town Meeting of the Air," broadcast from Atlantic City, January 23, 1941.
9. Benton to Hutchins, June 25, 1940. After Pearl Harbor, Bowles served in the Roosevelt administration as director of the wartime Office of Price Administration. Following Benton's lead, he sold his interest in Benton & Bowles and devoted his life to public sevice. He was elected governor of Connecticut, appointed ambassador to India by President Truman, and reappointed to that post by President Kennedy, whom he also served as under-secretary of state. Along the way he became a dedicated internationalist who came as close as any of his Democratic contemporaries to espousing a "One World" concept.
10. Hutchins to Benton, October 24, 1940.
11. Hutchins to Wilder, February 22, 1941. (Y)
12. Hutchins, "America and the War," National Broadcasting Company network, January 23, 1941.
13. Ibid.
14. Ibid.
15. Hutchins to Benton, January 29, 1941.
16. Douglas Stuart to Hutchins, May 3, 1941.
17. Herbert Hoover, "A Call to Reason," broadcast, June 29, 1941.
18. The press release listed only Hutchins as its source; he disassociated himself from the University by listing his home address as the site of his press conference, which was set for the following day, July 15, 1941.
19. Hutchins to Wilder, November 2, 1941. (Y)
20. Hutchins to Benton, November 1, 1941.
21. Stuart, mimeographed letter to "All Chapter Chairmen," December 8, 1941.
22. Stuart to Hutchins, January 3, 1942.

CHAPTER TWENTY-ONE

1. Hutchins, "The University at War," address to the faculty, January 7, 1942.
2. Ibid.
3. Ibid.
4. Ibid.
5. Ibid.
6. Ibid.
7. Hutchins, "The Relation of the University and Its Students to the War," address to the students, December 19, 1941.
8. Ibid.

9. Ibid.

10. Hutchins to Ickes, May 5, 1941. On May 7 Ickes replied, "It would seem that you have beaten the government to it."

11. Hutchins to Frank Knox, August 23, 1940.

12. Hutchins to Wilder, July 1, 1942. (Y)

13. John Gunther, *Chicago Revisited* (Chicago: University of Chicago Press, 1967), 58.

14. Ibid.

15. Minutes, University of Chicago faculty senate, January 23, 1942.

16. Minutes, College faculty, June 9, 1943.

17. Frodin, "Very Simple But Thoroughgoing."

18. John U. Nef, "An Established Interdisciplinary Faculty," unpublished address to the Visiting Committee on the Humanities, University of Chicago, October 9, 1970.

19. Ibid.

20. Ibid.

21. Ibid.

22. In interviews with the author, Nef, Shils, Grene, Bellow, and Tyler concurred in this appraisal of the role Hutchins played in faculty appointments to the Committee.

23. Hutchins, address, trustee-faculty dinner, January 12, 1944.

CHAPTER TWENTY-TWO

1. Hutchins, *Education for Freedom,* 39–40.

2. Ibid., 41–42.

3. Ibid., 20.

4. Ibid., 22–23.

5. Ibid., 58–59. At a Chicago trustees' dinner in January 1967, one of Hutchins's successors, George Beadle, attributed the demise of the reformed curriculum to the fact "that it was not accepted by other universities and, hence, that its early-awarded B.A. degree did not serve as qualification for graduate work. Even at Chicago, three-year M.A. programs designed to complement the early B.A. degree were never fully developed in all graduate areas.

"I was on a general educational policy committee at Stanford in the late thirties or early forties. Ray Lyman Wilbur, then president, argued for adopting the Hutchins plan there. But his proposal never got to the point of serious debate. I have often wondered what would have happened had it been implemented at Stanford. I think the plan then might have spread and become national. It is also possible that, if the plan had matured a half century earlier, in Harper's time, when it was first thought of and before the present junior-college movement had gained momentum, it might have spread very rapidly and widely."

6. Ibid., 65.

7. Hutchins, address, trustee-faculty dinner, January 13, 1943.

8. Ibid.

9. Hutchins, untitled memorandum to the board of trustees, March 10, 1943.

10. Hutchins, address, trustee-faculty dinner, January 12, 1944.

11. Ibid.

12. Ibid.

13. Ibid.

14. "Memorial to the Board of Trustees on the State of the University," memorandum adopted by the university senate, May 22, 1944.

15. Ralph Tyler, interview with the author.

16. *New York Times,* May 23, 1944; *Chicago Daily News,* April 2, 1944.

17. Benton to Hutchins, April 21, 1944.

18. Hutchins to Will Hutchins, June 5, 1944.

19. Hutchins, "The Organization and Purpose of the University," address to the students and faculty, July 20, 1944.
20. Ibid.
21. Ibid.
22. Ibid.

CHAPTER TWENTY-THREE

1. Hutchins to Nef, December 5, 1944.
2. "Report of the Committee on Instruction and Research to the Board of Trustees in Relation to Proposed Administrative Changes," December 18, 1944.
3. Edward Shils, "Presidents and Professors in American University Government," *Minerva* 8, no. 3, July 1970.
4. Hutchins, untitled address, trustee-faculty dinner, January 10, 1945.
5. Ibid.
6. Ibid.
7. Ibid.
8. Ibid.
9. Hutchins, "Education Asks No Profits," *Chicago Daily News*, February 17, 1944.
10. Milton Mayer, "Commando Hutchins," *The Progressive*, May 1, 1944.
11. *New York Herald Tribune*, July 9, 1944.
12. Francis G. Hutchins, Jr., letter to the author, April 27, 1987.
13. Hutchins, "The New Realism," address, University convocation, June 15, 1945.
14. Ibid.
15. James F. Byrnes, *All in One Lifetime* (New York: Harper & Brothers, 1958), 284–285.
16. "University of Chicago Roundtable of the Air," NBC broadcast, August 12, 1945.
17. Ibid.

CHAPTER TWENTY-FOUR

1. William T. Hutchinson, "The Department of History in Retrospect," unpublished manuscript, 1956.
2. Colwell to Hutchins, May 17, 1946.
3. Hyman, *The Lives of William Benton*, 247–248.
4. Ibid., 253.
5. Ibid., 254.
6. Ibid., 262.
7. Ibid.
8. Ibid.
9. Since *Britannica* had substantial sales in the British Commonwealth and had major editorial contributors in Great Britain, Sir Geoffrey (later Lord) Crowther, the chairman of the London-based *Economist*, was named vice chairman. Other additions to the board included Stanley Morison, a distinguished English historian and typographer, Adlai Stevenson, Beardsley Ruml, Norman Cousins, Clifton Fadiman, and Mortimer Adler.
10. Quoted in Hyman, *The Lives of William Benton*, 261.
11. Ibid., 287.
12. Adler, *Philosopher at Large*, 262.
13. Glenn T. Seaborg, "Premonitions after the Bomb," *Bulletin of Atomic Scientists*, December 1985.

14. Ibid.

15. Hutchins to Benton, telegram, March 1, 1946.

16. Richard P. McKeon and G. A. Borgese, memorandum to the Chancellor, September 17, 1945.

CHAPTER TWENTY-FIVE

1. Hutchins, untitled address, trustee-faculty dinner, January 9, 1946.

2. Benton to Hutchins, December 7, 1945.

3. Hutchins to Groves, October 6, 1945.

4. See note 1 above.

5. Ibid.

6. Rex Tugwell, *Tugwell's Thoughts on Planning*, Salvador M. Padilla, ed. (University of Puerto Rico Press, 1974), 26.

7. Ibid., 36–38.

8. Hutchins to Will Hutchins, July 31, 1946. (B)

9. See note 1 above.

10. Hutchins to Nef, March 3, 1943.

11. Minutes, discussion of proposed journal, Committee on Social Thought, June 14, 1948.

12. Hutchins to vonSimson, April 6, 1950.

13. Eliot to Hutchins, February 21, 1950.

14. Direct-mail subscription appeal, Henry Regnery Company, Publishers, announcing the Eliot series beginning in the December 1950 issue of *Measure*.

15. Hutchins to Nef, August 25, 1946.

16. James Sloan Allen, *The Romance of Commerce and Culture* (University of Chicago Press, 1983), 79.

17. Ibid., 145.

18. Ibid., 174.

CHAPTER TWENTY-SIX

1. Hutchins to Wilder, undated, 1947. (Y)

2. Hutchins to Nef, February 26, 1948.

3. Hutchins to Nef, January 31, 1949.

4. Hutchins to Nef, May 18, 1949.

5. Hutchins, "Statement to the Subversive Activities Commission of the Illinois State Legislature," in *Primer of Intellectual Freedom*, Howard Mumford Jones, ed. (Cambridge: Harvard University Press, 1949), 6–10.

6. David Broder, "The Chancellor — A Remembrance," *Washington Post*, May 19, 1977.

7. *Chicago Tribune*, November 17, 1947.

8. Foreword, *Preliminary Draft of a World Constitution*, by the Committee to Frame a World Constitution, Robert M. Hutchins, president (Chicago: University of Chicago Press, 1948), vi–vii.

9. Ibid., 44

10. Ibid., 83–84.

11. Ibid., 6.

12. George A. Bernstein, "Spelling Out World Government," *The Nation*, January 1, 1949.

13. McGeorge Bundy, "An Impossible World Republic," *The Reporter*, November 22, 1949.

14. *Preliminary Draft of a World Constitution*, vii.

15. Hutchins-Mayer interview, October 2, 1973.

16. Hutchins-Mayer interview, October 3, 1973.

17. Hutchins, convocation address, June 14, 1946.

18. William J. Hutchins, *The Preacher's Ideals and Inspirations* (New York: Revell, 1917), 160.

19. See note 17 above.

20. Robert M. Hutchins, *Morals, Religion and Higher Education* (Chicago: University of Chicago Press, 1950), 18.

21. Allen, *The Romance of Commerce and Culture*, 144–145.

22. Hutchins, "Goethe Bicentennial Address," July 12, 1949.

23. Allen, *The Romance of Commerce and Culture*, 168.

24. Ibid., 147.

25. The American participants, in addition to Hutchins and Borgese, included Robert Redfield, the Chicago anthropologist; William Ernest Hocking, the Harvard philosopher; and Thornton Wilder. Recruited from abroad were Stephen Spender, the English poet; Charles J. Burkhardt, a historian then serving as Switzerland's minister to France; Gerardus van der Leeuw, a professor of theology at the University of Groningen and the Netherlands' minister of education, arts and science; Barker Fairley, a Goethe authority at the University of Toronto; Halvadan Khot, a historian and former foreign minister of Norway; Jean Canu of France; Elio Gianturco of Italy; and Ernest Robert Curtius of the University of Bonn.

26. Sidney Hyman, *The Aspen Idea* (Norman, Okla.: University of Oklahoma Press, 1975), 47.

27. Ibid., 84

28. Allen, *The Romance of Commerce and Culture*, 195–196.

29. See note 22 above.

30. After Paepcke's death Robert O. Anderson, the chairman of Atlantic Richfield, became the Aspen Institute's principal patron. Headquarters were established in New York, and while the Executive Seminars continued at Aspen, programs were initiated elsewhere on the Environment and the Quality of Life; Communications and Society; Science, Technology and Humanism; Justice, Society and the Individual; Education for a Changing Society; and Foreign Affairs.

31. Hutchins to Nef, November 26, 1946.

32. Hutchins to Nef, October 4, 1947.

CHAPTER TWENTY-SEVEN

1. Ralph Tyler, interview with the author.

2. Hutchins to Francis Hutchins, January 11, 1945. (O)

3. Hutchins to Will Hutchins, January 11, 1945. (O)

4. *Newsweek*, June 19, 1944.

5. Hutchins to Adler, July 28, 1933.

6. Maxwell Geismar, introduction to Maude Hutchins, *The Elevator* (New York: William Morrow, 1962), viii.

7. Ibid., x.

8. Frances Logan to Hutchins, February 4, 1949.

9. Maude Hutchins, *Georgiana* (New York: New Directions, 1948), 59.

10. Geismar, introduction to Maude Hutchins, *The Elevator*, xix.

11. Hutchins to Will Hutchins, June 20, 1947.

12. Maude Hutchins, "Epigram," *Poetry*, December 1948.

13. Hutchins to his parents, undated, April 1947. (O)

14. Maude Hutchins to Will Hutchins, April 18, 1947. (O)

15. Hutchins to Will Hutchins, June 14, 1947. (O)

16. See note 11 above.

17. Hutchins to Nef, July 23, 1947.

18. Allen, *The Romance of Commerce and Culture*, 141.

19. Hutchins to Nef, undated, 1948.

20. Hutchins to Nef, undated, 1948.

21. Hutchins to Nef, March 14, 1948.

22. Hutchins to Will Hutchins, July 14, 1948. (O)

23. James Douglas, interview with the author.

24. Hutchins to Henry Luce, April 7, 1947. (T-L)

25. In addition to MacLeish, the Commission's members were, from Chicago, Charles E. Merriam and Robert Redfield; from Harvard, Vice Chairman Zechariah Chafee, Jr., professor of law, William E. Hocking, professor emeritus of philosophy, Arthur M. Schlesinger, professor of history; John M. Clark, professor of economics at Columbia; Reinhold Niebuhr, professor of ethics at Union Theological Seminary; John Dickinson, professor of law at the University of Pennsylvania; Harold D. Lasswell, professor of law at Yale; George N. Shuster, the president of Hunter College; and Beardsley Ruml, the chairman of the Federal Reserve Bank of New York. Foreign advisers were John Grierson, the former chairman of the Canadian Wartime Information Board; Huh Shih, the former Chinese ambassador to the United States; Jacques Maritain, the president of the Free French School for Advanced Studies; and Kurt Riezler of the New School for Social Research. In addition to Leigh, the staff included Llewellyn White, the assistant director, Ruth A. Inglis, and Milton D. Stewart.

26. Hutchins, *A Free and Responsible Press* (Chicago: University of Chicago Press, 1947), vi. In addition to the summary report, the Commission produced six other books, all published by the University of Chicago Press: *Government and Mass Communications* by Zechariah Chafee, Jr.; *Freedom of the Press: A Framework of Principle* by William Ernest Hocking; *Freedom of the Movies: A Report on Self-Regulation* by Ruth A Inglis; *The American Press and the San Franciso Conference* by Milton D. Stewart; *Peoples Speaking to Peoples: A Report on International Mass Communication* by Llewellyn White and Robert D. Leigh; and *The American Radio* by Llewellyn White.

27. Hutchins, *A Free and Responsible Press*, 55–56.

28. Ibid., 3.

29. Ibid., 80.

30. Ibid., 100.

31. Ibid., 102.

32. Louis M. Lyons, "The Press and Its Critics," *Atlantic Monthly*, July 1947.

33. Lippmann's comment was included in "Free for All: Freedom of the Press," *Fortune*, June 1947. Despite Henry Luce's reservations, the magazine published the entire report, less the last chapter's statement of principle, as a twenty-one-page insert. An accompanying editorial found flaws but did not dismiss the Commission's findings out-of-hand. *Time* carried a fairly straightforward two-page account that no doubt echoed Luce in its conclusion: "For the time and money, and the caliber of the men, it was a disappointing report."

34. *Hutchins Commission:* Freedom of Information Center Publication No. 69, School of Journalism, University of Missouri, January 1962. This excellent digest of the Commission's findings, the reaction of the press to them, and their subsequent neglect was prepared by Judith Murrill.

35. Frank Hughes, *Prejudice and the Press: A Restatement of Freedom of the Press with Special Reference to the Hutchins-Luce Commission* (New York: Devin-Adair, 1950), 4.

36. Ibid., 40.

37. Hutchins, "Freedom and the Responsibility of the Press: 1955," address to the American Society of Newspaper Editors, in *Freedom, Education and the Fund*, 58.

38. Richard Harwood was named ombudsman of the *Washington Post* in 1970, the first person to be designated as an independent critic of that newspaper's performance, whose findings would be published regularly on the editorial page. When he resumed the

office for a second stint eighteen years later, less than 2 percent of the nation's dailies had followed the *Post*'s lead in exposing itself to such critical examination. The quotation is taken from columns published on March 27 and April 3, 1988.

CHAPTER TWENTY-EIGHT

1. *Time*, November 21, 1949.
2. Hutchins to Nef, August 26, 1949.
3. Hutchins to Wilder, August 28, 1949. (Y)
4. Hutchins to Nef, May 18, 1949.
5. See note 3 above.
6. Hutchins, address, "International Intellectual Cooperation," Rectors' Conference, University of Frankfurt, May 19, 1948.
7. Hutchins to Paul Hoffman, December 23, 1949.
8. Hyman, *The Lives of William Benton*, 426.
9. Will Hutchins to Hutchins, January 9, 1940. (O)
10. Hutchins to Will and Anna Hutchins, telegram, December 19, 1950. (O)
11. Minutes, board of trustees' meeting, January 11, 1951.
12. F. Champion Ward recalled White's remarks in an interview with the author.
13. *The University of Chicago Magazine*, June 1951.
14. Ibid.
15. Ibid.
16. Ibid.
17. Ibid.
18. Ward, "Requiem for the Hutchins College," unpublished memoir made available in draft to the author.
19. Laird Bell, address, trustees' dinner, January 7, 1953.
20. Hutchins, address, alumni assembly, June 9, 1951.
21. Hutchins to Will Hutchins, September 22, 1937. (O)
22. Hutchins-Mayer interview, October 10, 1973. Hutchins also discussed with the author his impasse with the trustees over the issue of the encroaching ghetto.
23. On July 25, 1976, Kimpton, then living in retirement in Florida, forwarded to George Dell a taped response to questions that Dell had submitted to him in writing. He placed no restrictions on publication of his comments. The excerpts used here are from Dell's transcription of the tape, which he made available to the author.
24. Ibid.
25. F. Champion Ward, "Principles and Particulars in Liberal Education," in Arthur A. Cohen, ed., *Humanistic Education and Western Civilization* (New York: Holt, Rinehart & Winston, 1964), 121.
26. See note 15 above.
27. Donald Levine, *University of Chicago Alumni Magazine*, Winter 1985.
28. Among those who participated in the program with Tugwell were Melville C. Branch, Jr., Harvey S. Perloff, Edward C. Banfield, and Martin Myerson. After Tugwell's departure Perloff headed the program until it was discontinued in 1955.
29. Hutchins, "Farewell Address," trustees' dinner, January 10, 1951.
30. A. J. Liebling, *Chicago: The Second City* (New York: Alfred A. Knopf, 1952), 110–111.
31. Hutchins to F. Champion Ward, February 19, 1964.

CHAPTER TWENTY-NINE

1. Dwight Macdonald, *The Ford Foundation* (New York: Reynal & Company, 1956), 148.

2. The board of the Ford Foundation at the time Hoffman and Hutchins were appointed was made up of Henry Ford II, chairman; his brother Benson, a Ford Motor Company vice president; John Cowles, president of the Minneapolis Star and Tribune Company; Donald K. David, dean of the Harvard Business School; James E. Webber, vice president of the J. L. Hudson Company of Detroit; and Charles E. Wilson, director of Defense Mobilization.

3. Hutchins-Dell interview, January 6, 1975.

4. Macdonald, *The Ford Foundation*, 142.

5. *Report of the Study for the Ford Foundation on Policy and Program* (Detroit: Ford Foundation, 1949), 11.

6. Henry Ford II, foreword, *The Ford Foundation Annual Report for 1951* (Pasadena: Ford Foundation, 1951).

7. Memo to Rowan Gaither from Robert M. Hutchins, September 29, 1952. (F)

8. See note 6 above.

9. The other members of the board of the Fund for the Advancement of Education were Ralph J. Bunche, director of the Division of Trusteeship at the United Nations; Charles D. Dickey, a vice president of J. P. Morgan and Company; Mrs. Douglas Horton, a former president of Wellesley College; Philip D. Reed, the chairman of General Electric Company; Owen J. Roberts, a former associate justice of the U.S. Supreme Court; and James Webb Young, a consultant for the Ford Foundation.

The chairman of the board of the Fund for Adult Education was Alexander Fraser, a former chairman of the Shell Oil Company. The other members were Sarah Gibson Blanding, the president of Vassar College; Howard Bruce, a vice chairman of the Baltimore National Bank; the Reverend John J. Cavanaugh, the president of Notre Dame University; John L. Collyer, the chairman of the B. F. Goodrich Company; Clarence Francis, the chairman of the General Foods Corporation; Clinton S. Golden, a lecturer at Harvard Business School; Paul L. Helms, the president of Helms Bakeries; George M. Humphrey, the president of the M. A. Hanna Company; Allen B. Kline, the president of the American Farm Bureau; Charles H. Percy, the president of the Bell & Howell Company; Anna Lord Strauss, a former president of the National League of Women Voters; and James Webb Young.

10. Thomas C. Reeves, *Freedom and the Foundation: The Fund for the Republic in the Era of McCarthyism* (New York: Alfred A. Knopf, 1969), 13.

11. Hutchins to Patricia Hardesty, April 15, 1953. The article was to appear in the *Saturday Evening Post*.

12, 13, and 14. The original versions of the three poems were among the memorabilia that Martin Quigley took with him when he departed the Ford Foundation, shortly before Hutchins did. He made them available to the author.

15. Macdonald, *The Ford Foundation*, 144.

16. Robert M. Hutchins, "Matters for which I have responsibility in Area I," memo to Rowan Gaither and Dyke Brown, April 13, 1953. Ford Foundation Archives. Bernard Berelson of the University of Chicago faculty was the senior staff member for behavioral sciences; Jay Laughlin, the president of New Directions Press, created the Foundation's cross-cultural magazine, *Perspectives;* Ralph Tyler headed the Center for Behavioral Studies when it was established at Palo Alto; Edward Shils and Edward Levi received grants for projects carried out at Chicago.

17. Ibid.

18. Hutchins to Hoffman, December 21, 1950.

19. Clarence Faust, oral history transcript, page 11. (F)

20. Macdonald, *The Ford Foundation*, 54.

21. See note 13 above.

22. Robert Saudek, interview with the author.

23. Macdonald, *The Ford Foundation*, 78.

24. Alvin Eurich, interview with the author.

25. See note 23 above.
26. Macdonald, *The Ford Foundation*, 53–54.

CHAPTER THIRTY

1. Robert Lacey, *Ford: The Men and the Machine* (Boston: Little, Brown and Company, 1986), 408.
2. Ibid., 435.
3. Ibid., 437.
4. Westbrook Pegler, "Mystery of the Ford Foundation," *New York Herald American*, September 12, 1952.
5. Ibid.
6. Macdonald, *The Ford Foundation*, 78.
7. Victor Navasky, "The Happy Heretic," *Atlantic Monthly*, July 1966.
8. Reeves, *Freedom and the Foundation*, 22.
9. Macdonald, *The Ford Foundation*, 153.
10. Ibid.
11. W. H. Ferry, oral history transcript, page 24. (F)
12. Ibid., 25. Ferry apparently misinterpreted Taylor's perhaps ironic comment. At a dinner honoring Hutchins at the Waldorf-Astoria Hotel in New York on January 31, 1956, Taylor, after a light reference to his differences with Hutchins on educational matters, said, "I am proud to be associated on this occasion with Robert Hutchins, and to pay him my respects as a man of honor and integrity at a time when these are qualities of human character the more dearly prized in the scarcity of their public demonstration."
13. Clarence Faust, oral history transcript, pages 10–11. (F)
14. Lacey, *Ford: The Men and the Machine*, 459–460.
15. Martin Quigley, interview with the author.
16. Reeves, *Freedom and the Foundation*, 15.
17. Ibid., 26–27.
18. Ferry, oral history transcript, page 42. (F)
19. *Report of the Study for the Ford Foundation on Policy and Program*, 62.
20. Reeves, *Freedom and the Foundation*, 23.
21. Ibid., 26–27.
22. Ibid., 31.
23. Ibid., 32.
24. Charles T. Morrisey, interview with Robert M. Hutchins, oral history transcript, pages 16–17. (F)
25. Brownlee was a legal partner in the J. H. Whitney firm of New York; Cole was president of Amherst College; Griswold was dean of the Harvard Law School; Kestnbaum was president of Hart Schaffner and Marx of Chicago; Parten was president of Woodley Petroleum Company of Houston; Roper was a New York pollster and marketing consultant; Shuster was president of Hunter College; Mrs. Stevenson was the wife of the president of Oberlin; and Zellerbach was president of Crown Zellerbach Corporation of San Francisco. Bryan resigned after a single meeting. Membership of the founding board was completed two weeks later with the addition of Huntington Cairns, a prominent Washington lawyer; William Joyce, Jr., chairman of Joyce, Inc., of Pasadena; Russell Dearmont, counsel to the Missouri Pacific Railroad of St. Louis; and Albert Linton, the president of the Provident Mutual Insurance Company of Philadelphia.
26. Hutchins to Wilder, February 11, 1953. (Y)

CHAPTER THIRTY-ONE

1. Clarence Faust, oral history transcript, pages 11–12. (F)
2. Hutchins, oral history transcript, page 40. (F)

3. Hutchins to Wilder, undated, 1954. (Y)
4. Quigley to Gaither, May 16, 1954.
5. Quigley to Hutchins, June 5, 1953.
6. Hutchins to Wilder, undated, 1954. (Y)
7. Macdonald, *The Ford Foundation*, 171.
8. All of these lectures were published, in, respectively, *The Democratic Dilemma* (Stockolm: Alqvist & Wiksells Boktrycker, 1951); *Some Observations on American Education* (Cambridge: Cambridge University Press, 1956); *Some Questions about Education in North America* (Toronto: University of Toronto Press, 1952); *The University of Utopia* (Chicago: University of Chicago Press, 1953, 1964).
9. Hutchins, opening remarks, Great Books dinner, New York, April 15, 1952.
10. Dwight Macdonald, "The Book-of-the-Millennium Club," *The New Yorker*, November 29, 1952.
11. Dwight Macdonald, *Against the American Grain* (New York: Random House, 1962), 258.
12. James E. Colvin, letter to the author, August 3, 1987.
13. Reeves, *Freedom and the Foundation*, 38.
14. Ibid., 54.
15. Ibid., 56.
16. Hutchins to Thomas P. Lantos, January 27, 1954.
17. Hutchins to Alan Cranston, telegram, February 2, 1954.
18. Reeves, *Freedom and the Foundation*, 67.
19. Ibid., 60.
20. W. H. Ferry, oral history transcript, page 87. (F)
21. Reeves, *Freedom and the Foundation*, 76.
22. Ibid., 78.
23. Ibid., 39. The description is by Eric Goldman, a Princeton historian who became a consultant to the Fund.

CHAPTER THIRTY-TWO

1. Hutchins to Wilder, undated, 1954. (Y)
2. Hutchins, *Freedom, Education and the Fund*, 20–21.
3. Quoted in Reeves, *Freedom and the Foundation*, 72.
4. Ibid., 283.
5. Ibid., 284.
6. Ibid., 139.
7. The chairman of the Commission on Race and Housing was Earl B. Schwulst, president of the Bowery Savings Bank, New York. The board members were Gordon W. Allport, professor of psychology at Harvard; Elliot V. Bell, editor and publisher of *Business Week;* Laird Bell, a Chicago attorney; the Reverend John J. Cavanaugh, president of Notre Dame; Peter Grimm, chairman of the board of William A. White and Sons, New York; Charles S. Johnson, president of Fisk University; Charles Keller, Jr., president of the Keller Construction Company, New Orleans; Clark Kerr, chancellor of the University of California, Berkeley; Philip M. Klutznick, chairman of American Community Builders, Incorporated, Chicago; Henry R. Luce, editor-in-chief of Time, Inc.; Stanley Marcus, president of Nieman-Marcus, Dallas; J. C. McClellan, president of the Old Colony Paint Company, Los Angeles; Ward Melville, president of the Melville Shoe Corporation, New York; Francis T. P. Plimpton, a New York attorney; R. Stewart Rauch, Jr., president of the Philadelphia Savings & Loan Society; and Robert R. Taylor, executive director of the Illinois Federal Savings and Loan Association.
8. For an account of the Ashmore Project, see the author's *Hearts and Minds* (New York: McGraw-Hill, 1982). An updated version was published in 1988 by Seven Locks Press.

9. Reeves, *Freedom and the Foundation*, 94.

10. The consultants, in addition to Millis, Lazarsfeld, and Stouffer, were Frank Loescher, intergroup relations; Robert E. Cushman, civil liberties; Clinton Rossiter, studies of Communism in America; Howard Chernoff, television; John Cogley, blacklisting; George Overton, legal-assistance programs; Conrad Aronsberg, extremist groups; and Philip Woodyat, editorial competitions. Elmer Davis, the radio commentator, also served as a general consultant.

11. Quoted in Reeves, *Freedom and the Foundation*, 103–104.

12. Ibid., 104.

13. Ibid., 125.

14. Ibid., 138.

15. Ralph Tyler, oral history interview, page 277. University of California Archives.

CHAPTER THIRTY-THREE

1. Quoted in Reeves, *Freedom and the Foundation*, 120.

2. Ibid., 121.

3. Ibid., 124.

4. Ibid., 228.

5. Ibid., 227.

6. Ibid., 228.

7. Ibid., 151.

8. Hutchins to Members of the Board of Directors, memorandum, October 19, 1955. In an interview with the author, Harold Fleming, the head of the Southern Regional Council, recalled a conversation he had with Hutchins after the interracial organization became a major recipient of Fund grants. "What do you think, Mr. Fleming," Hutchins inquired. "Will your organization or ours suffer more damage from this association?"

9. Ibid.

10. Erwin Griswold, letter to the author, September 12, 1987.

11. Quoted in Reeves, *Freedom and the Foundation*, 161.

12. Ibid., 172.

13. Ibid., 173.

14. Ibid., 177.

15. William F. Buckley, Jr., "A Letter to Mr. Henry Ford," *National Review*, December 14, 1955.

16. Quoted in Reeves, *Freedom and the Foundation*, 181.

17. Paul Jacobs, *Is Curly Jewish?* (New York: Atheneum, 1965), 224.

18. Hallock Hoffman, interview with the author.

19. Quoted in Reeves, *Freedom and the Foundation*, 183.

20. Ibid., 184.

21. Ibid., 186.

22. Ibid., 189.

CHAPTER THIRTY-FOUR

1. The committee was made up of Elmo Roper, chairman, Charles Cole, J. R. Parten, and George Shuster.

2. Frank K. Kelly, *Court of Reason: Robert Hutchins and the Fund for the Republic* (New York: The Free Press, 1981), 73.

3. Ibid.

4. Ibid., 75.

5. Also interviewed by Wallace were Monsignor Francis J. Lally, the editor of the Boston archdiocesan paper *The Pilot;* Henry Wriston, the director of the American Assembly; Cyrus Eaton, a Cleveland tycoon; Arthur Larson, a Duke University law

professor; James McBride Dabbs, president of the Southern Regional Conference; Hutchins; and the author.

6. Reeves, *Freedom and the Foundation*, 193.

7. Ibid.

8. Ibid., 194.

9. Kelly, *Court of Reason*, 79.

10. Ibid., 81.

11. The Hollywood Ten were Adrian Scott, Edward Dmytryk, Lester Cole, Ring Lardner, Jr., Dalton Trumbo, John Howard Lawson, Albert Maltz, Alvah Bessie, Samuel Ornitz, and Herbert Biberman.

12. Quoted in Kelly, *Court of Reason*, 89.

13. Reeves, *Freedom and the Foundation*, 206.

14. Ibid., 207.

15. Kelly, *Court of Reason*, 99.

16. *New York Times*, July 13, 1956.

17. Quoted in Kelly, *Court of Reason*, 109.

18. Ibid., 110.

19. Ibid.

CHAPTER THIRTY-FIVE

1. Macdonald, *The Ford Foundation*, 79.

2. Reeves, *Freedom and the Foundation*, 285.

3. Ibid., 282.

4. Ibid., 291.

5. Macdonald, *The Ford Foundation*, 76.

6. Harry Kalven, *Journal of Legal Education* 10 (1957): 141–146.

7. Erwin Griswold, letter to the author, September 12, 1981.

8. Hutchins, "The Administrator Reconsidered," address, American College of Medical Administrators, September 19, 1955.

9. Ibid.

10. Ibid.

11. Hutchins to the Members of the Board of Directors, memorandum, May 4, 1956.

12. Hutchins, "The Academy Idea — The Center for Contemporary Thought," Fund for the Advancement of Education, August 10, 1953.

13. The participants at Princeton, along with Justice Owen J. Roberts, Paul Mellon, and Walter Lippmann of the board committee, were Huntington Cairns, Etienne Gilson, Charles Malik, Jacques Maritain, Robert Oppenheimer, Robert Redfield, Paul Tillich, Mortimer Adler, and Milton Katz. In London the board members were joined by Isaiah Berlin, Niels Bohr, Herbert Butterfield, Colin Clark, Sir Richard Livingstone, José Ortega y Gasset, Michael Polanyi, and R. H. Tawney.

14. Hutchins to William Benton, June 8, 1953.

15. Clarence H. Faust to H. Rowan Gaither, Jr., interoffice memorandum, Fund for the Advancement of Education, April 9, 1953.

16. Reeves, *Freedom and the Foundation*, 242.

17. Hutchins to the Board of Directors, memorandum, September 6, 1956.

18. Hutchins to the Board of Directors, memorandum, October 15, 1976.

19. Ibid.

20. David F. Freeman and Adam Yarmolinsky, "Memorandum on the President's Recommendations of October 15," October 31, 1956.

21. Quoted in Reeves, *Freedom and the Foundation*, 247.

22. Minutes, board of directors' meeting, May 16, 1957.

23. *New York Times*, June 19, 1957.

24. George Sokolsky, *New York Journal-American*, October 12, 1957.

CHAPTER THIRTY-SIX

1. Hutchins to William Benton, June 8, 1953.
2. Reeves, *Freedom and the Foundation*, 271. He cited the first four pamphlets as establishing the high standards that characterized the series: "Individual Freedom and the Common Defense," by Walter Millis; "Economic Power and the Free Society," by A. A. Berle, Jr.; "The Corporation and the Republic," by Scott Buchanan; and Clark Kerr's paper on the governance of trade unions.
3. Adler, *Philosopher at Large*, 275.
4. Quoted in Reeves, *Freedom and the Foundation*, 273.
5. Hutchins, "Reports and Recommendations to the Board," May 6, 1958.
6. Minutes, board of directors' meeting, November 19, 1958.
7. Hutchins, "Reports and Recommendations to the Board," May 7, 1959.
8. Vesta Hutchins, interview with the author.
9. Kelly, *Court of Reason*, 170.
10. Ibid.
11. Hutchins to Wilder, February 11, 1953. (Y)
12. Wilder to Hutchins, December 29, 1955.
13. W. H. Ferry, oral history transcript, pages 105–106. (F)
14. W. H. Ferry, "Robert Hutchins' Platonic Grove," *The Nation*, January 30, 1988.
15. Quoted in Reeves, *Freedom and the Foundation*, 277.

CHAPTER THIRTY-SEVEN

1. The quotation from the founder of the Benedictine Order, imprinted on cloth in ancient script, was presented to the Center, along with the bell, by John Cogley.
2. Hutchins to Ashmore, July 28, 1959.
3. Benton to Hoffman, May 6, 1959.
4. Hutchins to Hoffman, May 13, 1959.
5. Quoted in Harry S. Ashmore, ed., *Britannica Perspectives* (Chicago: Encyclopaedia Britannica, Inc., 1968), x.
6. Hutchins to Hoffman, May 13, 1959.
7. These financial arrangements were described to the author in interviews with Carl Stover, Hallock Hoffman, and Paul Armstrong.
8. *Report of the President for 1959–60*, Center for the Study of Democratic Institutions/ Fund for the Republic.
9. Hutchins to the Board of Directors, memorandum, November 7, 1960.
10. Quoted in Ashmore, *Britannica Perspectives*, xiv.
11. Ibid., xv.
12. Ibid., xv–xvi.
13. Ibid., xvi.
14. Ibid., xiv.
15. Ibid., xvi.
16. It was found in practice that the term "order" could not be applied in every case. The roof articles were finally identified as Nature, Human Nature, The Technological Order, The Legal Order, Mathematics and Logic, The Social Order, The Economic Order, The Political Order, Education, Linguistics, and The Fine Arts, with an Epilogue to provide historical overview.

CHAPTER THIRTY-EIGHT

1. Hutchins to John B. Elliot, July 30, 1959.
2. Among these were Robert M. Hutchins, *Two Faces of Federalism;* Harrison Brown and James Real, *Community of Fear;* W. H. Ferry, *The Economy under Law;*

Walter Millis, *A World without War;* William O. Douglas, *The Rule of Law in World Affairs;* William J. Brennan, Jr., *The Bill of Rights and the States;* Scott Buchanan, *Tragedy and the New Politics;* Aldous Huxley, *The Politics of Ecology;* and Jaime Benitez, *The U.S., Cuba, and Latin America.*

3. Recommendations to the Board of Directors, November 19, 1960.

4. Center press release, April 1961.

5. Participants in the American Character conference included the historian Henry Steele Commager; Justice William O. Douglas; Chancellor Louis Finkelstein of the Jewish Theological Seminary of America; Monsignor George C. Higgins of the National Catholic Welfare Conference; Irving Kristol, a vice president of Basic Books; Professor Perry Miller of Harvard; and Professor C. Vann Woodward of Yale.

6. A. B. Ruddock to Hutchins, February 23, 1961.

7. Hutchins to Ruddock, February 28, 1961.

8. See note 6 above.

9. Harry S. Ashmore, "The Thinking Man's Shelter," *Esquire*, April 1962.

10. Ibid.

11. Maurice Mitchell, interview with the author.

Chapter Thirty-Nine

1. Douglas to Hutchins, March 17, 1962. (LC)

2. Hutchins to Douglas, March 20, 1962. (LC)

3. Huxley to Hutchins, March 28, 1962.

4. New additions to the board included James H. Douglas, Jr., Hutchins's longtime friend and staunch supporter on the University of Chicago board; Ruth Field, the widow of Marshall Field; Crane Haussamen, a New York advertising executive; William C. Baggs, the editor of the *Miami News;* Edward Eichler, a California real-estate developer; the New York business leaders Ralph Ablon, the president of the Ogden Corporation, and Morris L. Levinson, the president of Associated Products, Incorporated; and Patrick Crowley, a Chicago attorney.

5. Quoted in Kelly, *Court of Reason*, 225–226.

6. Robert M. Hutchins, Scott Buchanan, Donald M. Michael, Chalmers Sherwin, James Real, and Lynn White, Jr., *On Science, Scientists and Politics*, Center occasional paper, 1963.

7. Hutchins to the Editor, *Los Angeles Times*, copy sent to Linus Pauling, October 11, 1963.

8. Hutchins, conversation with the author.

9. Hutchins to Stevenson, July 20, 1960. (P)

10. Stevenson to Hutchins, July 28, 1960.

11. Hutchins to Stevenson, September 12, 1960. (P)

12. Robert M. Hutchins, preface, *Pacem in Terris* (New York: Pocket Books, 1965), ix.

Chapter Forty

1. Ashmore, *Britannica Perspectives*, xviii.

2. Hyman, *The Lives of William Benton*, 579–580. *Perspectives* was distributed in 1968 as an anniversary bonus to buyers of *Britannica*. Some of the roof articles were published as separate volumes by the Praeger Publishing Company, which had been acquired by the Britannica company.

3. Warren Preece, interview with the author.

4. Norman Cousins, interview with the author.

5. Ashmore to Douglas, February 28, 1964.

6. Arrangements for the Wingspread planning session were made by Leslie Paffrath, the president of the Johnson Foundation, who later served as secretary general of the "Pacem in Terris" convocation. The participants included Senator Gaylord Nelson of Wisconsin; Brooks Hays, who in addition to his political connections was the president of the Southern Baptist Convention; Joseph E. Johnson, the president of the Carnegie Endowment for International Peace; Eugene Rabinowitch, the editor of the *Bulletin of Atomic Scientists;* Andrew Shonfield, the director of studies at the Royal Institute of International Affairs in Great Britain; John Tomlinson of the National Council of Churches; Nelson Glueck of Hebrew Union College; Chief S. O. Adebo, the Nigerian ambassador to the UN; Ahmad Al-Nakib, the deputy ambassador from Kuwait to the UN; Xavier Deniau of the French National Assembly; the Reverend John Cronin of the National Catholic Welfare Conference; Hudson Hoagland of the Worcester Foundation for Experimental Biology; Monsignor Luigi Ligutti, the Holy See observer at the Food and Agriculture Organization in Rome; Hans J. Morgenthau of the University of Chicago's Center for the Study of American Foreign Policy; and Livingston Biddle, representing Senator Claiborne Pell of Rhode Island.

7. Besides Willens, the other new members were Percy L. Julian, the head of Julian Laboratories in Chicago, the only black to serve on the board; Stanley Marcus, the Dallas department-store president; and two of Hutchins's former students, Bernard Weissbourd, the head of Metropolitan Structures, and Lyle Spencer, the president of Science Research Associates.

8. Quoted in Kelly, *Court of Reason*, 248.

9. Among the participants were Paul G. Hoffman, the director of the UN Special Fund; Adlai E. Stevenson, the US ambassador to the UN; Alex Quaisin-Sackey of Ghana, the president of the UN General Assembly; Abba Eban, the deputy prime minister of Israel; Vijaya Lakshmi Pandit, the governor of Maharashtra, India; Robert Buron, the chairman of the French National Committee on Productivity; Luis Quintanilla, Mexico's former ambassador to the Organization of American States; Philip C. Jessup, a judge of the International Court of Justice; Lord Caradon, the minister for foreign affairs of the United Kingdom; Alberto Lleras Camargo, the former president of Colombia; Kenzo Takayanagi, the chairman of the Japanese Cabinet Commission on the Constitution; Barbara Ward, a British economist and author; Abdul Monem Ria'i, Jordan's representative to the UN; Vida Tomsic, a member of the committee for foreign affairs of the Federal Assembly of Yugoslavia; Chief S. O. Adebo; Senator J. William Fulbright of Arkansas.

10. John K. Jessup, *Life*, March 5, 1965.

11. The three roundtable sessions were chaired by Henry Luce, Elmo Roper, and Norman Cousins, the editor of *Saturday Review*. Among the participants were James Farmer, the director of the Congress for Racial Equality; H. Stuart Hughes, the Harvard historian; James G. Patton, the president of the National Farmers Union; US Representative William Fitz Ryan of New York; Dagmar Wilson, the founder of Women Strike for Peace; Abram J. Chayes, the former legal adviser to the State Department; Marya Mannes, an author and critic; R. Paul Ramsey, a professor of religion at Princeton; Bayard Rustin, the executive secretary of the War Resisters League; Harold Stassen, the disarmament adviser to President Eisenhower; Steve Allen, the TV personality; Grenville Clark, the coauthor of *World Peace Through World Law;* Jerome Frank, a professor of psychiatry at Johns Hopkins; senators Eugene McCarthy and Claiborne Pell; Gerard Piel, the editor of *Scientific American;* Carl F. Stover, now the executive director of the National Institute of Public Affairs. Center associates George Shuster, Walter Millis, Stanley Sheinbaum, John Cogley, and Eugene Burdick also participated.

12. Quoted in Hutchins, *Pacem in Terris*, 93.

13. Ibid., 98.

14. Ibid., ix–x.

15. Ibid., 252.

16. Hubert Humphrey, conversation with the author.

17. Quoted in Hutchins, *Pacem in Terris*, 41.
18. Ibid., xx.
19. Quoted in Kelly, *Court of Reason*, 271.

CHAPTER FORTY-ONE

1. Quoted in Hutchins, *Pacem in Terris*, 144.
2. Ibid., 116–117.
3. Hutchins to Nef, January 31, 1949.
4. Carl F. Stover, "An Attempt at Perspective," unpublished address to the National Institute of Public Affairs, June 7, 1981.
5. Harry S. Ashmore and William C. Baggs, *Mission to Hanoi: A Chronicle of Double-dealing in High Places* (New York: G. P. Putnam's Sons, 1968), 3.
6. The weekly column "What Kind of World?" was syndicated to some twenty small and medium-sized newspapers but was not published in the parent paper, the *Los Angeles Times*. In the fall of 1969 Hutchins decided to discontinue writing it and suggested that I take it over. I wrote the column until 1976.
7. Quoted in Kelly, *Court of Reason*, 278.
8. Ashmore and Baggs, *Mission to Hanoi*, 4. Others at the Geneva planning session were Alastair Buchan, the director of the Institute for Strategic Studies in London; Mrs. Kiyoko Cho of the International Christian University in Tokyo; Justice William O. Douglas; Mohamed El-Zayyat, the under-secretary for foreign affairs from the United Arab Republic; senators Albert A. Gore of Tennessee and George McGovern of South Dakota; Manfred Lachs, a professor of international relations at Warsaw University; Dmitri D. Muravyev, the secretary-general of the Institute of Soviet-American Relations, USSR; C. V. Narasimhan, the chef de cabinet of the United Nations; Luis Quintanilla, a professor of international relations at the University of Mexico; Edgar Snow, the author of *Red Star over China;* and Sonn Voeunsai, Cambodia's ambassador to France.
9. Quoted in Kelly, *Court of Reason,* 281. Among the participants at the convocation were presidents Clark Kerr of the University of California and Rosemary Park of Barnard College; J. Douglas Brown, the dean of the faculty at Princeton; Sir Eric Ashby, the master of Clare College, Cambridge; President Detlev Bronk of the Rockefeller Institute; I. I. Rabi, the Columbia University Nobel laureate; and Jacques Barzun, the provost at Columbia.
10. Ibid., 280.
11. Ferry, "Robert Hutchins' Platonic Grove."
12. Ibid.
13. Robert M. Hutchins, *Zuckerkandl!* (New York: Grove Press, 1968). The expanded version was published in *Center Magazine*, September–October 1975.
14. Ibid.
15. Ibid.
16. Wilder to Hutchins, October 4, 1965.
17. Quoted in *Students and Society*, Center occasional paper, 57.
18. W. H. Ferry, "Farewell to Integration," *The Center Magazine*, March 1968.
19. Quoted in "The Dilemma of Black Studies," *Time*, May 2, 1969.
20. Paul Jacobs, *Prelude to Riot: A View of Urban America from the Bottom* (New York: Random House, 1967).
21. Quoted in *Students and Society*, 56.
22. Ibid.

CHAPTER FORTY-TWO

1. Ashmore, "The Public Relations of Peace," *Center Magazine*, October–November 1967.

2. Ashmore and Baggs, *Mission to Hanoi*, 34.
3. Ibid., 70–71.
4. Ibid., 76–77.
5. Ibid., 80.
6. William Baggs to Ashmore, March 27, 1967.
7. See note 1 above.
8. Ibid.
9. Ibid.
10. Justice Douglas presided at the opening session, which featured a televised address by U Thant, a message from Pope Paul VI (delivered by Charles Cardinal Journet of Fribourg), and a response by the Reverend Eugene Carson Blake, the general secretary of the World Council of Churches. Six panel discussions followed over two and a half days:

"Threats to Coexistence": General Said Uddin Khan of Pakistan, chairman; Senator Edward W. Brooke of Massachusetts; Galo Plaza Lasso, the former president of Ecuador; Arsene Usher Assouan, the foreign minister of the Ivory Coast; Roger Garaudy, of the Center for Marxist Studies and Research in Paris.

"Intervention: The Case of Vietnam": Ambassador Chester Ronning of Canada, chairman; Princess Tiao Moune Souvanna Phouma of Laos; Sonn Voensai, the Cambodian ambassador to France; Thanat Khoman, the foreign minister of Thailand; Nugroho, the Indonesian ambassador to North Vietnam; Jean Chauvel, an ambassador at large from France; Marian Dobrosielski, a counselor to the foreign minister of Poland; M. J. Desai of India, the chairman of the first International Commission for Vietnam.

"Confrontation: The Case of Germany": Olof Palme, the Swedish minister of communications, chairman; Wilhelm Wolfgang Shutz, a member of the praesidium of the Federal Republic of Germany; Gerald Gotting of the German Democratic Republic; Karol Malcuzynski, a foreign-policy expert for *Trybuna Ludlu* in Warsaw, Poland; Hubert Beuve-Mery, the editor of *Le Monde*, Paris; Sir Geoffrey de Freitas, a member of parliament from Great Britain and the president of the assembly of the Council of Europe.

"Beyond Coexistence": Vladimir Bakaric, a member of the Federal Assembly of Yugoslavia, chairman; Senator J. William Fulbright; Prince Jean de Broglie, a member of the French National Assembly and France's former minister of foreign affairs; Doudou Thiam, Senegal's minister of foreign affairs; and Paul Lin, a professor of history at McGill University in Canada.

"Interdependence": J. Kenneth Galbraith, the former US ambassador to India, chairman; Masamichi Inoki of the Center for Southeast Asian Studies at Kyoto University; J. L. Hromadka, a professor of theology and dean of the Comenius Faculty in Prague; Terence Nsanze, Burundi's ambassador to the UN; Silviu Brucan, a professor of social sciences at the University of Bucharest.

"Development": Chester F. Carlson, a Center board member, chairman; S. O. Adebo, the Nigerian ambassador to the UN; Paul Hoffman, the director of the United Nations Special Fund; Archbishop Dom Helder Camara of Brazil; E. R. Richardson, Jamaica's ambassador to the UN.

Among the Americans who spoke from the floor were the Reverend Martin Luther King, civil-rights leader and Nobel peace laureate; the Right Reverend James A. Pike, the former Episcopal bishop of San Francisco; Marya Mannes, an author and critic; senators Joseph Clark of Pennsylvania and Caliborne Pell of Rhode Island; and Pierre Renfret, a New York financier.

Others were Sean MacBride, the secretary general of the International Commission of Jurists; Risieri Frondizi, the former president of the University of Buenos Aires; Antoine M. B. Lacassagne, the director of biology at the Radium Institute in Paris; Edward Crowther, an Anglican bishop from the Union of South Africa; Norman Saint John-Stevas, a member of parliament in Great Britain; Monsignor Pietro Pavan of the Pontifical

Commission for Peace and Justice; Jules Moch, a French disarmament expert; André Philip, a former French finance minister.

Also Lord Ritchie-Calder, a Scottish author; Judge Luis Padillo Nervo of Mexico; E. F. Schumacher, a British philosopher; Father Gonzalo Castillo-Cardenas of Colombia; Canon François Houtart of Belgium; Father Paul Verghese of India; the Reverend Martin Niemoller of West Germany; Khushwant Singh, an Indian historian; Manduchehr Ganji of Iran; and Arnold Edinborough of Canada.

11. See note 1 above.

12. Quoted in Donald McDonald, "The Way It Was," *Center Magazine*, October–November 1967.

13. Ibid.

14. Ibid.

15. See note 1 above.

Chapter Forty-Three

1. Hutchins to Wilder, September 23, 1966. (Y)

2. Wilder to Hutchins, September 29, 1966.

3. See note 1 above. After the failure of two stormy marriages, Franja married Lou Binder and converted to his orthodox Jewish faith. Clarissa met her husband, Roddy Bronson, at the University of California, Davis, where she was attending law school. After serving a tour in the Peace Corps in Africa, they settled in Cambridge, where she practiced poverty law and served on the Harvard Law School faculty and he became a veterinary pathologist at Tufts Medical School. Joanna Blessing never found a satisfactory career. Barbara's marriage to Eugene Bailey did not survive the stress of his foreign-service career. After her divorce she earned a degree in architecture at UCLA and entered a successful career as a city planning official.

4. Wilder to Hutchins, December 12, 1964, recalling his comment on the loss of his residence.

5. Quoted in *Students and Society*, Center occasional paper, 1.

6. Ibid., 21.

7. Ibid., 61–62.

8. Vermont Royster, "Thinking Things Over: The Children's Crusade," *Wall Street Journal*, June 14, 1968.

9. Quoted in Kelly, *Court of Reason*, 340.

10. Ibid., 341.

11. Ferry, "Robert Hutchins' Platonic Grove."

12. Quoted in Kelly, *Court of Reason*, 349. Seeley turned the handwritten notes over to Ferry, who made them available to Kelly.

13. Ibid.

14. Ibid., 352.

15. Minutes, Center board of directors' meeting, May 19, 1969.

Chapter Forty-Four

1. Ashmore to Hutchins, memorandum, May 2, 1969.

2. Ibid.

3. Quoted in Kelly, *Court of Reason*, 400. The statements by Seeley were made in depositions taken in connection with a lawsuit brought by Ferry, challenging his dismissal from the Center.

4. Hutchins to Quigley, July 20, 1970.

5. Linus Pauling to Hutchins, June 20, 1969.

6. Ashmore to Joe Drown, memorandum, August 20, 1968.

7. Chester Carlson to Hutchins, August 13, 1968.

8. The other participants were Kenneth Boulding, a professor of economics at the University of Michigan; Raul Prebisch, an Argentinian economist and former secretary to the UN Commission for Latin America; Wilfred Sellars, a professor of philosophy at the University of London, and Jerome Weisner of MIT, a former science adviser to President Kennedy.

9. Hutchins to James H. Douglas, September 17, 1969.

10. Among the visiting fellows were the Swedish scholars Gunnar and Alva Myrdal; Arvid Pardo, a former Maltese ambassador to the UN; Silviu Brucan, a sociologist at the University of Bucharest; Ileana Marculescu, a science adviser to UNESCO; Nathan Rotenstreich, a professor of philosophy at Hebrew University in Jerusalem; Eduard Goldstucker, a Czech professor of history; Ronald Segal, a British social critic; and Paul T. K. Lin, an expert on the People's Republic of China at McGill University in Canada.

11. In addition to Utsunomiya, the Japanese delegation, all majority Liberal Democratic party members of the Japanese House of Representatives, was headed by Aiichiro Fujiyama, a former minister of foreign affairs, and included Munenori Akagi, a former minister of agriculture and forestry; Masumi Ezaki, a former director of the National Defense Agency; Ichitaro Ide, the chairman of the House Committee on Budget; and Shinuchi Matsumoto, a former ambassador to Great Britain.

Justice Douglas chaired the meeting, and the United States delegation included senators Alan Cranston of California; John Sherman Cooper of Kentucky; J. William Fulbright of Arkansas; and Mark O. Hatfield of Oregon; Representative Don Edwards of California; Arthur Goldberg, the former ambassador to the United Nations; and Edwin O. Reischauer, a former ambassador to Japan. Also present was Chester Ronning, the Canadian diplomat who was his country's ranking expert on China.

12. Hutchins to Wilder, May 5, 1971. (Y)

13. Hutchins to Center staff, memorandum, October 9, 1969.

14. Hutchins to Wilder, May 5, 1971. (Y)

15. Hutchins to Douglas, undated, January 1975. (LC)

16. Hutchins to Wilder, July 1, 1971. (Y)

17. Hutchins to Wilder, July 20, 1971. (Y)

18. Hutchins to Wilder, August 27, 1971. (Y)

19. Vesta Hutchins to Wilder, September 23, 1971. (Y)

20. Hutchins to Wilder, May 5, 1971. (Y)

CHAPTER FORTY-FIVE

1. Ashmore to Douglas, February 28, 1964.

2. Sidney E. Zion, "At 70, the 'Youngest' Justice of All," *New York Times*, May 26, 1969.

3. Quoted in "Douglas Resigns Foundation Post; Cites His Health," *New York Times*, May 24, 1969.

4. Quoted in "Douglas Says Tax Inquiry Aims to Get Him off Court," *New York Times*, May 26, 1969.

5. Ibid.

6. Peter C. Stuart, "Ouster of Douglas Doubted," *Christian Science Monitor*, April 8, 1970.

7. Douglas to Ashmore, December 23, 1969.

8. Ashmore to Douglas, December 30, 1969.

9. Hutchins, memorandum to the Joint Committee on Organization, March 4, 1970. The committee members were J. R. Parten, chairman, Arnold M. Grant, Hutchins, and Harold Willens.

10. Harvey Wheeler, memorandum appended to that cited in note 12 below.

11. John Cogley, memorandum appended to that cited in note 12 below.

12. Committee on Organization, summary report, submitted to the board of directors on May 15, 1970.

13. *Time*, January 24, 1969.

14. Felix Belair, "Constitution Building," *New York Times*, September 8, 1970.

15. "Constitutional Questions," *New York Daily News*, September 8, 1970.

16. Harry S. Ashmore, "Rexford Tugwell, Man of Thought, Man of Action," *Center Magazine*, September 1970.

17. Quoted in Karl E. Meyer, "Clark Rejects Bid by Tugwell for New Constitution," *Washington Post*, November 12, 1970.

18. Ibid.

19. Ashmore to Hutchins and Malcolm Moos, "The Center Communications Program," memorandum, December 12, 1973.

20. Hutchins to Wilder, March 1, 1972. (Y)

21. Hutchins to Wilder, January 18, 1973. (Y)

22. Norman Cousins, interview with the author.

23. Hutchins to Wilder, March 22, 1972. (Y)

CHAPTER FORTY-SIX

1. Hutchins to Wilder, August 14, 1972. (Y)

2. Hutchins to Wilder, June 9, 1972. The reference is to vandalism practiced on the Michelangelo sculpture. (Y)

3. Harrison, *The Enthusiast*, 267.

4. Hutchins to Wilder, September 19, 1972. (Y)

5. Hutchins to Wilder, September 17, 1973. (Y)

6. Wilder to Hutchins, March 14, 1972.

7. Hutchins to Wilder, July 14, 1972. (Y)

8. The Center fellows also participated in the conference, along with Blair Clark, the former director of CBS News and a Center board member; Lloyd Cutler, the Washington counsel to CBS; Reuven Frank, the former president of NBC News; Harry Kalven, a professor of law at the University of Chicago; James Loper, the president of KCET in Los Angeles and the former chairman of the Public Broadcasting Service; Newton Minow, a former chairman of the FCC; Paul Porter, another former chairman of the FCC; Lawrence H. Rogers II, the president of the Taft Broadcasting Company; Richard Salant, the president of CBS News; Antonin Scalia, the former general counsel of the White House Office of Telecommunications Policy; Eric Sevareid, the CBS commentator; Harold Willens, a Center board member and the codirector of Business Executives Move for Peace in Vietnam; and Thomas H. Wolf, a vice president of ABC News.

9. Harry S. Ashmore, *Fear in the Air: Broadcasting and the First Amendment: The Anatomy of a Constitutional Crisis* (New York: W. W. Norton, 1973), 179–180.

10. Hutchins to Wilder, April 27, 1972. (Y)

11. Sander Vanocur, interview with the author.

12. Quoted in *Center Report*, December 1973. Angus MacLean Thuermer, who was in the press section with Jim Anderson of UPI, recalled that as one of Kissinger's hecklers was being hustled out of the hall, he was heard demanding to be taken to Robert Maynard Hutchins: "Without breaking step or tempo, the 'Pacem in Terris' security man responded, as he passed by Jim and me, 'I am his surrogate.' Surrogate. Jim and I looked at each other in astonishment. 'Just for a change,' Jim said, 'it's nice to cover a riot that has a bit of class.' " There were in fact no security men; the hustler was Peter Tagger, the Center's staff fund-raising specialist.

13. Secretary Kissinger and Senator Fulbright were the keynote speakers. Among the others who spoke or served as panelists were Clark Clifford, the former secretary of defense; Marsall Shulman, the director of the Russian Research Institute at Columbia; Paul E. Warnke, a former assistant secretary of defense; the Reverend Theodore Hesburgh, the president of Notre Dame; former ambassadors John Kenneth Galbraith,

Edwin O. Reischauer, Sol M. Linowitz, Charles W. Yost, and Edward M. Korry; Bradford Morse, an under-secretary of the UN; Stanley Hoffman, a professor of government at Harvard; Herbert York, a science adviser to Presidents Eisenhower and Kennedy; Richard Barnet, the codirector of the Institute for Policy Studies; Robert W. Tucker, a professor of political science at Johns Hopkins; Hans J. Morgenthau, a professor of international relations at the City University of New York; John Paton Davies, a China policy expert; Peter G. Peterson, a former secretary of commerce; senators Frank Church, Abraham Ribicoff, Hubert H. Humphrey, Edmund S. Muskie, George McGovern, and Sam J. Ervin, Jr.; and James C. Thompson, Jr., the curator of the Nieman Foundation at Harvard. Among the journalists who served on the various panels were David Halberstam, Gloria Emerson, Frances FitzGerald, Peter Lisagor, Pauline Frederick, Leslie H. Gelb, Ronald Steel, and George F. Will.

14. Hutchins to Wilder, July 18, 1973. William Benton died March 18, 1973. Hutchins, who had had minor surgery to correct a hernia, wrote to Wilder on March 25, "I pulled myself out of bed and went to Bill Benton's funeral in Southport. The hydraulic engineers, who had failed me for weeks, saw me through this crisis. But I was so afraid of meeting Maude, a close friend of Helen Benton, that I was afraid of exploding at any time and got out of there as fast as I could." (Y)

15. Hutchins to Wilder, August 24, 1973. (Y)
16. Hutchins to Wilder, September 1, 1973. (Y)
17. Hutchins to Wilder, October 4, 1973. (Y)
18. Minutes, executive session of the board of directors, Fund for the Republic, Inc., October 8, 1973.
19. Ibid.
20. Kelly, *Court of Reason*, 510.
21. Ibid.
22. Hutchins to Wilder, November 5, 1973. (Y)

Chapter Forty-Seven

1. The board at the time of Moos's election was made up of Ralph E. Ablon, Joseph Antonow, Harry S. Ashmore, Blair Clark, Ramsey Clark, Patrick F. Crowley, Fagan Dickson, James H. Douglas, Jr., James C. Downs, Jr., Joseph W. Drown, Arnold M. Grant, Robert M. Hutchins, Vesta Hutchins, Francis J. Lally, Edward Lamb, Eulah C. Laucks, W. Price Laughlin, Morris L. Levinson, J. Howard Marshall, Frances McAllister, Stewart Mott, Paul Newman, Seniel Ostrow, Bernard Rapoport, J. R. Parten, Eleanor B. Stevenson, Bernard Weissbourd, and Harold Willens.
2. Kelly, *Court of Reason*, 511.
3. Ibid., 512. In his introduction to *Court of Reason* Kelly acknowledged that the book had been written with Parten's encouragement, "under the auspices of Boston University with a financial grant from the Parten Foundation."
4. Ibid., 508.
5. Ibid., 513.
6. Moos to Ashmore, November 23, 1973.
7. Ashmore to Moos, December 4, 1973.
8. Hutchins to Moos, December 5, 1973.
9. Ashmore to Hutchins and Moos, "The Center Communications Program," memorandum, December 21, 1973.
10. Kelly, *Court of Reason*, 529.
11. Ibid., 527.
12. Ashmore to Moos, January 21, 1974.
13. Quoted in Kelly, *Court of Reason*, 529.
14. Hutchins to Wilder, January 21, 1974. (Y)
15. Quoted in Kelly, *Court of Reason*, 531.

16. Ashmore to J. R. Parten, "Reorganization of the Center," memorandum, January 15, 1975.

17. Kelly, *Court of Reason*, 535.

18. Hutchins to Wilder, March 11, 1974. (Y)

19. The directors selected by Moos were L. Emmerson Ward, the chairman of the board of governors of the Mayo Clinic; Bernard H. Ridder, Jr., the publisher of the *St. Paul Pioneer-Dispatch;* and Arthur A. Burck, a Palm Beach management consultant.

20. See note 17 above.

21. Blair Clark, "The Future of the Center," resolution presented to the board of the Fund for the Republic, May 17, 1974.

22. Quoted in "Harvey Wheeler: Utopian in an Apocalyptic Age," an interview with Mary Harvey, *Center Report*, April 1971.

23. Ibid.

24. Quoted in Kelly, *Court of Reason*, 544–545.

25. Hutchins to Wilder, December 3, 1974. (Y)

26. Quoted in Kelly, *Court of Reason*, 574.

27. Hutchins to Wilder, April 23, 1975. (Y)

28. Hutchins to Wilder, March 24, 1975. (Y)

29. Quoted in the *Los Angeles Times*, May 16, 1975.

CHAPTER FORTY-EIGHT

1. Wilder to Hutchins, May 18, 1975.

2. Hutchins to Wilder, June 9, 1975. (Y)

3. Wilder to Hutchins, June 10, 1975.

4. *Center Magazine*, July–August 1975.

5. Ibid.

6. Hutchins to Wilder, undated, July 1975. (Y)

7. Among the headliners at "Pacem in Terris IV" were William Colby, the director of the CIA, who was teamed up with Charles Morgan, the executive director of the American Civil Liberties Union, and Vernon Jordan, the president of the Urban League; Roberto Guyer, the under-secretary of the United Nations, along with Daniel P. Moynihan, the outspoken American ambassador; George F. Kennan, the veteran foreign-policy expert; James S. Schlesinger, the former secretary of defense, and Admiral Elmo Zumwalt, the retired chief of naval operations; William E. Simon, the secretary of the treasury; James P. Grant, the president of the Overseas Development Corporation, and Robert O. Anderson, the president of Atlantic Richfield; and nine senators and seven representatives, including the ranking Republicans and Democrats on the key congressional committees. The panels were studded with such leading academic experts as Hans J. Morgenthau, Herbert York, Kenneth Thompson, and Robert E. Osgood.

The edited transcripts of the convocation were published in three paperback volumes: Fred Warner Neal, ed., *Pacem in Terris IV: American Foreign Policy at Home and Abroad in the Bicentennial Year* (Santa Barbara: Center for the Study of Democratic Institutions, 1976).

8. Minutes, board of directors' meeting, Fund for the Republic, April 13, 1976.

9. The Parten-Hutchins correspondence is excerpted in Kelly, *Court of Reason*, 612–616.

10. The new board members were Harold Fleming, the president of the Potomac Institute in Washington; Frederick M. Nicholas, a Los Angeles attorney; Maurine Rothschild, a New York civic activist; and four Chicagoans, Albert E. Jenner, an attorney, Philip M. Klutznick and Marshall Bennett, both real-estate developers, and J. Anthony Downs, a development consultant.

The holdover members were Joseph P. Antonow, Harry S. Ashmore, Ramsey Clark, James H. Douglas, Jr., Vesta Hutchins, Francis J. Lally, Edward Lamb, Eulah C.

Laucks, Frances McAllister, Stewart Mott, Paul Newman, Seniel Ostrow, Bernard Rapoport, Ralph W. Tyler, and Bernard Weissbourd.

11. Minutes, board of trustees' meeting, April 13, 1976.

12. Quoted in Kelly, *Court of Reason*, 637.

13. Quoted in "Get Ready for Anything," an interview with Robert M. Hutchins on the twenty-fifth anniversary of Hutchins's election as president of the Fund for the Republic, *Center Report*, June 1975.

14. Ibid.

15. Hutchins, "Why We Need World Law," *World Issues*, December 1976.

16. Hutchins to Wilder, December 14, 1971. (Y)

17. Hutchins to Wilder, April 27, 1972. (Y)

18. Hutchins, "The Great Anti-School Campaign," *The Great Ideas Today: 1972* (Chicago: Encyclopaedia Britannica, Inc., 1972), 220.

19. Hutchins, "Two Fateful Decisions," *Center Magazine*, January–February 1975.

20. Quoted in "Court OKs Fees to Ride School Bus: No Constitutional Right to Education, Justices Maintain," *Los Angeles Times*, June 25, 1988.

21. Quoted in Kelly, *Court of Reason*, 639.

22. Robert M. Hutchins, remarks, Thornton Wilder Memorial Service, Battell Chapel, Yale University, January 18, 1976.

23. Quoted in Harry S. Ashmore, ed., *The William O. Douglas Inquiry into the State of Individual Freedom* (Boulder: Westview Press, 1979), x. The contributors were twelve practicing attorneys and law professors who had been clerks for Justice Douglas. The essays served as background material for a two-day convocation in Washington on December 7 and 8, 1978. Although confined to a wheelchair, Justice Douglas was able to attend the dinner at which Chief Justice Warren Burger and other leading Washington figures paid him tribute.

24. Ibid.

CHAPTER FORTY-NINE

1. During his brief visit Adler had lunch with Clifton Fadiman, who had been an intimate friend since their undergraduate days at Columbia. Fadiman recalled that in the course of their gloomy reflections on the loss of Hutchins, Adler suddenly interrupted to say, "Of course I'll deliver the eulogy at your funeral, Kip, but who will deliver mine?" (Fadiman was born in 1904, Adler in 1902.)

2. The memorial addresses delivered in Rockefeller Chapel on June 8, 1977, were published in *Center Magazine* for September–October 1977, as were the quotations I read at the Santa Barbara memorial on May 20.

3. Ibid.

4. *Washington Post*, May 18, 1977.

5. Hutchins to Luce, August 8, 1949. (T-L)

6. Hutchins to Wilder, July 18, 1973. (Y)

7. In their extensive correspondence there is nothing to suggest that Wilder ever indicated his sexual preference or that Hutchins might have divined it — and I doubt that in any case it would have made any difference to their relationship. Gilbert A. Harrison, who had unrestricted access to Wilder's correspondence and journals and to his family and most intimate friends, wrote in his definitive biography,

> What we know of Thornton's most intimate companions is that any physical encounter was brief, awkward and left Thornton discomfited and probably remorseful. . . .
>
> Nowhere in his writing, private or public, is there any outright declaration about his sexual nature. . . .
>
> He had, of course, a reputation to protect, which dictated steering close to accepted decorum. Equally constraining was devotion to family — his own and

the idea of family. Any advertised act repugnant to the conventional sexual code would have been insufferable. One might be led into such acts by the necessities of one's makeup, but they had to be concealed. If he had been born thirty years later his story might have been different. Whether it would have been happier or more productive is unanswerable. (*The Enthusiast*, 167–169)

8. Ibid., 380.

9. See note 2 above.

10. The first phrase is from the obituary editorial in the *Washington Post*, May 18, 1977, the second from the *Washington Star* of the same date.

11. Hutchins, address, student convocation, University of Chicago, June 14, 1946.

12. Mrs. Luce was one of the celebrities converted to Catholicism by the noted evangelist Bishop Fulton J. Sheen, and like many converts she became an impassioned evangelist herself. Hutchins was highly amused by the no doubt apocryphal story that on her first visit to the Pope after she became ambassador to Italy, she was interrupted by His Holiness, who gently said, "You don't seem to understand, Mrs. Luce. I'm already a Catholic."

13. Hutchins to Luce, December 1, 1958. (T-L)

14. Arthur A. Cohen, "Robert Maynard Hutchins: The Educator As Moralist," in Cohen, *Humanistic Education and Western Civilization*, 11.

15. Hutchins, Bedell Lecture, Kenyon College, 1948.

16. Hutchins, "The Intellectual Community."

17. Ibid.

18. Ibid.

19. *Providence Journal*, May 17, 1977.

20. *Chicago Tribune*, May 19, 1977.

21. Nicholas von Hoffman, *Wilmington Morning News*, May 25, 1977.

22. Hutchins to Wilder, October 1, 1974. (Y)

23. Allan Bloom, *The Closing of the American Mind: How American Education Has Failed Democracy and Impoverished the Souls of Students* (New York: Simon & Schuster, 1987), 346.

24. Ibid., 344.

25. Russell Jacoby, "The Lost Intellectual: Relativism and the American Mind," *New Perspectives Quarterly*, Winter 1988.

26. Bloom, *The Closing of the American Mind*, 381.

27. See note 25 above.

28. Jeff Lyon, "The Last Pedagogue," *Chicago Tribune Magazine*, November 27, 1988.

29. Quoted in Adler, *The Paideia Proposal: An Educational Manifesto*, 6. Adler incorporated a "stinging critique" of Allan Bloom in "Great Books, Democracy and Truth," the prologue to a collection of his articles on liberal education and the Great Books, published over the years 1940–1988. He gave the book the pointed title *Reforming Education: The Opening of the American Mind* (New York: Macmillan, 1989).

30. Cohen, "Robert Maynard Hutchins," 7.

31. See note 16 above.

32. Quoted in "Eric Sevareid Televises Talk with Robert Hutchins," *Center Report*, June 1976.

33. Ibid.

Bibliographic Notes

When he prepared the "Bibliography of Robert M. Hutchins, 1925–50" for the *Journal of General Education*, Reuben Frodin included 299 entries, most of them citing scholarly publications. Hutchins, he noted, had "fulfilled more than eight hundred public engagements; and as must be the case with a university administrator, the writing done for these occasions forms the bulk of his publication."

Over the next quarter century Hutchins's secretary, Esther Donnelly, tried to keep the bibliography up to date, but it proved to be an all but impossible task. Until his last years there was no significant reduction in his speaking engagements, and texts of his speeches continued to be widely published and republished in academic and professional journals. From time to time he prepared selected speeches for publication in book form. The following titles are collections of this sort:

No Friendly Voice. Chicago: University of Chicago Press, 1936.

The Higher Learning in America. New Haven: Yale University Press, 1936.

Education for Freedom. Baton Rouge: Louisiana State University Press, 1943.

Education and Democracy. Chicago: University of Chicago Press, 1948.

Saint Thomas and the World State. Milwaukee: Marquette University Press, 1949.

Morals, Religion, and Higher Education. Chicago: University of Chicago Press, 1950.

The Democratic Dilemma: The Gottesman Lectures, University of Uppsala. Stockholm: Alqvist & Wiksells Boktrycker, 1951.

Some Questions about Education in North America: The Marfleet Lectures. Toronto: University of Toronto Press, 1952.

The Conflict in Education in a Democratic Society. New York: Harper & Brothers, 1953. This volume combines the Gottesman and Marfleet lectures.

The University of Utopia: The Walgreen Lectures. Chicago: University of Chicago Press, 1953.

Some Observations on American Education: The Sir George Watson Lectures. London: Cambridge University Press, 1956.

Freedom, Education and the Fund. New York: Meridian Books, 1956.

The following titles were written by Hutchins specifically for publication:

A Free and Responsible Press. Chicago: University of Chicago Press, 1947. While Hutchins is credited only with the foreword, this report of the Commission on Freedom of the Press was rewritten by him in its final form.

The Great Conversation. Chicago: Encyclopaedia Britannica, Inc., 1952. This is the introductory volume for those texts in the Great Books of the Western World series that were published under Hutchins's direction as editor in chief.

The Learning Society. New York: Frederick A. Praeger, 1968. This was originally written as a book-length essay for *Britannica Perspectives*, the three-volume work issued in 1968 to commemorate the two-hundredth anniversary of the encyclopedia.

Zuckerkandl! New York: Grove Press, 1968. This short version of Hutchins's satire on the followers of Sigmund Freud was illustrated with drawings taken from an art-film cartoon treatment. An extended version was published in *Center Magazine* for September–October 1975.

Along with Mortimer Adler, Hutchins served as co-editor of two volumes published in the Great Ideas Anthologies series:

The Humanities Today. New York: Arno Press, 1977.
The Social Sciences Today. New York: Arno Press, 1977.

There has been no previous biography of Hutchins, though a number of books deal in whole or in part with aspects of his career. The most important of these are:

Cohen, Arthur A., ed. *Humanistic Education and Western Civilization.* New York: Holt, Rinehart & Winston, 1965. This collection of essays was prepared as a tribute to Hutchins on his sixty-fifth birthday. The contributors were Mortimer Adler, Elisabeth Mann Borgese, Scott Buchanan, William O. Douglas, Philip Jessup, Bertrand de Jouvenel, Humayun Kabir, Milton Mayer, Richard P. McKeon, John Courtney Murray, S.J., David Reisman, Rexford G. Tugwell, F. Champion Ward, and O. Meredith Wilson.
Gideonse, Harry D. *The Higher Learning in a Democracy: A Reply to President Hutchins' Critique of the American University.* New York: Farrar & Rinehart, 1937.
Macdonald, Dwight. *The Ford Foundation: The Men and the Millions.* New York: Reynal & Company, 1956.
Purcell, Edward A., Jr. *The Crisis of Democratic Theory.* Lexington: University of Kentucky Press, 1973.
Reeves, Thomas C. *Freedom and the Foundation: The Fund for the Republic in the Era of McCarthyism.* New York: Alfred A. Knopf, 1969.
Tannler, Albert M. *One in Spirit: A Retrospective View of the University of Chicago.* Chicago: University of Chicago Library, 1973.
Taylor, Harold. *Students without Teachers.* New York: McGraw-Hill, 1969.
Ward, F. Champion, ed. *The Idea and Practice of General Education: An Account of the College of the University of Chicago.* Chicago: University of Chicago Press, 1950.

A number of biographical volumes devote significant passages to Hutchins:

Adler, Mortimer J. *Philosopher at Large: An Intellectual Autobiography.* New York: Macmillan, 1977.
Douglas, William O. *Go East Young Man: The Early Years.* New York: Random House, 1974.
Harrison, Gilbert A. *The Enthusiast: A Life of Thornton Wilder.* New York: Ticknor & Fields, 1983.
Hyman, Sidney. *The Lives of William Benton.* Chicago: University of Chicago Press, 1969.
Jones, Dorothy V. *Harold Swift and the Higher Learning.* Chicago: University of Chicago Library, 1985.
Kelly, Frank K. *Court of Reason: Robert Hutchins and the Fund for the Republic.* New York: The Free Press, 1981. This memoir deals with Kelly's experience as public-relations vice president of the Fund and his break with Hutchins after the appointment of Malcolm Moos as president.
Nef, John U. *The Search for Meaning: The Autobiography of a Nonconformist.* Washington: Public Affairs Press, 1973.
Russell, Carroll Mason. *The University of Chicago and Me, 1901–1962.* Privately

printed, 1982. This memoir by Mrs. Russell, a Chicago trustee's wife who grew up in the university community, is in the Special Collections of the University Library.

Smith, T. V. *A Non-Existent Man: An Autobiography*. Austin: University of Texas Press, 1962.

Other book-length publications quoted in the text are cited in the chapter notes.

PERIODICALS

In addition to his contributions to scholarly publications, Hutchins in the course of his tenure at Chicago began to write frequently for such magazines as *Harper's*, *Atlantic Monthly*, and *Saturday Evening Post*. At the request of his friend Henry Luce he even contributed a derogatory article on college football for the initial edition of *Sports Illustrated*.

The Fund for the Republic, which Hutchins took over in 1953, published a number of essay-style occasional papers and other publications to which Hutchins contributed. After he established the Center for the Study of Democratic Institutions, most of his written works appeared in its *Center Magazine*. Between 1967, when the magazine was launched, and his death in 1977, Hutchins is listed in the cumulative index (*Center Magazine*, January–February 1978) as the author of forty-nine articles. His work also appeared more than a score of times in *Center Report*, a less formal Center publication.

He was a frequent participant in the National Broadcasting Company's weekly radio broadcast "The University of Chicago Roundtable," which originated on the campus, and his remarks were transcribed and distributed by the network in pamphlet form. At the Center, which recorded and transcribed its "Basic Issues" dialogues, Hutchins's comments were included in published versions of the discussion. He can be heard on more than seventy edited audiotapes of these sessions, which were distributed in cassettes to radio stations, libraries, and individual purchasers.

Beginning in the 1930s he contributed special articles to the *New York Times*, the *New York Herald Tribune*, and the *Chicago Daily News*. For ten years after he established the Center in Santa Barbara he wrote a weekly column, "What Kind of World?," which was distributed to some twenty newspapers by the Los Angeles Times Syndicate. And of course, newspaper articles about Hutchins were published frequently throughout his career.

Sources for quotations from periodicals, newspapers, and transcripts are cited in the chapter notes.

UNPUBLISHED SOURCES

Far and away the most extensive repository of Hutchins's papers is the University of Chicago Archives, located in the Department of Collections at the University of Chicago Library. In addition to the official archives and the files from the president's office, he left behind papers he had accumulated as secretary of the Yale Corporation and as dean of the Yale Law School. The personal files he maintained after leaving the University have been given to the Library by his widow, Vesta Hutchins.

Other important sources in the Special Collections are the papers of Harold H. Swift, Robert Redfield, William Benton, and John U. Nef. Although they are not yet available, the papers of Mortimer Adler and Walter Paepcke are expected to be added. Unless otherwise identified, as indicated below, citations in the chapter notes are from sources at the University of Chicago Library.

Much of Hutchins's correspondence with his family is now at the Hutchins Library at Berea College, where his father and his brother Francis each served as president. These citations are designated "B."

Records of his elementary school and early college days are at the Oberlin College Library, designated "O."

Sources at Yale include material at the University Library, at the Law School Library, and at the Beinecke Rare Book and Manuscript Library, which contains Hutchins's extensive correspondence with Thornton Wilder. These are designated "Y."

Hutchins's correspondence with William O. Douglas is included in the Douglas papers at the Library of Congress, designated "LC."

Records from Hutchins's tenure at the Ford Foundation are in the Ford Foundation Archives, along with pertinent oral history interviews. These are designated "F."

When the Fund for the Republic closed its headquarters in New York, its archives were deposited with the Princeton University Library. There is also Hutchins correspondence in the Adlai Stevenson papers there. Material from Princeton is designated "P."

Correspondence with Henry Luce is in the Time-Life Archives, designated "T-L."

When the Center for the Study of Democratic Institutions was turned over to the University of California at Santa Barbara, its archives were transferred to the new location on the campus. After the Center was closed down in January 1988, these files were relocated in the UCSB Library. They are designated "UCSB."

INTERVIEWS

For more than a quarter of a century I discussed Hutchins's ideas and actions with his principal associates and supporters. Quotations derived from these sources are identfied in the chapter notes as "conversations." Those provided by the more than fifty persons whom I sought out during the preparation of this volume are cited as "interviews."

Transcribed interviews conducted by others have provided important source material, and excerpts from them are identified in the chapter notes.

Three lengthy interviews with Hutchins were conducted at the Center by Milton Mayer in 1973. These were never published, but transcripts were available in my files and are also in the Hutchins papers at the University of Chicago.

Transcribed interviews by George Dell with Hutchins, Ralph Tyler, Richard P. McKeon, and Lawrence Kimpton were made available to me and are now in the University of Chicago Archives.

Oral history interviews with Ralph Tyler are available at the Bancroft Library, University of California, Berkeley.

Oral history interviews with Hutchins, Clarence Faust, and W. H. Ferry are at the Ford Foundation Archives.

Acknowledgments

Two of Robert Hutchins's longtime associates were instrumental in persuading me to undertake his biography. Maurice Mitchell worked closely with Hutchins as president of Encyclopaedia Britannica Films and later as head of the parent publishing company, and after a decade as chancellor of the University of Denver, he succeeded him as the last president of the Center for the Study of Democratic Institutions. Clifton Fadiman, the distinguished editor and critic, was associated with Hutchins in the launching of Great Books of the Western World, served on the board of editors of *Encyclopaedia Britannica*, and became an associate of the Center after he moved to Santa Barbara. Mitchell offered to raise the funds required for research and travel, and Fadiman agreed to keep his discerning eye on the manuscript as it came into being.

Encyclopaedia Britannica, Incorporated, made a major grant, and I am personally indebted to Chairman Robert Gwinn for his assistance and encouragement. Others who responded to Mitchell's call were James H. Douglas, Alvin C. Eurich, Edward Lamb, Frances McAllister, Paul Newman, and Mr. and Mrs. Ralph Wagner (Louise Benton).

With one notable exception, all those whom I have called upon to share their memories and records have been generous in their response. W. H. Ferry replied, "I think that your book about Hutchins should contain the following lines: 'W. H. Ferry declined to help in the preparation of this book.' "

I have acknowledged my debt to the Hutchins family in the preface. Another invaluable source was Mortimer Adler, who made his personal files available to me, along with his advice and counsel. This was also true of James Douglas, who unfortunately did not live to see the work completed. Others to whom I am specially indebted are Paul Armstrong, Elisabeth Mann Borgese, James Colvin, Norman Cousins, Preston Cutler, Harold C. Fleming, Erwin N. Griswold, Hallock Hoffman, Barry D. Karl, Frank K. Kelly, Clark Kerr, Jay Laughlin, Elizabeth Paepcke, Warren Preece, Martin Quigley, George Martin, Myres S. McDougal, John U. Nef, Thomas Park, Robert Saudek, Mrs. Albert W. Scherer, Eric Sevareid, Edward Shils, Carl F. Stover, Peter Tagger, Angus MacLean Thuermer, Grace Tugwell, Ralph Tyler, and F. Champion Ward.

At the University of Chicago, where much of the research was centered, I have had the blessing of President Hanna H. Gray and of President Emeritus Edward Levi, as well as the indispensable support of Robert Rosenthal, the curator of Special Collections at the Joseph Regenstein Library, and his associate, Daniel Meyer. Rosenthal found, and made room for, Keith Tuma, my research assistant, who worked full-time there for more than a year and demonstrated that he is a discerning editor as well as an accomplished scholar. And at Chicago I also enjoyed the assistance and hospitality of Norton Ginsburg, retired professor of geography; Jerald C. Brauer, Naomi Shenstone Donnelley Professor at the Divinity School; and Sidney Hyman, William Benton's biographer.

At Berea, Francis Hutchins authorized me to examine the family files located in the library that bears his and his father's name. At Oberlin, Barbara Chalsma, the director of communications, provided assistance above and beyond the call of duty. At Yale,

Professor John G. Simon of the Law School was helpful in many ways, not the least being his putting me in touch with two of Hutchins's surviving New Haven contemporaries, Morris Tyler and James Cooper, to whom I am also indebted.

In the several libraries and archives where I have sought documentary material, the staffs have been cordial and helpful. I am specially grateful to Elaine Felsher at the Time, Inc., Archives, Sharon Bishop Laist at the Ford Foundation, Patricia C. Willis of the Beinecke Library at Yale, William Bigglestone, the Oberlin archivist, and Mrs. Malca Chall at the University of California's Bancroft Library.

My daughter, Anne Ashmore, a research librarian at the United States Supreme Court, went next door to search collections at the Library of Congress on my behalf. Patricia Douglas made her way through the unsorted files of the Center for the Study of Democratic Institutions, which have been deposited at the University of California at Santa Barbara.

I owe a special debt to four observers of Hutchins's career who made unpublished material available. F. Champion Ward, who served as dean of the undergraduate College at Chicago, allowed me to use excerpts from "Requiem for the Hutchins College: Recollections and Reflections," a memoir still in preparation. Edward Shils, Distinguished Service Professor at the University of Chicago, gave me access to an eloquent, discerning essay he wrote at the time of Hutchins's death. George Dell, now retired as professor of speech at San Francisco State University, turned over material he had compiled for an unpublished biography, including a number of transcribed interviews. Frank Keegan, the former president of Salem State College, also made available source material he had gathered in a similar endeavor.

Finally, the biography would not have been possible without the encouragement and good offices of my Little, Brown editors, Roger Donald, Ray Roberts, and Rick Tetzeli, and copyeditor, Dorothy Straight, who saw the manuscript through to print.

Index

ABC. *See* American Broadcasting Company
Academic freedom, 58, 61, 62, 185;
    Hutchins's views on, 54, 76, 113, 128–
    129, 153, 171, 242, 245, 248, 304, 305,
    330, 375, 536
Adler, Mortimer, 51–52, 90, 190, 217, 270,
    288, 367, 568n.13, 579n.1; at Aspen In-
    stitute, 285–286; Basic Issues program,
    388–389; Bloom vs., 539, 580n.29;
    at Columbia, 51–52, 85, 98, 103, 104;
    Encyclopaedia Britannica and, 430, 431,
    559n.9; Great Books and, 98, 99–100,
    101–102, 103, 118, 139, 147, 259, 285–
    286, 538, 551n.6; Great Books publishing
    project, 259–260, 336, 337, 408, 430,
    549n.6; Hutchins's death and, 528, 529,
    531; influence on Hutchins, 85–86, 97,
    98–99, 103–104, 110–111, 147, 171–
    172, 297, 531; Institute for Philosophical
    Research, 167, 319–320, 408, 431;
    liberal-arts college, plan for, 167–168,
    189; Maude Hutchins and, 52, 173–174,
    175; "Paideia Proposal," 539–540,
    554n.7; religion/Thomism, 139, 159–160,
    162, 167, 172, 531, 553n.15, 553n.25;
    St. John's College, 140, 189; at Univer-
    sity of Chicago, 85–87, 90, 93, 95–96,
    103–104, 105, 137, 138, 139, 167, 171–
    172, 189–190; at University of Chicago,
    Chicago Fight, 154, 157, 158, 166–167,
    169–170
"Administrator Reconsidered, The" (Hutchins
    speech), 378–379
Adult education, 70, 145–146, 246, 260, 273,
    388
AFL, 217. *See also* AFL-CIO
AFL-CIO, 389. *See also* CIO
Against the American Grain (Macdonald),
    337
Agar, Herbert, 206
Agnew, Spiro, 495

"Aims of Education, The" (Eliot lectures),
    272
Alamogordo, New Mexico, 252
Alerted Americans Group, 356
Alexander and Green, 36, 44
Allen, James Sloan, 273, 285–286
Allentown, Pennsylvania, 17, 18, 19, 23, 33,
    369
All in One Lifetime (Byrnes), 252
All Souls College, 380
Alpha Delta Phi, 27, 78, 110
Alumni Fund Association (Yale), 41
"America and the War" (Hutchins speech),
    215
America First Committee, 213–214, 217,
    218–219, 255–256; membership, 557n.7
American, 117, 128
Americana Hotel symposium, 421–422. *See
    also* "Prospects for Democracy" convo-
    cations
American Association of Colleges for Teacher
    Education, 322
American Association of University Professors
    (AAUP), 128, 143, 178, 191
American Baptist Education Society, 58
American Broadcasting Company (ABC), 321,
    367, 576n.8
American Catholic Philosophical Association,
    159
"American Century" (*Life*), 433
American Character study (Center for the
    Study of Democratic Institutions), 409–
    410, 417–418, 426; conference, 410 (par-
    ticipants, 570n.5)
American College of Surgeons, 144
American Committee for Cultural Freedom,
    362
American Dilemma, An (Myrdal), 421
American Friends Service Committee, 319,
    340, 350
American Individualism (Hoover), 130

American Institute of Architects, 268
American Legion, 130, 184; vs. Fund for the
    Republic, 340, 345, 352, 361, 373, 376
American Red Cross, 131
American Society of Newspaper Editors, 145,
    297
American Society of Planning Officials, 268
American Vigilant Intelligence Federation, 130
Amherst College, 104, 238, 260, 409,
    565n.25
Anderson, Robert O., 373
Anderson, Sherwood, 106
Andover Theological Seminary, 6
Angell, James Rowland, 48–49; Hutchins and,
    at Yale, 29–30, 38, 39, 40, 42, 44, 46,
    47, 48–49, 60; Institute of Human Rela-
    tions, 52, 53; at University of Chicago,
    49, 90
Anti-intellectualism, 235; scientific method
    and, 156, 157, 158, 161; of student
    protest movement, 448, 467
Anti-Semitism, 55, 183, 213, 250
Antonow, Joseph, 519, 577n.1, 578n.10
Aquinas, Thomas/Thomism, 139, 189, 320,
    409, 531, 553n.15; Hutchins and, 158–
    160, 162–163, 166, 170–171, 172, 240,
    297, 328, 337, 529, 553n.25
Arendt, Hannah, 230
Arens, Richard, 370, 371
Argonne National Laboratory, 266
Aristotle, 124, 139, 154; Hutchins's theories
    and, 117, 118, 158, 163, 166, 188–189,
    211, 280, 281–282, 297, 523, 532
Arkansas Gazette, 432; Ashmore and, 348,
    349, 359, 388; desegregation crisis and,
    388, 397
Arkansas State Teachers College, 348
Armance (Stendhal), 286
Armitage, John, 402
Armstrong, Paul, 403
Army Ambulance Corps, Oberlin unit, 17, 18,
    19, 22, 23
Army Corps of Engineers, 251
Army Specialized Training Program, 228
Arnold, Matthew, 36, 246, 522
Aron, Raymond, 430
Art and Prudence (Adler), 167
Asheville School, 23–24
Ashmore, Harry S., 347–348, 352, 418, 419,
    425, 465–466, 488, 572n.6; Basic Issues
    program, 387–388; with Center for the
    Study of Democratic Institutions, 396,
    397–398, 412, 415–416, 463–465, 470,
    471–472, 473, 474, 477, 478, 485, 48   6,

489–490, 495–496, 516, 536, 578n.10;
    Center under Moos, 505–509, 510, 512,
    513, 577n.1; civil-rights movement, 348–
    349, 388, 397, 399; *Encyclopaedia Bri-
    tannica* revision, 402–403, 406–407,
    416, 427, 428–430, 431, 442, 463; Fund
    for the Republic and, 347–349, 378, 383,
    567–568n.5; Hanoi trip, 453–458;
    Hutchins's memorial service, 528;
    "Pacem in Terris" convocations, 427,
    432, 442, 443–444, 452–458, 517–518,
    526; Parvin Foundation and, 411, 442,
    482, 484–485; press-commission project,
    397, 399–400; in Stevenson campaign,
    359, 360, 383, 402
Ashmore Report, 349
*Asian Dilemma: United States, Japan and
    China* (Center for the Study of Demo-
    cratic Institutions), 478
Aspen Company, 274, 283
Aspen Executive Seminars, 285, 561n.30
Aspen Institute for Humanistic Studies, 274,
    285–286, 522, 561n.30
Associated Press (AP), 365, 457
Association of American Law Schools, 46
Association of Motion Picture Producers, 369
Association of the Bar of the City of New
    York, 344
Astor, David, 292
Athens, 411–412
Atlantic Monthly, 173, 325
Atomic bomb. *See* Nuclear weapons
Atomic Energy Commission, 260, 266
Atomic Energy Control Conference, 260–262

Baggs, William C., 570n.4; Hanoi trip, 452,
    453, 455, 456, 458
Bailey, Walter K., 12
Baldwin, James, 448
Ball, George, 456
Baltimore Sun, 503
Baptist Union Theological Seminary, 58
Barden, John, 157
Barr, Stringfellow: Buchanan and, 104, 137,
    138–139, 473; Center for the Study of
    Democratic Institutions and, 429, 447–
    448, 463, 473; on Committee to Frame a
    World Constitution, 270; Great Books
    and, 99, 147, 260, 549n.6; at St. John's
    College, 140, 189; at University of Chi-
    cago, 99, 137, 138–139, 190; at Univer-
    sity of Virginia, 99, 137
Barrymore, Ethel, 99, 315
Barth, Karl, 394

Bartky, Walter, 251

Barzun, Jacques, 98, 404, 572n.9

Basic Issues program, 381–391; Athens dialogue, 411–412; at Center for the Study of Democratic Institutions, 391, 394, 395, 396, 398–399, 401, 403, 408, 409, 410, 411–412; criticism of/opposition to, 377, 382–385, 388–389; *Encyclopaedia Britannica* revision and, 403, 408, 409; origins of, 379–381, 386–387, 388–389; problems with, 388, 389–390; publications of, 387, 388, 389; residence for, 390, 391–392. *See also* Center for the Study of Democratic Institutions; Fund for the Republic

Bayer, Herbert, 283

Beaux Arts Institute of Design, 44

Bedell Lectures (Hutchins), 281

Bedford Presbyterian Church, 3, 4, 5

Bell, Laird, 217, 292, 306, 566n.7; University of Chicago reform, 237, 242, 244–245, 305, 309; Walgreen Case and, 130, 131

Bellman, Richard, 476

Bellow, Saul, 231

Belmont, Mrs. August, 65

Benedict, St., quoted, 398–399, 569n.1

Bennington College, 294

Benton, Elma, 185–186, 214

Benton, Helen, 181, 259, 293, 577n.14

Benton, William, 31, 179–186, 208, 254, 286, 288, 347, 425, 557n.9, 577n.14; *Encyclopaedia Britannica* and, 255–259, 378, 400, 401, 402, 403, 416, 426–427, 428, 430–431, 499; Ford Foundation and, 302–303; Great Books and, 259, 292, 336, 337; Hutchins and, 179, 180, 183–184, 185, 193, 262, 265, 288, 416, 428; press-commission project, 294, 397; as right-wing target, 325; at University of Chicago, 180–186, 202, 203, 241, 254, 255, 555n.13; World War II and, 206, 207, 214, 215, 217, 218, 219, 251

Benton & Bowles, 180, 181, 182, 557n.9

Berea College, 4, 25–26, 27, 34, 303, 314

Berelson, Bernard, 319, 564n.16

Berle, A. A., Jr., 384, 387, 388, 569n.2

Berlin, Isaiah, 230, 568n.13

Bernard, Claude, 156

Bernstein, George A., 279

Bessie, Alvah, 568n.11

"Best Physician Is Also a Philosopher, The" (Galen), 144

Bigelow, Dean, 85

Billings Hospital, 232, 247

Bill of Rights, 343, 344, 351, 355, 360, 369, 374, 375, 381, 495, 526. *See also* Constitution, US

Biltmore Hotel symposium/convocation, 421. *See also* "Prospects for Democracy" convocations

Bingham, Barry, 314, 379

Black, Hugo, 196, 410

Blacklisting study (Fund for the Republic), 345, 362, 367–372, 375, 379, 410, 567n.10

Black Muslims, 448

Blacks, 128, 216, 306–307, 376, 397; education and, 9, 25, 336, 341, 342, 346–347, 348–349, 359, 374, 388, 397, 483, 523–524, 538; militancy, and student protest movement, 441, 444, 445, 448–449, 450, 467. *See also* Civil rights/civil liberties; Civil-rights movement; Desegregation

Blair, Mildred, 12

Block, Herbert Lawrence. *See* Herblock

Bloom, Allan, 537–539, 580n.29

Bloy, Leon, 253

Bond Club of New York, 147

"Book-of-the-Millennium Club, The" (Macdonald), 337

Book-of-the-Month Club, 256

Boorstin, Daniel, 67, 230

Borgese, Elisabeth Mann, 160, 270, 284, 429, 477–478; Center for the Study of Democratic Institutions and, 456, 468, 473, 477, 516; "Pacem in Maribus" convocations, 477–478, 487

Borgese, Giuseppe Antonio, 116, 205–207, 270, 507, 550n.19; Goethe Bicentennial Celebration, 282, 283, 561n.25; world-government constitution, 262–263, 269, 277, 280

Bork, Robert H., 536

Bosch, Juan, 442

Boucher, Chauncey Samuel, 74, 75, 92, 93, 99

Boulding, Kenneth, 393, 575n.8

Bowles, Chester, 180, 181, 214, 347, 383, 557n.7, 557n.9

Brademas, John, 411

Brady, James, 395, 411

Brandeis, Louis Dembitz, 196, 197, 198, 488

Brandeis University, 445, 446, 449

Brewster, Kingman, 213, 490

Bridge of San Luis Rey, The (Wilder), 105

Bridges, Harry, 371

Britain: educational system, 149; "Pacem in
Terris II" and, 443; World War II and,
190, 204, 205, 210, 214, 216, 218
Broder, David, 114–115
Bronson, Clarissa. *See* Hutchins, Clarissa
Bronson, Roddy, 465, 574n.3
Brooke, Edward W., 456, 573n.10
Brooklyn, 3, 5, 8
Browder, Earl, 355, 357, 364
Brown, Harrison, 396, 421, 426, 569n.2; on
Hutchins at University of Chicago, 304–
305
Brownlee, James F., 332, 565n.25
Brown University, 70, 87
Brown v. *Board of Education*, 346, 348, 349,
374, 523, 525
Brüning, Heinrich, 283
Bryan, Malcolm, 332, 347, 565n.25
Buchanan, Scott, 104, 137–138, 167; Basic
Issues program, 384, 387, 388, 473,
569n.2; Center for the Study of Demo-
cratic Institutions and, 394, 447, 463,
569–570n.2; *Encyclopaedia Britannica*
revision, 405–406, 429; Great Books and,
98, 99, 260, 549n.6; influence on
Hutchins, 147; politics and, 440–441,
447; at St. John's College, 140–141; at
University of Chicago, 85–86, 99, 104,
137–139, 140, 190, 551n.6
Buckley, William F., Jr., 361, 457
Bulletin (Fund for the Republic), 367
Bunche, Ralph, 441, 564n.9
Bundy, McGeorge, 400, 456; on Hutchins and
world-government constitution, 279–280
Bundy, William, 453, 455
Burck, Arthur A., 512, 513, 578n.19
Burdick, Eugene, 384, 387, 413–414, 421,
571n.11
Burger, Warren, 494–495, 579n.23
Burns, Arthur, 421
Burton, Ernest DeWitt, 74
Burtt, E. A., 86–87
Bush, Vannevar, 265
Butler, Nicholas Murray, 50, 122, 168, 200
Byrnes, James F., 251–252

Cadenhead, Gary, 489, 500, 510, 511
Calabresi, Guido, 48
Calder, Ritchie. *See* Ritchie-Calder, Lord
Calhoun, John C., 347
California Institute of Technology (CalTech),
396, 414, 423, 424
Calvinism, 5, 6, 13, 26, 27, 33, 88, 210, 433,
532. *See also* Hutchins, Robert Maynard:

Puritan/Calvinist heritage; Presbyterian-
ism; Puritanism
Campaign Practices Act, 519
Campbell, William O., 411
Canham, Erwin, 337
Capp, Al, 354
Capps, Walter, 516
Carlson, Anton "Ajax" J., 158, 169–170,
217, 557n.7
Carlson, Chester F., 424, 433, 437, 442–443,
462, 463, 464, 474–475, 489, 511,
573n.10
Carnegie Foundation, 326, 350
Carpenter, Elizabeth, 432
Case, Clifford P., 345–346; Fund for the Re-
public president, 337–338, 339, 340, 341,
344, 347, 349, 359; "Prospects for De-
mocracy" symposium, 421
Castle, Elinor. *See* Nef, Elinor Castle
Castro, Fidel, 478
Catholicism, Roman, 167, 345, 409, 425;
Hutchins's views on, 159–160, 172, 327–
328, 533, 580n.12. *See also* Aquinas,
Thomas/Thomism
Catton, Bruce, 372, 387
Cavanaugh, Reverend John, 89, 160, 564n.9,
566n.7
CBS. *See* Columbia Broadcasting System
Céline, Louis Ferdinand, 447
Censorship, 146, 190, 289, 295, 369. *See also*
First Amendment; Nixon, Richard: anti-
media campaign; Press/media: freedom of
Center for Contemporary Thought, 379–381.
See also Basic Issues program: origins of;
Fund for the Advancement of Education:
Basic Issues/Center origins in
Center for the Study of Democratic Institutions, 391–400, 401, 403, 408–479, 482–
492, 496–522, 526, 527, 528; academic
program, 462, 468, 471, 472, 473, 474,
475, 485, 486, 501, 507, 508, 511, 516;
American Character study/conference,
409–410, 417–418, 426 (participants,
570n.5); Basic Issues program, 391, 394,
395, 396, 398–399, 401, 403, 408, 409,
410, 411–412; Chicago plan, 513, 514,
515–522; Comfort's lawsuit against, 519–
520; "communiversity," 509, 511–512,
513; Constitution, US, and, 466, 469,
476–477, 487–488, 489; constitution for,
468, 469, 471, 472, 475, 485; consultants, 575n.8; criticism, internal, 377,
382–384, 463, 486, 492, 508–509, 509–
510, 511, 512, 513; criticism, right-wing,

412–414, 415, 457; Douglas-Parvin controversy, 484–485; *Encyclopaedia Britannica* revision and, 401, 403, 407, 408, 409–410, 415, 416, 418, 426–427, 428, 430, 431; *Fail-Safe* controversy, 413–414, finances, 393–394, 409, 413, 414, 415–416, 417–423, 423–424, 437, 439, 442–443, 461, 462, 463, 474, 482, 489, 496, 497, 498, 505, 511, 512, 513, 514, 516, 517, 519, 522, 536; First Amendment conference, 495 (participants, 495, 576n.8); Ford Foundation and, 418–419, 420, 443; Fund for Peace and, 512, 517, 518, 521–522; Hutchins reinstated as president, 515–516; Hutchins's death and, 528, 536–537; Hutchins's successor, selection of, 461, 469, 471, 481, 482, 485, 489–491, 492, 496, 498–499, 500, 501–502; Japanese-American conference, 478–479 (participants, 575n.11); Kelly-Ferry debate, 412, 413; merger plans, 512, 521–522; as model university, 461–462, 533–534; under Moos, 499–502, 503–514, 515, 517, 519, 520, 521, 577n.1, 578n.19; organization of, 472, 486; origins of, 554n.10 (*see also* Basic Issues program: origins of); peace movement and, 439–440; permanence of, 520, 521, 522, 536–537; personnel/membership, 384, 394–396, 397, 408–409, 414, 417–418, 420, 423–424, 429, 433, 439–440, 440–441, 449, 468–469, 469–470, 471, 473, 474, 475–476, 489, 502, 506, 507, 509, 511, 514, 516, 517, 518–519, 522, 575n.10, 578–579n.10; projects and issues, 409, 410–412, 418, 444, 459, 468, 474, 476–478, 487, 488, 489, 495–496, 519; publications/communication program, 415, 462, 463–465, 471, 473, 474–475, 478–479, 489, 492, 494, 497, 506, 507, 511, 512, 516, 517, 569–570n.2; public relations, 410, 414, 440, 444, 497, 498, 511, 517, 518; purpose of, 421, 422, 426, 509–510; refounding/reorganization, 462–463, 464, 470, 471–474, 476, 485, 486, 496, 504, 507; St. Benedict's quotation, 398–399; setting, 391–392, 392–393, 399; student protest movement and, 447, 449–450, 466–468; tax-exempt status, 467; unilateral-disarmament controversy, 412–413; Wingspread conference, 433. *See also* Douglas Inquiry; Fund for the Republic; "Pacem in Terris" convocations; "Pros-

pects for Democracy" convocations; "University in America, The"
Center Magazine, 446, 464–465, 466, 478, 487, 516, 519, 523, 533, 537
Center Report, 478, 516, 519, 521. See also World Issues
Central Intelligence Agency (CIA), 457, 578n.7
Chamberlin, T. C., 72
Charles R. Walgreen Foundation for the Study of American Institutions, 132
Charles the Bold, quoted, 92
Charlotte News, 348
Chase, Stuart, 396
Chauvel, Jean, 443, 573n.10
Cheadle, Vernon, 414
Chester, C. M., 129
Chicago, Illinois, 68, 106, 112, 122, 127, 265; Center for the Study of Democratic Institutions' move to, 513; *Encyclopaedia Britannica* and, 416; as "second city," 69, 183, 310. See also Hyde Park
Chicago Club, 111, 353
Chicago Daily News: New Deal and, 127–128; on University of Chicago, 176, 178, 241; Wilder and, 225
Chicago Fight, 76, 169, 232, 300. See also Facts vs. Ideas controversy; University of Chicago: faculty vs. Hutchins
Chicago Magazine, 169
Chicago school, 90, 101, 170
Chicago Theological Seminary, 218
Chicago Times, 128
Chicago Tribune, 121, 457; anti-Communist campaign, 127–128, 129, 130, 276, 282; anti-Hutchins campaign, 128, 183, 276, 282, 296–297, 457, 487, 535; Hutchins's obituary, 535; reactionary viewpoint, 127–128; University of Chicago and, 87, 128, 129, 130, 183, 265; World War II and, 215
China, People's Republic of, 441–442, 443, 478
Christian Science Monitor, 337
Churchill, Winston, 121, 214, 215, 216
CIA. *See* Central Intelligence Agency
CIO, 118, 217, 325. See also AFL-CIO
City College of New York, 168, 371
City of Man, The (Borgese), 207
"Civilization of the Dialogue" (Center study), 477
Civil rights/civil liberties, 47, 129, 307, 338, 340, 362, 483, 524, 526; Bloom and, 538; Ford Foundation and, 324, 328,

Civil rights/civil liberties (*cont.*)
329–330; Fund for the Republic and, 330–331, 335, 341–342, 343–345, 346, 347, 350, 354, 358, 374, 376, 377, 381; right-wing opposition to, 324, 328, 329–330, 338, 339, 341, 344, 345–346, 346–347, 356, 376. *See also* Blacks; Constitution, US; Desegregation; Fourteenth Amendment

Civil-rights movement, 376, 399, 427, 441, 448, 450, 538. *See also* Blacks; Civil rights/civil liberties; Desegregation

Claremont Colleges, 396, 425

Clark, Bennett Champ, 219

Clark, Blair, 506, 509–510, 576n.8, 577n.1

Clark, Charles E., 39, 43, 49, 50, 53, 62, 197

Clark, D. Worth, 219

Clark, Joseph S., 421, 460, 573n.10

Clark, Ramsey, 489, 577n.1, 578n.10

Clark University, 47, 70

Clemson University, 347

Cleveland, Harland, 490

Cleveland Plain Dealer, 11

Clifford, Clark, 498, 576n.13

Closing of the American Mind (Bloom), 537–539

Coggeshall, Lowell, 308

Cogley, John, 429, 464–465; American Character study, 409–410, 417–418, 426, 570n.5; blacklisting study, 367–372, 375, 379, 410, 567n.10; Center for the Study of Democratic Institutions and, 394, 395, 412, 470, 472, 473, 486, 507, 569n.1, 571n.11

Cohen, Arthur, 533

Colby College, 70

Cole, Charles W., 332, 409, 565n.25, 567n.1

College Humor, 180

Collins, LeRoy, 442

Collins, Marjory, 439

Columbia Broadcasting System (CBS), 495, 503, 547n.8, 576n.8

Columbia Teachers College, 185

Columbia University, 78, 263, 265, 362; Adler and, 50, 52, 85, 98, 103, 104, 579n.1; Butler and, 50, 122, 167; faculty members, 50, 53, 87, 91, 226, 267, 344, 384, 404, 490, 562n.25, 572n.9; finances, 202, 306; "great books" course, 98; law school, 48, 50, 51, 53; McKeon and, 85, 104, 551n.6; student protest movement, 467–468; Van Doren and, 161, 260; Yale vs., 48, 49

Colvin, James E., 337

Colwell, Ernest C., 232, 254, 304

Comfort, Alex, 475, 476, 507–508, 514, 519–520

Commission on Freedom of the Press, 272, 397, 495–496; Hutchins's summary report, 293–298, 562n.26, 562n.33, 562n.34; participants, 562n.25. *See also* Press/media: freedom of

Commission on Race and Housing, 346, 375–376; participants, 566n.7

Committee for Economic Development, 185

Committee for the First Amendment, 369

Committee on Civilization, 229. *See also* Committee on Social Thought

Committee on Endowment, 475

Committee on Industrial Relations, 310

Committee on Instruction and Research, 237

Committee on Social Thought, 79, 158, 173, 229–231, 270–271, 272, 440, 538; participants, 558n.22

Committee on the Liberal Arts, 136–137, 138–140, 551n.6

Committee to Defend America by Aiding the Allies, 217

Committee to Frame a World Constitution, 263, 269–271, 282, 429, 522; draft charter, 276–280; *Tribune*'s conspiracy charges, 276–277. *See also* World government: constitution for

Common Cause, 270, 280

Commonweal, 370, 464

Communism, 215, 217, 435; campaign against/hysteria over, 128, 130, 133, 151, 269, 276, 296, 329, 330, 335, 338, 344, 345, 350–351, 352, 355–357, 369, 370, 373, 376, 425, 459, 487–488; Fund for the Republic study on, 341, 355, 375, 567n.10; Hutchins accused of, 47, 118, 128–132, 151, 276, 296, 297, 327, 338, 344, 359–361, 364; Hutchins's views on, 234; legality of, 360; Marxism vs., 362; University of Chicago accused of, 128–132, 151, 183. *See also* House Un-American Activities Committee; McCarthyism; Left wing; Right wing

Communist party, Polish, 435

Communist Party USA, 355, 362

Compton, Arthur, 226–227

Compton, Randolph, 512

Conant, James B., 226–227

Connelly, Matt, 251

Conscientious objectors, 17, 213, 330. *See also* Pacifism

Conservatism/conservatives, 42, 331, 337, 538; constitutional right to education and,

524–525; "pseudo-conservatism," 345–346; Republicans and, 122, 213; vs. Center for the Study of Democratic Institutions, 412–413; vs. Douglas, 483–485; vs. Hutchins, 127, 279; at University of Chicago, 269, 536. *See also* Right wing

Constitution, US, 277, 279, 341, 360, 396; Center for the Study of Democratic Institutions model, 466, 469, 476–477, 487–488, 489; education and, 341, 498, 523–525, 539, 540; freedom of the press and, 294, 295; Hutchins's views on, 439, 495, 498, 540. *See also* Bill of Rights; World government: constitution for

"Constitutionalization of Education, The" (Center study), 476–477

"Constitutionalization of Science, The" (Center study), 477

Container Corporation of America, 273

Continuing education, 497

Conway, Carl C., 192

Cooke, Alistair, 320

Coolidge, Calvin, 122

Cooper, James, 56

Corcoran, Tom, 199, 209

Cornell, Katherine, 99

Cornell University, 87, 321, 381

Cornfeld, Bernard J., 452, 460, 462

Cornwall College, 167

"Corporation, The" (Basic Issues study), 387

Court of Reason (Kelly), 366

Cousins, Norman, 284, 431, 490, 559n.9, 571n.11

Cowdery, Mr., 21

Cowles, Gardner, 257

Cowles, John, 257, 336, 564n.2

Cox, Eugene "Goober," 329

Craig, May, 360

Crane, Ronald, 343, 551n.6

Cranston, Alan, 339, 575n.11

Cressey, Donald, 516

Crime and Punishment (Dostoevsky), 100

Crisis of Democratic Theory, The (Purcell), 165

Crowther, Bishop Edward, 468, 528, 573n.10

Crowther, Sir Geoffrey (Lord), 403, 406–407, 430, 559n.9

Cukor, George, 315

Cushing, Cardinal, 372

Cutlip, Scott M., 66

Daily Maroon, 81, 115, 155–156, 157, 217

Danforth Foundation, 303, 353

Darien, Connecticut, 390

Dartmouth College, 325

Darwin, Charles, 13

Daughters of the American Revolution, 356

David, Donald K., 327, 333, 564n.2

Davis, Chester C., 312

Dean, Arthur H., 357

De Bakey, Michael, 479

Decline and Fall of the Roman Empire (Gibbon), 114

Defoe, Daniel, 116

Delacorte, George, 257

Dell, Floyd, 106

Dell, George W., 308, 552n.5

Dell Publishing, 257

Democracy, 278, 297, 357, 385, 518; education and, 28, 41, 101, 212, 301–302, 336, 538–539, 540; Hutchins on, 28, 211, 212–213, 216, 281–282, 301, 538–539

Democratic party, 42, 180, 207, 214, 325, 329, 359, 365, 389, 402, 452, 488, 557n.9, 578n.7; Hutchins and, 120, 194, 199, 208, 338, 426; Hutchins's "platform for youth" speech, 122–124, 125, 128

Deniau, Xavier, 443, 571n.6

Denver Post, 351

Depression, 126; effect on education, 140, 145, 149, 151; effect on University of Chicago, 112–113, 121, 134, 151, 173, 177, 178, 202, 222

Desegregation, 374, 388, 397, 523–524; southern opposition to, 326, 341, 342, 346–347, 348–349, 359, 483. *See also* Blacks; Civil rights/civil liberties; Civil-rights movement

Détente, 425, 518

Dewey, John, 49, 170, 171, 178, 322, 554n.7; Hutchins vs., 91, 157, 163–164, 165–167, 170, 326, 337, 362, 404; right-wing view of, 350; at University of Chicago, 49, 71–72. *See also* Facts vs. Ideas controversy

Diagrammatics (Adler/Maude Hutchins), 174

Dialectic (Adler), 139

Diary of Love, The (Maude Hutchins), 289

Dickens, Charles, 286

Dien Bien Phu, 443

Dilling, Elizabeth, 130

Divinity School (University of Chicago), 232, 254

Dobrosielski, Marion, 433, 573n.10

Dodge, John (Jack), 402, 428

Dominican Republic, 442

Donnelly, Esther, 116
Dostoevsky, Feodor, 286
"Dover Beach" (Arnold), 522
Douglas, Cathleen, 483
Douglas, James H., Jr., 130, 293, 314,
550n.14; Center for the Study of Democratic Institutions and, 476, 508, 570n.4,
577n.1, 578n.10; eulogy for Hutchins,
529
Douglas, William O., 367, 495, 522; Basic
Issues program and, 389; Center for the
Study of Democratic Institutions projects,
411, 418–419, 420, 421, 432, 452, 454,
478, 482, 484–485, 488, 569–570n.2,
570n.5, 572n.8, 573n.10, 575n.11,
579n.23; Hutchins's correspondence with,
192, 479–480; as Hutchins's supporter,
196–197, 198, 207, 208, 350, 367;
Parvin Foundation trustee, 411, 442, 482,
483–485; on Securities and Exchange
Commission, 191, 196, 197, 198; on Su-
preme Court, 198, 199, 482, 483–485;
University of Chicago and, 84–85, 197;
Yale and, 50–51, 53, 85, 197
Douglas Inquiry, 526
Drown, Joseph W., 422, 577n.1
Drown Foundation, 422, 497
Dubos, René, 429
DuPont, 266
Dworkin, Ronald, 490

Earl Newsom and Company, 316, 324, 325, 326
"Early Treatise on Education, An"
(Hutchins), 10–11, 544n.21
East European Fund, 314
Eaton, Cyrus, 392, 567n.5
Economic Cooperation Administration, 312
"Economic Order: The World after Keynes,
The" (Roll), 430
Economist, 403, 559n.9
Education: administrative duties in, 75, 76,
111–112, 378–379; anti-intellectualism
and, 156, 157, 158, 161, 235; case-study
method of, 32, 43, 49, 55, 305; Catholic,
172, 327–328; compulsory-attendance
laws, 135, 150, 523; Constitution and,
341, 498, 523–525, 539, 540; continuing,
497; democracy and, 28, 41, 101, 212,
301–302, 336, 538–539, 540; for disadvantaged, 25, 26; discrimination in, 55,
331, 523–525, 538; dropout rate, 147;
elitism in, 30–31, 41, 57, 101, 148, 538;
in Europe, 148–149, 150; federal aid for,
145; football and, 147, 200–202, 480,

556n.6; freedom in, 54, 58, 61, 62, 76,
113, 128–129, 153, 171, 185, 242, 245,
248, 304, 305, 330, 375, 536; general,
71, 72–73, 87, 92–93, 95, 134, 135, 137,
147, 148, 149, 158–159, 165, 166, 178,
187, 188, 228, 247, 265, 309; Great
Books curriculum, 98–99, 101, 103, 139,
140, 147, 231, 299–300, 537; libraries as
means of, 145–146; media and, 145–146;
metaphysics and, 99, 158–159, 160–161,
162, 163, 166, 211, 234, 246, 267, 268,
531; objects of, 149, 161, 381, 526, 532;
in postwar world, 233–236; progressive
movement, 90, 91; public, 134–135, 145,
147, 148, 149, 522–523, 539; public relations and, 66, 354, 554–555n.13;
religious/moral training and, 150, 160,
531, 532; Socratic dialogue method of,
43, 51, 99, 102, 462; specialization in,
72, 73, 92–93, 95, 101, 147, 153, 158,
187, 229, 247, 395, 401, 404, 423, 521,
526, 537; state of, 147, 149, 166, 238;
technology and, 146, 229, 234, 265, 444,
521, 537; television and, 320–321; values
in, 158–159; women and, 9, 77. *See also*
Adult education; Liberal arts; Universities/
colleges; University of Chicago;
Vocational/professional training
Educational reform. *See* University of Chicago: faculty/administrative reform;
Hutchins's effect on; as model for na-
tional reform; reform issues;
undergraduate/College reform
Education for Freedom (Hutchins), 233–235,
240, 243
"Education in a Democratic Society" (Ford
Foundation program), 313, 318
"Education: The Learning Society"
(Hutchins), 429
"Educator as Moralist, The" (Cohen), 533
Egeland, Margaret Rice, 11
Ehrlich, Paul, 476
Einstein, Albert, 226, 251, 268
Eisenhower, Dwight, 324, 331, 338, 344,
346, 373, 503, 538, 571n.11, 576–
577n.13; desegregation and, 342, 359
Elevator, The (Maude Hutchins), 289
Eliade, Mircea, 476
Eliot, Charles W., 73, 91, 171
Eliot, T. S., 191, 230, 271–272
Elliot, John B., Jr., 392, 408
Ellsworth, Maine, 6
Embree, Edwin R., 59
Emerson, Ralph Waldo, 521

Emory University, 477

Empey, Sergeant Arthur Guy, 18

Empiricism, 101

Encyclopaedia Britannica, 255–260, 522, 559n.9; Center for the Study of Democratic Institutions and, 401, 403, 407, 408, 409–410, 415, 416, 418, 426–427, 428, 430, 431; Chicago, relocation to, 416, 431; format, 406–407, 409, 428–429, 430; Hutchins and, 255, 256, 257, 258, 286, 288, 290, 292, 293, 315, 336, 337, 378, 400–402, 403–405, 429, 474, 498–499, 509; Revised Editorial Program (REP), 400–406, 428–431; "roof articles," 407, 409, 428–430, 569n.16, 570n.2; University of Chicago and, 255, 256, 257, 258, 260, 400–401, 474. *See also* Benton, William: *Encyclopaedia Britannica* and; Great Books of the Western World: publishing project

Encyclopaedia Britannica Films, Incorporated, 255, 258, 259, 314, 416, 536

Engberg, Edward, 464

Enthusiast, The (Harrison), 530

"Epigram" (Maude Hutchins), 290

Erskine, John, 98, 99, 100, 260, 286, 549n.6

Esalen, 449

Esquire, 415–416

"Establishment of Peace, The" (Ford Foundation program), 313, 318

Etean, 10

Ethics (Aristotle), 281, 532

Eurich, Alvin, 322, 348

Examiner: Red Terror campaign, 128, 129; Walgreen Case and, 131

Facts vs. Ideas controversy, 153–164, 165–167, 169–173. *See also* Chicago Fight; University of Chicago: faculty vs. Hutchins

Fadiman, Clifton, 98, 137, 336, 516, 534, 540, 559n.9, 579n.1; Hutchins interview, 520–521

Fail-Safe (Burdick and Wheeler), 413–414

Fair Deal, 345

Fantasia Mathematica (Fadiman), 137

Farrell, James T., 106

Faubus, Orval, 397

Faust, Clarence Henry, 187, 228, 231, 260, 309, 319, 333, 551n.6; Fund for the Advancement of Education president, 314, 320, 321, 327, 348, 381

Faust (Goethe), 98, 282

FCC. *See* Federal Communications Commission

Fear in the Air (Ashmore), 495–496, 497

Federal Communications Commission (FCC), 198, 421, 495, 576n.8

Federalist Papers, The (Hamilton, Madison, and Jay), 270, 487

Federal Republic of the World, 277

Federal Reserve Bank of New York, 270, 562n.25

Federal Reserve Board, 421

Federated Theological Faculty, 232

Federation of Institutes of Advanced Study (Stockholm), 476

Fermi, Enrico, 226

Ferry, Hugh, 325

Ferry, W. H. "Ping," 325–328, 329; Basic Issues program, 388; Center for the Study of Democratic Institutions and, 394, 395, 396, 427, 434, 436, 439, 466–467, 469, 470, 473, 569n.2; Ford Foundation and, 325, 326–328, 330, 340, 565n.12; Fund for the Republic and, 340, 355, 358, 364, 365, 366, 368, 473; minority rights/protest movement, 330, 340, 427, 444, 448–449, 466–467; unilateral-disarmament controversy, 412–413

Fifth Amendment Today, The (Griswold), 358

Figueres, José, 421

"Fine Arts: Modern Situations in the Arts, The" (McMullen), 430

Finnegan, Richard J., 357

First Amendment, 157, 295, 297, 331, 369, 371, 388; conference on, 495 (participants, 495, 576n.8). *See also* Commission on Freedom of the Press; Press/media: freedom of

Fleming, Harold, 521, 567n.8, 578n.10

Fleming, Joseph H., 130

Fleming, Robben, 490

Fletcher, C. Scott, 314, 319

Forbes, R. J., 429

Ford, Anne McDonnell, 323–324; Hutchins and, 327–328

Ford, Benson, 323, 331, 564n.2

Ford, Edsel, 323, 324

Ford, Gerald, 213, 483, 484, 485

Ford, Henry, I, 323, 324

Ford, Henry, II, 323–324, 325, 381; Ford Foundation and, 302, 311, 312–313, 316, 326, 329, 330, 333, 564n.2; Fund for the Republic and, 331, 332, 335, 359, 361, 368, 370; Hutchins and, 303, 322, 326, 327–328, 331, 332, 361–362; right-wing opposition to, 329, 345–346, 361

Ford, Josephine, 323
Ford, William Clay, 323
Ford Foundation, 302–304, 311–336, 503;
  board members, 564n.2; educational
  Funds, 318, 319–322, 326, 334, 535,
  564n.9; Ford Motor Company and public
  relations, 313, 316, 322, 323, 324, 330,
  334, 335, 347; Fund for the Republic
  and, 330, 331–332, 335, 341, 343, 349,
  359, 361, 368, 370, 379, 393; Fund for
  the Republic/Center funding, 418–419,
  420, 443; headquarters, Pasadena vs.
  New York, 311, 315, 318, 333, 334;
  Hoffman resignation/dismissal, 332, 333,
  335–336, 340; Hutchins, controversy
  and, 321–322, 325, 326–328; programs
  and issues, 312–315, 318–322, 326, 329–
  330, 335, 349, 358, 564n.16; as right-
  wing target, 324–325, 326, 328–331,
  335, 338, 350, 361; tax-exempt status,
  313, 329. See also Fund for Adult Edu-
  cation; Fund for the Advancement of Edu-
  cation; Fund for the Republic
Ford Foundation, The (Macdonald), 312
Ford Foundation Archives, 328
Ford Motor Company: Ford Foundation fund-
  ing, 313, 323; public image and Ford
  Foundation, 313, 316, 322, 323, 324,
  330, 334, 335, 347
Ford: The Men and the Machine (Lacey), 327
Foreign Affairs, 346
Fortas, Abe, 432
Fortune, 464
Fosdick, Reverend Harry Emerson, 218
Foster, F. H., 13
Fourteenth Amendment, 331, 524
Francis-Williams, Lord, 421
Frank, Jerome, 196, 571n.11
Frankfurter, Felix, 47, 350
Free and Responsible Press, A (Hutchins),
  294–298; media reaction to, 296–297,
  400. See also Commission on Freedom of
  the Press
Freedom. See Press/media: freedom of;
  Speech, freedom of
Freedom and the Foundation (Reeves), 326,
  376–377
"Freedom to See" (Mitgang), 388
Freeman, David, 337, 340, 364, 383, 385
Free Speech movement, 444. See also Speech,
  freedom of; Student protest movement
Freud, Sigmund/Freudians, 100, 289, 290,
  445, 532; Hutchins's satirization of, 445–
  447

Friday Club, 174
Friedman, Milton, 170, 269
Frodin, Reuben, 228
Fromm, Erich, 367
Frost, William Goodell, 25–26, 544n.2
Fulbright, J. William, 201, 421, 432, 444,
  458, 498, 556n.6, 571n.9, 573n.10,
  575n.11, 576n.13
Fuller, Lon L., 429
Fund for Adult Education, 314, 320–321, 327,
  348, 535; board members, 564n.9
Fund for Democratic Freedoms, 330. See also
  Fund for the Republic
Fund for Peace, 512, 517, 518, 521–522
Fund for the Advancement of Education, 320,
  328, 381; Adler's grant for Institute for
  Philosophical Research, 319–320; Ashmore Report, 348–349; Basic Issues/
  Center origins in, 379–381, 386–387,
  388–389; board members, 564n.9;
  Hutchins's influence on, 320, 321–322,
  535; teacher-education program, 321–322,
  348
Fund for the Republic, 330–332, 343–347,
  349–353, 354–355, 356–359, 360, 361–
  362, 363–390, 391; academic research,
  341, 344, 375; Basic Issues/Center for the
  Study of Democratic Institutions, as sole
  activity, 389, 392; Basic Issues program,
  381–385, 386–390, 391; blacklisting
  study, 362, 367–372; under Case, 337–
  338, 339, 340, 341, 344, 347, 349, 359;
  civil rights/civil liberties and, 330–331,
  335, 341–342, 343–345, 346, 347, 350,
  354, 358, 374, 376, 377, 381, 567n.8;
  Communism study, 341, 355, 375; consultants, 384, 475, 567n.10, 568n.13,
  575n.8; critics, internal, 358, 359, 360,
  363–364, 366, 368, 377–378, 382–383,
  473; critics, left-wing, 375; critics, right-
  wing, 335, 338, 340, 344, 345–346,
  350–352, 354, 355–358, 359–361, 364,
  366, 367–368, 369–372, 373, 374–375,
  381, 412; dissolution of, 536; effect of,
  374–377; Encyclopaedia Britannica, Center revision, 403; Ford Foundation and,
  330, 331–332, 335, 341, 343, 349, 359,
  361, 368, 370, 374, 379, 393, 418–419,
  420; grant-making function, 349, 350,
  352, 375, 376, 385; House Un-American
  Activities Committee vs., 330, 340, 351–
  352, 355, 357, 361, 364, 367–368, 369–
  372, 373, 374; leadership, 331–332, 337–
  338, 339, 341; in New York, 390;

personnel/membership, 331–332, 340, 345, 347, 372, 382, 383, 395, 408, 417–418, 420, 503, 508, 518–519, 565n.25, 570n.4, 571n.7, 577n.1, 578n.19, 578–579n.10; projects, 335, 350, 366, 375–377, 379; publications, 339, 350, 352, 354, 367–372, 375–376; public relations, 335, 350, 354–355, 358, 359–360, 363–364, 365–367, 370, 372–373, 376, 377, 400; reorganization, 363–364, 374, 377, 379–385, 389; role of, 339, 351, 358; tax-exempt status, 341, 357–358, 361, 373, 412. *See also* Basic Issues program; Center for the Study of Democratic Institutions

Gaither, H. Rowan, Jr., 312, 313, 334, 370
Galbraith, John Kenneth, 409, 490, 573n.10, 576n.13
Gale, Henry Gordon, 92
Galen, 144, 159
Galileo, 156
Gallup Poll, 218
Galsworthy, John, 28–29
Gardner, John, 490
Gardner, Richard, 490
Garst, Eleanor, 439
"Gate Receipts and Glory" (Hutchins), 201
Gavin, James M., 491
Geismar, Maxwell, 289, 290
Gellhorn, Walter, 396
General Education Board, 92
Geneva Accords, 443, 459
Georgiana (Maude Hutchins), 289
Germany, 16, 435; influence on American educational system, 135; in World War II, 210, 218, 226, 249, 250, 251
Germany, East, 282
Gibbon, Edward, 114, 550n.15
Gideonse, Harry D., 157–158, 162, 172, 178, 553n.24
Gifford Lectures (Niebuhr), 282
Gilkey, Reverend Charles W., 59, 89, 288
Gill, Samuel E., 218
Gill Poll, 218–219, 557n.19
Ginsburg, Douglas H., 536
Ginsburg, Norton, 486–487, 492, 500, 506, 507, 508, 516, 550n.18
Gish, Lillian, 99
Gladstone, William, 540
Goebbels, Joseph, 217
Goethe, Johann Wolfgang, 273, 282, 284, 285
Goethe Bicentennial Celebration, 273, 274, 275, 276, 282–285, 291; participants, 561n.25

Goheen, Robert, 411
Goldberg, Arthur, 389, 425, 426, 456, 458, 575n.11
Goldman, Eric, 352, 381, 384, 387, 388, 409, 432, 566n.23
Goldsmith, Arthur J., 338
Goldwyn, Sam, 315
Goliath (Borgese), 205
Gordis, Rabbi Robert, 89, 408, 409
Gorman, William, 408, 516, 551n.6
Gottesman Lectures (Hutchins), 336
Goucher College, 321
Gould, Samuel, 414
Government, world. *See* World government
Graham, Otis, 516, 519
Grant, Arnold M., 475, 489, 575n.9, 577n.1
Grant, George P., 404
Gray, Mrs. Horace, 391
"Great Anti-School Campaign, The" (Hutchins), 522
Great Books Foundation, 273–274, 314
Great Books of the Western World, 98–103, 119; at Aspen Institute, 285–286; criticism of, 99, 308; Hutchins and, 98–103, 118, 187, 259, 273, 286, 292, 320, 551n.6; as liberal-arts/general-education curriculum, 98–99, 101, 103, 139, 140, 147, 231, 299–300, 537, 580n.29; name/title, 100, 260; origin of, 98, 99, 100; publishing project, 101, 259–260, 286, 292, 336–337, 430 (advisory board, 549n.6); at St. John's College, 140, 189; *Syntopicon* (index), 259–260, 336, 337, 408, 549n.6; at University of Chicago, 98–103, 118, 139, 147, 187, 260, 273, 306, 538
Great Chicago Fight. *See* Chicago Fight
Great Conversation, The (Hutchins), 101, 549n.6
Great Ideas: A Syntopicon, The (Adler), 549n.6
Great Ideas Today, 522
Grene, David, 231
Griswold, Erwin N.: Basic Issues program, opposition to, 384; Ferry, opposition to, 358; Fund for the Republic and, 332, 389, 565n.25; Hutchins, opposition to, 358, 359, 363–364, 366, 377–378, 379, 383
Griswold, Whitney, 400
Groton, Massachusetts, 4, 40
Grove Press, 447
Groves, General Leslie, 252, 261, 262, 265, 266
Guerard, Albert Leon, 270

Guinan, Texas, 106
Gulliver's Travels (Swift), 447
Gunther, John, 226
Gustavson, Reuben G., 254

Haber, Bernard, 516
Hailsham, Lord, 421
Halas, George, 201
Hamilton, Alexander, 270, 496
Hammerstein, Oscar, II, 387
Hanoi, 443, 444, 453, 454, 455, 457, 459.
　See also Vietnam
"Happy Heretic, The" (Navasky), 325
Harding, Warren, 30, 122
Harper, William Rainey: academic achieve-
　ments, 57–58, 70; death of, 73; educa-
　tional program and theories, 58, 69–74,
　77, 87, 134, 135, 136, 147, 152; influ-
　ence on Hutchins, 66–68, 69, 70–71, 75,
　87, 88, 91, 96, 134, 135, 136, 147, 152,
　311; at University of Chicago, 57–58, 61,
　66–67, 69–74, 79, 80, 83, 85, 91, 203,
　232, 236, 311
Harper Memorial Library, 176
Harper's, 346
Harriman, Averell, 453
Harrington, Michael, 371, 410
Harrison, Gilbert, 106, 530, 579n.7
Harvard Club, 131
Harvard University, 179, 190, 201, 202, 226,
　321, 348, 481; Buchanan and, 104, 137;
　Commission on Freedom of the Press,
　562n.25; Committee to Frame a World
　Constitution and, 263, 270; Eliot, presi-
　dent of, 73, 91; *Encyclopaedia Britannica*
　and, 255; faculty members, 231, 279,
　283, 327, 344, 409, 429, 561n.25,
　564n.9, 566n.7, 570n.5, 571n.11,
　574n.3, 576–577n.13; Ford Foundation
　and, 327, 564n.2; Kelly and, 365, 425;
　law school, 43, 47, 48, 49, 270, 312,
　358, 483, 565n.25; Lyons and, 296, 400;
　University of Chicago vs., 78, 183. *See
　also* Nieman Foundation/Fellows
Harvey, Mary, 478, 516
Harwood, Richard, 298, 562–563n.38
Hatch, Stanley, 520
Haverford College, 218
Hayek, Friedrich von, 191, 230
Hays, Brooks, 432, 571n.6
Hays, Will, 190
Healy, John, 195
Hearst, William Randolph, 117, 118, 128,
　130, 132. *See also* Hearst newspapers

Hearst newspapers, 117; on Basic Issues pro-
　gram, 385; Ford Foundation, opposition
　to, 324–325; Fund for the Republic, op-
　position to, 340, 352; Hutchins, opposi-
　tion to, 128, 276, 296, 359; readership,
　128. *See also* American; Examiner;
　Pegler, Westbrook
Heffernan, Cathleen. *See* Douglas, Cathleen
Hegel, Georg, 163
Heidegger, Martin, 394, 538
Heiskell, J. N., 349
Held, John, Jr., 180
Henderson, Thomas W., 11, 12
Herblock (pseud. Herbert L. Block), 354
Herrick, Robert, 70
Herring, Reverend John W., 37
"Higher Learning, The" (Hutchins speeches),
　155–156
*Higher Learning in a Democracy: A Reply to
　President Hutchins' Critique of the Amer-
　ican University, The* (Gideonse), 162, 172
Higher Learning in America, The (Hutchins),
　161, 167, 234; controversy over, 161–164
Hill, James C., 6
Hilton, Conrad, 336
Hippies, 445, 449, 450. *See also* Student pro-
　test movement
Hiroshima, 252, 260, 267, 281
Hispanics, 524
Hitler, Adolf, 205, 211, 217, 250, 362
Ho Chi Minh, 453, 454, 455, 457
Hocking, William Ernest, 270, 561n.25,
　562n.25, 562n.26
Hoffman, Hallock: Center for the Study of
　Democratic Institutions and, 394, 403,
　413, 427, 449; Fund for the Republic
　and, 340, 363; as pacifist/American
　Friends Service Committee director, 340,
　413, 427; student protest movement and,
　449, 467
Hoffman, Nicholas von, 535, 537
Hoffman, Paul G., 571n.9, 573n.10; Basic
　Issues program, 381, 384, 387; Center for
　the Study of Democratic Institutions and,
　421; *Encyclopaedia Britannica* board
　member, 400, 402; Ford Foundation and,
　302–303, 311–312, 313, 315, 316, 319,
　320, 324–325, 326, 327, 329, 381,
　564n.2; Ford Foundation resignation/
　dismissal, 332, 333, 335–336, 340; Fund
　for the Republic chairman, 330, 331,
　332, 335, 337, 340, 357, 361, 363, 366,
　370, 372, 373, 381; as Hutchins's sup-
　porter, 360–361, 381; right wing vs.,

324–325, 329, 345–346, 352; at Stude-
baker Motor Company, 185, 302, 314, 336;
University of Chicago trustee, 185, 400
Hollywood Ten, 369, 568n.11
Holst, Hermann Von, 70
Homer, 100
Hook, Sidney, 362
Hoover, Herbert, 122, 125, 130, 218, 219,
283
Hopkins, Harry, 125, 196, 208–209
Hotchkiss, 42, 323
Houghton, Harry, 403, 416
House, E. M., 126, 193
House Un-American Activities Committee
(HUAC): Hollywood blacklisting, 368–
369; vs. Cogley, for *Report on Blacklist-
ing*, 367–368, 369–372; vs. Ford
Foundation, 329; vs. Fund for the Repub-
lic, 330, 340, 351–352, 355, 357, 361,
364, 367–368, 369–372, 373, 374; vs.
Hutchins, 329, 364
Howard, Nathaniel, 11
Howard University, 466
Howe, John, 182
HUAC. *See* House Un-American Activities
Committee
Hubley, Faith, 447
Hubley, John, 447
Hudson Institute, 437
Huggins, Charles B., 304
Hughes, Charles Evans, 130, 495
Hughes, Frank, 296–297
"Human Nature: Man and His Environment"
(Dubos), 429
Hume, David, 100–101
Humphrey, Hubert, 433, 436, 454, 456, 576–
577n.13
Hunter College, 394, 421, 562n.25, 565n.25
Huntington Hotel, 312, 340
Hutchins, Barbara (stepdaughter), 300, 315,
525, 574n.3
Hutchins, Anna Laura Murch (mother), 3, 4–
5, 18, 34–35, 300, 480
Hutchins, Clarissa (daughter), 116, 465,
574n.3
Hutchins, Fannie (aunt), 7
Hutchins, Francis, Jr. (nephew), 249, 544n.21
Hutchins, Francis (Frank) Sessions (uncle), 7,
23, 33, 34
Hutchins, Francis Stevenson (brother), 4, 6,
287, 303, 314
Hutchins, Franja (Mary Frances) (daughter),
52, 64, 78, 111, 174, 208, 300, 465,
574n.3

Hutchins, Isaac, 17
Hutchins, Joanna Blessing (daughter), 173,
465, 574n.3
Hutchins, Maude Phelps McVeigh (first wife),
62–65, 93–95, 287–291, 550n.6; ancestry,
34, 40; as artist, 34, 40, 44, 56, 78, 106,
173–174, 191, 288; health, 93–94, 95,
287, 288; marriage to Hutchins, 34–35,
79, 93–94, 100, 107, 173, 174–175, 191,
196, 204–205, 219, 286, 287–288, 290–
291, 292, 293, 575n.14; *Newsweek* on,
288; personality/behavior, 41, 52, 56, 65,
78–79, 93–94, 106, 107, 111, 173–175,
189; *Time* on, 111; as writer, 288–290
Hutchins, Nicholas, 4, 40
Hutchins, Reverend William James (father), 3,
4, 7–8, 12–13, 17, 94, 530, 550n.15; at
Bedford Presbyterian Church, 3, 4, 5; as
Berea College president, 4, 25–26, 544–
545n.2; correspondence with Robert, on
failing marriage, 287–288, 290–291, 293;
correspondence with Robert, on University of Chicago, 287–288, 307; correspondence with Robert, during World War I,
17–18, 19, 20, 21, 22–23; at Danforth
Foundation, 303, 353; income, 6, 7–8;
Maude Hutchins and, 34–35, 290; at
Oberlin Theological Seminary, 5–6; relationship with Robert, 17–18, 18–19, 22,
26–27, 88, 142, 269, 300, 352–353; on
speechmaking/public speaking, 26–27,
142; Vesta Hutchins and, 300
Hutchins, Robert Grosvenor (grandfather), 6,
7–8, 17
Hutchins, Robert Grosvenor, Jr. (uncle), 7, 8
Hutchins, Robert Maynard:
as administrator, 48, 60, 75, 76, 91–92,
109, 111–112, 149, 308, 378–379, 417,
418, 515, 517
ancestors, 6–7, 17, 34
awards and honors, 21, 27–28, 30, 41, 44,
143, 180
birthdate/birthplace, 3
career: Alexander and Green, 36, 44; Chicago Regional Labor Board, 126–127;
ministry, 37; National Recovery Administration, 194–195, 196, 199; New York
Stock Exchange, 191–192; NYSE board
of governors, 192–193, 198–199; in
politics/government, 120, 124, 125–126,
199, 207–208, 208–209, 302, 338–339;
Supreme Court appointment, 193–194,
195–196, 198, 199, 204, 208; Time,
Inc., 193. *See also* Basic Issues program;

Hutchins, Robert Maynard (*cont.*)
　　Center for the Study of Democratic Institutions; *Encyclopaedia Britannica;* Ford Foundation; Fund for the Republic; Great Books of the Western World; University of Chicago; Yale Corporation; Yale Law School; Yale University
　　childhood, 3–6, 8–9, 9–10
　　children of, 173, 293, 315, 465. *See also* Hutchins, Clarissa; Hutchins, Franja; Hutchins, Joanna Blessing
　　criticism of: for arrogance, 12, 39, 54, 109, 153, 360; for authoritarianism, 162, 163, 383; for elitism, 101, 148, 345, 351; by left wing, 84, 322, 337, 359, 362, 375, 415; by right wing, 34, 47, 118, 121–122, 127, 128–132, 133, 151, 247, 276, 296, 297, 325, 327, 338, 344, 345–346, 350–351, 352, 354, 355, 359–361, 364, 370, 371, 374–375; for scholasticism, 159, 162, 172, 188, 240
　　death of, memorials and obituaries, 526, 527, 528–529, 531, 534–535, 579n.1
　　education: at Oberlin Academy, 9–10, 12, 39; at Oberlin College, 10–17, 27, 33, 530, 544n.22; at Woodland Avenue public school, 9; at Yale, 24, 25, 26, 27–35, 36–37, 530; at Yale Law School, 32, 36, 39–40, 43–44
　　father, relationship with, 3, 4, 17–18, 18–19, 22, 26–27, 88, 142, 269, 300, 352–353, 544–545n.2, 550n.15
　　health, 22, 94, 479–481, 484, 492, 509, 516, 525, 526–527
　　income/salary, 24, 35, 37, 38, 40, 64, 113, 143, 292, 293, 315, 340
　　influence of/effect of, 55, 299–300, 378, 534, 535, 537–538, 540–541
　　influences on, 6, 13, 15, 90, 148, 521. *See also* Adler, Mortimer: influence on Hutchins; Harper, William Rainey: influence on Hutchins
　　language skills, 19–20, 264
　　life-style/social life, 33, 41, 56, 62–65, 78–79, 90, 94, 106, 111, 196, 315, 390–391, 465, 509, 512, 530
　　marriage to Maude Phelps McVeigh, 34–35, 37, 41, 52, 56, 93–95, 106, 107, 111, 173, 174–175, 189, 191, 196, 204, 219; failure of, 107, 286, 287–288, 289, 290–292, 293, 577n.14
　　marriage to Vesta Orlick, 300–301, 315, 334, 390–391, 466, 492–493, 501, 509, 512, 517, 525, 527, 528

　　maxims/quotations/mottoes, 92, 114, 117, 223, 227, 311, 331, 458, 550n.15
　　personality and style, 18, 27, 33, 40, 42, 52, 54, 58, 59, 60, 108–118, 120, 143, 168, 170, 179, 183, 184, 204, 248–249, 273, 275, 299–300, 326, 361, 363, 377–378, 378–379, 419, 462, 465, 490, 493, 494, 520–521, 530, 531; humor of, 29–30, 113–115, 131, 316; self-description, 88, 109, 274; use of irony, 28, 79, 91, 107, 117, 142, 167, 171, 215, 246, 249, 328, 343, 479, 540–541, 552n.5
　　physical description, 11, 17, 33, 78, 94, 108, 206, 299
　　Puritan/Calvinist heritage, 4, 5, 6, 8, 32, 33, 40, 48, 65, 84, 88, 89, 90, 105, 117, 160, 199, 249, 264, 273, 344, 471, 513, 515, 516, 525, 530, 531
　　reading habits, 19–20, 98, 100–101, 117, 231, 264, 282, 286, 494, 496
　　recreational activities, 205
　　religion/philosophy, 4, 8, 18–19, 26, 37, 58, 88–89, 146–147, 159, 160, 172, 213, 232, 280–281, 327–328, 471, 529–534; Catholicism and Thomism, 158–160, 162–163, 166, 170–171, 172, 240, 297, 327–328, 337, 529, 533, 553n.25, 580n.12
　　reputation/fame of, 78, 110, 114, 120, 183–184, 297, 299, 535, 540
　　residences, 3, 4, 41, 63–64
　　speechmaking/oratorical skill, 26, 27–28, 36–37, 41, 79, 81–82, 109, 111, 115, 142–147, 149, 200, 214, 219, 255, 336, 522, 528
　　women and, 18, 19, 33, 116
　　working style, 39, 44, 126, 275–276, 286, 300, 340, 366, 376–377, 384, 399, 451, 481, 525
　　during World War I, 17–24, 126, 211, 223
　　during World War II, 221–232, 252, 541
　　writing style, 115, 116, 120, 294, 442, 528; verses/doggerel, 10–11, 20, 29, 33, 56, 316–318
　　youth of/"boy wonder" image, 41, 42, 48, 50, 55, 57, 58, 59, 60, 78, 79, 84, 113, 114, 120, 126, 193, 299, 531
Hutchins, William Grosvenor (brother), 4, 24, 37; in World War I, 17, 18, 19, 20, 23
Hutchins, Vesta Orlick (second wife), 300–301, 328, 480, 527, 544n.21, 550n.19, 577n.1, 578n.10; health of, 334, 390, 465, 492–493, 501, 512, 516, 517, 525; Hutchins's death and, 528; life-style, 315, 390–391, 465–466, 492–493, 509

Hutchins Commission. *See* Commission on Freedom of the Press

"Hutchins Influence, The" (*University of Chicago Magazine*), 304

Hutchinson, William T., 254–255

Huttenback, Robert, 537

Huxley, Aldous, 315, 367, 396, 419, 421, 569–570n.2

Huxley, Julian, 230

Hyde Park (Chicago), 78, 306, 307; artists' community in, 105–106

Hyde Park High School, 110

Hyman, Sidney, 103, 186, 430–431

Ickes, Harold, 125, 194–195, 196, 197–198, 199, 209, 210, 224, 558n.10

Indianapolis Star, 457

Indiana University, 466

"Individual and the Common Defense, The" (Basic Issues study), 387

"Individual and the Labor Union, The" (Basic Issues study), 387

"Individual Behavior and Human Relations" (Ford Foundation program), 313

Industrial Relations Association of Chicago, 126

Inland Steel, 181

Innis, Harold A., 270

Inozemtsev, N. N., 434, 443

Institute for Advanced Study (Princeton), 380

Institute for Nuclear Studies (University of Chicago), 265

Institute for Philosophical Research, 167, 319–320, 408, 431

Institute for the Study of Metals (University of Chicago), 265

Institute of Experimental Psychology (Yale), 52

Institute of History of the Soviet Academy of Science, 434–435

Institute of Human Behavior. *See* Institute of Human Relations

Institute of Human Relations (Yale), 52–53, 60, 84

Institute of Military Studies (University of Chicago), 223–224, 225

Institute of Procedure (Yale), 49, 50

Institute of Radiobiology and Biophysics (University of Chicago), 265

Insull, Samuel, 68–69, 121, 122, 205

Integration. *See* Desegregation

"Intellectual Community, The" (Hutchins), 533

Intercultural Publications, Inc., 319

International Center for Advanced Studies in the Field of Journalism (University of Ecuador), 411

International Cooperation Year, 436

International Court of Justice, 41, 433, 571n.9

International Geophysical Year, 432

International Library of Philosophy, 51

International Rule of Law Year, 432

Investors Overseas Services Foundation (IOS), 452, 456, 460

Isherwood, Christopher, 315

Isolationism/isolationists, 205, 207, 208, 210, 213–214, 217. *See also* World War II: interventionists vs. anti-interventionists

Ittleson, Mrs. Henry, 167

Ivy League, 33; prep schools, 105, 144–145; University of Chicago vs., 69, 77, 129

Jacobs, Paul, 362, 371, 387, 394, 396, 410, 418, 449

Jacoby, Neil H., 254, 468, 470, 472, 476

Jacoby, Russell, 538–539

James, Henry, 247, 521

James, Lord of Rusholme, 421

James, William, 90, 157, 350

Janus, Christopher, 411

Japan, 438; World War II and, 219, 251, 252. *See also* Hiroshima; Nagasaki; Yokohama

Japanese Cabinet Commission on the Constitution, 438, 571n.9

Japanese-American conference, 478–479; participants, 575n.11

Jaspers, Karl, 394

Jay, John, 270

Jefferson, Thomas, 144

Jessup, John K., 433

Jessup, Philip C., 41, 571n.9

Jevons, William, 156

John Birch Society, 412, 415

Johns Hopkins, 57, 70, 501, 503, 571n.11, 576–577n.13

Johnson, Hugh S., 194, 196, 557n.7

Johnson, Lyndon, 432, 436, 441, 453, 454, 455–456; undermining "Pacem in Terris II," 454, 456–458, 460, 462

Johnson Foundation, 433, 571n.6

John XXIII, 425, 434, 435, 457

Jones, Wellington, 115, 550n.18

Jouvenel, Bertrand de, 475

Joyce, James, 286

Joyce, William, 343, 363, 565n.25

Joy of Sex, The (Comfort), 507, 514, 519, 520

J. P. Morgan and Company, 192, 564n.9

Judd, Charles H., 148, 552n.16
Judson, Harry Pratt, 73, 74
Julius Rosenwald Fund, 59
Jung, Harry A., 130
Jung, Kim Dae, 478

Kac, Mark, 429
Kahler, Erich, 270
Kahn, Herman, 437
Kalven, Harry, 157, 377, 576n.8
Kansas City Star, 365
Karl, Barry D., 155
Kass, Amy Apfel, 90
Katz, Milton, 312, 568n.13
Katz, Wilbur G., 230, 270
Katzenbach, Nicholas, 453, 456
Kelly, Frank K., 365–367; Basic Issues program, 388, 389; Center for the Study of Democratic Institutions public relations, 392, 394, 410, 411, 412, 413, 414, 468–469, 473, 497; Center under Moos, 501, 504, 506, 510; Fund for the Republic public relations, 365–367, 368, 372–373, 377; "Pacem in Terris" convocation, 425, 427
Kelvin, Lord, quoted, 154–155
Kennan, George F., 435, 578n.7
Kennedy, Devereaux, 467
Kennedy, Jackie, 416
Kennedy, John F., 409, 416, 425, 432, 452, 490, 491, 497, 557n.9, 576–577n.13
Kennedy, Robert, 421
Kent, Raymond, 218
Kenyon College, 281
Kerr, Clark, 384, 387, 394, 414, 566n.7, 569n.2, 572n.9
Kerwin, Jerome G., 241
Kestnbaum, Meyer, 332, 381, 387, 565n.25
Keynes, John Maynard, 170, 523
Khan, Said Uddin, 459, 573n.10
Khan, Zafrullah, 433
Kimpton, Lawrence, 305–307, 307–309, 310
King, Alexander, 476
King, Henry Churchill, 7, 8, 13, 16, 37
King, Martin Luther, 376, 459, 573n.10
Kinsey, Alfred, 350
Kissinger, Henry, 367, 498, 576n.12, 576n.13
Kleitman, Nathaniel, 182
Knight, Frank, 158, 170–171, 229, 271
Knight, John S., 336
Knowles, Mary, 355–357, 364
Knox, Frank, 127–128, 181, 224
Korean war, 312, 322
Kornienko, Georgi, 433

La Follette, Phil F., 219
La Follette, Robert, 125, 208
La Guardia, Fiorello, 268
Laboratory School, 71–72, 134, 136, 187
Lacey, Robert, 323, 327, 328
Laing, Gordon J., 74, 92
Lake Placid School, 37–38, 43
Lakeside, Michigan, 63, 78, 174, 204
Lalande, Monsignor Bernard, 426
Lally, Monsignor Francis J., 372, 567n.5, 577n.1, 578n.10
Lamont, Thomas, 192
Landis, James M., 270
Landman, Amos, 355, 357, 358, 364
Landon, Alf, 173, 180, 181, 219
Lantos, Thomas P., 339
Lapham, Roger, 360, 384
Larsen, Roy E., 314
Lasker, Albert, 256
Laucks, Irving, 439–440
Laughlin, J. Laurence, 70, 319, 564n.16
Laughlin, W. Price, 498, 577n.1
Laura Spelman Rockefeller Fund, 154
Lawrence, D. H., 286, 289
Lawrenceville, 37, 105
Lazarsfeld, Paul, 344, 375, 567n.10
Le Matin, 19
League of Nations, 123, 262, 278
Left wing, 434, 538; criticism of Hutchins, 84, 322, 337, 359, 362, 375, 415. *See also* Macdonald, Dwight; Student protest movement
"Legal Order: The Law — Its Ways and Byways, The" (Fuller), 429
Legal realism, 50, 53, 55, 162, 165, 553n.24
Lehman, Herbert, 372
Leigh, Robert D., 294, 562n.25, 562n.26
Lester, Robin D., 143
Levi, Edward H., 305, 319, 529, 564n.16
Levine, Donald, 309
Levinson, Morris L., 452, 518, 570n.4, 577n.1
Lewis, C. S., 286
Lewis, Fulton, 340, 352, 358, 359, 361, 373, 412
Lewis, John L., 219
Lewis, Sinclair, 207, 208
Lewis, Sir Arthur, 476
Liberal arts, 26, 32, 70, 90, 135, 149, 166, 167, 300, 314, 519, 531, 535, 539; Great Books and, 98–99, 101, 103, 139, 140, 147, 231, 299–300, 537; at Northwestern University, 152; in teacher education, 321; at University of Chicago, 92, 99, 105, 134, 136–137, 139, 147, 221, 228,

246, 532. *See also* Committee on the Liberal Arts; Education: general
Liberalism/liberals, 124, 198, 199, 208, 214, 362, 369; model US constitution and, 488, 489; McCarthyism vs., 344, 345–346, 369
Libraries, 145–146
Lichtman, Richard, 418
Liebling, A. J., 69, 310
Life, 218, 284, 433
Lilienthal, David, 260
Limbach, Arthur "Stump," 20, 21
Lincoln, Abraham, 116
Lindbergh, Charles, 214, 218, 219, 557n.7
Linn, James Weber, 131
Linton, Albert, 356, 363, 392, 565n.25
Lippmann, Walter, 296, 314, 379, 562n.33, 568n.13
Little, Arthur D., 491
Little Rock, Arkansas, 397
Llewellyn, Karl N., 49
Locke, John, 101
Logan Act, 457
Logical positivism, 381–382. *See also* Positivism
Look, 464
Lord & Thomas, 182
Los Alamos, New Mexico, 251
Los Angeles Times, 412, 423, 514, 572n.6
Los Angeles Times Syndicate, 442
Loti, Pierre, 19
Louisiana State University, 233
Louisville Courier-Journal, 314
Love, Donald M., 8–9, 13
Lovett, Robert Morss, 70, 130–131
Lucas, Scott, 365–366
Luce, Clare Booth, 325, 532, 580n.12
Luce, Henry, 31, 210, 256, 285, 325, 566n.7, 571n.11; Commission on Freedom of the Press and, 272, 293–294, 562n.33; Hutchins and, 193, 299, 529, 532–533; *Life* and, 218, 433; *Time* and, 120, 193, 299
Lyford, Joseph, 409, 417
Lyons, Louis M., 296, 400

McAllister, Frances, 510, 513, 577n.1, 578–579n.10
MacArthur, Douglas, 438
McCall's, 478
McCarran Bill, 329, 330
McCarthy, Eugene, 370, 432, 490, 571n.11
McCarthy, Joseph, 328, 329, 340, 374, 385. *See also* McCarthyism

McCarthyism, 276, 324, 330, 331, 338; decline of, 344, 345, 374; as populist movement, 345–346; supporters of, 345, 362. *See also* Right wing
McConaughy, James, Jr., 360
McCormick, Robert R., 121, 127, 128, 183, 296
McCracken, Henry Noble, 218
McDonald, Donald, 410, 465, 516
Macdonald, Dwight: on Ford Foundation, 312, 318, 335; on Fund for the Advancement of Education, teacher training, 322; on Fund for the Republic, 346, 375; on Great Books, 337; as Hutchins's critic, 322, 337, 359, 375, 377; on Ferry, 325
McDonnell, Anne. *See* Ford, Anne McDonnell
McDougal, Myres S., 162–163, 553n.25
McEvoy, J. P., 114, 120
McGovern, George, 432, 572n.8, 576–577n.13
McIlwain, Charles H., 270
McKeon, Richard, 104: Basic Issues program, 381, 411–412; Cornwall College and, 167, 217; *Encyclopaedia Britannica* and, 258; Great Books and, 98, 99; at University of Chicago, 85, 86, 99, 104–105, 109, 136, 137, 139, 200, 217, 231, 241, 551n.6; world government, 262–263, 269, 279
MacLeish, Archibald, 294, 562n.25
McMullen, Roy, 430
McNamara, Robert, 454–455
McVeigh, Frances, 289
McVeigh, Maude Phelps. *See* Hutchins, Maude Phelps McVeigh
Madison, James, 270
Magic Mountain, The (Mann), 206
Maguire, Ruth Swift, 61
Malcolm X, 448
Manhattan Project, 260, 261; origins of, in Metallurgy Project, 227, 251; scientists of, at University of Chicago, 265–266. *See also* Metallurgy Laboratory/Project
Mann, Elisabeth. *See* Borgese, Elisabeth Mann
Mann, Georg, 169
Mann, Horace, 135, 554n.7
Mann, Mrs. Thomas, 160
Mann, Thomas, 160, 206, 270, 283
Marder, Murray, 329
Marfleet Lectures (Hutchins), 336
Marin, Peter, 468, 470
Marina, Madeline, 394
Maritain, Jacques, 89, 191, 230, 336, 409, 562n.25, 568n.13

Marquette University, 410
Marshall, George C., 329
Marshall, J. Howard, 381, 577n.1
Marshall Plan, 302, 312
Martin, Joan, 483
Martin, William McChesney, 192
Marx, Karl, 163, 297, 385, 487, 525
Marxism, 125, 362, 369, 405, 418, 445, 532.
    See also Communism
Mason, Max, 74–75, 92
"Mass Media, The" (Basic Issues study), 387
Materialism, 32, 147, 246, 534, 537; Hutchins
    on, 233, 234
"Mathematics and Logic: Retrospect and Pros-
    pect" (Ulam), 430
Mayer, Milton, 117–119, 128, 130, 142, 173, 248
Maynor, Dorothy, 283
Mead, George H., 86–87, 90, 190
Measure, 271, 272, 464
Media. See Press/media
"Meet the Press," 360
Meiklejohn, Alexander, 260
Mellett, Lowell, 198
Mellon, Paul, 314, 379, 568n.13
"Memorial to the Board of Trustees on the
    State of the University," 240–243
Mendès-France, Pierre, 421, 443
Menjou, Adolphe, 19, 369
Merriam, Charles E., 59, 155, 194, 269, 305,
    562n.25
Metallurgy Laboratory/Project, 225–227, 251,
    261, 266. See also Manhattan Project
Metaphysics, 99, 158–159, 160–161, 211,
    246, 267, 268, 531; criticism of, 162,
    163, 166, 234. See also Facts vs. Ideas
    controversy
Metaphysics (Aristotle), 117, 118
Metropolitan Structures, 103, 571n.7
Meyer, Emma, 63–64
Meyer, Eugene, 180–181
Meyer, Fred, 63–64
Meyer, Katherine, 180
Miami Daily News, 452, 570n.4
Michelson, Albert A., 70
Michigan State University, 408
Middle East, 458
Mill, John S., 100, 523
Millay, Edna St. Vincent, 106
Miller, Francis, 140
Miller, Henry, 289, 315–316
Miller, William Lee, 408
Millis, Walter, 345, 360, 394, 395, 396, 412,
    418, 421, 567n.10, 569n.2, 569–570n.2,
    571n.11

Milstein, Nathan, 283
Milton, John, 143, 152, 445, 552n.7
Minneapolis Tribune, 503
Minow, Newton, 421, 576n.8
Mischel, Florence, 479
Mitchell, Maurice, 416, 430, 536
Mitgang, Herbert, 388
Mitropoulos, Dimitri, 283
"Model for Discussion, A" (Tugwell), 487
Modern Language Association, 282
Modern Library, Great Books editions, 259
Montaigne, Michel, 286
Moody, William Vaughn, 70
Moore, Underhill, 53
Moos, Malcolm, 503; Center for the Study of
    Democratic Institutions chairman, 499–
    502, 503–514, 515, 517, 519, 520, 521,
    577n.1; Center personnel, relationship
    with, 505, 506–508, 508–510, 511, 512–
    513, 518, 578n.19; Center reorganization,
    severance pay and dismissal, 514, 515;
    "communiversity" proposal, 509, 511–
    512, 513; Hutchins's views on, 503–504,
    508, 509, 512–513
Mordy, Wendell, 516
Morgan, J. P., 192
Morgan, Junius, 192
Morgenthau, Hans J., 65, 571n.6, 576–
    577n.13, 578n.7
Morini, Erica, 283
Morison, Stanley, 404–405, 559n.9
Morley, Felix, 218
Morris, John Godfrey, 102
Motion Picture Alliance for the Preservation of
    American Ideals, 369
Motion Picture Association, 190
Mott, John, 336
Mott, Stewart, 512, 577n.1, 578–579n.10
Mount Holyoke, 4
Moyers, Bill, 456
Mumford, Lewis, 206, 207, 421
Mundelein, Cardinal, 159, 553n.15
Munnecke, Wilbur C., 116, 274, 550n.19
Murch, Anna Laura. See Hutchins, Anna
    Laura Murch
Murch, Maynard Hale (grandfather), 6
Murch, Maynard Hale, Jr. (uncle), 6
Murphy, Arthur E., 86–87
Murphy, Michael, 449
Murray, Father John Courtney, 89, 408;
    Basic Issues program and, 381, 384,
    387
Mussolini, Benito, 163, 226, 487
Myrdal, Gunnar, 421, 575n.10

NAACP. *See* National Association for the Advancement of Colored People
NAB. *See* National Association of Broadcasters
Nabokov, Vladimir, 286
Nagasaki, 252, 260, 267
NAM. *See* National Association of Manufacturers
Narasimhan, C. V., 433, 441, 572n.8
Nation, 84, 279
National Advisory Council on Radio and Education, 146
National Association for the Advancement of Colored People (NAACP), 448
National Association of Broadcasters (NAB), 442
National Association of Manufacturers (NAM), 129, 217
National Broadcasting Company (NBC), 367, 421, 497, 576n.8
National Catholic Welfare Conference, 130, 570n.5, 571n.6
National Council of Churches, 130, 571n.6
National Education Association, 135
National Geographic Society, 463
National Institute of Arts and Letters, 131
National Labor Board, 126
National Merit Scholarship, 335
National Municipal League, 355
National News Council, 496
National Press Club, 350
National Recovery Administration, 194–195, 196, 199
National Review, 361
"Nature: Man and the Cosmos" (Calder), 429
"Nature of Man, The" (Adler lecture), 285
Navasky, Victor, 325
Nazism, 163, 213, 215, 217, 250, 538
NBC. *See* National Broadcasting Company
Neal, Fred Warner, 425, 476; "Pacem in Terris" convocations, 425, 433, 452, 456, 498, 517–518
Nef, Elinor Castle, 190, 191, 230
Nef, John Ulrich, 190–191; Committee on Social Thought chairman, 230, 231, 270–271, 272; Hutchins's letters to, 198, 200, 205, 244, 270–271, 272, 275–276, 286, 291–292, 292–293, 300, 301, 440–441; as Hutchins's supporter, 158, 173, 190, 191, 198, 217, 241, 292; Maude Hutchins and, 79; at University of Chicago, 190, 191, 198, 229–230, 231, 241

Negro and the Schools, The (Ashmore), 349
Neilson, William Allan, 206
Nenni, Pietro, 434
Neumann, John von, 230
New Deal, 125, 127, 193, 194, 312, 345, 384; Hutchins's views on, 125, 216; right-wing opposition, 128, 183, 350; Tugwell and, 269, 487, 488
New Directions Press, 289, 564n.16
New Haven, Connecticut, 26, 29, 50, 52, 56, 79
New Haven Civic League, 29
New Leader, 362
New Left, 445, 446, 447, 484. *See also* Student protest movement
Newman, John, 246
Newman, Paul, 422, 577n.1, 578–579n.10
New Perspectives Quarterly, 537
New Plan/Chicago Plan, 75, 92–93, 96, 97, 134, 135, 153, 169. *See also* University of Chicago: undergraduate/College reform
"New Realism, The" (Hutchins speech), 249–250
New Republic, 49
New School for Social Research, 270, 562n.25
Newsday, 387
Newsom, Earl, 324, 334, 340, 368
Newsom Company. *See* Earl Newsom and Company
Newspapers. *See* Press/media
Newsweek, 288, 296, 346
Newton, Isaac, 156, 268
New York Daily News, 457, 487
New Yorker, 69, 289, 310, 312, 337
New York Herald Tribune, 345, 402; black-population study, 397, 399; *Higher Learning in America* review, 161; on Hutchins, 84, 192–193, 217, 248–249
New York Post, 408
New York State College for Teachers, 234
New York Stock Exchange, 191–193, 198–199
New York Times, 23, 365, 388, 416, 464; on Ashmore-Baggs Hanoi trip, 454; on Center for the Study of Democratic Institutions, 489; on Commission on Freedom of the Press report, 296; on Douglas impeachment attempt, 483, 484; on Fund for the Republic, 385; *Higher Learning in America* review, 161–162; on HUAC, 371; on Hutchins, 84, 96, 124, 241; reactionary opposition to, 345–346; on University of Chicago reform, 96, 241
New York World Telegram and Sun, 360

Niebuhr, Reinhold, 89, 206, 282, 367, 394, 562n.25; American Character Conference address, 410; Basic Issues program, 384, 387; Center for the Study of Democratic Institutions and, 408, 409; Committee to Frame a World Constitution, 270, 279

Nielson, Elisabeth Burgess, 12

Nieman Foundation/Fellows, 296, 348, 365, 400, 411, 425, 576–577n.13

Nietzsche, Friedrich, 538

"Night Beat," 367

Nitze, William A., 272

Nixon, Richard, 114, 338, 426, 478, 517; anti-media campaign, 495, 497; Douglas impeachment attempt, 483, 484, 485; Supreme Court and, 494–495

No Friendly Voice (Hutchins), 143, 167

North Park College, 287

Northwestern University, 46; University of Chicago merger plans, 151–152, 153, 552n.23

Norton, Lucille, 129, 130

Notes Toward a Definition of Culture (Eliot), 271

Notre Dame, 89, 160, 564n.9, 566n.7, 576n.13

Nuclear weapons, 251–253, 260–262, 264, 267, 269, 277, 281, 438, 444, 540; development of, 225–227, 251–252, 260, 532; opposition to, at Center, 412–414, 427, 439, 455; Roosevelt and, 226, 251; scientists' attempt to stop use of, 251–252; world government to control, 252–253, 261, 436, 437, 477, 532. *See also* Atomic Energy Commission; Atomic Energy Control Conference

Nuremberg Trials, 250

Nyary, Nicholas, 518

Nye, Gerald P., 219

O'Brian, John Lord, 363, 383

O'Connor, Sandra Day, 525

Oberlin, Ohio, 5, 8–9, 33

Oberlin Academy, 9–10, 12, 39

Oberlin College, 4, 7, 8–16, 37, 188, 201, 356, 359, 490, 565n.25; Hutchins at, 10–17, 27, 31, 33, 36, 105, 282, 530, 544n.22; Puritan influence on, 8, 10–11, 13–15, 16, 31, 33; during World War I, 16–17

Oberlin Review, 11

Oberlin Theological Seminary, 5–6, 7, 13

Office of Scientific Research and Development, 265

"Official Bulletins" (Harper), 71

Ogburn, William F., 154

Ogden, C. K., 51

Ohio State University, 178, 201

Old Dominion Foundation, 314

"Omnibus," 320–321

"One World" theory, 210, 279, 557n.9. *See also* World government

"Operation Rolling Thunder," 436

Oppenheimer, J. Robert, 251, 568n.13

Oram, Harold, 419, 421

Origin of Species (Darwin), 13

Orlick, Barbara. *See* Hutchins, Barbara

Orlick, Vesta. *See* Hutchins, Vesta Orlick

Ortega y Gasset, José, 246, 284, 394, 568n.13

Ostrow, Seniel, 420, 421, 519, 577n.1, 578–579n.10

Other America, The (Harrington), 410

Other Side of Jordan, The (Ashmore), 399

"Our Contemporary Ancestors" (Hutchins speech), 27

Oxford, 104, 137, 138, 140, 161, 203, 258, 336, 461

"Pacem in Terris" ("PIT") convocations, 426–427, 440, 477, 478, 505, 506, 507, 571n.6; "PIT I," 425, 426–427, 431–437, 438–439, 441, 442, 451 (participants, 434–435, 571n.9, 571n.11); "PIT II," 441–442, 450, 451–460, 462, 468 (participants, 458–459, 573–574n.10); "PIT II" planning session, 443–444 (participants, 443, 572n.8); "PIT III," 497–500, 501, 517, 576n.12 (participants, 576–577n.13); "PIT IV," 498, 505, 507, 517–518 (participants, 578n.7); US undermining of, 454, 456–458, 460, 462. *See also* Center for the Study of Democratic Institutions; Wingspread conference

"Pacem in Terris" encyclical (John XXIII), 425, 426, 434

"Pacem in Maribus" ("PIM") convocations, 477–478, 487

Pacifism, 16, 23, 211. *See also* Conscientious objectors

Packer, Herbert, 375

Paepcke, Elizabeth, 174, 272–274

Paepcke, Walter, 272–274, 285, 301, 314, 336, 465, 561n.30; Goethe Bicentennial, 273, 274, 276, 283, 291

"Paideia Proposal" (Adler), 539–540, 554n.7

Palais des Nations, Geneva, 443, 451

Palme, Olof, 459, 573n.10

Palmer, Reverend Albert W., 218

Pankhurst, Emmeline, 11
Paradise Lost (Milton), 143
Park, Rosemary, 421, 572n.9
Parten, Jubal R., 332, 363, 370, 372, 373,
    432, 491, 565n.25, 567n.1; Center for the
    Study of Democratic Institutions and,
    418, 499, 509, 514, 518, 520, 575n.9;
    Moos controversy and, 501, 503–504,
    506, 508, 510, 511, 512, 513, 514,
    577n.1
Partisan Review, 271
Parvin, Albert B., 410–411, 482–483, 484.
    See also Parvin Foundation
Parvin Foundation, 411, 419, 442, 478, 482,
    482–485
Pascal, Blaise, 20
Patterson, Alicia, 336, 387, 390–391
Patterson, Hugh, 349
Patterson, Robert P., 265
Pauling, Linus, 414, 423, 424, 436, 440,
    473–474
PBS. *See* Public Broadcasting Service
Pearl Harbor, 219, 223, 252
Pegler, Westbrook, 99, 338, 340; conspiracy
    charges against Ford Foundation, 324–
    325
Pell, Claiborne, 432, 458, 571n.6, 571n.11,
    573n.10
People's Institute, 98
Perry, John, 442, 456, 463, 473, 474, 489
Perspectives, 430, 442, 564n.16, 570n.2
Peterson, Russell, 490
Phelps, Billy, 517
Phi Beta Kappa, 30, 104
"Philanthropic Stew" (Quigley), 316–317
Phillips Academy, 144
Piatigorsky, Gregor, 283
Piel, Gerald, 396, 571n.11
Pike, Bishop James A., 468, 573n.10
Pilgrim's Regress (Lewis), 286
Pilot, 372, 567n.5
"PIM." *See* "Pacem in Maribus" convocations
"PIT." *See* "Pacem in Terris" convocations
Pittsburgh Teachers Association, 145
Pius XII, 160
Plato, 98, 230, 280, 297, 462, 523, 538
Plymouth Monthly Meeting, 355, 356, 357
Pocket Books (publisher), 437
Poetry, 289, 290
Poetry and Mathematics (Buchanan), 104
Poincaré, Jules, 156
Poland, 443, 459
"Political Order: Democracy in a Revolution-
    ary Era, The" (Wheeler), 429

"Political Parties, Pressure Groups, and Pro-
    fessional Associations" (Basic Issues
    study), 387
Populism, 345
Portland Press Herald, 360
Portrait of the Artist as a Young Man (Joyce),
    286
Positivism, 101. *See also* Logical positivism
Potomac Institute, 521, 578n.10
Pravda, 434
Preble, Robert, 336, 337
"Preconditions of World Organization"
    (Hutchins speech), 522
Preece, Warren, 431
*Prejudice and the Press: A Restatement of the
    Principle of Freedom of the Press with
    Specific Reference to the Hutchins-Luce
    Commission* (Hughes), 296–297
Prelude to Riot (Jacobs), 449
Presburger, Josip, 433
Presbyterianism, 26, 58, 89, 281, 530. *See
    also* Calvinism; Hutchins, Robert May-
    nard: Puritan/Calvinist heritage; Puritan-
    ism
President's Report for 1959–69 (Center for
    the Study of Democratic Institutions),
    409
Press-commission study, 293–298, 352, 397,
    400, 495–496. *See also* Commission on
    Freedom of the Press
Press/media: Ashmore US-Vietnam disclosure,
    Vietnam policy, 457; blacklisting report
    and, 368, 371; bias of, 294–295; Center
    for the Study of Democratic Institutions
    and, 414–415, 422, 437, 458, 460, 462,
    487, 489, 495–496, 497, 498, 518,
    576n.8; educational role of, 145–146,
    320; Ford Foundation and, 324; freedom
    of, 272, 294, 295, 297, 330, 371, 495–
    496, 519; Fund for the Republic and,
    350, 355, 358, 359–360, 365, 367, 385;
    Gill Poll, 219; Great Books publishing
    project, 337; Harper's relationship with,
    66–67; Hutchins's obituaries, 529, 534–
    535; Hutchins's radio address on war in-
    volvement and, 217; Hutchins's
    relationship with, 41, 66–67, 84, 113,
    133, 143, 156, 165, 195, 201, 241, 276,
    300–301, 327, 359–360, 365, 366, 414–
    415; Hutchins's study on, 293–298, 352,
    397, 400, 495–496; mainstream, 338;
    Nixon's campaign against, 495, 497;
    Parvin Foundation controversy, 483–484;
    right wing, 128–129, 130, 133, 269, 276,

Press/media (*cont.*)
296, 324, 327, 329, 338, 355, 374, 376, 487; self-regulation, 496; University of Chicago–Northwestern University merger, 151. *See also* Commission on Freedom of the Press; First Amendment; *names of individual newspapers, magazines, radio and television shows;* Radio; Television
Pribham, Karl, 476
Price, Dick, 449
Princeton University, 226, 265, 380, 381, 409, 411, 423, 473, 568n.13, 571n.11, 572n.9
"Professor Is Sometimes Right, The" (Hutchins speech), 147
Progressive, 248
Progressive Education Association, 178
Progressive education movement, 90, 91
Progressive party, 440
"Prospects for Democracy" convocations, 420–422, 424, 427. *See also* Center for the Study of Democratic Institutions
Providence Journal, 534
Public Administration Clearing House, 224
Public Broadcasting Service (PBS), 497, 576n.8
Public education. *See* Education: public
Purcell, Edward A., Jr., 165
Purina Mills, 303
Puritanism, 4, 6, 8, 16, 25, 26, 31, 32. *See also* Calvinism; Hutchins, Robert Maynard: Puritan/Calvinist heritage; Presbyterianism

Quadrangle Club (University of Chicago), 79, 110, 111, 185
Quaker Oats, 181, 213
Quigley, Martin, 316–318, 334, 340, 564nn.12–14
Quintanilla, Luis, 453, 571n.9, 572n.8
Quito, Ecuador, 411

Rabi, Isidore, 384, 387
Racism. *See* Desegregation: southern opposition to; Hyde Park
Radio, 120, 295, 497. *See also* Press/media
Rainbow, The (Lawrence), 286
Random House, 174
Rapoport, Bernard, 499, 501, 577n.1, 578–579n.10
Rayburn, Sam, 370, 372
Rea, Thomas E., 11, 13
Reader's Digest, 257, 284
Reagan, Ronald, 524, 536, 538

Real, James, 418, 569n.2
Real Life of Sebastian Knight, The (Nabokov), 286
Redfield, Robert, 271, 319, 387, 561n.25, 562n.25, 568n.13; Basic Issues program and, 381, 384; Committee to Frame a World Constitution, 270; on Hutchins, 304; at University of Chicago, 229, 258, 304
Red Network (Dilling), 130
Reece, Brazilla Carroll, 338, 350–351
Reece Committee, 350–351
Reed, Edward, 388, 394, 464–465
Reed, Stanley, 196
Reeves, Thomas C., 325–326; Basic Issues program and, 382, 388; on Fund for the Republic, 349, 368, 375, 376; on right-wing campaign, 345–346, 352
Reflections (Pascal), 20
Reform. *See* University of Chicago: faculty/administrative reform; Hutchins's effect on; as model for national reform; reform issues; undergraduate/College reform
Regional Labor Board, Chicago, 118, 126–127
Regnery, Henry, 271, 272
Reischauer, Edwin O., 478, 575n.11, 576–577n.13
"Religion in a Free Society" (Basic Issues study), 387
"Religion: The Search for Final Meaning" (Cogley), 429
Religious News Service, 426
Report on Blacklisting (Cogley), 370
Republican party, 173, 180, 210, 213, 214, 219, 331, 338, 339, 456, 483, 536, 578n.7; Hutchins's opinion of, 120, 122–123, 124, 181; "un-Americanism" as issue for, 324–325
Research, 113, 147, 159, 242; Fund for the Republic and, 341, 344, 375; nuclear, 225–227, 251, 260, 262, 264–266, 267, 275; universities and, 113, 161, 163, 266; at University of Chicago, 57, 69–70, 72, 80, 83, 113, 147, 152, 153, 221, 222, 225–227, 236, 238, 251, 260, 261, 264–265, 266, 306
Research on Freedom: Report of Dialectical Discoveries and Constructions, 320
Reuther, Walter, 324, 421
Revolt of the Masses, The (Ortega y Gasset), 284
Richberg, Donald, 194–195
Rickover, Hyman, 421

Right wing: Bloom endorsed by, 538; First Amendment and broadcasting, 495–496; issues opposed to, 324, 328, 329–330, 338, 339, 341, 344, 345–346, 346–347, 350–351, 356, 376; patriotism as tactic of, 128; press/media and, 128–129, 130, 133, 269, 276, 296, 324, 327, 329, 338, 355, 374, 376, 487; vs. Center for the Study of Democratic Institutions, 412–414, 415, 457; vs. Ford Foundation, 324–325, 326, 328–331, 335, 338, 350, 361; vs. Fund for the Republic, 335, 338, 340, 344, 345–346, 350–352, 354, 355–358, 359–361, 364, 366, 367–368, 369–372, 373, 374–375, 381, 412; vs. Hutchins, 34, 47, 118, 121–122, 127, 128–132, 133, 151, 247, 276, 296, 297, 325, 327, 338, 344, 345–346, 350–351, 352, 354, 355, 359–361, 364, 370, 371, 374–375. *See also* Conservatism/conservatives; House Un-American Activities Committee; McCarthyism; White Citizens Councils

Rise of the British Coal Industry, The (Nef), 190

Ritchie-Calder, Lord, 429, 476, 507, 573–574n.10

Robert M. Hutchins Center for the Study of Democratic Institutions, 537

Roberts, Owen J., 349, 379, 564n.9, 568n.13

Rochester, Earl of, 525

Rockefeller, David, 336

Rockefeller, John D., 529; as University of Chicago benefactor, 57–58, 62, 66, 67, 68, 69, 80, 202, 232

Rockefeller, John D., Jr., 65, 202

Rockefeller, Nelson, 336

Rockefeller Chapel (University of Chicago), 59, 63, 89, 110, 204, 242, 528–529

Rockefeller Foundation, 53, 68, 74, 255, 326, 350

Rockefeller University, 429–430, 509, 511

Rogat, Yosal, 408

Roll, Sir Eric, 430

Rolz-Bennett, José, 441

Romance of Commerce and Culture, The (Allen), 273

Roosevelt, Franklin Delano, 127–128, 180, 198, 219, 267, 312, 325, 487, 488; Hutchins and, 124–125, 132, 193–194, 195, 196, 198–199, 207, 208, 209, 211, 215, 219; World War II and, 199, 205, 207, 210–211, 215–216, 218, 226, 251, 557n.9

Roosevelt, James, 452, 456

Roper, Elmo: Basic Issues program, 384, 388, 389; Center for the Study of Democratic Institutions projects, 418, 420, 571n.11; Fund for the Republic, 332, 339, 343, 363, 367, 368, 372, 384, 565n.25, 567n.1

Rosenberg, Ethel, 483

Rosenberg, Harold, 230

Rosenberg, Julius, 483

Rosenwald, Julius, 68, 255, 256

Rosenwald, Lessing, 256

Rossiter, Clinton L., 341, 355, 375, 381, 567n.10

Roullier Art Galleries, 288

"Roundtable of the Air," 120, 214, 252, 262

Rousseau, Jean, 116, 523

Royster, Vermont, 467

R. S. Maguire Fund, 61

Rubicam, Raymond, 336

Rubinstein, Artur, 283

Ruddock, A. B., 413, 414

Ruml, Beardsley, 110, 158, 270, 550n.6, 559n.9, 562n.25

Rush Medical College, 232

Rusk, Dean, 453, 456

Russell, Bertrand, 55, 156, 394

Russell, Carroll Mason, 78, 158, 191, 547n.3; on Maude Hutchins, 78, 93–94, 174, 204

Russell, Pete, 204

Russia. *See* Soviet Russia; Soviet Union

Ryerson, Edward L., 181

Ryerson, Martin, 203

Sacco, Nicola, 47, 59, 130

Sacco-Vanzetti case, 47, 59

Saigon, 458, 459. *See also* Vietnam

St. John's College, 100, 140–141, 189, 260, 270, 394

Salant, Richard, 495, 576n.8

Salinger, Pierre, 432

Salisbury, Harrison, 464

Salk, Jonas, 421

Sandburg, Carl, 391

Santa Barbara News-Press, 412, 467

Sarah Lawrence College, 165, 326

Sartre, Jean-Paul, 394

Saturday Evening Post, 201

Saturday Review, 284, 478, 490, 571n.11

Saudek, Robert, 321

Scalia, Antonin, 495, 576n.8

Schaff, Adam, 435

Scherman, Harry, 256

Schlegel, John Henry, 53

Schnabel, Artur, 191
Schoenberg, Arnold, 230
Scholasticism, 159, 162, 172, 188, 240
Schuman, Frederick, 128, 130
Schwab, Joseph J., 260, 516
Schweitzer, Albert, 284–285, 394
Science, 95, 101, 229, 264, 266; Hutchins
    and, 153, 156–158, 159, 160–161, 163,
    166, 304–305, 423; liberal education and,
    72, 531; methods of, 154–157, 158, 159,
    161, 163, 166, 222; social science vs.,
    86, 267. *See also* Facts vs. Ideas contro-
    versy; Social science
Scientific American, 396, 571n.11
Scott, Walter Dill, 151
Scottsboro Boys, 130
SDS. *See* Students for a Democratic Society
Seaborg, Glenn, 261
Search for Meaning (Nef), 190
Sears, Roebuck, 68, 192, 197; as *Encyclopae-
    dia Britannica* owner, 255, 256, 257, 258
SEC. *See* Securities and Exchange Commis-
    sion
Securities and Exchange Commission (SEC),
    51, 191, 196, 197, 198, 208, 460
Sedgwick, Ellery, 173
Seeley, John: Center for the Study of Demo-
    cratic Institutions and, 462, 463, 468,
    469, 470, 473, 486; student protest move-
    ment and, 449, 466, 467
Selective Service Act, 16
Senate Foreign Relations Committee, 444, 498
Senate Internal Security Committee, 355
"Sentimental Alumnus, The" (Hutchins
    speech), 14–15
Sevareid, Eric, 338, 540, 547n.8, 576n.8
Seymour, George Dudley, 40
Shakespeare, William, 98
Shannon, William V., 408
Sharp, Malcolm P., 172
Sheen, Monsignor Fulton, 323–324, 580n.12
Sheinbaum, Stanley, 408, 476, 496, 537,
    571n.11
Sherwood, Robert E., 208, 347, 356
Shidehara, Kijuro, 438
Shils, Edward, 102, 142, 230, 319, 564n.16;
    on University of Chicago reform/
    controversy, 158, 170–171, 173, 245
Shimer College, 119
"Should Institutions of Learning Be Abol-
    ished?" (Hutchins speech), 36
Simmons, Ellen French Vanderbilt, 557n.7
Shuster, George N., 332, 381, 394, 409,
    562n.25, 567n.1, 570n.11

Simmons, E. E., 192
Simon, James F., 85
Simon, Yves, 230
Sir George Watson Lectures (Hutchins), 336
Six Day War, 458
Slesinger, Donald, 53
Small, Albion, 73
Smellie, William, 402
Smith, Adam, 170, 269
Smith, T. V., 108, 109, 114, 125–126, 199
Smith College, 206
SNCC. *See* Student Nonviolent Coordinating
    Committee
Social Frontier, 163
"Social Order: The Promethean Dream —
    Society in Search of Itself, The" (Aron),
    430
Social science, 52, 70, 462, 511; controversy
    over, 86, 90, 153–156, 159, 160, 170;
    Hutchins and, 49, 53–54, 267, 423, 494,
    535–536. *See also* Facts vs. Ideas contro-
    versy
Socialist party, 125, 371
Sokolsky, George, 385
South Africa, 468, 573n.10
Southeast Asia, 436, 443, 454, 455, 457, 459.
    See also Vietnam
Southern Regional Council, 347, 376, 567n.8,
    567–568n.5
South Shore Country Club, 81–82
Southwest Conference, 201, 556n.6
Soviet Russia, 123, 128; World War II and,
    217. *See also* Soviet Union
Soviet Union, 282, 369; nuclear weapons and,
    261, 455; "Pacem in Terris" convoca-
    tion, 433, 434, 443, 458, 459, 478; US
    relations, 234, 341, 425, 426, 432, 435,
    459, 498, 518; world government and,
    270, 277. *See also* Soviet Russia
Spaak, Paul-Henri, 434
Specialization, in education, 72, 73, 92–93,
    95, 101, 135, 136, 147, 153, 158, 187,
    229, 247, 395, 401, 404, 423, 521, 526,
    537
Speech, freedom of, 185, 341, 413, 457–458,
    495–496, 497. *See also* Free Speech
    movement
Spivak, Lawrence, 360
Stalin, Joseph, 362, 435
Stanford Medical Center, 476
Stanford University, 218, 270, 305, 314, 466,
    473, 476, 558n.5
Stanford University Hospital, 525
Stein, Gertrude, 99–100

Stendhal (pseud. Marie-Henri Beyle), 286
Stephen Fitzgerald Agency, 365
Sterling, John W., 53
Stevens, John Paul, 485
Stevens, Robert, 48, 51, 55
Stevenson, Adlai, 122, 205, 325, 346, 359,
    360, 367, 383, 402, 421, 559n.9, 571n.9;
    Kennedy administration and, 425–426
Stevenson, Eleanor Bumstead, 332, 356, 357,
    363, 503, 565n.25, 575n.1
Stewart, Potter, 213
Stokes, Reverend Anson Phelps, 38
Stone, I. F., 344
Storke, T. M., 412
Storrs Lectures (Hutchins), 160. *See also*
    Higher Learning in America, The
Stouffer, Samuel, 344, 375, 567n.10
Stover, Carl, 403, 416, 426, 441, 571n.11
"Strengthening of Democracy, The" (Ford
    Foundation program), 313, 330
Stuart, John, 181
Stuart, R. Douglas, Jr., 213, 218, 219–220
Studebaker Motor Company, 185, 302, 314,
    336
Student Army Training Corps, 223
Student Nonviolent Coordinating Committee
    (SNCC), 466
Student protest movement, 441, 444–450,
    466–468; Hutchins's satirization of, 445–
    447
Students and Society (Center for the Study of
    Democratic Institutions), 467
Students for a Democratic Society (SDS), 466,
    484
Subversive Activities Control Board, 329
Summa Theologica (Aquinas), 320
Supreme Court, 213, 307, 389, 564n.9; deseg-
    regation, 336, 342, 346, 348, 349, 359,
    374, 523, 525; Douglas and, 51, 208,
    350, 411, 482, 483–485, 526; education,
    right to, 523–525; Hutchins's interest in,
    193–194, 195–198, 204, 208, 494–495;
    Reagan's anti-progressive crusade, 524,
    536; states' rights and, 523–524. *See also*
    Brown v. *Board of Education*
Supreme Court of California, 496
Supreme Judicial Court of Massachusetts, 47
"Survival and Freedom," 367, 567–568n.5
Sutherland, George, 196
Swan, Thomas W., 48, 49–50, 54, 55
Swift, Ann, 6
Swift, Charles, 61
Swift, Harold, 60–61, 78, 82, 106, 115, 181,
    305, 343; Hutchins and, 58, 59–60, 62–

64, 75, 129, 174, 204, 292; University of
    Chicago controversies and, 87, 129, 130,
    179
Swift, Ruth. *See* Maguire, Ruth Swift
Swift & Co., 61, 175
Syntopicon (Great Books index), 259–260,
    336, 337, 408, 549n.6. *See also* Great
    Books of the Western World: publishing
    project
Szilard, Leo, 226, 251, 252, 261

Taft, Robert A., 130, 213, 219, 325
Taft, William Howard, 47
Tagger, Peter, 500, 516, 519, 522, 576n.12
Takayanagi, Kenzo, 438–439, 571n.9
Tawney, R. H., 191, 291, 568n.13
Taylor, Harold, 165, 326–327, 565n.12
Taylor, Susan B., 11
Teachers/teaching, 91, 159, 224; education of,
    80, 81, 144, 148, 321–322, 348; salaries
    of, 145, 335. *See also* Education; Univer-
    sity of Chicago: faculty
Teague, Charles, 467
Technique of Controversy, The (Adler), 51
"Technological Order: The Conquest of Na-
    ture and Its Consequences" (Forbes), 429
Technology: education and, 146, 229, 234,
    265, 444, 521, 537; society, effect on,
    146, 266–267, 295, 427, 534
Television, 125, 320–321, 388, 474, 477,
    495, 497. *See also* Press/media
Television-Radio Workshop, 320–321
Temianka, Henri, 528
Temple University, 321
Temporary Committee on Information (Fund
    for the Republic), 364, 365, 567n.1
Tennessee Valley Authority, 260
"Termites of Capitalism" (Douglas speech),
    84
Thant, U, 433, 436, 458, 573n.10
Theophilus North (Wilder), 493
Thielens, Wagner, Jr., 375
Think tanks, 417, 537
Third World, 411, 478, 518
Thomas, J. Parnell, 369
Thomas, Norman, 125, 194, 371
Thomism. *See* Aquinas, Thomas/Thomism
Thompson, Dorothy, 207, 208
Thompson, Mrs. Samuel Ludlow, 35
Thompson, Ralph, 161–162
Thuermer, Angus MacLean, 110, 556n.8,
    576n.12
Tillich, Paul, 230, 434, 568n.13
Tillman, "Pitchfork" Ben, 347

Time, 31, 193, 346, 360, 487, 562n.33; on
  Hutchins, 115, 120, 195, 299–300; on
  Maude Hutchins, 111; on University of
  Chicago, 202, 203
Time, Inc., 193, 293, 314, 433; Commission
  on Freedom of the Press, 293
Time-Life, 325
Toklas, Alice B., 100
"Town Meeting of the Air," 213, 219
Toynbee, Arnold, 191, 405, 406, 434
Tran Van Do, 457–458
Traynor, Roger, 496
Trilling, Diana, 362
Trujillo, Molina, 442
Truman, Harry, 251, 275, 329, 366, 440,
  557n.9
Tuerck House, 315, 316, 320, 334, 340
Tufts, James H., 86, 90
Tugwell, Rexford Guy, 194, 267–269, 270;
  Center for the Study of Democratic Insti-
  tutions and, 463, 466, 473, 486, 507,
  516; right wing vs., 269, 487–488; US
  model constitution, 476, 477, 487–489; at
  University of Chicago, 268–269, 309,
  563n.28
Twentieth Century Fund, 496
Tyler, Morris, 39, 41, 56
Tyler, Mrs. Morris, 40
Tyler, Ralph, 178, 230, 241, 258, 287, 319,
  514, 516, 536, 564n.16, 578–579n.10

Ulam, Stanislaw M., 430
UN. *See* United Nations
UNESCO. *See* United Nations Educational,
  Scientific, and Cultural Organization
Union League Club, 79
Unions, labor, 126, 324, 387, 394, 396, 409,
  410, 569n.2
"Unions and Union Leaders of Their Own
  Choosing" (Kerr), 387
Union Theological Seminary, 4, 270, 372,
  562n.25
United Arab Republic, 443, 572n.8
United Auto Workers, 324, 421
United Jewish Appeal, 336
United Mine Workers, 219
United Nations (UN), 278, 346, 350, 373,
  389, 436, 456, 459, 478, 564n.9;
  Hutchins's views on, 262, 522; "Pacem
  in Terris" convocations and, 433, 434,
  441, 443, 571n.6, 571n.9, 573n.10, 576–
  577n.13, 578n.7; Stevenson and, 421,
  425, 426; world-government constitution
  and, 276, 277, 280

United Nations Educational, Scientific, and
  Cultural Organization (UNESCO), 302,
  575n.10
United States, 261; chauvinism of, 341, 425;
  Communism in, 341, 355, 360, 362, 375;
  democracy and human rights, 210, 211,
  212, 213, 215, 216, 250–251, 518; foreign relations, 441, 442, 478, 498, 518,
  533; Hutchins's views on, 28, 235, 250–
  251, 460, 533, 540; "Pacem in Terris
  II," undermining of, 456–458, 460, 462;
  Soviet relations, 234, 341, 425, 426, 432,
  435, 459, 498, 518; Third World and,
  518; Vietnam war, 436, 439, 441, 443–
  444, 450, 453–458, 459, 498, 517; in
  World War I, 16; in World War II, 199,
  210–211, 218, 221
United States Court of Appeals, 48
Universities/colleges, 6, 13, 37, 42, 135, 150,
  223, 444; ideal/role of, 161, 235, 243,
  246–247, 260, 266, 306, 381, 532. *See
  also* Education; *names of individual
  schools*
University Board of Examinations (University
  of Chicago), 96
University Club (Chicago), 100, 291
University College of North Staffordshire, 336
University Graduate School of the Claremont
  Colleges, 425
"University in America, The" (Center pro-
  gram), 444; participants, 572n.9
University of Amsterdam, 429
University of Arkansas, 201
University of Berlin, 319
University of Birmingham, 336
University of California, 396, 414, 512; Kerr
  and, 384, 387, 414, 566n.7, 572n.9;
  Berkeley, 384, 387, 394, 396, 408, 410,
  418, 444, 448, 449; Davis, 574n.3;
  Los Angeles, 468, 500, 574n.3; Santa
  Barbara, 396, 412, 419, 465, 516,
  519, 537; Southern California, 315,
  476
University of Chicago: adult education, 146,
  246, 260, 273; anniversary celebrations,
  67, 200, 202–203; architecture/buildings,
  69, 78, 79, 80, 81, 154, 232, 301, 306–
  307; benefactors, 59, 61, 62, 67, 68, 69,
  80, 202, 232 (*see also* finances/fund raising); Commission on Freedom of the
  Press and, 562n.25; Committee on the
  Liberal Arts, 136–137, 138–140; Committee on Social Thought, 79, 158, 173,
  229–231, 270–271, 272, 440, 538; Com-

munism, right-wing accusations of, 128–132, 151, 183; conservatism of, 269, 536; denominational ties of, 57, 58; Depression, effect of, 112–113, 121, 134, 151, 173, 177, 178, 202, 222; Divinity School, 232, 254; Economics Department, 269; *Encyclopaedia Britannica* and, 255, 256, 257, 258, 260, 400–401, 474; entrance examinations, 73, 96, 136, 187; faculty, 70, 77, 83–84, 84–86, 176–179, 225, 227–228, 237, 267, 304–306; faculty/administrative reform, 77, 83–84, 112–113, 227–228, 237–240, 242, 244–245, 247–248, 254, 264, 486; faculty salaries, 69, 80, 81, 83–84, 84–86, 86, 112, 113, 153, 177; faculty vs. Hutchins, 76, 95–96, 99, 109, 111, 135–136, 153–154, 155–158, 160, 166, 169–173, 176–179, 187, 188, 217, 236, 240–243, 244, 306–310; finances/fund raising, 66, 67–69, 78, 83, 111–113, 121, 129, 131, 151, 177, 184, 200, 202–203, 204, 222, 236, 256, 265, 275, 306, 307, 496 (*see also* benefactors); football, abolished by Hutchins, 200–202, 480; government projects/relations, 223–227, 228, 236–237, 264–266; graduate departments, 69, 74–75, 77, 80–81, 147, 151, 153, 190, 229–231, 246, 270–271; Great Books course, 98–103, 118, 139, 147, 187, 260, 273, 306, 538; history of/founding, 57–58; Hutchins's effect on, 299–300, 304–305, 308, 309–310, 535, 536, 558n.5; Hutchins's inaugural address, 80–81, 83, 548n.8; Hutchins's memorial service, 528–529; Hyde Park neighborhood, 78, 105–106, 306, 307, 563n.22; interdisciplinary programs, 80, 109, 268, 310; Ivy League competition, 69, 77, 78, 183; Laboratory School, 71–72, 134, 136, 187; Manhattan Project scientists at, 265–266; Medical School, 104, 152, 232, 247–248, 304, 308; Memorial, 240–242; Metallurgy Laboratory/Project, 225–227, 251, 266; as model for national reform, 135, 147, 299–300, 309, 532; Northwestern University merger plans, 151–152, 153, 552n.23; nuclear-weapons research, 225–227, 251, 260, 261, 264–265, 266; Philosophy Department controversy, 86–87, 90, 93, 103; planning program, 268, 309–310 (participants, 563n.28); public relations, 66–69, 111–112, 179, 180, 181, 182–185, 310, 554–555n.13; reform

issues, 83, 135, 136, 151, 171, 188, 200–202, 227–228, 235, 245–249 (*see also* undergraduate/College reform); reputation/ranking of, 69, 77, 183, 238; research, 57, 69–70, 72, 80, 83, 113, 147, 152, 153, 221, 222, 225–227, 236, 238, 251, 260, 261, 264–265, 266, 306; tenure controversy, 178–179, 191; trustee-faculty dinner addresses, 81–82, 133, 156, 171, 200, 232, 236, 237–240, 245, 264, 310; tuition, 112, 113; undergraduate/College reform, 73–75, 77, 80–81, 83, 87, 91, 92–93, 95–97, 134–137, 138–140, 146, 147–152, 153, 167, 171, 187–189, 221, 227–229, 235–236, 246, 304, 381, 445, 558n.5; University College, 77, 273; University/faculty senate, 73, 87, 92, 93, 109, 176, 178, 185, 191, 227, 237, 240–242, 244, 245; vocational/professional training and, 73–74, 137, 147, 221, 222, 236, 246; World War II and, 217, 221–232, 236
University of Chicago Magazine, 304
University of Chicago Press, 67, 260, 294, 562n.26
University of Colorado, 254, 430
University of Denver, 536
University of Ecuador, 411
University of Edinburgh, 203, 336, 402, 476
University of Frankfurt, 302, 319
University of Freiburg, 70
University of Hawaii, 490, 498
University of Illinois, 232
University of Louisville, 218
University of Manchester, 336
University of Michigan, 490, 575n.8
University of Minnesota, 498, 499, 501, 503, 506
University of North Carolina, 91
University of North Carolina Press, 349
University of Paris, 169
University of Puerto Rico, 411
University of Rochester, 218
University of Strasbourg, 284
University of Toronto, 270, 336, 561n.25
University of Virginia, 86, 201; Barr at, 99, 137; Buchanan at, 104, 138, 551n.6; Hutchins's Founder's Day speech, 144
University of the West Indies, 476
University of Wisconsin, 74
University of York, 421
Uppsala University, 336
Urey, Harold C., 226, 251
Utsunomiya, Tokuma, 478, 575n.11

Valentine, Alan, 218

Vandenburg, Arthur H., 219, 325

Vanderbilt, Alfred, 336

Vanderbilt, Cornelius, 64

Van Devanter, Willis, 196

Van Doren, Mark, 167, 260; Great Books and, 98, 99, 549n.6; *Higher Learning in America* review, 161, 162

Van Dusen, Henry Pitney, 372

Vanocur, Sander, 497, 505, 507

Vanzetti, Bartolomeo, 47, 59, 130

Vassar College, 70, 218, 564n.9

Vatican Council, 426

Veblen, Thorstein, 61–62, 70, 201

"Version XXXVII of a Model Constitution for a United Republics of America" (Tugwell), 487

Victor Emmanuel, King, 22

Vietnam: Ashmore-Baggs visit to, 453–456; "Pacem in Terris II" and, 443–444, 450, 453–458, 459; US bombing of, 436, 453–454, 459; US refusal to negotiate with, 454, 455–456; war in, 436, 439, 441, 442, 443–444, 450, 453–458, 459, 498, 517

Vocational/professional training, 135, 147, 149, 166, 235, 321, 401; at University of Chicago, 73–74, 137, 221, 222, 236

Voltaire, 385

vonSimson, Otto, 271

Wagner Act, 127

Walgreen, Charles R., 129–130, 131–132, 183, 552n.23

Walgreen Case, 129–132, 133

Walgreen Lectures (Hutchins), 336

Wallace, Dewitt, 257

Wallace, Henry, 209, 260, 440

Wallace, Mike, 367, 567n.5

Wall Street Journal, 201, 296, 372, 467–468

Walter, Francis, 351, 355, 357, 361, 364, 370, 371, 372, 373. *See also* House Un-American Activities Committee; McCarthyism

War and Peace (Tolstoy), 100

Ward, Barbara, 490, 571n.9

Ward, F. Champion, 309, 310; on Hutchins, 187–188, 188–189, 304, 309; on Kimpton appointment, 305–306

Warner, Irving, 421

Warren, Earl, 337, 341–342, 349, 374, 494, 495; right-wing attacks on, 346, 412

Washington Herald, 207

Washington Post, 180, 298, 329, 350, 354, 489, 562–563n.38; Hutchins's obituary, 529

Washington State, 50

Washington University, 466, 467

Watergate, 517

Watson, Thomas, Jr., 336

Watson, Victor, 128

Watson-Watt, Sir Robert, 421

Wayne State, 321

Weaver, Sylvester "Pat," 367, 421

Webster, Bethuel, 357, 369

Weil, George, 226

Weissbourd, Bernard, 103, 508, 513, 516, 519, 571n.7, 577n.1, 578–579n.10

Welles, Orson, 99

Wells, Thomas, 40

"What Kind of World?" (Hutchins), 442, 572n.6

What Maisie Knew (James), 247

"What the University Celebrates" (Hutchins speech), 204

Wheeler, Burton K., 219

Wheeler, Harvey, 412, 429, 448; Center for the Study of Democratic Institutions and, 414, 463, 470, 472–473, 476–477, 486, 520; description of/theories of, 510–511; as Moos's spokesman, 500–501, 504, 505, 506, 507, 508, 510, 511

White, Leonard, 269, 304

White Citizens Councils, 346, 347, 349, 397

Whitehead, Alfred North, 137, 156, 246, 481

White House Office of Telecommunications Policy, 495, 576n.8

Whitman, Walt, quoted, 311

Whitney, George, 192

Whitney, Richard, 191, 192

Wigmore, John Henry, 46, 51, 545n.3

Wigner, Eugene, 226

Wilbur, Ray Lyman, 218, 558n.5

Wilder, Thornton, 447, 462, 561n.25; career, 106–107, 394; Hutchins and, 4–5, 31, 105–107, 118, 195, 300, 462, 480, 494, 530, 555n.18; Hutchins's letters to, 215, 300, 334, 465, 501, 520, 530, 579–580n.7; Hutchins's letters to, on career, 94–95, 332, 334, 343, 494–495; Hutchins's letters to, on Center, 394, 461–462, 479, 481, 489–490, 490–491, 496, 498–499, 501–502, 508, 509, 512, 513–514, 515, 516, 517; Hutchins's letters to, on education, 522–523, 536; Hutchins's letters to, on health/mental state, 275, 479, 480, 492, 493, 517; Hutchins's letters to, on Maude, 94–95, 107, 173, 219, 577n.14; Hutchins's memorial address for, 525–526; religion/philosophy of, 31, 105, 106, 530–531; at University of Chicago, 105–106; during world wars, 16, 225

Wilhelm Meister (Goethe), 285

Wilkinson, John, 412, 473, 477, 507

Willens, Harold, 420, 433, 463, 571n.7, 575n.9, 576n.8, 577n.1

William Douglass White Lectures (Hutchins), 233

William Jeanes Memorial Library, 355

"William O. Douglas Inquiry into the State of Individual Freedom" (Ashmore), 526

Williams, Clay, 194

Williams, David W., 520

Williams, Lynn, Jr., 273

William the Silent, quoted, 92, 223

Willkie, Wendell, 210, 213, 214

Wilson, Charles E., 331, 564n.2

Wilson, Dagmar, 439, 571n.11

Wilson, Woodrow, 16, 126, 423

Wingspread conference, 433; participants, 571n.6

Winternitz, Milton C., 52, 55

Wirtz, W. Willard, 421

Wittgenstein, Ludwig, 55

Wolf's Head, 30–31, 41

Woltman, Frederick, 360

Women, education and, 9, 77

Women Strike for Peace, 439, 571n.11

Wood, Robert E., 192, 193, 197, 213, 219, 557n.7; *Encyclopaedia Britannica* and, 255, 256, 257

Woodland Avenue public school, 9

Woodstock College, 381

Woodward, Frederick "Fritz," 58

Wordsworth, William, quoted, 88–89

World Court, 123

World government, 262–263, 282, 319, 350, 522; constitution for, 262–263, 269–271, 276–280; for nuclear-weapons control, 252–253, 261, 436–437, 477, 532; organization of, 278–279. *See also* "One World" theory

World Issues, 522. *See also Center Report*

World War I, 16, 223, 281; Hutchins in, 16–24, 211

World War II, 23, 190, 199, 219, 205–207, 210–220, 221–232; atomic bomb, 251–252 (*see also* Manhattan Project; Metal-

lurgy Laboratory/Project); Hutchins's views on, 204, 211–213, 215–217; interventionists vs. anti-interventionists, 206–207, 213–220; postwar issues, 249–251; US involvement, 199, 210–211, 218, 221; University of Chicago and, 217, 221–232, 236. *See also* America First Committee

Wright, Frank Lloyd, 230, 391

Wright, Mrs. Quincy, 63

Wright, Quincy, 343

Wrigley, William, 68

Xerox Corporation, 424, 442, 475

Yale Club, 366, 530

Yale Club, Boston, 41

Yale Club, Chicago, 79, 81

Yale Corporation, 48, 50, 56; Hutchins and, 20, 30, 38–43, 75–76, 81

Yale Law Journal, 163

Yale Law Review, 47

Yale Law School, 45–56, 197; faculty, 50, 51, 52, 53, 54, 162, 490, 562n.25; Hutchins, as dean, 48–56, 60, 62, 66, 69, 75, 90, 114, 120, 154, 162, 305, 535, 545n.3; Hutchins, as instructor/professor, 44, 45–47, 49–50; Hutchins, as student, 32, 36, 37, 39, 40, 43, 44, 305, 521; reform of, 45, 49–55, 90, 154, 305, 535

Yale Record, 180

Yale University, 40, 202, 321, 400, 408, 490, 570n.5; alumni, 180, 273, 323, 345; Benton and, 31, 179–180; Douglas and, 50–51, 53, 85, 197; Harper and, 57, 58, 70; Hutchins attending, 24, 25, 26, 27–35, 36–37, 93, 105, 179–180, 273 (*see also* Yale Law School: Hutchins, as student); Hutchins family attending, 4, 37; Luce and, 31, 293; social biases of, 30–31, 41; University of Chicago vs., 78, 183; Wilder and, 31, 105, 525; World War II and, 213, 219. *See also* Yale Law School

Yale University Press, 161

Yarmolinsky, Adam, 345, 375, 383, 385

YMCA. *See* Young Men's Christian Association

Yokohama, 250

Young, James Webb, 321, 564n.9

Young Democratic Clubs, 122–124

Young Men's Christian Association (YMCA), 17, 18, 22–23; Hutchins on, 146–147

Young People's Society for Christian
 Endeavor, 89
Young Women's Christian Association
 (YWCA), 130
Yust, Walter, 259

YWCA. *See* Young Women's Christian Association

Zellerbach, James D., 332, 363, 383, 565n.25
Zhukov, Yevgenyi, 434
Zuckerkandl, Alexander, 445–447